SHOW ME YOUR
WAYS LORD

SHOW ME YOUR
WAYS LORD

GABRIEL BAPTISTE

Copyright © 2017 by Gabriel Baptiste.

Library of Congress Control Number:		2017916170
ISBN:	Hardcover	978-1-5434-5972-2
	Softcover	978-1-5434-5973-9
	eBook	978-1-5434-5974-6

All scripture quotations are from the Holy Bible, New King James Version (Authorized Version). The complete NKJV was first published in 1982.

Print information available on the last page.

Rev. date: 07/03/2018

To order additional copies of this book, contact:
Xlibris
1-888-795-4274
www.Xlibris.com
Orders@Xlibris.com
764223

Contents

Preface

A thrifty squirrel is busy burying acorns for the upcoming winter. How does his prudent investment compare to my nest egg (retirement saving)? A male Blue bird-of-paradise is putting on a fantastic display of a lifetime to impress his fussy mate. How does his romantic display relate to a man's ability to provide for his family? A young mother gray whale is nervously leading her growing infant calf to the rich buffet up North, but she must swim past a gantlet of hungry, rambunctious, and mischievous killer whales with dinner on their mind. It just doesn't make any sense at all. The black vulture is a model of monogamy; once paired, the group protects all new couples. Any would-be womanizer with adultery in mind is ferociously attacked and shown the exit door. Can we learn anything from our animal friends? Our two-year-old grandson, LaShawn, just had an accident on his mom's well-kept rug. Judging from the horror on her face, he sheepishly yelped his favorite words "Uh! Oh!"

Whether it is the gray whale, the thrifty squirrel, the bird of paradise, the black vulture, or little LaShawn, there is a wealth of spiritual nuggets to be gleaned from our friends in nature. God has benevolently implanted rich spiritual lessons in nature for our mental, spiritual, physical, emotional, and financial benefit. All that is required of us is to dig beyond the surface to unearth the treasures waiting to be discovered. Speaking under inspiration, the wise man Solomon counsels, "Go to the ant, you sluggard! Consider her ways and be wise" (Prov. 6:6). Did you get the hint? Can we really learn some valuable lessons from our friends in nature? I think we can. Do you know that, besides the Holy Spirit and the Word of God (the Bible), Mother Nature is our best teacher and that we have barely scratched the surface of her vast inventory of knowledge? If we are conscious, patient, curious, observant, and inquisitive, she will happily reward us and unravel her deep secrets to us. Having observed both human and animal behavior, I have compiled a few "oh oh" (surprise) moments and applied biblical principles to assist us in our walk with God. Happy reading, my dear friend, and may God bless you as you immerse yourself in this journal.

Acknowledgments

Thanks be to God Almighty for providing me the insight when I really did not know what I was doing. To you be the honor, glory, and praise. Amen. To my dear wife, Daisy, who endured the agony of ruined vacations, sleepless nights, and meaningless Sundays while I was engaged in this project, thank you. To my dear son, Lyonel, who provided critically needed electronic aid to my rather Stone Age software skills, thanks. To his gracious wife, Latoya, whose hospitality has been quite robust and charming, thank you. To my grandson, LaShawn, whose antics became the subject matter for much of this journal, thanks. To Elder George Atama, who constantly inquired about the publication date of this journal, thanks for keeping me focused and on track. To all my friends from Seabrook who were aware of this project and prayed for its success and timely entry into the market, thanks.

Thanks to my siblings, particularly Angie, who regularly checked to see how the writing project was going on. Thanks to Vickie, who unwittingly provided a wealth of material to me from her experiences in life. To my big brothers Hughes, Alucious, and Samson—all of whom I adore—and my sisters Victoria (Vickie), Angie, Rebecca, Rachel, and Mary Magdalene (Recelda), you all showered me with the best of affection. I love you all to death.

To the patient educators who enabled and sharpened my writing skill, I am eternally grateful. Thanks to Cavel Melbourne, who copyedited for me. Thanks to Drs. Bertram Melbourne, Marcia Gelfand, and Valarie Swan for their affirmation of this journal. Thanks to Salon Phillips, Esq., for his timely counsel.

Defender in Chief

God is our refuge and strength a very present help in time of trouble.
Therefore we will not fear; Even though the earth is removed, and the mountains are carried into the midst of the sea.

—Psalm 46:1–2

The Patriot missile battery system is made by the Raytheon Company, located in Huntsville, Alabama. It is classified as a surface-to-air missile, from which the acronym SAM is derived. It is feared by foes for its ability to take down other missiles, rockets, and any other heat-producing object. It is highly classified, and much of its characteristics remain a mystery.

Its first deployment in a theater of operation was during the 1991 Gulf War; however, analysts were not very happy with its performance then. Nonetheless, during the 2003 Iraq War, its success greatly improved because of a few tweaks here and there. With the threat of a nuclear conflict becoming more of a reality in our time, many countries are scrambling to make their purchase. The system has been deployed in many countries all over the world, and its presence in theaters of instability provides a relative sense of comfort and security for governments and their citizens (www.raytheon.com/capabilities).

God is our refuge and strength, and his shield is impenetrable to all incoming missiles. The enemy can get to us only with God's permission as Moses observes: "Have you not made a hedge around him, around his household, and around all that he has on every side?" (Job 1:10). Old Satan wanted to give Job a thrashing but was wise enough to ask permission. God placed a hedge around his people. "Because you have made the Lord, who is my refuge, even the Most High, your dwelling place, No evil shall befall you" (Ps. 91:9–10). God's promises to Israel of old are ours to appropriate and claim. God gathers to himself a people, whoever responds to his love; he enlarges their portion and builds a defensive wall around them. In Genesis 22:17, God promised Abraham, "I will multiply your descendants as the stars of the heaven and as the sand on the seashore." The apostle Paul improved on this statement a little further by stating that God "will call them My people, who were not My people" (Rom. 9:25).

Having severed ties with the kingdom of darkness, the believer finds himself in the crosshairs (gunsight) of Satan, but he is not left unprotected. God carefully weighs and measures the temptations confronting the Christian. Paul affirms, "No temptation has overtaken you except such as common to man; but God is faithful, who will not allow you to be tempted beyond what you are able, but with the temptation will also make a way of escape, that you may be able to bear it" (1 Cor. 10:13).

Has anyone won a championship by playing defense only? Shouldn't we go on the offensive for God? "Then Jonathan said to the young man who bore his armor 'Come, let us go over to the garrison of these uncircumcised; it may be that the Lord will work for us, For nothing restrains the Lord from saving by many or by few'" (1 Sam. 14:6). God is pleased when his children take bold steps to enhance his kingdom. Just as he shielded and strengthened Jonathan, he can and will do more than what we ask of him. Is he not our refuge and strength and a very present help in time of need? It is wise to plan, but we are in danger of spending too much time on planning and not enough time on the field of conflict, witnessing to others.

January 2

His Tender Care

Deliver us from the evil one.

—Matthew 6:13

On sale: Garden of Eden vegetables. Any takers? My sister Chal (name changed) has a green thumb; anything she plants grows vigorously. It came as no surprise that, while visiting her in New Jersey, we somehow ended up in her backyard garden. True to her nature, she proceeded to give my wife and me a tour of her garden. From there, she displayed her proudest achievement. My big sister was in her element. She absolutely loves gardening and has become an expert at it. She comes from a family with the ability to grow all kinds of plants.

While touring her garden, she briefed us on the progress of each species and its unique history. The cabbages were huge but under a withering attack by slugs and another vermin and needed quick relief, but the collards and tomatoes escaped their barrage unscathed. The broccoli, surprisingly, rushed ahead of their peers and yielded a cone ready for the pot. Having run the entire course of the garden, we retreated to the patio for a breather, and that was when a wonder of nature unfolded before our eyes.

A parent oriole, perched on the roof of an adjacent house, was busy issuing flying instructions to a chick that had not yet fully discovered the use of its wings. It was clumsy, running and bumping into obstacles. Its parent was obviously concerned about its prolonged time on the ground since it was getting dark. From her perch, she continued her barrage of encouragements and instructions. Undoubtedly, she had put generations of nestlings through flight school.

Her maternal care reminds me of our heavenly Father. How anxiously he watches as we bumble and stumble along the way through life! He often picks us up when we fall and dusts off the dirt from our faces. He rearranges circumstances and events and delivers us as he did David. Who is like unto our God? "Praise be to the Lord, the God of Israel, who has sent you today to meet me. May you be blessed for your good judgment and for keeping me from avenging myself with my own hands" (1 Sam. 25:32–33). Obviously, God sent an angel in the person of Abigail to quell and foil David's rash, hot anger. Does he not do the same for us? Not only does God care for his people but he also delivers them from evil, sometimes of their own creation. David realized all too well that it was God who shields and keeps us from temptation. Jesus, our Elder Brother and Maker, recognized our peril and asked the Father this special request on our behalf: "And lead us not into temptation, But deliver us from the evil one" (Matt. 6:13).

The soul that is weak but determined to resist evil will rise above sin and gain victory. God will empower, deliver, and save his children. "No temptation has overtaken you except such as is common to man; but God is faithful, who will not allow you to be tempted beyond what you are able, but with the temptation will also make the way of escape. That you may be able to bear it" (1 Cor. 10:13). Not only does God have our backs but he has our front covered as well. Someone once said, "We have nothing to fear except we forget the way the Lord has led us in the past." God will deliver us from every evil as long we are intent on being faithful to him. Does he not have a shield around you as he did Job? (Job 1:10). He most definitely does.

January 3

Long Live the Bride and Groom

Let us be glad and rejoice and give Him glory, for the marriage of the Lamb has come, and His wife has made herself ready.

—Revelation 19:7

There is a buzz of love in the air. Natalie and Andrew are getting married. Their long and much-anticipated wedding date has been set. An exquisite website has been created just for the purpose of issuing instructions and information to invited guests. This reflects the transition from the traditional snail mail invitation to the modern web invitations. Long live wedding invitations, whether antiquated or modern!

Natalie is funny, gregarious, virtuous, and outgoing. She is very sharp, sociable, and fun to be with. There is never a dull moment in her presence; she lights up everyone with her charm. Her smile is charismatic, infectious, and contagious, bringing joy and laughter to coworkers and friends alike. Andrew, on the other hand, is more reserved, more introspective, a thinker by all accounts. However, his résumé is very impressive; he's from New York and has come to the DC region to kick-start his educational aspirations.

Walking through their website is an adventure in itself. We were amazed at Andrew's creativity in popping up the magical question to Natalie. He had the plan all set up on his iPad, and quite casually, he enticed her into surfing the net. She immediately stumbled on the amazing marriage proposal. By this time, he was already on his knees with an engagement ring in hand, pleading, "Natalie, Natalie, will you marry me?" Can any woman resist such a romantic request?

Blushing shyly, she remarked, "Yes, Andrew, I will marry you."

The plan of salvation is similar to Andrew and Natalie's wedding. God has meticulously arranged a wedding to which everyone is invited. Matthew provides the details: "The Kingdom of Heaven is like a certain king who arranged a marriage for his son, and sent out his servants to call those who were invited to the wedding; and they were not willing to come. Again, he sent out other servants, saying, tell those who are invited, see I have prepared my dinner, my oxen and fatted cattle are killed, and all things are ready. Come to the wedding. But they made light of it and went their ways, one to his own farm, and another to his business. And the rest seized his servants, treated them spitefully, and killed them" (Matt. 22:2–6). The king represents God, his son is Jesus, and the wedding is salvation, and you have been cordially invited to the great feast.

Would you turn down an invitation from the president to his inauguration ball? You probably would not, but you are highly favored to have received such a prestigious invitation from God himself. The wedding invitation has been paid for at an immense cost to God. "For God so loved the world that He gave His only begotten Son, that whoever believes in Him should not perish but have everlasting life" (John 3:16). This wedding is very urgent; it cannot be ignored, made light of, postponed, or canceled. By saying yes to Jesus, we become invited guests to join God in celebrating the marriage between him and his people in the earth made new. Have you accepted and invited him into your life? If yes, great. Congratulations!

January 4

Send the Rain, Please, Lord

Then it came to pass the seventh time; that he said, there is a cloud, as small as a man's hand, rising out of the sea! So he said, go up, say to Ahab, prepare your chariot, and go down before the rain stops you.

—1 Kings 18:44

The year 2012 was a terrible year for farmers across the nation; they were hammered by a withering drought. When the rain finally descended, it came in torrents, but it was too late for many small farmers, and some went bankrupt. Ranchers raising livestock watched helplessly as the prolonged drought affected crop yield, increased the price of livestock feed, and decreased the market value of animals, and that left many farmers with wrinkles on their foreheads. Lawn businesses and other industries dependent on moderate rainfall all felt the pinch. My little backyard garden was demolished for lack of rainfall.

The lack of rain in the Bible economy is symbolic of the spiritual barrenness of God's people. Jesus delineates this point quite well: "Listen! Behold, a sower went out to sow. It happened, as he sowed, that some seed fell by the wayside; and the birds of the air came and devoured it. Some fell on stony ground, where it did not have much earth; and immediately it sprang up because it had no depth of earth . . . But other seeds fell on good ground and yielded a crop that sprang up, increased and produced; some thirtyfold, some sixty, and some a hundred" (Mark 4:3–5, 8). Acceptance of God's Word always represents fruitfulness, while rejection is symbolic of spiritual poverty and barrenness.

While farmers pray for rain to save their crop, we pray for a different kind of rain—the latter rain of the Holy Spirit. All of us, as God's people, are in dire need of the reign of the Holy Spirit in our lives. "And it shall come to pass afterward, that I will pour out My Spirit on all flesh; your sons and your daughters shall prophesy, your old men shall dream dreams, your young men shall see visions. And also on My menservants and on My maidservants I will pour out My Spirit in those days" (Joel 2:28–29). But that spiritual downpour will come only upon request. It must be diligently sought after and must be prayed for. It does not fall indiscriminately on everyone as your average spring shower.

Jesus referenced "good soil" in many of his parables and with good reason. Good soil is always reflective of productivity, and since productivity is welcomed by farmers and business establishments, will God expect any less from us? We must be engaged in productive Christian ministry to be filled by the Spirit. The Holy Spirit will not occupy the idle and slothful for service. They will be passed over in favor of those already engaged in ministry. God never entrusts his dynamic power to idle hands. Jesus's disciples were busy fishing when called. Many of those called to ministry by God were busy people: Amos, collector of nuts; Moses and David, shepherds; Paul, persecutor of God's people; and Peter and John, fishermen.

Can God do the same for me? Of course, he can. What can God do with me? How do I get started? The Lord may be saying to you, "What is in your hand? What are you good at? Can you cook? Then use cooking to lead others to Christ." If you have a pleasant personality and others are attracted to you, use that influence to guide others to the kingdom. Do you have a lovely voice? Use it to the glory of God. You cannot use what you do not have. If you have a talent and everyone does, then use it for Jesus.

January 5

It's Time to Come Home

O Jerusalem, Jerusalem, the one who kills the prophets and stones those who are sent to her! How often I wanted to gather your children together, as a hen gathers her chicks under her wings, but you were not willing.

—Matthew 23:37

In the animal kingdom, the mother hen should receive the Academy Award for her maternal care. She will send you packing if you stray too close to her chicks. Moments after her chicks hatch, maternal instinct kicks in. In defense of her precious investment, the mother hen goes on the offense by inflating her feathers when threatened. Looking much bigger than her normal size, she sends her enemies fleeing for their lives, but the unique aspect of her maternal care is her detection of threats. In typical chicken language, she chirps in a low-pitched cluck, which her chicks understand, and they dash to safety under her safe and fluffy breast. The rainy weather does not pose a problem; she loosens and spreads her waterproof feathers backward and voilà—an umbrella and an inviting warm body for her little chicks.

Jesus used the mother hen metaphor to describe both his frustration and yearning to provide comfort, security, and sustenance to his people in Israel. Regrettably, Israel rebuffed his overtures and frustrated him at every level by their apathy and intransigence. Are we in danger of repeating the same spirit of intransigence that caused Israel's downfall? "I have stretched out My hands all day long to a rebellious people, who walk in a way that is not good, according to their own thoughts: A people who provoke Me to anger continually to My face" (Isa. 65:2–3).

God's heart churns within him as the people whom he has ransomed by the shedding of his blood spurn his love and reject his grace. "How can I give you up, Ephraim? How can I hand you over, Israel? How can I make you like Admah? How can I set you like Zeboiim? My heart churns within Me; My sympathy is stirred" (Hosea 11:8). Admah and Zeboiim were wicked cities of the Old Testament era that resisted the Word of God and were destroyed. Did you hear the pathos in God's voice, the feeling, the emotion? Make no mistake about it. God is not going to save us against our will, but he is having a hard time allowing us to walk in the self-destructive path we have chosen.

Johnny was born with a "silver spoon in his mouth," a phrase used in my culture to describe inherited privileges, notably wealth and power. But can you imagine the horrific expression on a father's face when he discovers his son walked away from a wealthy inheritance in exchange for life on the streets as a panhandler? In many respects, we do the same thing to God. He owns the world and its bounty, but we have little esteem or appreciation for the great inheritance in heaven dangling before our very eyes.

It remains true: "You can take the horse to the water, but you can't force him to drink." And I am saying this in love: "For it would have been better for them not to have known the way of righteousness, than having known it, to turn from the holy commandment delivered to them" (2 Pet. 2:21). Lord, help us be faithful to you despite the distractions, the greed, and the evil of this age.

January 6

A Doer of the Word

For anyone who is a hearer of the word and not a doer, he is like a man observing his natural face in a mirror; for he observes himself, goes away, and immediately forgets what kind of man he was.

—James 1:23–24

In the epic fairy tale "Snow White and the Seven Dwarfs," legend reveals a wicked queen who owns a magic mirror and is infuriated when her mirror informs her that there is someone in the kingdom more beautiful than herself. Incidentally, the one prettier than the wicked old queen is her own stepdaughter, Snow White. She hates the child with a passion and embarks on a mission to eliminate her, but in her blind hatred to destroy the child, she ends up destroying herself (www.dltk-teach.com).

The law of God is like a mirror that reveals to us the condition of our body. It points out our defects and character flaws but is incapable of removing them. As transparent as a mirror may be, it can only reveal conditions present on the body; it cannot fix, remove, heal, or erase flaws in character. Likewise, God's law, the Ten Commandments, can neither save nor clean us up. Only Jesus saves.

At conversion, the child of God is saved by grace and is put on a course of obedience to God by the Holy Spirit. This course involves a life pleasing to God, which requires observance of the Ten Commandments. In essence, by abiding in Christ, one becomes a doer of the word and not a hearer only as the Bible states. "And those who are Christ's have crucified the flesh with its passions and desires" (Gal. 5:24). Paul did not leave us guessing what the works of the flesh entails. "Now the work of the flesh are evident, which are adultery, fornication, uncleanness, lewdness, idolatry, sorcery, hatred, contentions, jealousies, outbursts of wraths, selfish ambitions, dissensions, heresies, envy, murders, drunkenness, revelries, and the like; of which I tell you beforehand, just as I also told you in the past that those who practice such things will not inherit the kingdom of God" (Gal. 5:19–21). Once converted, the believer develops a distaste for these sinful behaviors of the flesh and seeks wholeheartedly what pleases God.

The good news of the Gospel reveals that God's grace is always sufficient and Christ's biddings always enabling. "Come to Me, all you who labor and are heavy laden, and I will give you rest. Take My yoke upon you and learn from Me, for I am gentle and lowly in heart, and you will find rest for your souls. For My yoke is easy and My burden is light" (Matt. 11:28–30). Fortunately, God's way—the path of obedience—is always better than the ways of the world. God's way may look difficult, but it is the best way. If the law of God is faithfully kept, it would effectively put an end to prisons, law enforcement agencies, security guards, locksmiths, and a host of health services.

God's law is very much relevant to today's civilization, and anyone teaching that his Ten Commandments are abolished, obsolete, irrelevant, and done away with is misinformed. At conversion, our will becomes subordinate to God's will; and like Paul, we submit, stop resisting, and ask, "Lord, what do you want me do?" (Acts 9:6). Hereafter, the path ahead becomes a life of compliance and obedience to God's will; it is only then that we will become happy doers of the word and not hearers only.

January 7

Can We Live Together?

But as for me, my feet had almost stumbled; my steps had nearly slipped. For I was envious of the boastful, when I saw the prosperity of the wicked.

—Psalm 73:2–3

Recent statistics have shown that the gap between the rich and the poor is growing and is the widest ever. This can be easily verified by the lucrative packages CEOs receive from their companies. Quite recently, the incentive for enticing a talented CEO to jump ship from one company to another has increased just a little bit more. It is also noteworthy to point out that the dedicated rank-and-file workers who labor devotedly to keep the company afloat have been denied an increase in wages. Needless to say, their meager income has forced them to hold several jobs to keep up with the rising cost of living. Management believes their low-level skill makes them expendable.

This is hardly anything new. The gulf that separates the rich and the poor has existed for millennia and has mystified the godliest of men throughout human history. Judas's false pretense for the poor is indicative of today's business rationale. "If we give the poor a raise in salary, we might have to cut staff to make up for lost revenue," they argue. But Judas and his modern-day counterparts are far from having any sympathy for the poor. "Why was this fragrant oil not sold for three hundred denarii and given to the poor? This said he not that he cared for the poor, but because he was a thief, and had the money box; and he used to take what was put in it" (John 12:5–6). Judas pretends to be a defender of the poor, but Jesus sees through it all and replies, "Let her alone; she has kept this for the day of My burial. For the poor you have with you always, but Me you do not have always" (John 12:7–8). Few genuinely care for the poor as Solomon observes. "The poor man is hated even by his own neighbor but the rich has many friends. But he who has mercy on the poor, happy is he" (Prov. 14:20–21).

The psalmist in our opening verse tried to figure out the wide disparity between the rich and the poor and almost lost his sanity. "When I thought how to understand this, it was too painful for me" (Ps. 73:16). In verse 7, he describes how the rich seems to have the magic touch: "They have more than heart could wish." Everything they lay their hands on seems to bloom and grow; their stocks and bonds do exceedingly well and above expectations. They are in vibrant health and have the best of medical care at their fingertips, but their standing is precarious.

The psalmist was permitted by God to see the whole picture, their end. He stopped envying their status when he realized their standing was fragile and precarious. "Until I went into the sanctuary of God then I understood their end. Surely You set them in slippery places; You cast them down to destruction. Oh, how they are brought to desolation, as in a moment! They are utterly consumed with terrors" (Ps. 73:17–19). How does the future look for the child of God? "Though a sinner does evil a hundred times, and his days are prolonged, yet I surely know that it will be well with those who fear God, who fear before Him" (Eccles. 8:12). Don't try to figure out the injustice in the world; it is too painful and mystifying for us. Jesus did not change the rich/poor equation; evil must be allowed to run its full course, and in the end, God will set things right. Whether we're rich or poor, if we are faithful to God, we will inherit eternal life.

January 8

Joy in a Jail Cell

Then the Philistines took him and put out his eyes, and brought him down to Gaza. They bound him with bronze fetters, and he became a grinder in the prison.
—Judges 16:21

Stanley "Tookie" Williams was as tough as shoe leather. He was leader of the Crips gang in Los Angeles. In 1981, he was convicted of the armed robbery of a convenience store, in which four people were slain. He was sentenced to death for his crime. Amazingly, while on death row, Stanley turned to God and began turning his life around, thanks in part to the diligent work done by volunteer religious groups and an insightful chaplain. Stanley apologized repeatedly and profusely to society for his criminal past, but this did not spare him the electric chair. He even wrote a book from his jail cell in an attempt to warn others and to clean up his criminal past, but after many attempts at clemency, Stanley "Tookie" Williams was executed in the year 2005 (www.biography.com/people/stanley).

Newspapers abound with stories of promising young men and women like Stanley who opt for life in the fast lane only to end up languishing in jail for the rest of their lives. Despite this, all is not lost; even while in jail, one can call on God and apply the spiritual discipline found in his Word to live a productive life. Yes, even while in jail and with Jesus abiding in the heart, one can be free as a bird and soar like an eagle.

Jails have become a last stop for many, as well as a classroom for grooming the world's next great leader. Was it not in jail that Samson rearranged his priorities and determined to live up to his full potential? Did not the Birmingham jail provide the platform for one of the most famous speeches ever, "I Have a Dream"? What did twenty-seven years of solitary confinement do to Nelson "Madiba" Mandela? Did it not refine him, purging him of bitter hatred to become the father of all races to his nation? Should we forget Joseph and the character transformation he underwent as a result of his prison encounter? Like Mandela, his prison adventure paved the way to the palace and the reins of power in the government.

Should we fear prison if our cause is just and noble? The day is looming fast when "they will put you out of the synagogues; yes, the time is coming that whoever kills you will think that he offers God service" (John 16:2). This is happening all around us; the righteous is being persecuted. "And the dragon [Satan] was enraged with the woman [the church] and went to make war with the rest of her offspring [last day saints], who keep the commandments of God and have the testimony of Jesus Christ" (Rev. 12:17). Looking down through the ages, Jesus foretold his church would be at odds with the authorities because of their allegiance to him: "But before all these things, they will lay their hands on you and persecute you, delivering you up to the synagogues and prisons. You will be brought before kings and rulers for My name's sake" (Luke 21:12).

The children of God have always been at odds with the sons of men controlled by the devil. Like John the Baptist, some of us might languish in jail because of our faith; or like Paul, some may even be executed, but a victor's crown awaits the overcomer. Be on the alert; you might be headed to jail for your faith someday.

January 9

When Little Becomes Much

There is a lad here who has five barley loaves and two small fish, but what are they among so many?

—John 6:9

With three hundred hungry orphans to feed and no food in sight, George Müller ordered the kids to sit at the table and say their grace (prayer). His wise old assistant thought he had gone off the deep end (mad), but faithful George had seen God at work several times before. While the children sat at the table, impatient and still hungry, there was a knock at the door. A baker whose sleep was interrupted by a mysterious urge to bake three extra batches of bread deposited the precious cargo at the orphanage. He had barely vacated the premises when a milkman's carriage broke down in front of the shelter. Sensing the milk would spoil after the long repair, the man contributed the tasty treat to the students. All went well. God is never rushed; neither is he delayed but is always on time, isn't he? Who thrives on taking little and making it much? Only God does (www.penneydouglas. com/2012/08/10/george-mueller-hungry-orphan-fed-miraclously).

"The word of the Lord came to him [Elijah], saying, arise, go to Zarephath, which belongs to Sidon, and dwell there. See I have commanded a widow there to provide for you" (1 Kings 17:8–9). God is full of humor. Did he say a widow, someone without a husband, without a job, and living in poverty? In biblical times, a widow was reduced to poverty when her breadwinning husband died. The woman was preparing her last meal when the prophet showed up with a demand: "Please bring me a little water in a cup that I may drink." And as she was going to fetch it, he called to her and said, "Please bring me a morsel of bread in your hand" (1 Kings 17:10–11).

Perplexed, the woman replied, "As the Lord your God lives, I do not have bread, only a handful of flour in a bin, and a little oil in a jar; and see, I am gathering a couple of sticks that I may go in and prepare it for myself and my son, that we may eat it, and die" (1 Kings 17:12). Was God testing her? Was he checking out her generosity? However, she passed the test by putting the interest of the stranger ahead of herself and her hungry son. Was she rewarded? Jesus highlighted her faith in the following parable: "When did we see you a stranger and take you in or naked and clothe you? Or when did we see you sick, or in prison, and come to you? And the King will answer and say to them, assuredly, I say to you inasmuch as you did it to one of the least of these my brethren, you did it to Me" (Matt. 25:38–40).

The believer must always be mindful that God owns everything, including the wealth of people and nations, and when we pray according to his will, he will appropriate their wealth to do his work. "The earth is the Lord's and its fullness, the world and those who dwell therein" (Ps. 24:1). God owns everything, including the little we possess, and he is eager to stretch it, if only we allow him. The widow of Zarephath would never have been on the biblical record if she was not willing to part with her meager ration. Little becomes much in the Master's hand. What was Christ able to do with the little boy's fish and bread? Did he not feed thousands? How far can he stretch your little piggy bank? You can't hold on to it if you expect him to use it. Should you not let it go? Give him your fish, and let him work his wonders with it. Dear Jesus, help us be unselfish with the resources you have placed at our disposal.

January 10

Being Connected

I am the vine you are the branches. He who abides in Me, and I in him, bears much fruit; for without Me you can do nothing.

—John 15:5

My neighbor was refurbishing his property for rent. Being a jack-of-all-trades, he did it all by himself. I watched with interest as he transformed his once-dilapidated house into a renter's delight. Not even the soil escaped his wrath. He rented an excavating machine and ripped the soil over, transforming it into a beautiful lawn with a few trees in the front and a garden to the backyard. Upon completion, he paused for a moment and, with a piercing gaze, realized to his horror that something was missing. *What am I doing?* he thought. *Where are the fruit trees? I must have fruit trees.*

He purchased two medium-sized peach plants to complement his project. He was gracious and generous in giving me the less favorable of the two. Over the next few months, I watched in envy as his peach tree accelerated in growth, while insects and slugs feasted regularly on mine. The insects were not deterred by my insecticide spray and seemed to be even more voracious and energetic in enjoying the tasty peach leaves. Totally frustrated by my inability to control them, I decided to allow nature to take its course about whether the plant would live or die.

By the third anniversary of the planting of the trees, my neighbor's tree was lush, luxuriant, healthy, and sturdy. In the following spring, his tree blossomed with a profusion of beautiful young peach fruits, while mine produced only three meager fruits. However, four weeks into spring, tragedy struck; my neighbor's tree, which showed much prospect, suddenly died. It simply shriveled up and died. I was horrified. *What happened?* I asked myself.

We may never know the reason behind the plant's sudden demise, but we are reminded of the wise counsel of Jesus in John 15:5–6: "I am the vine you are the branches. He who abides in Me bears much fruit; for without Me you can do nothing. If anyone does not abide in Me, he is cast out as a branch and is withered; and they gather them and throw them into the fire and they are burned."

My neighbor's tree represents those who begin walking with God. Over the years, they seem to be productive, but their love for God is eclipsed by their love for the world, and they give up. "Demas has forsaken me, having loved this present world and has departed for Thessalonica" (2 Tim. 4:10). Moreover, my tree, which did not show much promise at all, is very much alive today and represents those who remain and abide in Christ despite the odds and bear much fruit as a result. Fruit bearing is not a difficult undertaking; all it requires is total surrender to the will of God.

When every member of the body is fully yielded to Christ, fruit will blossom in great profusion without the believer's consciousness. "But the fruit of the Spirit is love, joy, peace, longsuffering, kindness, goodness, faithfulness, gentleness, self-control" (Gal. 5:22–23). These virtues (sap) flow from Christ to us as a result of abiding in him.

And here are examples of the fruits on display: "For I was hungry and you gave Me food; I was thirsty and you gave Me drink; I was a stranger and you took Me in; naked and you clothed Me, I was sick and you visited Me I was in prison and you came to Me" (Matt. 25:35–36). Go and do likewise. Produce some juicy fruits for Jesus, will you?

January 11

Divine Deliverance

The angel of the Lord encamps all around those who fear him and delivers them.
—Psalm 34:7

After a grueling day at the job, I jumped in my 1996 Mazda B3000 truck, slammed my foot on the accelerator, and headed for home. However, on the declining ramp from Route 695 to Highway 95 south, the entry lane was a curved steep downgrade. On a normal dry day, it would be tricky to negotiate the curve with speed of more than 40 mph. Yes, you guessed correctly. It was sleeting (wet snow). I soon found myself on the downgrade hedged in by a menacing eighteen-wheel tractor trailer to my right and an exit outlet going in the opposite direction to the left. To make matters worse, my wheels began hydroplaning (spinning) while going downhill at a speed of about 40–50 mph. I was in trouble. Several possibilities flashed through my mind: a rollover was a probability; I could sustain broken bones, neck, and back and could even die. Touching the brakes definitely was not an option; that could make matters even worse. There was no margin for error in this situation. Gabriel needed divine intervention—and fast.

Suddenly and quite mysteriously, a calm demeanor overtook me as an unseen hand negotiated the icy curve for me without any incident. I was awestruck. I just witnessed a moment no human should take credit for. God sent his angels to rescue his own. "Many are the afflictions of the righteous but the Lord delivers him out of them all" (Ps. 34:19). "The angel of the Lord encamps all around those who fear Him and delivers them" (Ps. 34:7). When we are powerless against the forces of evil, when the odds are stacked against us, when we are incapable of extricating ourselves from the mess of our own creation, God steps in and deliver us, his children. Glory! Hallelujah!

We have been warned in the scripture to be on guard because the devil is angry and is busy, on the prowl, destroying lives. Is he not in the war zones snuffing out lives without mercy? Where could he be found but on the street corners, poisoning both the mind and body of young men peddling drugs? Is he not in the dark alleys of abandoned buildings smiling as he assesses the grim evidence of his grisly work, the empty liquor bottles and discarded needles? He delights in nothing more than the entire destruction of the human race, but God, on the other hand, delights in mercy. He is full of love and delivers the willing from evil.

The raving demoniac is a typical example of what Satan has done to humanity. Hidden behind every tattooed and scarred body is a twisted mind crying out for deliverance. And that's precisely what Jesus came to do, to liberate and save (Mark 5:6–15). However, God is engaged in a greater deliverance than the mere rescue from physical danger; there is a greater danger facing humanity. Is it not the total destruction of the soul that Satan is after? He wants as many people as possible to share his fate in hell. That's why we must cooperate with God in rescuing our fellow humans from his grim fate. May God strengthen us as we cooperate with him in rescuing fallen humanity from total destruction.

January 12

All that Glitters Is Not Gold

Do not love the world or the things of the world, if anyone loves the world, the love of the Father is not in him.

—1 John 2:15

Nepenthes are plants with a delicate taste for insects and small game. This plant species lures victims to its dining room table with a tantalizing aroma to those with sensitive noses. Some species of this plant family employ clever incentives to lure unsuspecting victims to their parlor. Colorful entrances to their dining room are the most common of their guile. Most insects are swept off their feet by the dazzling beauty and tantalizing aroma leading to the dining room. The menu invites all to a delightful and delicious eat-all-you-can buffet, but there is a catch: the meal could be your last (www.carnivorous—plants.com/pitcher-plants.html).

Many are fooled and ultimately robbed of money they now possess by smooth-talking con artists. They promise easy cash with fantastic returns on their investments. Should we fall prey to their scheme as the dog who crosses a bridge, sees his reflection in the water with a bigger bone, and then drops his bone for what appeared to be a bigger one, only to lose both? Be on the alert for snake oil salesmen promising you lots of easy money. Show them to the door quickly. "All that glitters is not gold." "If it is too good to be true, it is probably not true." Should we believe anything that proceeds from the mouth of the father of deception? Consider the source.

"Again the devil took Him up on an exceedingly high mountain, and showed Him all the kingdoms of the world and their glory. And he said to Him, 'All these things I will give You if You will fall down and worship me'" (Matt. 4:8–9). What appeared to be glorious kingdoms were nothing but cities rife with crime and corruption. Thankfully, Jesus saw through the deception of Satan and replied, "Away with you Satan! For it is written, you shall worship the Lord your God, and Him only you shall serve" (verse 10).

While the devil lies, cheats, exploits, and deceives his subjects, God, on the other hand, operates under a different set of principles. He is honest and gives us precisely what is best for our needs. "If you then, being evil, know how to give good gifts to your children, how much more will your Father who is in heaven give good things to those who ask Him!" (Matt. 7:11).

Many are dazzled by the seductiveness of riches and are reluctant in following Christ, but may this never happen to the believer. "Jesus said to him, 'If you want to be perfect, go, sell what you have and give to the poor, and you will have treasure in heaven; and come and follow Me.' But when the young man heard that saying, he went away sorrowful, for he had great possessions" (Matt. 19:21–22). Of course, Jesus is not telling everyone to give away all their possessions. He is simply prescribing an individual diagnosis to this young man, who was dazzled by the deceitfulness of riches.

It is okay to pursue riches. After all, it is God who gives liberally to those who can manage it, but bear this in mind: "Do not trust in oppression, nor vainly hope in robbery; If riches increase, do not set your heart on them" (Ps. 62:10). "All that glitters is not gold," and many are discovering all too late the validity of this wise old saying. God is all sufficient and is ten thousand times better than gold or riches. Trust him today, make him your sufficiency, and you will have everything.

January 13

One Good Turn Deserves Another

Do not withhold good from those to whom it is due.

—Proverbs 3:27

Once upon a time, a little mouse was foraging on the African plain for his dinner. His diligent search led him to a hairy brown mound. Since the hill was cozy, hairy, and warm, the little mouse continued with his exploration. He noticed a twitch and then a yawn. It moved a little, groaned loudly, and shivered a bit, but the little mouse ignored his better judgment until he found himself being suspended by his tail into the jaws of a hungry lion. "Why did you disturb my nap?" the lion demanded, lowering the little mouse slowly into his gaping jaws.

"Please spare my life, and I will repay you someday," the little mouse retorted. The king of the beasts, wanting to be magnanimous to his little subject, granted him a reprieve. The little mouse scurried away as fast as he could.

Several days later, there was an agonizing roar on the plain, and the little mouse was quick to investigate. Upon arrival, he found the king caught fast in a trap. The more he tried to untangle himself, the more the ropes tightened securely around him. Tired, frustrated, and angry, the king gave up and resigned himself to his fate. The little mouse immediately recognized his benefactor and assured the king that he would soon set him free. "How can a little mouse like you free a great, big fellow like me?" he groaned.

"You watch." The little mouse nibbled away at the last rope that bound his friend, and soon the lion was free. They both parted ways after a big thank-you from his royal highness (www.planetozkids.com/oban/legends/lion-mouse-aesop-fable.htm).

This story, although an allegory, reminds us of our obligation to others, whether they deserve it or not. "We then who are strong ought to bear with the scruples of the weak, and not please ourselves. Let each of us please his neighbor for his good, leading to edification. For even Christ did not please Himself; but as it is written, 'The reproaches of those who reproached You fell on Me'" (Rom. 15:1–3).

Because the believer has been called in service to the world, his objective is interwoven with Christ's mission for the world. "The Spirit of the Lord is upon Me; because He has anointed Me to preach the gospel to the poor; He has sent Me to heal the broken hearted, to proclaim liberty to the captives and recovery of sight to the blind. To set at liberty those who are oppressed; to proclaim the acceptable year of the Lord" (Luke 4:18–19).

Like the lion caught in the trap, many of our neighbors, friends, and families are caught in various forms of confinements. Some are addicted to alcohol, gambling, drugs, pornography, homosexuality, illicit sex, tobacco, and other self-destructive habits. Should we ignore them? A thousand times no. We should, by the grace of God, go to work—as the little mouse did—in extricating them from these evil traps.

Do good to everyone, whether they deserve it or not, and by so doing, you will fulfill Christ's mandate. "But I say to you who hear: Love your enemies, do good to those who hate you, bless those who curse you and pray for those who spitefully use you" (Luke 6:27–28). Really? Oh yes. Leaving no doubt about the principles of his kingdom, the Savior continued: "But love your enemies, do good and lend, hoping for nothing in return, and your reward will be great, and you will be sons of the Most High. For He is kind to the unthankful and evil" (verse 35). Wow! What a mouthful! Go and do likewise.

Ugly Frog Becomes a Handsome Prince

Now Joshua was clothed with filthy garments, and was standing before the Angel. Then He answered and spoke to those before Him saying "Take away the filthy garment from him."

—Zechariah 3:3–4

Legend tells of a gorgeous prince who was cursed into becoming a hideous creature. His liberation could be achieved only if a beautiful maiden committed herself to him for better or for worse in his dreadful condition. Well, as it happened, love was stirring in the heart of a beautiful princess who took it upon herself to love this poor creature in spite of his pitiful condition. Was she ever rewarded? A simple "I love you" commitment transformed the horrible beast into a charming, handsome, likable mate and suitor. They lived happily ever after ("Beauty and the Beast").

When Adam sinned against his Maker, he incurred death—the just reward for his disobedience. "The soul that sins it shall die" (Ezek. 18:20). Although our fate looked bleak and grim, having incurred everlasting punishment for our sin, God instituted the plan of salvation to save us. "But God who is rich in mercy, because of His great love with which He loved us, even when we were dead in trespasses, made us alive together with Christ (by grace you have been saved)" (Eph. 2:4–5).

We probably wouldn't fully appreciate the fullness of God's love if we could assist him a bit in our salvation, but we were completely helpless, unable to save ourselves. "The Lord looks down from heaven upon the children of men, to see if there are any who understand, who seek God. They have all turned aside, they have together become corrupt" (Ps. 14:2–3).

God's anger is but for a moment, and we should be grateful. Many times, he would have been perfectly justified in destroying the whole human species, but his great compassion rushed ahead of his justice. "Nevertheless they flattered Him with their mouth, and they lied to Him with their tongue; for their heart was not steadfast with Him, nor were they faithful in His covenant. But He, being full of compassion, forgave their iniquity, and did not destroy them. Yes many a time He turned His anger away, and did not stir up all His wrath; for He remembered that they were but flesh, a breath that passes and does not come again" (Ps. 78:36–39).

God will always respond affirmatively to a contrite heart as evidenced during the captivity of Israel. "Take away the filthy garment from him . . . See I have removed your iniquity from you, and I will clothe you with rich robes" (Zech. 3:4). God always sees the best in us and lifts us from the pit of despair and misery, but he isn't through.

"For I know the thoughts that I think toward you says the Lord, thoughts of peace and not of evil, to give you a future and hope" (Jer. 29:11). God absolutely loves you and me and everyone who occupies this planet. Regardless of your past or present condition, God is highly interested in your well-being. The real question remains: will you accept the Savior's call to turn things around in your life? Not tomorrow but now. The promise is still outstanding. "Behold I stand at the door and knock. If anyone hears My voice and opens the door, I will come in to him and dine with him, and he with Me" (Rev. 3:20). Are you being invited to dine with the king? Wow! You simply can't pass up on this offer.

January 15

Jesus Loves Me at My Worst

Now it happened, as He was dining in Levi's house, that tax collectors and sinners also sat together with Jesus and His disciples; for there were many, and they followed Him.

—Mark 2:15

The ubiquitous, pesky, and much-maligned mosquitoes are creatures nobody loves, but the creatures of the Alaskan wilderness love them and look forward to their arrival. Migrating birds are easy to love, but who loves the mosquito? Alaskan fishermen greet the arriving whales with great pomp and ceremony and with good reason: their livelihood is timed to the whales' arrival. In a national park, a bird enthusiast jokingly remarked about a migrating bird from Mexico. "This one," he observed, "still has the taco smell on his breath."

Who looks forward to the arrival of mosquitoes? Who benefits from this much-misunderstood species? Ask the guppy, and he will tell you. While we loathe and despise mosquitoes, other creatures view them as manna falling from heaven. Guppies find their larvae (eggs) rather tasty. Dragonflies, purple martins, and a host of other birds time the raising of their family to this tasty mosquito buffet. Even if they chase us away from our backyard barbecues, this is no reason to hate them; their role in the food chain is absolutely necessary. We should look more favorably on this hated species. After all, they are a valuable food source that keeps many creatures healthy when food is scarce.

We despise people groups we consider beneath our social standard. In biblical times, sufferers of dreaded diseases were discriminated against and shunned by the public. Topping the list of undesirable subjects in biblical times were fishermen, shepherds, and a host of others; and first on the list of these untouchables were the hated tax collectors. They were viewed with disdain for their collaboration with Rome. They were called publicans (tax collectors), lumping them with all other notorious sinners.

Are the publicans still here with us? Of course, they are, except with nice modern names. We see them patrolling the street corners; some are camped under highway overpasses, and others abdicate their God-given gender for something more interesting. Yet these dear ones are magnetically drawn to the Savior. What do they see in Jesus? They see in his eyes a look of love and tender compassion. "I have not come to call the righteous, but sinners to repentance" (Luke 5:32). These snubbed ones seem to be very comfortable in the presence of one who is the epitome of purity and moral uprightness. He spoke their language. Do we speak the people's language? Do we offer to scratch where they itch? Do we have the heart of a good Samaritan?

God will allow certain crude people to cross our path to test our Christianity; it may bring out the good angel in us or the bad guy. If the truth be told, are we not all recovering addicts of some kind? Even the avowed enemies of Jesus who hardly said anything good about him conceded: "He is a friend of publicans and sinners" (Luke 7:34).

Jesus loves everyone, even the unlovely. Shouldn't we also love people of every class? We should see each person as a potential disciple for the kingdom of God. God's love transcends race, gender, national boundary, culture, social status, political affiliation, and national origin. May God help us as we look past our differences to what unites us.

January 16

Is This Really Love?

The thief does not come except to steal, to kill and to destroy. I have come that that they have life, and that they may have it more abundantly.

—John 10:10

Cynthia (name changed) was walking in fantasyland; she was in love. The singing birds, the ocean's rolling waves, and the rippling water of the nearby stream all seemed to confirm her fantasy. She was the center of attraction; everything seemed so nice and pleasant as she feasted on the generosity of her suitor. Her handsome admirer was on call 24/7, and the gifts came pouring in. She had a particular obsession for Kentucky fried chicken, and at the snap of her fingers, this particular delicacy came in by the buckets whenever she desired. Cynthia was on the proverbial "cloud nine." However, this 24/7 service came to an abrupt end after an illicit incident. This unfortunate incident left Cynthia distrustful of even well-intentioned friends. However, "There is a friend that sticks closer than a brother" (Prov. 18:24). Do you know him? Would you like to meet him?

We have absolutely nothing to fear from our Friend, Savior, and Admirer—the Lord Jesus Christ. He has guaranteed, "And lo, I am with you always even unto the end of the age" (Matt. 28:20). Our loving Father not only lavishes on us his affection and love but also has assured us that his abiding presence will be with us even during the most difficult periods of our life. When we are buffeted by life's bitter cup, it is comforting to know that God is with us. He is a friend who will stick with us when friends are few and the refrigerator is bare. In sickness and in health, in poverty and in wealth, God is with us.

Unlike Satan, who exploits his victims—robbing them of their health, innocence, vitality, and cognitive thinking—God treats his children very well. He gives life to all, even to the undeserving. "But God demonstrates His own love toward us, in that while we were still sinners, Christ died for us" (Rom. 5:8). The beauty of the Judeo-Christian faith hinges on the concept of a loving God reconciling his wayward creation to himself by incurring his own wrath to save us. "Who have believed our report? And to whom has the arm of the Lord been revealed?" (Isa. 53:1). This verse reveals the level of our skepticism in understanding the suffering of our Lord Jesus Christ. "He is despised and rejected of men; a man of sorrows and acquainted with grief: and we hid as it were our faces from Him; He was despised, and we esteemed Him not. Surely He has borne our grief and carried our sorrows; yet we esteemed Him stricken, Smitten by God and afflicted" (Isa. 54:3–4). Unless aided by the Holy Spirit, mortal man may never understand the length and breadth of God's love to sinful man.

God loves his creation dearly, including you and me, and is not about to consign us to our ignoble fate or surrender us to the vengeance of Satan. God wants to dwell with his people, and he yearns to unite the human family with his heavenly family. Like many of his prophetic counterparts, John picks up on Jesus's sense of urgency in uniting us with the heavenly family: "Let not your heart be troubled; you believe in God, believe also in Me. In My Father's house are many mansions; if it were not so, I would have told you. I go to prepare a place for you. And if I go to prepare a place for you, I will come again and receive you unto Myself; that where I am there you will be also" (John 14:1–3).

January 17

Too Much Energy

Behold, children are heritage from the Lord . . . Happy is the man who has his quiver full of them.

—Psalm 127:3, 5

Our one-and-one-half-year-old grandson is "energy on steroids." He is constantly in motion when he is awake. Recently, I was tapped to babysit while my wife, his grandma, was on a brief visit to South Carolina. I should have known that I would be undermanned; nonetheless, I accepted the challenge since we hadn't seen him in a while. His dad warned me that he had made significant strides in his mobility and that he was very fond of climbing over, into, and around things. I was in for a pleasant surprise when his parents pulled away from our driveway. Having slept during his voyage to our home, my grandson was well rested and ready for mischief.

LaShawn soon began his curious exploration. He was always one step ahead of me. Once in the kitchen, he pulled open the oven's lower drawer and began emptying it of its pots and pans. Having foiled his plan, he moved to the living room, where he flipped off the TV, blacking out everything. How did he know the correct Off button? It was intuition. While I was fiddling at damage control, he was already climbing into his feeding chair, which was something beyond his ability on a prior visit. He enjoyed repeating the parts of his adventure that brought him the most fun. While he was cranking up his activity, I was gradually being worn out.

Offering him food treats provided only temporary relief; I began wishing I had another pair of eyes on this child to relieve me. It was getting close to midnight, and young LaShawn was showing no sign of weariness. I scooped him up and headed for the bedroom, hoping the youngster would get the message and tone down his activity. Once on the bed, he began jumping while watching his image on a large closet mirror. I turned off the lights, hoping diminished vision would do the trick in slowing him down. It did not work. The TV provided some entertainment for me, but I shut it off since the little guy was getting comfortable watching TV. After the TV went silent, to my utter horror and amazement, the child began flipping over and doing somersaults in bed. I was close to a meltdown when, finally, he began showing signs of restfulness at about twelve thirty. I began gently rubbing his back, and slowly, he drifted into slumber. Relief came to me shortly afterward. In like manner, I succumbed to what was left of the night.

My grandson's foray is typical of what we all once were, bundles of energy. Moreover, the experience of my grandson speaks of the love, patience, devotion, and tolerance of mothers. Most of all, it gives us fresh insight into the patience, long-suffering, and love of our heavenly Father, who watches over us every day with his great love. Don't we bumble and stumble as we walk through life? "The Lord is merciful and gracious, slow to anger, and abounding in mercy. He will not always strive with us, nor will He keep His anger forever. He has not dealt with us according to our sins, nor punished us according to our iniquities. For as the heavens are high above the earth, so great is His mercy towards those who fear Him. As far as the East is from the West so far has He removed our transgressions from us" (Ps. 103:8–12). My grandson's antics have revealed to me how God views our antics and how patient he must be with us, his earthborn children.

January 18

Thinking of Quitting?

He that endures unto the end the same shall be saved.
—Matthew 24:13

He was born in abject poverty, and in spite of the incredible odds, with sheer guts and hard work, he clawed his way to the White House and the presidency.

In 1816 His family was forced out of their home. He had
to work to support them. In 1818 his mother died. In 1831 he
failed in business. In 1832 he ran for state legislature and lost.
He also lost his job. He wanted to go to law school but couldn't
get in. In 1833 he borrowed some money from a friend to begin
a business and by the end of the year he was bankrupt. He spent
the next 17 years of his life paying off this debt. In 1834 he ran
for state legislature again and won. In 1835 he was engaged to
be married, but his sweetheart died and his heart was broken. In
1836 he had a nervous breakdown and was in bed for six months.
In 1838 he sought to become speaker of the state legislature
and was defeated. In 1840 he sought to become an elector and
was defeated. In 1843 he ran for Congress and lost. He ran for
Congress again in 1846 and this time he won, went to Washington
and did a good job. In 1848 he ran for reelection to Congress
and lost. In 1849 he sought the job of land officer in his home
state, but was rejected. In 1854 he ran for Senate of the United
States and lost. In 1856 he sought the Vice–President nomination
at his party's national convention but got less than 100 votes. In
1858 he ran for U.S. Senate again and again he lost. In 1860 he
was elected president of the United States. (www.snopes.com/
glurge/lincoln.asp)

With this impressive string of defeats, a lesser man would have given up on
the attainment of political office but not Abe; he just kept his eyes on the prize
and moved on. Don't even think about quitting. You shouldn't. The stakes are
too high. There are souls to be saved, habits to overcome, battles to win, exams to
annihilate, mountains to climb, and rivers to cross. How can anyone think about
quitting? In hindsight, no one really cares how many times Old Abe lost or failed
at politics. What's most important is that he won the one that really mattered, the
big prize—the presidency of the United States. We should garner much strength
and inspiration from the dogged determination of Old Abe. Quitting was simply
not part of Abe's DNA, and because of his unrelenting determination, his bust is
etched in stone on Mount Rushmore among the other greats of the nation.

While some believers in biblical times have walked the straight path of integrity,
others have struggled mightily, but this is no reason for despair. "For a righteous
man may fall seven times and rise again, but the wicked shall fall by calamity" (Prov.
24:16). It matters not how many times we stumble and fail at moral uprightness;
when we fall, we must get up and prostrate ourselves at the feet of the loving and sin-
forgiving Savior. We know how the saga of sin will end; we will win because Christ
won. He defeated his rival, Satan, at Calvary. And because of Christ's great victory,
we can confidently exclaim, "I have been crucified with Christ; it is no longer I who
live, but Christ lives in me; and the life which I now live in the flesh I live by the faith
in the Son of God, who loved me and gave Himself for me" (Gal. 2:20).

The weakest of us can latch on to Christ's strength and overcome anything by
his great strength. "And they overcame him by the blood of the lamb and by the

word of their testimony, and they loved not their lives to the death" (Rev. 12:11). We shall overcome. When I am tempted to give up, I will remember it is Christ who strengthens me. Amen.

January 19

I Came, I Saw, I Conquered Part 1

I am He who lives, and was dead, and behold, I am alive for evermore. Amen. And I have the keys of Hades and of Death.

—Revelation 1:18

He burned down the gates of his enemies, humbled kings, and brought them back to Rome in chains. In describing the conquest of Pharnaces II of Pontus, Plutarch recorded Caesar saying to a friend, "I came, I saw, I conquered." The historian was being modest in his observation of Caesar since no one conquers the world without first defeating their enemies on their home soil, mastering the elements, and turning disadvantages into advantages. Caesar fought in all kinds of weather situations and under every condition favorable to his enemies and prevailed against them through his ingenuity. He built bridges to get to his enemies and destroyed them to his advantage. With his enemies defeated and would-be aspirants subdued, he returned to Rome to claim the wreath (crown) (www.venividivici.ch/julius_caesar.htm).

Like any successful conqueror, Jesus came, saw, and conquered a more insidious enemy—sin. "And she will bring forth a Son, and you shall call His name Jesus, for He will save His people from their sins. . . Behold a virgin shall be with child, and bear a Son, and they shall call His name Immanuel, which is translated, God with us" (Matt. 1:21, 23). Jesus's birth signaled his entry into our turbulent human family. He developed as any normal child of humanity would; he cried when wet, was very hard on his mom when he was hungry, and developed as a teenager facing all the pressures of the turbulent teen years and did not succumb to sin by one iota. At thirty, he entered his public ministry and in earnest began waging war on the kingdom of Satan.

Jesus saw the burden that sin had inflicted on humanity and shouldered the task of alleviating man's need. "And when Jesus went out He saw a great multitude; and He was moved with compassion for them and healed their sick" (Matt. 14:14). He rolled up his sleeve and started his mission of restoring the image of God in man. He taught by precept and example that God desires our good, while Satan oppresses and destroys lives. He was moved with compassion and restored the deceased to their grieving families. Whenever he saw suffering, he was moved to alleviate it. Is it any wonder he was called the friend of sinners, a title that sets him apart from other religious leaders?

After his death, the angel said to the disciples, "Do not be alarmed. You seek Jesus of Nazareth, who was crucified. He is risen! He is not here. See the place where they laid Him" (Mark 16:6). The resurrection of Jesus Christ sounded the death knell to Satan's kingdom. By his death, Jesus conquered death and sin, and a date was set for Satan's execution. No longer could Satan point an accusing finger at God because the evidence pointed to him as a criminal. The fact that he was the mastermind behind the death of the innocent Jesus was positive proof that he was indeed a "murderer from the beginning and abode not in the truth" (John 8:44).

Christ conquered where Adam failed and met the just requirements of God's law. He proved that God can pardon the sinner and be just at the same time because sin was punished in Jesus Christ. "For He made Him who knew no sin to be sin for us, that we might become the righteousness of God in Him" (2 Cor. 5:21). Jesus came, he saw, and he conquered. How about you? Are you conquering sin in your life? You can in Christ.

January 20

I Came, I Saw, I Conquered Part 2

Having disarmed principalities and powers, He made a public spectacle of them, triumphing over them in it.

—Colossians 2:15

Snake charmers fool the gullible with their hypnotizing craft. What you see, hear, or know might not necessarily be the whole truth; it must be compared with indisputable evidence and irrefutable facts. Some charmers cruelly extract the cobra's lethal fangs and fool us into believing the snake is deadly. Could this indeed be a form of cruel and unusual punishment to the cobra, which needs its fangs to hunt and defend itself in the wild? The fact that the snake is defanged allows the charmer to perform his craft with little or no danger to himself, but this is no trick; sin and Satan have been defanged by Jesus's death at Calvary.

"O death where is your sting? O grave where is your victory? The sting of death is sin, and the strength of sin is the law. But thanks be to God, who gives us the victory through our Lord Jesus Christ" (1 Cor. 15:55–57). By virtue of Christ's sinless life, death, and resurrection, he not only paid the price for the transgression of man's sins, meeting the just requirements of God's broken law, but he also brought the reign of sin, death, and Satan to a successful conclusion. In his conquest of sin, he received the keys to unlock the grave and empty it of all its prisoners. Everyone resurrected in both the Old and New Testaments were raised because of Christ's successful victory over sin. Jesus had to live a sinless life under the same conditions where Adam failed. And God had to be satisfied that he met the just requirements of the law and endorsed his conquest as fair and just.

Jesus defeated Satan on his home turf, planet Earth, where Adam failed. He conquered sin, death, and Satan in the garden where Adam stumbled. He gained victory over appetite, something disastrous to Adam but victorious to Christ (Matt.

4:3–4). Because he died a substitutionary death for sinners, we have unlimited access to God.

We noticed in yesterday's reading that a world-class conqueror must master the elements to achieve world dominion. He must plow through snow, drought, wind, and rain to attain his goal. Jesus did all of the above and more; even the elements were subject to his will. "So the men marveled, saying, who can this be, that even the winds and the sea obey Him?" (Matt. 8:27). Demonstrating his mastery over the elements, he not only proved his lordship over nature but he also solidified the faith of his terror-stricken disciples in him.

Something every military genius had to do in conquering the world was to turn disadvantages into advantages, and Jesus did this throughout his ministry by giving hope to the disenfranchised and marginalized. It was his delight to select the most horrible cases of human suffering and release people from their burdens (John 5:5–8). We all have been disadvantaged by sin. Some have been robbed of health, sanity, morality, and peace, but thank God because all that which was lost through the first Adam was restored by the second Adam and with greater dividends (1 Cor. 15:22). Have you taken advantage of what has been restored in Christ for your salvation? Forgiveness, grace, peace, joy, and temperance are yours to keep, and there is much more that we are not even aware of. Go out there and conquer the world for Christ. Be a conqueror of bad, naughty habits also.

January 21

The Keys

I am He who lives, and was dead and behold, I am alive for evermore. Amen. And I have the keys of Hades and of Death.

—Revelation 1:18

My grandson, who recently learned to use his legs, is fascinated by keys. He has already developed the uncanny ability to differentiate between his toy keys and his dad's real keys. He has already figured out that his toy keys get him nowhere, but his dad's keys are able to start the engine and unleash the horses of his Nissan Rogue. Only one and a half years old and unable to reach the doorknob, he grabs his dad's keys and drags him to the door. Once at the door, he looks intently at the doorknob and lets out a scream. He yearns to be released from the boredom of the living room to more interesting things on the outside. Keys are both a symbol of power and ownership, and nowhere is this recognized more than in Jesus's postresurrection declaration.

"I am He who lives and was dead and behold I am alive for evermore. Amen. And I have the keys of Hades and Death" (Rev. 1:18). After his resurrection, the victorious Savior plundered the grave and selectively raised from its prison house some of its most prominent prisoners. This scripture passage is almost never visited but is pregnant with promise. "And behold, the veil of the temple was torn in two from top to bottom; and the earth quaked and the rocks were split, and the graves were opened and many bodies of the saints who had fallen asleep were raised; and coming out of the graves after His resurrection, they went into the holy city and appeared to many" (Matt. 27:51–53). In every age, Satan has robbed us of the brightest, the noblest, and the most aspiring. Many were taken away from us before their goals and ambition came to fruition. With impunity and without apology, Satan snatches babies from their mothers' arms, husbands from their wives, and great leaders from the communities that endear to them. He has left generations of orphans through senseless endless wars and conflagrations. Now for the first time and after many generations, a Key (Jesus) has been found that will unlock the graves and set its prisoners free and certify Satan's doom.

"Behold I tell you a mystery: We shall not all sleep, but we shall all be changed—in a moment, in the twinkling of an eye, at the last trumpet for the trumpet will sound, and the dead will be raised incorruptible, and we shall be changed . . . So when this corruptible has put on incorruption, and this mortal has put on immortality, then shall be brought to pass the saying that is written: Death is swallowed up in victory. O death where is your sting? O Hades, where is your victory?" (1 Cor. 15:51–52, 54–55). This bold assertion can only be made by the trusting child of God. The child of God faces death with the confidence of a resurrected brand-new body like that of Jesus postresurrection. Do you have Jesus, the Pearl of great price, abiding in your heart? If not, why not? Pray with me. Dear Jesus, I invite you into my heart and life. Please forgive me for my sins and save me today. Amen.

January 22

Changing Things Around

Go therefore and make disciples of all nations, baptizing them in the name of the Father and the Son and of the Holy Spirit. Teaching them to observe all things that I have commanded you.

—Matthew 28:19–20

Meet the cleaning crew of Mzima Springs in Kenya, Africa. They are tough, thorough, meticulous, and efficient. Their next customer is a king—the dominant alpha bull hippo, who sports many battle scars to prove his status at the top of his clan. He has arrived early for a complete health manicure and spa. Being submerged, he stretches himself at full length, all nine feet of his huge frame; he raises his tail, gapes his jaws wide open, and allows the little guys to go to work. The cleaners (small cleaning fish) immediately go to work, dislodging pests, dead skin, and parasites from difficult and hard-to-reach places. A dental and gum inspection is all part of the health package. Sensing relief and free from the pesky parasites that plague plain creatures, the hippo lets out a wide yawn, expressing his approval for a job well done (*National Geographic*).

The rebellion of Lucifer brought undesirable change to our planet, which affected Adam and his children. This evil angel vowed to destroy all God's creation, and planet Earth became his chief priority. Ever since, he has been very busy breaking up homes, inciting wars, inflicting pain, instigating mistrust among brethren, and causing bloody revolutions, hatred, and confusion. He delights in destroying the young and vulnerable before they reach their true potential. His weapons of choice include war, drugs, alcohol, sex, and politics, but his real trump card is racism. It has worked well for him over the centuries, causing division and hatred among people, families, and nations.

Like the cleaning fish of the Mzima Springs, we have been tasked by Jesus to clean up the wounds of the bruised and afflicted. But how is this to be done? The Word of God is absolutely clear on this subject: "Go therefore and make disciples of all the nations, baptizing them in the name of the Father, the Son and of the Holy Spirit" (Matt. 28:19). The amazing thing about this command is our Lord tells us precisely how this task is supposed to be done. Ellen White, my favorite author, adds this comment, and I am paraphrasing: "Our Savior's method will bring the best outcome. The Savior mingled with the people. He empathized with them, supplied their needs, and then bade them to follow him" (*Ministry of Healing*, p. 143).

The great Martin Luther King referred to the poor as "the invisible poor." Why are they invisible? Is it because we ignore them and pretend they do not exist? But they do exist. We are supposed to see them. Stop avoiding them. Attend to their needs. Visit them in prison, and love them into the kingdom of God. Our Lord reminds us in this parable: "Assuredly, I say to you, inasmuch as you have done it to the least of these you did it to Me" (Matt. 25:45). We simply can't afford to ignore the poor any longer. We must be the hands, feet, and mouthpieces of Jesus in helping clean up our brothers and sisters degraded by sin. I was once in the gutter, bruised, and battered by sin until God rescued me. Did he rescue you at some point? Think about making a difference in the life of one disadvantaged person today. You'll truly feel the happiness of Francis of Assisi and Mother Teresa.

January 23

Staying in Formation

Not forsaking the assembling of ourselves together, as is the manner of some, but exhorting one another, and so much the more as you see the day approaching.
—Hebrews 10:25

If you live in the northeastern part of the United States, you've seen them before. Whenever these noisy neighbors take to the air, they quickly form a tight V formation. There are several benefits to be gained from maintaining this rigid discipline. They benefit from synergy. (The sum of the whole is greater than the individual part.) Mother Nature equips these geese to feed off the energy of one another while in flight, thus rewarding the flock with a longer flying range, something that would not have been possible by any individual bird. There is no problem if the leader tires; he just rotates to the rear while the closest bird takes over leadership. While in flight, these geese constantly quack, encouraging and affirming the tired, the young, and the fainthearted. This flying formation allows the Canada geese to migrate and proliferate successfully all over North America. Are there lessons to be learned from our feathery friends? Of course.

Even though our eyes are set on the prize—Jesus's Second Coming—we often squabble, fuss, and pick fights over nonessentials. Trivial squabbles that should have been resolved decades ago are still plaguing our spiritual growth. Oh, how I wish we were single-minded in our kingdom preparation, but alas, the church is plagued from within and without by spiritual and social maladies. Despite the church's apparent malaise, Paul reminds us that we are to exhort and encourage one another as we see the nearness of Christ's Second Coming. "Not forsaking the assembling of ourselves as some commonly do" (Heb. 10:25). Even though we are witnessing the unprecedented fulfillment of the Bible prophecy, there seems to be marked decline in our spirituality and church service attendance.

A recent survey revealed disappointing volunteer Bible study among evangelical Christians but most notably among Seventh-Day Adventists. That was a real eye-opener. The majority of us do not study our Bibles consistently every day. Need I reiterate that holy men paid the ultimate price translating the Bible from its original language to our modern languages? If they were still with us, would they not recoil in horror at our apparent lack of appreciation for their great sacrifice?

I encourage you, dear friend, to open the precious book at any given opportunity and allow God to speak to you through his Word. God has not changed his method of growing us in the faith: "As newborn babes, desire the pure milk of the word that you may grow thereby" (1 Pet. 2:2). The believer's growth is achieved only by hearing and receiving the Word of God. Jesus has other means of upholding the illiterate and those without the written word. But for those with several Bibles at home, the notion of not studying the Bible is inexcusable and unacceptable. It's comparable to starving oneself voluntarily. "Be diligent to present yourself approved to God, a worker who does not need to be ashamed, rightly dividing the word of truth" (2 Tim. 2:15). Lord, please help me and this reader avail ourselves of you and your Word today. Amen.

January 24

Forgiving My Enemies?

But I say to you, love your enemies, bless those who curse you, do good to those who hate you, and pray for those who spitefully use you and persecute you.

—Matthew 5:44

Harsh voices shattered the quiet peace on a Haarlem street in Holland. The gestapo commander ended his surveillance of Casper ten Boom's home. He had secretly observed all the visitors and activities in the home that day. He was ready as a bird of prey to swoop in and make his arrest. Corrie ten Boom and her family and friends, along with visitors and guests, were all arrested, carted away, and sent to various concentration camps, where most of them perished (https://www.ushmm.org/wic/mobile/en/article.php?moduleld=10006914).

Adolf Hitler, chancellor of Germany, was on a mad campaign of rounding up Jews all over Europe to be exterminated in gas chambers. Meanwhile, the Boom family was fully employed sheltering Jews from extermination, and that was a capital offense punishable by death. Unfortunately, they were betrayed, and all perished with the exception of Corrie, who was spared the death chamber by a clerical error. True to her faith in Jesus, Corrie freely confessed and proclaimed Christ to whoever would listen, even to her tormentors.

After the war, she received numerous awards for her outstanding bravery and work in saving Jews. She traveled worldwide, spreading the gospel of forgiveness and tolerance. One day while conducting a tour at the concentration camp where she was kept prisoner, she recognized a familiar face in the crowd. A prison guard who was instrumental in the demise of her family was there, and he recognized her also. Was he deserving of her forgiveness?

The scripture is replete with examples of painful family tragedies that warranted retaliation but were met with gracious forgiveness by the victim. Joseph forgave his brothers and repaid them with good for their evil (Gen. 50:15–20). Jephthah forgave his brothers and the elders of Gilead for their mistreatment toward him (Judg. 11:7–11). David freely forgave Saul for attempting to murder him on numerous occasions (1 Sam. 26:20–24). Jesus, our Lord and Savior, while being brutally tortured by the very people he came to save, uttered these eternal words: "Father forgive them for they know not what they do" (Luke 23:34). Being our example in everything, Jesus suffered and died for our sin and sinners of all time. He calls on us to do the same by forgiving those who assault us, assassinate our character, and infringe on our rights.

Being human, Corrie recalled all the painful memories and hesitated. She froze and shivered as she remembered the terrible days at the concentration camp, but something jolted her forward, and she grasped the outstretched hand of her former tormentor, now a believer himself (James Dobson, *When God Doesn't Make Sense*). The love of Christ absolutely conquers hatred. Is there someone who has tormented you, violated your body, assaulted your character, and insulted your integrity? If such a person who has robbed you of your peace of mind exists, I invite you to lay that person at the feet of Jesus, and you will have much-needed peace. Hate will consume the lives of those who harbor it. "Love your enemies, bless those who curse you, do good to those who spitefully use you and persecute you that you may be sons of your Father in heaven" (Matt. 5:44–45).

How Big Is Your Closet?

Two things I request of You. Remove falsehood and lies far from me;
Give me neither poverty nor wealth; Feed me with the food allotted to me;
lest I be full and deny You, and say, who is the Lord?
Or lest I be poor and steal, and profane the name of my God.

—Proverbs 30:7–9

The psychologists who swear allegiance to the food industry have devised clever methods to make us spend more money than we really want to. Television commercials are creatively doctored to convince us that we need everything they recommend. We even take loans for vacations at the request of these smooth-talking snake oil salesmen. Their doctrine, which retail and department stores have adopted and implemented with great success, has given rise to generations of superconsumers. The store owners strategically pack milk and other breakfast staples at the very last aisle of the store. You must walk the entire length of the store just to get a loaf of bread. Is this mere coincidence or a strategic plan to empty our wallets? Also, to squeeze the last cent from our pockets, the checkout counters are loaded with eye-popping gossip magazine and tasty sweet treats just within reach of goggle-eyed kids. Sweet, soft, and mellow music entertain shoppers, creating an environment that makes shopping pleasurable and relaxing. Eager, smiling, and helpful attendants are virtually everywhere, offering their services to transport your merchandize to your car. They even personalize their use of the product, dispelling all our doubts about its reliability. The attendants seem to have all the answers to our problems. Do they really, or are they after your dollars?

Recent statistics reveal Americans owe a staggering amount of debt. The average credit card debt per person is $16,748. The average mortgage debt is $176,222. The average student loan per person stands at $49,905. The total American consumer debt is a whopping $12.58 trillion (https://www.nerdwallet.com/blog/credit-card-data). Are we beginning to see how the wool is being pulled over our eyes by corporate America? I must admit candidly that I am still in debt; however, I have embraced a rigid, realistic plan that will make me debt-free in about two years. Do you have a plan for your financial freedom? Bear in mind that "the borrower is servant to the lender" (Prov. 22:7). Have you realized we spend too much on things we don't need? Get yourself a reality check; take a look at the size of your wardrobe and your shoe stack. Do you wear all what's in there? Besides the snow shovel and the other necessary tools, do you need all the other expensive accessories? Probably not.

A word of advice from the wealthiest man who ever existed is still relevant today: "Give me neither poverty nor wealth; feed me with the food allotted to me" (Prov. 30:8). In modern-day vernacular, Solomon articulates, "Give me only what I need, Lord." If we do not need the exquisitely huge closet, the elaborate, fancy kitchen, the expensive toys, and the state-of-the-art automobile, why don't we accumulate the proceeds and donate it to the Red Cross, 3ABN, Adventist World Radio, or the Salvation Army? Some of these organizations are evangelistic Christian electronic networks that spread the gospel of Jesus Christ globally. Can we, in all honesty, live with less of the clutter that chokes our spiritual walk with Christ? Can we? Oh yes, we can by God's grace.

January 26

Marriage—What Is It?

Woe to those who call evil good, and good evil; who put darkness for light, and light for darkness, who put bitter for sweet and sweet for bitter!

—Isaiah 5:20

The nation's highest court has spoken. They have just invalidated the 1996 Defense of Marriage Act (DOMA) and have rendered it unconstitutional. DOMA, which empowered states against recognizing same-sex marriage, has been ruled unconstitutional by the Supreme Court. Have they given the green light to same-sex marriage? Polls taken by various organizations have discovered a seismic shift among Americans on the institution of marriage. This shift was facilitated by the Supreme Court's landmark decision on marriage. Five of the nine distinguished jurists on the Supreme Court found DOMA unconstitutional. What repercussion will their decision have on our biblical definition of *marriage*?

The Bible makes it abundantly clear that marriage was instituted by God and is a union entered into by members of the opposite sex (Gen. 2:24). Jesus further elaborated on this issue with this statement: "But from the beginning of the creation, God made them male and female. For this reason a man shall leave his father and mother and be joined to his wife, and the two shall become one flesh; so then they are no longer two, but one flesh" (Mark 10:6–8). Marriage is a sacred institution given by God to mankind for the following reasons: procreation, companionship, family cohesiveness, harmony, unity, and social stability. And it is symbolic of his intimate relationship with his people.

Who then should get married? From the early dawn of human civilization, this principle has been unequivocally clear: marriage is and should be between consenting male and female adults. "Then the rib which the Lord God had taken from man He made a woman, and He brought her to the man, And Adam said this is now bone of my bones and flesh of my flesh; she shall be called Woman because she was taken out of a man" (Gen. 2:22–23). Man and woman should approach marriage from different and separate genders to be joined together by mutual agreement to love and care for each other till death. There is no doubt about the distinctiveness of the two persons; the Genesis account states they are different in gender for a purpose. The female anatomy was designed by the all-wise Creator to bear and nurse children, while the male—by virtue of his muscular frame and superior strength—was the provider, protector, and leader of his family.

Times and social mores are constantly changing, but God's Word is firm, decisive, irrevocable, and unchangeable. The Ten Commandments, the fabric on which every human law originates, are not subject to amendments or human tinkering. God's law cannot be improved on because it is perfect, and it is the foundation on which his government is built. "Righteousness and justice are the foundation of your throne. Mercy and truth go before your face" (Ps. 89:14).

Even though ethics, social mores, laws, and morals are crumbling before us, we are called on to uphold the bloodstained banner of our Prince, Immanuel. "Heaven and earth will pass away, but My words will by no means pass away" (Matt. 24:35). We are called on to uphold the truth, even though the heavens fall apart. "And we ought to obey God rather than man" (Acts 5:29).

January 27

One More Chance

But he answered and said to him; sir let it alone this year also, until I dig around it and fertilize it. And if it bears fruit, well. But if not, after that you can cut it down.
—Luke 13:8–9

The young girls were grinning with excitement as they raced toward their dancing partners. For many months, they had dreamed of this special moment, and it had finally come at last. On the waiting end of this special moment were their prison dads, men who had made serious mistakes in their lives. They were incarcerated for various crimes, ranging from drug distribution to armed robbery. Dressed in gorgeous three-piece suits with bow ties and shiny black shoes, these prisoners danced themselves back into their daughters' hearts and lives. One emotional inmate who was serving time for distribution of drugs confessed, "I thought I needed material things to make my daughter happy when what I needed was right in front of my face." All the inmates who experienced this moving moment with their daughters swore upon release never to return to this horrible place. Special thanks to the kindhearted folks who labored behind the scene for showing us how much we owe our daughters and for giving these fine gentlemen another chance at fatherhood (www.npr.org/2014/04/25/301828303/a-father-daughter-dance-in-prison).

This event, put together by many people and with much planning, gives us a little insight into the magnanimity of the God we serve. How deserving are we to be afforded a place at the Master's table? We are not at all deserving, yet he has called us friends. "You are My friends If you do whatever I command you. No longer do I call you servants, for a servant does not know what his master is doing; but I have called you friends, for all things that I heard from My Father I have made known to you" (John 15:14–15).

The centurion speaks eloquently for us all: "Lord, do not trouble Yourself, for I am not worthy that You should enter under my roof. Therefore I did not think myself worthy to come to You. But say the word, and my servant will be healed"

(Luke 7:6–7). Maybe it hasn't dawned on us yet how insignificant we are in God's eyes, but amazingly, we are the object of his love. And it is not because of who we are but because of who he is. Tiny Earth—a speck in the universe, the smallest of the planets in our solar system—has become the object of God's love and attention. "When I consider Your heavens, the works of Your fingers, the Moon and the stars, which You have ordained, what is man that You are mindful of him, and the son of man that You visit him" (Ps. 8:3–4).

The fact that God has placed value and esteem on the rebels of Earth is indicative of his great love. "The Lord is merciful and gracious, slow to anger, and abounding in mercy. He will not always strive with us, nor will He keep His anger forever. He has not dealt with us according to our sins, nor punished us according to our iniquities. For as the heavens are high above the earth, so great is His mercy towards those who fear Him; As far as the East is from the West, so far has He removed our transgressions from us. As a father pities his children, so the Lord pities those who fear Him" (Ps. 103:8–13).

We are without excuse if we despise the grace of our loving God. Do you despise the riches of his goodness, not knowing that the goodness of God leads you to repentance? (Rom. 2:4). God simply wants us to be with him in heaven and is giving us multiple chances and opportunities to make it there.

January 28

On Holy Ground

Then He said, do not draw near this place, take your sandals off your feet, for the place where you stand is holy ground.

—Exodus 3:5

The bush erupted in flames but was not consumed. Moses stood transfixed by this amazing sight. Of course, being a shepherd, he was used to seeing lightning bolts ignite clusters of dry bush in the wilderness; but unlike other bushes, this one was different because the fire did not consume its host. Moses's curiosity got the better part of him, and he decided to take a peek, and from the bush, he heard the voice of God: "Take your sandals off your feet, for the place where you stand is holy ground" (Exod. 3:5).

The throne room of God gives us the closest insight into his holiness. "In the year King Uzziah died, I saw the Lord sitting on a throne, high and lifted up, and the train of His robe filled the temple. Above it stood seraphim; each one had six wings: with two he covered his face, with two he covered feet and with two he flew. And one cried to another and said: Holy, Holy, Holy, is the Lord of host; the whole earth is full of His glory" (Isa. 6:1–3).

God's throne room is saturated with glory and majesty, and that glory illuminates everything that is close to him. His glory is brighter than ten thousand noonday suns; Moses's face had to be veiled after his encounter with the Almighty on Mount Sinai (Exod. 34:35). The angels never failed in exclaiming, as they flew back and forth, "Holy, holy, and holy is the Lord of Hosts." These holy creatures glowed in radiance in the immediate presence of the One who is altogether lovely.

John the Revelator, who was exposed to the same vision, exclaimed, "God is light and in Him there is no darkness at all" (1 John 1:5).

Because God is absolutely radiant, holy, magnificent, and wonderful, shouldn't we approach him with utmost reverence, joy, gladness, and thanksgiving? The psalmist gives us a clue. "Enter into His gates with thanksgiving and into His courts with praise. Be thankful to Him, and bless His name, for the Lord is good; His mercy is everlasting and His truth endures to all generations" (Ps. 100:4–5). When we approach God, like the angels, we must do so humbly yet conscious that he is merciful and approachable.

Praising God is a voluntary act of worship; no creature is ever coerced or forced into this exercise. Are the angels ever bored or listless in praising God? Of course not. In the presence of God, there is virtue, love, joy, happiness, life, vigor, and vitality. How could anyone be bored in the presence of the One who manufactures joy? Alas, our present sinfulness hinders our total appreciation of eternal things. What a revelation it will be on resurrection morning when the scales are lifted from our eyes! God will give us a new perspective of eternal things when the human family leads the chorus around God's throne, singing this song: "Moses the servant of God and the song of the Lamb" (Rev. 15:3). Then the angels will listen with folded wings as we sing the song of how God delivered us from sin and degradation; we will sing how you and I made it over into heaven.

To be with Jesus in heaven, we must practice holy living down here. God dwells in the temple of our hearts. Every day we must erect the family altar and worship him. Have you erected an altar for him in your heart?

January 29

Facts from Fiction

My son, if sinners entice you, do not consent . . . My son, do not walk in the way with them, keep your foot from their path.

—Proverbs 1:10, 15

Great men and women who become successful are quick to point out that their achievement is in part due to the help they have received from their father, mother, spouse, teachers, advisors, and friends. Having said that, it becomes absolutely necessary for rulers to surround themselves with advisors who will give them honest and wise counsel, regardless of how difficult the advice is to digest. However, advisors sometimes find themselves under great stress trying to speak words that must be pleasing to their king, boss, or CEO. Why would anyone want to be in disfavor with the one who signs their paycheck, have total control over their life, or is the founder of the company? The wisdom of the ages dictates, "Faithful are the wounds of a friend, but the kisses of the enemy are deceitful" (Prov. 27:6). Would you keep a doctor who hides, withholds information, or misleads you regarding the state of your health? Not even liars enjoy being lied to.

Israel's king Rehoboam had some tough political decisions to make. His kingdom was falling apart, and he needed some urgent advice to contain the spread of a revolution in his kingdom. He convened a conference of his advisors, and notably present were some old holdovers from his father's administration. But he brought along a new group of advisors about his age and asked them their opinion. Regrettably, the youthful advisors took him on the path of least resistance; they gave him a rosy picture, telling him precisely what he wanted to hear. However, the old, more experienced, and cautious advisors told him to listen to the voices of the people and redress their grievances. Tragically, and to his detriment, he chose the unwise counsel of the inexperienced young leaders and suffered the consequence he desperately sought to avoid (1 Kings 12:9–17).

In another instance of rejecting wise counsel, King Ahab of Israel and his counterpart Jehoshaphat of Judah agreed on joint military operations to recover lands stolen by Syria. They convened a hastily called conference of court prophets for advice on battle operations. Without exception, all the prophets predicted an overwhelming victory for Israel and Judah, but Jehoshaphat did not like what he heard and requested input from a prophet of God. The prophet Micah was fetched, but his message from God ran contrary to that of the other court prophets. His message was obviously rejected, and the kings went into battle. Of course, disaster ensued. King Ahab was killed in battle, and a dispirited Jehoshaphat cried mightily to God and was saved (1 Kings 22:4–9).

Life surrounds us with friends and well-wishers who are eager to advise us on matters of critical importance. How do we handle these well-intentioned advisors without offending them? Are we wise enough to seek second opinions, especially from someone much older? Maybe we should do as our Quaker friends: form a "clearness committee" of friends to help us separate facts from fiction and truth from error. When in doubt, stop and ask, "Is the Lord with me in this matter?" "My son, do not forget my law, But let your heart keep my commands; for length of days and long life and peace they will add to you" (Prov. 3:1–2). It behooves us to be acquainted with the voice of the Holy Spirit; he gives the best counsel, which amazingly is always correct and absolutely free.

January 30

Dual Citizenship Part 1

For he waited for the city which has foundation, whose builder and maker is God.
—Hebrews 11:10

Lady Liberty stands 151 feet and 1 inch tall. The pedestal on which she stands is 154 feet tall, making her 305 feet and 1 inch tall. She wears a crown with seven sharp points, symbolic of the seven oceans and seven continents from which one must navigate to get to her. In her uplifted right hand is a lit torch, beaming enlightened ideas to the world. Her left hand firmly grips a tablet of significant importance, the Declaration of Independence. Strategically located in the bay where all incoming immigrants can see her, the grand old lady stands with a somber look, beckoning the poor, rich, tired, politically oppressed, and religious exiles to her shores (www.libertyellisfoundation.org/statue-history).

They come here from every country on earth. While some come seeking refuge from repressive regimes who wish them much harm, others take shelter because their religious convictions had become odious to their rulers and society at large. And a third class, economic migrants, simply want a better future for themselves and their children. We are eternally grateful to this generous nation, which has flung its doors wide open to us. To this, we all say, "Thank you very much, America."

About four thousand years ago, another migrant was seeking a land of opportunity. Our father Abraham was searching diligently for a city that had godly foundations. He looked far and wide, and it seemed, at every turn, he met bitter disappointment and frustration. His brief stay in Egypt was a humiliating disaster when he said Sarah was his sister to protect his life from those interested in her, but God was very close to his erring prophet and kept him despite his moral failings (Gen. 12:12–19). Abraham's quest for the eternal city of God brought him to many lands, but his diligent search materialized nothing.

We look forward to a different city—one where God is the supreme ruler, a place where peace and harmony will never cease, where the sun will never set, the roses never fade, and the inhabitants will not say, "I am sick." Overpopulation, climate change, hurricanes, tornadoes, and wintry days will be a thing of the past. Loved ones from all ages will be there, as well as those who sealed their testimonies with their blood, never to see or hear from their tormentors again.

God has left no stone unturned in preparing a home for his people. "Now I saw a new earth for the first heaven and the first earth had passed away. Also there was no more sea. Then I, John saw the holy city, New Jerusalem, coming down out of heaven from God, prepared as a bride adorned for her husband. And I heard a loud voice from heaven saying, Behold, the tabernacle of God is with man, and He will dwell with them and they shall be His people. God Himself will be with them and be their God" (Rev. 21:1–3). Don't you want to be a citizen of this fair country? I look forward to this place. How about you? If you desire to be there where the Savior is now preparing mansions for his people, pray this prayer with me: Lord, please forgive me for my sins, save me from this evil world, and prepare me for your kingdom. Amen.

January 31

Dual Citizen Part 2

But now they desire a better, that is, a heavenly country. Therefore God is not ashamed to be called their God, for He has prepared a city for them.

—Hebrews 11:16

The anxious appointments, tedious correspondence, and agonizing wait were behind him; Gabriel's (that's me) citizenship dream was becoming a reality. He was informed by mail to meet with immigration officials regarding his citizenship request. His big moment was here at last. He was up before the birds, checking out his commute route for any traffic hiccups. To secure parking, he headed out two hours in advance of his appointment. Fortunately, the procedure went very well, better than expected. The once-dreaded immigration officials actually smiled and became friendly after all. It was all over after a brief quiz on the history of the United States. With oath administered and photos taken, Gabriel became a brand-new citizen, but here's the sweetest part—his green card (identity card), always in his wallet, was shredded, not needed anymore.

Natural-born citizens may not fully appreciate the exhilaration wrapped up in this moment. Now new citizens can actually vote and fully participate in local, regional, and national affairs. They can travel without any hassles. They are no longer aliens, outsiders, or strangers but full-fledged citizens with all the rights and privileges of a member of the USA.

However, nothing here on earth is comparable to heavenly citizenship. Upon accepting Jesus as Savior and Lord, the believer instantly transitions from sinner to saint and becomes a citizen of the kingdom of God: "Now therefore, you are no longer strangers and foreigners, but fellow citizen with the saints and members of the household of God" (Eph. 2:19). What an awesome and wonderful feeling to be called a child of the King! God is beaming with delight and stands ready to welcome anyone who turns to him from sin to a life of righteousness. "But the father said to his servants, bring out the best robe and put it on him, and put a ring on his hand and sandals on his feet, and bring the fatted calf here and kill it, and let us eat and be merry; for this my son was dead and is alive again; he was lost and is found and they began to be merry" (Luke 15:22–24).

There is no joy on earth comparable to life in Jesus Christ. Toys fade away and lose their luster; even our best tasting foods lose their savor and become unappetizing in time, but the joy of the believer is renewed daily and never fades away. "But you are a chosen generation, a royal priesthood, a holy nation, His own special people, that you may proclaim the praises of Him who called you out of darkness into His marvelous light; who once were not a people but are now the people of God" (1 Pet. 2:9–10).

Is there a greater privilege than to be a citizen of the richest, greatest, and most freedom-loving nation on earth? Yes. Our heavenly citizenship is first and foremost, and it takes priority over all earthly attainments. And if we live only for this life, then "we are of all men the most miserable" (1 Cor. 15:19). Everything materialistic around us will fade away. Only one thing won't fade away—the things done in faith for Jesus.

While it is nice to belong to this great nation, it is much more important to be a citizen of the heavenly land where God is King and where everlasting joy, peace, health, and life are the order of the day. Have you filed your request for citizenship yet? Have you accepted Jesus as the Savior and Lord of your life? Great.

February 1

Dual Citizenship Part 3

But as it is written: eye has not seen, nor ear heard, nor have entered into the heart of man the things which God has prepared for those who love Him.
—1 Corinthians 2:9

My wife and I love to travel, and she becomes like a kid in a candy store especially when traveling to foreign countries. On our first trip to Europe, we buzzed past the Versailles Palace and walked where Marie Antoinette and Napoleon took their evening strolls and met their demise. We posed for photos under the Eiffel Tower, a wonder of the modern era. Germany was particularly interesting with its towering cathedrals, magnificent autobahns, and squeaky-clean train stations. Britain, our point of entry and temporary home, was simply majestic with its rustic old castles (dating back to antiquity), bustling cities, and lush green countryside. The friendliness of Europeans touched our souls to the core; we were in paradise (so we thought).

But wait. No place on earth, however beautiful, is comparable to what John saw on the isle of Patmos. "And he carried me away in the Spirit to a great and high mountain, and showed me the great city, the holy Jerusalem, descending out of heaven from God, having the glory of God. Her light was like a most precious stone, like a jasper stone, clear as crystal" (Rev. 21:10–11). This is your future home, and it absolutely defies human description. John described the city as similar to the design of his era with gates and walls, but should we put a limit on God's artistic creativity and the surprise he has in store for his children? "The twelve gates were twelve pearls; each individual gate was of one pearl. And the street of the city was pure gold, like transparent glass" (Rev. 21:21). But wait a minute, aren't the golden streets and gorgeous foundation the main feature? "But I saw no temple in it, for the Lord God Almighty is its temple. The city had no need of the sun or of the moon to shine in it, for the glory of God illuminated it. The lamb is the light" (Rev. 21:22–23). This is our future home, people, and it is as real as tomorrow's sunlight. Go ahead and imagine yourself already in your future home. Would you prefer, like Rahab, to live on the high wall to view the countryside and see who's coming in and going out? Nothing wrong with that. After all, we will be in a sinless environment.

However, before the reward of the saints can be materialized, Jesus must come to rescue us from this sin-cursed planet. And that time of deliverance is near at hand. We can almost hear the Father saying, "Gather My saints together to Me, those who have made a covenant with Me by sacrifice" (Ps. 50:5). The writer of Hebrews shares this sentiment. "But now they desire a better, that is, a heavenly country. Therefore God is not ashamed to be called their God, for He has prepared a city for them" (Heb. 11:16).

And that's the precise reason for Christ's Second Coming, to bring his people home to live eternally with him. Has it dawned on you that Jesus is coming very, very soon? Real soon. The signs of the end foretold by the prophets are being fulfilled with rapid frequency and accuracy. Have you made your calling and election sure? Have you invited Jesus into your heart to live for him daily? "Behold, I stand at the door and knock. If anyone hears My voice and opens the door, I will come in to him and dine with him, and he with Me" (Rev. 3:20). Lord, use my heart, my life, my all and do with me according to your purpose. Amen.

February 2

The Eagle Has Landed!

Therefore the Lord himself will give you a sign; Behold, the virgin shall conceive and bear a Son, and shall call His name Immanuel.

—Isaiah 7:14

On July 20, 1969, three brave Americans changed the world as they set foot on a neighboring planet. The world held its breath as Apollo 11 (the *Eagle*), with a crew of three, descended on the Sea of Tranquility on the moon. A beaming president relaxed in his chair at the White House as he watched with pride the American flag being pounded into the moon's surface. Man had conquered a new frontier, and Kennedy's daring campaign pledge to put humans on the moon paid great dividends by completely revolutionizing the world.

In the quiet little town of Bethlehem, a different revolution was unfolding in Manger Square. A baby boy was born to a virgin girl, but he was no ordinary baby. He was the King of the universe: "But you, Bethlehem, Ephrata, though you are little among the thousands of Judah, yet out of you shall come forth to me the One to be ruler in Israel, whose goings forth are from of old, from everlasting" (Mic. 5:2). The King landed on our planet and made his abode with men. He quickly went to work in restoring the disfigured image of God in mankind. Relieving physical pain by miraculous healing was the gateway to man's great spiritual need, and he pursued this mission with relentless passion. An irresistible power drove him to human need and tragedy. He restored an only son to a grieving widow, healed a forty-year-old man paralyzed from birth, cleansed lepers, and interacted with sinners. Why was he doing this?

Adam, the father of our race, doomed our planet to sin and death by his disobedience to God. According to God's righteous law (the Ten Commandments), we were condemned to death. "The soul that sins shall die" (Ezek. 18:4). "For the wages of sin is death, but the gift of God is eternal life through Christ Jesus our Lord" (Rom. 6:23). Our loving Father couldn't endure the destruction of his creation; therefore he offered his only Son, part of himself, to suffer the penalty of his own law. The King and Creator of the universe came to our planet to die in our place and rescued man from the tyranny of sin and Satan. The moment he arrived, Satan was waiting, working through civil and religious leaders to thwart, derail, and destroy the plan of salvation. But Satan's gloat that man was his possession and beyond restoration was premature. The cross redeemed man back to God.

The Savior's death vindicated the just character of God and ripped the mask of hypocrisy off Satan's face by revealing, to a watching universe, the love and justice of God. In one single act, God pardoned the sinner through Christ while enduring the pain (penalty) of sin in his own body.

By virtue of Jesus's vicarious death, many Old Testament prophecies met their fulfillment in him. "Mercy and truth have met together, righteousness and peace have kissed. Truth shall spring out of the earth and righteousness shall look down from heaven" (Ps. 85:10–11). Your soul is priceless to God, and that's why Jesus died to redeem us from sin. Have you invited him in your life already?

February 3

Light Shining in Darkness

Then Jesus spoke to them again, saying, I am the light of the world. He who follows Me shall not walk in darkness, but have the light of life.

—John 8:12

A convoy of ships is being battered and jostled by the angry Atlantic. Day gives way to night without relief from the raging surf. The captain is a seasoned veteran, but his crew—a rowdy bunch of hardened criminals (granted a reprieve)—is restless and on the verge of revolt (casting him overboard). The lookout man peers through the darkness and observes a faint, flickering light. Jubilantly, he shrieks an alarm the captain and crew are desperately praying for: "A light! A light! A light! A light!" (Joaquin Miller, "Columbus").

Light is unquestionably the most precious commodity on earth. Was it not the very first item on God's Creation agenda? Can we exist without it? Light is the building block required by plants to make food. It provides warmth to us and even emboldens us to do a little extra work during the day, does it not? But many people simply do not know the true significance of light.

We learned of this funny story in grade school: A native person desperately wanted to dry his clothes, so he hung them in his tent and went outside with a large bowl, catching as much sunlight as possible, and then returned repeatedly to pour it on his clothes, hoping they would dry. Some people ignore the significance light plays in their daily life, but Jesus made it abundantly clear that he is the Light. "I am the Light of the world, he who follows Me shall not walk in darkness" (John 8:12).

For all the reasons stated above and more, Jesus is the reason why this world functions. Light is symbolic of knowledge, enlightenment, and progress. He who abides in Jesus will not walk in darkness because he is plugged into the source of all light. "You are the light of the world. A city that is set on a hill cannot be hidden" (Matt. 5:14). In the workplace, in the barbershop, in the supermarket checkout line, at the bank, in the airport lounge, and yes even on the highways, we are light bearers, and our lives must reflect this fact. Should we then seek every opportunity to point others to Jesus, the true Light? Absolutely. Are we expected to be examples to society by virtue of who we are and who we know? Failure to do just that will inevitably result in eternal ruin.

This is not a time to be timid and apologetic about who we are and who we represent. "You are My witnesses, says the Lord; and My servants whom I have chosen that you may know and believe me" (Isa. 43:10). For crying out loud, we are God's ambassadors, his representatives in this sin-infested world. And Jesus is very blunt in regard to our witness. "Let your light so shine before men, that they may see your good works and glorify your Father in heaven" (Matt. 5:16). We adamantly believe we are saved by grace and grace alone. But James makes it abundantly clear that "faith without works is dead" (James 2:17). He continues, saying, "Show me your faith without your works, and I will show you my faith by my works" (James 2:18).

Since walking in the light produces good works, the Christian's good work touches his neighbor, friend, relative, and spouse. A life dedicated to God produces lots of juicy Spirit-filled works. Are you walking in the light or still groping in darkness? Please ask Jesus to flood your path with his light today.

February 4

Mates for Life

Drink water from your own cistern, and running water from your own well.
—Proverbs 5:15

In an age where monogamy and marital purity are despised and ridiculed by the media and other liberal organizations, we can learn a few lessons from our feathered neighbors. The black vulture is a model worthy of our study for its monogamous lifestyle. Rigorous studies of this species have discovered that black vultures are uniquely monogamous in their relationship. They don't tolerate others playing around with another's mate; there is no office romance or moments of indiscretion among them. They have been observed, in some instances, attacking would-be philanderers (womanizers) in their midst. Promiscuity (illicit sexual intercourse) is not to be tolerated among clan members. While many other animal species adopt this excellent lifestyle, the black vulture remains a model of fidelity (https://www.allaboutbirds.org/guide/Black_Vulture/id).

Since the marital institution is under constant abuse and being attacked by both friendly and hostile forces, we must pause a little and highlight the virtues that make up a successful marriage. Although the landscape is littered with failed marriages, some couples have managed to have successful marriages by following sound, commonsense principles. Having pledged yourself, like the black vulture, to only one partner, here are some measures you can take to strengthen your union and keep you out of trouble. Incidentally, I write this excerpt—and I give glory to God—on June 29, our twenty-seventh wedding anniversary. Hooray! These principles have kept us faithful to each other.

1. Put Jesus at the center of your marriage and keep others out.
2. Dispose of all memorabilia of former suitors (e.g., photos, videos).
3. Stay away from salacious materials (e.g., pornography, toxic and lustful e-mail).
4. Repeatedly affirm, pray for, and compliment each other.
5. Remember anniversaries and birthdays. Apologize repeatedly if you forget.
6. Make breakfast in bed often, especially on holidays.
7. Go on vacations, if affordable.
8. Enjoy drinking from your own cistern.
9. Invent some of your own. They will stimulate your marriage.
10. Forgive each other every day.

In the natural world, young animals copy the behavior of their parents and elders. The same is true of humans. Isn't it time to pass on to the upcoming generation a healthy, stable, and exemplary marriage? The best legacy parents can hand down to their offspring is a successful marriage. Remember, we are their teachers, and they are still watching us. If you desire a mate, hopefully one of the opposite sex, that's a good thing. However, ask for a mate who loves God more than they love you, and you do the same. Ask for a godly man, not a perfect man. Pray that he will love and cherish you even as you grow old together. I wish you Godspeed with your choice.

February 5

Why Did It Happen? Part 1

The beauty of Israel is slain on your high places! How the mighty have fallen?
—2 Samuel 1:19

Barry (name changed) was a vibrant and vivacious young man with upward mobility wired in his bones. He blasted his way into his school's athletic record books. Blessed with a lean, mean, and healthy body, he gobbled up track and field but did not intend to make sports a career. He set his sights on a career in dentistry. We were delighted and already looking forward to the day when we would welcome in our ranks the first family physician. The University of North Carolina, with its impressive academic and sports history, lured him into its sporting program. He was a kid every mom would dream of having as her son.

Just one day after his enrollment, Barry went into the university bookstore to pick up his books for his classes. Tragically, he collapsed to the floor; and within minutes, he was pronounced dead—a victim of cardiomyopathy, a weakening of the heart muscle. His mom went into shock. "No, it couldn't have happened," she said with tears streaming down her cheeks. "Not to my Barry. I just dropped him on campus a few days ago." She repeated this over and over. His death was a bitter pill for us to swallow.

But families all over the world are experiencing similar tragedies every day. They perform the grim task of burying young family members who held out much promise but were denied the fulfillment of their dreams by death. Why must the icy tentacles of death rob us of the service of the very best and talented among us? Americans and people all over the world are grappling with this age-old question. Why did it happen?

Toward the end of a grinding civil war, the nation was robbed of the steady and capable hand of Abraham Lincoln. Civil rights leaders were confident that momentum and public opinion had finally swung in their favor, and then the unthinkable happened. Martin Luther King Jr. was gunned down on the porch of a motel in Tennessee, the victim of an assassin's bullet. Why all this senseless violence? Can't we all live in peace? Why should babies be robbed of their parents and parents their babies?

"Help Lord, for the godly man ceases! For the faithful disappear from among the sons of men" (Ps. 12:1). The psalmist is still in the doldrums and wonders how long God will continue to ignore his suffering. But does God really ignore the suffering of his children? "How long, O Lord? Will You forget me forever? How long will You hide Your face from me?" (Ps. 13:1). It is worth repeating that the second "how long" denotes the psalmist's sense of urgency and near desperation. But all is not lost, though, as surely as day follows night, light follows darkness, and a calm is after a storm; there is a brighter day coming.

"Behold I tell you a mystery: we shall not all sleep, but we shall all be changed, in a moment, in the twinkling of an eye, at the last trumpet. For the trumpet will sound, and the dead will be raised incorruptible, and we shall be changed" (1 Cor. 15:51–52). We may never completely understand the perplexities plaguing our lives down here; however, we look forward with eager anticipation to Christ's Second Coming, when all our doubts will be resolved and our questions answered. Are you looking forward to that great day, or do you dread that his coming might interrupt your agenda? I hope and pray the former is true. Ask Jesus to keep you faithful unto the day of his coming.

February 6

Why Did It Happen? Part 2

How the mighty have fallen! Tell it not in Gath, Proclaim it not in the streets of Ashkelon—least the daughters of the Philistines rejoice, least the daughters of the uncircumcised triumph.

—2 Samuel 1:19-20

Brushing aside his mischievous adolescence, Barry was the dream child every parent would be proud to have as a son. Being the only boy in his home, he constantly offered his help to his mom, who was operating a small business. He busied himself with cleaning chores long after the last customer left. At the funeral, his pastor spoke in glowing terms about his zeal in helping operate a homeless feeding program. His relationship with Jesus was real and deep. The young adults in his church had a big brother in Barry, who affirmed and encouraged them. His smile was warm as the morning sunlight and melted the hearts of those whom he was called on to serve. You couldn't miss him in a crowd; his great height was an easy giveaway. He was smart, sharp, affectionate, and handsome. College colleagues were equally powerless in resisting his charm offensive. At his funeral, one young lady remarked that she was swept away by his charm on the very first day of his entry into the university. What can we learn from the passing of this lovely butterfly who never had the opportunity to unfurl his majestic wings and soar on the swirling currents of the wind?

"The righteous perishes, and no man takes it to heart; Merciful men are taken away, while no one considers that the righteous are taken away from evil" (Isa. 57:1). In his misunderstanding of the saga of human suffering, Job tried to figure it out: "I will say to God, do not condemn me; show me why you contend with me; does it seem good to You that You should oppress, that You despise the work of Your hands, and smile on the counsel of the wicked?" (Job 10:2–3). Oops! Was Job accusing God of being the cause of his suffering? Did God really smile on the counsel of the wicked? Did he? There are lots of things we do not understand about our great God, but he is merciful and understands and even wipes our tear-filled eyes. He understands grief unlike any other. After all, was not his Son brutally slain by wicked men before his very eyes? God is still working with his erring people even when we question his sovereignty.

"The Lord answered Job out of the whirlwind and said: . . . 'Where were you when I laid the foundations of the earth? Tell me, if you have understanding. Surely you know! Or who stretched the line upon it? To what were its foundations fastened? Or who laid its cornerstone?'" (Job 38:1, 4–6). Poor Job, he finally got it. "Therefore I have uttered what I did not understand, things too wonderful for me, which I did not know" (Job 42:3).

We must be careful in not giving reasons for human suffering because the Bible does not give one. We simply do not have the mental capacity to understand the mystery behind human suffering here on earth. Job did not get an explanation from God either but was simply told in eloquent terms, and I am paraphrasing, "Trust me, I am in control of the universe." Even when you do not understand all the crazy stuff taking place around you, are you willing to trust God and let him work what is best in your life? Thanks for allowing God to work things out in your life even when you do not understand. We lost Barry, but we are confident we will see him again. Come quickly, Jesus and resurrection morning.

February 7

Winning the Big One

And everyone who competes for the prize is temperate in all things. Now they do it to obtain a perishable crown, but we for an imperishable crown.

—1 Corinthians 9:25

The roar of the crowd was thunderous as Andy won it big for the Brits. In the parks, in the bars, at the stadium, on huge screens across city streets, even near the iconic London Bridge, they all watched as their homeboy champion Andy Murray made British history. With a flick of a racket, he ended the Brits' seventy-seven-year drought in world-class tennis. After many close finish to the top, ole Andy won the championship in commanding fashion. He obliterated his opponent Novak Djokovic, 3–0. Murray received commendations from the Queen, the prime minister, legislators, members of the nobility, sportsmen, and women around the nation, not forgetting his grateful tennis fans the world over. As incredible as his feat was, however, and every point was keenly contested over, it is nothing in comparison to the inheritance of the saints. Tell me, how do we go about winning the big prize, the eternal one?

"And they overcame him by the blood of the Lamb and by the word of their testimony, and they did not love their lives to the death" (Rev. 12:11). Our victory over sin is tied to Jesus's victory over Satan and death, and this necessitates daily mortification (death) of the flesh (unconverted nature). Our good intentions that are very much like Peter's oath of never betraying Christ prove that they are no guarantee of faithfulness to God under stress (Matt. 26:35). Total surrender of the will and all members of the human anatomy is what's required for victory. The blood of Christ must permeate our souls just as it did over Israel's doorpost and secured those on the inside. Are you covered by the blood of Jesus Christ, the Lamb of God?

How can I be covered by the blood or clothed in the righteousness of Christ? The journey of the Christian begins with a simple step, obedience to the voice of the Holy Spirit. "Your ears shall hear a word behind you saying, 'This is the way, walk in it'" (Isa. 30:21). And we should be obedient to that voice and walk in the path outlined by the Holy Spirit. "My sheep hear My voice, and I know them, and they follow Me" (John 10:27).

Here is the sequence of steps for winning big in Christ: hear, believe, and trust.

1. Hear: "My sheep hear My voice and follow me" (John 10:27).
2. Believe: "Believe on the Lord Jesus and you will be saved" (Acts 16:31).
3. Baptize: "And now, why are you waiting? Arise and be baptized" (Acts 22:16).

These simple steps, along with a daily surrender to Jesus, will result in overcoming sin by God's grace. A crown that never perishes awaits all those who gain victory over sin. However, the overcomer in Christ would rather die, if necessary, than compromise her or his faith or disobey God. Are you willing, by God's grace, to overcome sin, even the darling ones, the ones we find pleasurable? Do you have the faith to lay down your life in defense of your faith in Jesus if called on? Lord Jesus, please give your servants the power to overcome sin and live for you. Amen.

Mischief Never Pays

Whoever digs a pit will fall into it, and he who rolls a stone will have it roll back on him.

—Proverbs 26:27, NKJV

Off the east coast of Angus, Scotland, lay a perilous reef called the Inchcape Rock. It posed great danger to mariners navigating their ships during dark, starless nights and stormy weather. A kindhearted gentleman, the abbot of Arbroath, installed a bell mounted on a buoy to warn sailors of the imminent danger. On many a dark and windy night, its clanging gong would be a blessing to mariners, warning them to steer clear of the perilous rock. The good abbot received numerous acknowledgments from grateful seamen for his good works, insight, and generosity.

Then came a mischievous pirate named Sir Ralph the Rover with wickedness oozing from his bones. Bent on undoing the kind work of the abbot of Arbroath, Sir Ralph ordered his men to take him to the Inchcape Rock. Upon arrival, he literally cut the bell from the buoy to which it was attached and dropped it into the ocean. A gloating Ralph flashed a sinister smile as the bell splashed into the sea with its last clanging gong.

A day or two later and on a very dark night, a furious storm caught Sir Ralph in its grip. "Oh, how I wish I could hear the Inchcape bell," Ralph groaned. On that very night, his ship was jolted by a gashing, violent crash, and he ran smack into the Inchcape Rock. "The devil below was ringing his bell" (Robert Southey, "Inchcape Rock"). This poem brings to mind Haman's evil plot to have Mordecai hanged on a fifty-foot gallows he built with the specific purpose of destroying his avowed enemy, Mordecai (Esther 7:9). He was hanged on the very gallows he built for Mordecai. "Whoever digs a pit will fall into it, and he who rolls a stone will have it roll back on him" (Prov. 26:27).

Jesus puts it succinctly in Luke 6:31: "And just as you want men to do to you, you also do to them likewise." Intentionally devising evil against a friend, a spouse, a neighbor, or even an enemy is not the way to go and runs contrary to the spirit of Jesus. God always does a better job of avenging his righteous people. Daniel was quite aware of the evil machinations of his so-called friends; he just kept on doing his job and allowed God to take care of his back. Daniel's enemies, like Haman, were taken care of in quite a dramatic fashion; they were caught in their own trap, thrown into the lions' den (Dan. 6:23–24).

If your enemies are breathing down your neck, it may be that God, in his mercy, is developing the fruits of his spirit in your life. He may allow you to share space with a cantankerous person to bring out the true gems hidden inside of you. Could he be preparing you for entry into his museum of character building? The process of making a pearl is not easy for oysters. They are continually trying to dislodge from their shell grains of sand, which cause them great discomfort. They release mucus around the sand to isolate and evict them. As time passes by, the mucus hardens, and a beautiful pearl is formed from that irritation. The Lord is willing to make a great pearl from your hot temper, your sharp tongue, your weakness, and your slothfulness. Will you allow him? Are you willing to say, "Lord, you are the Potter, and I am the clay. Do with me whatever you deem necessary"? Amen.

February 9

No Other Way

There is no one like the God of Jeshurun, who rides the heaven to help you.
—Deuteronomy 33:26

Some animals put their mates through a grueling fitness test to determine their eligibility to reproduce the next generation. Those chosen may have to dance flawlessly, sing melodiously, swim gracefully, fly furiously, or fight ferociously. They all must follow the rule laid down by Mother Nature in ensuring that their offspring will have the best dad to take care of the kids. You would think this makes perfect sense to us humans, but some dads totally negate the concept of helping moms with child-rearing. Why bother with child-rearing when there is a whole lot of fun to be had out there? How sad.

Not so with our God, the God of Jeshurun (Israel). Since he is our Creator, Savior, Provider, and Defender, he will move heaven and earth to save us. "Because they did not believe in God, and did not trust in His salvation. Yet He commanded the clouds above, and opened the doors of heaven, had rained down manna on them to eat, and given them of the bread of heaven. Men ate angels' food; He sent them food to the full" (Ps. 78:22–25). Are we deserving of God's mercy and kindness?

Despite Israel's unbelief and ungratefulness, God continued to supply their needs in a very barren and inhospitable environment. That's why we should spend more time thanking God for his many blessings to us not because we are deserving but because he is kind, merciful, and forgiving. Even when we are not granted the toys we request, it is still a good thing to give thanks to the Lord, for he is our God. "Oh give thanks to the Lord, for He is good! For His mercy endures forever. Let the redeemed of the Lord say so, Whom He has redeemed from the hands of the enemy, and gathered out of the lands, from the East and from the West, from the North and from the South" (Ps. 107:1–3).

Who hasn't experienced divine deliverance from the Lord? I recall the multiple times the grim reaper had me in his sight. Had it not been for the mercy and intervention of my God, I would have sunk into silence. How can we not thank God every day? The devil is hot on our trail daily, seeking to destroy us, but God delivers us. We concur with Jeremiah that it is because of God's mercy that we are not destroyed. "Through the Lord's mercies we are not consumed, because His compassions fail not. They are new every morning; great is your faithfulness" (Lam. 3:22–23). And Peter begins where Jeremiah left off: "Be sober, be vigilant; because your adversary the devil walks about like a roaring lion, seeking whom he may devour" (1 Pet. 5:8). This warning is no idle threat; the devil wants to destroy us. "Therefore rejoice, O heavens, and you who dwell in them! Woe to the inhabitants of the earth and the sea! For the devil has come down to you, having great wrath, because he knows that he has a short time" (Rev. 12:12).

But God is always up to the task of taking care of his own. "And it shall come to pass that before they call I will answer; and while they are still speaking I will hear" (Isa. 65:24). That's the kind of God we serve, and there is no one like him. All the so-called gods are really nothing but mere mute and dumb toys, the work of human creativity. Worship God, for he alone is worthy of our praise. After all, he made you and me, and should we devote our worship to another?

February 10

Get Ready, Here I Come

For nation shall rise against nation, and kingdom against kingdom. And there will be famines, pestilences, and earthquakes.

—Matthew 24:7

He has built a multimillion underground compound preparing for doomsday, but will he survive it when it comes? Mr. X and others who share his belief spend their fortune building fortresses complete with modern amenities for what they think will be the end of the world. The lighting, furniture, and plumbing are state-of-the-art. A surveillance camera at the property's entrance relays the movement of approaching intruders to a command-and-control center. Mr. X is armed to the teeth and is convinced that the world is going to be engulfed in some kind of nuclear conflict. He and his family train rigorously every day for just such an event. *Doomsday Preppers* have become a popular reality show across the nation and have captivated audiences and inadvertently shed some light on biblical last day events.

Yes, the Bible does prophesy of an end-time global conflagration; yes, it also speaks of wars, violence, famines, pestilences, and earthquakes. However, these events will not bring an end to the world. Only Jesus Christ's Second Coming will stop the clock on human civilization. In light of these facts, should we pack up our belongings, like the preppers, and head for the hills? No, of course not. Who will then evangelize the cities? "So he called ten of his servants and said to them, 'Do business till I come'" (Luke 19:13). The old King James Version, which I grew up reading, renders the following text: "Occupy till I come." The inference from this saying can be interpreted this way: continue doing business until I come.

We are admonished to "be ready for the son of Man is coming at an hour you do not expect" (Matt. 24:44). Our safety lies in us being ready. We may not be able to run away from the calamities that afflict our world, nor can we run from the government whose reach is everywhere, but we can make Jesus our "refuge and strength" (Ps. 46:1). But here's the juicy part: "For in the time of trouble He shall hide me in His pavilion; in the secret place of His tabernacle He shall hide me; He shall set me high upon a rock" (Ps. 27:5). Don't you want to be in God's pavilion when the authorities turn hostile and friends begin acting strangely? I sure want to be in his pavilion. How about you?

Did God not promise that our bread and our water will be sure when difficult times arise? "He who walks righteously and speaks uprightly, he who despises the gain of oppressions, who gestures with his hands, refusing bribes . . . He will dwell on high; his place of defense will be the fortress of rocks; bread will be given him, his water will be sure" (Isa. 33:15–16). The child of God need not worry where his next meal will come from. Just as God fed Elijah, the prophet, by ravenous ravens, he will take care of the needs of his children. We only have to reflect on his sustenance of Israel in the desert to determine his ability to take care of us. Did he not set a table before them in the wilderness and split rocks to quench their thirst? Can he not do the same for us?

Will he make a way for his last day people, whom he has redeemed by his own blood? You need not build yourself an underground bunker or train in the use of firearms to defend yourself; let God be your refuge and shield, your sure foundation. "No weapon formed against you can prosper" (Isa. 54:17). Make him your defense, Savior, and Sanctuary today.

February 11

Perpetually Hungry

And Jesus said to them, I am the bread of life he who comes to Me shall never hunger, and he who believes in Me shall never thirst.

—John 6:35

Utilizing corn to make fuel sparked violent worldwide protest and anger against the United States. No one anticipated that such a simple, self-serving action would have such devastating consequences. With the surging price of oil on the international oil exchange market, the United States government—in seeking ways to increase its domestic fuel production—touched the hungry stomachs of many in the Third World. Deciding to process corn into fuel-based ethanol to lessen its dependence on foreign oil, the United States inadvertently cut its corn export to some nations. The result was swift and furious. Severe food shortages and rising prices resulted, driving waves of angry rioters into deadly rampages in city streets all across the world. One observer bluntly remarked, "While we are worrying about filling our gas tanks, some are struggling to put food in their stomachs." The carnage that ensued sent world leaders scrambling for answers in hastily called conferences (www.examiner.com/article/global-food-crisis-forcast-crisis).

Sweeping his eyes over a multitude of people hungry for a better way, Jesus declared, "I am the living bread which came down from heaven. If anyone eats of this bread, he will live forever; and the bread that I shall give is My flesh, which I shall give for the life of the world" (John 6:51).

Bread was, and still is, an essential staple in the diet of the ancient world; and by comparing himself to bread, Jesus was, in essence, saying, "I am the source of your daily sustenance. But Jesus was not through and continued. "This is the bread which came down from heaven, not as your fathers ate manna, and are dead. He who eats this bread will live forever" (John 6:58).

There is a profound hunger ravishing the soul of man. And many are clueless about how to satisfy this deep craving for something lasting, something more satisfying than the mundane things of this life. People fill sports stadiums and shuttle back and forth from Las Vegas, gambling in casinos, searching to quench the thirst of the soul, but alas, it's fruitless. However, "Jesus is the answer for the world today. Above him, there's no other. Jesus is the way," says the songwriter. And I concur with the writer; Jesus is certainly the way, not a way but the only way.

While many are seeking the thrills of the amusement parks and others bury themselves in their jobs, let us tell them in creative ways, "We have a friend so precious, so very dear to us. He loves us with a tender love. He loves us faithfully, and so we dwell together, our Lord and us" (L. Shorey, "My Lord and I," paraphrased). We are obligated to tell everyone of God's amazing love to them.

The bread of life wants to fill your hungry soul today; will you let him in your heart today? The things of this world are transient, passing away. Only Jesus and his kingdom will not pass away. The God space within us cannot be filled by alcohol, pleasures, gambling, sporting events, wealth, sensual pleasures, exercises, traveling, or anything else. Only Jesus can satisfy the soul. And he is waiting on you right now to invite him into your life as your Lord and Savior.

February 12

When It Rains, It Pours

While he was still speaking, another also came and said, the Chaldeans formed three bands, raided the camels and took them away, yes, and killed the servants with the edge of the sword; and I alone have escaped to tell you.

—Job 1:17

It was a splendid sunlit Sunday morning, a perfect day for a beach party. Suddenly, there were some moving black specks in the sky, and then all hell broke loose as the bombs began falling indiscriminately everywhere. The United States was under attack as waves of Zero fighters dropped their deadly cargo indiscriminately on military and unsuspecting civilian targets. When the dust finally cleared, 8 battleships were damaged, 4 sunk, 3 cruisers lost, 188 aircrafts destroyed, 2,403 dead, and 1,100 wounded. All this happened while Japanese ambassadors were talking peace in Washington. Fortunately for the United States, the prized aircraft carriers, the linchpin of U.S. offensive power, were out at sea and escaped the onslaught unscathed (www.history.com/topics/world/war-ii/pearl-habor). Was the United States stronger before or after the attack?

There are days when everything that could go wrong will go wrong. While some cave in under the withering attack of the enemy, others seem to thrive under pressure. It is only when the gold is heated to its melting point that the dross and impurities are burned off. Trials and afflictions are God's chosen method of purifying his saints. "It is good for me that I have been afflicted, that I may learn Your statues" (Ps. 119:71).

Before Pearl Harbor, the United States was a regional power on the level of Great Britain, France, and Germany. The war, however, forced improvisation that unleashed an explosion of industry, innovation, experimentation, know-how, science, and technology. The United States grew stronger from the conflict. Likewise, Job emerged from his test stronger, a precious jewel worthy of imitation. The believer's spiritual muscles must be tested time and again by trials and tribulations; otherwise, they might get flabby and useless, and they might lose focus on Jesus. If a boat remains forever in the safety of the harbor, it may never be proved seaworthy. It is only when it is taken to face the fierce headwinds of the ocean that is it declared seaworthy. Are we stronger before a test or after the test? The latter is correct.

Jesus has promised that he will never allow us to be tempted above that which we are able to bear but will in every situation make a way of escape for us. "No temptation has overtaken you except such as is common to man; but God is faithful, who will not allow you to be tempted beyond what you are able, but with the temptation will also make the way of escape, that you may be able to bear it" (1 Cor. 10:13). Let the words go forth that heaven stands ready to unleash, at our request, battalions of angels, but we must first desire to please God and renounce all sin and evil.

Moses's charge to Joshua is equally applicable to us as we stand on the threshold of our heavenly Canaan. "Be strong and of good courage, for you must go with this people to the land the Lord has sworn to their fathers to give them, and you shall cause them to inherit it. And the Lord, He is the One who goes before you. He will be with you, He will not leave you nor forsake you; do not fear nor be dismayed" (Deut. 31:7–8). We must conquer through Christ the sins and bad habits that threaten to destroy us. "I can do all things through Christ who strengthens me" (Phil. 4:13). Absolutely, through Christ, we can and must conquer the darling little sins that threaten to destroy us.

February 13

Let Bygones be Bygones

Then Peter came to Him and said, Lord, how often shall my brother sin against me, and I forgive him? Up to seven times?

—Matthew 18:21

Nelson "Madiba" Mandela emerged from twenty-seven years of prison with his dignity intact, a bright smile, spirit soaring, and his right hand clenched and held high for the world to see. International sanctions and world boycotts were biting hard at the economic engine of South Africa. The nation was on the brink of implosion. Crime, violence, and social upheaval were tearing the nation apart. A steady hand was desperately needed to navigate the nation from this internal convulsion. The world looked on with both interest and anticipation, wondering what Mandela would do. Of course, he was swept into office by the overwhelming black majority, voting for the very first time. Rolling back centuries of injustice, discrimination, and inequality wasn't going to be easy, but it was accomplished when victims and victimizers understood that hate only destroys, and breeds mistrust. Establishing a truth and reconciliation committee provided the forum to address hideous crimes committed by the state against its own people. The rule was quite simple: if you confess it, it will be forgiven; if you don't, be prepared to face swift prosecution and punishment. This setting paved the way for racial harmony in South Africa, which resulted in people of all races living in peace and harmony today. Nelson "Madiba" Mandela achieved for his nation what most multiracial societies aspire but are unwilling to make the necessary sacrifice to achieve.

Someone once remarked that the hardest words to come out of the human lips are the words "I am sorry, please forgive me." Why is it so difficult to make this admission? Pride is the chief culprit. Some view admission of misdeeds as a sign of weakness. Others view it as being too embarrassing to perform and beneath their dignity. A third class believes that requesting forgiveness puts one in the role of a supplicant begging for mercy.

But forgiveness is the only vehicle by which we achieve family harmony, racial equality and national unity. The Savior, in his teaching on the Mount of Olives, affirmed, "Forgive us our debts, as we forgive our debtors" (Matt. 6:12). Personal grievances, however painful, must be brought to the table for redress. We will achieve mental and spiritual wholeness only as we seek to resolve these difficult issues. Jesus continues: "Therefore if you bring your gift to the altar, and there remember that your brother has something against you. Leave your gift there before the altar, and go your way. First be reconciled to your brother, and then come and offer your gift" (Matt. 5:23–24). Oh how much peace we often forfeit because we ignore this time-tested rule.

It really doesn't matter how many times we are offended, whether by the same person or another; we are admonished to forgive. Having forgiven his tormentors, Nelson Mandela established an astonishing precedent for forgiveness. By taking the higher road, he walked in the footsteps of our Lord and Savior. Are there relationships in your life that are crying out for redress? Even if you have been abused, don't carry the extra burden of hate; ask God to give you a forgiving spirit. And I do not know the extent of your pain, but this I know: there is not a disease that the great Physician cannot heal. He has an excellent healing record. Not one patient has expired on his watch. Are you willing to let Jesus heal your broken heart today? Thank you for allowing him to do it.

February 14

Can He Dance?

A little sleep, a little slumber, a little folding of the hands to sleep, so shall your poverty come on you like a prowler and your need like an armed man.

—Proverbs 6:10–11

A furious dance is on display, and the dancer has only one chance to get it right. His self-esteem and privilege to procreate depends on a skillful performance. Choosing the right spot for his dance is crucial; it must be accessible to his intended lady. Birds of paradise come in many varieties. There are the dancers who must impress their suitors with flawless precision and choreography. Not to be outdone by the dancers, the singers sing their way into the hearts of their partners with their mesmerizing love songs. Their sweet melodies must strike the right chord; otherwise, rejection could be quite painful. Succeeding the singers are the handsome ones; with their dazzling beauty, they wow the audience with their exotic sparkling colors. This class of performers is outfitted with a dazzling array of colorful feathers, which when intentionally displayed could hypnotize a fussy lady. They need not dance or sing; beauty is their chief asset. Our last class of performers is the designers, and they are rather interesting. Some undertake the arduous task of building an intricate and elaborate nest to please their picky mate. One particular species of designers choose not to build at all but to design. They import classy objects from out of town. Colorful artifacts are carted in, and with meticulous care and precision, they arrange in order colorful stones, plastic spoons, and anything they deem pleasant to win the nod of their mate (David Attenborough, *Paradise Birds*).

Most animals, particularly mammals, require this rigorous test to certify that the applicant matches his résumé. Should ladies require any less in a potential suitor? What should be the criteria for selecting a husband? We have been instructed in the Bible on the criteria in the selection of bishops, elders, deacons, pastors, and yes life mates as well, but what foremost quality should a lady look for in a potential husband?

Hunter-gatherer cultures have taught us much. Skilled hunters, fishermen, craftsmen, and farmers have had little problem attracting mates. He who feeds his clan is indispensable to his community. Beauty and brute strength must give way to skill, wisdom, and craftsmanship. These pastoral communities love their providers; their lives depend on them. "Then he said, Behold now, I am old, I do not know the day of my death. Now therefore, please take your weapons, your quiver and your bow, and go out to the field and hunt game for me. And make me savory food, such as I love, and bring it to me that I may eat, that my soul may bless you before I die" (Gen. 27:3–4). Another reference cites the importance of hunters to their clan: "Cush begot Nimrod; he began to be a mighty one on the earth. He was a mighty hunter before the Lord. Therefore is it said, Like Nimrod the mighty hunter before the Lord" (Gen. 10:8–9).

The ancients required of young men the ability to display industry, skill, and craftsmanship—requirements necessary in making successful husbands and fathers. The animal kingdom instinctively follows these timeless principles. Should the modern culture require any less from our young men? The apostle Paul puts it bluntly. "For even when we were with you, we commanded you this: if anyone will not work, neither shall he eat" (2 Thess. 3:10). And I concur. Get a job before the baby event, will you? Amen.

February 15

Swimming against the Tide

But you are a chosen generation, a royal priesthood, a holy nation, His own special people, that you may proclaim the praises of Him who called you out of darkness into His marvelous light.

—1 Peter 2:9

Wang (name changed) grew up in a tough crime-infested neighborhood, but Jesus caught him before his life began spinning out of control. At a very tender age, he learned the dos and don'ts of street discipline. To survive the mean streets, he had to toughen up. It goes without saying that exposure to the daily menu of profanity, drugs, violence, and robbery had an obnoxious effect on him, and he became a willing participant in vile activities. He climbed quickly through the ranks of his criminal enterprise to become the leader of his gang. Utilizing the tools of the crime trade, he became ruthless and heartless. Just when he had accomplished total dominance over the other competing gangs, there was a persistent knock on his door; someone was calling. Was it an old enemy paying him a visit?

In the moving of divine providence, Wang was invited by the persistent knocker (a friendly former gang member) to a neighborhood meeting. Reluctant at first, the tough guy decided to give it a hearing. *What do I have to lose?* he mused to himself. Once seated, he became transfixed by what transpired under the tent. The tough gangbanger began falling apart under the subduing grace of God. His formerly proud and heartless spirit gave way to the tender wooing of the Holy Spirit. He began shedding his old nature for a new one. Metamorphosis was taking place and fast; the tough crime chief was shedding his old nature for a brand-new one. He was being transformed into a brand-new creature.

"Therefore, if anyone is in Christ, he is a new creation; old things have passed away; behold, all things have become new" (2 Cor. 5:17). Wang immediately discovered he could not be the CEO of his criminal enterprise and a child of God at the same time. He submitted his resignation to the criminal enterprise and embarked on a campaign of sharing the love of Jesus to everyone he encountered.

"A dead fish drifts with the tide, but a living fish swims against the tide." One thing is characteristic of all humans: "For all have sinned and fall short of the glory of God" (Rom. 3:23). This pronouncement from Paul puts us all drifting downward with the tide of popular culture and ultimately toward eternal condemnation and death. But when touched by the wondrous grace of God, we learn to swim against the tide of sin and popular culture. We must admit this sometimes puts us in awkward situations with spouses, families, friends, and the society at large. But that's precisely what Christians are supposed to do—stand for counterculture, stand against all that is loved and endeared by the world. "Do not love the world or the things in the world. If anyone loves the world, the love of the Father is not in him" (1 John 2:15).

A clear line of demarcation is undoubtedly drawn when one joins the army of God. As the text implies, "Old things are passed away, and behold, all things have become new." Let us thank God that we are no longer slaves to sin but slaves by choice to our Lord and Savior, Jesus Christ. "For My yoke is easy and My burden is light" (Matt. 11:30). Do you want to submit yourself for the rest of your life to the will of the Father? Lord, please give your child the strength and courage to follow through with her or his decision to serve you.

February 16

The Power of a Smile

A merry heart does good, like medicine, but a broken spirit dries up the bones.
—Proverbs 17:22

The pain was unbearable, but after baby Joey emerged, the smile on her face said it all. Mary had just given birth to her first child over at the city's medical center. Being a first-time mom, she was thoroughly briefed on the childbirth experience, but no amount of coaching prepared her for what was to come. The pain was sharp, unrelenting, and excruciating; but the moment baby Joey was placed on her tummy, her pain evaporated and gave way to great joy and relief. The returning troops from the battlefield come home, bubbling over with it long before they make physical contact with their loved ones. Happily married couples use it extensively after they've been proclaimed man and wife. Children playing on school playgrounds cannot have enough of it. What's in a smile that makes it such a potent and infectious emotion?

"I will praise You, for I am fearfully and wonderfully made; marvelous are Your works, and that my soul knows very well" (Ps. 139:14). The smile is a powerful instrument to affirm, to enjoy things, to show approval, to encourage, to greet, to welcome, and yes even to make fun of. Presidents use it on occasions to poke fun at themselves. The crowd goes wild with laughter, and this relaxes the president from the burden of the office. It shouldn't be any surprise to us that TV network comedians are paid exorbitant salaries just to make folks laugh. And thousands stay up late at night, with baggy eyes the next morning, just to have a good laugh. Laughter then must be a good thing.

The old adage "Laughter is the best medicine" has been corroborated both in and out of the lab. "A merry heart does good, like medicine, but a broken spirit dries up the bones" (Prov. 17:22). Smiles are in abundance everywhere. There's plenty of it to go around; don't limit yourself to just a few. Take as much as you want, and remember, use it only on your face. Smiles have not been proved to work on other body parts. Use them profusely and extravagantly, and don't limit them only to family members. Greet everyone you meet with them—the strangers, the undeserving, the destitute, the elderly, and even your dreaded boss. We simply cannot exhaust the source of the smile because "every good gift and every perfect gift is from above, and comes from the Father of lights with whom there is no variation or shadow of turning" (James 1:17).

What can a smile do? It can stabilize the mind of a nervous worker. It can inspire a failing student to try just a little harder for that satisfactory grade. It can say to a recent divorcee, "The sky has not fallen, and the sun will shine again. There is life after a divorce." Even if you received undesirable news from your doctor, force yourself to smile because "it's good for you" as mom would say to us when administering bitter medicine. God is still our Shield and Protector. Let his will be done in your life. He always has our best interest at heart. If it is still hard for you to smile, call in a clown or a funny friend to make you laugh. It takes more facial muscles to frown than it does to smile. The songwriter sings, "You can smile when you can't say a word, you can smile when you cannot be heard, you can smile when it's cloudy or fair, you can smile anytime, anywhere." God be with you with your new weapon. Smile.

February 17

Words and Their Effects

Even so the tongue is a little member and boasts great things. See how great a forest a little fire kindles!

—James 3:5

An anonymous poet wrote, "There are four things that come not back: the spoken word, the sped arrow, the past life, and the neglected opportunity." Words have the power to kill, as well as to empower.

Sitting in the Oval Office with a blazing fire in the background, a calm president Franklin D. Roosevelt blurted out bluntly, "A date which will live in infamy." He was referring to the bombing of Pearl Harbor by the empire of Japan. The steely words of the president galvanized the nation into a massive industrial revolution.

Words build. Young Abraham was born in a poverty-stricken family and had a very harsh life but found a soul mate in his stepmother, Sarah Bush Lincoln. Being illiterate herself, she constantly affirmed and encouraged young Abe to follow his dreams and passion for reading. Her counsel found fertile soil in Abe as he burned the midnight oil poring over books borrowed from friends. Despite having had little formal education, Abe read himself into law school and ultimately into the presidency of the United States.

Words bind. Part of the U.S. war doctrine stipulates, "No comrades left behind." This principle is best illustrated in the war monuments all over the country depicting wounded and fallen comrades being carried by their colleagues while being shot at. The words of drill instructors bind and hold together some raw, nervous recruits into effective fighting men/women.

"We build men," they proudly boast.

Conversely, words can also have devastating effects on people. A Chinese master called his students around him, and in his hand was a pillow stuffed with fine bird feathers. He cut the pillow open and vigorously shook its contents into the wind until the sack was empty. He then ordered his students to collect the feathers and return them to the sack. "Impossible! The feathers have drifted in a million directions," a student remarked.

"So likewise," the wise old master retorted, "you cannot retrieve your words once they are spoken." The notion that "sticks and stones can break my bones but words can do me no harm" is a fallacy born out of ignorance. Words that are carelessly, willfully, and maliciously spoken can harm, maim, and even destroy lives.

After all, we're in the character-building business, aren't we? "A word fitly spoken is like apples of gold in settings of silver" (Prov. 25:11). Have you sprinkled a few golden nuggets on someone lately? They may not deserve the commendation, but it can be an incentive for them to attain loftier ideals. My mom played this game with me; she was very generous with her commendations when I drew anything. In her view, I was Michelangelo. Though I did not become an artist, her kind affirmation gave me lots of confidence to do other things. Can we be more generous in our compliment and affirmation of others? A warning to all: never toot your own horn. "Let another man praise you, and not your own mouth; a stranger, and not our own lips" (Prov. 27:2). By uplifting others, we get noticed by our Father, who sees in secret. Lord, I realize I may have been a little stingy with my commendation of others. Please strip me of pride, and help me see the best in others. Help me be like Barnabas, one who encourages. Amen.

February 18

Are You Wide Awake or Asleep?

Watch therefore for you know neither the day nor the hour in which the Son of Man is coming.

—Matthew 25:13

With his firearm loaded and ready, he kept the vigil as long as he could and then fell asleep; the thief came in as usual and had a grand feast again. A jaguar was on the prowl tonight and was checking out the neighborhood for some tasty fresh meat for dinner, but before he got his meal, he must get past a gantlet of weary villagers. He was patient, methodical, and calculating. On a moonless night, he pounced, snatched a hapless victim, and disappeared into the jungle. The villagers were obviously furious at their loss and determined to capture and punish the robber. An appetizing young goat was tied to a pole as bait for the thief, but a volunteer was needed to stand guard, rifle in hand, ready to eliminate the thief. However, hours of watchfulness gave way to yawns and finally slumber. When the watchman awoke, the rope was still attached to the pole, but the goat was nowhere to be found. The jaguar had struck again (my dad's travel adventure story).

"But know this, that if the master of the house had known what hour the thief would come, he would have watched and not allowed his house to be broken into" (Matt. 24:43). Sleeping on guard is a serious offense, which compromises the safety of any army. Because it puts the army at risk, punishment for sleeping on guard is usually swift and harsh. History confirms the watchmen on the walls of Babylon as being both drunk and sleepy. General Cyrus, their Persian archenemy, didn't have to shoot an arrow at Babylon; he simply walked in past the sleepy and drunken guards with his army.

Those responsible for the safety of others should remain awake and alert. "And you son of man: I have made you a watchman for the house of Israel; therefore you shall hear a word from My Mouth and warn them for Me" (Ezek. 33:7). Besides being God's modern-day watchmen on the walls of today's society, we have also been tasked to be our brother's keeper. "Then the Lord said to Cain, where is Abel your brother? He said I do not know. Am I my brother's keeper?" (Gen. 4:9). Oh yes, we all are our brother's keeper. By virtue of seniority, the elder child becomes the protector of the younger and is usually held accountable if she or he leads the younger into mischief. Likewise, being custodians of the everlasting gospel, we are responsible and obligated to lead others to Christ.

At conversion, the believer becomes accountable to those with whom he interacts. And he must carry out this assignment by warning men of the imminent coming of our Lord. Being awake entails being in a state of readiness to meet emergencies, helping others get ready, and upon seeing a threat alerting others to steer clear of it.

As modern-day watchmen, we are in mortal danger of becoming drowsy and sleepy at a time of earth's greatest crisis. "When I say to the wicked, O wicked man, you shall surely die! And you do not speak to warn the wicked from his way, that wicked shall die in his iniquity; but his blood I will require at your hand. Nevertheless if you warn the wicked to turn from his ways, and he does not turn, he shall die in his iniquity; but you have delivered your soul" (Ezek. 33:8–9). Some business owners use guard dogs to watch their establishment, but what good is a guard dog if it cannot bark or is always asleep? Are you a watchman? Are you awake or fast asleep? Jesus is coming soon. Wake up.

February 19

Sweet Life Is No Long Life

And I will say to my soul, Soul, you have many goods laid up for many years; take your ease; eat, drink, and be merry. But God said to him, "Fool! This night your soul will be required of you."

—Luke 12:19–20

Do not set your affection on the pleasures of this life; they are deceptive. In a folktale, staggering under the weight of his heavy burden, Brutus the Donkey made his way to his master's residence. Nearing the end of his journey, he stumbled on his old buddy Porky the Pig. "Why do you have such a hard life? Why do you have to work so hard?" Porky quipped with a tinge of sarcasm. "Your master is working you to death." He continued. "See, I live in absolute luxury. My master brings me the best food, even from his table." Poor Brutus, he didn't have much to say; he just went about his business, carrying his burden. The following day, he was on his way to his master's farm when he heard a horrendous shriek. Quickly, he made his way to the direction of the commotion. Brutus discovered his friend Porky being prepared for slaughter.

Sweet life is no long life, Brutus mused, and I concur.

"Why does the way of the wicked prosper? Why are those happy who deal so treacherously? You have planted them, yes, they have taken root. They grow, yes, they bear fruit. You are near in their mouth but far from their mind. But You, O Lord, know me; You have seen me, and You tested my heart toward You. Pull them out like sheep for the slaughter, and prepare them for the day of slaughter" (Jer. 12:1–3).

Some have mistakenly held the notion that everyone is entitled to the material blessings stipulated under the terms of the covenant to Israel, but God is more interested in ensuring that we are faithful in the least to be trusted with the most. "But as for me, my feet had almost stumbled; my steps had nearly slipped, for I was envious of the boastful, when I saw the prosperity of the wicked" (Ps. 73:2–3). But their apparent success is precarious and short-lived. "When I thought how to understand this, it was too painful for me, until I went into the sanctuary of God; then I understood their end. Surely You set them in slippery places; You cast them down to destruction" (Ps. 73:16–18).

Being puzzled by what he could not understand, the psalmist goes into the sanctuary (the temple, church, or synagogue), and then he understands the plan of God more fully. He learns that service to God is far better than material possession. He also learns to trust God and respect his decision to distribute resources to whomever he wills. He has new insights from God's Word, the Bible: "Do not lay up for yourselves treasures on earth, where moth and rust destroy and where thieves break in and steal; but lay up for yourselves treasures in heaven, where neither moth nor rust destroys and where thieves do not break in and steal" (Matt. 6:19–20). This world's pleasures are seductive and intoxicating; had they not been, Satan would not have offered them to Jesus in the wilderness temptation (Matt. 4:8–9). Jesus outshines anything this world has to offer.

The world and its pricey resorts, amusement parks, entertainment industry, and illustrious sports establishments will eventually pass away and be thrown to the flames, but only the things that are done for Jesus will last. We should choose to serve Jesus rather than enjoy the pleasure of sin for a season. I trust that you have made the decision not to lay your affection on the things of this life. Trust Jesus. He offers more than the treasures of this life.

February 20

Who Will Go for Us?

Sacrifice and offering You did not desire, but a body You have prepared for Me. In burnt offering and sacrifices for sins You had no pleasure. Then I said, Behold, I have come in the volume of the book it is written of Me, to do Your will O God.
—Hebrews 10:5–7

Who will tie a bell around the cat's neck? Who has the guts? Legend tells of a hastily called meeting that is under way; a serious matter is being addressed by senior delegates. Someone is stalking members of the community, and everyone seems to be irate and jittery over the issue. The chairman calls for calmer and cooler heads to prevail in deliberating over this thorny issue. One thoughtful member proposes installing a bell around the neck of the perpetrator to warn community members of approaching danger. The members cheer wildly at this brilliant suggestion. The chairman then calls for a volunteer to perform this dangerous assignment, but there is a deafening silence; no mouse is brave enough to undertake the assignment of tying a bell around the cat's neck.

But not so with the Son of God. Before the creation of mankind, even before sin made its ugly entrance to planet Earth, in the council of heaven, Jesus willingly risked it all to save humanity. And he really did. In eternity past, an all-seeing God foresaw the emergence of evil on planet Earth. A sad cord of disobedience and eventual death was struck in God's universe, and a volunteer was needed to rescue man from eternal death and ruin. Consequently, the brave and compassionate Son of God stepped forward to assume the body and identity of Jesus Christ to save mankind. "For God so loved the world that He gave His only begotten Son that whoever believes in Him should not perish but have everlasting life" (John 3:16).

It was love for his creation that motivated Jesus to volunteer for this dangerous assignment. He risked everything in the colossal battle to reconcile man to God. Failure, ruin, and eternal separation from his Father were real practical possibilities. Only the Creator could be the Redeemer of mankind. No angel's life could bridge the gulf caused by man's sin before a holy and righteous God; only the Creator could be man's Savior.

God's eternal law dictates, "The wages of sin is death, but the gift of God is eternal life in Jesus Christ our Lord" (Rom. 6:23). God's law could not be amended, modified, or changed; it could not be swept under the carpet, nor could it be ignored. It must be obeyed implicitly. The perpetrators had to be held accountable, and the guilty race was powerless to save itself. That's when God stepped in and incurred his own wrath on behalf of mankind for the violation of his righteous law. "For what the Law could not do in that it was weak through the flesh, God did by sending His own Son in the likeness of sinful flesh, on account of sin: He condemned sin in the flesh, that the righteous requirement of the law might be fulfilled in us who do not walk according to the flesh but according to the Spirit" (Rom. 8:3–4).

"Jesus paid it all, all to Him I owe; sin had left a crimson stain He washed it white as snow" (Elvina M. Hall). I concur. Jesus indeed paid it all. Glory be to God. Jesus did not shrink from the enormous risk in saving mankind. Where there is no risk there is no gain. Coming to this sinful planet and inheriting man's fallen nature while being bombarded every day by Satan's temptations said it all. "If that isn't love, then the ocean is dry, and the sparrows can't fly" (Heritage Singers). Thank you, Jesus, for saving us.

February 21

Power in the Word

For the word of God is living and powerful, and sharper than any two-edged sword, piercing even the division of the soul and spirit, and of joints and marrow, and is a discerner of the thoughts and intents of the heart.

—Hebrews 4:12

Sitting under the shade of a mango tree at the height of the Pacific noonday sun, Max was approached by a curious tourist. Upon seeing Max reading his Bible, the visitor remarked sarcastically, "Why are you reading this old, obscure, and obsolete book?"

"You ought to be grateful I am reading this old, obscure, and obsolete book," replied Max. "Had it not been for the Bible, you, my dear friend, would have been toast on my grill right now." Of course, cannibalism was endemic among some indigenous people of the Pacific before the introduction of Christianity there.

The Word of God is alive, active, and transformational with the power to turn sinners into saints, and the believers of the early church were beneficiaries of that power. "Now when the apostles who were at Jerusalem heard that Samaria had received the word of God, they sent Peter and John to them, who, when they had come down prayed for them that they might receive the Holy Spirit" (Acts 8:14–15). And Paul did not leave the Colossians wanting either: "Let the word of Christ dwell in you richly in all wisdom, teaching and admonishing one another in psalms and hymns and spiritual songs, singing with grace in your hearts to the Lord" (Col. 3:16). The Word of God is needed now more than ever before. With the sheer insanity of human degeneracy swirling around us, the Word of God is the only refuge that provides hope, shelter, and security in this world.

Nowhere is the power of the Word of God more evident than in the prisons. Condemned criminals well beyond reform and too dangerous to live among their peers melt under the sweet, inviting voice of the Holy Spirit. Some openly confess of the peace and freedom they now have, which eluded them for most of their lives. And though many may never walk again in society as free men, they are saved and have the assurance of being citizens of the new world coming—a world where all things will be restored, where there will be no more crimes, no more jails, no more lawlessness. God will write his law in the hearts of his people.

The Word of God is a powerful, dynamic force with creative and recreative power. "And the Spirit of God was hovering over the face of the waters. Then God said let there be light; and there was light" (Gen. 1:2–3). God called the world into existence by the dynamic power of his Word, and interestingly enough, that same Word who created the world, opened deaf ears, reversed blindness, healed the sick, and cleansed lepers will penetrate the grave and awake the sleeping saints. "Behold, I tell you a mystery; we shall not all sleep, but we shall all be changed, in a moment, in the twinkling of an eye, at the last trumpet. For the trumpet will sound, and the dead will be raised incorruptible, and we shall be changed" (1 Cor. 15:51–52).

If you are not secured, sheltered, and protected in Jesus, you certainly will neither hear nor recognize his voice on resurrection morning. However, if you are obedient, compliant, and familiar to the voice of Jesus, your sleep will be interrupted by the voice of the Life Giver. Continue being faithful, dear friend; a crown of life awaits you.

February 22

A Tiny Setback but a Major Comeback

For a righteous man may fall seven times and rise again, but the wicked shall fall into mischief.

—Proverbs 24:16

A flawless liftoff ended in disaster, but it was only a minor setback; the space program must go on, and it was here to stay. The engineers were ready at the controls as state officials took their front row seats for the countdown to liftoff. Sitting atop an unmanned Soyuz-U rocket was a payload of supplies and equipment for the International Space Station. The blastoff was impeccable, but about 325 seconds into the flight, something horrible went wrong. The rocket veered off its intended trajectory and exploded into a spectacular fireball. What went wrong was on everybody's mind (www.spacedaily.com/news/launchers-02p.html).

Judy is from a hardworking middle-class family. Her parents pour into her all the resources necessary for academic success. Judy is thriving academically and plays defense on her school's soccer team. She has earned the respect of opponents and has gained a fearful reputation for ruining the day of would-be goal scorers. While attending a friend's party one evening, she comes into contact with drugs and alcohol; and under intense peer pressure, she buckles and gives in. Oh how she wishes she could erase this terrible moment from her memory, but the consequences of the evening's indiscretion are just beginning to unravel. Her belly has a bulge; Judy is pregnant. Her rocket, destined for a smooth takeoff, warbles and disintegrates soon after liftoff. What should she do? How are her parents going to digest the news?

"My little children, these things I write to you, so that you may not sin. And if anyone sins, we have an Advocate with the Father, Jesus Christ the righteous" (1 John 2:1). Regardless of the mud and mire we wallow into, God is right there waiting with outstretched arms, ready to lift us if we call on him. No situation is too grave or beyond his ability to mend, restore, and make whole. Jesus invites, "Come unto me, all you who labor and are heavy laden, and I will give you rest. Take My yoke upon you and learn from Me, for I am gentle and lowly in heart, and you will find rest for your souls. For My yoke is easy and My burden is light" (Matt. 11:28–30). Those are the sweetest and most comforting words any offender could ever hear. The Lord has never been in the condemning business and welcomes the vilest of sinners with open arms. "This is a faithful saying and worthy of all acceptance, that Christ Jesus came into the world to save sinners, of whom I am chief" (1 Tim. 1:15).

Fortunately for Judy, she has a loving family, who completely encircled her wagon. "For all have sinned and fall short of the glory of God" (Rom. 3:23). No one can claim exemption from moral lapses, for we all have sinned one way or the other. The Lord has been very patient and merciful to us; shall we not extend love and sympathy to the erring? Jesus remains our only perfect example and bids us to sympathize with the weak and bind up their wounds. Bear in mind that the army of Christ should never shoot its wounded but rather seek them out and heal their wounds. If you have been wounded by an unsympathetic or misguided person, know that our Lord and Savior stands by your side to heal, cleanse, and make you whole again. Will you allow him to do so today?

February 23

Dig Deep Within

And so it was, when Moses held up his hand, that Israel prevailed; and when he let down his hand, Amalek prevailed. But Moses' hands became heavy; so they took a stone and put it under him, and he sat on it. And Aaron and Hur supported his hand.

—Exodus 17:11–12

The 2011–12 NFL season began with a splash for the New York Giants. Quarterback Eli Manning and his men ruined the dreams of their many opponents by imposing their will on their adversaries. By midseason, they had six wins and two losses—an excellent position to be in—but three losses in a row jolted their resolve and questioned their ability to win. Badly humiliated by the string of defeats, they limped their way to the end of the regular season barely qualifying for a playoff spot. They went on record as being the only team with a nine-win-seven-loss season to win the Super Bowl. How did they do it?

The twists and turns, ups and downs of a big game may be too much for a faint heart to bear, but the game of life is much more serious and demands our full attention. We are all actors in the theater of life, and who hasn't been knocked down and trampled over by the enemy, Satan? We all have, haven't we? We take courage from the words of Paul: "We are hard-pressed on every side, yet not crushed; we are persecuted, but not forsaken; struck down, but not destroyed" (2 Cor. 4:8–9). The three Hebrew captives were firm in their belief that God is just a prayer away and declared, "Our God whom we serve is able to deliver us from the burning fiery furnace and deliver us from your hand, O king" (Dan. 3:17). God is more than able to deliver us from whatever the enemy throws at us. The important question remains: do you wish to remain on the canvas when knocked down, or do you prefer to get up and fight? We should get up and fight knowing that, once we step out in faith, God will give us the strength to defeat the enemy. Did he disappoint David, who stood up to the formidable and undefeated Goliath with nothing but a slingshot for a weapon?

With their season hanging by a thin thread, the New York Giants dug deep within their innermost souls and unleashed the championship spirit deep down within. And of course, the rest was history; they became world champions of Super Bowl XLVI. Do you have this championship spirit within you? I pause for your answer. Jesus Christ defeated Satan on Calvary's cross. His victory is ours to claim. When buffeted and jostled by the fiery darts of the enemy, we can claim the promises of Jesus. "No temptation has overtaken you except such as is common to man; but God is faithful, who will not allow you to be tempted beyond what you are able, but with the temptation will also make the way of escape, that you may be able to bear it" (1 Cor. 10:13). Wow! Thank you, Jesus.

Victory is never in doubt for the child of God; through the strength of Jesus Christ, we can overcome whatever the devil throws at us. The Savior's conquest over sin at Calvary made it possible for the weakest of saints, like you and me, to overcome sin in his strength, not in our puny strength but in the mighty power of Jesus Christ. Do you wish to overcome the little sins that ruin your day and cause you to stumble? Thank you for your affirmative response. Lord Jesus, please give your children the power to overcome sin.

Finishing the Race Strong

I returned and saw under the sun that, the race is not for the swift, nor the battle to the strong.

—Ecclesiastes 9:11

He began the race and pulled a hamstring; he staggered, rolled over, got up, and hobbled to the finish line. Derek Redmond was favored to bring home the gold for Great Britain. His speed record was very impressive. He gobbled up the 400 m sprint and the 4 × 400 m relay effortlessly. At the 1992 Olympic event in Barcelona, Spain, Derek was ready to go. At the blast of the gun, he zoomed forward at breathtaking speed; but a few minutes into the race, the unthinkable happened. Derek grimaced in agony and pain as he clutched his right hamstring. He knew all too well what had happened, and it wasn't good. Coming to a stop, he hastily rolled over, still grabbing his hamstring while grimacing in pain and agony. What happened next was absolutely unpredictable and was etched in the annals of Olympic history. Derek got up and began hopping toward the finish line. The pain was unbearable, but he had come too far to allow this fall to derail his ambition. But wait a minute. Someone in the crowd has broken through the security barrier and was running toward the hopping athlete. Could this be his dad? Yes, it was. Derek's dad, motivated by his son's indomitable spirit, threw his arms across his son's shoulder and helped him across the finish line. In one of the most moving scenes in Olympic history, father and son crossed the finish line together and locked themselves in an emotional embrace. They were oblivious to the applause of the crowd and the sound of clicking, roving cameras around them (en.espn.co.uk/athletics/sports/story/146713html).

Derek's fall is typical of the believer's struggle. We fall, and some choose to stay fallen, but most get up and—with a hand from Jesus, the Father, and the Spirit—hobble to the finish line. "For a righteous man may fall seven times and rise again, but the wicked shall fall by calamity" (Prov. 24:16). Irrespective of the pain, we must get up; there's a race to win and a battle to conquer. Paul brings home this sobering thought: "I press towards the goal for the prize of the upward call of God in Christ Jesus" (Phil. 3:14). Amen. We can't win anything by looking back or giving in to fear, fatigue, or discouragement. Victory for the Christian is guaranteed by virtue of Christ's death, but it requires perseverance, abiding in Christ, and walking hand in hand with him day by day.

Nearing the end of his race and perceiving the approaching dark clouds, Paul reflects, "For I am already being poured out as a drink offering, and the time of my departure is at hand. I have fought the good fight, I have finished the race, and I have kept the faith. Finally, there is laid up for me the crown of righteousness, which the Lord, the righteous Judge, will give to me on that day, not to me only but also to all who have loved His appearing" (2 Tim. 4:6–8).

Jesus is the best coach anyone could have. He enables the weakest to overcome. It does not matter how many times you may have fallen; what matters most is crossing the finish line. And like Derek's dad, Jesus will help all those determined to overcome and make it to the finish line. If we keep our eyes on Jesus, we will overcome just as Peter and Ruben overcame despite their shortcomings. We can win despite the adversity life throws at us. "I can do all things through Christ who strengthens me" (Phil. 4:13).

February 25

Marriage Supper of the Lamb

Then he said to me, write: blessed are those who are called to the marriage supper of the Lamb! And he said to me, these are the true sayings of God.
—Revelation 19:9

Food preparation comes naturally to us as we watch Mom work her magic in the kitchen, but her pots are nothing compared with heaven's delicacies. Cooking as an art is embedded in my culture. Growing up in the '60s, the average kid did some kind of home cooking. Fridays bring back nostalgic memories of childhood cooking adventures. It was a fun time at school on Fridays as the girls played house, while the boys experimented with culinary art. Kids were encouraged to bring to class rice, ingredients, a pot, usually an open tin can, salt, and bananas, and off we went to the hills to try things out. We threw everything into one pot, and—kaboom!—out came a salty mess. Kids usually don't get things right the first time anyway, and even though we couldn't eat our salty mess, the experiments motivated us to perfect our culinary skills later on in life.

Cooking is celebrated in every culture on planet Earth; from the hunt to the celebration of historic events, we all enjoy good cooking. Rice, being a staple for many, is prepared in a variety of ways with rather interesting finger-licking results. Hats off to our Jamaican neighbors for sharing with us their delicious bean-and-rice formula, which I absolutely love. The Trinidadian roti brings to us the tantalizing taste of India with its finger-licking effects. Of course, it's quite natural for every Caribbean national to exaggerate her or his own national dish. Quite often and out of courtesy, we feel obliged to thank and compliment cooks profusely for sharing with us their rich national dish.

The International Food Festival has become a grand event at my church. Months of meticulous preparation culminate in a feast fit for royalty. Dishes from almost every continent and ethnicity are displayed and sampled; you simply purchase a ticket and taste all the delicious ethnic niceties. As tasty as some national cuisines may be, and some really are, God has something better in store for his people, and it boggles the imagination in scope.

"Eyes have not seen, not ear heard, nor have entered into the heart of man the things which God has prepared for those who love Him" (1 Cor. 2:9). Can you imagine sinking your teeth into a juicy mango and feel the invigorating sensation pulsating from your taste buds to the rest of the body? This, my friend, is just an appetizer; the best is yet to come. "In the middle of its street, and on either side of the river, was the tree of life, which bore twelve fruits, each tree yielding its fruit every month. The leaves of the tree were for the healing of the nations" (Rev. 22:2).

I often wonder why I did not receive an invitation to the most recent wedding at my church. Well, it might have slipped their minds. However, there is an invitation we can't afford to turn down. "Then he said to me, 'write! Blessed are those who are called to the marriage supper of the Lamb'" (Rev. 19:9). By the grace of God, I plan to attend this grand wedding prepared for the saved of all the ages. Have you pledged allegiance to the Bridegroom, Jesus Christ? Have you purchased your wedding garment (the righteousness of Christ)? Have you been washed in the blood of the Lamb? I pray you have been. If not, pray this prayer with me: Lord, please forgive me of my sins. Come into my heart and save me. Amen.

February 26

The Uh-Oh Moments of Life

When I was a child, I spoke as a child, I understood as a child I thought as a child; but when I became a man, I put away childish things.

—1 Corinthians 13:11

Our one-and-a-half-year-old grandson is developing rapidly in intelligence and perception. His latest escapade has sent us scratching our heads in wonder. Being wet in liquid of one's creation is no fun at all, and little LaShawn is still searching for the correct step in the bathroom procedure. He is aware that adults visit the bathroom intermittently but can't figure out quite yet what goes on in there.

One evening little LaShawn pulled down his diaper and allowed the fluid to flow freely on his mom's well-kept rug. When called to account for his action by his stern-faced mom, he yelped sheepishly, "Uh! Oh!" LaShawn was unable to speak but was somehow capable of distinguishing unacceptable behavior with his favorite exclamation—oh, oh!

John was recently released from a state penitentiary for possession of methamphetamine and was driving out of town when his worst fear became a reality; the flashing blue and orange lights were trailing him. Pulling his car to the side of the road, John tried very hard to keep his composure, but he was nervous. He was keenly aware of the illegal substance he had recently purchased and broke down during interrogation. John wept bitterly that his brief moment of freedom was about to expire. Was he contrite about his drug addiction or sorry that he got caught and would soon be back in jail?

We all have had our "oh-oh" moments in life, haven't we? "The Lord looks down from heaven upon the children of men, to see if there are any who understand, who seek God. They have all turned aside, they have together become corrupt. There is none who does good, No not one" (Ps. 14:2–3). Sin has infected every member of the human family, and without the grace of God, we are powerless to disentangle ourselves from sin's deadly embrace. We simply cannot attain God's righteous standard by our own strength and standards. We need help. "Behold, I was brought forth in iniquity, and in sin my mother conceived me" (Ps. 51:5). Is there any hope for the professional and closet sinner? Yes, of course. There is hope as long as there is contrition for sin.

God's solution to the sin problem came in the form of a little baby boy born in the town of Bethlehem. "But when the fullness of the time had come, God sent forth His Son, born of a woman, born under the law. To redeem those who were under the law, that we might receive the adoption as sons" (Gal. 4:4–5). The Father loved his human creation to the extent that he devised a plan for their salvation even before they sinned. Jesus became the Lamb of God slain from the foundation of the world. In eternity past, well before the creation of the world, God foresaw the emergence of sin and its terrible consequences and provided a remedy in the cross of Jesus Christ. Sin's infection cannot be healed by the ablest psychologist, heart surgeon, or neurosurgeon. We sinners, dear friend, can only be healed as we repent of our sins, turn away from them, and invite the Lord Jesus Christ into our heart.

Some think they must change first and then come to Jesus Christ. Oh no. You come as you are and allow Jesus to clean you up. He did it for me, and there is no doubt he can do it for you also. Dear Savior, please save me right now. Amen.

February 27

Witness Number One, Rise. Speak!

For there are three that bear witness in heaven: the Father, the Word, and the Holy Spirit; and these are one.

—1 John 5:7

Unlike the Epic of Gilgamesh and other ancient literature that speculate about the creation of the earth, the Bible emphatically states what actually happened. "In the beginning God created the heavens and the earth. The earth was without form, and void; and darkness was on the face of the deep. And the Spirit of God was hovering over the face of the waters. And God said, let there be light and there was light" (Gen. 1:1–3). This empirical evidence comes not from speculation but from the Creator himself. The Creation documented in Genesis is the only credible and authentic account of the origin of life. This truth must be accepted without doubt or equivocation; to do otherwise would amount to an outright rejection of the truth and the acceptance of a lie. Paul's letter to the Thessalonians authenticates this point. "Because they did not receive the love of the truth, that they might be saved. And for this reason God will send them strong delusion, that they should believe the lie" (2 Thess. 2:10–11). Believing the big bang theory is a monumental work of faith in itself; one has to gobble up all the inconsistencies, speculations, modifications, miscalculations, and outright fallacies.

"For without faith it is impossible to please Him, for he who comes to God must believe that He is, and that He is a rewarder of those who diligently seek Him" (Heb. 11:6). Those flying across the nation and the world trust the FAA to ensure that airline pilots are vetted, certified, and well qualified to operate an aircraft. We exercise our faith in this department to the extent that we never question whether a pilot is licensed or not. Likewise, God calls on us to exercise unquestioning faith in his word and actions. If one begins to question the integrity of the scripture, she or he is undermining the very definition of faith, which is "the substance of things hoped for, the evidence of things not seen" (Heb. 11:1). We must trust every word in the scripture because they are God inspired. "For prophesy never came by the will of man, but holy men of God spoke as they were moved by the Holy Spirit" (2 Pet. 1:21). Peter's bold declaration is a call to accept the integrity of the scripture. Unlike the evolutionists who make wild speculations about things they do not understand, God gave his prophets a detailed account of his creative activity.

There is unanimous harmony among Bible writers pointing to God as the undisputed Creator of this world. From Moses to John the Revelator, the Bible writers all speak loudly and with one accord. "For in six days the Lord made the heavens and the earth, the sea, and all that is in them, and rested the seventh day. Therefore the Lord blessed the Sabbath day and hallowed it" (Exod. 20:11). Moses, of course, was not an eyewitness to Creation since man was created last of all, but under divine inspiration, he received a step-by-step revelation concerning God's creative work. John the Revelator's remarks about Creation sums it up nicely: "Fear God and give glory to Him, for the hour of his judgment has come; and worship Him who made heaven and the earth, the sea and springs of water" (Rev. 14:7).

The scripture confirms the creation of the world was the collaborative effort of all three members of the Godhead (Gen 1:1, John 1:1). God the Son, Jesus, is the undisputed Creator of the world. Do you believe this with all your heart? God bless you.

February 28

Witness Number Two, Rise. Speak!

For by Him all things were created that are in the heaven and that are on earth, visible and invisible, whether thrones or dominions or principalities or powers. All things were created through Him and for Him.

—Colossians 1:16

"In the beginning was the Word, and the Word was with God, and the Word was God. He was in the beginning with God. All things were made through Him, and without Him nothing was made that was made" (John 1:1–3). Jesus, the Word, in collaboration with the Father and the Holy Spirit, created the world in six literal days. "For He spoke, and it was done; He commanded, and it stood fast" (Ps. 33:9). Paul adds in on the subject. "For by Him all things were created that are in heaven and that are on earth, visible and invisible, whether thrones or dominions or principalities or powers. All things were created through Him and for Him. And He is before all things, and in Him all things consist" (Col. 1:17). Addressing the Jewish leaders who were in denial about his divinity, Jesus remarked, "Most assuredly, I say to you, before Abraham was I am" (John 8:58). "I am" denotes self-existence. It means "I am God, I am before all things, I created all things, and I owe my existence to no one." No wonder the Jews attempted to take his life because they fully understood the enormity of his claim.

Jesus exercised mastery over nature as no other being could, and nature recognized its Creator and complied with his command. "Then He arose and rebuked the wind, and said to the sea, 'Peace, be still!' and the wind ceased and there was a great calm. And they feared exceedingly, and said to one another, who can this be, even the wind and the sea obey Him" (Mark 4:39, 41). The greatest evidence of Jesus's creatorship was his ability to restore life. "Jesus said to her I am the resurrection and the life. He who believes in Me, though he may die, he shall live. And when He had said these things, He cried with a loud voice, Lazarus, come forth!" (John 11:25, 43).

Even the demons (fallen angels), once-loyal ministering angels created by Jesus ("Since in Him all things consist" [Col. 1:17]), recognized Jesus's divinity. "And when He stepped out on land, there met Him a certain man from the city who had demons for a long time. And he wore no clothes, nor did he live in a house but in the tombs. When he saw Jesus, he cried, fell down before Him, and with a loud voice said, 'What have I to do with You, Jesus, Son of the Most High God? I beg You, do not torment me'" (Luke 8:27–28).

The most convincing aspect of Jesus's divine identity came from his own lips. "Therefore My Father loves Me, because I lay down My life that I may take it again. No one takes it from Me, but I lay it down of Myself. I have power to lay it down, and I have the power to take it again. This command I have received from My Father" (John 10:17–18). No one except God can make such a claim. All creatures derive life from God; therefore it is beyond anyone's capacity to resuscitate oneself after death. Jesus's miraculous birth, life, and death proved beyond a shadow of a doubt that he is indeed who he claimed to be, the Most High God. He is so huge that the heaven of heavens cannot contain him yet so small that he can dwell in our hearts. Have you accepted him as Lord and Savior of your life? Is there any room in your heart for him?

Witness Number Three, Rise. Speak!

And the Spirit of God was hovering over the face of the deep. Then God said, "Let there be light," and there was light.

—Genesis 1:2–3

The Holy Spirit is the third member of the Godhead but certainly not lesser in significance or equality. All three entities are one God, and Moses illustrates this point beautifully with this statement: "Hear O Israel; The Lord your God is one!" (Deut. 6:4). This is a concept one should neither analyze nor dispute but simply accept by faith. To aid us in understanding this concept of faith, the writer of Hebrews asserts, "By faith we understand that the Worlds were framed by the Word of God, so that the things which are seen were not made of things which are visible" (Heb. 11:3).

Faith plays a significant part in our business transactions. We use it more often than we are aware of. For instance, when we order an item on eBay, we pay by credit card and wait in faith for the package to appear in the mail, trusting that the manufacturer will follow through. The same is true of the concept of theology (the study of God); we must trust God absolutely and believe everything the Bible says about him. We must, by faith, accept his existence, study his Word daily, and accept and believe every word that proceeds from the mouth of God.

The Holy Spirit was an active agent in the creation of the world. "The earth was without form, and void; and darkness was on the face of the deep. And the Spirit of God was hovering over the face of the waters" (Gen. 1:2). Finishing his work of creating on the fifth day, God said to the other members of the Trinity, "Let Us make man in Our image according to Our likeness" (Gen. 1:26). Who comprise the "us" and "our" being referenced here? God the Father, God the Son, and God the Holy Spirit planned and executed the creation of man and the universe. The Holy Spirit is a Cocreator, along with the other two members of the Godhead as cited in Genesis 1:1 and John 1:1.

Tasked with the birth, operation, and development of the early church, the Holy Spirit's role has been more visible to us now than ever before. "I will pray the Father and He will give you another Helper, that He may abide with you forever, the Spirit of Truth, whom the world cannot receive, because it neither sees Him, nor knows Him but you know Him, for He dwells with you and will be in you" (John 14:16–17). Having completed his mission on earth, Jesus ascended to heaven to intercede on our behalf, while the Holy Spirit was tasked with leading, guiding, and equipping the church for ministry. "As they ministered to the Lord and fasted,

The Holy Spirit said, 'Now separate to Me Barnabas and Saul for the work to which I have called them'" (Acts 13:2). Someone appropriately remarked that the book of Acts should be called the book of the Holy Spirit. Everywhere in the book, the Spirit is seen choosing, organizing, coordinating, and empowering believers for mission both at home and abroad.

Besides the administrative work of the Holy Spirit, he is the active agent in leading the penitent sinner to Christ. "And do not grieve the Holy Spirit of God by whom you were sealed for the day of redemption" (Eph. 4:30). The Holy Spirit leads and guides the sinner to the truth. "When He the Spirit of truth is come He will guide you into all truth" (John 16:13). Is the Holy Spirit leading you to embrace doctrines outlined in the Bible that are not being practiced in your church? Follow wherever the Spirit leads you.

March 1

Fully Protected

Therefore take up the whole armor of God that you may be able to withstand in the evil day, and having done all, to stand.

—Ephesians 6:13

Modern warfare has intensified the killing power of weaponry, and the U.S. Army has adapted quite well. It has given its fighting men and women a relatively good chance of surviving severe battle injury that would otherwise have killed them. Over the years, it has developed a tried and proven battle-tested uniform for its armed forces. Let's take a look at the outfit. Headgear comes in a wide assortment of style depending on the occasion the service member is preparing for. The chief headgear is the Kevlar helmet, made from a lightweight material five times stronger than steel. It can be equipped with sophisticated instruments for night adventures and other operations (www.military.com/join-armed-forces/military-uniform).

The upper-body apparel may comprise a coat, shirt, T-shirt, or blouse, but the most indispensable part of the upper-body gear is the bulletproof vest, which is optional, depending on the task to be completed. The vest has lived up to its usefulness in cutting down battle fatalities, saving thousands of lives. The belt, though small and may seem insignificant, holds everything together. Besides holding an assortment of essentials, it keeps the fighter balanced and connects the upper and lower tunic into a complete uniformed soldier. Boots are always worn by service members, and it is unthinkable to venture on the battlefield without them. Not only do they protect the feet but they also provide warmth, comfort, and balance in all kinds of weather to do rigorous work. How can we forget the soldier's staple, the M16 rifle and its offensive capabilities?

In ancient warfare, clubs, arrows, stones, and swords were the offensive arsenal used in military campaigns. Modern militaries utilize a wide assortment of offensive weaponry. Drones, among many, have become the weapon of choice to advanced militaries. Lazars are currently being tested and may soon be deployed to neutralize the offensive capability of enemy forces, but no weapon is comparable to the Word of God.

Christians wear a formidable armor that is impregnable to all incoming missiles. When the child of God is fully clad in it, "no weapon formed against you shall prosper" (Isa. 54:17). Being shackled to a Roman soldier in prison, Paul highlighted the strength of Christ's armor at the disposal of every Christian. He interjected, "Stand therefore, having girded your waist with truth, having put on the breastplate of righteousness, and having shod your feet with the preparation of the gospel of peace; above all, taking the shield of faith with which you will be able to quench all the fiery darts of the wicked one. And take the helmet of salvation, and the sword of the Spirit, which is the word of God" (Eph. 6:14–17).

The armor of God comes in a complete package and must never be taken off but be worn every day. One is not safe if one unit of the uniform is neglected or discarded. The armor is equipped with both defensive and offensive capabilities. The sword of the Spirit, which is the Word of God, has both offensive and defensive capabilities and must be used every day. Jesus used it very effectively in his encounters with the Jewish leaders and in his temptation by Satan, (John 8, Matt. 4:1–10). Do you avail yourself of the study of God's Word, the Bible? Is it part of your daily menu? Keep on studying the Bible; it is good for you.

March 2

Smelling Your Roses

Therefore a man shall leave his father and mother and be joined to his wife, and they shall become one flesh.

—Genesis 2:24

We gave Mom and Pop the privilege of smelling their roses while they were still alive to appreciate it. There was a buzz of excitement in the air, and the wedding bells were chiming. Invited guests were waiting expectantly. Preparations for this exciting event were being executed a continent away with military-style precision, but the bride and groom seemed very relaxed despite the buzz of activity all around them. The day arrived with the flowers and decorations all resplendent with beauty and elegance as the groom waited in eager anticipation for his gorgeous bride. A delightful note exploded from the organ as the beautiful bride slowly made her entry to stand by her waiting groom. She wore an elegant, well-designed off-white dress and was accompanied and attended to by a retinue of bridesmaids (her grown girl children). They were in the company of family, friends, and well-wishers. Eden and Emilia Baptiste (our parents) celebrated their fiftieth wedding anniversary by renewing their vows in the presence of smiling children, grandchildren, and other family members. We gave our parents the awesome gift of smelling the fragrance of their flowers while they were still alive, and they deserved every bit of it.

"Honor your father and your mother, that your days may be long upon the land which the Lord your God is giving you" (Exod. 20:12). There are many ways in which we can honor our parents. Here is a short list. Of course, you can improve on it.

1. If it is at all possible from a medical perspective, invite them to live with you. We owe it to them. They raised and took care of us. Honoring them entails taking care of them when they are old and are unable to care for themselves.
2. If they choose to be independent of us, and that's their right, we can make their final days honorable by doing things with them that bring them joy.
3. We should always affirm them and remind them how much we love them.
4. Always remind your children of their grand privilege of having their grandpa and grandma living with them and sharing their rich experience with them.

There are many more ideas that can make the golden days of our parents a pleasurable experience. Aging is a process we all must confront someday, and how we treat our parents will determine how we will be treated when we get old someday. The cycle of life unfolds around us: we are born, grow up, marry, reproduce, age, and then die, and the cycle is completed. What goes around comes around. How you treat others determines how you will be treated in turn. For emphasis, treat your parents honorably, and you will receive the same treatment when you grow old yourself.

The only commandment with a promise compels us to care for our parents. If we do, we are promised long life. One of Jesus's last words on the cross was "Woman behold your Son! Then He said to the disciple, Behold your mother! And from that hour that disciple took her to his own home" (John 19:26–27). Even in death, Jesus ensured that his mother would be properly cared for. What have you done for your mom or pop lately? It is never too late to give them their flowers while they can still smell and appreciate them. Go out there and surprise them with your kindness and love.

March 3

A Time for Everything

A time for every purpose under heaven: A time to be born, and a time to die . . . A time to embrace, and a time to refrain from embracing . . . a time to love, and a time to hate.

—Ecclesiastes 3:1–2, 5, 8

You probably heard their music before. How could you have missed it? On October 9, 1965, their song was on Billboard's top 100 songs. By December 4, it was number one. "Turn! Turn! Turn!," with its biblical lyrics, blasted its way to number one and stayed there for three full weeks. The Byrds came to fame with one of the most inspirational proverbial songs of all time. "To everything there is a season, a time for every purpose under heaven. A time to be born and a time to die" (Eccles. 3:1–2).

Solomon strongly recommends remembering God the Creator in the days of our youthfulness. He begins with knowing and serving God before the onset of the difficult days. What are the difficult days? Whether the difficult days are the turbulent teenage years, midlife crisis, or unseen hardships, having a relationship with God will spare us much unnecessary pain and sorrow. As the body ages over time, and it will with the passage of the years, the relationship we have developed with God during our youth will sustain us in difficult times. Needless to reiterate, the very system that motivates us and causes us to enjoy life begin to fail as we age. "Then the dust will return to the earth as it was, and the spirit will return to God who gave it" (Eccles. 12:7).

What then should we do with the time allotted to us down here on planet Earth? The writer of Ecclesiastes gave us some useful hints. "Remember now your Creator." Whether you are young or old, this is good advice. For some, it is refreshing to know that the Lord has had possession of their body throughout their entire lives, but let's not kid ourselves. God accepts everyone in any condition as long as there is a desire to renounce their life of sinfulness. "All that the Father gives Me will come to Me and the one who comes to Me I will by no means cast out" (John 6:37). Jeremiah is very clear on this subject: "Let not the wise man glory in his wisdom, let not the mighty man glory in his might, nor let the rich man glory in his riches; But let him who glories glory in this that he understands and knows Me" (Jer. 9:23–24).

We were created by God to reflect his glory. Regrettably, some are unwilling to come to this conclusion. Knowing and serving God is the best gift we can offer him, and it is a theme woven throughout the Bible. Having experienced life on both sides of the fence, Solomon came to the sobering conclusion that serving God is all that really matters in life. Having tried everything his deep pocket could afford, in the end, Solomon declared the experience as total madness, chasing after the wind, a life of trouble and regret. Serving Jesus really pays. We really don't need to incur the terrible battle scars that service to Satan brings when Jesus beckons, "Come unto Me, all you who labor and are heavy leaden, and I will give you rest, take My yoke upon you, and learn of Me . . . For My yoke is easy and My burden is light" (Matt. 11:28–30). Will you happily surrender your life today to Jesus? If you have done so already, I commend you for your bold decision. Serving Jesus really pays.

March 4

Are We There Yet?

Then they will see the Son of Man coming in the clouds with great power and glory. And then He will send His angels, and gather together His elect from the four winds; from the farthest part of earth to the farthest part of heaven.

—Mark 13:26–27

My little passengers in the back seat intermittently poked their heads up between naps with a weary inquiry. "Dad, are we there yet?"

"Not quite," I replied. "We still have some ways to go." The trip to Niagara Falls seemed like an eternity to my two youngsters, who wondered what was taking Dad so long. Their young minds could not process the length of time it takes an automobile traveling at about 70 mph from New Jersey to the Canadian side of Niagara Falls. The people of God, through the centuries, have asked this same rhetorical question. Are we there yet? How long, Lord?

"And one said to the man clothed in linen, who was above the waters of the river, how long shall the fulfillment of these wonders be?" (Dan. 12:6). We frequently ask the same questions as we see the signs of the end of the world being fulfilled around us daily. God dwells beyond the realm of time and is not affected by its passage, nor is he encumbered by time as we are. "But, beloved, do not forget this one thing, that with the Lord one day is as a thousand years, and a thousand years as one day" (2 Pet. 3:8). Our perception of time and God's are quite different since we are mere mortals, and God dwells beyond the realm of time. How should we react to the perceived delay of Christ's coming?

"Therefore be patient, brethren, until the coming of the Lord. See how the farmer waits for the precious fruit of the earth, waiting patiently for it until it receives the early and latter rain" (James 5:7). James emphasizes the farmer's patience in the planting cycle. Once he sows the seed, the development of the plant is beyond his control; he cannot rush or delay the process but must wait on God to fulfill his part in the continuation of the growth cycle. He must wait on the former rain, which moistens the soil, releasing the much-needed nutrients for the seeds' growth and development. The former rain accelerates growth, while the latter rain matures and ripens the crop for harvest, but the farmer still has a job to do. He cannot just stand idly by; in the interim, he must tend the crop by suppressing weeds and eliminate vermin, which threaten the growth of his crop.

Like the farmer, we wait patiently for the coming of Christ; but while we are waiting, there are a few chores that we must do to be fully prepared for this glorious event. First, we must pray for an infilling of the Holy Spirit. Second, we must get busy and stay busy. But busy doing what?

God has entrusted to us the salvation of our fellowmen. "Go therefore and make disciples of all nations, baptizing them in the name of the Father and the Son and the Holy Spirit" (Matt. 28:19). This injunction applies to everyone. We cannot fulfill this commission in our power; we must—I reiterate, must—pray for the anointing of the Holy Spirit. Like the farmer who patiently waits for the latter rain, we must sincerely pray for it to motivate us. Bear in mind the Holy Spirit is not drenching everyone as some think. Only those who earnestly pray for its infilling will receive its life-giving showers. Are you praying for the outpouring of the Holy Spirit?

March 5

Lift Him

And I, if I am lifted up from the earth will draw all peoples to myself.
—John 12:32

Among the many monuments on display in Washington, DC, the flag-raising marines on Mount Suribachi is the most sacred. The history behind this monument is profound and legendary. A squad of battle-hardened leathernecks is seen grasping the pole of Stars and Stripes and thrusting it into the dirt of Mount Suribachi. It sends a chilling message to the world that the United States of America will spend blood, sweat, and tears in the defense of freedom and its values. The flag fluttering in the wind means the villains are vanquished, the battle is won, and victory is here to stay.

There is a more potent symbol of victory than a flag fluttering in the wind. In the Exodus experience, Moses was instructed by God to erect a bronze serpent and attach it to a pole (Num. 21:8). Israel had sinned grievously against God, and the Lord had temporarily withdrawn his protection from them. Hordes of venomous serpents invaded the camp and zeroed in on the offenders with lethal accuracy. The camp was filled with agonizing cries from dying people. However, quick to show his people that God was their only source of healing, Moses erected a fiery bronze serpent (symbolic of Christ at Calvary) in the center of camp. Anyone stung and dying must look up to the serpent for healing. Many in disbelief failed to look up and perished in their sins. However, those convicted of their waywardness looked in faith and received healing from their suffering. There was no healing virtue in that lifeless serpent; it was faith in the shed blood of Jesus Christ that provided the cure for the stricken sinners.

"Now as Jesus passed by, He saw a man who was blind from birth . . . When He had said these things, He spat on the ground and made clay with saliva; and He anointed the eyes of the blind man with the clay. And He said to him, go wash in the pool of Siloam. So he went and washed, and came back seeing" (John 9:1, 6–7). Again, the water at the pool was not the agent of change; it was obedience to Jesus and faith in his word that enabled this man to see.

"And I, if I am lifted up from the earth will draw all peoples to Myself" (John 12:32). Jesus's Crucifixion on Mount Calvary provides healing to all who are sick and dying from the infection of sin. According to Roman records, Jesus died as a revolutionary and an enemy of the state; but according to God's record, he is the "Lamb slain from the foundation of the earth" (Rev. 13:8). Jesus is symbolic of every Passover lamb faithfully eaten by all the believing children of God (John 1:36). He is also symbolic of the manna eaten by Israel during their Exodus wandering (John 6:49–51). He is the Rock from which they drank in the wilderness (1 Cor. 10:4).

The vilest instrument of torture ever invented (the cross) was transformed into a life-giving stream to satisfy man's thirst. Jesus, our Savior, conquered sin, triumphed over death, plundered the tombs of the dead, and by virtue of his sinless life and sacrificial death met the just requirements of God's law. God's character stands vindicated; he punished sin in the person of Jesus and saved the sinner in the same process. What a mighty God we serve! Have you been washed in his blood? Thank God that you have been.

March 6

A Brand-New Heart

I will give you a new heart and put a new spirit within you; I will take the heart of stone out of your flesh and give you a heart of flesh.
—Ezekiel 36:26

Dorothy's health was deteriorating fast; she simply didn't have the energy to do simple tasks around the house anymore. A visit to her family doctor confirmed her worst nightmare; her heart was degenerating rapidly. She needed immediate surgery. Thanks to a skilled team of physicians, Dorothy Fischer was given a brand-new heart with twelve more years of service. God promises free heart transplants to anyone who senses their spiritual depravity. Have you had your transplant yet? (www.sahistory.org.za/dated-event/first/sa-wonan-receives-heart-transplant)

"Then I will give them one heart, and I will put a new spirit within them, and take the stony heart out of their flesh, and give them a heart of flesh" (Ezek. 11:19). Will any heart patient refuse a healthy, functioning heart? Yet the people of God (you and me) are sometimes hesitant in requesting such a gift, even though it's absolutely free.

Having made the transition from sinner to saint, the babe in Christ goes on the operating table. The physician is quite safe and reputable. He has never made an unnecessary incision with his scalpel. Under the anesthesia of the Holy Spirit, the Master Physician goes to work. He chips away at immorality first because it can spread rapidly if not contained immediately. Next, he cuts hate. Hate kills slowly, and it consumes us insidiously from within, making monsters of good, decent people. But wait a minute, he's not finished yet. The patient seems a little impatient and restless and even threatens to abort the operation. The surgery has taken a little more time than anticipated, but God is faithful, and the procedure is a complete success.

Someone once remarked, "Sanctification [the act of getting right with God] is the work of a lifetime." One never gets off the operating table during his or her lifetime; God is continually at work in us, suppressing the carnal (evil) nature.

Here's a sample of what actually exists outside the operating room. "It is actually reported that there is sexual immorality among you, and such sexual immorality as is not even named among the Gentiles, that a man has his father's wife!" (1 Cor. 5:1). O Lord, please continue your good work in us despite our protest. Save us, O Lord God, from ourselves. Our vision of heavenly things is limited. We see only the here and now, but you see the whole picture.

"Look, I go forward, but He is not there, and backwards, but I cannot perceive Him; when He works on the left hand, I cannot behold Him; when He turns to the right hand, I cannot see Him. But He knows the way that I take; when He has tested me, I shall come forth as gold" (Job 23:8–10). The testing, the scalping, the cutting, the trimming, the chiseling, and the culling are all necessary in making us showpieces for God's art gallery. It wasn't easy or comfortable for Job, but he made it into the Hebrews Faith Hall of Fame. Are you being a compliant patient while on the operating table? Do you trust the Master Physician to do what is necessary for you to make it into his kingdom? The cutting may be uncomfortable, but hang in there; one day we all will thank God for giving us the ultimate makeover to triumph over sin.

March 7

Faithful Friend

Faithful are the wounds of a friend, but the kisses of an enemy are deceitful.
—Proverbs 27:6

Marcus Brutus, Judas Iscariot, and Benedict Arnold have much in common, but one trait distinguishes them from the rest of humanity; they betrayed their best friend. Marcus Brutus casually led his friend Julius Caesar into a waiting mob of merciless dagger-wielding assassins. The same is true of Judas Iscariot, who led a vengeful mob to Christ and betrayed him with a kiss on the cheek. Benedict Arnold's conspiracy differs a bit; his treacherous action cost this nation dearly in blood, tears, and treasure.

But not so with our forever friend and Savior, Jesus Christ; we are admonished to trust him fully and completely. Christ is the embodiment of trustworthiness. "A man who has friends must show himself friendly, But there is a friend who sticks closer than a brother" (Prov. 18:24). Being social creatures, we take great risks when we allow people to gravitate into our inner circle. We welcome them into our space, seeking their companionship, but often, we get hurt by their unkind words and unthoughtful actions. Hurts are painful and difficult to get over. They sting particularly hard, especially when inflicted by friends, but they are nothing compared with the kiss of an enemy. Having been betrayed by friends and foes alike, it came as no surprise that David chose to be chastised by God rather than man for his sin of indiscretion. "Please let us fall into the hand of the Lord, for His mercies are great; but do not let me fall into the hand of man" (2 Sam. 24:14).

Who hasn't been stung by the inappropriate words and callous behavior of friends? The ancients are correct: "bushes do have ears" (ability to hear unkind things spoken by friends). Is the microphone on or off? Ah yes. Many have had to make profuse apologies for unkind words spoken about a best friend. Others wish they could retrieve thoughtless and unkind words, but once spoken, words are irretrievable. You may not be able to put the proverbial genie back in the bottle. But there is a friend who sticks closer than a brother, and he can keep a secret—your secret. Would you like to meet him? He knows all our intimate secrets, and he will never embarrass us.

"Fear not for I have redeemed you; I have called you by your name; you are mine. When you pass through the waters, I will be with you; and through the rivers, they shall not overflow you. When you walk through the fire, you shall not be burned, nor shall the flame scorch you. For I am the Lord your God, The Holy One of Israel, your Savior" (Isa. 43:1–3). We claim the promise that God is with us even when we are unaware of his presence. Are not his angels continually accompanying us in our daily vocation?

Jesus is my forever friend. Is he your friend also? "No longer do I call you servants, for a servant does not know what his master is doing; for all things that I heard from My father I have made known to you. You did not choose Me, but I chose you and appointed you that you should go and bear fruit and that your fruit should remain, and that whatsoever you ask the Father in My name He may give you" (John 15:15–16). With Jesus as our friend, we will never be alone, nor should we fear being alone. Jesus is our sufficiency.

March 8

Growing, Growing, Growing

As newborn babes, desire the pure milk of the word that you may grow thereby.
—1 Peter 2:2

Grow in grace and electronic toys? Several months ago, my wife and I were tasked with babysitting our energetic twenty-one-month-old grandson. His joyous entry at home was soon short-lived. It became apparent our grandson LaShawn was totally bored after about five minutes with us. He wandered aimlessly from room to room. What was he searching for? Nothing we tried with him seemed to work. His parents occupied his interest with an array of push-button electronic gadgets. We had none of those toys. To save the day, we scrambled to Walmart to purchase a few things to occupy his interest. It worked magnificently, and we were spared another sleepless night.

LaShawn's boundless energy reminds me very much of my early conversion experience. When Christ found me in the spring of 1969, my appetite for spiritual things was insatiable and relentless. I read everything in sight. I spent early mornings and late evenings poring over biblical material. My mentor drafted me as a junior

Bible study partner, and off we went to the neighbors with the good news. I grew fat on the Word.

The milk formula used for babies works well on believing infants also. "As new-born babes, desire the pure milk of the word, that you may grow thereby" (1 Pet. 2:2). Whether we are grown-ups in Christ or mere infants, the Bible is our only source of nourishment. Jesus affirms, "This is the Bread which comes down from heaven that one may eat of and not die. I am the living Bread which came down from heaven, if any one eats of this Bread, he will live forever, and the Bread that I shall give is My flesh, which I shall give for the life of the world" (John 6:50–51). The Bible, with its life-giving formula, is nourishment for the Christian's growth. Failure to delve into its sacred pages (if literate) will result in spiritual malnutrition and, eventually, starvation and death.

Not only does the Word nourish the believer but it also starves the carnal nature that is antagonistic to Christian growth. "Your word I have hidden in my heart that I might not sin against You" (Ps. 119:11). Familiarity with the words of the Bible will deter us from adventurous wandering and sinning presumptuously against the Lord. The Word of God truly serves as a "lamp to my feet and a light to my path" (Ps. 119:105).

In nursing a child, there is always the danger of overfeeding the infant; no such thing exists for the Christian babe. You can eat and drink as much as you want from God's Word. The Bereans of the book of Acts were commended for their tenacity in reading and checking out the scripture. "These were more fair-minded than those in Thessalonica, in that they received the word with all readiness, and searched the scriptures daily to find out whether these things were so" (Acts 17:11). We tip our hats to the noble Bereans. Are you checking and double-checking out the scriptures to determine if your footing is secure on biblical principles? Thank you, Bereans, for your sterling example of rigorous Bible study. Do you have a regular time for Bible study, or is it a haphazard thing? Do you enjoy the Word even when it goes against your best wishes and craving? Mom used to say to me about bitter medicine, "Take it, it's good for you." Enjoy the scripture; it's good for you, even when some of it is rather difficult to digest.

March 9

Ready for Service Lord

So he, trembling and astonished said, "Lord, What do you want me to do?" And the Lord said to him, "Arise and go into the city, and you will be told what you must do."
—Acts 9:6

Breaking the will of an Asian elephant for a life of servitude is not a work for the fainthearted, but when done, a lifelong bond develops. The adventure begins with the selection of a fine young specimen from the wild. Using domesticated elephants, trainers called mahouts chase and isolate an individual young beast and lead it to camp. At camp, it undergoes the breaking process. It is chained by the leg and denied food, water, and sleep. It is poked with rods relentlessly, denied rest, and provoked for as long as it takes until its will is broken. It then falls helplessly in total submission at the feet of its tormentor. The tormentor now takes on a new role; he becomes a trusted friend. He pats and strokes the beast and whispers soothing niceties in its ears. He offers it food and water and wins over its trust. The beast is now broken and knows who is boss. He is now ready for a lifetime of unquestioned servitude to his master.

This method of training is not relegated to the training of elephants only. The training of the United States Marines follows a similar course. Upon arrival at various training installations, the new recruits disembarking from their sleepy long bus trip run through a gantlet of mean, angry snapping, barking drill instructors. They make life miserable, hard, and uncomfortable for the poor kids who, just days ago, were being doted over and serenaded by family and friends. Many drop out, but the few who endure benefit from an improvement in voice tone, encouragements, rewards, and other helpful treatments. A U.S. marine has been made to guard the interest of the nation.

Similarly, God utilizes an identical method in training his most ardent and trusted leaders. Moses, upon being called, was not yet fit for leadership, so he was commissioned to boot camp. In the desert of Midian and under the tutelage of God and nature, he began showing traits that would eventually grow him into a leader fit to confront the world's most formidable tyrant. After tending sheep for forty years, Moses was ready for service (Exod. 2:15–22, 3:1–2). Paul had a similar obstacle course in preparation for his ministry. After his call and under the direction of the Holy Spirit, he was trained and equipped for ministry (Gal. 1:15–18). In the desert of Arabia, Jesus visited his penitent and humble servant and outlined to him his evangelical assignment.

Some leaders received their calling with a baptism by fire as in the case of Martin Luther King Jr. During his confinement in the Birmingham jail, he penned his most inspirational speech, "I Have a Dream." Being confined on Robben Island in solitary confinement, Nelson Mandela became a leader reborn, shaped, and sharpened under the crucible of affliction. He accomplished through confinement what he couldn't achieve through the muzzle of a gun. God's top-notch leaders all went through the crucible of trials to test the limits of their endurance and their capability to lead men to God.

God carefully selects his leaders and develops their character by fiery trials. Are you a leader in God's service? Do you gripe and complain when things don't go according to plan? Do you still wish to continue the leadership course? Why not?

March 10

The Last Race

Do you not know that those who run in a race all run, but one receives the prize?

Run in such a way that you may obtain it.

—1 Corinthians 9:24

Alaska's Iditarod Race is the most grueling race on earth, yet many have succeeded in being champion multiple times. This grueling 1,049-mile dogsled race in blinding snow and in the most inhospitable conditions tests the limit of human endurance. It begins in Anchorage, Alaska's largest city, and ends in Nome. The usual duration of the race ranges from ten to fourteen days. It is a dangerous ordeal; one could be swallowed up in the deep crevices hidden beneath the snow. Dogs could also freeze to death, rendering the musher (transport powered by dogs) stranded in below freezing temperature. A blinding blizzard could disorient the competitor, sending him chasing after an imaginary finish line. Many other hazards lay hidden along the way.

One thing is crucial for success in this race: the musher must develop a close relationship with his dogs; his life depends on them. He is careful not to overwork them. At set periods, he feeds them and checks them out for signs of distress. Everything he needs for survival is on that sledge; he is on his own with no support or backup staff. In the bone-shivering cold, he relentlessly pursues one objective, the finish line. After many tireless days, he finally glimpses the familiar landmarks of Nome, Alaska, the finish line, and his reward. With the cheering crowds and flashing cameras, he enters the domain where few have trod. Many begin the race, but there is room for only one winner (iditarod.com).

Paul likens the believer's race to the Greek marathon, where the athletes rigorously train to compete in the games. The years of training, discipline, and self-sacrifice will be put on trial during the games. In the end, the winners all receive a crown (wreath) and a place in the record books.

Believers are in a similar race for something much bigger, more enduring, and eternal. We are in life's race with Jesus as our trainer and the Holy Spirit as our coach, and over at the finish line, the Father is waiting to welcome us into his kingdom. As we scale the obstacles in life, hidden dangers are everywhere; but with the aid of the Holy Spirit, we are able to detect, identify, and overcome problems. God has given us beeping signals through his Word about where the mines and snares of the enemy are hidden. "Your word is a lamp unto my feet and a light unto my path" (Ps. 119:105).

After every hard-fought race, there is an exhilarating reward, and the race of the believer is no exception. "And after these things I looked, and behold, a great multitude which no one could number, of all nations, tribes, peoples, and tongues, standing before the throne and before the Lamb, clothed with robes and palm branches in their hands, and crying out with a loud voice, saying, Salvation belongs to our God who sits on the throne, and to the Lamb" (Rev. 7:9–10). Can you picture yourself in that number? Are you confident of victory even when you stumble? Absolutely. With Christ walking with us, we can do all things. We can and will make it if we keep our eyes on Jesus, who is the Author and Finisher of our faith. Keep your eyes on the prize—Christ Jesus—and never look back; we are minutes from eternity, and this is not the time to get weary.

March 11

Wait Patiently on the Lord

But those who wait on the Lord shall renew their strength; they shall mount up with wings like eagles, they shall run and not be weary, they shall walk and not faint.
—Isaiah 40:31

Stanford University psychologist Walter Mischel conducted a scientific experiment on patience and instant gratification. The results sent many scientists scratching their heads in shock and amazement. Children were given a choice between a marshmallow now and two after a fifteen-minute break. The children who exercised discipline and waited for the two marshmallows after the fifteen-minute break period moved on to be more successful in life than their other counterparts, who opted for instant gratification. Delayed enjoyment was a huge factor for success in the kids who waited for the second marshmallow. Does patience play a pivotal role in one's life and success? (jamesclear.com/delayed-gratification)

Hunters, fishermen, and snipers are world-renowned for their extraordinary patience. They wait patiently in concealment for just the right moment and then pounce on their hapless victim. An annoying fly on the tip of the nose is ignored in favor of focus and concentration. At the precise moment, the hook is ripped, the shot is fired, and the desired objective is attained.

Instant gratification gained the better part of Esau, and he wept bitterly when he realized he sold his inheritance for a bowl of lentil soup (Heb. 12:17–18). Saul lost patience at the very last moment and foolishly encroached on the priest's sacred office (1 Sam. 13:9–11). Abraham and Sarah acted irrationally by not waiting for the fulfillment of God's promise. They tried to facilitate the process, and did they regret their meddling?

"I waited patiently for the Lord; and He inclined to me, and heard my cry. He also brought me up out of the horrible pit, out of the miry clay, and set my feet upon a rock, and established my steps" (Ps. 40:1–2). David was anointed the future king of Israel at about age seventeen and probably was in his late thirties or early forties when he was crowned king. During this period, he was hunted like a wild beast but was patient in waiting on the Lord, even though his life was almost snuffed out from him on numerous occasions. Can premarital sex wait till after the "I do" moment?

Joseph displayed extraordinary patience by allowing events to unfold, even when he could have forced the issue of betrayal by his brothers. He waited patiently for signs of remorse and repentance from his brothers before he revealed his identity to them. "Then Joseph said to his brothers, I am Joseph; does my father still live? But his brothers could not answer him, for they were dismayed in his presence. And Joseph said to his brothers, please come near to me. So they came near. Then he said: I am Joseph your brother, whom you sold into Egypt" (Gen. 45:3–4). What a beautiful example Joseph left us of self-restraint and of how to treat those who harm us or wish to do us harm.

We are required to have patience; it is a fruit of the Spirit and is essential in the fight against evil. "But the fruit of the Spirit is love, joy, peace, longsuffering, kindness, goodness, faithfulness, gentleness, self-control" (Gal. 5:22–23). Patience is one of the many juicy fruits of the Spirit. Do you have it growing on your tree? If not, why not? You won't be able to handle your difficult and cranky neighbor without it. Get it now. It's free for the asking from the one who manufactures it, the Lord Jesus Christ.

March 12

I Love You Much

Husbands love your wives and do not be bitter toward them.

—Colossians 3:19

Romeo is tough, sharp, jovial, exciting, and extremely smart, but he has a dark past. Vincia (my grandniece) thinks he is responsible for Juliet's demise. At five thirty every morning, he brightens the home with his keyless tunes and sharp chirps. Romeo is a cockatiel, a native bird of Australia. He once had a beautiful companion, Juliet. But don't be fooled; he is not as romantic as his name implies. His low self-esteem led him to harass Juliet to the extent that she lost all interest in eating her favorite food, scrumptious Brazilian nuts. Vincia thinks he should be banished to some penal bird colony for his crime, but her bigger sister, Penny, yawns at the whole idea. But Romeo has much to learn from his feathery neighbors, the emperor penguin and the black vulture, who mate for life and dote over their companions with love and fondness.

The Bible calls on believing couples everywhere to lavish love without restraint on each other. "Behold you are fair, my love! Behold you are fair! You have dove's eyes" (Song of Sol. 1:15). Where have all the lovely courtship words gone? Not very far. We must bring ourselves to repeat them continuously to the ones we love. "I am my beloved's, and my beloved is mine. He feeds his flock among the lilies" (Song of Sol. 6:3).

Christian believers have every reason to be the most loving and romantic couples on planet Earth since Jesus is the embodiment of love and since we talk about love more than any other religion on planet Earth. Regrettably, because of failed relationships, past and current, our witness is muffled. However, this is no excuse to have a pity party for oneself; the scripture is replete with steamy, healthy, and exciting monogamous relationships. Boaz and Ruth are prime examples; they couldn't have enough of each other. It probably was love at first sight, but it developed into a healthy, sparkling, and fruitful relationship (Ruth 2:14–15). Isaac and Rebecca are not to be forgotten; although their marriage was prearranged in keeping with the cultural motif of their day, they enjoyed a monogamous, stimulating, and fruitful union. Little is said about Joseph's marital relationship, but considering the blow he inflicted on Mrs. Potiphar's ambition, we can safely assume he also had a healthy marriage.

Someone remarked, "Love is the most abused word in the English language." I reluctantly concur, but we can make it beautiful, stimulating, pleasant, and meaningful once more. We can say what we mean and mean what we say. Let me emphasize: if you love me, show it. Action speaks louder than words. While some may be very romantic with words, shouldn't their actions speak louder than their lofty words? We are very fortunate that God's actions speak louder than his words, and he loves us with an unconditional love, whether we are good or bad.

"I have loved you with an everlasting love; therefore in loving-kindness I have drawn you" (Jer. 31:3). Yes, even if you have been starved of true love, God loves you personally anyway. He really does, and you can count on his word. He will never stop loving us, regardless of what we do or may not do. He loves us unconditionally. God loves you, and so do I.

March 13

Needle in a Haystack

For the Son of Man has come to seek and to save that which was lost.
—Luke 19:10

As Grandma Freda became less mobile, sewing became her obsession, and threading her needle became a real challenge as her vision faded. However, it was not a problem; her grandson was usually within hearing distance anyway. Granny's tone of voice became frantic whenever she dropped her needle. Her inflexible knees would not allow her to bend and search for it. Young eyes would have difficulty locating the needle in the proverbial haystack of a wooden floor riddled with crevices. The needle was usually found after a diligent short search, and Granny would be happy for another day.

Is someone searching somewhere for a runaway teen, a spouse, a dad, a mom, or some other loved one? David's trouble-prone son Absalom murdered his big brother Amnon and fled to his grandpa, a neighboring king. "And King David longed to go to Absalom. For he had been comforted concerning Amnon, because he was dead" (2 Sam. 13:39). Paternal love would not allow David to rest comfortably, even though he had many other sons, including his heir apparent, Solomon. David was indeed a poor example of fatherhood, having multiple wives and failing to discipline his errant children for their misbehavior, but he was exemplary in demonstrating true love for his children. Jesus certainly was not ashamed of being called the Son of David. David yearned and prayed for his children in spite of his shortcoming.

God is searching the nightclubs, the casinos, the gay bars, the political convention centers, and even the churches for a lost son and a wayward daughter. Not everyone may be willing to come back home, but his everlasting love is relentless, and it drives him on. He issues us this invitation: dinner is ready. "Tell those who are invited, see, I have prepared my dinner, my oxen and my fatted cattle are killed, and all things are ready. Come to the wedding" (Matt. 22:4). The invited guests, who include everyone who hears the small still voice of the Holy Spirit, make fun of the urgency of the invitation. "But they made light of it and went their ways, one to his own farm, and another to his business. And the rest seized his servants, treated them spitefully, and killed them" (Matt. 22:5–6).

In the big cities, the rural villages, in the Kalahari Desert, in the Alaskan wilderness, in the jungles of uncivilized cultures, even on cruise ships, wherever men are, Jesus invites them, "Come unto me." He doesn't save en masse but one individual at a time. The haystack is being turned inside out to find that son or daughter who is desirous of coming back home. The prodigal story displays God's unrelenting yearning for his wayward children to come home. "But when he was still a great way off, his father saw him and had compassion, and ran and fell on his neck and kissed him" (Luke 15:20).

Have you received your invitation yet? Are you determined to come to the wedding? Are you bringing an invited guest along with you? What in the world are you waiting for? Come on, hurry before it's too late and the gate is shut.

March 14

Heroes Indeed

For scarcely for a righteous man will one die; yet perhaps for a good man someone would even dare to die. But God demonstrates His own love towards us, in that while we were still sinners, Christ died for us.

—Romans 5:7–8

While others are running away from the flames, they are rushing toward it. They are the brave firemen and women all over the world who put others' safety ahead of their own. The tragedy of 9/11 revealed the self-sacrificing spirit of this elite group. They race up stairways of burning buildings while panic-stricken folks are hustling down. Firemen are at their finest when tragedy strikes. With little thought of their own safety, they even save pets whenever possible. Putting out fires is only one aspect of their many calls to service; they deliver babies, perform CPR, treat wounds, and mentor kids. They pay a heavy price on their dangerous assignments, and we all grieve when they perish on duty.

The Christian missionary has much in common with the fireman. They both have devoted their lives to saving others from fire. However, the missionary's work is of a spiritual nature; he has dedicated his life to save others from another kind of fire. They forsake the comfort of home and family to embrace another culture of their choosing, where they become teacher, doctor, nurse, consultant, counselor, and preacher to others. Like their master Jesus, they seek no attention to themselves and prefer to work in obscurity. Immersing themselves into the social life of their subjects, they seek opportunities to inject the love of Jesus in their host. For inspiration, they call to memory the Missionary who came down to our planet about two thousand years ago. He became one of us and made his abode with us. He walked our streets, attended social gatherings, ate our food, slept under our roofs, and died to save us all. In essence, we are all missionaries to the world. The Lord has called not some but all his people to ministry, and we may very well incur what Paul was privileged to encounter.

> In labors more abundant, in stripes above measure, in prisons more frequently, in deaths often. From the Jews five times I received forty stripes minus one. Three times I was beaten with rods; once I was stoned; three times I was shipwrecked; a night and day I have been in the deep; in journeys often, in perils of waters, in perils of robbers, in perils of my own countrymen, in perils of the Gentiles, in perils in the city, in perils in the wilderness, in perils in the sea, in perils among false brethren, in weariness and toil, in sleeplessness often, in hunger and thirst, in fasting often, in cold and nakedness, besides the other things, what comes upon me daily: my deep concern for all the churches. (2 Cor. 11:23–28)

Are you prepared for this assignment? Jesus can prepare you for it.

As we witness the closing signs before the return of Jesus to this earth, God is calling on all to a life of service to others. We have the solution to this world's ill, and if we remain silent, something evil might befall us. "Then they said to one another, 'We are not doing right. This day is a day of good news, and we remain silent. If we wait until morning light, some punishment will come on us. Now therefore, come, let us go and tell the king's household'" (2 Kings 7:9). You and I have been commanded to spread that good news. How are you spreading the good news? It is very simple: just tell someone what God has done in your life and leave the rest to the Holy Spirit.

March 15

Hold Your Tongue

A soft answer turns away wrath, but a harsh word stirs up anger.
—Proverbs 15:1

Once upon a time, the fable goes, the wind and sun were in a heated argument. They vigorously debated which one had the power and wit to force a traveler to shed his coat. Wind was the first to go. He huffed and he puffed, but the traveler held his coat ever so tightly around his body. Then came the sun with its balmy warmth. It didn't do much; it just shone. And to everyone's amazement, the traveler began shedding his coat; a few degrees more, and off came the shirt and hat also. What could not be accomplished by brute force and bulging muscle was easily accomplished through gentleness, thoughtfulness, and calculation.

"He who is slow to anger is better than the mighty, and he who rules his spirit than he who takes a city" (Prov. 16:32). Mom had a secret weapon, her soft-spoken voice, which she used quite effectively on us. It was firm, persuasive, and commanding. In many respects, she reminds me of Jesus. While soft-spoken, affirming, and gentle to the repentant, he was uncompromising and stern to the haughty Pharisees. He dispensed blessings on the poor being crushed by their oppressors but hurled woes on their heartless exploiters (Matt. 23:13–18).

"For every kind of beast and bird, of reptile and creature or the sea, is tamed and has been tamed by mankind. But no man can tame the tongue. It is an unruly evil, full of deadly poison" (James 3:7–8). How can we tame the tongue? "Finally, brethren, whatever things are true, whatever things are noble, whatever things are just, whatever things are pure, whatever things are lovely, whatever things are of good report, if there is any virtue and if there is anything praiseworthy mediate on these things" (Phil. 4:8). Dwelling on positive things is a perfect antidote for an untamed tongue, and it comes straight from the Word. "A good man out of the good treasure of his heart brings forth good; and an evil man out of the evil treasure of his heart brings forth evil. For out of the abundance of the heart his mouth speaks" (Luke 6:45).

While it is easy and convenient to dwell on the negative, we must take the higher route and fiercely resist the urge to go negative. When the Lord looks at his children, he sees what we can become in him and not who we are at present. Can we intentionally begin to affirm everyone with whom we come in contact? "Oh, that dress is simply gorgeous. Where did you buy it?" And a friend is made; it is that simple. Remember, we are kingdom-minded people; every contact we make must be saturated with love. Is there anyone who doesn't want to be loved? Not one. Everyone loves compliments; therefore let's be generous with it. When maligned and provoked, take the higher road. If you are verbally assaulted, start counting from one to ten and pray for the aggressor. By the time you arrive at ten, the Lord will have injected some Christian civility in you. Let's be intentional about brightening the corner where we are. "Even a fool is counted wise when he holds his peace" (Prov. 17:28). Don't waste your breath on unnecessary remarks; consider the source and take the higher road.

March 16

The Chariots of Israel

And Elijah saw it, and he cried out, my father, my father, the chariot of Israel and its horsemen! So he saw him no more. And he took hold of his own clothes and tore them into two pieces.

—2 Kings 2:12

Lockheed Martin's F-22 Stealth Raptor is a fine lady with lots of fancy, glittering moves; she evades radar with impunity. The aircraft is virtually invisible to radar and can knock at the gates of her enemies unannounced and without being detected. The technology composing her makeup is mind-boggling, which makes it a coveted secret. Its primary purpose is to win the nation's battles and discourage would-be opponents from ever encountering her. Military analysts have declared her the best fighter aircraft ever built. The unit price per fighter is a whopping $360 million. Can you afford one? (http://www.lockheedmartin.com/us/products/f22/f-22-sustainment.html)

Chariots were the weapon of choice in ancient warfare, primarily used to intimidate and defeat opponents, but Israel's God of Hosts was her strength and refuge. "No king is saved by the multitude of an army; a mighty man is not delivered by great strength. A horse is vain hope for safety; neither shall it deliver any by its great strength" (Ps. 33:16–17). The Lord constantly reassured his people, "Have I not commanded you? Be strong and of good courage; do not be afraid, nor be dismayed, for the Lord your God is with you wherever you go" (Josh. 1:9). God was the tip of the arrow in Israel's defense. In battle, they plowed through and defeated nations mightier and better equipped because the Lord was their buckler and shield.

Similarly, believers in God have nothing to fear from false friends and the legions of demons that harass them: "If God is for us, who can be against us?" (Rom. 8:31). At present, the people of God are more dependent on the police and national armies for protection from those hostile to them. However, the time is coming when the angels holding back the winds of strife will be told to let loose their restraints, and the hellish forces, now restrained, will aim their weapons on God's people. At such a moment, this precious promise will come to pass: "Listen, all you of Judah and inhabitant of Jerusalem, and you, King Jehoshaphat! Thus says the Lord to you: Do not be afraid nor dismayed because of this great multitude for the battle is not yours, but God's" (2 Chron. 20:15). An attack against you is an attack against God.

The believer must be confident that, in the battle against sin, he has an ally in Jesus who has never lost a battle against evil. We should do well to remember a military contingent was sent to arrest the prophet Elisha only to be destroyed by an angel. The prophet's servant was concerned about a second military unit sent to accomplish the task that the first failed to do. "And Elisha prayed, and said, Lord open his eyes that he may see. Then the Lord opened the eyes of the young man, and he saw. And behold, the mountain was full of horses and chariots of fire all around Elisha" (2 Kings 6:17).

We do not need to worry. God will deliver his people as in the past. "And Moses said to the people, stand still, and see the salvation of the Lord, which He will accomplish for you today. For the Egyptians whom you see today, you shall see again no more forever" (Exod. 14:13). "God is our helper and strength a very pleasant help in time of trouble therefore we will not fear even though the earth be removed" (Ps. 46:1–2).

March 17

Saving for Rainy Days

How long will you slumber, O sluggard? . . . A little sleep, a little slumber, a little folding of the hands to sleep. So shall your poverty come on you like a prowler, and your need like an armed man.

—Proverbs 6:9–11

A Sabbath walk in our favorite park reveals a resident squirrel furiously digging and burying acorns for the approaching winter. He is oblivious of the presence of two curious observers checking out his hard work. Instinct has kicked in; his supply of acorns must be adequate, or he might starve during the lean, cold days of winter. Unlike his rural neighbors in the western states whose supply may be raided periodically by ever-hungry grizzly bears, his storehouse here is secure since there are no such acorn thieves over here in Washington, DC. "Make haste while the sun shines" is his motto. He scurries here and there burying seeds, doing what generations of squirrels and other seed collectors have done, collecting the abundance of nature, and storing it up for the hard, lean times ahead. Instinct has taught him not to depend on the generosity of humankind; that might tamper with his ability to provide for himself and his family.

Similarly, humans should work hard while youth and health are vibrant to ensure a more pleasurable existence in old age. The story of the "talents" in Matthew 25:15–30 reveals the validity of this principle: The stewards who received five and two talents, respectively, invested their master's money and made more money upon return. Of course, they were commended for their industry. However, the servant with the one talent paid no attention to his companions' thriftiness but instead lounged around, wasting his opportunities. The day of reckoning revealed his utter slothfulness and eventual doom. "Therefore take the talent from him, and give to him who has ten talents. For to everyone who has, more will be given, and he will have abundance; but from him who does not have, even what he has will be taken away. And cast the unprofitable servant into the outer darkness. There will be weeping and gnashing of teeth" (Matt. 25:28–30).

Although human productivity peaks at various ages, modern science and technology have given many a second chance to make amends for wasted years. However, to offset the unfortunate experience of living on limited income in old age, one can learn a lot from our industrious little friends in nature. "Go to the ant, you sluggard! Consider her ways and be wise, which, having no captain, overseer or ruler, provides supplies in the summer, and gathers her food in harvest. How long will you slumber, O sluggard? When will you rise from your sleep?" (Prov. 6:6–9).

Coming from a hardworking family, we didn't have to look very hard for an exemplary work role model. Father worked hard and retired comfortably according to cultural standards of his day but not before providing his children a good head start in life. Are you doing what is necessary by collecting acorns (money) for the lean, hard days of old age and diminished health? If going back to school is an option, then do it. Do you still have a few more productive years of gathering acorns? Then go for it. Are you satisfied with a supplemental income even if you are healthy and can still gather a few more acorns for retirement?

March 18

Learning to Walk

For a righteous man may fall seven times and rise again, but the wicked shall fall by calamity.
—Proverbs 24:16

A little toddler no more than a year old was trying out his newly discovered legs in the park. He galloped a few steps and then stumbled; he got up and immediately plopped back down on his posterior. Somehow he gathered himself again, but balance and coordination were off, and he stumbled sideways. Not discouraged by his past failures, he dug deep down and bolted forward toward the outstretched arms of his dad. Amazingly, not once did the little guy doubt his ability to walk. He fell, got up, fell again, and bounced back up instantaneously. Instinct was driving him on; he must continue trying if he seriously intended to walk upright.

In the mind of every toddler is the struggle to push on and conquer new frontiers; that's all part of growing up. Apparently, he's grown tired of crawling around on his knees and is ready for new challenges ahead. We applaud this toddler for his bold spirit of adventurism. We all, without exception, have gone through the struggle of staying with the status quo or moving ahead to something more interesting. Something in us, like an idea whose time has come, just keeps pushing us onward, forward till we get it right no matter how many times we may have tried and failed. In our struggle for buoyancy, we may fall, but should we stay fallen?

Believers fall also. Oh yes, we do, but here's the antidote (remedy) for when we fall. "If we confess our sins He is faithful and just to forgive us our sins and to cleanse us from all unrighteousness" (1 John 1:9). Sin is offensive to our holy and righteous God; therefore immediately upon consciousness of sin, we must throw ourselves at the mercy seat of God, pleading for forgiveness. We must not wait till we get home, when we simmer down, or when we arrive at our destination; we must confess immediately upon consciousness of sin. We cannot cancel or delay asking for forgiveness. "Lord, I am sorry. Forgive me." That's all it takes. Of course, if injury is inflicted on someone, whether physical or emotional, this might necessitate a verbal, public, or written apology.

God's ideal for his children is that they sin not, but having inherited a corrupt nature from birth, every human from Adam has sinned. But wait, help is on the way. "My little children, these things I write to you, so that you may not sin. And if anyone sins, we have an Advocate with the Father, Jesus Christ the righteous" (1 John 2:1). What a blessed thought to know that we do not have to live in sin or die in its grisly embrace. If we keep our eyes fixed on Jesus Christ, it is possible not to sin. As the experience of Peter reveals, as long as he had his eyes on Jesus, he was doing okay. A single glance away from the source of perfection sent him plummeting in the deep.

"Now to Him who is able to keep you from stumbling, and to present you faultless before the presence of His glory with exceeding joy, to God our Savior, who alone is wise, be glory and majesty dominion and power both now and forever" (Jude 24–25). Only Jesus can keep us from sinning, and this happens when we lock our steps in his will. When we yield ourselves daily on the altar of sacrifice, we will walk with God as Abraham, Enoch, Moses, and Elijah did. Do you desire to walk with God today?

March 19

You Bore My Pain

Then the king was deeply moved, and went up to the chamber over the gate, and wept. And as he went, he said thus: O my son Absalom, my son, my son Absalom, if only I had died in your place! O Absalom my son, my son. —2 Samuel 18:33

My grandson LaShawn is back with us again; his parents are having a candlelit dinner date without him. He's a whole lot more mobile now than previously. However, he has not yet developed the skill of negotiating obstacles in his way. Upon entry into our home, you climb seven steps to the living room, where a piano sits, protruding slightly into the hallway. To the left is a walkway leading to the other rooms; to the right is the living room. Little LaShawn uses this long hallway to do his fifty-meter dashes.

One Saturday night, during one of his speedy lapses, he bumped his head into the piano. Oh, how it hurt! Did you feel it? We felt it from the intensity of his writhing cries. Oh, how I wish I could bear the hurt and pain for my little grandson, but it was not to be. I was helpless as he squirmed in pain, resting on my bosom. God was in a similar predicament.

Several centuries ago, the Father stood helplessly as Jesus was being worked over by a satanic mob. They mocked and whipped him, slapped him in the face, spat on him, stripped him naked, and forced a crown of prickly thorns on his head; and finally, to add insult to injury, they crucified him. How could the Father stand by and not intervene? As most parents are aware of, you cannot hold down a bully while your child pummels him with kicks and punches. This is illegal. God must allow the watching universe to see the true character of evil and its dire consequences. Jesus had to fulfill all the prophecies concerning his handling of the sin question. "I have trodden the winepress alone, and from the peoples no one was with Me" (Isa. 63:3). Even his closest friends forsook him and fled. "But this was done that the Scripture of the prophets might be fulfilled. Then all the disciples forsook Him and fled" (Matt. 26:56).

David's problematic son Absalom murdered his half-brother Amnon, and he, in turn, was devoured by the sword. Oh, how David wished he could have absorbed the punishment for his wayward son, but the law stipulates that the father cannot be held accountable for the son's sin. "The son shall not bear the guilt of the father, nor the father bear the guilt of the son. The righteousness of the righteous shall be upon himself, and the wickedness of the wicked shall be upon himself" (Ezek. 18:20). Justice also dictates that "all who take the sword will perish by the sword" (Matt. 26:52). Absalom had met his just reward for murdering his brother, but what did our Lord Jesus do to deserve this atrocious punishment? "For He made Him who knew no sin to be sin for us, that we might become the righteousness of God in Him" (2 Cor. 5:21). As an innocent lamb had to be slain for the atonement of the guilty sinner, likewise, Jesus—the innocent Lamb of God—volunteered to suffer the wrath of God in our place. What love!

Jesus absorbed in his body the bumps and bruises we deserved for transgressing God's holy law. We deserved death, but he died in our place so that we might obtain the life that was his. And this, my friend, we must accept by faith as we fall at the foot of the cross and plead for forgiveness. Jesus is the Lamb slain from the foundation of the world. Have you accepted his atonement for your sins?

March 20

The Coming Kingdom

Then I John saw a new heaven and a new earth, for the first heaven and the first earth had passed away. Also there was no more sea. Then I, John saw the holy city, New Jerusalem, coming down out of heaven from God, prepared as a bride adorned for her husband.

—Revelation 21:1–2

A boy was fishing in his favorite spot. When asked how many fish he had caught, he retorted with a smile, "When I have caught this one and two more, I shall have three."

The news emanating from the media has been depressing lately; we need some good news every now and then to keep functional. But where can one's spirit be rejuvenated except in the Word of God? Besides teaching a superior lifestyle, the Bible speaks of a glorious future for all who are looking forward to Christ's coming kingdom. Among its chief feature is a brand-new world with a dazzling capital city now under construction. Even as we speak, real homes are being matched to individual names, all purchased by the blood of Christ. How much do they cost? Don't worry about the price; it's all been paid for. When can I move in? "Let not your heart be troubled; you believe in God believe also in Me. In My Father's house are many mansions; if it were not so, I would have told you. I go to prepare a place for you. And if I go and prepare a place for you, I will come again and receive you to Myself; that where I am, there you may be also" (John 14:1–3).

Pilgrims throughout the ages have written about this amazing space city. John Bunyan, in his classic *Pilgrim's Progress*, wrote extensively about it. Saint Augustine of Hippo wrote about it in his famous work *City of God*. The Protestant reformers and succeeding church leaders referenced the coming kingdom in their writings. In Matthew 24, Jesus enumerated a series of climatic events that would befall this world just before the emergence of the coming space city.

The boy in our opening story hadn't caught any fish yet but was very confident about grabbing a few from the ocean. Believers in Christ Jesus need to be very optimistic and passionate about the coming kingdom. The promises of God are more certain than tomorrow's sunrise. "By faith he [Abraham] dwelt in the land of promise as in a foreign country, dwelling in tents with Isaac and Jacob, heirs with him of the same promise; for he waited for the city which has foundations, whose builder and maker is God" (Heb. 11:9–10).

What type of mansion do you anticipate inhabiting? Do you prefer living in a country house surrounded by lush green meadows and pristine lakes? Since the city is a perfect square, would you opt for a condominium with the lofty transparent walls for a more perfect view of the countryside? To those who love gold, diamond, and all sorts of precious materials, these are the building materials of this great city.

A sign by the forest reads, "Absolutely no tree cutting or excavation of soil." That's right, everything has been prepared for the righteous. There will be no need to cut or destroy plants in that blissful land, for cutting and killing are things of the past; all things have become new. Since sin will be vanquished forever, a long category of professions will become extinct. Undertakers, doctors, health care providers, and reminders of our broken health system will be out of service. The leaves and fruits of that land are tasty and life enhancing. "In the middle of the street and on either side of the river, was the tree of life, which bore twelve fruits, each tree yielding its fruit every month. The leaves of the tree were for the healing of the nations" (Rev. 22:2). Is any place on earth comparable to heaven? I dream of a city called heaven. Are you planning to be there? Are your bags packed and ready to go? Do you have your ticket, the Lord Jesus Christ?

March 21

Till Death Do Us Part

And He answered and said to them, have you not read that He who made them at the beginning made them male and female; and for this reason a man shall leave his father and mother and be joined to his wife, and the two shall become one flesh?
—Matthew 19:4–5

Having awakened from his nap on the sixth day of Creation, Adam gazed into the face of his Creator, who helped him to his feet. But wait, who is this beautiful, gorgeous lady standing next to God? Could she be his? Yes, she is. Eve, his soon-to-be mate for life, blushed shyly and inched her way toward Adam. Standing together in the presence of their Creator and surrounded by the curious animals already paired, Adam and Eve exchanged vows and pledged allegiance to each other for life.

Singular male and singular female (emphasis on *singular*) is the sacred order of marriage. God intentionally created the man with a muscular physical body not only to distinguish him from his mate but also to care, protect, and provide for his wife. Eve, on the other hand, was wired up a little bit more complex. She was designed to give birth, nurse, love, hold the family together, and do all the interesting things men could only dream of but simply can't do.

To establish his home, the man must leave his doting parents and establish his own family. The primary love that he had for Mom and Dad is transferred to his new love, his wife. He does not love his parents any less, but to have a successful marriage, he must elevate his mate above all competing interests, including his parents.

Love is the main ingredient in marriage; it gives and gives and keeps on giving. When illness strikes to test one's devotion to the other, love hangs in there. Even in hard times, when the paycheck can't cover all financial obligations, love hangs in there. For better or for worse, in sickness and in health, in poverty and in wealth, we should hang in there, period. Marriage is like a flight with no escape parachutes except if one dies or a mate refuses to stay married.

Jesus showed his appreciation for marriage by accepting a wedding invitation, and he blessed the couple by performing his first miracle at that occasion. Conversely, he showed his utter disdain for divorce with these words: "Therefore what God has joined together, let not man separate" (Matt. 19:6). Running into stiff resistance from the religious leaders, the Savior was equally forceful and emphatic in the defense of marriage: "He said to them, Moses, because of the hardness of your hearts, permitted you to divorce your wives, but from the beginning it was not so" (Matt. 19:8).

Someone described marriage as a fire that must be tended constantly. The logs must be pushed against each other regularly to generate heat; when one log burns alone, the fire goes out quickly. Married partners, primarily the man, should ignite and maintain the spark in the relationship. Why should the burden fall on the man? The man initiated the whole thing in the first place; he proposed, didn't he? Isn't he the instigator of the whole affair? It is incumbent on him, being the senior partner, to ensure the health and success of his marriage.

Marriage is still the glue that keeps families together. It creates a beautiful fragrance in the home. Are you giving your best in your marriage? Are you finding it extremely hard to apologize? Do you always have to have the final word? Do you enjoy building or tearing things down in your marriage? God bless you in your relationship.

In the Name of Jesus

And whatever you ask in My name, that I will do, that the Father may be glorified in the Son. If you ask any thing in My name, I will do it.

—John 14:13–14

Johnny (name changed) is tormented by evil spirits; he is demon possessed. His loved ones stand helplessly as demons torment him continuously. Such attacks usually send him into convulsions, causing him to foam at the mouth and utter unintelligible sounds. Just when it seems likely that Johnny is destined for a life of ruin and degradation, a team of evangelists descends on his village. They canvass the neighborhood and, upon finding Johnny's family, learn of his terrible affliction. The family promptly requests Bible study, and in the name of Jesus and by the power of the Holy Spirit, the demons are evicted and sent packing. To the relief of the family, the young man goes on to live a normal life, free from any further demonic molestation.

Jesus said to his disciples, "Most assuredly, I say to you, he who believes in Me, the works that I do he will do also; and greater works than these he will do, because I go to My Father" (John 14:12). This promise is at the disposal of every believer in Jesus Christ. Knowing full well the possessive nature of evil, the Savior gave this command to his followers: "And as you go, preach, saying, the kingdom of heaven is at hand. Heal the sick, cleanse the lepers, and raise the dead, cast out demons. Freely you have received freely give" (Matt. 10:7–8).

God will not impose his will on any human sufferer; there must be an intense desire for deliverance from the affliction that shackles the soul. The desire for liberation must outweigh the pleasure derived from sinful indulgence. When a decision for a better life is made, God puts that person on a collision course with the messengers of heaven (human witnesses). "By faith the harlot Rahab did not perish with those who did not believe, when she received the spies with peace" (Heb. 11:31). Was it by chance or coincidence Rahab was delivered from her night profession, or was there an intense desire for a better life?

The loving Father scans the world over, looking for those who desire a way out of their sinful life. We are prime examples of this fact, are we not? We are saved now, but before, we were career thieves, adulterers, liars, blasphemers, and Sabbath breakers, were we not? Thanks be to God for instilling in us a desire for a better way. Paul recognized God's hand in the lives of humans with this statement. "Or do you despise the riches of His goodness, forbearance, and longsuffering, not knowing that the goodness of God leads you to repentance?" (Rom. 2:4).

Deliverance is promised to anyone who wishes to break away from his or her sinful life, and there is abundant grace and mercy to match the level of one's depravity. "But where sin abounded, grace abounded much more" (Rom. 5:20). The Savior beckons, "Behold I stand at the door and knock. If anyone hear My voice and open the door, I will come in to him and dine with him and he with Me" (Rev. 3:20). What an invitation! Are you hearing the voice of the Holy Spirit inviting you to a better life? Do you desire victory over the passions of the flesh? Is obedience to Jesus more important than continuing to walk in sin and disobedience? Lord Jesus, please give us victory over sin.

March 23

Best Friend

And lo, I am with you always, even to the end of the age.
—Matthew 28:20

A tribunal is in session in the courts of heaven; the judge, defense attorney, and prosecutor are all seated. The attention of the court is focused on a poor defendant who is in deep trouble. Let's listen. "Then he showed me Joshua the high priest standing before the Angel of the Lord, and Satan standing at his right hand to oppose him. And the Lord said to Satan, The Lord rebuke you, Satan! The Lord who has chosen Jerusalem rebuke you! Is this not a branch plucked from the fire?" (Zech. 3:1–2).

Jesus is our best friend and walks with us throughout our lifetime. Has he not promised? "And lo, I am with you always, even to the end of the age" (Matt. 28:20). Not only does Jesus walk with us but he also sympathizes with us when we are burdened with life's heavy load. After all, did he not put on a human body to completely identify with our lot? "For we do not have a High Priest who cannot sympathize with our weakness, but was in all points tempted as we are, yet without sin" (Heb. 4:15). When neighbors are unsympathetic and friends are few, Jesus is always there with outstretched arms, ready to lift us.

Joshua, our biblical high priest in the book of Zechariah, is in deep trouble; he had fallen on hard times (Zech. 3:1–10). As he stands before God in filthy, tattered garments, Satan—the prosecutor and accuser—is pointing a finger of ridicule and condemnation at him. The fact that Joshua is clad in a filthy garment is indicative of his current state of sinfulness. Poor Joshua, he cannot defend himself against such a powerful prosecutor who knows every slip he had made in life.

Let's compare a modern-day Joshua with the biblical one cited above. Court evidence against our modern character is staggering, and his criminal profile leaves much to be desired. On Christmas Day, he was caught and arrested for drunk driving. He paid a fine and served time in jail. His wages has been garnished because of inconsistent child support payments. He was also arrested for driving while his license was suspended. Our modern-day character throws himself at the mercy of the court but he still has to pay his debt to society.

But let's return to our biblical character for a minute; the defense attorney is addressing the court. "And the Lord said to Satan, 'The Lord rebukes you, Satan! The Lord who has chosen Jerusalem rebuke you! Is this not a brand plucked from the fire?' Then He answered and spoke to those who stood before Him, saying, 'Take away the filthy garments from him.' And to him He said, 'See, I have removed your iniquity from you, and I will clothe you with rich robes.' And I said, 'let them put a clean turban on his head.' So they put a clean turban on his head, and they put the clothes on him" (Zech. 3:2–5).

Unlike our modern-day Joshua, when we throw ourselves at the mercy of our Lord Jesus Christ, we will find forgiveness. God will forgive us for our sins no matter how grievous the offense may be, but God's forgiveness does not cancel our debt to society if we have committed offenses against the state. We all have stumbled and have fallen short of God's perfect law, but if we confess our sins, we have our High Priest currently representing us in the courts of heaven. Those who have accepted the plan of salvation will have a friend and defender in Jesus. "What a friend we have in Jesus, all our sins and griefs to bear" (Brad Paisley). Aren't you glad we have a friend in heaven? Thank God for such a friend. Have you taken advantage of the mediation of Jesus on your behalf before the tribunal of God? I have. Have you?

March 24

Let My People Go

Today if you will hear his voice do not harden your hearts as in the rebellion.
—Hebrews 3:15

The sun melts butter, but it also hardens clay. The Holy Spirit, very much like the sun, has the same effect on the hearts of men. If we are willing and desirous to know God and do his will, our hearts will melt into compliance with his kingdom-building program. Conversely, if the heart is stubborn and resistant to the wooing of the Holy Spirit, it will harden and be devoid of compliance to the will of God. Consequently, a heart controlled by Satan—the enemy of souls—will not only get harder but will also become a willing tool against God's kingdom-building enterprise.

Staring the world's most powerful dictator in the face, Moses demanded, "The Lord God of the Hebrews has sent me to you, saying, 'Let My people go, that they may serve Me in the wilderness; but indeed, until now you would not hear'" (Exod. 7:16). The playbook of the evil one has not changed with time. He busies himself by ordering his subordinates to repress and harass the people of God, saddling them with heavy burdens, placing obstacles in their way, and inhibiting their access to Jesus. Bent on the destruction of God's kingdom since his fall, Satan causes his earthbound followers to be hostile to the good news of the gospel wherever it is preached. He causes them to view with suspicion and scorn the very good news that can save men. His sinister plan calls for cluttering the lives of believers with so much stuff that there will be little room left for the Savior and salvation. And of course, with those who do not know God, he is satisfied by allowing them to perish in ignorance, fanaticism, and darkness.

Under the guise of family unity and social stability, Satan uses close relatives, friends, and even government authorities to punish anyone about to desert his ranks. He causes spouses to harass and mistreat their believing counterpart to woo them back to his service. The sacred bonds of love once cherished by family members are turned into blind hatred whenever one accepts Jesus as Savior and Lord. Neighbors who seek the better way of salvation have become objects of scrutiny, ridicule, and punishment by their former friends.

Their only crime is seeking a nobler path. Any decision for Christ is contested and fought by Satan and his disciples. Should we be surprised? "If the world hates you, you know that it hated Me before it hated you. If you were of the world, the world would love its own. Yet because you are not of the world, but I chose you out of the world, therefore the world hates you" (John 15:18–19).

Today the call to be part of God's last day people is still being heard. "The Lord God of the Hebrews has sent me to you, saying, 'Let My people go, that they may serve Me in the wilderness'" (Exod. 7:16). Don't let some pharaoh stand in your way of yielding to the Master's call for service. You are the master of your own destiny. God is building his kingdom in the hearts of men, and you are part of that kingdom. Let no man hinder you from yielding to the urgency of that call. "Today, if you will hear His voice, do not harden your hearts as in the rebellion" (Heb. 3:7–8). Can you hear God's voice amid the noise and distraction of today's hustle and bustle? Yes, I can. That's a good sign. Thanks for your affirmative response. May the Lord bless and keep you.

March 25

God is Able

Yet in all these things we are more than conquerors through Him who loved us.
—Romans 8:37

Lisa is a cheerful and prayerful young woman in her thirties. However, she carries with her a painful burden. She's afflicted with sickle cell anemia, along with many other health challenges. Pain is her constant companion. The hospitals in the area are very familiar with her, and over the years, she has been a regular patient to their wards. Those of us who are close to her are continually requesting God's healing on her behalf. During a recent testimony service, she described her normal day like this: "Apart from my regular pain, I am all right." Since she has developed a high tolerance to pain, we have some idea of what she means by her regular pain. Lisa does not like pain but has come to accept it as a normal part of her life.

How should the believer cope with pain, whether physical, spiritual, or emotional? Paul knew pain very well, having been beaten by rowdy mobs, stoned regularly, imprisoned constantly, and left for dead on many occasions. He wrote to the suffering believers, "And lest I should be exalted above measure by the abundance of the revelations, a thorn in the flesh was given to me, lest I be exalted above measure. Concerning this thing I pleaded with the Lord three times that it might depart from me. And He said to me 'My grace is sufficient for you, for My strength is made perfect in weakness.' Therefore most gladly I will rather boast in my infirmities, that the power of Christ may rest upon me" (2 Cor. 12:7–9). Can a thorn in the flesh yield eternal benefits?

Blessed are those like Job who are called on to bear the full brunt of Satan's fury. God is glorified by their suffering; their reward is eternally secure. God assures us in his word: "No temptation has overtaken you except such as is common to man; but God is faithful, who will not allow you to be tempted beyond what you are able, but with the temptation will also make the way of escape, that you may be able to bear it" (1 Cor. 10:13). We have been told that "where there is no pain, there is no gain." It hurts while we're going through excruciating pain and debilitating trials, and no one understands it quite like Jesus, who walks with us and bears all our pain.

At the grave site of his friend Lazarus, the record states, "Therefore, when Jesus saw her weeping, and the Jews who came with her weeping, He groaned in the spirit and was troubled" (John 11:33). Although he knew he would raise Lazarus, he "groaned and was troubled." Does he really see and understand our pain, weaknesses, and struggles? Absolutely. "For we do not have a High Priest who cannot sympathize with our weaknesses, but was in all points tempted as we are, yet without sin" (Heb. 4:15).

As in the story of the traveler who confronted God about his absence when things were tough, "Where were you when I was being crushed by life's ills? Where were you?" To this, the Savior replied, "I was carrying you when you were too weak to walk."

At every turn in life lurk unseen dangers, hidden obstacles, pitfalls, and the fear of the unknown. But Jesus is right there with us as our Pilot, and with his steady hand, he guides our path around the minefields we can't see and leads us safely to our destination. When the pain strikes again, remember Jesus suffers with us and understands our lot. May God bless you and give you adequate strength that corresponds to your pain and suffering.

March 26

Not Perfect but Still Striving

Wash me thoroughly from my iniquity, and cleanse me from my sin . . . Purge me with hyssop, and I shall be clean; wash me and I shall be whiter than snow.
—Psalm 51:2, 7

A well-meaning parishioner declared to his pastor, "I no longer want to be enlisted in the church membership."

"What's wrong?" asked the pastor, raising his eyebrows.

"I smoke terribly, and I fear the odor may be a distraction to the membership."

"My dear friend," the wise pastor remarked, "we all have some kind of odor emanating from us. If odor had colors, we would have a rainbow coalition in the pews." We are all recovering sinners, aren't we?

We can take comfort from the stalwarts of the faith. Those included in Hebrews 11 Hall of Faith had serious character flaws. To name a few, Abraham was a habitual liar. It is no disservice to him; the Bible record is factual. It records the saints' heroics as well as their weaknesses. Isaac, the son of Abraham, was a liar as well (Gen. 26:7). The fruit never falls far from the tree. Jacob, Isaac's son, was a consummate deceiver. Samson had perpetual problems with members of the opposite sex. David was an adulterer/murderer, and his house was in a continuous state of disarray, but he and the above-mentioned men of God overcame, not in their own strength but by the grace of God.

The good news of salvation entails God calling people away from sin into his kingdom. Amazingly, he is obliged by his love to work with us in spite of our weaknesses. "For as the heavens are high above the earth, so great is His mercy toward those who fear Him; as far as the east is from the west, so far has He removed our transgressions from us" (Ps. 103:11–12). And the news only gets better: "As a father pities his children, so the Lord pities those who fear Him. For He knows our frame; and remembers that we are dust" (Ps. 103:13–14). What can be expected from dust? Not much, but God allows us to mature and develop, and when we falter and fall on our face or deviate from the straight and narrow path, he remembers that we are just dust.

However, "For God so loved the world that He gave His only begotten Son, that whoever believes in Him should not parish but have everlasting life" (John 3:16). This promise can be claimed by the vilest criminal. In the words of our Master Jesus Christ, if we fall on the Rock, (Jesus) repentant and compliant, we will receive mercy. But if unrepentant and uncompliant, the Rock will eventually fall on us and crush us.

God's love is as great as his mercy. David realized this wonderful attribute of God and literally flung himself headlong into the arms of the sin-pardoning Savior. Having inadvertently pronounced on himself the most hideous punishment, David sorrowfully confessed, "Have mercy upon me, O God according to Your loving-kindness; according to the multitude of Your tender mercies, blot out my transgression" (Ps. 51:1). There is no little or big sin with God; all sin is offensive to him. Jesus's death took care of all sin. When the sinner surrenders to Christ, his slate is wiped "clean as a whistle," and he is a new creature. Have you been washed from your sins, or are you still carrying the heavy baggage of sin? Remain blessed in Jesus.

March 27

Fearfully and Wonderfully Made

For as the body is one and has many members, but all the members of that one body, being many, are one body, so also is Christ.

—1 Corinthians 12:12

When we were kids in school many moons ago, we were taught this poem: "If all the eyes in the land were but one eye, what a great, big eye that would be. And if all the hands in the land were but one hand, what a great, big hand that would be!" The object of this saying is obvious: one great hand can neither serve nor function as a body. There is unity in diversity. The body is made up of many parts, all with different functions. All body parts are uniquely important, regardless of how small or limited their role may seem.

Christ's body, the church, operates under the same principle as our physical body. In his infinite wisdom, God assigned specific roles to each individual member. We all probably love singing, but few can skillfully carry a note, and fewer still can actually sing professionally to earn a living. Please don't waste your time doing a job you are not called to do. God has equipped you with special capabilities that no one else can utilize as efficiently as you. Know your limits. Go ahead and do what you are good at.

The church operates as a finely tuned military organization, and in essence, it is. "And God has appointed these in the church: first apostles, second prophets, third teachers, after that miracles, then gifts of healing, helps, administration, varieties of tongues" (1 Cor. 12:28). Again, the operation of the church is amazingly similar to that of the body. The eye has its specific task to perform and should not compete with the nose in trying to sniff out things. Let the eye concentrate on seeing and the nose on smelling.

"Are all apostles? Are all prophets? Are all teachers? Are all workers of miracles? Do all have the gifts of healing? Do all speak in tongues? Do all interpret?" (1 Cor. 12:29). The answer to these questions is a resounding no. All cannot and should not compete against one another in the church; otherwise, chaos will ensue.

Henry Ford introduced the assembly-line-style production to the world, and we give tribute to him for his insight and ingenuity, but he borrowed this concept from the scripture. More can be achieved if one specializes in their area of giftedness. What if the conveyor belt, which transports finished goods to their respective packaging point, breaks down? Yes, you've guessed it. A great pileup and disruption of the entire system result. How important then is the conveyor belt? Tiny but very useful. So is the role of the least-esteemed member.

"And those members of the body which we think to be less honorable, on these we bestow greater honor; and our unpresentable parts have greater modesty, but our presentable parts have no need. But God composed the body, having given greater honor to that part which lacks it, that there should be no schism in the body, but that the members should have the same care one for another" (1 Cor. 12:23–25).

Though the janitor receives little attention, his role is indispensable to the smooth functioning of the church. His role may be overlooked by many but is absolutely necessary. Have you found your place or niche in the church? Are you discouraged because you do not play a greater role as Mr. and Mrs. X? Play your instrument faithfully and skillfully to your best, and the orchestra (the church) will do just fine.

March 28

Under the Weather Lately?

Then the Lord said to him: Go return on your way to the wilderness of Damascus; and when you arrive, anoint Hazel as king over Syria . . . Jehu the son of Nimshi as king over Israel. And Elisha the son of Shaphat . . . you shall anoint as prophet in your place.

—1 Kings 19:15–16

Elijah, the prophet, stood up defiantly against King Ahab and his hundreds of false prophets but fled when threatened by Queen Jezebel. Elijah had a spectacular ministry as a prophet of God, but in an unguarded moment, a threat from the queen sent him wallowing in depression. What happened? The prophet's résumé was very impressive; he stared down 450 royal prophets of Baal and slew them in the name of the Lord. At his word, the clouds withheld their moisture, and a blistering drought ensued for about three and a half years. What then caused such a fearless stalwart to buckle and flee at a mere threat from Jezebel?

All the great heroes of the faith have had their peaks and valleys, their ups and downs, and Elijah is no exception. David sums it best in his struggle to overcome depression, which incidentally was the main cause of Elijah's breakdown. "Why are you cast down, O my soul? And why are you disquieted within me?" (Ps. 42:5). Some have the ability to lift themselves when adversity comes knocking, while others depend on close friends, family, or a therapist for help. A third class is simply crushed by the adversity and may never recover by themselves from their adverse circumstance.

No saint is immune from the physical ailments that beset mankind; we are all vulnerable to depression, discouragement, and adverse situations of life. Let's hear this candid admission from the apostle Paul: "For the good that I will to do, I do not do; but the evil I will not to do, that I practice. Now if I do what I will not to do, it is no longer I who do it, but sin that dwells in me" (Rom. 7:19–20). Paul displays a rare moment of frustration at being overcome by the weakness of the flesh. Did this admission come from Paul, the prince of the apostles? Yes, it did, and it is only by the grace of God that we all are not crushed and overwhelmed by evil.

Everybody has had bad days at work when everything that could go wrong went wrong. Job had such days when he wished his mom had forever remained pregnant and never given birth to him (Job 3:11). Habakkuk protested vigorously to God: "Why did you cause me to see all this injustice?" (Hab. 1:3). Jeremiah wished his eyes were a flowing fountain so he could weep for the abominations of his people (Jer. 9:1). God's strong men were not without their vulnerabilities. This should give us hope and comfort that past generations overcame their struggles, and so can we with God's help.

"God is a present help in trouble" (Ps. 46:1), not some of the times but all the time. "The name of the Lord is a strong tower; the righteous run to it and are safe" (Prov. 18:10). The words of a heathen monarch make this point even more succinct. "For He is the living God, and steadfast forever; His kingdom is the one which shall not be destroyed, and His dominion shall endure to the end. He delivers and rescues, and He works signs and wonders in heaven and on earth, who has delivered Daniel from the power of the lions" (Dan. 6:26–27). "Now to Him who is able to do exceedingly abundantly above all that we ask or think, according to the power that works in us" (Eph. 3:20). Are you aware that when we are weak, we can be made strong?

March 29

Standing up when It Matters

For if you remain completely silent at this time, relief and deliverance will arise for the Jews from another place, but you and your father's house will perish. Yet who knows whether you have come to the kingdom for such a time as this?
—Esther 4:14

He went to the Colosseum to make a point, and he did but was slain by the angry mob. Mysteriously moved by an inner voice, the little monk followed the crowd to the Colosseum, where the games were held. Two gladiators were locked in mortal combat, and one had to die. The monk had seen enough. He quickly made his way into the arena, shouting as he went, "In the name of Christ, forbear!" trying to put a stop on the games. Unfortunately, he was slain by the angry mob for his interruption of their favorite pastime. But Telemachus's death was not in vain; it set in motion a chain of events that led to the outright ban of this macabre blood sport. He dared to stand when everyone else sat (www.google.com/amp/s/jesseleeproject.com/2010/01/31/in-the-name-of-jesus-stop).

Pollsters are constantly gauging public behavior and refining their latest polls, but the biblical values that we hold sacred are not up for public referenda, recalls, or amendments. Ethical values and long-held social mores have given way to shifting immoral standards. Virtue is being ridiculed, while vice and immorality on and off the screen are gradually accepted as normal behavior. We need Telemachus now, but alas, he is dead and long gone. Where are the modern standard bearers of truth? Where are they? Who will stand up for the Lord and state his case of moral purity? Can the Lord count on you and me?

The Jews in the kingdom of Medo-Persia were caught between a rock and a hard place; genocide was staring them in the face. A legal edict crafted by the wicked Haman lay on king Ahasuerus's desk. The wicked Haman was determined to exterminate the entire Jewish population because of a grudge against one individual Jew, Mordecai. Standing under the shadow of extinction, Mordecai gave Queen Esther this ultimatum: "If you remain completely silent at this time, relief and deliverance will arise for the Jews from another place, but you and your father's house will perish" (Esther 4:14).

It is comfortable to remain silent and not create waves. Why rock the boat? Why disturb the peace? But that's precisely what we are called to do, and Jesus's words are explicit on this subject. "Do not think that I came to bring peace on earth. I did not come to bring peace but a sword. For I have come to set a man against his father, a daughter against her mother, and daughter-in-law against mother-in-law, and a man's enemies will be of his own household" (Matt. 10:34–36). The gospel always breeds trouble and is a challenge to social mores. It troubled cannibalistic cultures, whose tradition called for feasting on the scalp of their enemies. It challenged the blood sport in Roman gladiatorial combat. It equalized the boardrooms for women and minorities. It gave a voice to the voiceless and hope to the downtrodden. Should we then be silent at such a time as this when right is on the scaffold and wrong sits forever on the throne?

It is a challenging time to be alive when ethical standards are shifting beneath our feet and when polls are being taken to gauge immorally accepted behavior. But we have been called on to make a difference in society by demonstrating God's love to mankind, as well as pointing them to Jesus, who can make the sinner whole. Remember, Jesus said, "Neither do I condemn you, go and sin no more" (John 8:11).

March 30

The God of All People

Then the king of Assyria commanded, saying, send there one of the priests whom you brought from there; let him go and dwell there, and let him teach them the rituals of the God of the land.

—2 Kings 17:27

Legend has it that six sightless men of India wanted to know what an elephant looks like. A friend took them to experience their lifelong dream. Drawing close to the great beast, the first blind man took hold of the elephant's front leg and affirmed to his companions that it was just as he thought—a tree trunk. Succeeding him, the second man felt the belly and declared the beast was really like a wall. The third man touched the sharp tusk and tried to convince his other friends that the elephant was indeed like a spear. Not daunted by his companions' assertion, the fourth man grabbed the beast's curly trunk and adamantly stated it was like a slithering snake. Approaching the animal from the rear, the fifth man made contact with the hairy end of the tail and was convinced that the beast was like a rope. The sixth man gently touched the beast's large ear, and as he felt the wafting air from the fanning motion, he excitedly exclaimed, "The elephant is a fan!" Interestingly, they all assumed the entire beast was exactly like the body part they touched; but in reality, the elephant is much more than their limited perception of it.

"You are My witnesses, says the Lord, and My servant whom I have chosen" (Isa. 43:10). As a group of missionaries was ministering to the health and educational needs of a poverty-stricken community, one villager was touched by the service of a particular missionary and remarked, "Thank you for your kindness. You brought God to us today." Well, our service, thoughtfulness, kindness, and overall behavior may be the only glimpse some people might have of the God we serve. "Philip asked Jesus, 'Lord, show us the Father, and it is sufficient for us.' Jesus said to him, have I been with you so long, and yet you have not known Me, Phillip? He who has seen Me has seen the Father; so how can you say, show us the Father?" (John 14:8–9).

Actions speak louder than words, don't they? The world looks at our conduct for evidence of God indwelling in our hearts. "By this all will know that you are My disciples, if you have love for one another" (John 13:35). God is relying on his last day people to convince a skeptical world that he really loves them, does exist, and has their best interest at heart. Jesus exemplified what God is like to his generation. He demonstrated in action what God is doing about hunger, infirmity, and social inequality. He healed the sick, cast out demons, forgave sins, raised the dead, and comforted the heavily burdened—all characteristics of a loving God.

The baton has been passed to us by retiring generations to uphold the torch of God's love to a skeptical public. Is your Christian witness one that demonstrates that God indeed loves, forgives, and is altogether merciful? "Whom shall I send and who will go for Us? Then I said, here am I, send me" (Isa. 6:8). Let us ask God to give us the will to serve him, to alleviate the needs of humanity, and to represent him well in public. Are you a living witness for God?

March 31

Praise Him

And some of the Pharisees called to Him from the crowd, Teacher, rebuke Your disciples. But He answered and said to them, I tell you that if these should keep silent, the stones would immediately cry out.

—Luke 19:39–40

Nature works wonderfully and cooperatively in executing God's will, while man—its overseer—is being dragged, kicking and screaming to join the universal chorus in praising God. The trees busy themselves multitasking, converting carbon dioxide into oxygen for both man and beast. They, in turn, rely on the clouds for intermittent downpours to refresh themselves. The forest, home to a wide diversity of creatures, is a generous host, providing take-home meals to its many residents. The oceans, rivers, and lakes abound with creatures great and small, all glorifying God in their unique functions. But mankind—the crowning masterpiece of God's Creation, the one designed to worship and glorify his Creator—rebelled and, by virtue of his sin, ruined creation.

The first worship experience that should have been a rapturous burst of thanksgiving by the first couple became a terrifying retreat to the fig tree grove. With their innocence shattered, guilt, shame, and fear became uninvited tormentors. Since man could no longer behold his Maker face-to-face, an alternate method of worship was instituted. Man's face-to-face communion with God was replaced by the altar, which gave way to the sanctuary, synagogue, and ultimately church worship service. But all was not lost; the psalmist gives us a hint of what true worship constitutes. "Praise God in His sanctuary; praise Him in His mighty firmament! Praise Him for His mighty acts; praise Him according to His excellent greatness! Praise Him with the sound of trumpet; praise Him with the lute and harp! Praise Him with the timbrel and dance; praise Him with the stringed instrument and flutes! Praise with the loud cymbals; praise Him with the clashing cymbals! Let everything that has breath praise the Lord. Praise the Lord!" (Ps. 150:1–6).

In describing the scene around God's throne, which consists of continuous worship, the prophets of old could not find adequate words in describing the praise and melody of heaven. "Then I looked, and I heard the voice of many angels around the throne, the living creatures, and the elders; and the number of them was ten thousand times ten thousand, and thousands of thousands, saying with a loud voice: worthy is the Lamb who was slain to receive power and riches and wisdom, and strength and honor and glory and blessing!" (Rev. 5:11–12).

Human beings have not been left out in the worship service in heaven. Yes indeed, we are represented. John sees a vast multitude, in Revelation 7:9–15, of all nations, tribes, peoples, and tongues standing around the throne clothed in white and with palm branches in their hands thanking God for washing them clean in the blood of the Lamb. Yes, from all the continents of the earth, the children of God—with bright smiles on their faces and waving palm branches—will thank the Creator for saving them. We will cast our crowns at Jesus's feet and worship him for enduring the cross even when his body was saying to him, "Let this cup pass away from me. Nevertheless, not my will but yours."

Like Thomas, we will gaze at the nail-scarred hands and wounded side and gasp, "My Lord and my God." Thank you, dear God, for salvation so full and free in Christ Jesus.

April 1

I Want to Live

And whatsoever you ask in my name, that I will do, that the Father may be glorified in the Son. If you ask anything in my name, I will do it.
—John 14:13–14

Samuel (name changed) was discharged from a medical institution and sent home to die in dignity, but he had no interest in dying quite yet. He wanted to live. His grandniece visiting from London who attended our old year night service placed an urgent request for the church to visit her uncle. He was slipping away fast, and every moment spent with him was precious. Fortunately, our Sabbath school class jumped at the opportunity and visited Sam and his lovely wife, Gill. We brought them a small sampling of our worship service, complete with testimonies, songs, and a Bible reading. Samuel could barely walk, but with the support of his charming wife, he came to worship with us. With Jesus in the midst to bless, each Sabbath, we sang, prayed a little, testified, and conducted a mini–Bible study. What transpired thereafter is for the ages. We watched in wonder and amazement every Sabbath as our prayers for a miraculous turnaround became reality before our eyes.

With each passing week, Samuel's steps grew stronger and sturdier, until he broke the sound barrier and began speaking again. He even surprised his wife by volunteering to take the lead in family worship again, his first sound since his bout with his illness. He also gained some much-needed weight and began doing little chores here and there around the house. Sam is fully on the mend. Glory be to God and tribute to faithful friends. "Jesus said to her, 'I am the resurrection and the life. He who believes in Me though he were dead yet shall he live'" (John 11:25). Were we overwhelmed when Sam finally made it to church to fellowship with his church family? Sam is a living testimony of what happens when God's children petition his throne on behalf of others.

This is what the Lord desires: "Ask, and it will be given to you; seek, and you will find; knock, and it will be opened to you. For everyone who asks receives, and he who seeks finds, and to him who knocks it will be opened" (Matt. 7:7–8). God is more willing to bestow good gifts on his children than their ability to request them. It is his desire to lavish on his people all the essentials required in the conflict against evil, but it must be requested. Why would he pour his precious resources on one who has not requested it, is unprepared for it, or worse has little esteem for it?

We prayed for our friend and brother, and God heard our prayers and granted our petition. God will honor the prayers of his people when they seek to promote his interest here on earth. But will he grant a request he knows could be injurious to his children's welfare? "You ask and do not receive, because you ask amiss, that you may spend it on your pleasures" (James 4:3). We are admonished by our Lord to pray in harmony with God's will, and that is the very basis of the Lord's Prayer: "Your kingdom come. Your will be done on earth as it is in heaven" (Matt. 6:10).

In our quest to live, we should focus more on the quality of life rather than the quantity of life. After all, what good is life down here if it does not appreciate the saying "Well done good and faithful servant; you were faithful over a few things, I will make you ruler over many things. Enter into the joy of your Lord" (Matt. 25:23).

April 2

Love Dwells Here

Entreat me not to leave you, or to turn back from following after you; for wherever you go I will go; and wherever you lodge, I will lodge; your people shall be my people, and your God, my God.

—Ruth 1:16

Abandoned by his master, Jolly hollered, croaked, and screeched for four full days and nights until he was rescued. His owner's property went into foreclosure, and they left in a hurry, leaving poor Jolly in a cage to fend for himself. Locked up and with no access to food and water, Jolly began letting everyone in his neighborhood know he was hungry with his incessant chirps and croaks. An observant neighbor who sensed the home was without window drapes (an indication of vacancy) decided to take a peek and discovered Jolly's plight. Once the proper agency was called in, Jolly's status improved significantly. From abandonment to celebrity, Jolly is now a retiree feasting on delicious nuts in his new home.

Just like Jolly's owner, Naomi's family had fallen on hard times, victim of a terrible drought. With starvation becoming a real possibility, the family of four packed their belongings and moved to Moab, a neighboring country. Once there, things went from bad to worse. Naomi's breadwinning husband, Elimelech, died suddenly; and her two sons, Mahlon and Chilion, followed their dad to the grave in quick succession, leaving her without the social support necessary for survival. She turned to her two grief-stricken daughters-in-law and encouraged them to return to their respective families since she was now a widow and could not afford the expense of having them around. Naomi was pleasantly surprised by what transpired next. "Entreat me not to leave you, or to turn back from following after you; for wherever you go I will go; and wherever you lodge, I will lodge; your people shall be my people, and your God, my God" (Ruth 1:16). What an example of unselfish, inseparable love, loyalty, and friendship between these two women!

God's love is more enduring than anyone else's. He is the founder and CEO of love. He continually reassures his skeptical people of his abiding love and continuous presence among them. "Be strong and of good courage, do not fear nor be afraid of them; for the Lord your God, He is the one who goes with you, He will not leave you nor forsake you" (Deut. 31:6). God has never abandoned or neglected his people when they sin. He brandishes the chastening rod when necessary or allows their enemies to chastise them to bring them back to repentance, but he is ever watchful, waiting for signs of true repentance and reformation from them. Does he do the same with us?

"Can a woman forget her nursing child, and not have compassion on the son of her womb? Surely they may forget, yet I will not forget you. See I have inscribed you on the palms of My hands" (Isa. 49:15–16). Yes, while it is true that men and women have abandoned their children to pursue their selfish ambitions, God will never abandon or forsake the people whom he has redeemed. Lord, your love is simply overwhelming, too wonderful for me to comprehend. Please accept us and wash us thoroughly in your blood and save us from sin.

April 3

Repairing Life's Potholes

Come let us reason together, says the Lord, though your sins are like scarlet, they shall be as white as snow; though they are red like crimson, they shall be as wool.

—Isaiah 1:18

"Humpty Dumpty sat on a wall, / Humpty Dumpty had a great fall; / All the king's horses and all the king's men / Couldn't put Humpty together again" (https/www. poetryfoundation.org/poems-and-poets/poems/detail/46951). This most popular of English rhymes is truthful about one thing: man's great moral fall and his inability to extricate himself from the mess of sin, something of his own creation.

Every year, millions of pilgrims converge on holy sites around the world in an attempt to cleanse their souls from impurities. The devout ones fast from food and liquids. The most extreme and pious inflict physical punishment on their person to appease their god. Over here in the West on New Year's Day, we make fantastic resolutions never again to practice certain lewd behaviors we detest. But do these self-atonement rituals really work? "Can the Ethiopian change his skin or the leopard its spots? Then may you also do good who are accustomed to do evil" (Jer. 13:23). No. Absolutely not. We need divine assistance in turning our lives around.

Since we are incapable of making ourselves acceptable to God's holy standard of righteousness, can anyone do it for us? "For He made Him who knew no sin to be sin for us, that we might become the righteousness of God in Him" (2 Cor. 5:21). No one needs to go on any expensive long pilgrimage anywhere; the price of our salvation has been paid in full by Jesus on Calvary. Christ became sin for us. He suffered the wrath of God in his body. Our Creator became our Savior by trading places with us. He incurred the everlasting death we deserved and gave us his eternal life in return. The consequence of Adam's sin was enormous, which resulted in spiritual death and eternal separation from God, but Jesus turned that around. When Jesus cried on Calvary's cross, "My God, My God, why have You forsaken Me?" (Matt. 27:46), at that moment, he actually became our sin bearer. The iniquity of humanity, down to the very last sinner of the age, was dumped on him. The separation that sin initially caused in the Garden of Eden was remedied by Jesus in the garden of Gethsemane. What Adam lost in the Garden of Eden was gained in the garden of Gethsemane.

And that which the king's horses and men could not do in putting Humpty (us) back together again Jesus did. No amount of pilgrimages to holy sites can atone for man's violation of God's holy law. The lighting of candles and prayers to deceased saints will not do; no amount of fasting or self-flagellation (hitting oneself with a whip) will do either. It is only by submitting oneself broken at the feet of Jesus that will do. "Come to Me, all you who labor and are heavy laden, and I will give you rest. Take My yoke upon you and learn from Me, for I am gentle and lowly in heart, and you will find rest for your souls. For My yoke is easy and My burden is light" (Matt. 11:28–30).

Though we cannot fix the potholes in our lives, there must be a willingness to have them fixed. We must yearn for a better life—a life beyond the empty pursuits now holding us captive. Let us be willing to be directed to the foot of the cross, where we can find grace and mercy. Jesus is always there, waiting to receive the penitent sinner. You have nothing to lose but your sins and have everything to gain by coming to Jesus.

Ambassadors for Christ

But you are a chosen generation, royal priesthood, a holy nation, His own special people, that you may proclaim the praises of Him who called you out of darkness into His marvelous light.

—1 Peter 2:9

Andrei Sakharov was hailed as a hometown hero by the Soviet masses but denounced by the ruling elites as a pain they could do without. Andrei was an avowed atheist, human rights activist, and father of the Soviet Union's nuclear bomb. Defying arrest, prison, and exile, he fought for civil rights and basic human dignity for his people. Sakharov became a painful thorn the authorities wished would just go away, but he wasn't going anywhere. He felt it was within his right to voice his dissent, and consequently, he was denounced and relentlessly persecuted for his views. Undaunted by the persecution, Andrei employed the same relentless passion that drove him to achieve nuclear status for his nation into his human rights campaign. Despite his confinement, he devoted the rest of his life fighting for a society where people could speak their mind without fear of a knock on their door at midnight or, worse, disappearing completely.

The army of Christ is looking for a few good men and women like Andrei who are not swayed or intimidated in confessing Christ, even in hostile territories. Lest we forget, Jesus still beckons us, "Go therefore and make disciples of all nations, baptizing them in the name of the Father and of the Son and of the Holy Spirit, teaching them to observe all things that I have commanded you and lo, I am with you always, even to the end of the age" (Matt. 28:19–20).

As ambassadors for Christ, we represent him in our work environment, at school, at home, on the playground, in the checkout line, on the bus, in the train, at the airport check-in line, and at home. The early church turned the Roman Empire upside down because they took the story of Jesus everywhere they went, and so must we. "Therefore those who were scattered went everywhere preaching the word" (Acts 8:4). Persecution proved to be a blessing for the gospel; it caused the church to be scattered, paving the way for the gospel to make inroads into new communities and cultures.

"You are our epistle written in our hearts, known and read by all men; clearly you are an epistle of Christ, ministered by us written not with ink but by the Spirit of the living God, not on tablets of stone but on tablets of flesh, that is of the heart" (2 Cor. 3:2–3). That's very true. We are indeed read like books and are being studied by our colleagues, mates, and friends. Since we are under such microscopic scrutiny, we would do well to guard our footsteps and quickly apologize when we offend or make a misstep in our Christian walk. Should we apologize profusely when we offend someone? Of course. We represent the King of the universe. Why shouldn't we?

Are we perfect? No, at least not yet. But even in our imperfections, our friends should see in us a willingness to attain a better mode of conduct. When we apologize to someone we have wronged, it demonstrates to that person how Christians operate with one another and with the world at large. Are you too proud to admit fault? "You are my witnesses," says the Lord. God has called you, with all your imperfections, to be his ambassador. Are you willing to do his will and go where he sends you? Great.

April 5

I Don't Understand

For My thoughts are not your thoughts, nor are your ways My ways, says the Lord. For as the heavens are higher than the earth, so are My ways higher than your ways, and My thoughts than your thoughts.

—Isaiah 55:8–9

Why should the bully have the last laugh? She is just leading her slow-moving calf from the birth nursery to the rich feeding ground up north when suddenly she has company, definitely not the type she hopes for. Orcas are the bullies of the ocean, and they live up to their fearful reputation. Upon detecting a nursing gray whale with calf, the pod immediately sets out to separate the mom from her calf. Once this is done, they take turn exhausting and harassing the little guy; and when they knock the wind out of him, they drown him. With their grim work done, they eat only the tongue and lower jaw, less than 1 percent of the entire weight of the calf. After their brief snack, they jubilantly hurry off to another address where they think their service is needed (*National Geographic*).

There are lots of things we just do not understand. Why do the innocent suffer? Why do the rich get richer? Why do villains usually live long lives? Why does the drunk driver somehow survive while his victim dies? Why was Brian robbed of the opportunity of playing baseball with his dad? Why did Susie lose her mom to breast cancer?

There are no explanations for these human tragedies. The narratives of human suffering are too painful to dwell on. "Why do you show me iniquity, and cause me to see trouble? For plundering and violence are before me; there is strife, and contention arises. Therefore the law is powerless, and justice never goes forth. For the wicked surround the righteous; therefore perverse judgment proceeds" (Hab. 1:3–4). Sounds like CNN nightly news. Is anything new under the sun?

Ever since the emergence of sin on our planet, families have had to grapple with these very complex issues. Jesus himself groaned in spirit after the death of a close friend. "Therefore his sisters sent to Him, saying, Lord, behold, he whom You love is sick" (John 11:3). Apparently, Jesus was a frequent visitor to this family that the sisters of the sick man could have made this claim. The sick man grew worse and eventually died; the sisters were devastated that Jesus was so casual about the whole thing. Was he? "Therefore, when Jesus saw her weeping, and the Jews who came with her weeping, He groaned in the spirit and was troubled. And He said, where have you laid him?" (John 11:33–34).

Every loss of life, every untimely death, every suicide, every fatal illness, every divorce, and every disability draws a similar groan from our sympathizing friend and Savior. "For we do not have a High Priest who cannot sympathize with our weaknesses, but was in all points tempted as we are, but without sin. Let us therefore come boldly to the throne of grace, that we may obtain mercy in time of need" (Heb. 4:15–16). God hurts more than us when he sees his children suffering.

A day is coming when all mysteries will be solved, when all wrongs will be righted, and when judgment will be meted to the wicked and unrepentant. We cannot understand all the terrible calamities of life, nor can we solve them. However, we can pray and ask God to place us in someone's path to make a positive difference in their life.

April 6

Jacob's Ladder

And he dreamed, and behold a ladder was set up on the earth, and its top reached to the heaven; and there the angels of God were ascending and descending on it.
—Genesis 28:12

With smoke billowing from a high-rise, thirteen-floor apartment building in New York City, a maintenance worker was trapped with nowhere to go. He dangled perilously on a repair platform outside a window as the raging flames were closing in. His situation grew from bad to worse. Some urged him to jump from the thirteen-story platform where he was trapped; others shouted just about anything. The heat was becoming unbearable, and the thick, billowing smoke only added to the urgency of his ordeal. Sensing the worker's desperate plight, Rosendo Lopez— the building superintendent—grabbed his ladder and created a bridge between his building and the victim. The trapped man, assisted by other rescuers, stepped on the firm ladder platform and walked away to freedom. The whole episode was caught on film by a CBS 2 News crew.

Ladders lie idle in our garages and on the side of buildings, but don't you ever discard them. Your life may depend on them one day. Jesus is the Link, the Bridge, the Ladder between heaven and earth, between God and man. He is the symbolic Ladder that connects heaven and earth in Jacob's dream (Gen. 28:12). In many Old Testament prophecies, he is observed inserting himself into human history, connecting man back to God. Isaiah proclaimed that he would be born of a virgin (Isa. 7:14). Moses declared that he would bruise the head of the serpent Satan (Gen. 3:15). Isaiah again stated that he is Immanuel, "God with us," and John confirmed regrettably that he would be rejected by his own people—us (John 1:11). Moses asserted that he would be called a prophet (Deut. 18:15), while the psalmist portrayed him as being betrayed by his close friend (Ps. 41:9). In every detail and without failure, Jesus fulfilled the hundreds of Messianic prophecies concerning himself. He even enlightened his audience from the scriptures about when and where specific prophecies were to be fulfilled concerning himself.

In his hometown of Nazareth, when given a portion of the scripture to read from the book of Isaiah, which was about him, he read it and reminded his audience, "Today the Scripture is fulfilled in your hearing" (Luke 4:21). In the latter part of his ministry, he pointed out to his betrayer his macabre assignment, something prophesied in the Psalms but transacted only by Judas Iscariot (Mark 14:18–21).

God had salvation wonderfully planned. Man's mortal Fall did not find God napping or scrambling for answers; it was foreseen by the Godhead, and contingency plans were put in place to save mankind. "The next day John saw Jesus coming towards him, and said, Behold! The Lamb of God who takes away the sins of the world!" (John 1:29). Our salvation was not an afterthought; it was meticulously planned and executed with flawless efficiency by the Godhead. As Ellen White puts it, "It was a plan laid too deep to fail." "Jesus said to them, I am the way the truth, and the life. No one comes to the Father except through me" (John 14:6). We must climb the Ladder that is Jesus to get to God. Where are you on that Ladder? Have you begun climbing?

April 7

I Need You

For none of us lives to himself and no one dies to himself.

—Romans 14:7

Naval Station Norfolk churns out another Nimitz superclass aircraft carrier, but just like a little baby, it will need a lot of help from others for its safe operation. Officials believe that aircraft carriers are the pride of the United States Navy and are an extension of U.S. diplomacy. The ship is being dedicated in honor of the forty-first president, George Herbert Walker Bush. It is the tenth and final Nimitz superclass aircraft carrier. It is both immense and impressive and will depend on a convoy of naval support ships for its defense, operation, and supply needs. Its battle group consists of guided missile cruisers, antiaircraft warships, antisubmarine destroyers, and other machines lying beneath the depths. Of course, the carrier and its battle group are joined periodically by supply ships carrying goodies, fuel, mail, food, and munitions. The support ships recognize their role and fulfill them flawlessly for the smooth operation of the carrier. No one ship acts independently by itself; they all act in concert with one another (www.cnn.com/2009/US/01/10/bush.ship.commissioning/index.html).

When a pebble is dropped into a pond, it causes an immediate ripple that is felt throughout the length and breadth of the body of water. Likewise, the life we live—whether good or bad—has a ripple effect on others. As in the game of basketball, which is an excellent team sport, a prolific scorer can enhance his game by passing the ball to his supporting cast and getting them involved. Though he can score at any moment, he usually passes the ball, creating easy layups to his teammates, building their confidence and affirming their supportive role. Someone once said, "When the tide rises, it lifts all boats." Believers are called on to build up the lives of others around them by investing in their growth, health, and welfare. Jesus set the supreme example for us to follow.

Christians need one another; we cannot live our lives in isolation. We are admonished to bear the burdens of our weaker brethren (Rom. 15:1). David needed Jonathan when his spirit was low and required affirmation and refreshment. Naomi needed Ruth and vice versa; they complemented each other well. Paul needed the physician Luke. His hard life of absorbing much punishment needed medical care. On the final day of ministry, our Lord selected three of his intimate friends to encourage him and share in his passion. "Then Jesus came with them to a place called Gethsemane, and said to His disciples, sit here while I go and pray over there. And He took with Him Peter and the two sons of Zebedee, and He began to be sorrowful and deeply distressed" (Matt. 26:36–37). Even the Son of Man needed human companionship and support. Would we be daring enough to believe that we can make it to heaven all on our own?

Everything in nature is interdependent. If we carelessly break the food chain, a host of creatures are affected, and some may never recover. We need one another, and the singing band America illustrates this point succinctly with their signature song "I Need You": "I need you like the flower needs the rain . . . You know I need you like the winter needs the spring. You know I need you. I need you." Somewhere I read, "We'll either stand together or die divided." There is no division in Christ. "In Christ, there is no east or west nor north or south." Is Christ divided? No, of course not. In Christ, we are just one big family.

April 8

We Have Found Him

Phillip found Nathanael and said to him, "We have found Him of whom Moses in the law, and also the prophets, wrote—Jesus of Nazareth" . . . Phillip said to him, "Come and see."

—John 1:45–46

We arrived at Heathrow Airport without a clue about how we would be identified, let alone be picked up, but my big brother left nothing to chance; our pickup was well coordinated. My brother lived in Liverpool to the north, and London—our port of entry—was to the south. It was out of his way to pick us up; therefore he had his best buddy do the pickup for him. I missed telling my brother about the clothes I was wearing to be identifiable for pickup, but he had everything figured out. This was his description of me to his friend: "Look for someone who looks exactly like me." Of the thousands of travelers hustling out from Heathrow's busy concourse terminals to their various transit points, I was identified with pinpoint accuracy by my brother's friend. Wow! "How did you find me?" I asked.

"Simple," he replied jokingly. "I looked for someone who looks exactly like your big brother."

The Bible abounds with numerous prophecies identifying Jesus as the Messiah. His address and tribal lineage were no secret: "But you, Bethlehem Ephrathah, though you are little among the thousands of Judah, Yet out of you shall come forth to Me the one to be Ruler in Israel Whose goings forth are from of old, from everlasting" (Mic. 5:2). Those who knew about his mission and were casual about the event were passed over and left in the dark. However, shepherds—regarded by the ruling elites as ignorant, uninformed, and spiritually blind but nonetheless anxiously waiting for the event—were tapped and brought to the very doorsteps of the Messiah. The wise men from the East, guided by a mysterious hand, embarked on a mission to find the Christ. They found him, worshipped him, and following the custom of their time emptied their deep pockets with gifts befitting a king.

God has made himself very convenient and available to those seeking him. "And as He walked by the Sea of Galilee, He saw Simon and Andrew his brother casting a net into the sea; for they were fishermen. Then Jesus said to them, follow Me and I will make you become fishers of men" (Mark 1:16–17). It was by no coincidence that Jesus, walking by the sea, called ordinary working people to discipleship. Why did he not go to the local rabbinical school for recruits? Could it mean that these men were handpicked because they were pliable? Who wants to work with brittle and uncooperative material?

The selection process continues. Jesus is still seeking "jewels for his kingdom" as the song affirms. But the scripture is emphatic about the selection process: "Nevertheless the solid foundation of God stands, having this seal: the Lord knows those who are His" (2 Tim. 2:19). Not only does God know who are his but he also actively seeks them wherever they are and arranges events and circumstances to woo them to him. The truth of the matter is we do not find God; he finds us. Paul stated to the Athenians that "He [God] is not far from each one of us" (Acts 17:27). But some of us are playing hide-and-seek with God. Do you really want to be found? "And you will seek Me and find Me, when you search for Me with all your heart. And I will be found of you, says the Lord" (Jer. 29:13–14). Are you sincerely searching for God?

April 9

Forgiven Much, Loves Much

Therefore I say to you, her sins which are many, are forgiven for she loved much. But to whom little is forgiven, the same loves little.

—Luke 7:47

An angel in human personality is helping women kick their bad habits and find their true self-worth. After twenty-one bouts with law enforcement, Kathryn had had enough. She cleaned up at a drug rehab program and eventually fought for legislation in her state, imploring officials to place emphasis on rehabilitation as opposed to imprisonment. She won and founded We've Been There Done That, an organization dedicated to restoring the dignity and self-worth of these beautiful women. With hugs, affirmation, personal testimonies, and presentations at court hearings, she is bringing aunts, mothers, sisters, and daughters back into being productive members of society. Oh, how we wish she could be divided and sent to all fifty states (http://hereandnow.legacy.wbur.org/2013/08/15/former-prostitute-program).

The good little resident in us is inspired and developed only by the power of the Holy Spirit. "Without Me ye can do nothing" (John 15:5). "For I know that in me (that is, in my flesh) nothing good dwells; for to will is present with me, but how to perform what is good I do not find. For the good that I will to do I do not do; but the evil I will not to do, that I practice" (Rom. 7:18–19). Satan has an agenda for our lives, and it is not good, but thanks be to God who plucked us from certain destruction. "And the Lord said to Satan, the Lord who has chosen Jerusalem rebuke you! Is this not a brand plucked from the fire?" (Zech. 3:2). We can replace Jerusalem with our names. Were you plucked from the fire of prostitution, alcoholism, drug addiction, or any other affliction? The Lord who has chosen Mark, Fred, Judy, and Alice rebukes you. The grand design the devil had for your life and mine was foiled because God loves us, and we responded to his love.

Have you ever questioned God's love for you when the chips were down? We all have. However, the Bible has many antidotes for doubters. "The Lord has appeared of old to me, saying: Yes, I have loved you with an everlasting love; therefore with loving kindness have I drawn you" (Jer. 31:3). No one can doubt the sincerity of this charm offensive because it originates from the Creator of love. Others may love for ulterior motives, but God's love is genuine and unconditional. Did he not empty heaven of its most priceless gift on our behalf? If anyone knows a thing or two about love, it is God. "He who does not love does not know God, for God is love" (1 John 4:8).

God's love is magnified even more through weak, willing, and compliant human vessels. Mary, the woman of our memory verse, was moved by the tender touch of Jesus in reaching out to her from the street corners, where she plied her trade. She mustered all her resources and purchased the most expensive (imported) ointment to anoint the feet of her benefactor, Jesus. She was forgiven much, and this was evidenced by her generous deed of appreciation. But Jesus reprimanded his host Simon, whom he cleansed from leprosy but didn't think to provide the very basic service of foot washing to the King of the universe. While Mary unknowingly paid homage to the King of kings, Simon denied him the honor befitting an ordinary invited guest. What have you done lately for Jesus in showing your appreciation for saving you from sin and yourself?

God, My Provider

Give us this day our daily bread.

—Matthew 6:11

Celebrate the dance, but give credit to the real rainmaker, God. A celebratory dance complemented by drums is on full display as colorful Pueblo Indians dance to invoke the spirits for some much-needed rain. Among many Native American tribes and particularly among the Pueblo people, whenever rain is much needed, a rain dance becomes necessary. Other cultures around the world employ interesting methods of inducing rain from the gods. Some observe the structure of dry bones to predict the wet stuff. But how safe and reliable are these crystal ball tactics? Could talking to a friendly unknown spirit advisor be talking to the devil? Who provides for our basic needs anyway?

"And it shall be that if you earnestly obey my commandments which I command you today, to love the Lord your God and serve Him with all your heart and with all your soul, then I will give you the rain for your land in its season, the early rain and the latter rain, that you may gather in your grain, your new wine, and your oil" (Deut. 11:13–14). God is the Creator of the universe and supplies all the needs of his creatures. He provides adequate snacks along the routes of migrating animals and fills them with enough goodies for their journey. Humans are not neglected. It would have been to their benefit had his people, Israel, complied with his will, but even in their noncompliance, he was gracious and honored the covenant he made with Abraham, our father. He supplied them with their daily necessities in spite of their waywardness.

God is an incredibly loving and impartial Being. He has no favorite children, nor has he any grandchildren; he treats everyone equally. He even satisfies the needs of those who hate him. "But I say to you, love your enemies, bless those who curse you, do good to those who hate you, and pray for those who spitefully use you and persecute you, that you may be the sons of your Father in heaven; for He makes His sun rise on the evil and on the good, and sends rain on the just and on the unjust" (Matt. 5:44–45). Everyone, including the wicked, is dependent upon our heavenly Father for sustenance (Matt. 6:11).

No shaman, priest, weather forecaster, magician, or so-called rainmaker can induce a drop of rain from the skies, however impressive the dance or ceremony may be, but we certainly can influence the hand of God and of nature by our prayers. "When the heavens are shut up and there is no rain because they have sinned against You, when they pray towards this place and confess Your name, and turn from their sin because You afflict them, then hear in heaven, and forgive the sin of Your servants Your people Israel that You may teach them the good way in which they should walk; and send rain on Your land which You have given to Your people as an inheritance" (1 Kings 8:35–36). The antidote for a drought is still prayer—fervent, sincere prayer.

Jesus's prayer "Give us this day our daily bread" shows not only God's provision for all his creatures but also our utter reliance on him for our daily needs. In our rush to work and to get there on time, we sometimes forget it is God who gives us the power to earn income. "And you shall remember the Lord Your God, for it is He who gives you power to get wealth" (Deut. 8:18). Thanks for the employment, boss, but God gets the honor for using you as a vessel to channel my blessings to me.

April 11

When Pain Is an Afterthought

For we know that the whole creation groans and labors with birth pangs together until now. Not only that, but we also who have the Spirit, even we ourselves groan within ourselves, eagerly waiting for the adoption, the redemption of our body.
—Romans 8:22–23

Little four-month-old baby Morgan (name changed) lies heavily sedated on her little bed hooked to sophisticated medical equipment. We have been told she has been a little cranky lately and with good reason. Her only comfort, a pacifier, has been taken from her to prepare her for upcoming surgery, and she is not happy. At another medical institution, Candy's body racks with pain from another bout with sickle cell anemia. She is temporarily distracted from her pain to greet an incoming couple who happen to be her first visitors of the day. The longing in her voice for familiar company is quite obvious. We prayed, administered Holy Communion to her, and departed. Another family is battling pain of a different kind; this disease involves blank stares, long periods of silence, and loss of memory. Familiar friends and family are hardly recognizable anymore.

What do all three cases have in common? All the families and friends of these wonderful, dear ones and others not mentioned long for the redemption and wellness of their loved ones, and regrettably, this may not be possible here on this earth. While we pray and fervently ask God to heal, restore, and relieve pain, we must be cognizant of the fact that only God sees the entire picture. He alone knows the end from the beginning. God will never hurt his children needlessly or lead them astray. Even in our human anguish and sorrow and between sobs, we must submit to the Father's wise counsel as Jesus did. "O My Father, if it is possible, let this cup pass from Me; nevertheless, not as I will, but as You will" (Matt. 26:39). The body may be groaning for liberation, but the Spirit is insisting on sticking to God's agenda. Father knows best.

The apostle Paul described himself as having a thorn in the flesh that caused him tremendous discomfort. He sought three times in agonizing prayer to have it removed, only to be told, "My grace is sufficient for you, my strength is made perfect in weakness" (2 Cor. 12:9). This may not have been the answer the apostle was seeking, but it was the one he got from an all-wise God.

Things are murky down here; our limited insight does not allow us to see the entire picture, and that's where we must submit to the higher authority, God. The Father is more anxious than us to have this whole sin problem wrapped up, but he sees and knows everything, and we must submit to his all-wise counsel and judgment. On that fateful Thursday night, Jesus could not see beyond the cross but wisely submitted his life into the hands of an all-caring God. Can we always make sense of the mass confusion around us?

As we grapple with pain, joy, sorrow, births, deaths, accidents, and anniversaries down here, we may not always know how to make sense of them, but we await a brighter day when God will make all things right. "And God will wipe away every tear from their eyes; there shall be no more death, nor sorrow nor crying. There shall be no more pain, for the former things have passed away" (Rev. 21:4).

April 12

Letting off Steam

Be angry, and sin not: do not let the sun go down on your wrath.
—Ephesians 4:26

We've all seen it before, angry ballplayers shattering their sports gear, venting rage on opposing fans, behaving badly in public, attacking referees, even inflicting injury on their person. Is it really worth it? In the end, if they hope to continue their careers, they will have to apologize to their fans, coaches, and the general public. Unrestrained anger could cost you your life. It's not worth it. Get a hold of your temper if you're thin-skinned or quick-tempered.

It's okay to be angry; very much like love, anger is a legitimate human emotion. Some of our most admired biblical heroes were angry and used their anger to glorify God. Some were angry and sinned mightily, while others directed their anger at the source of iniquity. Israel had fallen prey to Balaam's wicked plan and was induced into idolatry and fornication. Phinehas—son of Eleazar, son of Aaron, the high priest—was infuriated about the widespread iniquity. He was righteously indignant that his fellow Israelites prostituted themselves and dishonored God when they were at the very gates of the Promised Land. They fell prey to the cunning plot of Balaam. In his anger and zeal for God's honor, he took a javelin and impaled a prominent couple who were still in the illicit act of copulation. His quick action and righteous indignation stopped the plague. "Phinehas the son of Eleazar, the son of Aaron the priest has turned back My wrath from the children of Israel, because he was zealous with My zeal among them, so that I did not consume the children of Israel in My zeal" (Num. 25:11).

Jesus was angry when his house (the temple) was turned into a stock exchange for pricing animal sacrifice. "And He found in the temple those who sold oxen and sheep and doves, and the money changers doing business. When He had made a whip of cords, He drove them all out of the temple, with the sheep and the oxen, and poured out the changers' money and overturned the tables. And He said to those who sold doves, 'Take these away! Do not make My Father's house a house of merchandise!'" (John 2:14–16).

Jonah was furious at God and wished for death because God had saved the Ninevites, Israel's archenemy. "For I know that You are a gracious and merciful God, slow to anger and abundant in loving kindness, One who relents from doing harm. Therefore now, O Lord please take my life from me, for it is better for me to die than to live" (Jonah 4:2–3). Poor Jonah. It was misdirected anger. Is this not what salvation is all about—saving the lost? Doesn't the prophetic office call for ministering to the lost?

David's eldest son, Amnon, sexually abused his little sister, Tamar, a crime punishable by death by stoning, according to Levitical law. King David, a scholar of the law himself, chose to do absolutely nothing besides just being angry (2 Sam. 13:21). As a result of his inaction, he lost not only one son but many from the carnage that ensued.

"Nothing is new under the sun." Road rage and fistfights have been with us ever since the first sin. Cain initiated the first fistfight and murdered his brother Abel (Gen. 4:8). How can we handle this hot passion called anger? Simple. "A soft answer turns away wrath, but harsh words stir up anger" (Prov. 15:1). It works. It really does. Try it on your best friend or spouse, and you'll see the results. If that fails, it's time to back off. "Be angry and do not sin, do not let the sun go down on your wrath" (Eph. 4:26).

April 13

Battered but Still Resilient

We are hard-pressed on every side, yet not crushed; we are perplexed, but not in despair; persecuted but not forsaken; struck down, but not destroyed—always carrying about in the body the dying of the Lord Jesus, that the life of Jesus also may be manifested in our body.

—2 Corinthians 4:8–10

My father had a fabulous green thumb (grows everything). Everything he touched grew vigorously, but I did not learn the green thumb secret before he passed. I absolutely love fruit trees and planted some, hoping one day to munch on their delicious offerings, but just as the trees began budding their leaves, an army of insects attacked the trees with much zeal and ferocity. Applying insect repellant and insecticide only served to energize the little pests. They chose to ignore the abundance of vegetation all around them and zeroed in on my fruit trees, showing no mercy to the struggling plants. Anxious to save my plants, I went to the store and purchased a mosquito net and encircled the plants with its covering. Would you believe a determined few found their way in? Despite the assaults to their foliage, the plants are thriving and will bear fruit one day.

"Every branch in Me that does not bear fruit He takes away; and every branch that bears fruit He prunes, that it may bear more fruit" (John 15:2). Pruning can be a painful process, but it is necessary for a healthy plant and a more bountiful harvest. Pruning entails the removal of diseased, nonproductive parts, which put strain on the economy of the plant. Pruning has positive benefits. The process allows the gardener to control the shape and maintain the plants, all in an effort of increasing the harvest yield. The plants benefit from the pruning process, however uncomfortable it may be. They become healthier and yield more fruit, and the farmer gets a more robust harvest.

What the farmer does to the vine with his pruning knife, God does to our heart. He takes his scalpel and makes cuts and incisions to remove diseased body parts, such as hate and racism. Sometimes he makes grafts, infusing people in our lives to mentor us in matters of morals, doctrine, and spiritual uprightness. "When Aquila and Priscilla heard him, they took him aside and explained to him the way of God more accurately" (Acts 18:26). Here is a classic case of a graft, a mature couple gently pulling aside a budding young talent and instructing him in the way of the Lord more fully.

Pruning is never a painless procedure, and no one understood this better than God himself. "As for Saul, he made havoc of the church, entering every house, and dragging out men and women, committing them to prison. Therefore, those who were scattered went everywhere preaching the word" (Acts 8:3–4). With the church being persecuted and believers scattered all over the place, the desired effect God intended was achieved. The gospel went to the ends of the earth. The pruning of the church really works.

Even when pruning invites persecution, God is right there with us. "Who shall separate us from the love of Christ? Shall tribulation, or distress, or persecution, or famine, or nakedness, or peril, or sword?" (Rom. 8:35). Nothing can separate us from the love of God, which is in Christ Jesus. God is working in us, and though at times we may be battered by the fierce winds of persecution, just hang in there. God has your back. "No weapon formed against you shall prosper" (Isa. 54:17).

April 14

Fall Afresh on Us

It is the Spirit who gives life; the flesh profits nothing. The words that I speak to you are spirit and they are life.

—John 6:63

The last puddle of moisture in the lagoon is disappearing fast; survival instinct kicks in. The bullfrog knows what to do; he must take evasive action. He burrows his way deep down into the mud, cocoons himself into a ball of mucus, and waits as long as needed, maybe years, for the life-giving rains. The grass, devoid of moisture and nutrients, has turned dry and yellow, so the migrating animals have no choice but to move on and seek greener pastures. Lions, though, find migrating too labor-intensive and are forced to eke out an existence on less desirable meals while waiting for the rains to bring back their prey. Months of blistering heat pass, and the bullfrog patiently waits. Then suddenly, there's a flash of lightning; dark gray clouds heavy with moisture collide, causing a thunderous blast, and the showers come cascading, sending the good news to plain residents far and wide (*National Geographic*).

The rain has changed everything. The burrowing bullfrog, safe inside his cocoon, receives the news with great delight. He gently pushes and wiggles his way out to a nearby pool already full of gleeful residents (mostly his kind). The lions are grateful also. Their meager diet has been complemented with choice steak and prime ribs, but the feast that resulted from the rain is possible only through the providence of God. The seed and roots that lie dormant during the hot summer respond to the moisture by absorbing and exploiting it. With this metaphor, Jesus illustrated the interaction among seed, productivity, and soil. "Most assuredly, I say to you, unless a grain of wheat falls into the ground and dies, it remains alone; but if it dies, it produces much grain" (John 12:24). The seed must die the death of a seed before it can grow, let alone produce food. Must we die to sin and self before we can be productive in God's service?

The Father, Son, and Holy Spirit all work in unison to bring the spiritually dead back to life just as the dormant seed made its transition back to life upon contact with water. Likewise, we begin to live when we respond to the still, soft voice of the Holy Spirit. This process is called conversion, and it ushers in the death of the old nature of sin and gives birth to a new nature in Christ Jesus. The sinful old habits give way to a new creature with godly desires and aspirations.

Though the new birth is complete, God is not finished with us quite yet. Like a little baby, and that's what we are at conversion, we must depend on the Holy Spirit for growth, nutrition, and development. And who does this job better than the Holy Spirit? It is his task to grow, nurture, and develop our muscles so we can walk and talk as Christ. The Spirit will lead if we don't resist to a life of prayer, Bible study, and witnessing to others.

"But the Helper, the Holy Spirit, whom the Father will send in My name, He will teach you all things, and bring to your remembrance all things that I said to you" (John 14:26). Holy Spirit, be my teacher and my guide. I have much yet to learn. Please teach me all I should know so that I can be an effective witness for you. Make plain to me what I should do once I am convinced of a truth I am not currently practicing. Make me be obedient to your will. Amen.

Not a Sprint but a Marathon

I returned and saw under the sun that the race is not for the swift, nor the battle for the strong, nor bread for the wise, nor riches to men of understanding, nor favor for the men of skill; but time and chance happen to them all.

—Ecclesiastes 9:11

Legend tells us that a tortoise and a hare argued bitterly about who could run the fastest mile. The animals in attendance set up a starting point and a finish line. At the crowing of the rooster, the runners were off. The hare intentionally delayed his takeoff so as to embarrass his slower competitor, and then he zoomed past him with a smirk of arrogance on his face. Nearing the finish line, he decided to take a short nap in a tree shade, confident he would wake up in time to stroll across the finish line, but he overslept. When he awoke and to his utter dismay, his lumbering competitor was just crossing the finish line. Despite his great speed, the hare lost the race, and the issue was settled once and for all—the tortoise was indeed the faster of the two runners. What an irony, the slowest creature ever winning a race against a seasoned speedster. "The race is not for the swift, nor is the battle for the strong" (Eccles. 9:11).

The Christian race is not a sprint; it never has been. It's a marathon.

> For the kingdom of heaven is like a landowner who went out early in the morning to hire laborers for his vineyard. Now when he had agreed with the laborers for a denarius a day, he sent them into his vineyard. And he went out about the third hour and saw others standing idle in the marketplace, and said to them, you also go into the vineyard, and whatsoever is right I will give you. So they went. Again he went out about the sixth hour and the ninth hour, and did likewise. And about the eleventh hour he went out and found others standing idle, and said to them, why have you been standing here idle all day? They said to him, because no one hired us. He said to them, you also go into the vineyard, and whatever is right you will receive. (Matt. 20:1–7)

The early birds complained bitterly, claiming they worked the hardest, while their counterparts worked for just one hour and received the same pay as them. The owner reminded them, "Take what is yours and go your way. I wish to give to this last man the same as to you. Is it not lawful for me to do what I wish with my own things? Or is your eye evil because I am good? So the last will be first, and the first last. For many are called, but few are chosen" (Matt. 20:14–16).

Paul reminded his Corinthian brethren that they, together with us, are in a real race: "Do you not know that those who run in a race all run, but one receives the prize? Run in such a way that you may obtain it" (1 Cor. 9:24). Interestingly, every one of us can make it to the finish line, but here is a word of caution: "Therefore let us not sleep, as others do, but let us watch and be sober" (1 Thess. 5:6). Sleeping could imply having one foot in the church and the other in the world. We must guard against the tendency to get lax and careless as we approach the finish line, but let us keep our eyes fixed on Jesus, who is the Author and Finisher of our faith. Are you getting tired of waiting and watching for the coming of the Lord? Paul admonishes us to stay awake. Every child of God can finish the race in Christ's strength. "But he that endures to the end the same shall be saved" (Matt. 24:13). It is not how you begin a race that matters but how you end it.

April 16

Undoing What Is Convenient

Nevertheless the solid foundation of God stands, having this seal: the Lord knows those who are his. And let everyone who names the name of Christ depart from iniquity.

—2 Timothy 2:19

Sally rewarded her hairy white terrier with a bubble bath since he was so well-behaved during his vet visit. Just after his exciting bubble bath, he couldn't resist running outside and refreshing himself with a fine, good old dust bath by wallowing in the dirt. Dogs do what comes naturally to dogs. Maybe the dust bath releases some inner stress, eases pain and discomfort, or simply satisfies some natural behavior unknown to us.

The pleasure of a dust bath after a refreshing bubble bath is typical of dogs. Is our behavior any different? We offend in identical fashion. "God looks down from heaven upon the children of men, to see if there are any who understand, who seek God. Every one of them has turned aside; they have together become corrupt; there is none who does good, no not one" (Ps. 53:2–3).

I couldn't help but notice the natural man on full display at my job. Every few words of my unbelieving work companions are laced with profanity and debasing and obscene gestures. Lewd, degrading jokes and jests are the order of the day. No wonder the scripture referenced Lot as being vexed by the lewd conduct of the wicked. "And delivered righteous Lot, who was oppressed by the filthy conduct of the wicked for that righteous man dwelling among them, tormented his righteous soul from day to day by seeing and hearing their lawless deeds" (2 Pet. 2:7–8). Let's not get carried away by thinking we are more righteous than anyone. It is the grace of God that makes us different. Paul understood this and exclaimed in frustration,

> For I know that in me (that is in my flesh) nothing good dwells; for to will is present with me, but how to perform what is good I do not find. For the good that I will to do, I do not do; but the evil I will not to do, that I practice. Now if I do what I will not to do, it is no longer I who do it, but sin that dwells in me. I find then a law, that evil is present with me . . . O wretched man that I am! Who will deliver me from this body of death? (Rom. 7:18–21, 24)

Like any descendant of Adam, Paul was having a mighty struggle with the natural man embedded under his skin. Do you share Paul's struggle of suppressing the natural man?

David had his struggles with covetousness and made this candid confession after his sin with Bathsheba: "Behold I was brought forth in iniquity and in sin did my mother conceive me" (Ps. 51:5). The natural man, commonly referred to in Paul's epistles as the "flesh" (unconverted nature), is constantly at war with our spiritual nature, but we must suppress it daily to be victorious.

"Have mercy on me, O God, according to Your loving kindness; according to the multitude of Your tender mercies, blot out my transgressions. Wash me thoroughly from my iniquity and cleanse me from my sin" (Ps. 51:1–2). Though familiar with David's confession, Paul asked the poignant question: "Who shall deliver me from this body of death?" Paul, Jesus can and will. By virtue of his sinless life and death, Jesus made it possible for us to conquer sin in his strength, not in our weakness. He offers his spotless and perfect righteousness to our vile and sin-riddled life. Should we pass off on such a magnificent offer?

April 17

One More Chance

Sir, let it alone this year also, until I dig around it and fertilize it. And if it bear fruit, well. But if not, after that you can cut it down.

—Luke 13:8–9

Every year we hope this time would be its breakout year; its leaves were resplendent, verdant, and green, but it never delivered anything, never rewarded our patience with any precious fruits. Mangoes do very well in tropically dry climates with a moderate amount of rainfall. However, our tree grew in the cold interior of the country and was struggling against the odds to be productive. Every year it went through the elaborate process of sporting new leaves and lovely flowers, which never delivered anything to us but disappointment and frustration. We were never able to sink our teeth into its juicy fruit. It was barren, occupying precious space but yielding nothing in return. Understandably, it had to be destroyed to make way for profitable and productive trees.

"My well beloved has a vineyard on a very fruitful hill. He dug it up and cleared out its stones, and planted it with the choicest vine. He built a tower in its midst, and also made a winepress in it; so He expected it to bring forth good grapes, but it brought forth wild grapes. And now, O inhabitants of Jerusalem and men of Judah, judge, please, between Me and My vineyard. What more could have been done to My vineyard that I have not done in it?" (Isa. 5:1–4).

The Master Gardener evaluates the potential of every plant, and he liberally bestows opportunities on all vegetation to be fruitful and productive. He selected a fertile hill and established his vineyard. Jerusalem was strategically situated on the ancient trade route of world commerce. It was prime real estate where traveling pilgrims could learn and be acquainted with Israel's God. More opportunities were given to that blessed nation after the Babylonian captivity. "Sir, let it alone this year also, until I dig around it and fertilize it. And if it bears fruit, well. But if not, after that You can cut it down" (Luke 13:8–9). Divine forbearance lingered with the unrepentant nation for a little longer until they rejected their Redeemer and persecuted God's messengers among them. God's effort to revitalize his vineyard was rebuffed and rejected by Israel and her ungodly leaders. "O Jerusalem, Jerusalem, the one who kills the prophets and stones those who are sent to her! How often I wanted to gather your children together, as a hen gathers her chicks under her wings, but you were not willing" (Matt. 23:37).

All the wonderful promises and opportunities given to Israel of old apply to us, and like them, we are in danger of squandering them away. He has invested in us all the necessary essentials to healthy spiritual growth. His blessings are innumerable. He has planted us in a blessed and fruitful land with a world-class economy and has made us the envy of other nations. He redeemed us and gave us a country respecting the rule of law. What more could we ask for? What more could he have done that he hasn't done already? But the question persists. What are we doing with the opportunities given to us?

Let us take heed, lest we repeat Israel's sins of unproductivity. My father's favorite proverb affirms: "If your companion's beard catches fire, sprinkle yours." He who fails to learn from history is doomed to repeat it. Let us spread the good news of a sin-pardoning Savior. Jesus is coming soon. Are you getting ready to receive him?

April 18

We Struck Gold

Your word is a lamp to my feet and a light to my path.

—Psalm 119:105

With some fancy footwork, a few wiggles of his abdomen, and buzzing wings, he describes the location, distance, and quality of the upcoming feast. Honeybee colonies send scouts to the surrounding neighborhoods to check things out. They see who is out there, where food is available, and the quality of the food and bring it home to feed the family. Upon discovering a promising find, the scout is overcome with sheer delight and hurries back to the hive. He engages in a dazzling, elaborate dance that gives the location, distance, and quality of the find. He then leads his fellow workers to the feast, and the hive is sustained for another day. God's Word is even sweeter than honey.

"The entrance of your words gives light; it gives understanding to the simple" (Ps. 119:130). To cultures and people stuck in tradition and long-held cultural mores, the Word of God is truly a light in a very dark place. Health and longevity have improved and increased as a result of the introduction of the Bible and its life-enhancing principles. Demonic strongholds have been demolished as long-held beliefs in the spirits have waned and crumbled with the introduction of the Bible in society. Schools and medical establishments have replaced the witch doctor as spiritual advisor to the culture.

Tribal warfare that decimated populations has been replaced by an invasion of another kind, the preaching of the everlasting gospel to neighbors and friends. Knives, spears, stone axes, pistols, bow and arrows—once tools of aggression—have been replaced by textbooks, Bible studies, Bibles, scripture scrolls, DVD videos, transistor radios, and computers all in a bid to advance the spread of the gospel. The results of the introduction of the Bible into these cultures are nothing short of miraculous.

Even in advanced societies, the effects of the Word of God can be seen. The rule of law has been patterned after the Bible. Legislative bodies, school boards, corporate boards, and educational establishments derive their constitutions from the creed set by biblical standards. What a great treasure we have in earthen vessels. "For it is God who commanded light to shine out of darkness, who has shone in our hearts to give the light of the knowledge of the glory of God in the face of Jesus Christ. But we have this treasure in earthen vessels, that the excellence of the power may be of God and not of us" (2 Cor. 4:6–7). "This treasure in earthen vessel" is Jesus living in us. What a privilege it is to have the King of the universe dwelling and abiding in us as sinful as we are!

We give thanks to God for the transformation that has been wrought in our lives as a result of the Word of God. We were all lost, swimming in darkness, trespasses, ignorance, and sin, and Jesus's love lifted us from darkness into his marvelous light. The Bible is a hidden treasure. When found, everything else becomes secondary to it. "How sweet are Your words to my taste, sweeter than honey to my mouth? Through Your precepts I get understanding; therefore I hate every false way" (Ps. 119:103–104). Thanks for your word of life, dear God, and thanks for Jesus, the Word.

April 19

Am I My Brother's Keeper?

Then the Lord said to Cain, where is Abel your brother? He said, I do not know. Am I my brother's keeper?

—Genesis 4:9

A fire is raging in the neighborhood, but there is no fire department in town, no fire trucks, no emergency numbers, and certainly no cell phones. What do you do? Let's rewind the tape of the lives of real people living in a culture outside the affluence of the Western world. Father was a self-declared watchman turned announcer who sounded the alarm when someone's house caught on fire. In this part of the world, fire usually occurred at night when lamps and burning candles were knocked over. When a full-blown fire was raging, Father went on the offensive. From the vantage point of his two-story building towering over the little rickety wooden shacks in the neighborhood, he bellowed, "Fire! Fire! Fire!" Immediately, a bucket brigade was formed from a coalition of the willing. They rushed to the site, buckets in hand, to douse the inferno.

Once assembled, they used a running water pipe (a public water facility where villagers collected water) to douse the flames. The survival of the house and its occupants was always dependent on the quick response and easy access to water. The beauty of this volunteer call to service coalition (fire brigade) enabled neighbors to fight the common enemy, fire. Someone once said, "Fire is a good servant but a terrible master." I agree completely.

Are you aware there is an enemy more insidious, more destructive than fire prowling our streets and snatching victims from homes in the cities of our nation? This enemy is, of course, the evil and enraged devil, and Peter classifies him as very dangerous. "Be sober, be vigilant; because your adversary the devil walks about like a roaring lion seeking whom he may devour" (1 Pet. 5:8). Who hasn't seen his carnage? It includes wasted and diseased bodies, ruined lives, premature death, infant mortality, school shootings, wars, broken homes, truancy, unnatural affection, and the list is endless. When we see his signature on the lives of people all around us, it is time to jump into action as the volunteer fire brigade to rescue the perishing.

"So you, son of man: I have made you a watchman for the house of Israel; therefore, you shall hear the word from My mouth and warn them for Me. When I say to the wicked, O wicked man, you shall surely die! And you do not speak to warn the wicked from his way, that wicked man shall die in his iniquity; but his blood I will require at your hand" (Ezek. 33:7–8). It couldn't be said any plainer. We are accountable to those in our immediate sphere of influence. Tell them of God's amazing love.

We often think of the difference the gospel might make in the lives of the unreached, faraway residents, but we fail to see the difference it can make in the life of our next-door neighbors suffering in silence. Let us be bold and proactive as Jonathan. "Then Jonathan said to the young man who bore his armor, 'Come let us go over to the garrison of these uncircumcised; it may be that the Lord will work for us. For nothing restrains the Lord from saving by many or by few.' So his armor bearer said to him, 'Do all that is in your heart. Go then; here I am with you according to your heart'" (1 Sam. 14:6–7). If we are willing, God will supply the courage. Be your brother's keeper, and spread the good news of a loving and forgiving Savior to those near you.

April 20

A Hedge around Us

Have you not made a hedge around him, around his household, and around all that he has on every side? You have blessed the work of his hands, and his possessions have increased in the land.

—Job 1:10

Surrounded by a thick hedge of prickly plants, the beautiful orange and red marigolds were safe from hungry deer and swinging coats. A Sabbath potluck dinner invitation led us past a beautiful garden full of vibrant colorful marigold plants. Bees busied themselves flying from one flower to another, collecting their daily ration of nectar. In the process, they involuntarily returned the favor by cross-pollinating the plants.

What was quite obvious was the design of the gardener. She intentionally planted diverse marigolds, which were very colorful, and surrounded them with a hedge of prickly, thorny plants, probably to sting and ward off hungry deer. There, they were safe and secure with a buffer and shield between them and an array of potential enemies.

God employs the same strategy in the defense of his children; even Satan acknowledges that. "Have you not made a hedge around him, around his household, and around all that he has on every side?" (Job 1:10). The protection afforded Job is given to every trusting believer in Jesus Christ. We are covered by an impenetrable shield.

In the analogy of Psalm 23, the shepherd leads his sheep where the pasture is green and luxuriant. He scans the landscape for danger from predators. If they show interest in his sheep, he is ready with rod in hand to meet the threat. "I am the Good Shepherd. The Good Shepherd gives His life for His sheep" (John 10:11).

Not only will the Good Shepherd give his life for his sheep but he also is wary of anyone intent on hurting them. "For thus says the Lord of Host: He sent Me after glory, to the nations which plunder you; who touches you touches the apple of His eye" (Zech. 2:8). If someone is rubbing you wrongly, don't fret. God is not blind. He'll take care of you. Was Jacob unguarded when he fled from Laban with nothing for defense but his walking stick? And even when Esau approached with his squad of four hundred heavily armed warriors to exact revenge for the birthright issue, didn't God give him a change of heart? "But Esau ran to meet him, and embraced him, and fell on his neck and kissed him, and they wept" (Gen. 33:4). Isn't God superamazing? He turned a revenge encounter into a friendly, grand old family reunion. "Behold, He who keeps Israel shall neither slumber nor sleep" (Ps. 121:4).

God's eyes are riveted on the righteous, and nothing can penetrate his all-searching gaze. "The eyes of the Lord are on the righteous, and His ears are open to their cry" (Ps. 34:15). We should walk in confidence even in the darkest hours of midnight, in troubled situations, in pending court hearings, and in tough hot spots in school and at home. "God is our refuge and strength, a very present help in trouble. Therefore, we will not fear, even though the earth be removed, and though the mountains be carried into the midst of the sea; though the waters roar and be troubled, though the mountains shake with its swelling . . . God is in the midst of her, she shall not be moved" (Ps. 46:1–3, 5).

April 21

Dust to Dust

In the sweat of your face you shall eat bread till you return to the ground, for out of it you were taken; for dust you are, and to dust you shall return.
—Genesis 3:19

The singing group Kansas summed up death pretty nicely with their 1978 hit single "Dust in the Wind." Kerry Livgren reminds us of the briefness of our human existence on planet Earth. With his melancholy acoustic song, he says to us, "Get your priorities in order. Tomorrow is promised to no man."

The song goes, "I close my eyes only for a moment, and the moment's gone. All my dreams pass before my eyes, a curiosity. Dust in the wind, all they are is dust in the wind." Indeed, we are dust in the wind.

This song coincides with the proverbial saying of King Solomon: "Whatever your hand finds to do, do it with all your might; for there is no work or device or knowledge or wisdom in the grave where you are going" (Eccles. 9:10). Mortal man, God is more precious than anything you are pursuing. Why settle for the inferior when the superior beckons and is within easy grasp?

God has gone out of his way in preparing the best eternal package for his children. There is an indescribable reward awaiting the believer in contrast to what this troubled world has to offer. "If in this life only we have hope in Christ, we are of all men the most pitiable" (1 Cor. 15:19). This world, however dazzling, should not hold our affection. I have tried to understand the rationale behind the Black Friday (day after Thanksgiving) madness; to camp overnight at the store and trample on others in a rush to purchase discounted electronic equipment is sheer insanity. Well, probably, believers are not part of this riotous mob. The standard "what would Jesus do?" applies to believers everywhere in all situations. Christians walk a middle road charted by the Lord Jesus Christ. We must neither be dull nor be flamboyant; a happy median is preferable.

We came naked into this world and will take nothing away when we make our exit. Having said that, it is incumbent on us while living to use our influence and resources to make others happy by alleviating their pain and suffering. Be mindful, only the things that are done in faith for Jesus will last. In Christ's parable of the final judgment, those on his left hand will be called to account for their stewardship, and they will make this unfortunate remark: "Lord when did we see You hungry or thirsty or a stranger or naked or sick or in prison, and did not minister to You? Then He will answer them, saying, assuredly, I say to you in as much as you did not do it to one of the least of these, you did not do it to Me" (Matt. 25:44–45).

We are likened to pilgrims unfolding our tents for a brief stop here on earth; therefore it behooves us to focus on our relationship with our heavenly Father. Paul, sensing his impending death, focused on what was really important—his relationship with God. "The time of my departure is at hand. I have fought a good fight I have finished the race, I have kept the faith. Finally, there is laid up for me a crown of righteousness, which the Lord, the righteous Judge will give to me on that day, and not to me only but also to all who have loved His appearing" (2 Tim. 4:6–8).

April 22

Freedom in Releasing

Cast your bread upon the waters, for you will find it after many days.
—Ecclesiastes 11:1

The Kalahari bushman has devised an ingenious method of catching his favorite prey, the baboon. From his observation post, he waits until a curious animal strays close to a termite mound. He approaches the mound and makes a small hole large enough to get his fist through. The primates, being keen observers, watch with curiosity and interest. The hunter drops some tasty treats into the hole, probably delicious nuts, and withdraws at a distance. The baboon goes over to check things out. He grabs a handful of the tasty stuff but soon discovers that his clenched fist will not allow him to free his hand from the tight-fitting hole. He is trapped; impending captivity looms in his future or, worse, his demise. He groans, pulls, winches, and stomps but does not have the intelligence to release his bounty and walk away free (*National Geographic*).

In similar ways, we sometimes selfishly clench our fist, refusing to share with others what God has blessed us with, thus limiting God's overall blessings on us. We can only receive when, unlike the baboon, we unclench our fist, allowing our fingers to unfurl to receive blessings from the Giver. Job's generosity to his neighbors is legendary, enabling God to bless him even more so that he could refresh others. "I was eyes to the blind, and I was feet to the lame. I was a father to the poor, and I searched out the case that I did not know. I broke the fangs of the wicked, and plucked the victim from his teeth" (Job 29:15–17). When Job said he searched the case he did not know, was he saying here that he hired a law firm at his own expense to investigate corporate crimes that always tend to disenfranchise the poor? He sure did.

God stands ready to unleash heaven's bounty on his people, but they must be proved generous and trustworthy. We rob God when we are stingy and tightfisted with the resources with which he has blessed us. "Will a man rob God? Yet you have robbed Me! But you say, in what have we robbed You? In tithes and offering. You are cursed with a curse, for you have robbed Me, even this whole nation. Bring all the tithes into the storehouse, that there may be meat in My house and try me in this, says the Lord of Host, if I will not open for you the windows of heaven and pour out a blessing that there will not be enough room to receive it" (Mal. 3:8–10). Is the payment of tithe an afterthought to you? Do we meet all our financial obligations first and give God the leftovers, or do we separate the tithe and offering first and do our bills after we have given God what belongs to him? I hope we put God first in all our transactions.

The Lord is asking his people to prove him and determine for themselves whether their status will improve as a result of their faithfulness to him. A word of caution here: do not associate blessings to material gain only. For what benefit would a fat bank account be to you if you do not have health to enjoy it? Which would you prefer, money in the bank or the health of your body? I assume you would opt for the latter. Only God can decide which is best for us. Not everyone has the capability to handle wealth and health at the same time. Could it be that God gives us resources proportionate to our ability to dispense with them wisely for his glory and honor? Let us pray that the Father will give what is best for us. "Your kingdom come, Your will be done on earth as it is in heaven" (Matt. 6:10).

April 23

When God's People Pray

And Enoch walked with God; and he was not, for God took him.
—Genesis 5:24

At 365 years of age, Enoch was considered a young adult according to the longevity of his ancestors; however, he walked and talked with his Maker so much that God took him away. God also enjoyed the walk and talk, so he took Enoch to heaven to continue the relationship. The word used to describe Enoch's walk with God is the Hebrew verb *halak*, which means "to go on habitually." God is always the first at initiating conversations. He spoke to Adam, didn't he? "Can two walk together, unless they are agreed?" (Amos 3:3). The walk described here is more than a casual stroll. It denotes intimacy, friendship, mutual understanding, sharing, love, and trust.

Face-to-face communication with God became a terrifying ordeal after the entrance of sin. Adam hid himself among the bushes at the approach of God (Gen. 3:8). Moses's request to see God's face was a simple request but with grave ramifications. "But He said, you cannot see My face; for no man shall see Me and live . . . So it shall be, while My glory passes by, that I will put you in the cleft of the rock, and will cover you with My hand while I pass by. Then I will take away My hand, and you shall see My back, but My face shall not be seen" (Exod. 33:20, 22–23).

Other great men of the Bible have reached the pedigree of Enoch and Moses in open communication with God through prayer. Daniel walked with God and was reminded by the angel that he was highly favored. Listen as Daniel prays, "Now therefore, our God, hear the prayer of your servant, and his supplications . . . O my God incline Your ear and hear; open Your eyes and see our desolations, and the city which is called by Your name; for we do not present our supplications before You because of our righteous deeds, but because of Your great mercies" (Dan. 9:17–18).

The prayer of Ezra pleading for God's mercy on his rebellious countrymen meets the threshold of one who walks closely with God. Paul's constant prayer for wayward Israel, the growing church, and his demanding schedule puts him in the category of those who enjoy intimate fellowship with God. Stephen's short life of service and his prayer for his enemies while he was being stoned to death meets the threshold of one who walks with God. Of course, no one enjoyed more of an unbroken communication with God than Jesus Christ. "Now in the morning, having risen a long while before daylight, He went out and departed to a solitary place; and there He prayed" (Mark 1:35).

The great men/women who achieved the seemingly impossible spent much time with God in prayer. It became such a joy to them that communication with God superseded every earthly function or interest. Some are too busy to pray today. Are we too busy to talk to the Creator of the universe while we hustle to meet our earthly boss, a fellow creature that God created? Now wait a minute, shouldn't God come first and then others? Give him the first and best of everything, including yourself. "If My people who are called by My name will humble themselves, and pray and seek My face and turn from their wicked ways, then I will hear from heaven, and will forgive their sin and heal their land" (2 Chron. 7:14). Are you driven to your knees only by emergencies? Think about it.

April 24

The Victory Parade

They have seen Your procession, O God, the procession of my God my King, into the sanctuary. The singers went before, the players on instruments followed after; among them were the maidens playing the timbrels. Bless God in the congregations, The Lord, from the fountain of Israel. There is little Benjamin, their leader, the princes of Judah and their company, the princes of Zebulun and the princes of Naphtali.

—Psalm 68:24–27

We may have seen images of the victory parade in Times Square at the conclusion of World War II. Wasn't it wonderful? Thank God that the forces of good triumphed over evil. Incidentally, nobody puts on a parade quite like New Yorkers. With their tall skyscrapers dropping harmless confetti on revelers down below, who can duplicate that?

Processions and parades were part of the ancients' victory celebrations. When Israel marched against the city of Jericho, the priests bearing the ark led the way, followed by the military and the people. "So it was, when Joshua had spoken to the people that the seven priests bearing the seven trumpets of rams' horn before the Lord advanced and blew the trumpets, and the ark of the covenant of the Lord followed them. The armed men went before the priests who blew the trumpets, and the rear guard came after the ark, while the priests continued blowing the trumpets" (Josh. 6:8–9).

But this system was not relegated to military operations only; these parades were standard operating procedures whenever the ark of God was being moved. "And so it was, when those bearing the ark of the Lord had gone six paces, that he sacrificed oxen and fattened sheep . . . So David and all the house of Israel brought up the ark of the Lord with shouting and with the sound of the trumpet" (2 Sam. 6:13, 15).

Since the procession always precedes the victory parade, we will liken the procession to the preparation we must make before the final victory. The procession calls on us to confess all sins and totally surrender the body to the will of God. "Therefore do not let sin reign in your mortal body, that you should obey it in its lust. And do not present your members as instruments of unrighteousness to sin, but present yourselves to God as being alive from the dead, and your members as instruments of righteousness to God" (Rom. 6:12–13).

To those who think we might be celebrating prematurely, listen to this: We can shout "hallelujah" that righteousness triumphed over evil, that Christ rose from the dead, and that salvation is available to anyone who desires to know God. We can thank God for battles won and blessings in the pipeline. We must begin the celebration down here because heaven is a real place, and our salvation is secure. When we consider the filth from which we were plucked, we must shout and praise God. Who can remain silent when God has delivered us from the many snares of the devil? When we think of the cost of our salvation to God, his dear Son, Jesus Christ, who can remain silent? When we see the evils we've been spared by simply abiding in Christ, who can remain silent? When we consider the fate of the wicked and the glory that awaits the saints, who can remain silent? It is a good thing to give thanks to the Lord. Let the celebrations begin. God is good to them who call on his name, and salvation is within the grasp of everyone.

April 25

The Answer Is Behind the Doorknob

Peter was therefore kept in prison, but constant prayer was offered to God for him by the church.

—Acts 12:5

If you've prayed to God for something of great importance to you and the answer was instantly given and you had difficulty believing it, you're not alone. It happened to the early disciples. James, the twin brother of John the Revelator, was killed by Herod for no justifiable reason but "because he saw that it pleased the Jews" (Acts 12:3). The church was caught off guard by the slaying of James, but they were not about to allow lightning to strike the same spot twice. With Peter arrested and about to be executed, they (the church) called for an all-night prayer service and began petitioning God on Peter's behalf, but what transpired next is both amazing and humorous.

While they were still in prayer, God sent a rescue team to snatch Peter from the executioner's ax, but the saints had trouble believing Peter was actually free, even when told that he was knocking at the door. "But they said to her, 'You are beside yourself!' Yet she kept insisting that it was so. So they said, it is his angel. Now Peter continued knocking; and when they opened the door and saw him, they were astonished" (Acts 12:15–16). "It shall come to pass that before they call, I will answer; and while they are still speaking, I will hear" (Isa. 65:24).

Our God is patient, understanding, and full of humor. He did not castigate, rebuke, or reprove his doubtful saints overwhelmed by the rapidity of his response to their prayer. Peter himself had no appetite for reproving his astonished brethren for keeping him knocking a little longer than normal.

Keep praying for that son/daughter in prison. Keep praying that God will strengthen you to continue making payments to the various loans you are obligated to. Keep praying that God will change you before he changes your partner. Oh yes, before we forget, the commitments you made to God are still doable and achievable; and by his grace, they must be kept.

Now that we know the answer to our prayer lies just beyond the doorknob, are you ready to grasp the reality of the response? Our sons and brothers might never walk the streets as free men again, and they may very well die in prison, but there is hope for them in Jesus. While God delights in answering prayers, he also respects the decisions his intelligent children make to live with him or without him. Our prayers for friends and family members are contingent on their cooperation with the heavenly agencies sent to save them. Lot and his family were saved by cooperating with the angels to flee Sodom (Gen. 19:15–16).

Concerning our duty to repay financial commitments into which we entered, let common sense and fairness prevail. Every creditor should honor payment depending on the debtor's willingness and ability to pay an agreed-upon sum. God is big on honoring agreements. "When you make a vow to God, do not delay to pay it; For He has no delight in fools. Pay what you have vowed" (Eccles. 5:4). But if one is unable to repay his/her debts, this calls for the drastic step of declaring bankruptcy, and that is biblical also (Deut. 15:1–23). The concept of bankruptcy originates from the Bible and allows the debtor to be released from his financial obligations.

Lest we forget, God answer prayers even before we reach for the doorknob. Isn't God good? He continues to work wonders in our lives and in the lives of our loved ones.

April 26

Not Peace but a Sword

Do not think that I came to bring peace on earth. I did not come to bring peace on earth but a sword. For I have come to set a man against his father, a daughter against her mother, and a daughter-in-law against her mother-in-law.
—Matthew 10:34–35

I was a mere teenager, probably fifteen, when I had a spiritual awakening. This awakening necessitated me to forsake the traditional religion of my family to accept Jesus as my personal Savior and Lord. My decision to forsake the established church did not go very well with Father, who was a very devout deacon in his church. He dutifully woke us up at 5:00 a.m. to attend early Mass at our parish church, and he had us perform all the necessary rituals required for being good Christians at his church. However, when I became of age, I had many questions for which the church had no plausible answers; neither did they have solid biblical reasoning for their doctrines. Needless to say, I became extremely frustrated and began looking elsewhere for answers to my Bible questions. Of course, Father became infuriated and disappointed that his investment in my religious upbringing did not satisfy my spiritual yearning; but through the intervening years, he resigned himself to the fact that everyone should be the master of their destiny.

God has ingenious ways of reining in the curious. A neighbor's little girl reading her Sabbath school quarterly (religious material) caught my attention. The lessons were child-appropriate material, but they satisfied my yearning. I kindly asked the little girl permission to read the material, which she happily obliged. I devoured the Bible lessons and requested more. I exhausted her little supply and was still hungry for more. Soon after, I was linked to a Bible instructor who owned a modest library, and this quenched my appetite for a while.

While engaged in studying my newfound beliefs, I was gradually drifting away from the established family religion to the consternation of Father; he repeatedly warned me that he would tolerate no other religions in his home. However, I was undeterred; and after some study, I scheduled a date for my baptism in my newfound faith. On a sunny Sunday morning and with a handful of well-wishers in attendance, I was transformed by baptism into a new person. "Therefore, if anyone is in Christ, he is a new creation; old things have passed away; behold, all things have become new" (2 Cor. 5:17).

In every age, whenever one desires to move away from superstition to worship the one and only true God, he or she is met by fierce opposition. The forces of evil have always sought to do harm to the force for good. "Then they will deliver you up to tribulation and kill you, and you will be hated by all nations for My name's sake" (Matt. 24:9). But in Christ, we have this hope: "When my father and my mother forsake me, the Lord will take care for me" (Ps. 27:10).

The gospel of Jesus Christ, while it brought sweet peace to my heart, divided our home. Father and I obviously had a strained relationship over the incident and never actually became the best of friends, but I forgave him and love him dearly. The little inconvenience I encountered is nothing compared with those who risk life and limb for the cause of the gospel. Pastors and members are sitting in cruel jail cells because they chose a path that put them in collision with family and the authorities.

In hindsight, it was worth it all, and I would do it all over again for my Lord, who gave so much for me. "He who loves father or mother more than Me is not worthy of Me. And he who loves son or daughter more than Me is not worthy of Me. And he who does not take his cross and follow after Me is not worthy of Me" (Matt. 10:37–38).

April 27

Survival of the Fittest?

Can you hunt prey for the lion or satisfy the appetite of the young lions when they crouch in their dens, or lurk in their lairs to lie in wait?

—Job 38:39–40

Male lions have terrible table manners. They relax during hunts, allowing the females to do the heavy lifting. When prey is brought down, they muscle their way to the feast by brute force, chase the females away, and gulp down the lion share of the meal. This type of behavior may be tolerable in the animal kingdom but certainly not acceptable in human society. While it is true that the stronger in society stand a better chance of survival than the weaker, we should work diligently to reverse that trend. God loves his children, all of them, even the vulnerable ones like the orphans, the old, and the weak, and has instituted laws for their protection. "When you reap the harvest of your land, you shall not wholly reap the corners of your field when you reap, nor shall you gather any gleanings from your harvest. You shall leave them for the poor and for the strangers. I am the Lord your God" (Lev. 23:22).

Bill Gates is leading the way in convincing his billionaire friends of this simple truth. "For everyone to whom much is given, from him much will be required; and to whom much has been committed, of him they will ask the more" (Luke 12:48). While the well-to-do are dragging their feet in implementing this biblical concept, Mr. Gates is fully employed in his charitable organization, lifting millions out of poverty.

God is the ultimate provider to all our needs, but he has entrusted those with the ability to accumulate wealth the sacred trust to relieve the needs of their weaker brethren. The sooner one comes around in acknowledging that what he owns is not actually his but on loan from the Lord, the better he will dispense wisely the resources placed under his stewardship. "The earth is the Lord's and all its fullness. The world and those who dwell therein" (Ps. 24:1). Job recognized the fragility of wealth with this statement: "Naked I came from my mother's womb, and naked shall I return there. The Lord gave and the Lord has taken away; blessed be the name of the Lord" (Job 1:21).

The people of the rain forest whom some consider not enlightened understand this concept beautifully. Whether the hunt is meager or bountiful, everyone gets a taste. The hunter-gatherers share their bounty with everyone—the old, the infirmed, and the very young. Of course, God has implanted this concept of being my brother's keeper in every culture, even in groups untouched by civilization. No one is excused if he fails to provide what is necessary for his brother's need if he is in a position to do so.

Social programs have their origin in the law of God. The law states, "Love your neighbor as yourself" (Mark 12:31). The Golden Rule, which is embraced by every faith on earth, is this: "Do unto others as you would have them do unto you" (Luke 6:31). Proponents of the "survival of the fittest" theory claim that nature ensures that the strongest survive. Consider the source. This principle is not compatible to the Word of God. It is a concept straight from the playbook of Satan. God wants all his children to thrive and survive, including the poor. They must have enough to eat and enjoy life. We look forward to the day when the playing field will be even and sin will be eradicated once and for all from our planet. Don't you long for that day?

April 28

It's Always There

Through the Lord's mercies we are not consumed, because His compassions fail not. They are new every morning; great is Your faithfulness.

—Lamentations 3:22–23

The exploding electrical fireball was inches from our bed. With my wife leading the way, I grabbed my computer and made a hasty exit out of the house. Our electrical system was compromised, causing us constant power interruption. Simply turning on the microwave while the toaster is on would trigger a power interruption, sending us scrambling to the garage to flip on a trip switch. At 1:00 a.m. on a cold December morning, we were sent packing into the street in our pajamas in the wake of an electrical explosion inches from our bed. Within minutes, the fire department was at our doorsteps. Their analysis team called in BGE, our local electrical supplier, to investigate the matter. BGE's diagnosis turned up a severed ground cable. Work commenced immediately, and by nightfall, we had uninterrupted power once more, minus Internet service.

The speedy response of the fire department is worthy of commendation, and we are grateful to them. They put their lives on the line every day. They respond to emergencies irrespective of one's race, social status, or gender. Whether you're delinquent on your taxes or not, that's not their concern; their calling is to put out fires and save lives. They serve their community faithfully. What would we do without them?

God's love is like that; it is always there. As someone once said, "It will outrun you and overtake you." God's love does not discriminate, does not play favorites, and is totally inclusive of everyone. "The thief does not come except to steal, and to kill and to destroy. I have come that they may have life, and that they may have it more abundantly" (John 10:10). God's love shields us from evil even when we are blissfully unaware of it.

Jeremiah remarks, "Through the Lord's mercies we are not consumed, because His compassions fail not" (Lam. 3:22). While Satan seeks to destroy us all, God shields us from his evil plans. "The name of the Lord is a strong tower; the righteous run to it and are safe" (Prov. 18:10).

"In this the love of God was manifested towards us, that God has sent His only begotten Son into the world, that we might live through Him" (1 John 4:9). Who are we to command so much attention from God? "When Jesus heard that He said to them 'Those who are well have no need of a physician, but those who are sick'" (Matt. 9:12). We are all sick and infected by sin and need much love and attention by our heavenly Father. God's love is there every morning. His very nature is love; he created beings so that he could lavish on them his tender care and affection. Love would not be love if there was nothing to love, and as long as there are creatures to love, God's love will always be there.

"In this is love, not that we loved God, but that He loved us and sent His Son to be the propitiation for our sins. Beloved if God so loved us, we also ought to love one another" (1 John 4:10–11). Love is at its finest when it is lavished on those undeserving. Think about it. Have you tried to love someone who is completely unlovable and has not made it easy for you to love them? That's what God did to us. "While we yet were sinners Christ died for us" (Rom. 5:8). Thank you, God, for loving us despite ourselves.

Staying Calm during a Storm

In the world you will have tribulation; but be of good cheer, I have overcome the world.

—John 16:33

As the world inches toward calamity and uncertainty, politicians love to assure us that our best days are ahead of us. Are they? The newspaper headlines of any large city in the United States would include the following stories: record profits for wealthy corporations, politics, entertainment, sport scandals, climate change, crime, and unemployment. There are times one might be tempted to bury his or her head in the sand and not wake up for at least a few weeks to avoid the steady dose of bad news. But reality dictates we make good out of bad situations and survive through the power of Christ.

Staying positive in tumultuous situations is the primary and foremost trait of a Christian. Fire instructors train their students to remain calm during life-threatening circumstances. Many lives depend on their split-second decision making. To make decisive decisions under difficult situations, one must be calm. The military also stresses being calm and relaxed under stress to make lifesaving decisions. Decisions made while angry or agitated are usually bad and regretted later.

A casual boat ride turned violent as a horrific storm burst on the lake from out of nowhere. The disciples of Christ turned frantic as their valiant effort to stabilize the boat yielded no benefit. Overcome with fear, they gasped, "Teacher, do you not care that we are perishing?" Jesus was sleeping peacefully. Was he teaching a lesson even by taking a nap? But of course. Nothing Jesus did is insignificant. By falling asleep during a catastrophic storm, he trusted his life into the safekeeping of his Father. It really didn't matter how horrific the storm was. Where God is, there is perfect peace. "Then He arose and rebuked the wind, and said to the sea, 'Peace be still!' And the wind ceased and there was a great calm" (Mark 4:39).

We are admonished by Paul to have that same positive attitude even when facing the turbulent storms of life. The brain simply cannot operate and make correct decisions in a confused state of mind. "Let this mind be in you which was also in Christ Jesus" (Phil. 2:5). Despite the uncertainties of the economy and the constant drumbeat of war, we can have hope and peace because they come from a secure source. "Peace I leave with you, My peace I give to you; not as the world gives do I give to you. Let not your heart be troubled, neither let it be afraid" (John 14:27).

The peace that Jesus gives is permanent, it triumphs over distress, and it overcomes sickness and looks forward toward recovery, if not in this life, then in the one to come. It gives hope to the hopeless and brings relief to the oppressed, even though their situation may not improve in this lifetime. Quite candidly, we do not expect this world to improve; it will get progressively worse. However, we place our trust and confidence in the One who controls and operates the universe, our Lord and Savior, Jesus Christ. "But evil men and imposters will grow worse and worse, deceiving and being deceived" (2 Tim. 3:13). Only in Jesus can we place our trust and have hope in times of uncertainties.

April 30

Stop! Stop! Incoming Traffic

There is a way that seems right to a man, but its end is the way of death.
—Proverbs 14:12

You've probably seen it before on television, offenders running away from the law, with sirens blaring, red and blue lights flashing, and lawmen in hot pursuit; they have few options left, but surrendering peacefully is not an enterprising thought. They do what most irrational people do under stress, break more laws. With all escape routes cut off and law enforcement closing in on them, they do the unthinkable, driving in the direction of oncoming traffic. The Bible is replete with folks who drove in the direction of oncoming traffic. Metaphorically, I think we all have, at some point, done the same thing, drive in the direction of oncoming traffic.

"Now Dinah the daughter of Leah, whom she had borne to Jacob, went out to see the daughters of the land [bad idea] . . . And Jacob heard that he had defiled Dinah his daughter. Now his sons were with his livestock in the field; so Jacob held his peace until they came" (Gen. 34:1, 5). This unfortunate experience of a young adult weary of family worship and in search of something more stimulating is typical of the human dilemma, but God has not left the highway of life without flashing red light warning signs.

"He has shown you, O man, what is good; and what does the Lord require of you but to do justly, to love mercy, and to walk humbly with your God?" (Mic. 6:8). Someone once said, "The road of life is paved with good intentions," but it takes more than good intentions to live in peace with one's neighbor. Love others and treat them as you would like to be treated. If this truth were universally practiced and adhered to, one would think twice before driving into oncoming traffic. Oncoming traffic could be any situation that could cause harm and destruction to you and others who share the road of life with you. Everyone is conscious of this truth, treating others as you expect to be treated. "For the grace of God that brings salvation has appeared to all men, teaching us that, denying ungodliness and worldly lust, we should live soberly, righteously, and godly in the present age" (Titus 2:11–12). This truth has been made clear to everyone at some point.

One does not have to be a blatant troublemaker to be driving in the direction of oncoming traffic. Simply ignoring the best path, the way of God, could put one on the path of oncoming traffic. "And if it seems evil to you to serve the Lord, choose for yourselves this day whom you will serve, whether the gods which your fathers served that were on the other side of the River, or the gods of the Amorites, in whose land you dwell. But as for me and my house, we will serve the Lord" (Josh. 24:15).

The choice is decisive and stark; serving a little god made by God doesn't make sense at all. Joshua challenged his fellow Israelites to serve the God who worked wonders in the land of Egypt in their behalf, but if they so choose to serve another, he and his family would serve God. The Bible issues the same challenge to us. The glitter of amusements and the delicacies of this world will fade away, leaving us empty and searching for something more fulfilling, but the way of God satisfies all our longings.

"By faith Moses, when he became of age, refused to be called the son of Pharaoh's daughter, choosing rather to suffer affliction with the people of God than to enjoy the pleasures of sin, esteeming the reproach of Christ greater riches than the treasures in Egypt; for he looked to the reward" (Heb. 11:24–26).

May 1

Where Is God?

And it happened the next day, the second day of the month, that David's place was empty. And Saul said to Jonathan his son, why has the son of Jesse not come to eat either yesterday or today?

—1 Samuel 20:27

"You're sitting on the horse and asking for it." Chomping on his cigar with a look of frustration on his face, my boss made no effort in concealing his disgust when I fumbled the ball by asking for something that was right before my eyes. We do this more often than we think, looking for something that is front and center before our face.

Saul was the undisputed ruler over all Israel, but he was constantly looking over his shoulders to destroy David, his potential rival to the throne. He made several attempts to kill David, a man who defended Israel when everyone else, including Saul himself, was too scared to challenge Goliath, the Philistine champion. Saul grudgingly gave David a seat around the royal table, and when David was absent, because of the king's recent attempt to take his life, Saul amazingly exclaimed, "Where is David, the son of Jesse?" (1 Sam. 19)

To a lesser extent, we ask the same question when jostled by life's fierce, troubled winds. "Where is God?" we ask. Many sad incidents in life have given occasion to this inquiring refrain. "Where were you when my child was burning with a fever?" "You allowed me to contract this deadly disease even though I prayed earnestly to you for healing." "My house went into foreclosure, and all my hard work went down with it." "My marriage crumbled before my very eyes even when I prayed most earnestly to you." These and many other life-crushing ordeals leave us grappling with the question where is God when we need him the most? After all, did he not promise that he would be with us always, even to the end of the world?

Worshippers of false gods carried their gods with them. They thought these little gods had peculiar strengths and weaknesses. For instance, the god of fertility might not give you victory in battle since this is not his function. Nor would the god of the hills ensure you success on the high seas. This necessitated serving multiple gods to meet one's need, but the God of Daniel is "something else" as acknowledged by the heathen Nebuchadnezzar, king of Babylon. "The king answered Daniel, and said, 'Truly your God is the God of gods, the Lord of kings, and a revealer of secrets, since you could reveal this secret'" (Dan. 2:47). The wise man Solomon makes this observation: "The eyes of the Lord are in every place keeping watch on the evil and the good" (Prov. 15:3).

God is not blind, nor is he oblivious to the plight of the righteous. The promises God made to ancient Israel are applicable to spiritual Israel (the church) as well. "Because he has set his love upon Me, therefore I will deliver him; I will set him on high, because he has known My name. He shall call upon Me and I will answer him; I will be with him in trouble; I will deliver him and honor him" (Ps. 91:14–15). It is not within the grasp of mortals to explain or understand the acts of an all-knowing God. We cannot explain why God delivered Peter from prison and allowed John the Baptist to die in jail. But one thing is certain: he has our back. "But He knows the way that I take; when He has tested me, I shall come forth as gold" (Job 23:10). Keep trusting God; he is with us every step of the way, even when we cannot detect his presence.

May 2

Doing It Jesus's Way

So they told him that that Jesus of Nazareth was passing by. And he cried out, saying, Jesus, Son of David, have mercy on me! Then those who went before warned him that he should be quiet; but he cried all the more, Son of David, have mercy on me!
—Luke 18:37–39

They come in trickles at first to an auditorium ornately decorated with Christmas trimmings, homemade meals, and gifts ready for the taking. Our friends from Downtown Washington, DC, are regulars at our Christmas Day program. We feed them every second and fourth Saturdays, while a sister church fills in for us with the first and third Saturdays. Every Thanksgiving and Christmas holiday, we bus them from DC to our auditorium in Maryland, where they feast on turkey, sweet potatoes, and other niceties. We've come to know them quite well, and some of them have interesting backgrounds. We've encountered ex-musicians, poets, writers, veterans, and other interesting characters. We are humbled by their profound appreciation for our services. After all, we constantly remind ourselves we are only a few paychecks from being homeless ourselves.

In the animal kingdom, the weak, old, and infirmed are swiftly dealt with by predators, which raises an interesting insight about what sin has done to God's once-beautiful world. Humans, being social and intelligent beings, should not have to be reminded to care for their weaker and less fortunate brethren; even some animals do that. However, we live in a sinful and selfish world, and someone has to take the initiative to restore the dignity of our friends who are voiceless and, more often than not, are suffering in silence. That's what Jesus has called his modern-day disciples to do.

"And as you go, preach, saying, the kingdom of heaven is at hand. Heal the sick, cleanse the lepers, and raise the dead, cast out demons. Freely you have received, free give" (Matt. 10:7–8). It is the care and compassion for the sick, needy, and disenfranchised that will show the watching world who God really is. We demonstrate to the world by our actions that our God is loving, kind, and compassionate to those in need. A picture is worth more than a thousand words. We are God's hands and feet to the lost.

Jesus was derided by the religious leaders for spending too much time in the company of sinners (the marginalized), but it is primarily to these people that he came to give hope. "And the Scribes and the Pharisees complained against His disciples, saying, why do you eat and drink with tax collectors and sinners? Jesus answered and said to them, those who are well have no need of a physician, but those who are sick. I have not come to call the righteous, but sinners, to repentance" (Luke 5:30–32).

The devil is constantly destroying and ruining the lives of people, but God calls on us to comfort, restore, affirm, heal, visit, and help in any way we can to point sufferers to their loving, kind, and compassionate Father. "But where sin abounded, grace abounded much more" (Rom. 5:20). We cannot abandon the inner cities and ghettos to the tender mercies of Satan. With the spirit of the Lord, we must go and make a difference in the lives of our fellow citizens, or else we won't hear a welcoming commendation from Jesus. Go out there, join a volunteer group, and make a difference in the life of someone. The person you help the most might be yourself.

May 3

The Best Thing Ever

But when the fullness of the time had come, God sent forth His Son, born of a woman, born under the law, to redeem those who were under the law, that we might receive adoption as sons.

—Galatians 4:4–5

Gladys Knight spoke for humanity with her 1974 hit song, which went to number three on the Billboard top 40. Although the song was written with romantic sentiments, it perfectly describes God's love and goodness to mankind. "If anyone should ever write my life story, ah, for whatever reason there might be, oh you'll be there between each line of pain and glory 'cause you're the best thing that ever happened to me." Is God the best thing that has ever happened to you, even when you're hurting?

Everyone born into this world becomes infected with sin even before consciousness is developed. David sums it up best with these words: "Behold, I was brought forth in iniquity, and in sin my mother conceived me" (Ps. 51:5). Adam's sin has been transmitted to all his descendants through choice. Every child born into this world is born with the propensity to sin, including Jesus, who chose not to sin. Amen, amen, and amen.

Having said that, man was not left to grapple with the sin problem without divine assistance; neither did God let the clock wind down to the very last minute before he took action. Was God taken by surprise? No. God foresaw the Fall of man in eternity past; before Adam was created, Jesus Christ became the Lamb. "The next day John saw Jesus coming toward Him, and said, 'Behold! The Lamb of God who takes away the sins of the world'" (John 1:29). No one can earn salvation by her or his own merit, nor can anyone achieve reconciliation with God except through the blood of Jesus Christ. "Let it be known to you all, and to all the people of Israel that by the name of Jesus Christ of Nazareth, whom you crucified, whom God raised from the dead, by Him this man stands here before you whole. 'This is the stone which was rejected by you builders, which has become the chief cornerstone.' Nor is there salvation in any other, for there is no other name under heaven given among men by which we must be saved" (Acts 4:10–12).

On a personal note, many of us have been born in very adverse situations. Some of us have had the misfortune of being born and raised in dysfunctional situations. Child abuse is leading the way as the Black Death of the twenty-first century. Poverty abounds everywhere with no respect to class, age, gender, nationality, or race; and with it comes the temptation to soothe our woes with sex, drug addiction, and alcohol abuse.

Let us give thanks to God that "where sin abounded, grace abounded much more" (Rom. 5:20). God is very near to those handed the worst fate by the enemy, and many have responded to the amazing grace of God, including you and me. Still, there are so many yet to hear and know that Jesus is the only way out of their sin dilemma.

"Then I heard the voice of the Lord, saying: 'Whom shall I send, and who will go for Us?' Then I said, 'Here am I! Send me.' And He said, 'go and tell this people'" (Isa. 6:8–9). Are you already telling others of the amazing grace of Jesus? This news is too good to keep secret any longer. Go out there and tell somebody, everybody about his amazing love and mercy to them. God goes with you, my friend.

May 4

Passing on the Baton

Likewise, exhort the young men to be sober minded, in all things showing yourself to be a pattern of good works; in doctrine showing integrity, reverence, incorruptibility.

—Titus 2:6–7

Scientists at South Africa's national park were mystified when rhinos were being found dead with their prized ivory tusk intact and no bullet wounds to show injury, but with horrific gaping wounds on their bodies. Someone or something was killing Africa's most endangered white and black rhinos. The assassins continued their grisly work, leaving little or no clues except for gaping wounds on their victims. Who or what could inflict such horrible bodily injury to such massive beasts? A break came after many hours of tedious surveillance. Orphaned juvenile elephants, never having been taught by their elders, were the culprits. Since they grew up without adult supervision on how to be good, law-abiding members of the ecosystem, they took it upon themselves to terrorize residents in their neighborhood. The white rhino and, to a lesser extent, its black counterpart bore the brunt of their fierce wrath (*National Geographic*).

Hooray! Mystery solved? No, not really. Having been raised by humans without clan supervision, they came early into musth (infusion of testosterone); and not being able to control their ecstasy, they vented their rage on their rivals, the rhino. Before the situation was brought under control, about sixty-three rhinos perished. To mitigate the situation, a bold plan was called for before the species' population plunged further. A group of no-nonsense muscular bulls were carted in, and without any protest, the young delinquents immediately submitted their arrogance at the feet of their elders. Hooray to the elders! Problem solved, no more unsolved mystery killings.

Young adults in the faith and, to a greater degree, children need elders to teach them how to successfully navigate life's tricky turns and bends. As children learn by imitating their parents, baby Christians can learn by the good example set by their spiritual mentors. An elder—by virtue of his wisdom, age, and experience—should be seasoned with wise counsel and knowledge, ever ready to make himself accessible to his younger and less experienced juveniles in the faith.

However, the bar set by the scripture for elders is an exceedingly high one and deservedly so because the young need guidance, and who should they look up to but their elders? "A bishop [elder, pastor] must be blameless, the husband of one wife, temperate, sober-minded, of a good behavior, hospitable, able to teach; not given to wine, not violent, not greedy for money but gentle, not quarrelsome, not covetous; one who rules his own house well, having his children in submission with all reverence" (1 Tim. 3:2–4). I must admit I am where you are, below the bar, but still reaching toward the high calling in Christ.

The more we look on Jesus, the closer we become like him in character. Once we become like him, his image in us is reflected to others. We really don't have to say much; our lives will tell his story. Someone rightly said, "I rather see a sermon than hear one." Elders, the world is watching you. Be an example.

May 5

He Is Almost Here

Watch therefore, for you do not know when the master of the house is coming, in the evening, at midnight, at the crowing of the roster, or in the morning—lest, coming suddenly, he finds you sleeping. And what I say to you, I say to all: Watch!
—Mark 13:35–37

The wait was unbearable, but the guests stuck to their seats, confident that the guest of honor would most certainly show up. At the time appointed, the announcement was made. "Ladies and gentlemen, the prime minister is here. Rise to greet him." Everyone stood up in recognition of this momentous event. The prime minister walked into the packed audience and was greeted with a thunderous applause. As he made his way to the podium, he shook hands with some eager nationals. Accompanying him to this special dinner were his UN ambassador and two cabinet ministers. The atmosphere was elegant and cheerful; the guests were gorgeously dressed and a little rowdy, some already showing signs of intoxication. After recognizing guests of unique distinction, the master of ceremony turned the spotlight to the prime minister and his progress report.

His address highlighted inheriting a government on the brink of financial collapse, with creditors calling regularly about overdue loan payment. He spoke with nostalgia of his government accomplishment in health, social programs, foreign policy, road rehabilitation, and his vision for the future. He was interrupted intermittently by standing ovations and thunderous applause. However honest and well-intentioned this head of state may be, several variables could derail his dreams from becoming reality.

Our dream is a reality; Jesus is coming soon. How soon? Very soon. Do we know when he is coming? No, but the signs of the times speak for themselves. During his ministry on earth, Jesus admonished his disciples to be always in a state of readiness. The parable of the talents of Luke 19:13 illustrates it best. A noble man delivered various sums of money to his servants and told them to use it wisely on the money exchange market. Two of the three gentlemen returned handsome investments and were rewarded for their industry. However, the third manager did absolutely nothing and was quickly put out of commission by his boss. A reflection on the obedient servants' work ethics reveals that they did their master's bidding by being resourceful and were commended for their faithfulness. They invested as they were told and reaped the rewards thereof.

Likewise, Jesus left us careful instructions that will wrap up the work and hasten his coming. Are you familiar with his marching order that will effectively bring the world as we know it to an end? "Go therefore and make disciples of all nations, baptizing them in the name of the Father and of the Son and of the Holy Spirit" (Matt. 28:19). How do we know that Jesus will come after the gospel has been preached to every nation, kindred, tongue, and people? "And this gospel of the kingdom will be preached in all the world as a witness to all the nations, and then the end will come" (Matt. 24:14). God wants to give everyone a fair opportunity of choosing to live for him and inherit everlasting life or the opposite, which is to enjoy this present life and reap eternal doom and death. I trust you have chosen the former. God bless you and your choice.

May 6

Being on Fire for God

Then there appeared to them divided tongues, as of fire, and one sat upon each of them. And they were all filled with the Holy Spirit and began to speak with other tongues, as the Spirit gave them utterance.

—Acts 2:3–4

They worked themselves into a frenzy, chanting unintelligible words while darting back and forth on red-hot coals of fire. People around the world have used the art of fire walking to impress their peers and to demonstrate the possession of some superior power. Bursting with curiosity, renowned anthropologist Loring Danforth decided to peer into this ancient mystery. He scrutinized several theories forwarded by some of his counterparts, but this quotation caught his attention: "What controls [the ability of the fire walker] is more than physics, it's your state of mind" (*National Geographic*). Do you know who possesses the mind of the fire walkers and protects them from burns?

"Behold, I send the promise of My Father upon you; but tarry in the city of Jerusalem until you are endued with power from on high" (Luke 24:49). Jesus had just established the infant church, and its leaders needed the unction of the Holy Spirit for ministry and unique leadership capabilities. The Holy Spirit fulfilled this function by equipping the disciples with power to work miracles, speak in unknown tongues, solve problems, and plant the gospel in foreign lands. Can you distinguish which of the two groups possesses the Holy Spirit? Is it the fire walkers or the disciples?

The Holy Spirit is an equal partner of the Godhead, and his operation dates back to the first day of Creation. "The earth was without form, and void; and darkness was on the face of the deep. And the Spirit of God was hovering over the waters. And God said let there be light and there was light" (Gen. 1:2–3). The Holy Spirit possessed Old Testament believers just as he did in the New Testament. "And the Spirit of the Lord came mightily upon him, and he tore the lion apart as one would have torn apart a young goat, though he had nothing in his hand" (Judges 14:6). The Holy Spirit empowers the children of God to accomplish their mission as long as it is compatible to God's work.

Satan, the great counterfeiter, does the same to his followers; he equips them with abilities as well, a false spirit. "Now it happened, as we went to prayer, that a certain slave girl possessed with a spirit of divination met us, who brought her masters much profit by fortunetelling. This girl followed Paul and us, and cried out, saying, 'These men are servants of the Most High God, who proclaim to us the way of salvation.' And did this for many days. But Paul, greatly annoyed, turned and said to the spirit, I command you in the name of Jesus Christ come out of her. And he came out that very hour" (Acts 16:16–18). Not all spirits are from God as we just discovered. "Beloved, do not believe every spirit, but test the spirits, whether they are of God; because many false prophets have gone out into the world" (1 John 4:1).

Lord, imbue us with your Holy Spirit, and remove anything from us that will prevent the full operation of the Holy Spirit in our lives. Divest from us the dross of worldliness, and equip us for service in your vineyard. Is this your earnest prayer? Supplicate with God, wait on him, stay busy telling others of his wonderful works in your life, and you will be filled with the power of the Holy Spirit without realizing it.

May 7

Wash Me Clean

Then He came to Simon Peter, and Peter said to Him, Lord, are you washing my feet? Jesus answered and said to him, what I am doing you do not understand now, but you will know after this.

—John 13:6–7

The president of the United States is fully employed today, dishing out food at a soup kitchen. Yes, it happened on September 10, 2011, at the DC Central Kitchen. The president was promoting his community service initiative to commemorate the anniversary of 9/11. Serving others at a soup kitchen may not be the defining moment of anyone's presidency, but this is precisely what Jesus was calling attention to by his foot washing ceremony—service to others.

"For even the Son of Man did not come to be served, but to serve, and to give His life a ransom for many" (Mark 10:45). This foot-washing service that Jesus instituted emphasizes humility and equality. In Christ, no one is superior to his brother; at the foot of the cross, we are all equal. Jesus illustrates this point with this statement: "You know that the Gentiles lord it over them, and those who are great exercise authority over them. Yet it shall not be so among you; but whoever desires to become great among you, let him be your slave" (Matt. 20:25–27). Is Jesus suppressing egotism here? Yes, absolutely. No church leader should take credit for any achievement accomplished in God's service. "And whatever you do in word or deed, do all in the name of the Lord Jesus, giving thanks to God the Father through Him" (Col. 3:17).

Knowing his disciples were constantly jockeying for temporal position, Jesus put them to a test. "After that, He poured water into a basin and began to wash the disciples' feet, and to wipe them with the towel with which He was girded. Then He came to Simon Peter. And Peter said to Him, Lord, are You washing my feet?" (John 13:5–6). "No way," Peter remarked.

Jesus, looking at his confused disciple, said, "What I am doing now you do not understand, but you will in the end. But if I don't wash your feet, you will have no part with me." It finally dawned on Peter, at that moment, that to be a leader in God's cause, you must first be a servant. To be great, one must first be humble. Being a leader in God's cause entails serving the people you are leading as Jesus demonstrated in the foot-washing ritual. "If I then, your Lord and Teacher, have washed your feet, you also ought to wash one another's feet. For I have given you an example, that you should do as I have done to you" (John 13:14–15).

Foot washing is a liberating experience. We wash each other's feet not because their feet are dirty but because we want them to know we love them, care for them, and harbor no malice toward them. This act also divests one of selfishness and pride and instills a spirit of acceptance to the recipient. And of course, this is an excellent forum for the confession of past sins to God. You don't have to say a word; the act itself does all the talking. By choosing to wash the feet of your rival or archenemy, you are saying, "Let's bury the hatchet and let bygones be bygones." If your church has not been practicing this excellent service of humility, ask your pastor to initiate it. Jesus instituted it and said we should do it to our fellow brothers.

May 8

Arrested for Doing Good

Then Jesus came out, wearing the crown of thorns and the purple robe. And Pilate said to them, Behold the man.

—John 19:5

Though spotless in character, Jesus was condemned to death by both Jewish and Roman laws for being a model citizen. Governments and businesses the world over motivate their subjects and workers to be productive and be good model citizens, and Christ Jesus did just that, yet he was arrested and later executed for helping his community.

"Then Jesus answered and said to them, 'Have you come out, as against a robber, with swords and clubs to take Me? I was daily with you in the temple teaching, and you did not seize Me. But the Scriptures must be fulfilled'" (Mark 14:48–49). We know of no one in history whose character was absolutely spotless yet killed solely on the basis of doing good. Society usually honors and recognizes those who serve others in the field of medicine, science, politics, education, and humanitarian service, yet Jesus was killed solely for doing good.

Jesus was more than a miracle worker, a good teacher, or a civil rights advocate. He was the world's Creator and Messiah, and the people who should have known this allowed blind bigotry, nationalism, and prejudice to gain the better part of their thinking. To illustrate the ignorance of the religious leaders in reference to his mission, Jesus chided Nicodemus—a leader of the Sanhedrin (Jewish legislature)— for not knowing what he should have known. "Jesus answered and said to him, are you a teacher of Israel and do not know these things?" (John 3:10). What were Nicodemus and the Jewish Sanhedrin ignorant of?

"The Spirit of the Lord God is upon Me, because the Lord has anointed Me to preach good tidings to the poor; He has sent Me to heal the brokenhearted, to proclaim liberty to the captives, and the opening of the prison to those who are bound; to proclaim the acceptable year of the Lord, and the day of vengeance of our God; to comfort all who mourn in Zion and to give them beauty for ashes and the oil of joy for mourning, the garment of praise for the spirit of heaviness" (Isa. 61:1–3). How did the Jewish leaders miss this glaring prophecy that Jesus read in the synagogue concerning himself? How did they miss it? "Today this Scripture is fulfilled in your hearing" (Luke 4:21).

Nevertheless, Jesus went about doing his Father's will by imparting light to both Jews and Gentiles. "The people who sat in darkness have seen a great light, and upon those who sat in the region and shadow of death Light has dawned" (Matt. 4:16). Jesus came to save all mankind, even those outside Israel. "And I, if I am lifted up from the earth, will draw all peoples to Myself" (John 12:32). Was the nation prepared for its Messiah? "He came to His own and His own did not receive Him. But as many as receive Him, to them He gave the right to become children of God, to those who believe in His name" (John 1:11–12).

In doing his Father's will, Jesus was never far from the shadow of death. "Then the Jews took up stones again to stone Him. Jesus answered them. 'Many good works I have shown you from My Father. For which of those do you stone Me?'" (John 10:31–32). But God gave the hardened nation one more chance. "And you will seek Me and find Me, when you search for Me with all your heart" (Jer. 29:13). They, however, did not seek God but chose a thief and a murderer in place of the One who came to save them.

May 9

I Will Grow

But grow in the grace and knowledge of our Lord and Savior Jesus Christ.
—2 Peter 3:18

Pumping her little fist in the air and kicking and screaming at the top of her lungs, she demanded from her mom her long-awaited meal. Ah yes. That's how little babies grow. They wake us up at inconvenient hours of the night, demanding our care. By screaming loudly, they tell us they don't feel well; are cold, too warm, or lonely; need changing; or are hungry. They even show their displeasure if we're too slow as well. That's how they develop both mentally and physically. Christians begin life as babes and grow in like fashion.

Your boss gives you a tongue-lashing whether you deserved it or not. What do you do? Reciprocate? Return the favor? Absolutely not, not if you value your job. You profit from the experience by asking the following question: Did I deserve it? And if you did, how can you improve and not repeat this unfortunate behavior? You are running late for an appointment, traffic is going nowhere (sounds familiar), and someone intentionally cuts in front of you. What do you do? Call down fire and brimstone on him? "Repay no one evil for evil. Have regard for good things in the sight of all men. If it is possible, as much as depends on you, live peaceably with all men" (Rom. 12:17–18).

We develop the fruits of the Spirit by turning adversities into opportunities and by doing good works. You notice that the line you're in is backing up, while the other lines are moving quite well. To your utter horror, you discover that the cashier is a rookie and is having a bad day. What do you do? Say an encouraging word or castigate him or her for slothfulness? Guilty! Guilty! Guilty! We have all fallen in this trap, haven't we?

We simply don't grow in good times. Just as a ship must go out and face the fierce headwinds of the oceans to be seaworthy, likewise, our faith is tested and grows when we encounter fiery trials. "But it happened about this time, when Joseph went into the house to do his work and none of the men of the house was inside; that she caught him by his garment, saying, 'lie with me.' But he left his garment in her hand, and fled and ran outside" (Gen. 39:11–12). Where was the place of most growth for Joseph? Was it in the comfort of his father's house or in the dungeon in Egypt? Obviously, in prison in Egypt. Not only did he grow and become a shrewd businessman but he also became a savior to his family, Israel, and the nation of Egypt.

On their departure from the land of Egypt and during their wilderness experience, the Lord gave the Israelites many opportunities to grow, but they were all squandered. They thought that the Lord was too hard on them and didn't love them. "And the people thirsted there for water, and the people complained against Moses, and said, why is it you have brought us up out of Egypt, to kill us and our children and our livestock with thirst?" (Exod. 17:3). They did not believe the God who made the world could cause a spring to gush out of dry ground. Are we in danger of repeating the mistakes of ancient Israel by not trusting in the God who has plucked us from many troubles?

"The Lord is near to all who call upon Him, to all who call upon Him in truth. He will fulfill the desire of those who fear Him; He also will hear their cry and save them" (Ps. 145:18–19). We grow as we depend on God to supply our needs.

May 10

Go, Cross the Jordan

And it shall come to pass as soon as the soles of the feet of the priests who bear the ark of the Lord, the Lord of all the earth, shall rest in the waters of the Jordan, that the waters of the Jordan shall be cut off, the waters that come down from upstream, and they shall stand as a heap.

—Joshua 3:13

With neither money nor business experience and absolutely no idea how to make ice cream, this particular entrepreneur became successful at ice cream making. His love and passion for the creamy white stuff led to his financial success. Those who traverse the terrain of financial success tell us, "Find something that interest you and become an expert at it, and then sell it" (http://www.lazyway.blogs.com/ lazy way/2005/10/how to start a /comments/page/2/). That thing or passion that should interest every Christian is faith. "Without faith it is impossible to please Him, for he who comes to God must believe that He is, and that He is a rewarder of those who diligently seek Him" (Heb. 11:6).

Unlike the entrepreneur who must believe in himself and depend on his ability and creativity to be successful, Christians must believe in God and his overall will to do as he pleases with their life. The airwaves abound with well-meaning motivational preachers who are passionate about financial success. But do they tell us to seek what is God's will for our lives? If God is moving you in a particular direction of service to him, then go for it. It might not necessarily involve being fabulously wealthy, but it will bring fulfillment to you and those whom you will be called on to serve.

Paul had a passion for carrying out assignments, albeit for the wrong master, but God channeled his passion in the right direction. Luke writes, "Indeed I myself thought I must do many things contrary to the name of Jesus of Nazareth. This I also did in Jerusalem, and many of the saints I shut up in prison, having received authority from the chief priests; and when they were put to death, I cast my vote against them. And I punished them often in every synagogue and compelled them to blaspheme; and being exceedingly enraged against them, I persecuted them even to foreign cities" (Acts 26:9–11). That's being passionate about the wrong cause. Let's see what Paul did when his passion was redirected. "But rise and stand to your feet, for I have appeared to you for this purpose, to make you a minister and a witness both of the things which you have seen and of things which I will yet reveal to you . . . To open their eyes, in order to turn them from darkness to the light and from the power of Satan to the God" (Acts 26:16, 18).

In confirmation of this marvelous encounter, Paul reminded King Agrippa, "I was not disobedient to the heavenly vision" (Acts 26:19). God calls us to different vocations in life. He called Mother Teresa to the slums of Calcutta, Martin Luther King to civil rights and ultimately to the Birmingham prison, and Nelson Mandela to the jail in Robben Island. They all made the world a better place by responding to their call. Is God calling you today?

To enter the Promised Land, we must cross the Jordan (any formidable obstacle). Your Jordan might be a broken relationship that you must muster the strength to get over. It might be ill health, unpaid bills, an impending court hearing, financial ruin, or any other unknown. God is saying to you, "Step into the water to cross the Jordan." "Stand still and see the salvation of the Lord, which He will accomplish for you today. For the Egyptians whom you see today, you shall see again no more forever" (Exod. 14:13). He who waits till all obstacles are removed will never make any progress.

May 11

A Little Child's Faith

So Jesus said to them, because of your unbelief; for assuredly, I say to you, if you have faith as a mustard seed, you will say to this mountain, move from here to there, and it will move; and nothing will be impossible for you.

—Matthew 17:20

They missed their flight from Baltimore to Haiti, and dreams of their long-planned vacation were fading fast. There was a possibility they could go from Atlantic City, New Jersey, to Haiti if they could get there on time. Jerry (name changed) pleaded with the ticketing agent; he put on his best begging performance, but it got him nowhere. The family of five stood hopeless and dejected before the check-in desk. Dad was almost ready to pull out his hair when his ten-year-old son said, "Daddy, let's pray." Well, after the prayer, things began coming together for the little family. They were booked, confirmed, and on their merry way to Haiti.

When God's people pray, amazing things happen. "If my people who are called by my name will humble themselves, and pray and seek My face, and turn from their wicked ways, then I will hear from heaven, and will forgive their sin and heal their land" (2 Chron. 7:14). So many times, we fail to remember God is present with us in all our trials and tribulations and is waiting for us to enlist his help. As King Ahaziah who fell and hurt himself, we exhaust all other avenues before turning to God.

Now Ahaziah fell through the lattice of his upper room in Samaria, and was injured; so he sent messengers and said to them, go inquire of Baal-Zebub, the god of Ekron, whether I shall recover from this injury. But the angel of the Lord said to Elijah the Tishbite, arise, go up to meet the messengers of the king of Samaria, and say to them, it is because there is not a God in Israel that you are going to inquire of Baal-Zebub, the god of Ekron. Now therefore, thus says the Lord: you shall not come

down from the bed to which you have gone up, but you shall
surely die. (2 Kings 2:1–4)

"Now faith is the substance of things hoped for, the evidence of things not seen"
(Heb. 11:1). Faith is easier to cultivate than doubt. When we fly, we may never see
the pilot, but we believe that he is board certified. We have faith in the FAA, don't
we? Most of our financial transactions are done purely on the merit of faith that the
other party on the other end will follow through with his end of the bargain. "By faith
Noah, being divinely warned of things not yet seen moved with godly fear, prepared
an ark for the saving of his household, by which he condemned the world and
became heir of the righteous which is according to faith. By faith Abraham obeyed
when he was called to go out to the place which he would receive as an inheritance.
And went out, not knowing where he was going" (Heb. 11:7–8). Wow! That's faith.

Now it's our turn to exercise faith. How is faith acquired? Believe in God
without doubt. Faith alone will not get you anywhere. James has some wise counsel
for us. "What does it profit, my brethren, if someone says he has faith but does not
have works? Can faith save him? . . . Show me your faith without your works and I
will show you my faith by my works" (James 2:14, 18). Faith and works go hand in
hand. Have you practiced some faith with works lately?

May 12

The Battle Is Not Yours

O our God, will you not judge them? For we have no power against this great
multitude that is coming against us; nor do we know what to do, but our eyes are
upon you.

—2 Chronicles 20:12

Briefed on the attack on the North Tower and a subsequent attack on the South
Tower, a steely president Bush stiffened his resolve but remained calm before his
kindergarten students. At precisely 8:46 a.m., an American Airlines plane—hijacked
by terrorists—slammed into the World Trade North Tower. While the president was
still sitting with the students at a Florida elementary school, another plane struck
the South Tower at 9:03 a.m. In the chaos that ensued, no one thought of another
attack, but it happened again. The Pentagon was struck at 9:37 a.m., and a fourth
plane en route to strike the White House was taken over by heroic passengers and
crashed in Shanksville, Pennsylvania. The nation was under attack (http://www.
cnn.com/2016/09/11/us/9-11-events/index.html).

All eyes turned to the commander in chief for leadership as the nation stood
in shock in the wake of the attack. A special service was called the following day for
quiet reflection. It was attended by dignitaries from every branch of the government

and the military. It was refreshing to see the nation tuning to God at such a time of national crisis.

Israel was facing a crisis of similar proportion. Its national existence was being threatened by neighborhood bullies. King Jehoshaphat assessed the situation and determined, like David, that his enemies were not only fighting against Israel but were, in essence, also fighting against God himself. God is never far away when his people are threatened, and he always sends his prophets to speak words of comfort to them. "And he said, listen, all you of Judah and you inhabitants of Jerusalem, and you King Jehoshaphat! Thus says the Lord to you: do not be afraid nor dismayed because of this great multitude, for the battle is not yours, but God's" (2 Chron. 20:15).

The great red dragon of Revelation 12:17 is constantly threatening to harm God's people. His threats are not idle. Peter portrays him as a roaring lion seeking whom he may devour (1 Pet. 5:8). The world was populated with only four people when Satan incited Cain to murder his righteous brother, Abel. Ever since, Satan has made it his chief objective to harass and destroy all those who call on the name of Jesus Christ.

When the devil has turned friends, family, coworkers, spouses, and total strangers against us, don't be alarmed; let us claim this promise: "God is our refuge and strength, a very present help in trouble. Therefore we will not fear, even though the earth be removed, and though the mountains be carried into the midst of the sea; though its waters roar and be troubled, though the mountains shake with its swelling. There is a river whose streams shall make glad the city of God, the holy place of the Most High" (Ps. 46:1–4).

We must always remember there is nothing that can overtake the child of God for which God has not made a way of escape. If you are hemmed in by circumstances or situations beyond your control, it's time to pray and "stand still and see the salvation of your Lord, which He will accomplish for you" (Exod. 14:13).

May 13

Bless the Lord, O My Soul

Bless the Lord, O my soul, and all that is within me, bless his holy name! . . . Who satisfies your mouth with good things, so that your youth is renewed like the eagle's.
—Psalm 103:1, 5

It looks old, ugly, and sluggish, but give it a few days of seclusion; nature will reward it with a new makeover, and it will be transformed into a brand-new creature. Eagles undergo what is to us a midlife crisis. As they age, their feathers become oily and worn-out. Their talons become dull by constant wear and tear. They become sluggish and unable to hunt effectively. At this point, they seek seclusion in the lowlands and begin plucking off their feathers. They spare no effort in smashing their beaks against rocks or tree branches to get rid of the clumsy stuff. Their talons are rubbed against hard objects until they disappear. At this stage, the bird is completely vulnerable and is virtually at the mercy of a benevolent companion for protection and sustenance. But nature steps in and rewards the eagle's effort with an amazing makeover. It is vigorously restored, emerging with new strength and will for its new life ahead.

God does the same to his children who have been battered and oppressed by sin. In reflecting on the goodness of God, Moses wrote, "Your garments did not wear out on you, nor did your foot swell these forty years" (Deut. 8:4). Besides providing the daily ration of manna and drinking water for well over a million people, God was very much involved in their spiritual health as well.

We will bless the Lord because he has given us hope in very difficult times. Even though the financial forecast may look grim, we are confident that he who feeds the little sparrows and provides snacks along the way for migrating animals is more than capable of taking care of us. We will bless the Lord, "who heals all your diseases, who redeems your life from destruction, who crowns you with loving kindness and tender mercies, and who satisfies your mouth with good things" (Ps. 103:3–5).

We will continue to bless the Lord, who puts good things in our mouths. No longer will we swear, cheat, and abuse others. He has transformed our minds; now we lead others to the Light, who has vanquished the darkness that surrounded us. Once tools in the service of the enemy, now we are instruments in the hands of the mighty God.

To those once held in the prison house of sin (that includes us all), there is a sense of exhilaration that comes from being redeemed. No longer are we imprisoned by our past. We confidently look forward to a brighter day and future where the flowers never fade and time as we know it will be no more. The song lyric "Jesus took my burden and rolled them in the sea, never to retrieve them anymore," brings relief and closure to our turbulent earthly life. I have booked my reservation in the first resurrection train leaving the earth to the kingdom of heaven. Have you purchased your ticket yet?

May 14

Dear Mom

Moreover his mother used to make him a little robe, and bring it to him year by year when she came up with her husband to offer the yearly sacrifice.

—1 Samuel 2:19

The animal kingdom is replete with amazing moms. The crocodile jaws can clamp down on prey at a force of 3,700 pounds per square inch, yet that fearsome jaw gently scoops up its young in a pouch in its lower jaw specially designed for such a purpose. Despite their amazing feats at motherhood, they are moved only by instinct. Snakes, on the other hand, totally abandon their young at birth without much of a second glance at them and with good reason; they might devour their babies. Not so with human mothers; they are totally different. They can love, kiss, and whisper sweet lullabies to their young.

Mother was simply amazing; she wore many titles: protector, provider, nurse, cook, playmate, disciplinarian, teacher, judge, and comforter, to name a few. How did she make it when times were tough and Father was away in search of gold? Driven by love, duty, and a passion to raise her kids well, Mom saddled her donkey each morning and headed for the hills to tend her garden. She came back, sometimes late in the evenings, bearing a variety of tropical niceties, including delicious yams and ripe bananas.

Not having attended school herself, she put great emphasis on us attaining an education. Her work in raising us was continuous in the absence of microwave, washing machines, toaster ovens, and refrigerators. Need I emphasize that she did all these chores manually? She affirmed us continuously, knowing we faced many cruel challenges from our community. In her presence and in the comfort of home, we grew strong in confidence and self-affirmation. She did so much with so little. Thanks, Mom. You're the greatest.

> Who can find a virtuous wife? For her price is far above rubies. The heart of her husband safely trusts her; so he will have no lack of grain. She does him good and not evil all the days of her life. She seeks wool and flax, and willingly works with her hands. She is like the merchant ships, she brings her food from a far. She also rises while it is yet night, and provides food for her household, and a portion for her maidservants. She considers a field and buys it; from her profits, she plants a vineyard. She girds herself with strength, and strengthens her arms. She perceives that her merchandise is good. (Prov. 31:10–18)

Solomon perfectly describes you, Mom. You are everything articulated in these verses and even more.

Thanks, Mom, for your watchful vigilance over us when we were vulnerable. Oh, lest I forget, thanks for the gallons of delicious fresh, warm milk from your breast and your tireless and watchful vigilance around my bed. Thanks for kissing my scrapes and bruises. Thanks for singing me to sleep with sweet, melodious lullabies. Oh, one more thing, Mom, thanks for teaching me about our loving, heavenly Father. Like Hannah, you poured yourself into us, and we became exactly what you envisioned us to be.

"Can a woman forget her nursing child, and not have compassion on the son of her womb? Surely they may forget, yet I will not forget you. See I have inscribed you on the palms of My hands; you are continually before Me" (Isa. 49:15–16). Can anyone love more than our God or show more compassion than him? Dear God, thanks for loving us even more than our moms do.

May 15

A New Thing

Behold, I will do a new thing, now it shall spring forth; shall you not know of it? I will even make a road in the wilderness and rivers in the desert.

—Isaiah 43:19

Electronics companies are constantly developing new gadgets; they have to in this competitive climate. Who wants to go the way of the dodo bird and the dinosaur? I was particularly impressed with the 2013 rechargeable LED reading glasses. Besides magnifying images, it allows you to read leisurely in low light and can deliver an electric charge that can last 2.5 hours.

While the electronic field is buzzing with competition, God has zero competition in his creative and innovative department. Why is this so? He is the Creator and origin of knowledge and does all things right the first time. It becomes necessary, every once in a while, to remember that God has no limit to his massive frame. "Remember the former things of old, for I am God, and there is no other; I am God, and there is none like Me, declaring the end from the beginning, and from ancient times things that are not yet done, saying, My counsel shall stand, and I will do My pleasure" (Isa. 46:9–10).

"I will even make a road in the wilderness" (Isa. 43:19). The wilderness, home to scorpions and venomous snakes, is a dangerous neighborhood. You probably would prefer safer accommodations for residence. Yet God has promised to make a highway out of this hostile environment. Has he come to the rescue of his people in many sticky situations? When Israel crossed the Red Sea on dry land, the condition changed drastically for the pursuing Egyptian army. "And He took off their chariot wheels, so that they drove them with difficulty; and the Egyptians said, 'Let us flee from the face of Israel, for the Lord fights for them against the Egyptians'" (Exod. 14:25).

That new thing being referenced here isn't really new at all, for God has always been hard at work providing for his people's needs and delivering them when trouble strikes. When the storm clouds gather and we are hemmed in on all sides, he sends his holy angels to make a way of escape for his children. "Now behold, an angel of the Lord stood by him, and a light shone in the prison; and he struck Peter on the side and raised him up, saying, 'Arise quickly' and his chains fell off his hands" (Acts 12:7). Can he do the same in our time? Of course, he can. The question that begs an answer remains, will we allow him to do it for us? Nothing is really new to God. He is the same yesterday, today, and forever. He has seen it all.

"I will make rivers in the desert." A desert, as was referenced earlier, is usually an inhospitable living space; and most animals, except for the most versatile, choose to live elsewhere. Spiders, scorpions, and a few determined mammals eke out an existence where others fail. Our God has promised to irrigate the deserts and make them fruitful again. Can he do the same in our lives by creating rivers of hope and springs of faith? Before coming to faith in Jesus, our lives were wicked, barren, and fruitless; but thanks to the abiding presence of the Holy Spirit, we are fruitful now. "For you were once darkness, but now you are light in the Lord. Walk as children of light" (Eph. 5:8).

May 16

Penetrate Society

You are the salt of the earth; but if the salt loses its flavor, how shall it be seasoned? It is then good for nothing but to be thrown out and trampled upon.
—Matthew 5:13

What we grew up believing as kids is now confirmed by medical science: salt has healing properties. The standard local remedy for the common cold in the part of the world where I grew up was a good old sea bath. When feeling tired and worn-out, the beach is never too far away for a refreshing dip. Salt performs multiple functions in daily life.

Quite recently, salt has been taking a beating largely because of its overuse in food production, but that should not detract from its critical importance as a stimulant to our taste buds. Without salt, a meal would be equivalent to a visit to the dentist, something dreaded rather than enjoyed. Salt has other uses as well; it preserves. Until the invention of the refrigerator, salt was key in food preservation. Codfish would not have assumed its royal title as King Cod had salt not elevated its status to that of royalty. Salt became a currency of exchange to nomadic tribes across the Sahara Desert and may still be in use there. In snowy weather, you may have gone to your local hardware store and purchased a few bags yourself. Just think of what the highways would look like in a blizzard without salt—not very pretty. The ancients used it to seal deals and cement agreements because of its stabilizing and unchanging nature.

Knowing the above properties of salt and the many that we are unaware of, Jesus says to us, "You are the salt of the earth." If salt is to give flavor to the pot, it just can't remain in a corner and hope to permeate the pot with its flavor. No, it must traverse the entire length and breadth of the pot, releasing its taste-enhancing qualities until the food is transformed by it. Should we then penetrate every club, every civic institution, every sport establishment, every political party, every culture, every nation, and every sector of society with the life-giving message of the gospel?

Jesus led the way in showing us how this is done. To reach all classes, he became one of us, a child of humanity. His obscure birth and occupation marked him as belonging to the lower class. This, not accidental, gave him the legitimacy to identify with the masses, who were mightily oppressed by the rich and powerful. He identified with those caught in the web of iniquity and did not castigate them but offered them a way out. He forgave the sins of the woman caught in the very act of adultery. "When Jesus had raised Himself up and saw no one but the woman,

He said to her, 'Woman where are those accusers of yours? Has no one condemned you?' She said, no one, Lord. And Jesus said to her, 'neither do I condemn you; go and sin no more'" (John 8:10–11).

If Jesus did not condemn folks caught in the web of iniquity, neither should we. Remember, he came to seek and save the lost, and his gentle arms are still outstretched, welcoming all classes, even those we think are undeserving. What kind of fisherman would go fishing with an unattractive bait? The fish would laugh at him and pay him no attention. But if he makes the bait attractive, the fish will show interest. Are we making the gospel of Christ attractive to sinners so they will bite our bait? We are both salt and fishermen at the same time. Go, permeate society, and win the lost for Christ by your gentle and kind words. While you are on your way, wear a smile on your face also.

May 17

Freed from Bitterness

And forgive our debts, as we forgive our debtors.

—Matthew 6:12

Her ex-husband, who brought her much grief and sorrow, was remarried and enjoying his new family, while she remained trapped in bitterness and hate. Mary (name changed) admitted she was too angry to forgive her ex-husband for the lies, the double-dealing, and the outright hurt that he inflicted on her. She described the pain of reliving the terrible experiences as if they were but yesterday. Her personal appeal to those hurt by the callous deeds of others was "Let it go. Why imprison yourself to the memory of someone who no longer cares about you?"

In his autobiography *The Sunflower*, Simon Wiesenthal was called in by a nurse at the request of a dying Nazi SS camp guard. The man wanted forgiveness for the horrible pain he inflicted on the Jews. Simon listened to his lengthy detailed confession but left the room in silence, refusing to forgive him on behalf of all his people who were murdered. Some argue that one person (Simon) does not have the right to act on behalf of the millions who were systematically murdered at the hands of their killers.

"For if you forgive men their trespasses, your heavenly Father will also forgive. But if you do not forgive men their trespasses, neither will your Father forgive your trespasses" (Matt. 6:14–15). We do more injury to ourselves by harboring ill feelings toward an archrival. The best therapy against abuse and mistreatment of any kind is forgiveness.

Forgiveness is a theme that runs through the Old and New Testaments. How can anyone miss it? "Who is a God like You pardoning iniquity and passing over the transgression of the remnant of His heritage? He does not retain His anger forever, because He delights in mercy. He will again have compassion on us and subdue our iniquities. You will cast all our sins into the depths of the sea" (Mic. 7:18–19).

The psalmist gives us further insight into the patience and mercy of God. "But He being full of compassion, forgave them of their iniquity, and did not destroy them. Yes, many a time he turned His anger away, and did not stir up all His wrath; for He remembered that they were but flesh, a breath that passes away and does not come again. How often they provoked Him in the wilderness, and grieved Him in the desert! Yes, again and again they tempted God, and limited the Holy One of Israel. They did not remember His power" (Ps. 78:38–42).

That same God who exercised mercy to Israel speaks eloquently in the New Testament. "If your brother sins against you, rebuke him; and if repents, forgive him. And if he sins against you seven times in a day, and seven times in a day returns to you saying, 'I repent,' you shall forgive him" (Luke 17:3–4).

God's kingdom is based on love, compassion, and forgiveness. How can we not forgive another when God has forgiven us so much? The cross of Christ is the very definition of God's love, mercy, and forgiveness toward sinners. "And when they had come to the place called Calvary, there they crucified Him, and the criminals, one on the right hand and the other on the left. Then Jesus said, 'Father, forgive them, for they do not know what they do'" (Luke 23:33–34). If God forgave us for killing his Son, should we not forgive others who infringe on our rights?

May 18

The Passover

Now the blood shall be a sign for you on the houses where you are. And when I see the blood, I will pass over you; and the plague shall not be on you to destroy you when I strike the land of Egypt.

—Exodus 12:13

The twelve-year-old Jesus watched as the high priest handed the knife to Jacob, the offender. Would he have the audacity to take the life of the innocent little lamb to atone for his offense? He did. Attending the Passover feast with his parents, it began to dawn on the mind of the young Jesus that one day he would be the sacrificial Lamb slain for the sins of the world, including yours and mine. He observed with deep interest as the little lamb, without a struggle, was slain by the sinner, and its blood was carried by the high priest to the holy place.

"But He was wounded for our transgressions, He was bruised for our iniquities; the chastisement for our peace was upon Him, and by His stripes we are healed. He was oppressed and He was afflicted, yet He opened not his mouth; He was led as a lamb to the slaughter, and as a sheep before its shearers is silent, so He opened not his mouth" (Isa. 53:5, 7). Through the vivid illustration of the ceremonial law, God was revealing to the Israelites and to a growing Jesus that one day the lamb would not be a mere sheep but Christ himself.

The purpose of the blood on the doorpost and the eating of the Passover lamb was to demonstrate faith in a powerful, living God who is saving his people from moral and physical bondage. This sacrificial lamb was literally slain by every patriarch, from Adam to the last sinner before Calvary. It basically pardoned the guilty sinner and transferred his sins to the lamb, which is symbolic of the righteousness of Christ on our behalf. "For He made Him who knew no sin to be sin for us, that we might become the righteousness of God in Him" (2 Cor. 5:21). Having met its fulfillment in the life of Christ, the Passover feast transitioned into what Jesus instituted as the Lord's Supper.

"And as they were eating, Jesus took bread, blessed and broke it, and gave it to the disciples and said, 'Take, eat, this is My body,' then He took the cup, and gave thanks, and gave it to them, saying, 'Drink from it, all of you. For this is My blood of the new covenant, which is shed for many for the remission of sins'" (Matt. 26:26–28). Having met its fulfillment in the death of Christ, after Calvary, the Passover feast became irrelevant to the plan of salvation and was replaced by the Communion.

All the signpost and traffic signals of the Old Testament rituals pointed in the direction of Calvary. No longer were the saints to look forward to a Savior to come but back to a Savior who died at Calvary, was risen, and is at the right hand of God at this very moment, representing humanity in the heavenly court. "Seeing then that we have a great High Priest who has passed through the heavens, Jesus the Son of God, let us hold fast to our confession. For we do not have a High Priest who cannot sympathize with our weaknesses, but was in all points tempted as we are, yet without sin" (Heb. 4:14–15). Aren't you happy we have one of us (Jesus) interceding on our behalf in heaven? Are you taking advantage of this reality? Do you have his blood over your doorpost? Are you washed by his blood?

May 19

Forgetting the Past

Do not remember the former things, nor consider the things of old.
—Isaiah 43:18

It was a bonanza for the West when Soviet pilot Viktor Belenko flew his MiG-25 "Foxbat" to Hakodate, Japan, during the height of the Cold War. He brought with him many precious gifts, including a manual of the secretive MiG-25 and prized intelligence worth many bags of gold. He was immediately granted political asylum by Pres. Gerald Ford. Usually, a prized defector (one who gives up his country for another) is given a new identity and a handsome pension, but Viktor was quickly employed by his new country for his valuable contribution. However, he would do well to forget his past if he was to be successful in his new country of adoption (https://theaviationist.com/2016/09/06/the-story-of-the-soviet-pilot-who-defected-to-japan-with-a-secretive-mig-25-foxbat-40-years-ago-today/).

"Plenty fishes in the sea," we were told when growing up. If one gets away, just keep on fishing, and you will catch another. Well, the stock market crisis of recent months left many in worse financial shape than before, but even when we fall, we get up, don't we? If you were hit by the financial crisis, I urge you to move on. Please do not dwell on the past; it will only weaken your resolve. Successful business firms absorb many financial setbacks and move on, and so can we. Candid entrepreneurs will admit that preliminary failures only stiffened their resolve to achieve greater success.

We are told to forget the former things. What former things should we forget? Defeat comes to mind. Who wants to remember being beaten up, being punched on the nose, or losing a game? Past misdeeds are already forgiven and are buried in the farthermost part of the ocean; therefore it is not necessary to go fishing and retrieve them again. Being annoyed by the contention at the Corinthian church, Paul intimated, "For I determined not to know anything among you except Jesus Christ and Him crucified" (1 Cor. 2:2).

Life brings us more good memories than bad, and we should remember and dwell on the good ones. Here are some good ones. "Brethren, I do not count myself to have apprehended; but one thing I do, forgetting those things which are behind and reaching forward to those things which are ahead, I press towards the goal for the prize of the upward call of God in Christ Jesus" (Phil. 3:13–14). Many races have been lost by runners who looked back to eye their nearest competitors. Football players have been told by their coaches, "When you have the ball, run with it and don't look back."

We have spent much time forgetting the bad things; here are some pleasant things we should definitely remember. "Finally, brethren, whatever things are true, whatever things are noble, whatever things are just, whatever things are pure, whatever things are lovely, whatever things are of good report, if there is any virtue and if there is anything praiseworthy, meditate on these things" (Phil. 4:8). Good thoughts breed good works; wicked thoughts breed wicked actions. Think positive thoughts. Go and do likewise.

May 20

On the Potter's Workbench

Arise and go down to the potter's house, and there I will cause you to hear my words.
—Jeremiah 18:2

With only a high school education and no inheritance from wealthy relatives, he changed the world. Malcom McLean revolutionized global trade with his inventions of containerized shipping and motorized trucking. What started as a family affair with no input from wealthy investors developed and became a huge giant, and world trade benefited immensely from McLean's other pet project, containerized shipping. These two key inventions changed the course of commercial business in the world, and shipping and world commerce have never been the same ever since (hbswk.hbs.edu/item/the-truck-driver-who-reinvented-shipping).

While some assume credit for their inventions—and deservedly so—God has a unique way of keeping the ego of his people in check. "The word which came to Jeremiah from the Lord saying: Arise go down to the potter's house, and there I will cause you to hear My words. Then I went down to the potter's house, and there he was, making something at the wheel. And the vessel that he made of clay was marred in the hand of the potter; so he made it again into another vessel, as it seemed good to the potter to make" (Jer. 18:1–4). An important lesson leaps at us from this verse: the clay is completely at the potter's discretion to use as he sees fit. He may choose to make whatever he desires from the clay with no input from it. It is always a good sign when our children, early in their life, choose a career with little meddling from us eager parents. However, we should stand ready to guide them into choices of noble professions if they err in judgment and deviate from the straight and narrow way. God does the same with us. Very often, it becomes necessary to break our will and reshape us into something better when we deviate from his chosen path.

Consequently, if by any means the vessel is misshapen, the potter reserves the right to recycle it into an altogether different vessel, again with no input from the clay. The potter knows from experience which utensil is best suited to be made from a particular lump of clay. Does God know which profession can have the most impact in his service? If he does, shouldn't we give him the prerogative to choose for us in every area of our decision making?

"O house of Israel, can I not do with you as this potter? Says the Lord. Look, as the clay is in the potter's hand, so are you in My hand, O house of Israel!" (Jer. 18:6). The Lord is amazing, isn't he? Although he has unlimited power over everything, he respects the power of choice of his intelligent creation. He will not violate our will; he respects the decisions we make. Like a frustrated parent, many times he watches and waits for a call for help in our troubled affairs but to no avail. "I have stretched out My hands all day long to a rebellious people who walk in a way that is not good, according to their own thoughts" (Isa. 65:2). God is gracious and merciful, and he is always there to help, even when we are intent on having our own way. May the Lord have mercy on us. "Lord, I believe; help my unbelief" (Mark 9:24).

May 21

Overcoming the Grasshopper Syndrome Part 1

There we saw the giants (The descendants of Anak came from the giants); and we were like grasshoppers in our own sight and so we were in their sight.
—Numbers 13:33

For twenty-two years, he spied for the Soviet Union against his own country. The Justice Department described his activities as the worst intelligence disaster in modern history. On February 18, 2001, Robert Philip Hanssen's career as an FBI agent came to an abrupt end when he was caught spying for Russia. Why did he do it? For a fistful of dollars and some diamonds, Hanssen betrayed his own country— the country he swore to defend. Spying is as old as sin and has been around for some time (http://www.cnn.com/2013/03/25/us/robert-hanssen-fast-facts/).

"The Lord spoke to Moses, saying, send men to spy out the land of Canaan, which I am giving to the children of Israel; from each tribe of their fathers you shall send a man, everyone a leader among them. And see what the land is like: whether the people who dwell in it are strong or weak, few or many; whether the land they dwell is good or bad; whether the cities they inhabit are like camps or strongholds; whether the land is rich or poor, and whether there are forests there or not" (Num. 13:1–2, 18–20).

The twelve spies were leaders of their tribes who witnessed God inflict twelve withering plagues on a stubborn Egyptian nation that refused to set Israel free. They witnessed the parting of the Red Sea by Moses at the direction of God. Barren, hostile deserts became hospitable to Israel, and dry rocks gushed out water before them at the word of God. Nations superior to them militarily trembled in fear at their silent approach. The Lord was with them in a cloud by day for cooling and a pillar of fire by night for heating. His abiding presence was with their army. Israel instilled fear in opponents and rendered their armies ineffective. But ten of the twelve spies sent to survey the land doubted the power of God to deal with their enemies as he had done in the past.

Are we any different from the spies if we doubt God's ability to redeem us from traumatic situations? An abuse may have taken a terrible toll on your self-esteem but be patient with yourself; your healing may come in stages. Never doubt; it will come. Maybe you are struggling with a weakness you wish you didn't have, but it's there, staring at you in the face. Don't give up, and just keep on praying; you will overcome in his strength. "And they overcame him by the blood of the Lamb and by the word of their testimony and they did not love their lives to the death" (Rev. 12:11).

Our strength in overcoming the giants of life lies not in our ability but in the strength of the One who once walked in our shoes and overcame. "For we do not have a High Priest who cannot sympathy with our weaknesses, but was in all points tempted as we are, yet without sin. Let us therefore come boldly to the throne of grace that we may obtain mercy and find grace to help in time of need" (Heb. 4:15–16).

Simply put, we can defeat the "grasshopper syndrome" by asking God for strength to shore up our weakness. God is renowned for giving courage to the fainthearted. Can you slay a giant? I pause for your answer. Oh yes, you can, and you must; otherwise, it will destroy you. All we have to do is say, "Lord I believe; help my unbelief" (Mark 9:24).

May 22

Overcoming the Grasshopper Syndrome Part 2

Then Caleb quieted the people before Moses, and said, let us go up at once and take possession, for we are well able overcome it.

—Numbers 13:30

At sixty-five years old and with two previous failed efforts under his belt, Sir Ranulph Fiennes overcame his fear of climbing to scale the world's most formidable obstacle, Mount Everest (http://www.dailymotion.com/video/x46army_highest-mountain-sir-ranulph-fiennes-obe-guinness-world-records-60th-anniversary_fun). His first attempt to climb the mountain was abandoned after suffering a heart attack, and his second attempt failed after fatigue and exhaustion settled in. But Sir Ranulph wasn't done with the mountain quite yet; he invoked the champion within him and triumphed where many others stumbled. He succeeded and triumphed over the mountain in his third attempt.

When God's name is being vandalized by the wicked, righteous men should recoil in horror as David did when Goliath defiled God's holy name (1 Sam. 17:10). Jonathan felt that righteous indignation also and challenged his armor bearer to join him in destroying an elite well-equipped Philistine garrison (1 Sam. 13:14). Caleb had seen enough; he challenged his fellow men to overcome their fear of the unknown and engage the enemy (Num. 13:30). To get to Canaan, they must overcome and get past their enemies.

Likewise, to get to our heavenly Canaan, there are many Goliaths (trials, habits) we must slay and overcome. Looming ahead of the pack is a formidable fighter called appetite. He has a deadly left hook and must be approached carefully. He has knocked out cold many good folks. Following him is a lesser known fighter but an equally competent boxer known simply as weight. Doctors fear him; he has a bad reputation of robbing them of their patients. And of course, following weight is the silent knockout king himself, inactivity. He may be silent but has a violent temper and is known to put out of commission anyone who refuses to exercise and cooperate with the laws of good health.

So far, we have enumerated only three bad-tempered giants, but there are many more. Let's see how we can overcome these with the help of the Almighty. The original diet for man that is best for our health can be found in Genesis 1:29. After the entrance of sin, some foods became unfit for human consumption. A list of these unclean foods can be found in Leviticus 11:1–30 and Deuteronomy 14:1–21. God's method of preventive health is always better than the costly hospital bills anyway, and who can argue with that?

By properly controlling the appetite in consuming wholesome foods and measurably limiting the quantity of food consumed, we can bring our weight under control with moderate exercise. Some unfairly blame the invention of the TV remote control for their exercise woes. We remain inactive by choice if there are no physical limitations to our bodies.

The giants may threaten, but by the grace of God, "I can do all things through Christ who strengthens me" (Phil. 4:13). A sister text that can shudder the approach of any incoming giant is this one from Ephesians: "Now to him who is able to do exceedingly abundantly above all that we ask or think, according to the power that works in us" (Eph. 3:20). By faith and works, move on in faith, and slay those naughty giants.

May 23

Overcoming the Grasshopper Syndrome Part 3

Therefore we also, since we are surrounded by so great a cloud of witnesses, let us lay aside every weight, and the sin which so easily ensnares us, and let us run with endurance the race that is set before us, looking unto Jesus the author and finisher of our faith.

—Hebrews 12:1–2

Usain Bolt leisurely galloped his way to the finish line, easily outdistancing his hustling competitors as he sprang his way into history. Winner of the one-hundred-meter and two-hundred-meter races, Bolt became the first man to hold this coveted distinction. At 6'5", Bolt has wowed the athletic world by tearing down just about every record in Olympic history. And he might be around to shatter many more records since he just turned twenty-eight.

We are striving to enter a different record book—the Book of Life. "He who overcomes shall be clothed in white garments, and I will not blot out his name from the Book of Life; but I will confess his name before My Father and before His angels" (Rev. 3:5). Tremendous emphasis is placed on overcoming in Jesus; every biblical writer highlights this important message. What is so important about overcoming? Sin is odious (extremely unpleasant) in God's sight. He has vowed to eradicate sin, both the root (Satan) and the branch (followers). Therefore it goes without saying that if we desire to live in eternity with God, we must allow him to cleanse us from sin.

What's encouraging about walking with Jesus is that "we are surrounded by so great a cloud of witnesses." Imagine this: the men and women who walked with God in ages past were saddled with grave defects, like you and me. The twelve patriarchs struggled with their own brand of weaknesses as well. It was said of Reuben, "You are my firstborn . . . Unstable as water, you shall not excel Because you went up to your father's bed; then you defiled it—he went up to my couch" (Gen. 49:3–4). Despite Reuben's incestuous relation with his stepmother, he overcame in the end and was saved. He represents those who will overcome despite their flaws.

Samson, like Judah, had his problems with prostitutes. "Then his father and mother said to him, 'Is there no woman among the daughters of your brethren, or among all my people, that you must go and get a wife from the uncircumcised Philistines?' And Samson said to his father, 'Get her for me, for she pleases me well'" (Judg. 14:3). Did Samson finally get it right? Well, he is in the Hebrews Faith Hall of Fame. Surely, he made his peace with God after his eyes were gouged out, his hair was sheared, and he was thrown in jail. He overcame and represents those who will make sincere last-minute deathbed confession.

Isn't God merciful and wonderful? He saves us despite our weakness. "For God did not send His Son into the world to condemn the world, but that the world through Him might be saved" (John 3:17). As long as there is a will to be saved, God sets in motion a chain of events to bring us to the foot of the cross. It may not be not be pretty, but he reserves the prerogative to use any means necessary to save us. Some folks may never see the outside of a prison wall again, but it doesn't matter; what's really important is knowing Jesus as Savior and Lord.

We are involved in a real-life drama in which we are being cheered on by spectators (unfallen, sinless beings) and our coach (Jesus). We can make it. "Have I not commanded you? Be strong and of good courage; do not be afraid, nor be dismayed, for the Lord your God is with you wherever you go" (Josh. 1:9).

May 24

A Brand-New Body

Then He who sat on the throne said, behold, I make all things new. And He said to me write, for these words are true and faithful.

—Revelation 21:5

Most faucets usually shut down after being turned off, but my friend's is different; it kept dripping all day long. Sitting in her living room chair and glancing at a bouquet of lovely flowers, I saw her leaky faucet. While a leaky faucet barely raises an eyebrow anymore, it reveals some interesting realities. A leak always carries unintended consequences and usually costly repair bills. Everything that carries liquid or air will leak eventually. Automobiles develop leaks in tires, engine, muffler, and other components and if not attended will increase your fuel consumption, resulting in costlier bills. Wherever a line is conducting fluid under pressure from one point to another, there exists the possibility of a leak.

Are humans immune from this pestilent leaky problem? Not really. Gray hair invades faces and heads, and our body shows sign of aging. The once-resilient valves that shut and open doors for the passage of fluids are less reliable and vigilant than before. The valves to the heart are the most critical and can't afford to leak, but they often do. But wait, don't despair; the psalmist has already petitioned God on our behalf. "Do not cast me off in the time of my old age; do not forsake me when my strength fails." He continues his petition on our behalf. "Now when I am old and gray-headed, do not forsake me, until I declare your strength to this generation, and your power to everyone who is to come" (Ps. 71:9, 18). Did you notice the request of the psalmist for you? He aspires for you the opportunity of telling the younger generation of God's amazing love, even as you age. What an astonishing request. Can we appropriate this promise? Why shouldn't we? Don't you want to see your granddaughter's children?

It should bring a great deal of comfort to those of us making the transition into seniority that we have much-needed resources and wisdom to pass on to the upcoming generation. Age has endowed us with much wisdom, which we should liberally share with anyone who will listen. We cannot afford to take to the grave the pioneering achievements of our lifetime. What good will it do down there? My memory goes back to an aunt who did not impart her fragrant, mouthwatering cake recipes to the next generation. Once in a while, I sniff the imaginary delicacies she once made, but can I taste them? Of course not. What good is that to me?

When we are cognizant enough to recognize the onset of failing health, then it is time to set our house (relation with God) in order and look forward to our brand-new bodies.

> Behold I tell you a mystery: we shall not all sleep, but we shall all be changed, in a moment, in the twinkling of an eye, at the last trumpet. For the trumpet will sound, and the dead will be raised incorruptible, and we shall be changed. For this corruptible must put on incorruption, and this mortal must put on immortality. So when this corruptible has put on incorruption, and this mortal has put on immortality, then shall be brought to the pass the saying that is written: "Death is swallowed in victory." O death where is your sting? O Hades where is your victory? (1 Cor. 15:51–55)

I look forward to eternal life with Jesus and the occupation of my brand-new body. Do you?

May 25

Be Ready Always

Preach the word! Be ready in season and out of season, convince, rebuke, exhort, with all longsuffering and teaching.

—2 Timothy 4:2

Genghis Khan was particularly harsh to sentries who fell asleep on duty; they paid dearly with their lives. The Romans weren't gentler either. Pilots, air traffic controllers, lawmakers, motorists, and even police officers have been caught taking a little snooze while on duty, so what's the fuss about a soldier napping while working? They have been entrusted with the nation's defense, that's why. Sleeping on guard is unacceptable. Sleeping and watching are incompatible; they are mutually exclusive, and they cancel each other out. You invite the enemy in by sleeping on guard. Christians should always be wide awake in the fight against evil.

"So we labored in the work, and half of the men held the spears from daybreak until the stars appeared. At the same time I also said to the people, let each man and his servant stay at night in Jerusalem that they may be on guard by night and a working party by day. So neither I, my brethren, my servants nor the men of the guard took off our clothes except that everyone took them off for washing" (Neh. 4:21–23). The threat to Nehemiah and his colleagues was real; their enemies did not want a restored and fortified Jerusalem. The enemy, under the leadership of Satan, sought every opportunity to harass, frustrate, stop, and inflict bodily harm on the workers, but God foiled their plans, and the work prevailed. The work prospered because the workers exercised vigilance and prudence. Can we afford to do any less? Since the enemy has not changed his mode of operation, should we relax our vigilance?

On the night of his travail, Jesus brought with him Peter, James, and John, hoping to draw strength from their prayers and solidarity from their company, but they fell asleep. "Then He came to His disciples and found them sleeping, and said to Peter, 'What? Could you not watch with Me one hour? Watch and pray, lest you enter into temptation. The spirit indeed is willing but the flesh is weak'" (Matt. 26:40–41). The battle is fierce, and the game is real. Satan is lulling a lot folks to the sleep of death. If we do not attempt to remain alert with a prayer in our hearts and sword in hand (the Bible), we might be lulled into sleep from which there is no awaking.

The Plains Indians developed a highly successful means of harvesting buffalo. They drove an unsuspecting herd to what they assume to be happy gallop but instead led them to the edge of the cliff. By the time the frontline beasts realized their mortal danger, the momentum of the arriving rear guard plunged many to their deaths. We should be watchful with a keen sense of discernment to detect the devil's tricks and temptation so that we are not swept away like the buffalo herd into total destruction.

Being awake entails preaching the Word, being ready in season and out of season, convincing, exhorting, and teaching with long-suffering. Christ gave this same mandate in Matthew 28:19–20. "Go and make disciples of all nations" is now being reiterated by Paul to his young pastor son in the faith. "Preach the word! Be ready in season and out of season, convince, exhort and rebuke." I want to be awake and active when God is pouring his Spirit on his people during Earth's final days. How about you? Are you awake or half-asleep?

May 26

Is God with Us?

And they said to one another, did not our hearts burn within us while He talked with us on the road, and while He opened the Scripture to us?
—Luke 24:32

Mao Zedong is the Chinese Communist revolutionary leader who put China on the geopolitical map. He is better known as Chairman Mao. Chinese revere him and with good reason. He broke the yoke of colonialism and championed the rights of the little people. To the masses, he could do no wrong, even though he had many missteps in his path to leadership. "No man is perfect," we often say, but we serve a God who is altogether perfect, and he chose to make his abode with us, even in our imperfection (tps://www.google.com/amp/www.biography.com/amp/people/mao-tse-tung-9398142).

"Behold, a virgin shall be with child, and bear a son, and they shall call His name Immanuel, which is translated, God with us" (Matt. 1:23). Just as McDonald's and Walmart are part of the American landscape, Jesus is part of our human family. Yes, he really did exist, and since he was not born in the United States, we cannot go downtown to verify his birth certificate. I have a better idea. Let us go through the greatest book ever written and verify his origin. Let's see what it says. "And it came to pass in those days that a decree went out from Caesar Augustus that all the world should be registered . . . For there is born to you this day in the city of David a Savior, who is Christ the Lord" (Luke 2:1, 11).

As sure as the residents of Shaoshan claimed Mao as one of them—and indeed he was—in like manner, we claim Jesus as 100 percent human and 100 percent God at the same time. "In the beginning was the Word, and the Word was with God, and the Word was God. He was in the beginning with God. All things were made through Him, and without Him nothing was made that was made" (John 1:1–3).

Even though he is not physically present with us, his indwelling Spirit, the Holy Ghost, lives and abides with us. "And I will pray the Father, and He will give you another Helper, that He may abide with you forever" (John 14:16). The "forever" indwelling of God with us is indicative of many of God's promises to Abraham and the patriarchs. "Behold, I am with you and will keep you wherever you go, and will bring you back to this land; for I will not leave you until I have done what I have spoken to you" (Gen. 28:15). The promises made to the patriarch are binding on his children since in Abraham we all are blessed. Again, we see God reiterating his promise that he will abide with us for all time.

God created our planet and planted a beautiful garden for our first parents, Adam and Eve. It was his intention to unite them with the universal family after a period of probation, but they had to pass the test of obedience if they hoped to be eternally secure. Tragically, they sinned, and God's causal company became a terrifying retreat to the fig tree grove. However, though sin separated us from God, he loved us so much that he created new methods in communicating with us.

Besides his indwelling presence in us, he talks to us in other ways. "If there is a prophet among you, I, the Lord, make Myself known to him in a vision; I speak to him in a dream. Not so with My servant Moses, he is faithful in all My house. I speak to him face to face" (Num. 12:6–8). Has God spoken to you in a dream or through a friend? When did you last hear God's voice? Was it through reading the Bible? Oh yes, that's the one. Keep on reading. God is still speaking to his people. Are you listening?

May 27

Nothing Is Free

For God so loved the world that He gave His only begotten Son that whoever believes in Him should not perish but have everlasting life.

—John 3:16

The delicious flowers are there for the taking. They are simply delightful, the aroma tantalizing, but they come at a cost. The insects must be willing participants in cross-fertilization. The plants advertise their spectacular offering to entice insects in spreading their pollen far and wide. The pollen must be transported to species of the opposite sex, and the insects' hairy legs are perfect for the job; their abdomen, hairy also, has been specially designed for just such a transaction. The plants benefit by reproducing more of themselves while the insects enjoy a tasty treat. Both plant and insect derive mutual benefits. Nothing is free.

The cost of salvation to mankind came at a very high cost to God but is absolutely free to humans. The Godhead has been inseparable from eternity past. They exist as a unit, and to be separated was a first, which was caught in this agonizing utterance from a dying Savior. "My God, My God why have you forsaken Me? Why are you so far from helping Me, and from the words of My groaning? O My God, I cry in the daytime, but You do not hear; and in the night season, and I am not silent" (Ps. 22:1–2).

The Bible states that God allowed Adam's children (us) to incur the curse that sin brought—alienation from God. But Jesus, the second member of the Trinity, determined to take the fall for us. He became sin for us. God allowed Jesus to suffer death in the flesh, in his humanity. "God made Him who knew no sin to be sin for us, that we might become the righteousness of God in Him" (2 Cor. 5:21). When humanity sinned, God was in a precarious position. He had to punish sin to be just. He couldn't gloss over sin, not even when they were laid on Jesus. "Surely He has borne our grief and carried our sorrow; yet we esteemed Him stricken, smitten by God, and afflicted. But He was wounded for our transgressions, He was bruised for our iniquities, the chastisement for our peace was upon Him and by His stripes we are healed" (Isa. 53:4–5).

Our salvation came at a heavy price to God. He could not spare his own Son once he volunteered to become our Savior. God could not hold back the hands of the Roman soldiers who were pounding the nails into the hands of the Savior. Nor could he silence the gloating priests who were taunting Jesus as he lay dying. To remain impartial, God must allow Jesus to tread the winepress alone; but in the cover of this unusual noonday darkness, God was right there with Christ, even if he did not recognize it. While the Father wholeheartedly supported the Son, Jesus had to bear the cross alone. "He trod the winepress alone" (Isa. 63:3).

Isaiah portrays an intimate God involved in the affairs of his people. "When you pass through the waters, I will be with you, and through the rivers, they shall not overflow you. When you walk through the fire, you shall not be burned, nor shall the flame scorch you" (Isa. 43:2). God was with Christ every step of the way, and he is here with us as well.

When I sin, it grieves me to think that my sins cause God, Christ, and the Holy Spirit so much pain. Lord, help me not to sin, and give me the power to overcome it when I do. Amen.

May 28

Here We Stand

Behold the proud, his soul is not upright in him; but the just shall live by his faith.
—Habakkuk 2:4

With a hammer, a few nails, and a scroll with some words written therein, he sent shock waves through the papal establishment. Possessed by a strong, indomitable resolve to find the true path and walk in it, Martin Luther calmly walked up to the church in Wittenberg, Germany, and hammered his Ninety-Five Theses on the cathedral's door so all could see. The content of this scroll distraught the papal establishment, which claimed to have primacy over the interpretation of the scripture (http://www.history.com/this-day-in-history/martin-luther-posts-95-theses).

It was called the Dark Ages with good reason. The masses were illiterate, and the church was very happy about that. The scripture was locked in a language not spoken by the common people, and the church was delighted. According to the church, only the pope, friars, priests, and bishops could interpret the Bible; but in reality, they were the most ignorant of its sacred truths. The people were at the mercy of the state church for salvation.

The long masses and costly pilgrimages to Rome brought in much-needed revenue to the coffers of the church. The people languished and yearned for spiritual light but could not get beyond the carefully worded fables of their parish priest. Then came the bold and conscientious Martin Luther with his passion, hunger, and thirst for knowing and doing God's will. The church did not have biblical answers for his many questions, and he was shocked and horrified when the church decided to excommunicate him rather than defend its belief from the holy scriptures.

Thank God for the Lutheran revolution. Men are saved by faith in Jesus and not by some creed, pilgrimage, intercession of saints, or some holy mother. The Bible is its own interpreter and can be understood by anyone desirous of knowing the truth. The decrees of councils and conventions are subordinate to the teachings of the scriptures. Jesus is our only intermediary as evidenced in the scripture. These tenets were the foundation of the Protestant Reformation. Long-forgotten Bible texts were unearthed and understood by sincere truth seekers. "Seeing then that we have a great High Priest who has passed through the heavens, Jesus the Son of God, let us hold fast our confession. For we do not have a High Priest who cannot sympathize with our weaknesses, but was in all points tempted as we are, yet without sin" (Heb. 4:14–15).

We must never depend on the intercession of deceased saints or ask forgiveness from anyone other than God and the one we offend. To continue this practice will undermine the ministry of Jesus, who is our real High Priest in the heavenly courts. Only God has the divine prerogative to forgive sins; the person we offend can forgive us, but only God can absolve one from guilt through the blood of Jesus Christ. Any attempt or claim to absolve one from sin is blasphemy.

The Protestant Reformation, initiated by God through the ministry of godly men, shed much light on the path corrupted by false teachings and teachers over a long period. Thank God for the Protestant Reformation. When we avail ourselves of daily study of the Bible, bear in mind that it cost some of these reformers their lives to bring us the clear, undiluted words from the scripture. Keep on reading the scriptures; it's good for you.

May 29

Freedom in Christ

Stand fast therefore in the liberty by which Christ has made us free, and do not be entangled again with a yoke of bondage.

—Galatians 5:1

Things had gone terribly wrong for the Union army of Pres. Abraham Lincoln at the Battle of Bull Run. The army was defeated, deflated, and in disarray; the nation was restless and chaotic, and someone needed to step up to the plate to heal the wounds of the nation. Then came the Gettysburg Address, which transformed a war-weary nation into the envy of the world. Lincoln's three-minute address—with its emphasis on all men being created equal, the preservation of the Union, honoring the fallen braves, the emancipation of slaves, and the government of the people, by the people not perishing from the earth—transformed the nation and made it a beacon of hope for mankind. It was a shot in the arm for a war-weary nation teetering on the brink of national catastrophe. The boiling cauldron of venom, hate, rage, revenge, and despair was averted and simmered down to a quiet halt as President Lincoln lifted the nation back to its strength (http://www.abrahamlincolnonline.org/lincoln/speeches/gettysburg.htm).

What Lincoln's speech accomplished in saving the nation from disintegration and anarchy cannot be compared with Christ's victory at Calvary. Our Savior's victory accomplished much more; it reconciled man and God. Sin enslaves its victims, but Jesus grants freedom and victory to anyone desirous of casting off the yoke of sin. "Therefore do not let sin reign in your mortal body, that you should obey its lusts. And do not present your members as instruments of unrighteousness to sin, but present yourselves to God as being alive from the dead and your members as instruments of righteousness to God" (Rom. 6:12–13). The repentant sinner can overcome sin regardless of how deep his addiction may be. "My grace is sufficient for you, My strength is made perfect in weakness" (2 Cor. 12:9). Christ stands ready to deposit tons of grace into your account. Are you ready to receive it? "But where sin abounded, grace abounded much more" (Rom. 5:20). Regardless of how mired the sinner may be, Jesus can restore and make whole again.

Not only does the cross liberate one from sin but it also equalizes the playing field. The early church had not fully come to grips with the equality of all believers in Christ, but the Holy Spirit was ahead of the game. "Men and brethren, you know that a good while ago God chose among us, that by my mouth the Gentiles should hear the word of the gospel and believe. So God, who knows the heart, acknowledged them by giving them the Holy Spirit, just as He did to us, and made no distinction between us and them, purifying their hearts by faith" (Acts 15:7–9). Bear in mind that the Jews still considered themselves the favorites of heaven, but the gospel of Christ did many wonderful things for the downtrodden. It restored the dignity of women as equals—something that was a little hard for men to swallow—and installed the brotherhood of all believers regardless of one's birth, social status, or national origin. In essence, the grace of Christ destroys all feelings of bigotry and superiority. "There is neither Jew nor Greek, there is neither slave nor free there is neither male nor female for you are all one in Jesus Christ" (Gal. 3:28).

What are you struggling with? What is binding you—a false sense of superiority, a little bigotry, a little racism? "Therefore He is able to save to the uttermost those who come to God through Him, since He always lives to make intercession for them" (Heb. 7:25).

May 30

Honesty, the Best Policy

For we all stumble in many things. If anyone does not stumble in word, he is a perfect man, able also to bridle the whole body.

—James 3:2

It has long been observed that animals employ trickery to survive in dangerous neighborhoods, but the hognose snake has taken trickery and deception to a new level. When threatened, it rolls over with jaws gaping and tongue hanging and waits perfectly still until the threat is gone. When the all-clear signal is detected, the snake rights itself up and carries on with its business as usual. Deception is strictly forbidden to the child of God.

Disciples of Christ should not practice deception, not in thoughts, words, deeds, glances, or nods. Even if it means incurring a fine, imprisonment, or death, they should stand on the solid foundation of truth, which is Jesus Christ. "And they overcame him by the blood of the Lamb and by the word of their testimony, and they did not love their lives to the death" (Rev. 12:11). The discipline of truth telling is not an occasional, on-and-off, haphazard incident of convenience. Truth telling is a lifestyle; it is the hallmark of the Christian's integrity. Jesus is still the Truth, the Way, and the Light. When asked by Pilate, "What is truth?" Pilate should have known of an earlier discourse in which Jesus empathetically stated, "I am the way, the truth, and the life no one comes to the Father except through me" (John 14:6).

Because we are ambassadors of the Truth (Christ) and represent him in every aspect of life, our life, conduct, association with friends, and business dealing must be above reproach. Abraham set us a sterling example of dealing with conflict even when it seems to be at our disadvantage. God can turn disadvantages into advantages when he sees fit. "So Abraham said to Lot, please let there be no strife between you and me, between my herdsmen and your herdsmen; for we are brethren. Is not the whole land before you? Please separate yourself from me. If you take the left, then I will go to the right; or if you go to the right, then I will go to the left . . . Then Lot chose for himself all the plain of Jordan [Sodom and Gomorrah], and Lot journeyed east. And they separated from each other" (Gen. 13:8–9, 11). Although Lot chose what he deemed the better choice, his decision had disastrous consequences for his family. Abraham, on the other hand, who settled for the leftovers, inherited what is now Israel, the Land of Promise.

Righteousness and evil cannot coexist. The devil injects a little lie with truth when it is convenient for him to cheat and deceive. God, on the other hand, never mixes truth with error; the truth must be completely 100 percent truth and nothing but the truth. The devil used deception in approaching Eve, the mother of all living. "Has God indeed said, you shall not eat of every tree of the garden? . . . Then the serpent said to the woman, you shall not surely die [half-truth]. For God knows that in the day you eat of it your eyes will be opened, and you will be like God, knowing good and evil" (Gen. 3:1, 4–5).

We live in an age where truth speaking has become a liability in business; a little inside information gets you ahead of the competition. Not so with the child of God. We walk a different route and report to a higher authority, God. We cannot and must not dabble in lies. Truth telling is always nobler than telling a little white lie. May God bless us as we aspire to grow in this area of Christian integrity.

May 31

Yes, You Can

Now to Him who is able to keep you from stumbling, and to present you faultless before the presence of His glory with exceeding joy to God our Savior, who alone is wise, be glory and majesty dominion and power, both now and forever amen.
—Jude 24–25

Only a handful of college players make it to the NFL. If you're battling a disability, the odds are mightily stacked against you making it to the NFL, but don't tell this to Derrick Coleman of the Seattle Seahawks, who will be contending with his team for a chance to win the Super Bowl. Coleman has been hearing-impaired since childhood but had determined early in life to excel over his disability (http://www.cnn.com/2015/08/06/health/derrick-coleman-seahawks-deaf/).

His high school prowess on the field left opponents scratching their heads and college scouts cheering wildly. He frustrated opposing players with his quick moves and fancy footwork. Teams that snubbed him because of his handicap paid a heavy price against a determined Coleman intent on punishing them for snubbing him. They became the objects of his wrath on the field. When asked how he anticipates plays since he is hearing-impaired, he simply remarked, "When the ball moves, then I move." Obviously, Coleman keeps his eyes on the ball, and who can argue with that? Very smart, Coleman, very smart. Derrick is a motivating example to us all; we can make it if we keep our eyes on Jesus. Are you determined like Coleman to overcome the obstacles in your way?

Our God can do anything, including breathing new life into his broken vessels. "The Jews from Antioch and Iconium came there; and having persuaded the multitudes, they stoned Paul and dragged him out of the city, supposing him to be dead. However, when the disciples gathered around him, he rose up and went into the city. And the next day he departed with Barnabas to Derbe" (Acts 14:19–20). Was Paul discouraged? Nah.

God stands ready to bestow on us the very resources we stand in need of, but the question persists: will we use them? You use it or lose it. He has promised to give us everything needed for our continuous spiritual development. "For the Lord God is a sun and shield; the Lord will give grace and glory; no good thing will He withhold from those who walk uprightly" (Ps. 84:11). Not only has the Lord given us the tools we need for success but he also has guaranteed our success if we stick to the job and faint not. He helps us when we get weary, refreshes us when we stumble, and supports the weak to the finish line. If we have the will to win, in Jesus, we can make it. Never quit.

The classic saying "You can take a horse to the water, but you can't force him to drink" stands true in the Christian life. God can do everything except force our will. "When Jesus saw him lying there, and knew that he already had been in that condition a long time, He said to him, 'Do you want to be made well?'" (John 5:6).

That would be a violation of one's will if he or she is saved against his or her wish. Even God must receive our permission to save us.

Once the will is made to be saved or remain lost, God goes into action whether to save us or respect our decision to live apart from him. And of course, knowing that he has done everything he could to save us, he seals our decision for heaven or hell. I trust your decision for him is in the affirmative, to live with him forever. There is no reason to be lost. Go out there and conquer your disabilities in Christ's strength.

June 1

Jesus in My Mess

And a great windstorm arose and the waves began to beat into the boat, so that it was already filling. But He was in the stern, asleep on a pillow, and the disciples said to Him, Teacher, do you not care that we are perishing?

—Mark 4:37–38

A dashing young prince with a dazzling future ahead of him walked away from the throne and its privileges to become a servant to his afflicted people. Being raised in the royal palace, Moses was groomed for leadership, possibly the throne one day, but he walked away from it all to suffer with and lead his people from Egypt to the Promised Land. "By faith Moses, when he became of age, refused to be called the son of the Pharaoh's daughter, choosing rather to suffer affliction with the people of God than to enjoy the pleasures of sin. Esteeming the reproach of Christ greater riches than the treasures in Egypt; for he looked to the reward" (Heb. 11:24–26).

Moses is hardly unique in his example of self-sacrifice. About two centuries ago, a plan etched in eternity past unfolded at Bethlehem's Manger Square. Let's hear Paul's version of the event. "But when the fullness of the time had come, God sent forth His Son, born of a woman, born under the law, to redeem those who were under the law, that we might receive the adoption as sons" (Gal. 4:4–5). Did you hear what I just heard about being adopted as sons in God's universal family? This is too good to be true, but it is true.

Jesus could no longer remain in his ivory palace while his children wasted away in degradation and sin. He jumped right into the boat with us and became one of us, suffering with us and carrying our burdens. It pained him to see our degradation by sin; he was moved with compassion and healed many of our diseases. But man's physical disease was only a symptom of the greater wretchedness afflicting him. Adam, the father of our race, had sinned, and so he plunged our planet into total rebellion against God. "Therefore, just as through one man sin entered the world, and death through sin, and death spread to all men, because all have sinned" (Rom. 5:12).

Every human life is of infinite value to Christ. His precious blood was spilt for the Asians; Europeans; Africans; Australians; North, South, and Central Americans;

and the islanders of the sea. Whatever condition we find ourselves in, God is right there with us. He has demonstrated his kinship with us. The title *Immanuel*, meaning "God with us," also implies God is among us. By choosing to clothe himself with humanity, Jesus inherited all our baggage, our limitations, our confinement to time, our afflictions, and even our sins. "For He made Him who knew no sin to be sin for us, that we might become the righteousness of God in Him" (2 Cor. 5:21).

It is almost unthinkable to fathom that Jesus jumped into the gutter with the drug addicts, the gamblers, the blue- and white-collar criminals, the prostitutes, and the pedophiles, but that's precisely what he did. He became one of us to save us. "Therefore He is also able to save to the uttermost those who come to God through Him since He always lives to make intercession for them" (Heb. 7:25). Are you in a mess? Do you want to get out? Jesus is right there with you, ready to help you find your way to God.

June 2

Imprinted on His Hand

See I have inscribed you on the palms of My hand; your walls are continually before Me.

—Isaiah 49:16

A seal gives birth to a bouncing little noisy pup, but the colony is overcrowded with hundreds of young look-alikes. What is Mom supposed to do, and how does she recognize Junior from his buddies? Conditioning and imprinting are all good, but seal moms recognize their young by sound. Even when they return from frequent feeding trips to the ocean to stock up on food, they have no problem identifying the voice pitch of their pup from among the thousands. Scientists call this process imprinting, the learning or recognition between the mom/dad and offspring.

Lest we forget—and sometimes we do—God has his own method of imprinting. He has inscribed our names on the palm of his hand. Of course, God never forgets; but in the human vernacular, it means "You are very special to me, and I have placed you where I can see you very often." When we walk into someone's office, we usually see the pictures of loved ones, children, spouses, and even pets. Likewise, God wants us to know that he loves and treasures us, even when we get messy at times or a little stubborn.

We all love our children dearly, and their bad behavior does not dictate the quality of our love to them. We even seem to love the problematic ones more and spend extra time with them because they may need more individual care than the others. Now if we as humans can react this way, can you imagine the patience, tolerance, prodding, and affirmation God lavishes on us daily?

"Can a woman forget her nursing child, and not have compassion on the son of her womb? Surely they may forget, yet I will not forget you" (Isa. 49:15). God is stating that the most intimate human bond between a mom and her baby may fail, but his compassion, love, and goodness to us will never fail. One-year-old toddlers get into everything. They are constantly exploring (my grandson included). You need to have your eyes hovering over them all the time to keep them from trouble. Likewise, God never slumbers or sleeps, not just because we are prone to trouble but because he loves us.

"Roll back the curtains of memory now and then. Show me where you've brought me from and where I could have been. Just remember, I'm a human, and humans forget. So remind me. Remind me, dear Lord." Alison Krauss jolts our minds to remember what we were before we came to Christ. Because of our short memories, we need constant reminders, but God never fails in his paternal care of us.

Of the tons of swirling debris around our planet, there is no record of any civilization being wiped out of existence from these so-called asteroids. Many times our superpowers came dangerously close to igniting a nuclear catastrophe, but God intervenes as always. Since we have been inscribed on the palm of his hand, we can rest secure no evil can befall us. "Because you have made the Lord, who is my refuge, even the Most High, your dwelling place, no evil shall befall, nor shall any plague come near your dwelling, for He shall give His angels charge over you, to keep you in all your ways" (Ps. 91:9–11). Don't you worry, and don't despair. God has you covered.

June 3

Let Everything with Breath Praise Him

Lift up your heads, O you gates! And be lifted up, you everlasting doors! And the King of glory shall come in. Who is this King of Glory? The Lord strong and mighty, The Lord mighty in battle.

—Psalm 24:7–8

Criminal investigators enjoy finding a motive for crimes in which the criminal left no clues. Likewise, the motive behind the writing of these awesome Psalms gives us some insight into the lives of the people who wrote them. What was the motive behind the writing of Psalm 24? Israel had suffered a humiliating defeat at the hands of the Philistines who captured the ark of the covenant. Did it get that bad? It did.

With the Philistines amassing on their border, the Hebrews presumptuously carried the ark of the covenant with them in battle, hoping its presence would intimidate the enemy and give them victory. Needless to say, the battle was a disaster. God allowed the ark to be taken to teach his people a lesson—that he is their protector and not the ark.

Of course, the ark was too hot to handle as the Philistines found out and were very eager to return it to Israel. "But the hand of the Lord was heavy on the people of Ashdod, and He ravaged them and struck them with tumors, both Ashdod and its territory. And when the men of Ashdod saw how it was, they said 'The ark of the God of Israel must not remain with us, for His hand is harsh towards us and Dagon our god'" (1 Sam. 5:6–7). After paying a heavy price for tampering with the very symbol of God's identity, the Philistines sent the ark back to Israel with a respectable trespass offering.

The ark was brought to the house of Abinadab of Kirjath Jearim (1 Sam. 7:2, 2 Sam. 6:4) and remained there for some time until David decided to bring it to Jerusalem, his capital city. This transfer to the city included a parade by David and the military, and it set the stage for the writing of Psalm 24. The imagery he used for the ark being carried to its new home is typical of the King of kings being welcomed by two opposing choirs of angels after his victory over sin and Satan. "Lift up your heads, O you gates! And be lifted up, you everlasting doors! And the King of glory shall come in. Who is this King of Glory? The Lord strong and mighty, the Lord mighty in battle" (Ps. 24:7–8).

To intensify the moment, the psalmist commands the gates to lift their heads, but gates are inanimate and lifeless. Nevertheless, he calls on the occupants of the Holy City to prepare themselves to receive their King. If the gates are commanded to anticipate this glorious moment, how about us? "And some of the Pharisees called to Him from the crowd, 'Teacher, rebuke Your disciples.' But He answered and said to them, 'I tell you that if these should keep silent, the stones would immediately cry out'" (Luke 19:39–40).

The last phrase of Psalm 24:8–10 gives the reasons why we should worship the great King. First, he is strong in battle, having defeated Satan and the host of evil at the cross. Second, he is the Lord of Hosts, Commander of the heavenly angels. Third, he is deserving of our worship. "Worthy is the Lamb who was slain to receive power and riches and wisdom, and strength and honor and glory and blessing! . . . Blessing and honor and glory and power be to Him who sits on the throne, and to the Lamb, forever and ever" (Rev. 5:12–13).

June 4

The Cross, The Cross

But He was wounded for our transgressions, He was bruised for our iniquities; the chastisement for our peace was upon Him, and by His stripes we are healed.
—Isaiah 53:5

It was too late to do anything but to throw himself on the live grenade, smothering its deadly blast with his body. Navy tech Mike Monsoor was awarded the Congressional

Medal of Honor (posthumously) for exceptional bravery by President Bush. Mike is no longer with us, but his outstanding self-sacrifice to save his fellow SEALs gave him entrance into an elite class of men and women who gave up their life to save others. A live grenade thrown at them was just seconds from exploding when Mike did the unthinkable. He threw himself on the grenade and smothered its destructive blast. At his funeral, in a tribute befitting his valor, his fellow Navy SEAL buddies formed a row on each side of his casket; and in a moving ritual, each man removed his trident insignia and laid it on his casket as homage to one who paid the ultimate price (http://www.nbcnews.com/id/24017137/ns/us_news-military/t/bush-awards-medal-honor-navy-seal/#.WNgL1uk2yB0).

With certain destruction hanging over our heads for the transgression of God's holy law, Jesus took our place at the execution block and died in our place, smothering the sting of eternal death for mankind. The transgression of God's law results in eternal death. "The soul who sins shall die" (Ezek. 18:20). No one should be rewarded for lawlessness, although some have, but their day of reckoning is coming. Martin Luther King cites, "The arc of the moral universe is long, but it is bent towards justice." Justice demanded the death of the transgressors of God's righteous and holy law, but mercy said no, and Jesus stepped in and absorbed the full impact of the wrath of God on our behalf.

"Who has believed our report? And to whom has the arm of the Lord been revealed? For He shall grow up before Him as a tender plant, and as a root out of dry ground. He has no form of comeliness; and when we see Him, there is no beauty that we should desire of Him. He is despised and rejected by men" (Isa. 53:1–3). The road to Calvary was a long and grueling one. Our Lord faced continuous scorn by his nation's leaders. His virgin birth was an object of constant ridicule and his good works maligned and criticized even while he lay dying.

To culminate the price of our salvation, "He was oppressed and He opened not His mouth; He was led as a lamb to the slaughter, and as a sheep before its shearers is silent, so He opened not His mouth" (Isa. 53:7). Reflecting over the brutal barbarity of Caesar's death, the famous Mark Antony lamented, "O Justice, thou art fled to brutish beasts, and men have lost their reason" (Shakespeare, *Julius Caesar*). Israel's leaders lost not only their reason but their souls as well. All who despise and reject the cross of Christ will deem themselves unworthy and unfit to live with him in glory.

We need to be reminded time and again what it cost God to purchase our salvation. God's hands were tied proverbially. He could not intervene and save his Son because Satan would cry foul. Nor could he spare him the consequence that was ours. He did what only God could do—cover the cross with a cloak of darkness and encourage and comfort his beloved Son, Jesus Christ. Thank you, Jesus, for dying in our place.

June 5

Teach Us How to Pray

Now it came to pass, as He was praying in a certain place, when He ceased, that one of His disciples said to Him, Lord, teach us to pray, as John also taught his disciples.
—Luke 11:1

With her fingers firmly grasping every individual bead of her rosary, Grandma Freda invoked Mary and the saints to ask Jesus to help her. When pain became her constant companion, Grandma's prayers became a huge part of her spiritual discipline. I was very impressed by her praying vigil, but sleep was more important to a growing young teenager back then. And quite frankly, I wasn't able to keep up with her prayerful discipline. After I left the big church to become an evangelical Christian, it finally dawned on me why Grandma spent huge chunks of her time in prayer. It was to talk to God about matters of concern to her.

Someone described *prayer* as an intimate conversation with a friend, and of course, that friend is our heavenly Father. As I grew in the faith, I discovered that prayer should be directed to God alone and not to any other earthly person. Jesus taught this model prayer in response to his disciple's request to teach them to pray. "Our Father in heaven, hallowed be Your name. Your kingdom come. Your will be done on earth as it is in heaven" (Luke 11:2). We should always approach God in endearing terms as we would our father, mother, or other respected elders.

Before bombarding him with our list of needs, we should spend quality time thanking him for all his many blessings to us. Since prayers should always be unselfish in substance, we present to him the needs of others, including our own. The health and welfare of our spouses, children, neighbors, coworkers, and kingdom-related materials should be prudently petitioned. Should we miss praying for our local, national, and international leaders? Of course not. We are admonished to pray for those who rule over us. "Therefore I exhort first of all that supplications, prayers, intercessions and giving of thanks be made for all men, for kings and all who are in authority, that we may lead a quiet and peaceable life in all godliness and reverence" (1 Tim. 2:1–2). After presenting our petitions to the Father, we should always conclude with the words "In the name of Jesus."

Prayers are diversified to suit the occasion; whether called on to say grace over a meal, open a Bible study, or give a closing prayer, the format can still work with fewer words. The Bible contains a long list of effective prayers that turned the hand of God and decided the fate of people and empires. These prayers attracted God's attention and evoked a speedy response from him. Take a look at Daniel 9:4–20 and a prayer of intercession for the people in Ezra 9:6–15. Jesus's prayer of intercession for his followers and Stephen's prayer for his executioners belong to the ages (John 17:1–26, Acts 7:60). These holy men of God put the interest of their fellowmen and even of their enemies ahead of their own and changed the destiny of people and nations.

As for my grandma, she prayed with sincerity and devotion, and I believe Jesus accepted her worship. We cannot differentiate between sincerity and hypocrisy; only God can read the heart. Neither are we called on by God to judge others. Someone once said, "Heaven will be filled with surprises. Some people you'd expect to be there won't be, and those you'd expect not to be there will be there." Pray that you get there.

June 6

Houston, We've Got a Problem

Now in those days, when the number of disciples was multiplying, there arose a complaint against the Hebrews by the Hellenists, because their widows were neglected in the daily distribution.

—Acts 6:1

A toilet malfunction is a serious problem here on earth, but if you're an astronaut on the International Space Station, the problem is magnified a thousand times over. You've probably experienced one of those days when everything that could go wrong went wrong, and so it was with the astronauts and cosmonauts on board the space station orbiting the earth. A critical cooling pump malfunctioned, shutting down the power to half the space station, affecting even the bathrooms. Needless to say, that problem was top priority; but thankfully, the situation was resolved after much anxiety, and the bathrooms became operational for business once more (space.com).

Problems are nothing new to our world; sin caused major problems that cost God dearly. Have you ever had major problems? Probably not. Let's assume you are problem-free. Ha ha! But let's see how God's people dealt with their problems in times past. Discrimination is nothing new; it popped its ugly head in the early church, and the apostles themselves were not free from it either. The Hellenists (non-Jews) were being overlooked for resources in favor of the Jewish believers. "There arose a complaint against the Hebrews by the Hellenists because their widows were neglected in the daily distribution" (Acts 6:1). Problems, problems! When they do arise, they provide us an opportunity to evaluate, take introspection, and adjust to changing circumstances around us. Could there be an opportunity for growth when problems arise? Obviously. The discrimination of the Hellenist widows gave rise to a better and smoother church organization. Do we become more efficient after solving a problem or less efficient? Of course, we get better at solving problems. Could problem-solving offer opportunities for growth? Sometimes we operate best under difficult situations.

Problems continued plaguing the early church, but the church grew exponentially, and the Holy Spirit was always one step ahead of the problems with fresh innovations for the growing church. "And He Himself gave some to be apostles, some prophets, some evangelists, and some pastors and teachers, for the equipping of the saints for the work of ministry, for the edifying of the body of Christ, till we all come to the unity of the faith and of the knowledge of the Son of God, to a perfect man to the measure of the stature of the fullness of Christ" (Eph. 4:11–13).

Some problems are good to have; more often than not, they shed light on issues that would otherwise be swept under the rug. If we ignore the symptoms of a disease, we run the risk of contracting the disease itself or, worse, dying from it. Which would you prefer, dealing with the symptoms or the disease itself? Problems usually point to situations that need redressing. When our automobile misfires, brakes scratch, or a red light pops up on the dashboard, if we ignore the warnings, be sure it will cost us later.

With this new approach on problem-solving, stop cursing the darkness, and search for the light switch. Lord, thanks for the occasional problems. They keep us on our knees and closer to you. God be with you, my friend, with your new problem-solving attitude.

June 7

Help Me, Somebody, Anybody!

Then He said to His disciples, the harvest truly is plentiful, but the laborers are few. Therefore pray the Lord of the harvest to send out laborers into His harvest.
—Matthew 9:37–38

For nine days, it lay trapped without water or food, and how it survived is still a mystery. The tornado that flattened Washington, Illinois, destroyed the home of Dexter, a little puppy. Going through the debris, which once were beautiful homes full of urban residents, a life was detected. A faint moan was enough to scramble rescuers to the spot. Dexter was discovered, but he had to be coaxed out of his prison with a few tasty hot dogs. His owner giddy with delight and Dexter unable to control his wagging tail made a happy ending to this catastrophic event (https://www.theguardian.com/world/2013/nov/29/illinois-tornado-dog-rescue-owner).

Dexter's moan for help reflects the condition of our world, including our neighbors and friends. It hurts real bad to hear of a suicide, but it stings enormously if we know that person personally. We often ask ourselves what mental anguish could have occupied the thoughts that precipitated the fatal step. Many will silently and steadily march toward this grim fate unless we stand in their way and do something about it. We must tell them of a loving, kind, compassionate, and amazing God. I have grown to appreciate my next-door neighbors who unfortunately are living in an illicit same-sex relationship. I do not condone their lifestyle but seek opportunities to befriend them and tell them of our amazing God. Throwing stones at them won't help; it will only draw us further apart.

Jesus's method is still the best tool for evangelism, and it has not been improved on ever since. Our Lord befriended people. He genuinely made friends with all classes of people, seeking their company. Is it any wonder he was called "the friend of sinners"? After befriending them, he sympathized with them, and who wouldn't? You're a friend now. You have won their confidence. You are no longer on the porch or standing beyond the fence or in the rain; you are in their living room now. He supplied their needs. Of course, being in the home opens your eyes to the genuine need of the person, whether they are physical or spiritual. After their needs are met, you bid them to follow Jesus (*Ministry of Healing*, p. 143, paraphrased).

This method of disciple making is very cheap, cost-effective, and long-lasting. Everybody benefits; lasting friendships are formed, the church grows, and costly soul-winning budgets are funneled to other critical church programs. Very few people walk with a sign on their chest stating, "Help me, somebody, anybody," but in reality, if the mask is torn from the occasional half smile or half-hearted hello, we will discover a patient in need of immediate surgery. Therefore we must be living witnesses ready to lend a helping hand to everyone with whom we come in contact. "I charge you therefore before God and the Lord Jesus Christ, who will judge the living and the dead at His appearing and His kingdom: preach the word! Be ready in season and out of season. Convince, rebuke, exhort, with all longsuffering and teaching" (2 Tim. 4:1–2).

Go out there, and make a difference in the life of somebody. The life you save might be your very own. God goes with you, my friend.

June 8

Who Is My Neighbor?

And a vision appeared to Paul in the night. A man of Macedonia stood and pleaded with him, saying, Come over and help us.

—Acts 16:9

Tribal wars and sectarian conflicts are positive proof that your neighbor may not necessarily be the one who lives across the street from you but those who live in faraway places who need your help. This summer, the nation of Kenya will be welcoming a new group of thrill seekers with a mission on their mind. They hope to engage the local village children in vacation Bible school, institute health programs in the community, and preach the gospel of Jesus. Let's see if they will meet the biblical definition of *neighborliness*.

"A certain man went down from Jerusalem to Jericho, and fell among thieves, who stripped him of his clothing, wounded him, and departed, leaving him half dead" (Luke 10:30). The wounded man was ignored by a priest, probably in a great hurry to deliver the morning sermon and could ill afford to be late, or so he thought. The Levite had important temple duties to perform as well and was too busy to assist, and besides, the robbers could be still lurking around. *Why risk my safety?* he must have thought. Then came a complete stranger, someone from another ethnicity and of another nationality, who just happened to pass that way.

He was moved with love and compassion and immediately attended to the wounded man. Let's run and catch the ending of the story: "On the next day when he departed, he took out two denarii, gave it to the innkeeper, and said to him, 'Take care of him; and whatever more you spend when I come again, I will repay you.' So which of these three do you think was neighbor to him who fell among thieves?" (Luke 10:35–36). It goes without saying, the Samaritan.

The Savior's parable pokes holes in the popularly held belief that your neighbor is the one who lives next to you. Your neighbor is anyone who needs your assistance. So where do we begin by being good neighbors? Ah yes, you're right, first at home. Why not? What benefit would it bring to you if you assist others in building their homes and yours is an absolute disaster? "If a man does not know how to rule his own house, how will he take care of the church of God?" (1 Tim. 3:5). You've probably heard the saying at some point "Charity begins at home," and who doesn't wish the best for the folks at home? It is a true saying that you cannot fool the folks at home; they see through you from miles away. I do not recommend wearing a hypocritical mask with the folks at home.

I still ask God, "How can I be a better husband, a better father, a better man, and a better neighbor?" We are constantly growing and adjusting to a changing world, and the roles and dynamics of the family are constantly evolving. How do we adjust? The empowerment and skills of the amazing feminine species have grown exponentially. How do we men adjust to this situation without surrendering our manhood and dignity? A good neighbor anticipates changes, as in the case of the good Samaritan story, and makes the necessary adjustments to affect the neighbor for the better. We are still heads of households but much wiser and efficient and less belligerent. Go out there, my friend, and be a good neighbor.

June 9

Eyes on the Prize

For I consider that the sufferings of this present time are not worthy to be compared with the glory which shall be revealed in us.

—Romans 8:18

A quick sniff in the air reveals a bounty for the taking, but honeybees don't release their precious investment without a fierce fight. If the honey badger desires to feast in delight, he must first get past hundreds of short-tempered guard bees. He charges the hive but runs into a frontal assault on his vulnerable snout. He retreats to lick his wounds, take a pause, and prepare for his next attack. Salivating over the sticky stuff and more determined than ever, he charges into the hive again; this time, he rips the cones open with his sharp claws, and dinner is served. The bees scatter in confusion, and the badger dines with delight. Reward outweighs present suffering (*National Geographic*).

The eternal reward of the saints is too exciting to be silent about. Someone once said that spectators at a game (us included) scream at the top of their lungs, but when talking about spiritual things, they maintain a hush-hush attitude. The ball games are temporal, and the players, along with their historic achievements, will fade away, but the things of God are eternal and will never pass away. "While we do not look at the things which are seen, but at the things which are not seen. For the things which are seen are temporary, but the things which are not seen are eternal" (Rom. 4:18). We have every reason to be cheerful, excited, and elated about our future because it is real.

The sheer bliss, joy, and happiness spoken of by the prophets fill us with great anticipation for our future home while giving us hope to cope with disappointments, sicknesses, pain, and suffering in this present life. Should we not keep our focus on the eternal things as Abraham? "By faith he dwelt in the land of promise as in a foreign country, dwelling in tents with Isaac and Jacob, the heirs with him of the same promise; for he waited for the city which has foundations whose builder and maker is God" (Heb. 11:9–10).

Abraham saw that beautiful city that John saw on the isle of Patmos, and he was content to continue living in tents until his Lord called him home. Moses also saw the glorious heavenly city that made the glamour of Egypt pale in contrast. "By faith Moses, when he became of age, refused to be called the son of Pharaoh's daughter, choosing rather to suffer affliction with the people of God than to enjoy the passing pleasures of sin, esteeming the reproach of Christ greater riches than the treasures of Egypt; for he looked to the reward" (Heb. 11:24–26).

As the finish line becomes more discernable, our feet may get a little tired and weary, but this is no time to quit, be discouraged, or lose focus. Be careful, dear friend; it will become very challenging as we approach the finish line. We have been warned that fears and doubts will arise to test our resolve, but we have nothing to fear except we forget the One "who is able to keep you from stumbling, and to present you faultless before the presence of His glory with exceeding joy" (Jude 24). In case we miss the point, John reminds us, "Be faithful until death, and I will give you the crown of life" (Rev. 2:10). Has God ever reneged on his promises? Absolutely not. Be faithful.

June 10

Imprisoned but Free

Rejoice in the Lord always. Again I will say rejoice.

—Philippians 4:4

With the executioner's ax staring him in the face, Paul kept himself very busy comforting the discouraged, writing the scripture, and winning Caesar's household to Christ. Citizenship has its privileges. A Roman citizen could not be scourged, could not be crucified, could travel anywhere unhindered, was entitled to a fair trial, could invoke citizenship privileges, and could appeal his sentence all the way to the supreme emperor. As a native-born citizen of the Roman Empire, Paul invoked all of these rights, but he had exhausted all his appeals; his mission on earth was drawing to a close. Having accomplished his gigantic mission, God was calling him to rest from his labor.

Even during his long trials, which spanned many years, Paul's heart was with the churches he helped start. It became apparent from the many epistles he wrote from jail that his prison cell had replaced Jerusalem as the headquarters of the infant church. Though confined, he received a steady stream of visitors and correspondence concerning the growth, status, and health of the churches. Interestingly, his prison became the source of many of his transformational epistles, including Ephesians, Philippians, and 2 Timothy. But now he had exhausted all his court appeals. The handwriting was on the wall; a date had been set for his execution. "For I am already being poured out as drink offering, and the time of my departure is at hand. I have fought a good fight, I have finished the race, and I have kept the faith. Finally, there is laid up for me the crown of righteousness, which the Lord, the Righteous Judge, will give to me on that Day, and not to me only but also to all who have loved His appearing" (2 Tim. 4:6–8).

Though imprisoned and chained to a Roman guard, Paul was liberated by the peace that comes only from knowing Jesus Christ as Lord and Savior. God was calling his faithful witness to rest, but he still had some unfinished business to do. Far from being restrained by chains and prison walls, Paul converted his successive jailors to faith in Christ and spread the gospel even to Caesar's household. His imprisonment turned into full-blown, active correspondence with the churches now that he was deactivated from the battlefield.

We may be enslaved to a long list of creditors, but in Christ, we are free. We may not be particularly proud of still paying student loans, mortgages, and credit card debts, but we are free in Jesus, who has canceled our debt of sin. Even if we may never be free from the circumstantial restrains that confine us, we can still claim freedom in Jesus, who will one day liberate us from these circumstances. Some are trapped in sickly bodies, but I have good news for you, dear friend. One day and very soon, we will inherit a glorious imperishable body. To the brothers and sisters confined in penal institutions, though you may never see the free world again, Christ's coming will set you free.

We have much to be thankful for; we simply cannot allow our surroundings or circumstances dictate our joy in Christ. Paul and Silas were beaten to a pulp, but they were singing and praising God. The jailors and prisoners were a little bit confused; they were accustomed to hearing swearing and complaining from condemned prisoners, but these men were actually thanking God for being counted worthy to suffer for him. Do you desire such faith? If you are currently suffering for Jesus, just say no to these trial lawyers offering you lots of cash.

June 11

Walking Where Jesus Walked

Yes, and all who desire to live godly in Christ will suffer persecution.
—2 Timothy 3:12

His police record was squeaky-clean; not even a citation was found. No one could point an accusing finger at him, yet he was tried, declared innocent, flogged, condemned guilty, and executed. No one on earth fits this profile except Jesus, the Son of the Most High God. Everyone, at some point, has been guilty of some misconduct, a little lawbreaking of some sort, but no one can accuse Jesus of any wrongdoing. Speaking to his disciples one day, Jesus candidly admitted, "The ruler of this world is coming, and he has nothing in Me" (John 14:30). No human dare make such a declaration. Satan could not claim Christ as a victim of his guile and sophistry. Jesus did not succumb to sin by any thought, word, or deed. Not even a glance of indifference or a nod of contempt was found in him, yet we are called to walk in his shoes. How can this ever be achieved?

Here is the secret: "I have been crucified with Christ; it is no longer I who live, but Christ lives in me; and the life which I now live in the flesh I live by faith in the Son of God, who loved me and gave Himself for me" (Gal. 2:20). God's biddings are always enabling. He has made it possible for anyone who desires to live a morally upright life to overcome sin and live soberly and righteously in this world. You may say, "Boy, that's a tall order," and it is. While it is true we have been completely deformed by sin and that the way of righteousness seems a daunting challenge, remember the words of Paul: "It is no longer I who live, but Christ lives in me." When Christ lives in the heart, his bidding becomes enabling. He enables us to be victorious in his great strength.

Yes, the way to God is daunting and challenging; had it not been, many more would be on that path, but it is because of its restrictions that only a few choose to remain on that course. "Enter by the narrow gate; for wide is the gate and broad is the way that leads to destruction, and there are many who go in by it. Because narrow is the gate and difficult is the way which leads to life, and there a few who find it" (Matt. 7:13–14). Don't be fooled; even Jesus admitted that the way to God has restrictions. You simply can't continue drinking vodka and smoke Marlboro and expect to slide into heaven.

The way of Christ calls for a life of obedience, self-discipline, and restraint. Paul nods in affirmation: "You therefore must endure hardship as a good soldier of Jesus Christ. No one engaged in warfare entangles himself with the affairs of this life, that he may please him who enlisted him as a soldier. And also if anyone competes in athletics, he is not crowned unless he competes according to the rules" (2 Tim. 2:3–5). He must abide by the rules, and that's what most people are running away from—the rules, the Ten Commandments. If we throw the rules out, what kind of game do we have without rules?

Abiding in Jesus entails walking by faith and obeying his commandments. If it were easy, the churches would be packed, but everything is achievable through Christ, who strengthens us. How many things can I do through Christ, who strengthens me? All things. Now go out there and do likewise. Walk where Jesus walked by having faith in him and obeying his Word just as he kept his Father's will and abode in his Word.

June 12

I Pledge Allegiance

Let us be glad and rejoice and give Him glory, for the marriage of the lamb has come, and His wife has made herself ready.
—Revelation 19:7

"Ladies and gentlemen, please rise to your feet to welcome the bride." The doors swung wide open, and all eyes are riveted on the stunningly beautiful bride. There she was, wearing an exquisite long white dress with an extended train dragging behind her. She slowly made her way to the altar, where her anxious prince charming was waiting. He gently extended his strong hand to assist her in climbing the steps to the altar. With their backs to the audience, they took the solemn vow to love each other till death.

Did you know that upon accepting Jesus as Savior and Lord, we become members of his body, the church? And are you aware that the body of Christ, the church, which includes you and me, is in fact the bride of Christ? "So continuing daily with one accord in the temple, and breaking bread from house to house, they ate their food with gladness and simplicity of heart, praising God and having favor with all the people. And the Lord added to the church daily those who were being saved" (Acts 2:46–47).

The vow we take in our baptism pledging to be faithful to our Lord (the Groom) is equivalent to a marriage vow. Since we have pledged ourselves to him for life, we will reject the advances of all potential suitors, regardless of how enticing their offerings appear to be. Israel, God's beautiful bride, had a problem with suitors, for she had delicate eyes. "Return, O backsliding children, says the Lord; for I am married to you, I will take you, one from a city and two from a family, and I will bring you to Zion" (Jer. 3:14). God loved his wayward bride (Israel) and was constantly wooing her back from her adulterous ways, but Israel had an obsession for her idols and was oblivious of God's love until it was too late. "When Israel was a child, I loved him, and out of Egypt I called My son. As they called them, so they went from them; they sacrifice to the Baals, and burned incense to carved images" (Hosea 11:1–2).

We no longer bow down to idols; we're too sophisticated for that, but there are modern equivalents. Can we name a few? "Better not mess with me during the NFL, NBA, and NHL playoffs. The Miami Heat game is coming on tonight." "Mm, I think

I'll skip prayer meeting tonight. Target is having a sale on shoes. I'll see what they have to add to my collection." Modern idols can take insidious forms, but one thing is predictable: if they occupy the center of our attraction, they take the place of God.

Nevertheless, the Groom (Christ) is patiently waiting. What can the bride (us) do to be ready for the wedding (Second Coming)? "The night is far spent, the day is at hand, therefore let us cast off the works of darkness, and let us put on the armor of light. Let us walk properly as in the day, not in revelry and drunkenness, not in lewdness and lust, not in strife and envy" (Rom. 13:12–13). The coming of the Lord is near at hand, and it doesn't require rocket science to figure it out; the signs are everywhere. His bride, the church (you and me), must repent and pray, ask for the baptism of the Holy Spirit, and tell others of his wonderful love. And this, my friend, will get us ready for the wedding.

June 13

Late Again but Made It

Therefore you also must be ready for the Son of Man is coming at an hour you do not expect.

—Matthew 24:44

Sally (name changed) lived very close to the school she attended, so close that she could peer into the classrooms from her bedroom window, yet she was perpetually late for class. Sally is not alone in her tardiness to honor time obligations. We live within about ten- to fifteen-minute drive to Baltimore-Washington International (BWI) Airport and actually created a nightmare scenario for ourselves by being late for our much-anticipated vacation to the Bahamas. We were destined to depart BWI via U.S. Airways to Charlotte, where we were to take our connecting flight to Miami, but all our fantastic plans were about to evaporate in thin air as we stood begging at the flight gate for a slot on the next flight departing BWI. Our headaches had just begun.

The flight attendants had seen it all before, and we were completely at their mercy. However, my wife is not the type who usually takes no for a final answer. She has a knack for wiggling her way out of sticky situations. Our lucky break came when she hinted to the agent that our cruise coincided with her birthday; fortunately for us, the agent shared the same birthday, and the rest was for the history books. We were on our merry way, but we were not out of the woods yet. We still had a connecting flight to catch in Charlotte to make it to Miami. We had to be at the cruise terminal one hour before departure. God is simply amazing. He actually smiled on us, and we made it, with just a few minutes to spare. Tired and exhausted, we slumped into our chairs. How much trouble we could have spared ourselves if only we had been on time?

Our Lord Jesus is all too familiar with this sort of tardiness—mortals waiting to the very last second to make life's most important decisions. Noah's friends and neighbors made light of his preaching while the wild animals, mysteriously guided by unseen hands, marched into the ark two by two and in pairs of sevens. When the lightning flashed and dark clouds began unleashing their cargo in furious torrents, the crowd made a hasty attempt to enter the ark, but it was too late; the door was shut by God himself. Father used to tell us, "You can never be too early, but you can always be too late." Why did I not heed Father's advice by being early for my flight since I live very close to Baltimore-Washington International Airport?

"Watch therefore, for you do not know what hour your Lord is coming" (Matt. 24:42). The blessing of not knowing the day and hour of Jesus's coming allows the people of God to be sincere and intentional in their service to him. In other words, we certainly don't want to party, as Noah's generation, to the very last minute and then hasten to church to repent. No. We want to live godly every moment of the day so others can see Jesus in us. The parable of the ten talents is a reminder to us that we should occupy till he comes. "So he called ten of his servants, delivered to them ten minas, and said to them, do business till I come" (Luke 19:13). Doing business for Jesus entails investing in the kingdom by helping others get ready for that great and glorious day.

"And this gospel of the kingdom will be preached in all the world as a witness to all the nations and then the end will come" (Matt. 24:14). I have learned my lesson on time consciousness, and by God's grace, I shall not be late for his Second Coming.

June 14

Don't Forget

You shall teach them to your children, speaking of them when you sit in your house, when you walk by the way, when you lie down, and when you rise up.
—Deuteronomy 11:19

The grandmother of a neighborhood friend tied a little cord to his pinky finger to remind him what particular grocery item to purchase at the store, but guess what happened when he got to the store? He forgot what he came to purchase. Regrettably, my childhood buddy preoccupied himself with many nonessentials to the extent that he forgot what was essential. Grandma was obviously furious when he came back without the grocery, imploring her to repeat the purchase order.

God's memory is vast and needs no reminding. He foresaw the forgetfulness of his people and instructed Israel to teach his words to the new and upcoming generation. "You shall teach them diligently to your children, and shall talk of them when you sit in your house, when you walk by the way, when you lie down, and when you rise up. You shall bind them as a sign on your hand and they shall be as frontlets between your eyes" (Deut. 6:7–8). Someone once said, "Give me your young children from zero to ten, and I will make them Catholics for life." Does godly childhood training really pay? Of course, it pays great dividends.

Hannah understood this principle very well. She taught young Samuel all she could and then delivered him to the high priest Eli. Although he witnessed the wickedness and profanity of Eli's sons, his mother's training kept him pure (1 Sam. 2:11–18). Having won the favor of the pharaoh's daughter to raise her very own son, Jochebed taught Moses about God, the garden misfortune, the flood, and the patriarchs Abraham, Isaac, and Jacob (Exod. 2:7–10). The scribes and Pharisees admitted Jesus did not attend their schools yet was full of wisdom, thanks to his early training by Mary and Joseph (John 7:15). Early childhood training works, and it pays great dividends.

Wherever Abraham, Isaac, and Jacob went, they dotted the landscape with altars, leading their families in worshipping Jehovah, the only true God. "And he went on his journey from the South as far as Bethel to the place where his tent had been at the beginning, between Bethel and Ai, to the place of the altar which he had made there at first. And there Abraham called on the name of the Lord" (Gen. 13:3–4).

Erecting family altars are quite different now from biblical times, but the principle remains the same—starting and ending the day with God. I love this little anecdote: If Jesus were passing through your neighborhood early this morning, would he hear the beautiful songs of Zion wafting from your home? How long does he have to wait for his chosen people to pick up their Bibles and read from his holy Word? Or better yet, would we be aware of his presence? Or would he have to turn away because of the altars erected to the gods of this world? Those who are in tune with the divine will sense his presence and invite him in.

"Train up a child in the way he should go, and when he is old he will not depart from it" (Prov. 22:6). Our son, who has returned to the faith from the far country, is testimony to the truthfulness of this text. Do your part every day, keep the family altar fire lit, and let God do what he does best—saving our children.

June 15

A Little Child Shall Lead Them Part 1

But Isaac spoke to Abraham his father and said, my father! And he said, here I am, my son.
Then he said, look, the fire and the wood, but where is the lamb for a burnt offering?
—Genesis 22:7

He was told he was a child of promise, that the family inheritance would someday be his, but now he must grapple with the thought of dying young before the fulfillment of that promise. We do not know how old Isaac was, maybe seventeen, but old enough to carry a pack of wood. What transpired next is a story for the ages (Gen. 22:6). After asking his father for the lamb and being told that he was in fact the lamb, Isaac willingly obliged. What a triumph for parental upbringing and child obedience and compliance! God taught Abraham the greatest story ever taught, that Isaac is symbolic of Jesus, who would lay down his life for the sins of the world.

"Therefore My Father loves Me, because I lay down My life that I may take it up again. No one takes it from Me, but I lay it down of Myself. I have power to lay it down, and I have power to take it again. This command I have received from My Father" (John 10:17–18). There must have been a very close bond between Abraham and Isaac to have caused him to forgo his future inheritance for the spur-of-the-moment decision by his father. Likewise, there exists a oneness among God the Father, the Son, and the Holy Ghost that we may not fully understand but must accept by faith. "And now, O Father, glorify Me together with Yourself, with the glory which I had with You before the world was. . . . Father, I desire that they also whom You gave Me may be with Me where I am, that they may behold My glory which You have given Me; for You loved Me before the foundation of the world" (John 17:5, 24).

As Isaac submitted himself to Abraham, his father, likewise, Jesus subordinated his will to that of his Father. The strong young man who could have rebelled against his father's command completely submitted his will to that of his wise, godly father, even though he did not understand what his dad was doing. Childlike trust—that's what it takes, and we are called on to exercise that type of trust in God. Jesus emphasizes the point: "Assuredly, I say to you, unless you are converted and become as little children, you will by no means enter the kingdom of heaven" (Matt. 18:3). Here it is again, childlike trust. Children are trusting, very trusting, and they have to be because they cannot fend for themselves and are dependent on others for sustenance. God wants us to trust him in like manner.

Are children pliable? Can you mold and shape them into something you desire? Of course. God loves to fashion us like children into his masterpiece. Children are forgiving; you spank them now, and the next moment, they're back in your arms. When we are chastened by God, we hold no grudges, right? Children are brutally honest. Remember the saying "My mother told me to tell you she is not home." Oh yes, they tell it like it is, and so should we. With all these wonderful childlike qualities, God wants his people to possess the traits and faith of little children. However, he wants us to grow up. Of course, little children grow up. Are you growing in faith and in the knowledge of Jesus Christ? Do you have the childlike trust it takes to have Jesus give you a makeover?

A Little Child Shall Lead Them Part 2

And said, assuredly, I say to you, unless you are converted and become as little children, you will by no means enter the kingdom of heaven.

—Matthew 18:3

Long before I knew the definition of the word *counselor*, I found myself often mediating disputes between my parents. This often put me in a difficult position in being counselor one moment and an obedient son the next. Clearly, I had no idea what I was doing; but since I embraced Christianity in my midteens, the Lord God Almighty saw it fit to use me to heal frictions in my parents' relationship.

"Before I formed you in the womb I knew you; before you were born I sanctified you; I ordained you a prophet to the nations" (Jer. 1:5). Several children were born destined to become leaders before they even had a choice in the matter. "Then she made a vow and said, 'O Lord of host, if You will indeed look on the affliction of Your maidservant, and remember me, and not forget Your maidservant, but will give Your maidservant a male child, then I will give him to the Lord all the days of his life, and no razor shall come upon his head'" (1 Sam. 1:11). Thank God for praying mothers. Moses's childhood took a similar course as Samuel's: "By faith Moses, when he was born, was hidden three months by his parents, because they saw he was a beautiful child; and they were not afraid of the king's command" (Heb. 11:23). Parents do decide the destiny of their children. How sad it is today that parents are surrendering their children to Hollywood film directors for training.

We are probably familiar with the story of the family going for a drive on a beautiful sunlit day. Halfway into the drive, the wife remarked, "Honey, I think we are going in the wrong direction." Confidently, her husband assured her that everything was under control. The wife was puzzled. "Honey, I think we should have been there by now. Turn around. We are going in the wrong direction."

It takes courage to admit you're on the wrong course and even more courage to turn around, and of course, we must admit this does not come naturally. "Every good gift and every perfect gift is from above, and comes down from the Father of Lights, with whom there is no variation or shadow of turning" (James 1:17). To admit failure, guilt, or admission of sin is a childlike and godly attribute. This brings into focus Jesus's saying, "Assuredly, I say to you, unless you are converted and become as little children, you will by no means enter the kingdom of heaven" (Matt. 18:3).

Everyone enters the spiritual kingdom as a newborn babe, which means you grow and develop into a child and ultimately adulthood. Jesus made this point absolutely clear to Nicodemus. "Most assuredly, I say to you, unless one is born again, you cannot see the kingdom of God" (John 3:3). We grow by faith in God, and faith is not automatic. It does not grow on trees, and we don't receive it by drinking some mixed cocktail brew, nor is it attained by dieting. How then is faith attained? It must be believed, accepted, and practiced. My friend's ten-year-old son said to him, "Daddy, I think we must pray." We must believe God as little children trust their parents and see him go to work in our behalf.

June 17

In the World but Not Part of It

I have given them your word; and the world has hated them because they are not of the world, just as I am not of the world.
—John 17:14

American wolves are extremely social animals despite their bad publicity by uninformed observers. Wolves live in packs headed by an alpha male and his mate. They have strict rules governing pack behavior; repeat offenders of these rules are punished harshly and may even be banished from the pack for life. For example, when the dinner bell is rung, a strict pecking order comes into play. His and her royal highness must eat to their full first before all others, and then other pack members follow in order of seniority. This, of course, is to ensure the health of the breeders and the continuation of the species. Should any member, however hungry, disturb the royal couple at the table, punishment is usually swift and harsh, and banishment from the pack is a likely possibility.

Though the believer is not banished from society yet, someday we may very well be. In some parts of the world, believers are already being viewed with much suspicion, especially by those emboldened in lawlessness. Jesus was not optimistic about his followers' acceptance in the world. "They are not of the world, just as I am not of this world" (John 17:16). Although the believer has deep genetic and familial ties and must conduct human relations, social functions, and business dealings with others, he really does not belong to the world. Let me clarify: "Do not lay up for yourselves treasures on earth, where moths and rust destroy and where thieves break in and steal; but lay up for yourselves treasures in heaven, where thieves do not break in and steal. For where your treasure is there your heart will be also" (Matt. 6:19–21).

Like the banished wolf that may look like his comrades and have all the distinguishing qualities of the other pack members but does not belong to the pack, likewise, the believer shares similar physical qualities with his unbelieving friends but does not belong to this world. The song by Jim Reeves puts it succinctly: "This world is not my home. I'm just a-passing through. My treasures are laid up somewhere beyond the blue. The angels beckon me from heaven's open door, and I can't feel at home in this world anymore." Like a nomad who pitches his tent temporarily for the night, the pilgrim passes through this life aware that a better country awaits him or her. "But now they desire a better, that is, a heavenly country. Therefore God is not ashamed to be called their God, for He has prepared a city for them" (Heb. 11:16).

Since your heavenly home is real and is not far away, are you anticipating what will soon be yours—an eternal residence, an immortal body, and life in the presence of God? Where will you choose to dwell? Is it in the countryside or in the city? Do you plan to do interplanetary travel and meet other members of the unfallen worlds? How about meeting your guardian angel and asking him about the many times he pulled you from the brink of disaster? During my early Christian experience, I had tons of questions to ask Jesus; but with maturity, they have all but disappeared. They've been answered down here. I long for the heavenly Canaan, don't you? Work as we know it will be a thing of the past and every aspiration attempted achieved. See you up in heaven.

June 18

Dear Dad

You have seen what I did to the Egyptians, and how I bore you on eagle's wings and brought you to myself.

—Exodus 19:4

While his friends were out socializing and having fun with one another at the bar, Dad chose to spend quality time with us, his family. Happy is the home where Dad spends quality time with his family and Mom works magic with the cooking pots. Who could ask for anything better? Dad was a product of his time: stern, rugged, funny, industrious, and delightfully sociable. Mother, on the other hand, was the softer of the two but no pushover either. Dad spared no effort in drilling hard work and a military-type discipline into us. How prophetic were his words: "What I am doing now you may not appreciate, but later down in life, you will thank me for it." Boy, was he ever so correct! Regrettably, I did not have the insight then to fully appreciate his training for life's difficult moments.

In spite of his love and charm offensive to us, I chose a path of rebellion and resentment against his authority. I avoided him like a plague, communicated very little with him, and counted the days when I would be free from his authority. Needless to say, that wish came back to haunt me for the rest of my life. With the passage of time, I grew up and migrated to the United States, and his letters and Christmas cards found their way to my door wherever I wandered. I was somewhat grateful but did not fully appreciate his affection for me until he was no longer with us. Oh, how I missed him when he was no longer there!

In hindsight, I deprived myself of his encyclopedic memory. The knowledge and history of past generations, which he would have been happy to share with me, was forever gone. I missed the opportunity of a father-and-son relationship, which would have been mine to enjoy. My loss was incalculable, but all was not lost; what I failed to gain directly from him I learned indirectly. In retrospect, I learned some very valuable lessons by observing this remarkable man God placed in my life. How true are the words "You never miss the water until the well runs dry."

Besides his genetic gifts, I have been spared much trouble and heartache by walking in the footsteps of this remarkable man. His character traits are embedded in us. His work ethics, love for family, social skills, and generosity to others I embrace with gratitude. Thanks be to God for the stable home, part of his legacy to us, that provided the foundation for my own home. Thanks, Dad, for staying married to Mom, giving me the example and discipline to be married and to stay married. I wish I could have thanked you in person for all the kind gestures and overtures that went by unappreciated. I thought I was punishing you by spurning your love, but in essence, I was "cutting off my nose to spite my face." Even though I did not appreciate you in my youth and later the oceans separated us, you left me a rich legacy that is above monetary value. Everything I am today, Dad, I owe it all to you. You are truly my hero.

"When Israel was a child I loved him, and out of Egypt I called My son. . . . I taught Ephraim to walk, taking them by the arms, but they did not know that I healed them" (Hosea 11:1, 3). God pursues us with his amazing love and kindness; even when we spurn his love and despise his overtures to us, he loves us anyway. I love you, Dad.

June 19

I Find No Fault in Him

Pilate then went out again, and said to them, behold, I am bringing Him out to you, that you may know that I find no fault in Him.

—John 19:4

The Romans bragged about being a nation of law and order, yet Pontius Pilate, governor of Judea and proficient in Roman law, went on record, saying, "I find no fault in Him." Nevertheless, they crucified our Lord Christ Jesus without a shred of guilt found in him. The false charges brought against Jesus Christ should have been summarily dismissed, but through a system rife with corruption, Jesus was tried, condemned, and executed even when declared innocent by a judge under Roman law.

Pilate was not the only one who was unable to find fault in Jesus; no one else could, not even his enemies. He made a conscious decision not to sin. Stepping down from the bosom of the Father and the Holy Spirit, Jesus clothed himself in the garment of Adam's fallen nature. He successfully fended off all the attacks of the devil and conquered sin, where Adam failed. Adam disobeyed God and sinned through his unrestrained appetite and lack of appreciation for the Word of God. Christ, on the other hand, when tempted to turn stones into bread to satisfy his hunger, had an altogether different response, choosing instead to trust his Father and abide by his Word. "Now when the tempter came to Him, he said, if you are the Son of God, command that these stones become bread. But He answered and said, 'Man shall not live by bread alone, but by every word that proceeds from the mouth of God'" (Matt. 4:3–4). Christ triumphed over sin by putting God's Word ahead of his own physical needs. Should we do the same? Can we actually live on the Word of God? Had Adam remembered this scripture verse, things could have been altogether different.

Before Pilate made his infamous declaration of Jesus's innocence, the Father had already declared his favor in Christ: "When He had been baptized, Jesus came up immediately from the water; and behold, the heavens were opened to Him, and He saw the Spirit of God descending like a dove and alighting upon Him. And suddenly a voice came from heaven, saying, 'This is My beloved Son, in whom I am well pleased'" (Matt. 3:16–17). Christ himself declared he did not need the affirmation of men. What really mattered to him was the Father's approval of his work and ministry. "Now when He was in Jerusalem at the Passover, during the feast, many believed in His name when they saw the signs which He did. But Jesus did not commit Himself to them, because He knew all men. And had no need that anyone should testify of Him, for He knew what was in men" (John 2:23–25).

Satan threw everything at Christ, including the kitchen sink. Utilizing the religious leaders who had just condemned the innocent Lamb of God, Satan continued using them to hurl insults against Christ. But one thing stands true in their mockery: "himself he cannot save." Having thrown himself at the mercy and will of his Father, to have saved himself would have shown distrust in his Father's providence. Remember his saying "Father, if it is Your will, take this cup away from Me; nevertheless not My will but Yours, be done" (Luke 22:42). The just requirement of God's law was met by Christ's sacrifice. "For He made Him who knew no sin to be sin for us, that we might become the righteousness of God" (2 Cor. 5:21). Are you covered by the blood?

June 20

We Shall Behold Him

Then the sign of the Son of Man will appear in heaven, and then all the tribes of the earth will mourn, and they will see the Son of Man coming on the clouds of heaven with power and great glory.

—Matthew 24:30

Coming out of a disastrous 2012 losing season, nobody expected the Boston Red Sox to win their division, let alone be the 2013 World Series champions. Having had a losing season and intent on shaking the box, management fired the coach and hired new players. The Sox quickly turned things around and silenced their many critics. When the dust all settled, Bostonians turned out in droves to celebrate their hometown heroes, who made them forget the sad events of the devastating bombing. We were all Bostonians on that memorable day as the champions rode in town to a ticker-tape parade. Crowds waved wildly as confetti rained down on the champs.

One day very soon, a little cloud will appear in the east. It will enlarge itself as it makes its way to the earth, and it will explode in dazzling glory as Jesus will make his appearance to this earth to gather his people. "Behold, He is coming with clouds, and every eye will see Him. Even those who pierce Him. And all the tribes of the earth will mourn because of Him. Even so, amen" (Rev. 1:7).

The newspapers and television networks jockey among themselves at predicting breaking news even if they have to retract their errors the next day, but no one is interested in touching this awesome news—the nearness of Christ's Second Coming. "Now learn this parable from the fig tree: When its branch has already become tender and puts forth leaves, you know that summer is near. So you also, when you see all these things, know that it is near, at the doors!" (Matt. 24:32–33). The wars, senseless killings, crimes, political upheavals, natural disasters, and violence against the poor all point to Jesus's coming and the climactic end of the world.

We don't want to be the ones who will mourn at Christ's coming; we want to be the ones rejoicing at his presence. "And it will be said in that day: Behold, this is our God; we have waited for Him, and He will save us. This is the Lord; we have waited for Him; we will be glad and rejoice in His salvation" (Isa. 25:9). These words should be music to our ears because one day we are going to repeat these beautiful words at Christ's coming.

We can almost hear the rumbling of the approaching storm. "And do this, knowing the time, that now it is high time to awake out of sleep; for now our salvation is nearer than when we first believed. The night is far spent, the day is at hand. Therefore let us cast off the works of darkness, and let us put on the armor of light. Let us walk properly, as in the day, not in revelry and drunkenness, not in lewdness and lust, not in strife and envy. But put on the Lord Jesus Christ, and make no provision for the flesh, to fulfill its lusts" (Rom. 13:11–14). Are you ready for Christ's coming, getting ready, or not ready at all? I pray you will be ready for that great day when he will eradicate sin once and for all and usher in his reign of righteousness.

June 21

A God Close at Hand

On the last day, that great day of the feast, Jesus stood and cried out, saying, if anyone thirsts, let him come to Me and drink.

—John 7:37

Her calf stumbles and crashes to the ground from dehydration. Mom gives him a gentle nudge with her foot to urge him on, but it's too late; he has lost the will to live. Under the blistering heat of the Sahara Desert, an elephant mom and her infant son are making their way through a hostile and dry desert to fetch a drink. Although the journey is risky, she has no other choice but to get some water to help replenish her meager milk reserve, but Junior has a problem. He is getting weaker and lagging behind as time passes by. He finally succumbs to his thirst and is unable to go any further. Mom is torn between quenching her own thirst and comforting her dying son (*National Geographic*).

The calf's thirst reflects the plight of humans; we are thirsty but don't seem to appreciate the drink that can quench our thirst. While some are drinking from false cisterns that make them thirstier than before, Jesus offers the water of life: himself. Jesus is the drink that satisfies, and many simply don't know who he is or where he can be found. However, Jesus is very near and convenient to those who genuinely seek him. He makes himself available to them. "Then the Spirit said to Philip go near and overtake this chariot. So Philip ran to him, and heard him reading the Prophet Isaiah, and said, do you understand what you are reading? And he said, how can I, unless someone guides me? And he asked Philip to come up and sit with him" (Acts 8:29–31).

God knows all those who are desirous of salvation and moves heaven and earth to find them. The Ethiopian eunuch, being a sincere seeker of truth, apparently purchased a copy of the scripture in Jerusalem but did not understand the Jesus talk there. He needed someone to personally introduce him to Christ. Before you think of going to China, India, Africa, or some other faraway field, there is a mission field sitting right before your eyes. My old boss usually told me when I went searching for something sitting under my nose, "You're sitting on the horse and asking for it." The mission fields staring at you every day are the people you interact with.

"And I heard the voice of the Lord, saying: Whom shall We send, and who will go for Us? Then I said, here am I! Send me. And He said, go and tell this people" (Isa. 6:8). We must be in tune with the Holy Spirit to sense the need to evangelize. God will not use idle and unwilling hands, and he has a million ways of accomplishing his purposes without us, but he wants us to be instruments in the salvation of our fellow men.

Where do I begin in evangelizing those around me? Start by praying for the person closer to you. If the person is grouchy, that's even a better start. Seek an opportunity to do them a good favor. Seldom will someone return a good favor with evil, and even if they do, the Bible says to pray for them anyway because it is the right thing to do. Attending to the needs of another person changes their attitude toward us and hopefully to Christ for their good. There is an awesome work to be done; enlist God's help in your witnessing campaign, and someday shoot me an e-mail or text me about it.

Forbid Them Not

But Jesus said, let the little children come to Me, and do not forbid them, for of such is the kingdom of heaven.

—Matthew 19:14

It had all the trappings of an extravagant wedding—the atmosphere was ornate and elegant, the guests had arrived, and the long wait was over finally. The words rang out: "The birthday girl is here. Please rise to greet her." Mom and Dad were beaming with delight as they directed the proceedings for Sonia's (name changed) coming-of-age birthday celebration at sixteen. Her young friends strode into the ballroom hand in hand, elegantly dressed with a smile of pride on their faces. They stopped briefly midway, bowed, and flashed a smile to a waiting camerawoman. They then took their place in a two-line formation along gender lines. Finally, everyone rose to their feet in applause as the birthday girl made her appearance, much to the delight of the glowing audience.

"Behold, children are a heritage from the Lord, the fruit of the womb is a reward, like arrows in the hand of a warrior, so are the children of one's youth. Happy is the man who has his quiver full of them" (Ps. 127:3–5). Children pass through this corridor of youthfulness only once, and every opportunity should be maximized to make their childhood as pleasant and memorable as possible. Do meaningful things that your children will appreciate as they grow older and look back through memory lane. It doesn't have to be a grand ball; it could be a simple sleepover properly supervised.

Today's children are tomorrow's leaders; the values we instill in them will determine how they lead and shape the church and the nation when we gracefully make our exit from the earth. Jesus understood the importance of little children and took time out with the little ones. He made many references to little children, and his message was simple enough for them to understand. Since they were part of his audience, it is unthinkable to assume that he did not create special stories to suit their needs.

A war is waging for the allegiance of children. Everybody seems interested in them; after all, they will be tomorrow's consumer. Their path is mined with many destructive instruments. The entertainment industry corrupts their young minds. Musicians point their lewd lyrics and crafts at this vulnerable population. Electronic engineers have them hooked to their amazing machines. Should we just stand by idly while our children are being enslaved by these demonic masters? No. We should pray for them and stand in the gap for our youth and children. How much more should we fill the lives of these dear ones with good and positive experiences to fend off these demons?

Shouldn't we be the guardians of all the children around us? But of course. Because of their innocence, criminals have them in their crosshairs (gunsight), and Satan will spare no effort in enticing them to himself. Should we not make them a priority in our prayers to lead them to the Pearl of great price, the Lord Jesus Christ?

"Train up a child in the way he should go, and when he is old he will not depart from it" (Prov. 22:6). Spend quality time with your children, hug them often, affirm them continuously, ask them which famous figure in history is their role model, and remind them there is still time to attain their aspirations. Hang portraits of famous people in their rooms; remember, Christopher Columbus was influenced by a picture of a ship in his room. God be with you in raising your children or grandchildren.

June 23

Proving God in Difficult Times

What shall I render to the Lord for all His benefits towards me?
—Psalm 116:12

My one-and-one-half-year-old grandson, LaShawn, is very generous sometimes. When he's in a good mood, he gives Grandpa everything in sight, including his favorite toys. His sour side is quite predictable; he stops giving and focuses inward, on himself.

LaShawn's attitude reflects the behavior of most mortals. We give to God's work when we're in the mood, when times are good, when it is convenient, when there is a surplus or a demand. Sad to say, such a giving pattern stunts our growth and does nothing to prepare us for the difficult days ahead. Thank God for the examples given in the scripture that can build our faith. The widow of Zarephath, though poor, was tested and is an excellent example to us in the department of stewardship and selflessness.

"So she said, 'As the Lord your God lives, I do not have bread, but only a handful of flour in a bin, and a little oil in a jar; and see, I am gathering a couple of sticks that I may go in and prepare it for myself and my son that we may eat it, and die.' And Elijah said to her, do not fear; go and do as you have said, but make me a small cake from it first, and bring it to me; and afterward make some for yourself and your son" (1 Kings 17:12–13). Did you hear that? What principle is being highlighted here? First, God and his kingdom are primary; they come first. Second, faithfulness to God begins in that which is least. To be trusted with much, it must be proved that we can be faithful in that which is least. This is worthy of repetition; if we squander and mismanage the little we have in our hands, shall we not do the same with the much we hope to acquire? Here is the true test of faithful giving, and passing this test qualifies us to manage larger things in life. "He who is faithful in what is least is faithful also in much; and he who is unjust in what is least is unjust also in much" (Luke 16:10).

The woman of Zarephath was down to her last handful of flour but was willing to advance the interest of God's work and put another's need ahead of her own. But where can we find such opportunities? They are all around us. Everyday opportunities present themselves to us to help us exercise our faith muscles. What we do with these opportunities determines how muscular and vibrant our faith muscles are or, conversely, how flabby and weak they are. God wants us to grow in our liberality, and he has given us every incentive to do so.

"Bring all the tithes into the storehouse, that there may be food in My house, and try Me now in this says the Lord of Host, if I will not open for you the windows of heaven and pour out for you such blessing that there will not be room enough to receive it" (Mal. 3:10). Is God asking us to try him in this sensitive area of financial stewardship? Are you up to the challenge? I am already discovering God's blessings in this area. Am I a millionaire? No, but God has blessed me with a healthy body and a creative mind, and for this, I am grateful. Some count their riches in terms of their financial portfolio, but I prefer to count my riches in terms of good health and a creative mind. How useful is money then if you do not have the health and sanity to enjoy it?

What can I render to the Lord for all his blessings? Once Jesus has all your heart, he will have our wallet/purse and treasure. "For where your treasure is there your heart will be also" (Matt. 6:21).

June 24

No Pain, No Gain

Therefore we also, since we are surrounded by so great a cloud of witnesses, let us lay aside every weight, and the sin which so easily ensnare us, and let us run with endurance the race that is set before us.

—Hebrews 12:1

Cheyanne fantasizes winning the U.S. Open Tennis Championships and hoisting the glittering trophy over her head while still in her teens. Go, Cheyanne, go! She has the athleticism and skill, but only time will tell if she has the mental discipline to power her way past determined opponents. We share Cheyanne's dream of hoisting a trophy over our heads one day, except that ours will be a heavenly one, a crown that never fades away.

"Do you not know that those who run in a race all run, but one receives the prize? Run in such a way that you may obtain it. And everyone who competes for the prize is temperate in all things, now they do it to obtain a perishable crown, but we for an imperishable crown" (1 Cor. 9:24–25). We are all runners in the race of life, and Jesus successfully ran the tracks ahead of us, leaving us a marked trail to follow. He showed us by example how to navigate life's difficult curves and obstacles. After his ascension into heaven, the Holy Spirit became our Coach and stands at the sidelines as both Coach and Comforter. He dutifully whispers comforting words in the ears of the weary and fainthearted while refreshing the spirit of the exhausted.

However, the track is teeming with hidden dangers, but they have all been clearly marked to alert runners of the danger. One section of the tract is called "the entertainment industry." It has distracted many well-intentioned runners and thrown them off course. Its agenda stands opposed to kingdom building, and its programs are filled with sleazy and profane material. Its TV producers have become their own regulators, injecting any and everything harmful to families and detrimental to kids. Succeeding the entertainment industry by half a lap is the cool, jazzy world of "secular music." Be careful as you accelerate this lane; if your footing is not secure on Jesus Christ, you may lose your way and be lulled into its seductive embrace. Upon clearing the jazzy world of secular music, looming ahead is "the major world of sports" with all its dazzling and highly paid athletes. But don't be fooled and be careful; if addicted, the *Monday Night Football* could deaden your spiritual perception.

But who doesn't like a good game of any competitive sport? However, here is a perplexing dilemma. Can *Monday Night Football* and other ball games consume so much of our time that they take us away from our spiritual formation (e.g., prayer, Bible study, and other profitable work ventures)? Lord, help us! "Brethren, I do not count myself to have apprehended; but one thing I do, forgetting those things which are behind and reaching forward to those thing which are ahead, I press toward the goal for the prize of the upward call of God in Christ Jesus" (Phil. 3:13–14).

Life's track is without a doubt very challenging and filled with distractions, but we can make it with Jesus as our running mate, the Holy Spirit as our coach, and God the Father at the finish line urging us to persevere unto the end. Don't' worry, if like me you have not yet won anything in life, you can win in this race with God. "Now to Him who is able to keep you from stumbling, and to present you faultless before the presence of His glory with exceeding joy, to God our Savior, who alone is wise, be glory and majesty, dominion and power, both now and forever. Amen" (Jude 24–25).

June 25

Hidden in Christ

For in the time of trouble He shall hide me in His pavilion; in the secret place of His tabernacle He shall hide me; He shall set me high upon a rock.

—Psalm 27:5

Oskar Schindler had no kinship to his Jewish employees but spent his entire fortune saving them from Nazi concentration camps. His initial motive was just protecting his business interest by shielding his employees from harm, but it soon became his obsession as Hitler began losing his mind, and more Jews were being destroyed. As the Final Solution (the destruction of Jews from Europe) went into full gear, Oskar had to provide larger bribes to Nazi officials to protect his workers from the gas chambers. His passion for saving Jewish lives drove him bankrupt by war's end. Having failed at other businesses after the war, he subsisted in his retirement on the generosity of the people whom he helped rescue. In retrospect, his heroism in saving the Jews, at the peril of his life and that of his family, won him worldwide acclaim posthumously (http://www.jewishvirtuallibrary.org/oskar-schindler).

To our brothers and sisters who are going through the fierce fires of persecution, this promise is pregnant with hope. "And do not fear those who kill the body but cannot kill the soul. But rather fear Him who is able to destroy both soul and body in hell" (Matt. 10:28). The purposes of God are beyond our understanding, and we do not understand why he allows some to perish while he delivers others. However, we confidently trust him in all his ways, knowing that his motives toward us are pure and for our own benefit. "For I know the thoughts that I think toward you, says the Lord, thoughts of peace and not evil, to give you a future and a hope" (Jer. 29:11).

"When the wicked came up against me to eat up my flesh . . . They stumbled and fell." David composed Psalm 27 while on the run from Saul, who was determined to take his life. Through his firm dependence on the Almighty, he was sheltered from harm to lead God's people. Interestingly enough, God led a tired Saul to take a nap in the very cave where David and his men were hiding. Was this accidental or providential? Is God showing us how to deal with those in leadership position who do not favor us or those who wish us harm? David spared Saul's life because he was God's anointed. Our lives are hidden in God; anywhere is safe when God is with us. The most dangerous place with Jesus is safe, and the safest place without Jesus is dangerous.

The Bible predicts a time of great trouble against God's people perpetrated by satanic led forces. The devil has never lost his zeal to destroy God's children. "For then there will be great tribulation, such as has not been since the beginning of the world until this time, no, nor ever shall be" (Matt. 24:21). The gathering storm of the persecution of believers is real and is taking place right now in some nations around the world. Soon, our tolerant and friendly neighbors will turn against us as the Bible predicts. "Then they will deliver you up to tribulation and kill you and you will be hated by all nations for My name's sake" (Matt. 24:9). Righteousness is always a rebuke to evil; therefore evil has always sought to eradicate righteous living, but in the final analysis, righteousness will triumph. Amen.

In times of hardship, God has always provided a haven for his people. Are you hidden in Christ? When persecution for your faith arises at your job, will you seek your lawyer, or will you let God's name be glorified in you? "Blessed are they who are persecuted for righteousness' sake for theirs the kingdom of heaven" (Matt. 5:10).

June 26

Thank God for Suffering

And not only that, but we also glory in tribulations, knowing that tribulation produces perseverance; and perseverance, character, and character, hope.

—Romans 5:3–4

Approaching her final hours and clutching her Bible with both hands, Sue (name changed) confessed, "If I had not contracted AIDS, I would not have known God." Touched by the tender love and warmth of her caretakers who restored to her the dignity that others had stolen, Sue made her peace with God before slipping away. In Bible study, she discovered she no longer had to appease the spirits with expensive offerings or be terrified by them. Even though her frail body was being ravaged by a disease in a part of the world where medical care was nonexistent, she latched on to the hope of receiving a brand-new body on resurrection morning.

Sue's confession is an admission every rational child of God must candidly admit. "Had it not been for this or that situation, I would not have known God." The process of character purification is intense and sometimes painful. Saving one's soul sometimes necessitates sending that person behind bars for the rest of his or her natural life to get his or her act together. In other instances, a prolonged illness, loss of physical health, loss of material assets, or the death of a loved one may be enough for one to put their spiritual house in order. If we are intent on being saved, God will use whatever means possible to save us, including whacking us upside the head. Jacob had a permanent limp (Gen. 32:25), and Paul suffered from visual problems (Acts 9:3–9)—wounds received to help turn them around. The divine Refiner who sees and knows all things allows his people to undergo character purification in whatever form he sees fit for their spiritual development. He often calls some home to rest after reaching their spiritual peak, while leaving others in the furnace for further cleansing.

Every once in a while, the Lord jolts us with a mild shock of affliction to remind us we are in continuous war with evil. And that shock, of course, is usually some mild affliction. "Yes, and all who desire to live godly in Christ Jesus will suffer persecution" (2 Tim. 3:12). How are you holding up under your persecution? Can we ask Paul how he made it out of his hardships?

In labors more abundant, in stripes above measure, in prisons more frequently, in deaths often. From the Jews five times I received forty stripes minus one. Three times I was beaten with rods; once I was stoned; three times I was shipwrecked; a night and a day I have been in the deep; in journeys often, in perils of waters, in perils of robbers, in perils of my own countrymen, in perils of the Gentiles, in perils in city, in perils in the wilderness, in perils in the sea, in perils among false brethren; in weariness and toil, in sleeplessness often, in hunger and thirst, in fasting often, in cold and nakedness, besides the other things, what comes upon me daily: My deep concern for the churches. (2 Cor. 11:23–28).

Compounded with an impending court hearing, Paul declares, "Therefore I take pleasure in infirmities, in reproaches, in distresses, for Christ's sake. For when I am weak, then I am strong" (2 Cor. 12:10). Can you cherish this text when the little cloud of persecution comes your way next time? Have faith, dear friend, in God. He is developing your character for heaven.

June 27

Please, Don't Hurt Me!

But if you are without chastening, of which all have become partakers, then you are illegitimate and not sons. Furthermore we have had human fathers who corrected us, and we paid them respect. Shall we not much more readily be in subjection to the Father of the spirits and live?

—Hebrews 12:8–9

Ms. Suzan (name changed), one of my teachers, perfected the art of corporal punishment by sending us out to fetch and choose the size and thickness of the whip she would use to thrash our buttocks. The assignment, she hoped, would give us enough time for behavior modification. Later in life and as we grew older and wiser, we understood her motive. Thanks, Ms. Suzan, for looking out for our best interest; we applaud you. I never told her because of sheer embarrassment, but in hindsight, I truly appreciated every bit of her thrashing; it kept me on the straight and narrow path. "My son, do not despise the chastening of the Lord, nor be discouraged when you are rebuked by Him; for whom the Lord loves He chastens, and scourged every son whom He receives" (Heb. 12:5–6).

We may not always appreciate the chastening rod of the Lord. In essence, it is painful and sometimes a little embarrassing, especially if there are onlookers around. Who enjoys chastisement anyway? Do you? I sure don't. Let's see how David responded to the chastening rod of the Lord. "Then the Lord spoke to Gad, David's seer saying, 'Go and tell David saying, thus says the Lord: I offer you three things; choose one of them for yourself, that I may do it to you'" (1 Chron. 21:9–10). God uses any means possible to get our attention, but in this instance, he gave David the prerogative to choose the form of chastisement by which he would be punished. It is a humbling experience having to choose your form of punishment, but David wisely conceded: "I am in great distress. Please let me fall into the hand of the Lord, for His mercies are very great; but do not let me fall into the hand of man" (1 Chron. 21:13).

Punishment is no doubt very painful, uncomfortable, and humiliating, but here are a few compelling reasons why we should cope and not grumble about the Lord's chastisement. "Now no chastening seems to be joyful for the present, but painful; nevertheless, afterward it yields the peaceable fruit of righteousness to those who have been trained by it" (Heb. 12:11). As painful and humiliating as it may seem, we should neither complain nor murmur while God is reconstructing his image in us. "Shall the clay say to him who forms it, what are you begetting?" (Isa. 45:9).

In hindsight, David reflects on God's evenhandedness and surmised, "It is good for me that I have been afflicted, that I may learn Your statutes" (Ps. 119:71). Here, we observe one positive result of chastisement, although there are many: "That I may learn Your statutes." Chastisement offers other benefits, such as behavior modification, which is the desired objective anyway and one that I have grown to appreciate. Should that fail to achieve God's ideal for one's life, the alternative may be undesirable but necessary. "He who is often rebuked, and hardens his neck, will suddenly be destroyed, and that without remedy" (Prov. 29:1). After repeated warnings and behavior modifications are resisted, God has no choice but to endorse the decision we've made. I trust that your decision for Christ has been favorable and that final destruction will not be on your record.

June 28

Died in My Place

For Christ also suffered once for sins, the just for the unjust, that He might bring us to God, being put to death in the flesh but made alive by the Spirit.
—1 Peter 3:18

Inmate DeLuna vehemently proclaimed his innocence to the legal establishment but was executed, while the real culprit roamed free and kept himself busy committing more horrendous crimes. On December 7, 1989, the state of Texas executed Carlos DeLuna by lethal injection despite the overwhelming body of evidence proving that he didn't and couldn't have committed the crime he was charged with. He was nowhere near the crime scene. Evidence collected at the crime scene did not associate Mr. DeLuna to the crime, while proof that could have exonerated him were ignored. Even his death row chaplain conceded. Unlike some death row inmates who protest their innocence but, as the end approaches, usually confess and set the record straight, DeLuna tried to lift his head under the hood one last time to protest his innocence to anyone with ears (https://thewrongcarlos.net/).

Carlos Hernandez, the real criminal of the gas station attack, continued to brag about the killing during his many prison adventures. However, after his death of natural causes, his family decided to break their silence and admit that their son and brother was indeed the killer of Wanda Jean Lopez. That didn't help Carlos DeLuna one bit. He had already been executed, another innocent man paying for the crime of a guilty party.

Unlike the heartless Hernandez who allowed another man to go to his death while he, the real criminal, remained free, Jesus voluntarily took the fall for us. He died in our place. "Behold we are going to Jerusalem, and the Son of Man will be betrayed to the chief priests and to the scribes; and they will condemn Him to death and deliver Him to the Gentiles; and they will mock Him, and scourge Him, and spit on Him, and kill Him. And the third day He will rise again" (Mark 10:33–34). This is a science that will be studied by intelligent creatures throughout the ceaseless ages of eternity: how God became man and died as a criminal to save his creation. The eternal God and Creator became our Savior.

Could Jesus have aborted his death? Could he have walked away from the rescue operation? But of course. Just remember, dear friends, he was "in all points tempted as we are, yet without sin" (Heb. 4:15). Abandonment of the human race was a real possibility since he was tempted in all points as we are. His human body shrank from the massive ordeal about to overwhelm his soul, but his love for wayward humanity prevailed, and he surrendered his body to be crushed, the price for our atonement. "O my Father, if it is possible, let this cup pass from Me; nevertheless, not as I will, but as You will" (Matt. 26:39).

Thank you, dear Lord, for staying the course even in the wake of the excruciating pain. Thanks for willingly dying that we might live. You could have abandoned the whole rescue operation and walked back to the pearly gates and to the adoration of the angels, but your love for us would not allow you to do that. We just want to say thanks again and again.

A Native American, upon hearing of the plan of salvation and what it cost God to redeem mankind, did what was typical of his culture. He wanted to give God something special for his love to the tribe; therefore he gave what was precious and very dear to him, his bow and arrow. Lord, here's my life. Take it and use it according to your will.

June 29

Buried in Christ

Therefore we are were buried with Him through baptism into death, that just as Christ was raised from the dead by the glory of the Father, even so we also should walk in newness of life.

—Romans 6:4

Fourteen days after he was buried alive by tons of rubble, Rico Dibrivell was pulled out from the earth, weak and dehydrated but very much alive. The earth shook, buildings crumbled, and tens of thousands instantly met their end in Haiti. Rescuers and their dogs rushed to a site where a faint moan was heard. After removing a ton of debris, a live human was pulled from the twisted rubble. What is remarkable about the recovery of Mr. Dibrivell is that he defied the odds. Recovery experts don't expect survivors to make it without food and water beyond the fifth day, but Mr. Dibrivell survived fourteen days buried alive under tons of rubble. Analysts credit this miracle to the human spirit to survive but leave God out of the equation. Even in the midst of the Haitian tragedy, we all can rejoice at any life that was rescued (http://www.cnn.com/2010/WORLD/americas/01/17/haiti.earthquake.rescue/).

The believer experiences a burial at conversion, in which the old nature is put to death. Baptism buries what the Bible calls the "carnal nature" (the unconverted old you and me). When we emerge from the water after baptism, we are transformed into brand-new creatures in Christ. Baptism is symbolic of all three aspects of Christ's sacrifice: his death, burial, and resurrection. "Therefore we were buried with Him through baptism into death; that just as Christ was raised from the dead by the glory of the Father, even so we also should walk in newness of life. For if we have been united together in the likeness of His death, certainly we also shall be in the likeness of His resurrection. Knowing this, that our old man was crucified with Him that the body of sin might be done away with, that we should no longer be slaves of sin" (Rom. 6:4–6). At baptism, the old nature is crucified; during emersion (while underwater), the old nature, including hideous past sins, is buried and forgotten, and the new person emerges from the water, rejoicing in Christ's resurrection. The resurrection gives one the renewal of life complete with joy and hope. Baptism sets the believer on a new course, a journey to everlasting life and happiness.

What a beautiful analogy Jesus gave us to celebrate our new birthday in him. "Therefore, if anyone is in Christ, he is a new creation; old things are passed away; behold, all things have become new" (2 Cor. 5:17). The burial of sinful past practices makes the believer a brand-new babe in Christ, but babies are very fragile and delicate and must be handled with utmost care and tenderness. They must be cleaned, checked on, looked after, and fed continuously. The same is true of the new believer. Let us not assume they will just grow; we must take care of them as we would the little ones.

We thank God for our Lord Jesus Christ, who did not need the rite of baptism, having never sinned, but being our example, he subjected himself to it. "Permit it to be so now, for thus it is fitting for us to fulfill all righteousness, then he allowed Him" (Matt. 3:15). Jesus did not need baptism but submitted to the rite anyhow to be an example for you and me; therefore I will humbly submit myself to him by burying my life with him in baptism.

June 30

God Showed Up Big-Time

Cast your burden on the Lord, and He shall sustain you;
He shall never permit the righteous to be moved.

—Psalm 55:22

The date of their dream vacation was approaching fast, and their son's passport was still unaccounted for. In utter desperation, she made one final call to the embassy, and—bingo!–it was issued. Madlyn booked her family's vacation online, only to discover the passport of her son Jamal had expired. The embassy assured her that the procedure would take between four and six weeks. After the sixth week, she called in to express her concerns and was informed there was a minor error that needed correction. With their vacation deadline looming fast, Madlyn decided to take her situation to the ambassador in chief, Jesus Christ. Would you believe it? On the very day of their departure, her son's passport became available. Thanks be to God for his sense of timing and the prayers of the saints.

"Call to Me, and I will answer you, and show you great and mighty things, which you do not know" (Jer. 33:3). God controls the minutest detail of our life. Our Savior knows everything that ails us, but He waits till we muster enough faith to seek his favor. "Look at the birds of the air for they neither sow nor reap nor gather into barns; but yet your heavenly Father feeds them. Are you not of more value than them?" (Matt. 6:26).

Oh, we of little faith, why do we not take everything to God in prayer? God can do anything, except fail. My wife was turning the house upside down looking for a much-needed tax document. I could tell she was getting exasperated and suggested to her, "Honey, let's pray about it." After a brief prayer, my eyes zeroed in on the document. "Am I a God near at hand, says the Lord, and not a God afar off? Can anyone hide himself in the secret places, so I shall not see him, says the Lord; do I not fill the heaven and the earth? Says the Lord" (Jer. 23:23–24). "What a friend we have in Jesus, all our needs and sins to bear! What a privilege to carry everything to God in prayer! Oh, what peace we often forfeit. Oh, what needless pain we bear, all because we do not carry everything to God in prayer!" (Joseph M. Scriven).

Why we do not want to seek the help of the God who runs the universe remains a mystery. David was renowned for his constant seeking for God's advice. One of his often repeated sayings is coined this way: "Lord, shall I go up there? Will you deliver my enemies into my hands?" We must develop the practice of involving God in every aspect of our lives. "I waited patiently for the Lord; and He inclined to me, and heard my cry. He also brought me up out of the horrible pit, out of the miry clay, and set my feet upon a rock and established my steps. He has put a new song in my mouth, praise to our God" (Ps. 40:1–3).

Shall we use the convenience of our God as a fire escape to use only when needed and, after the emergency passes, never again call on him for service? "But those who wait upon the Lord shall renew their strength; they shall mount up with wings like eagles, they shall run and not be weary, they shall walk and not faint" (Isa. 40:31).

July 1

Persistence Pays

And he will answer from within and say, do not trouble me; the door is now shut, and my children are with me in bed; I cannot rise and give to you. I say to you, though he will not rise and give to him because he is his friend, yet because of his persistence he will rise and give him as many as he needs.

—Luke 11:7–8

With every rejection, his knocks grew louder and more determined, until the door finally cracked open to him. Mr. Chew had unexpected guests one night. A friend on a cross-country sightseeing tour decided to drop in. His guests were hungry, and the closest store in the neighboring town was about twenty miles away. Since he could not offer his friend his leftovers from last night's meal, his thoughts turned to his neighbor's well-stocked refrigerator. However, waking his moody neighbor in the middle of the night was not an enterprising thought, but it was his only alternative. His knocking became a test of persistence and determination, but after an agonizing wait, the door finally swung open. Standing there was a sleepy neighbor holding a bagful of goodies. Jesus continues the story: "I say to you, though he will not rise and give to him because he is his friend, yet because of his persistence he will rise and give him as many as he needs. So I say to you, ask, and it will be given to you; seek, and you will find, knock and it will be opened to you" (Luke 11:8–9).

The spider's web won first place over the weaver bird in my reckoning on home building. Although the weaver bird's nest is more intricate and seems better designed, the spider's web is a marvel of engineering, strength, durability, and persistence. Spiders hardly build their mansion in one single attempt. To some species, it's extremely labor-intensive and takes several attempts to get that horizontal strand attached. The vertical strand is the easy part, but getting the horizontal strand across necessitates working against the law of gravity. It takes hard work to achieve anything of value. Are you up to the task of working hard to achieve your gains and goals in life?

Ringo Starr of the Beatles coined these words: "It don't come easy. You know it don't come easy." Any worthy achievement, including a closer walk with God, demands effort, dogged determination, and sacrifice. Ask the Olympic athletes who strain every muscle training just to qualify to represent their country and must put a greater effort to win the championship trophy. They do it for an earthly crown but we a heavenly.

Our spiritual walk with God follows the same formula. Our spiritual muscles are developed by studying the Word of God and daily prayer. It is shocking how little time is devoted to Bible study when compared with other daily activities. Some folks don't read their Bibles anymore. Fortunately, technology has come to the rescue for the sluggish; the Word of God comes to us in many forms, which we can easily utilize. It can be installed on your smartphone or be inserted into your DVD player even while driving, and there may be many other listening devices of which I am unaware. Fortifying yourself in the Word of God will pay great dividends and will come to your aid when needed. You cannot get from the bag what is not stored in there.

Should we not develop a hunger for the Word of God and a dedication to prayer? Remember, "it don't come easy." You must put in a determined effort to achieve the desired returns. May God bless you in your renewed prayer life and Bible study.

July 2

The Midnight Knock

Today, if you will hear His voice; do not harden your hearts, as in the rebellion.
—Psalm 95:7–8

They came in at midnight to create minimum disturbance to neighbors and sleeping families, but their grisly work left many women widowed and children fatherless. Aleksandr Solzhenitsyn, in his classic *The Gulag Archipelago*, described in horrifying detail the terrifying knock on the door at midnight. With tips from neighbors, hundreds of thousands of sons and fathers went missing. They were dragged from their beds in the dead of night, hastily tried on trumped-up charges, and sent to the labor camps, where they perished from forced labor, bone-chilling cold, starvation, overwork, and disease. Do not fear; there is a knock that is recognizable and quite friendly.

"Behold I stand at the door and knock. If anyone hears My voice and open the door, I will come in to him and dine with him, and he with Me" (Rev. 3:20). While this message was given to Laodicea, the last church of the apostolic era, it has relevant application to us, the last day church of the modern era. A distinct and firm knock can be heard above the noise, the distractions, amid the busy and hectic existence of today's modern world. It is the knock of the Savior. Can you hear his voice?

It is a knock to come apart and find some quiet space, a secluded place, and spend quality time with the God of the universe. You may have to drop your tools momentarily, put your computer on Sleep mode, turn off the TV, stop, or pull over your car to a safe place and plug into the divine. "I will lift up my eyes to the hills from whence comes my help? My help comes from the Lord, who made heaven and earth" (Ps. 121:1–2). Today "hill" implies any place dedicated to worshipping God, including the side of the road, a parking lot, the park, or even your car.

Hearing the knock is fine, but responding to it is quite another experience. David requests of God, "Keep back your servant also from presumptuous sins; let them not have dominion over me. Then I shall be blameless, and I shall be innocent of great transgression" (Ps. 19:13). Ah yes, presumptuous sins could be the darling little sins we love and knowingly commit or omit from confession.

Nature hates a void. Any empty space will be automatically filled with something either good or bad; therefore filling the day with pleasant things is of paramount importance as we see the day of the Lord approaching. "Finally, brethren, whatsoever things are true, whatever things are noble, whatever things are just, whatever things are pure, whatever things are lovely, whatever things are of good report, if there is any virtue and if there is anything praiseworthy, meditate on these things" (Phil. 4:8).

I am responding to the gentle knock of the Savior by igniting worship service in the morning (preferable) or evening before I retire for the night. I will be more selective in what I watch on TV, and I will say no to the bad videos I intend to rent and the questionable music I tend to listen to. Dear Jesus, please look beyond my good intentions, and give me the power to do your will. Amen.

July 3

Who Are We?

When I consider Your heavens, the work of your fingers, the moon and stars, which You have ordained, what is man that You are mindful of him and the son of men that You visit him?

—Psalm 8:3–4

The once vibrant and bouncing puppy had transitioned into a lethargic old friend. The sparkle in his eyes was all gone, the wagging tail was no more, and he moved when he must with great difficulty and discomfort, but his master loved him even more. My old boss described the relationship between him and his dog as deep and enduring. They were inseparable; wherever he went, his dog Shadow followed. It came as no surprise to anyone that, as his dog aged and could no longer muster the energy to hop into his truck, the boss spent a small fortune trying to restore his old friend's health.

God has a better abiding relationship with the human family, and the psalmist was mystified in trying to understand it. "When I consider Your heavens, the work of Your fingers, The moon and the stars, which You have ordained, what is man that You are mindful of him, and the son of man that You visit him?" (Ps. 8:3–4). When we ponder the vastness of space, the galaxies in their continuous motion, the beauty and serenity of the moon, the dazzling splendor of the stars, who are we that you take so much interest in us considering the many headaches we've caused you?

"The Lord has appeared of old to me saying: Yes, I have loved you with an everlasting love; therefore with loving kindness I have drawn you" (Jer. 31:3). Since God's love is everlasting and everything he created is absolutely gorgeous, humans—the crowning act of his Creation—are dotted over with his love and attention. God is the embodiment of love, and he showers the rebels of earth (us), undeserving as we are, with his choicest love. He gives and gives and just keeps on giving.

We are totally undeserving of such priceless showering of affection, considering the cost to God in redeeming us to the family of heaven. "Even when we were dead in trespasses, made us alive together with Christ (by grace you have been saved), and raised us up together, and made us sit together in the heavenly places in Christ Jesus, that in the ages to come He might show the exceeding riches of His grace in His kindness toward us in Christ Jesus" (Eph. 2:5–7). We cannot fully understand God's unconditional love. It is priceless and so freely given to all regardless of nobility, social standing, race, or national origin.

Even when we choose to reject God's gracious love and mercy, he reluctantly respects the choice of his intelligent creatures. He does not use force or coercion in his dealings with his creatures but stamps the decisions we make. "And if it seems evil to you to serve the Lord, choose for yourselves this day whom you will serve, whether the gods which your fathers served that were on the other side of the River, or the gods of the Amorites, in whose land you dwell. But as for me and my house, we will serve the Lord" (Josh. 24:15).

There is no one quite like you in all the universe, and that's the reason why God is madly in love with you and wants you to spend the rest of eternity with him. Do you want to be with him also?

July 4

The Birth of a Nation

And the Lord said to Moses, go to Pharaoh and say to him, Thus says the Lord: let My people go, that they may serve Me.

—Exodus 8:1

The National Mall and neighboring parks are teeming with activity as revelers are gathered to celebrate the Fourth of July holiday. Some have brought blankets, others barbecue grills, but all come prepared for the fireworks display, which will follow after sunset. Who should miss this spectacular display of exploding fireworks in every direction in the sky? The day itself is reminiscent of a historic event when fifty-five radicals, as they were referred to by the British, put their lives on the line by revolting against their colonial master, Great Britain. They declared the United States a free and independent nation. John Hancock and his fellow revolutionaries were fully aware that by attaching their names to this historic document, they were making themselves voluntary candidates for the gallows, but a greater force was driving them on. In a bold act of defiance, they took this sacred oath: "We mutually pledge to each other our lives, our fortunes, and our sacred honor" (www.redstate.com/diary/sunshinestatesarah/2012/07/04). All fifty-five delegates of the thirteen colonies signed the historic document, and the others not present affixed their signatures at a later date (*American Heritage*).

Several centuries ago, the nation of Israel demanded its independence from its colonial master, Egypt. However, the Egyptians—having enslaved Israel and benefiting immensely from their free labor—were in no mood to let this lucrative labor force go free. In defiance to the God of the universe, the ruler of Egypt arrogantly declared, "Who is the Lord, that I should obey His voice to let Israel go? I do not know the Lord, nor will I let Israel go" (Exod. 5:2). The famous Martin Luther King once declared, "Freedom is never voluntarily given by the oppressor. It must be demanded by the oppressed."

We celebrate this Fourth of July mindful of several important achievements in the life of the believer; chief among many is his or her relationship with Jesus. As we celebrate anniversaries and other milestone events, we sometimes overlook our spiritual birthday, the day we were delivered from a life of sin to the service of the living God. No other celebration is equal in importance; it is even more important than one's natural birth. Jesus emphasized its importance with these words: "Most assuredly, I say to you, unless one is born again, he cannot see the kingdom of God" (John 3:3). To enter the kingdom of heaven, you must experience the new birth in Christ Jesus.

Equally important on the list of anniversaries is our relationship with Christ. A couple would be missing out on a whole lot of fun if they only celebrate their anniversary while ignoring the fun that preceded it. I often remember the hundreds of miles I drove from the Bronx, New York, to New Jersey to see my sweetheart. Memory will not allow me to forget the long drives to New Jersey in a sputtering Volkswagen Beetle. And the windy George Washington Bridge did not make life any easier for me, jostling my little Volkswagen Beetle from one lane to another, but it was worth it all. The memories help stabilize our marriage.

We should always recall that glorious day when Jesus saved us from sin, and that calls for constant celebration. We may not have had a dramatic conversion experience as Paul, but God has been good to us. Considering where he found us and where we are now headed is reason enough to shout (is anybody watching?), "Hallelujah! Praise the Lord!" Thank you, Jesus, for saving a wretched sinner like me.

July 5

Corresponding Strength for the Burden

My God shall supply all your needs according to His riches in glory by Christ Jesus.
—Philippians 4:19

Garry (name changed) is going through a terrible marital nightmare; his spouse is seeing someone else. At night, he wishes for the daylight to alleviate the pain; and when the day arrives, he wishes for the night to sleep it off. On weekends, he dons his jogging shoes and takes to the tracks to keep his sanity. While running, Garry is overwhelmed by a reassuring feeling of calm and serenity; he senses the presence of a friendly running mate whom he cannot see but who seems to say everything will be okay. "When you pass through the waters I will be with you; and through the rivers, they shall not overflow you. When you walk through the fire, you shall not be burned, nor shall the flame scorch you for I am the Lord your God, the Holy One of Israel, your Savior" (Isa. 43:2–3). Garry instantly recognizes that God is reassuring him that he will get through this nightmare and that everything will be all right no matter how nasty things may turn out.

Trouble is the common lot of mankind, but God has never abandoned fallen man to the tender mercies of the devil. "Cast your burden on the Lord, and He shall sustain you; He shall never permit the righteous to be moved." Annie J. Flint wrote, "He giveth more grace as the burden grows greater. He sendeth more strength as the labors increase; to added afflictions He addeth His mercy, to multiplied trials, His multiplied peace." Is God ever caught off guard by the trials of the righteous?

Have you ever been driving or walking and heavily engaged in thought only to arrive at your destination wondering, *Wow, how did I get there?* Have you ever been challenged by some excruciating perplexities, only to discover that you sailed through the turmoil with minimum discomfort? Give glory to God; your guardian angel was at the helm driving or placing your feet in the right spot. God's children are still being delivered by their guardian angels as in times of old. Sometimes they appear in the form of neighbors and familiar friends or may choose to remain completely anonymous.

However, we should not expect angels to extricate us from the mountain of debt in which we bury ourselves. Sometimes God allows us to learn from our mistakes the hard way. It has been proved that hard knocks and bitter experiences are the best teachers. God never punishes his children unnecessarily. He is always faithful and has promised never to leave us or abandon us, even in situations of our own creation. He assures, "Fear not, I am with you; be not dismayed, for I am your God. I will strengthen you, yes I will help you, I will uphold you with My right hand" (Isa. 41:10).

Are you hesitant in asking for God's help? Do you sometimes feel frustrated doing the same things you asked forgiveness for yesterday? Well, that's a healthy feeling; it urges us to seek help outside of ourselves. It confronts us with a sense of our inadequacy and makes us flee to the all-sufficient Rock, Christ Jesus. Remember, Jesus always increases the strength as the burden gets greater.

July 6

Where Were You?

You asked, who is this who hides counsel without knowledge? Therefore I have uttered what I did not understand, things too wonderful for me, which I did not know.

—Job 42:3

The lammergeier vulture is a bone-crushing specialist. He does with ease what others can't and feeds exclusively on rich, fat-laden, juicy bones. On his feeding forays, he scans the landscape for carrion. If the dinner table is crowded, he patiently waits for his turn until the carcass is picked clean, and then he goes to work. Instinctively, he selects a bone with the highest concentration of marrow.

Taking to the air, he finds a rocky ledge and drops the bone to expose its fat-laden contents. He then gulps down the entire bone and its marrow. His highly acidic stomach is thoroughly equipped to handle such a package and reduces everything to a neat, crisp pulp by the next day. God's creation is marvelous, isn't it? (mentalfloss.com/article/58253/11-facts-about-bone-eating-bearded-vulture).

Man has made impressive gains in the field of science and technology, but there is so much we do not know. As admitted by scientists themselves, "We have only discovered the tip of the iceberg in terms of the vast body of knowledge that is out there." Looking at the immensity of the ocean and realizing we have accessed a very limited portion of it, the tip of the iceberg, should humble us in terms of our limitation to exploit the vastness out there. Putting a tiny spacecraft into orbit in an infinite universe was a terrific human achievement, but we are clueless about the vast unknown. Do we have any information about life on any other planet? While we applaud the scientific community for the vast body of knowledge they have gleaned over the centuries, are we aware of our human limitations? We do not know everything, and since we don't, everything—including science—must be measured by the Word of God.

"Where were you when I laid the foundation of the earth? Tell me, if you have understanding. Who determined its measurements? Surely you know! Or who stretched the line upon it?" (Job 38:4–5).

And so it was, after the Lord had spoken these words to Job, that the Lord said to Eliphaz the Temanite, "My wrath is aroused against you and your two friends for you have not spoken of Me what is right as My servant Job has. Now therefore, take for yourselves seven bulls and seven rams, go to My servant Job and offer up for yourselves a burnt offering; and My servant Job shall pray for you. For I will accept him, lest I deal with you according to your folly; because you have not spoken of Me what is right, as My servant Job has." (Job 42:7–8)

The scientists are dead wrong on the theory of evolution and are creating bigger lies to cover their initial lie, the big bang. "In the beginning God created the heavens and the earth. The earth was without form, and void, and darkness was upon the face of the deep and the Spirit of God was hovering over the waters. And God said let there be light and there was light" (Gen. 1:1–3). The Bible says God literally created the heaven and earth, and I believe it, and that is good enough for me. Do you believe it also? How blessed you are!

Overwhelmed by Love

In this is love, not that we loved God, but that He loved us and sent His Son to be the propitiation for our sins.

—1 John 4:10

At the tender age of thirteen, Jimmy Butler was abandoned by his mom, and his dad wasn't a good option either. With no permanent place to call home, Jimmy spent nights with friends until he wore out his welcome. But don't count little Jimmy out just yet; he is as resilient as one could ever get. After being challenged by a freshman to a three-pointer basketball contest, Jimmy and Jordan Leslie (his challenger) became the best of friends. He was a regular at their home. His charm, good behavior, and likability set in motion his being adopted into a family at last. With Mom Michelle Leslie as both coach and advisor, Jimmy became a prolific scholar and a sportsman. He embarrassed opponents at will on the basketball court and made his way to the NBA with the Chicago Bulls (http://sportmockery. com/2014/11fromhomelesstonbastar/).

We have much in common with Jimmy Butler. As the Leslie family adopted him into their family, likewise, we have been adopted into the commonwealth of Israel by virtue of God's magnanimity. "Therefore remember that you, once Gentiles in the flesh, who are called un-circumcision by what is called the circumcision made in the flesh by hands, that at that time you were without Christ, being aliens from the Commonwealth of Israel and strangers from the covenant of promise, having no hope and without God in the world. But now in Christ Jesus you who were once far off have been brought near by the blood of Christ" (Eph. 2:11–13).

Having been adopted, we must remain humble and not flaunt our weight around at the expense of the natural-born children. We must accept our place at the table with gratitude and humility. We owe a lot of respect and affection to our brothers and sisters, the Jews and Muslims. Remember, Father Abraham has many sons and daughters. "But Abraham gave gifts to the sons of the concubines which Abraham had; and while he was still living he sent them eastward, away from Isaac his son, to the country of the east" (Gen. 25:6). We must love our brothers and sisters of other faiths and not vaunt ourselves above them but genuinely seek them out with love and sincerity to win them over to the family of God.

Lest we forget, we are not the natural branch; the Jews and the Ishmaelites (Muslims) are. "And if some of the branches were broken off, and you . . . were grafted in among them, and with them became a partaker of the root and fatness of the olive tree, do not boast against the branches. But if you boast, remember that you do not support the root, but the root supports you" (Rom. 11:17–18).

God has many other children of other faiths who love him just as much as we do and are sincerely worshipping him with the limited light given to them. "And other sheep I have which are not of this fold; them also I must bring, and they shall hear My voice, and there will be one flock and one shepherd" (John 10:16). When Elijah thought he was the only one serving God, he was gently rebuked to the contrary. "Yet I have reserved seven thousand in Israel, all whose knees have not bowed to Baal, and every mouth that has not kissed him" (1 Kings 19:18). We should work with great sensitivity with Abraham's other children in bringing them back into the family. Whether you were part of the natural branch or grafted in, God loves you anyway. God is love.

July 8

It's Okay, I Understand

Then the scribes and Pharisees brought to Him a woman caught in adultery. And when they had set her in the midst, they said to Him, Teacher, this woman was caught in adultery, in the very act . . . But what do You say?

—John 8:3–5

Like many others before her, she was caught and condemned, while her partner in crime was allowed to walk away, a freeman. The Jewish law made provision for both male and female offenders to be penalized for the sin of adultery, but more often than not, the woman was punished, while the man slithered away with his dignity still intact. Our God is not impartial on the question of sexual immorality and infidelity. The scripture quotes, "If a man is found lying with a woman married to a husband, then both of them shall die, the man that lay with the woman, and the woman; so you shall put away the evil from Israel" (Deut. 22:22). Fortunately for us, Jesus died in our place, neutralizing the death sentence of the law.

Jesus specifically states that he did not come to judge or condemn. He came to save as John observes. "When Jesus had raised Himself up and saw no one but the woman, He said to her, Woman, where are those accusers of yours? Has no one condemned you? She said, no one, Lord. And Jesus said to her, 'Neither do I condemn you; go and sin no more'" (John 8:10–11). Interestingly, Jesus could have condemned her. After all, he is God, and it was his law that was broken. Being altogether sinless, he had every right to condemn her, but he didn't. He sympathized with her. "Go and sin no more." What a God we serve—merciful, just, understanding, and forgiving. The embodiment of righteousness and justice looks in pity on a weak, fallen child of humanity and says in today's vernacular, "It's okay, I understand. We'll work it out together."

Oh, what a Savior is Jesus, our Lord! Jesus took the sting of death so that we might live. Of course, the chief reason why the woman caught in adultery was not stoned, even while deserving of that punishment, is that Jesus absorbed the punishment for sin in his body. The guilt that is ours he took upon himself so that we might be clothed in his righteousness. Is it any wonder the prophet Isaiah asked in sheer horror, "Who have believed our report?" (Isa. 53:1)? It is almost too good to be true, but it is true. God became man and died for our sins, not just an ordinary death but an ignominious death—the death of a common criminal—in our place. The cross became "foolishness to the Greeks and a stumbling block to the Jews" (1 Cor. 1:23). The great Greek thinkers could not analyze intellectually how a defeated, condemned criminal—so they thought—could achieve victory in death, nor did the Jewish leadership believe one of such humble origin could be the promised Deliverer.

But to every contrite and repentant sinner, Jesus seems to say, "It is okay, I understand." Zacchaeus read acceptance on Jesus's face and repented; the adulterous woman saw that sympathizing face and repented also. After making eye contact with Jesus, Peter also saw sympathy. The centurion who presided over the crucifixion read forgiveness and acceptance on the face of Jesus. Even doubting Thomas, who humiliated the Savior by refusing to believe the resurrection account, saw compassion on the Savior's face and gasped, "My Lord and my God" (John 20:28).

Jesus remains sympathetic to the sinner and has made ample provision for all who are willing to turn away from sin, but the rejecters of his mercy will be left without excuse.

July 9

The Glory of the Lord

As for the likeness of the living creatures, their appearance was like burning coals of fire, like the appearance of torches going back and forth among the living creatures.
The fire was bright, and out of the fire went lighting.

—Ezekiel 1:13

Every year wildfires make their unwanted appearance on the hills of California, bringing grief to many homeowners and chewing up thousands of acres of prime real estate. While we are terrified of fire down here, it seems to be the building material around God's throne. "For our God is a consuming fire" (Heb. 12:29). The visions of Isaiah, Zachariah, Ezekiel, and John all confirm God is surrounded by balls of glowing, red-hot fire. Ezekiel describes Lucifer walking "back and forth in the midst of the fiery stones" (Ezek. 28:14). John saw the victorious saints standing on a sea of glass mingled with fire. Isaiah's lips were touched with a live coal from the altar (Isa. 6:7). Moses was hidden in a rock for his safety to shield him from the intense fire that issued from the presence of God (Exod. 33:22). The mountain of Sinai was engulfed in flames as God descended to deliver the Ten Commandments to Moses (Exod. 19:18). Elijah was translated to heaven in a blazing chariot of fire (2 Kings 2:11). What is so fascinating about fire?

Fire absolutely destroys humans. Then how can we endure the flames that surround God's throne since we are a people of "unclean lips"? How then can we stand in God's presence? David beckons. "Come let us worship and bow down; let us kneel before the Lord our Maker. For He is our God, and we are the people of His pasture, and the sheep of His hand" (Ps. 95:6–7). But we are still terrified by the glowing, hot flames that surround his presence. However, Paul encourages, "Let us come boldly to the throne of grace, that we may obtain mercy and find grace in time of need" (Heb. 4:16). But we feel a sense of unworthiness, like the centurion. "Lord I am not worthy that You should enter under my roof, but only speak the word and my servant will be healed" (Matt. 8:8).

"Oh magnify the Lord with me, and let us exalt His name together. I sought the Lord, and He heard, and delivered me from all my fears . . . This poor man cried out and the Lord heard him, and saved him out of all his troubles" (Ps. 34:3–4, 6). The Lord has been good to us because he has drawn us to himself with loving-kindness. We will praise God because he has given us peace in a turbulent and crime-infested world.

It is a good thing to give thanks to and praise the Lord, and here's the reason why: "Praise God in His sanctuary; Praise Him in His mighty firmament! Praise Him for His mighty acts; Praise Him according to His excellent greatness! Praise Him with the sound of the trumpet; Praise Him with the lute and harp! Praise Him with the lute and dance! Praise Him with the timbrel and harp. Praise Him with stringed instruments and flute! Praise Him with loud cymbals! Praise Him with clashing cymbals! Let everything that has breath praise the Lord" (Ps. 150:1–6). We agree with the psalmist and join all the creatures around the universe in worshipping and praising God because he is worthy of praise. While we still have breath, it is good to praise the Lord, isn't it? "The dead do not praise the Lord, nor any who go down into silence" (Ps. 115:17). It is quite obvious; when we are dead, we sink into silence. Should we not praise the Lord while we are still alive to make much noise to his name?

July 10

I Can See Clearly Now

Now as Jesus passed by, He saw a man who was blind from birth. And His disciples asked Him, saying, Rabbi, who sinned, this man or his parents, that he was born blind?

—John 9:1–2

Blindness came on her in her senior years, but it did not put a damper on her creativity in the kitchen. Determined not to let visual impairment dictate her passion for cooking and life in general, KC kept busy improving on her well-respected culinary skill. The aroma from her delicacies could be sniffed far and wide as neighbor and friends came calling. When she wanted to identify someone near and dear to her, she would ask them to sit beside her and gently run her delicate hands over their face and upper body to determine their physical features. Though sightless, she reminded everyone who came close to her how beautiful they were. She utilized her creative imagination to affirm and build others. In essence, she saw what others did not care to see, the beauty in us all.

Jesus once called the pastors and teachers of the synagogue blind guides. Though sighted, they closed their eyes to the needs of others (Matt. 23:24). Truly, no one is as blind as one who refuses to see. Shall we ask God to open our eyes to see the good in others and affirm and encourage them? Can we accentuate the positives and eliminate the negatives? Coaches get the best from their players by affirming, commending, building, and encouraging them. Barnabas was such a coach. "And Joses, who was also named Barnabas by the apostles (which is translated Son of Encouragement), a Levite of the country of Cyprus, having land, sold it, and brought the money and laid it at the apostles' feet" (Acts 4:36–37). Not only did Barnabas set a trend of selfless giving in the early church but he also saw the good in others when it was not obvious to the most discerning.

"Now Barnabas was determined to take with them John called Mark. But Paul insisted that they should not take with them the one who had departed from them in Pamphylia, and had not gone with them to the work. Then the contention became so sharp that they parted from one another. And so Barnabas took Mark and sailed to Cyprus, but Paul chose Silas and departed" (Acts 15:37–40). Barnabas was determined to give this young deserter another chance, but Paul would have none of it. This sharp disagreement caused a split among these close friends. But Paul later admitted in a letter to Timothy, "Only Luke is with me, get Mark and bring him with you, for he is useful to me for ministry" (2 Tim. 4:11). Did Paul really say that Mark, the deserter, is useful to him for ministry? Thank God Barnabas gave the young deserter another chance. Mark went on to become the author of the second gospel. Take another hard look at that trouble-prone teenager of yours, and be generous with your affirmations. He might just be the next Albert Einstein, Bill Gates, Barack Obama, Mark Finley, or C. D. Brooks.

Do you see the good in others, especially our mistake-prone, troubled teenagers? Do we pounce on their foibles while ignoring the good we see in them? Remember, we were once where they are right now—young, thoughtless, and reckless. Give them a break. Pray for them and encourage them instead; they will eventually turn around. Did you not turn around yourself? God bless you, my friend. Keep encouraging everyone.

July 11

A Person of Interest

The Spirit of the Lord is upon Me, because He has anointed Me to preach the gospel to the poor;
He has sent Me to heal the broken hearted. To proclaim liberty to the captives and recovery sight to the blind to set at liberty those who are oppressed.
—Isaiah 61:1

Someone is causing quite a stir in communities across the land of Judah, and the authorities are obviously concerned. News reaching the Sanhedrin reveals that the dead are being raised, demon possessed liberated, leapers cleansed, and entire villages have had their sick healed by a man choosing to remain anonymous. Upon receiving the news, Jewish leaders are poring over Isaiah's prophecy to determine the accuracy of the report. They have hauled in for questioning a number of people and are closely examining the miraculous reports to determine if indeed the long-promised Messiah had arrived.

All the suspects, including John the Baptist, have flatly denied being the promised Messiah. "Pilate therefore said to Him, are you a king then? Jesus answered, you say rightly that I am a King. For this cause I was born and for this cause I have come into the world, that I should bear witness to the truth. Everyone who is of the truth hears My voice" (John 18:37). It is by no accident or coincidence that you are reading the Bible, for it says, "He who is of God hears God's words; therefore you do not hear, because you are not of God" (John 8:47).

The person of interest who perfectly fits the Isaiah profile is none other than our Lord Jesus Christ. The demons knew it and confessed. "Now there was a man in their synagogue with and unclean spirit. And he cried out, saying, Let us alone! What have we to do with You, Jesus of Nazareth? Did You come to destroy us? I know who You are, the Holy One of God" (Mark 1:23–24). The demons knew better and quickly affirmed the divinity of Jesus Christ. After all, they were once righteous angels who chose to be deceived by Satan.

Though the Jewish leaders tried to suppress the truth about Jesus's true identity, the common people knew their Messiah was among them by virtue of the works that accompanied his ministry. "Then as He was now drawing near the descent of the Mount of Olives, the whole multitude of the disciples began to rejoice and praise God with a loud voice for all the mighty works they had seen, saying: 'Blessed is the King who comes in the name of the Lord! Peace in heaven and glory in the Highest'" (Luke 19:37–38). Again, this was a prophecy being fulfilled in their presence, but the Jewish leaders chose to ignore it: "Rejoice greatly, O daughter of Zion! Shout, O daughter of Jerusalem! Behold, your King is coming to you; He is just and having salvation, lowly and riding on a donkey, a colt, the foal of a donkey" (Zech. 9:9).

With the mounting body of evidence, we therefore agree with the prophets that Jesus is indeed who he said he was, the Messiah and King, the promised One by God to save the world from sin. Did the Jews recognize him as such? "He came to His own, and His own did not receive Him. But as many as received Him, to them He gave the right to become children of God, to those who believe in His name" (John 1:11–12).

Have you accepted Jesus into your life? Aren't you happy to be accorded the privilege to be called a child of God? Aren't you also happy there is everlasting life awaiting all those who serve God faithfully?

Delightfully Refreshing

On the last day, that great day of the feast, Jesus stood and cried out saying, "If anyone thirst, let him come to Me and drink."

—John 7:37

Water manufacturers think their particular brand of bottled water is the absolute best, but in this day and age, companies knowingly use deceptive advertisements on their labels and opt to pay a fine if ever caught. In a 2003 documentary published by the *Environment* magazine, it was discovered that the claims made by water companies are neither true nor safe. While water is essential and absolutely necessary for life, someone is profiting from these deceptive advertisements. Can anyone help us consumers?

However, Jesus promises water of a different kind to anyone who is thirsty. "On the last day, that great day of the feast, Jesus stood and cried out saying, 'If anyone thirsts, let him come to Me and drink. He who believes in Me, as the Scripture has said, out of his heart will flow rivers of living water'" (John 7:37–38). Everyone, at some point or another, gets thirsty and must find water to quench their thirst, and they will inevitably get thirsty again and again, but Jesus is the true thirst quencher, and the water he dispenses is eternal life. "And all drank the same spiritual drink. For they drank of the spiritual Rock that followed them, and that Rock was Christ" (1 Cor. 10:4). Paul is here referencing the children of Israel's journey to the land of Canaan. Although Israel drank from the water that is symbolic of Christ, they did not allow him to transform their stony hearts to a heart of flesh; their condition remained unchanged and unsaved.

While some are conscious of the origin of the purest water, others dismiss him with disdain, but the Spirit-led are diligently searching for that pure source. "Jesus answered and said to her, if you knew the gift of God, and who it is who says to you, give Me a drink; you would have asked Him, and He would have given you living water" (John 4:10). Jesus had just piqued the woman's curiosity about a source of water that cancels thirst. "Whoever drinks of this water will thirst again. But whoever drinks of the water that I shall give him will never thirst. But the water that I shall give him will become in him a fountain of water springing up into everlasting life" (John 4:13–14).

Who in their right mind would refuse such a delightful drink? "The woman said to Him, Sir give me this water, that I may not thirst, nor come here to draw" (John 4:15). Although the water is free, it comes at a high price. The price is total surrender of our lives to God, and the benefits we will inherit from this investment are priceless when compared with the alternative.

While hanging on the cross for our sins, your sins and mine, Jesus said, "I thirst." The One who made the rivers and fountains of water could not pour himself a drink but was dependent on his Father, who did not quench his thirst. He had to die thirsty to quench our thirst. He willingly took upon himself our nature and all its limitations and liabilities. He had to, like us, depend on the tender mercies of his Father. His thirst, though not quenched by water, was quenched by the Father's approval of his sacrifice. Are you daily drinking of that spiritual water? Is it flowing in your veins?

July 13

Can't Wait

And while they looked steadfastly toward heaven as He went up, behold, two men stood by them in white apparel, who also said, men of Galilee, why do you stand gazing up into heaven?

—Acts 1:10–11

Nothing prepared my grandson, LaShawn, for his first day at day care. He clung tightly to his dad's strong shoulders and would not let go. When he was finally coaxed into taking his place among the sea of strange faces in class, he became cranky and was miserable all day. You can appreciate the smile and relief on his face when his dad returned from work to pick him up. He literally leaped into the waiting arms of his dad.

Like little LaShawn, we are tempted to remain in the friendly and familiar confines of home, but there is a lot of work to be done before we are called home or see our Lord come again in glory. However, there is also the growing-up phase, which we all desperately need to mature and grow in Christ. "As newborn babes, desire the pure milk of the word, that you may grow thereby" (1 Pet. 2:2). Admittedly, that process of growth is usually painful and is a lifetime of character development.

The Lord grows us in areas where we are deficient. If we are lacking in love, he crosses our path with someone who is in dire need of that commodity. Are you lacking in patience and temper management? No problem, he'll set up your next-door neighbor or workplace buddy to lend some assistance. How about being a spoiled child who usually gets his or her way? That too can be fixed by an outright denial of selfish dreams and ambitions. "You ask and do not receive, because you ask amiss, that you may spend it on your pleasures" (James 4:3).

And while we are growing in Christ, there are other important kingdom-building jobs to be done. "Be diligent to present yourself approved to God, a worker who does not need to be ashamed, rightly dividing the word of truth" (2 Tim. 2:15). The old King James Version of the text reads, "Study to show thyself approved unto God a workman that needs not be ashamed, rightly dividing the word of truth." There is no virtue in being ignorant; we must devote huge chunks of our time to the study and spreading of God's Word. Remember, we cannot extract from our memory a Bible text that wasn't implanted there in the first place. We cannot get out of the bag that which was not put there. If we wish to memorize the scripture as our Lord did, then we must engage in a systematic study of the Bible.

The final part of our growing-up experience is the sharing of our faith with others. "And when He got into the boat, he who had been demon possessed begged Him that he might be with Him. However, Jesus did not permit him, but said to him, 'Go home to your friends, and tell them what great things the Lord has done for you, and how He had compassion on you'" (Mark 5:18–19). The experience of sharing our faith has many benefits to us who are doing the witnessing and to the church, which will grow numerically as a result of our witnessing. It is only by telling others of the good things the Lord has done for us that we can bring to fruition the words the angels revealed to the disciples. "This same Jesus, who was taken up from you into heaven, will come in like manner as you saw Him go into heaven" (Acts 1:11). I can't wait for him to come again. How about you? Will his Second Coming interrupt your splendid program?

July 14

When Memory Fails

Remember His marvelous works which He has done, His wonders, and the judgments of His mouth, O seed of Abraham His servant, you Children of Jacob, His chosen ones!

—Psalm 105:5–6

On a very cold winter night, my wife and I went to a nearby Walmart to pick up a few items; but after the brief shopping, we could not locate our vehicle. Sounds familiar? We spent about ten minutes in the bitter cold wandering aimlessly in the congested parking lot, trying to find our vehicle. We thought, *It couldn't be stolen* (worst-case scenario). We pressed the remote control button, hoping that the alarm would sound off, but nothing seemed to work. The chill was biting and bone numbing, and we were too embarrassed to ask for help. After all attempts failed, we decided to retrace our entry into the huge parking lot; and finally, after a long search, we breathed a sigh of relief. We located our vehicle. Next time, we will remember where we park.

"Remember now your Creator in the days of your youth, before the difficult days come" (Eccles. 12:1). Satan is delighted when we choose to forget God's mighty acts in our lives, but we simply cannot allow this to happen. "When they went from one nation to another, from one kingdom to another people, He permitted no one to do them wrong; yes He rebuked kings for their sakes" (Ps. 105:13–14). While we are blissfully unaware, God is removing obstacles in our way and unlocking or blasting doors open for us, which would otherwise remain shut. Even while we are asleep, he keeps us safe by shielding us from illness and other catastrophes. The refrigerator, the single and most important piece of property in the home, he keeps well stocked with a marvelous diversity of good things. While on the road, we are oblivious to the dangers whizzing past us at 55 mph to 100 mph, and we arrive home in time for dinner and don't give much of a second thought about God's providence. Praise him for his goodness to us.

We hear of terrible things occurring to people in faraway places, and without a second thought, we dismiss them as being unrelated to us and our loved ones. However, the 9/11 experience taught us how small and interconnected our world really is. What happens in faraway lands can actually affect my peace with God and my fellow human beings. Can we offer a prayer to God in behalf of victims of violence with whom we may never cross path? The old folks usually say, "What affects the nose also affects the eyes."

"They did not remember His power: the day when He redeemed them from the enemy, when He worked His signs in Egypt, and His wonders in the field of Zoan" (Ps. 78:42–43). We run the risk of forgetting the many benefits the Lord has lavished on us. Why complain about what we do not have? Why don't we thank God for what we do have? Would you prefer a bigger bird in the bush you do not possess or the small one you now have in your possession? While many are thanking God for the many blessings he bestowed on them, I thank him for denying me the disastrous things I craved but were denied.

Go ahead and praise God for all his goodness toward you. If your neighbors or work buddies are a little bit cranky and difficult to live with, give thanks anyway. "Oh, give thanks for He is good! For His mercy endures forever" (Ps. 106:1). Let the redeemed of the Lord say so.

July 15

Respect Your Leaders

He permitted no one to do them wrong; yes, He rebuked kings for their sakes, saying, "Do not touch My anointed ones, and do My prophets no harm."
—Psalm 105:14–15

A lone gunman armed with rage, hate, and resentment calmly walked up to the balcony where Pres. Abraham Lincoln was viewing a play and ended his life right there, on the spot. Life has not been the same in the United States since this cowardly act was perpetrated. Respect for leadership is gradually eroding, and that is incompatible to the Word of God. Wherever authority is established—whether civil, religious, or tribal—it is responsible for the smooth functioning of civilization, and any attempt to threaten, undermine, or overthrow it becomes an assault on the very government of God.

"Then Miriam and Aaron spoke against Moses because of the Ethiopian woman whom he had married; for he had married an Ethiopian woman" (Num. 12:1). There's a lot to chew on in this verse, but we won't go there today, and it is a sticky issue anyway. Big sister Miriam and brother Aaron were unhappy with Moses's choice of a black Ethiopian for a wife and aired their displeasure in public, which was interpreted as a challenge to their brother's leadership. "Suddenly the Lord said to Moses, Aaron, and Miriam, come out, you three to the tabernacle of the meeting! So the three came out . . . Then He said, 'Hear now My words: if there is a prophet among you, I, the Lord make Myself known to him in a vision; I speak to him in a dream. Not so with My servant Moses; he is faithful in all My house. I speak with him face to face, even plainly, and not in dark sayings . . . Why then were you not afraid to speak against My servant Moses?'" (Num. 12:4, 6–8).

Spiritual leaders are not the only ones deserving of our respect; corporate leaders, civic leaders, tribal elders, elders in general, and even political leaders— undeserving as they may be—must be respected. We must not only respect the office but the holder of the office as well. "Let every soul be subject to the governing authorities. For there is no authority except from God, and the authorities that exist are appointed by God. Therefore whoever resists the authority resists the ordinance of God and those who resist will bring judgment on themselves" (Rom. 13:1–2).

Of course, many of us dare not openly take up arms to do harm to our leaders, but we may be guilty of something more sinister, such as backbiting and undermining their leadership. "But I say to you that whoever is angry with his brother without a cause shall be in danger of the judgment. And whoever says to his brother, 'Raca!' [stupid or good-for-nothing] shall be in danger of the council. But whoever says, 'you fool!' shall be in danger of hell fire" (Matt. 52:22). We should pray for our leaders, especially as they are erring.

"And seek the peace of the city where I have caused you to be carried away captive, and pray to the Lord for it; for in its peace you will have peace" (Jer. 29:7). It is a hard thing to pray for someone who has just stolen your lunch, but Jesus says to pray for him anyway, and that settles it for me. Should we even bother pray for a corrupt and repressive government or person? Yes. Jesus said it, and I believe him.

July 16

Fishers of Men

And Jesus, walking by the Sea of Galilee, saw two brothers, Simon called Peter, and Andrew his brother, casting a net into the sea; for they were fishermen. Then He said to them, Follow Me, and I will make you fishers of men.
—Matthew 4:18–19

In the icy Bering Sea, they ply their dangerous trade, catching crabs. They cast their fish traps and nets overboard and occasionally catch a fish or two but plenty of crabs. Yes, they are fishermen, and to make a living, they must outsmart these weary little creatures by enticing them into the traps. All creatures love a free lunch, and to the ocean dwellers, a free lunch is irresistible, even if it means getting caught.

But how do we catch smart, sophisticated modern fish intent on not being caught, intent on despising the simplicity of the gospel in favor of carefully devised fables? "Nothing is new under the sun." Paul confronted this very situation at Mars Hill in Athens, Greece. Men despise the simple truth in favor of the more complicated hoax. However, even when presenting the truth, we must be "wise as serpents and harmless as doves" (Matt. 10:16). Present the truth and allow the Holy Spirit to do the convicting.

"Where is the wise? Where is the scribe? Where is the disputer of this age? Has not God made foolish the wisdom of this world? For since, in the wisdom of God, the world through wisdom did not know God, it pleased God through the foolishness of the message preached to save those who believe" (1 Cor. 1:20–21). "The foolishness of preaching"—how can we, as sinners, tell other sinners to live a sinless life? It may not sound logical, but this is not for us to figure out. When we tell men the beautiful story of the life and death of Jesus, the Holy Spirit goes to work by bringing about conviction.

A smart fisherman will never throw a rock at the fish he intends to catch. Having been called to catch men puts us in a unique position to genuinely love all people, especially the ones we hope to win to Christ, and if we are not sincerely interested in their well-being, they will rip apart our mask and see through our hypocrisy. The fisherman also appeals to the fish's sense of smell, sight, and taste. Nice juicy cutlets of bait or a tantalizing sparkling lore usually does the trick. To attract others to the Pearl of great price, shouldn't we exhibit the choice gifts of the Spirit through these marvelous evangelical tools: adult education (teaching English to new immigrants), counseling, computer skills, money management courses, simple car repairs, and health awareness?

If anyone intends to catch fish, he must go where the fish are since the fish will never come to him. Smart fishermen usually go where the fish gather in schools; this, of course, maximizes their catch. Paul and the early disciples practiced this type of fishing. They conducted evangelistic campaigns in large cities where the masses lived. Jesus commands us to go to every nation, kingdom, tongue, and people, including the residents of Amazonia, Papua New Guinea, and beyond.

Have you been fishing lately? Have you caught anything yet? Are you being successful in attracting fish? If one bait isn't working for you, try another, and ask God to help you in your endeavor. It is not rocket science. Jesus usually told his hearers, "Go home to your friends, and tell them what great things the Lord has done for you and how He has had compassion on you" (Mark 5:19). That's all it takes; it's that simple. Leave the rest to the Holy Spirit. Happy fishing, my friend. May you have the catch of a lifetime.

July 17

Jesus Loves Me, This I Know

In this is love, not that we love God, but that He loved us and sent His son to be the propitiation for our sins.

—1 John 4:10

Love is in the air on the Galápagos Islands. A male frigate bird is putting on a fantastic display on land for the lady of his dream. He inflates his puffy red pouch and vigorously displays a delicate dance, chirping sweet lullabies as he flutters his wings. If she's impressed, she'll descend from her aerial hovering and join him in raising a family. Fantastic stories abound of how modern-day Romeos meet their Juliets, but none is more fascinating than God's relationship with his bride, Israel. How did this one-sided relationship work? Did it really work at all? How did it end?

"When Israel was a child, I loved him, and out of Egypt I called My son . . . I taught Ephraim to walk, taking them by their arms . . . I drew them with gentle cords, with bands of love" (Hosea 11:1, 3–4). What a beautiful imagery of God's passionate affection for his people of Israel. God doted on Israel, his bride-to-be, and led her to the fertile green land of Goshen. However, the pharaoh had other plans for Israel, enslaving them to build his public works infrastructure, but things went from bad to worse for the Egyptian nation as God rained down plagues on them and delivered his people with signs and great wonders. "Egypt was glad when they departed, for the fear of them had fallen upon them. He spread a cloud for a covering, and fire to give them light in the night" (Ps. 105:38–39). At Sinai, God and Israel consummated their marriage with these solemn words: "Now therefore, if you will indeed obey My voice and keep My covenant, then you shall be a special treasure to Me above all people . . . And you shall be to Me a kingdom of priest and a holy nation . . . So Moses came and called for the elders of the people; and laid before them all these words which the Lord commanded them. Then all the people answered together and said, 'All that the Lord has spoken we will do.' So Moses brought back the words of the people to the Lord" (Exod. 19:5–8).

The honeymoon was hardly over when the pleasure-loving and adventurous bride went searching for greener pasture. Did God give up on his thrill-seeking bride in light of her unfaithfulness? Absolutely not. The Lord's love and mercy went into high gear trying to woo unfaithful Israel back to him. "My people are bent on backsliding from Me . . . How can I give you up, Ephraim? How can I hand you over, Israel? How can I make you like Admah? How can I make you like Zeboiim? [cities destroyed by the Lord for their wickedness] My heart churns within Me; My sympathy is stirred. I will not execute the fierceness of My anger; I will not again destroy Ephraim" (Hosea 11:7–9).

Regrettably, Israel was no longer interested in being faithful to God, and she became addicted to her idols. "When I saw that for all the causes for which backsliding Israel had committed adultery, I had put her away and given her a certificate of divorce; but her treacherous sister Judah did not fear, but went and played the harlot also" (Jer. 3:8). He loves us even more despite our unfaithfulness. "But where sin abounded, grace abounded much more" (Rom. 5:20). Aren't you grateful for God's unconditional love with no strings attached? We come to him messed up, and he makes us whole with no question asked and without exposing our hideous past. I am grateful for such tender love.

July 18

Jesus Wept

O Jerusalem, Jerusalem, the one who kills the prophets and stones those who are sent to her!
How often I wanted to gather your children together, as a hen gathers her chicks under her wings, but you were not willing!

—Matthew 23:37

Mrs. Gibson (name changed) peeps into her son's bedroom to see whether he's home. The bed is neatly made, and the room is tidy, but Arnold is not home. She worries and with good reason. Heroin has been making a comeback in upscale middle-class neighborhoods. Her worst fears are confirmed: Arnold, a straight A student, has been failing his classes at a plush, elite college. His speech is slurred, his weight has dropped precipitously, and his hygiene is an afterthought. Mrs. Gibson is silently weeping as any mother would, but she does something beyond weeping. She confronts Arnold, who admits his affliction and volunteers to be treated at a rehab center.

Jesus wept the same way over a nation in denial of its addiction to idolatry. "For you were hypocrites in your hearts when you sent me to the Lord your God, saying, pray for us to the Lord our God, and according to all that the Lord your God says, to declare to us and we will do. And I have this day declared it to you, but you have not obeyed the voice of the Lord your God, or anything which He has sent you by me" (Jer. 42:20–21). Are we also blameless for the many promises we have made to God and miserably failed in fulfilling? God is merciful, isn't he? Jeremiah loved his people and shared in their fate and suffering, and even when his loyalty was questioned, he remained patriotic, loyal, and faithful. "Oh, that my head were waters, and my eyes a fountain of tears, that I might weep day and night for the slain of the daughters of my people!" (Jer. 9:1).

If Jesus were here in person, would he weep over our addiction for the nonessential things of this world? Some pat themselves on the back, surrounded by their expensive toys. "Soul you have many goods laid up for many years; take your ease; eat drink, and be merry. But God said to him, Fool! This night your soul will be required of you" (Luke 12:19–20). At whose expense do we amass all these wasteful toys? Shouldn't we "seek first the kingdom of God and His righteousness and all these things shall be added to [us]" (Matt. 6:33)? Do we really need the expensive fast cars and all those glittering electronic gadgets? Do we really?

If Jesus were here today and proceeded toward the refrigerator, what would greet his sight? Well, we know wine and liquor would not be in there, but how about the sodium-laden, overprocessed foods? What would he find in there? Would he be able to recognize anything in there? Would he find collard greens (one of my favorites), broccoli, carrots, apples, and Kedem grape juice (another of my favorites) in there?

If Jesus were here today and took a look at your computer hard drive, what would he find on it? If he proceeded to the living room table and took a look at the cash receipts of your recent credit card purchases, would he compliment you or be horrified at the terrific waste and questionable payments you made to business organizations? Some people call it putting money in a pocket full of holes, but let's call it what it really is—madness. "Why spend your money for what is not bread, and your wages for what does not satisfy? Listen carefully to Me, and eat what is good" (Isa. 55:2).

July 19

Prepare Me a Body

Sacrifice and offering You did not desire, but a body You have prepared for Me. In burnt offerings and sacrifices for sin You have no pleasure. Then I said, behold, I have come, in the volume of the book it is written of Me to do Your will, O God.
—Hebrews 10:5–7

Yang (name changed) traded his law enforcement uniform for a motorbike, a black leather jacket, and a bad attitude to infiltrate a criminal mob enterprise. Although he came under intense suspicion many times and was nearly killed, Yang was able to convince the crime boss that he was rough and tough as any other gang member. But how he navigated the gang initiation process, which involved committing a brutal crime, remained a mystery. In the end, the gang was infiltrated, mysterious and cold case crimes were solved, and many gang members were arrested, tried, and sentenced to long prison terms (http://www.lamag.com/culturefiles/the-cop-who-infiltrated-southern-californias-most-notorious-biker-gangs/).

The role of a double agent has never been easy, and many good men have perished in trying to serve two masters, but Jesus was no double agent as defined by the counterintelligence manual; he was fully God and fully man at the same time. "In the beginning was the Word, and the Word was with God, and the Word was God. He was in the beginning with God" (John 1:1–2). Jesus is coequal with God the Father and God the Holy Spirit. They have always been together and owe their origin to no other being or force. They are self-existent and have always been there, but something interesting happened that made Jesus take upon himself human nature. Do you know what?

"Therefore rejoice, O heavens, and you who dwell in them! Woe to the inhabitants of the earth and the sea! For the devil has come down to you, having great wrath, because he knows that he has a short time" (Rev. 12:12). Planet Earth and its human occupants became victims of the enraged fallen angel (Lucifer) cast out from heaven. However, God was not caught napping, and the plan that was devised in eternity past, before the foundation of the earth was laid, went into effect.

"And the Word became flesh and dwelt among us, and we beheld His glory, the glory as of the only begotten of the Father full of grace and truth" (John 1:14). No one wore the human body as proudly as Jesus. Despite being God in every respect and having the keys to all the prerogatives of God, he chose to proudly identify himself as the Son of man, instead of the Son of God. "Foxes have holes and birds of the air have nest, but the *Son of Man* has nowhere to lay His head" (Matt. 8:20, emphasis mine). The one who crafted and designed the universe did not have a place to call home.

God's love for humanity is indescribable. Nothing written, sung, or composed can adequately help us comprehend the depth, height, and width of God's love. A little boy was asked to describe his dad's love for him. He stretched both hands horizontally, as far as they could go, and said, "This much." God loves us that much and more. "O love that will not let me go, I rest my weary soul in thee; I give thee back the life I owe, that in thine ocean depth its flow may richer, fuller be" (George Matheson). We can never fully understand the full dimension of God's love for us; it will be a science to be studied throughout the ceaseless ages of eternity. Dear God, thank you for loving me, even when I am unlovely.

July 20

News of His Demise

And Jesus cried out again with a loud voice, and yielded up His spirit.
—Matthew 27:50

Although he predicted it would happen, no one really believed him; but when it did, it shook the nation to its very core. On April 4, 1968, Martin Luther King Jr. was assassinated by James Earl Ray at the Lorraine Motel in Memphis, Tennessee. In his last speech at the Mason Temple in Memphis, Martin lamented, "Like anybody else, I would like to live a long life, but longevity has its place. But I'm not concerned about that now." Also, in his "I Have a Dream" speech and throughout his career as a civil rights advocate, Martin Luther King predicted his death as he became public enemy number one to the establishment. "Then they said to one another, look, this dreamer is coming! Come therefore, let us now kill him and cast him into some pit; and we shall say, some wild beast has devoured him. We shall see what will become of his dreams!" (Gen. 37:19–20).

Another dreamer predicted his demise, but no one listened to or believed him, not even the ones hatching the plot to kill him. "Why do you seek to kill Me?" (John 8:40). The people answered and said, "You have a demon. Who is seeking to kill you?" Despite masking their true purpose with trash-talking, they did succeed in killing the Lord of glory. "Most assuredly, I say to you, unless a grain of wheat falls into the ground and dies, it remains alone; but if it dies it produces much fruit" (John 12:24).

But the Savior's death produced much fruit, and what an abundant harvest it was! The grain of wheat, symbolic of the death of Jesus Christ, saved every soul that repented, from Adam down to the last repentant sinner before the close of this age. If Jesus hadn't died, there would have been no resurrection for Lazarus, no translation for Enoch and Elijah. If Jesus hadn't died, Moses would not have been resurrected from the grave. If Jesus hadn't died, the demons would have laughed at Elisha resurrecting the Shunamite's son. If Jesus hadn't died, the graves would have remained perpetually shut and would have been the permanent home of mankind. If Jesus hadn't died, mankind—including you and me—would have been eternally lost. The news of his death had been greatly exaggerated by Satan and his demons. "I am He who lives, and was dead, and behold, I am alive forevermore. Amen! I have the keys of Hades and of Death" (Rev. 1:18).

The significance of Christ's death is mind-boggling. Here's a sample of what Christ's death accomplished for us: eternal life for the saved, gaining the keys from God to unlock the grave and liberate the saved held captive by death, an end to the reign of sin, the demise of Satan, the restoration of the rebellious earth back to the family of the universe, and the relocation of God's throne from heaven to the new earth.

"Then I, John saw the holy city, the New Jerusalem, coming down out of heaven from God, prepared as a bride adorned for her husband. And I heard a loud voice from heaven saying, behold, the tabernacle of God is with men, and He will dwell with them, and they shall be His people. God Himself will be with them and be their God. And God will wipe away every tear from their eyes; there shall be no more death, nor sorrow, nor crying. There shall be no more pain, for the former things have passed away" (Rev. 21:2–4).

July 21

Leaders Are Not Born; They're Made

Now therefore, please let your servant remain instead of the lad as a slave to my lord and let the lad go up with his brothers. For how shall I go up to my father if the lad is not with me, lest perhaps I see the evil that would come upon my father?
—Genesis 44:33–34

Qualifying for the Olympics was the easy part as grueling as it was; then came the illness and the magnanimous decision to relinquish her spot on the team to her sister, Lanny. Tracy and Lanny Barnes were inseparable sisters and training partners for the U.S. biathlon team. Training involved a twenty-kilometer cross-country hike on ski and in snow while shooting at targets with a rifle, but after qualifying for the

U.S. team, Tracy became seriously ill and missed three important practice events. The true Olympian came out of her when she coerced her sister into taking her place at the Sochi Olympic. Her little sister strongly protested, but Tracy would have none of it. "You're going to represent the nation in my place," she insisted. Who can argue with that? (https://www.usatoday.com/story/sports/olympics/sochi/2014/01/14/olympic-athlete-biathlon-gives-spot-to-twin-sister/4475535/).

Judah and his brothers were not the firebrands they once were as young adults, but Joseph needed proof to be convinced of the change he had noticed in them. He had one more trick up his sleeve. At his command, his drinking cup was placed in the grain sack of Benjamin, his younger brother, and what took place thereafter is a selfless act for the ages. Judah, not knowing that he was talking to his younger brother Joseph—the one whom he and the other brothers had sold into slavery a few decades before—decided to become a personal slave to Joseph instead of Benjamin, in whose sack the cup was found. His humility and magnanimity melted Joseph's heart. Joseph was stunned and overcome with emotion by Judah's selfless act. "Then Joseph could not restrain himself before all those who stood by him, and he cried out, 'Make everyone go out from me!' So no one stood with him while Joseph made himself known to his brothers" (Gen. 45:1).

As impressive as Tracy's selfless act of surrendering her place on the national team to her sister, Lenny, and Judah in becoming a slave to Prime Minister Joseph to shield his younger brother Benjamin from the rigors of slavery, there is an act that is unparalleled in the annals of the earth's history. "Sacrifice and offering You did not desire, but a body You have prepared for Me. In burnt offerings and sacrifices for sin You had no pleasure. Then I said, behold, I have come, in the volume of the book it is written of Me, to do Your will, O My God" (Heb. 10:5–7). Did you capture the moment? He has prepared a body like ours. Oh what love! The Master and Maker of the universe became like one of us. The little good in us is pale in comparison to the great sacrifice Jesus did on our behalf. Is it any wonder that the cross of Christ will be a study that will occupy the minds of the righteous saints, the angels, and all the intelligent universe for the rest of eternity?

It must have been a very tough decision for God to give up the One who was in his very bosom for naughty sinners like you and me, but he did. "In this the love of God was manifested towards us, that God has sent His only begotten Son into the world, that we might live through Him. In this is love, not that we loved God, but that He loved us and sent His Son to be the propitiation for our sins" (1 John 4:9–10). Thank you, God, for loving us in all our mess, and thank you, Jesus, for dying in our place. Thank you again.

The Rush Is On

But as the days of Noah were, so also will the coming of the Son of Man be.
—Matthew 24:37

They stand in line with boarding passes in hand, eyes riveted on the ticket agent at the boarding gate. They're going somewhere, just about everywhere. Some are going on dream vacations or visiting loved ones in faraway places, others on business trips, but most are just doing what regular people do every day—traveling from one place to another. A gentleman is on his way to attend his daughter's wedding and anticipates a bonanza of memorable events. A soldier in full battle attire, with his backpack at his feet, is anxiously anticipating his homecoming and the sweet aroma of homemade dinners and kisses from his wife. He has not held his nine-month-old son because of his Afghanistan deployment. A mother of three toddlers has her hands full in corralling her troops in line on their way to see Grandma. Everybody seems busy these days.

Nothing will change leading to the Second Coming of Jesus Christ; everybody will be busy doing something. "For as in the days before the flood, they were eating and drinking, marrying and giving in marriage until the day that Noah entered the ark, and did not know until the flood came and took them all away, so also will the coming of the Son of Man be" (Matt. 24:38–39). The scripture is quite emphatic about the behavior of society leading to the Second Coming of Christ. Quite obviously, people will arise and do the regular things they are accustomed to doing with little thought of the climatic and social changes taking place all around them. Should the people of God be blissfully unaware of the times and seasons leading to the Second Coming of Jesus Christ?

"Now learn this parable from the fig tree: when its branch has already become tender and puts forth leaves you know that summer is near. So you also, when you see all these things, know that it is near—at the doors" (Matt. 24:32–33). Peering through the corridors of time, Jesus predicted the social, political, and military climate that would precede the destruction of Jerusalem. Now prophecy has dual application; though written for the first-century church, it speaks eloquently to our days. The natural disasters, political upheavals, senseless violence, unprovoked shootings, unnatural affections, sports crazes, and callous indifference to God's Word will precede the Second Coming of Christ. This type of behavior, which was typical of Noah's civilization, will serve as a prelude to Christ's Second Coming. As we see the events foretold by Jesus and the prophets being fulfilled from the comfort of our living rooms, we must spend quality time consolidating and building up our relationship with God. To be forewarned is to be forearmed. May God help us not repeat the fatal behavior of Noah's generation.

"Therefore brothers establish your hearts for the coming of the Lord is at hand" (James 5:8). Jesus wants his people to live in a constant state of preparedness;

understanding the seriousness of the times will enable us to walk closer and more circumspectly with God. "Now our salvation is nearer than when we first believed" (Rom. 13:11). As the day of the Lord approaches, the only safe and secure place to be is in God's pavilion. I want to be where God is. Don't you?

July 23

I Will Arise and Build

Therefore whoever hears these sayings of mine, and does them, I will liken him to a wise man who built his house on the rock: and the rain descended, the floods came, and the winds blew and beat on that house; and it did not fall, for it was founded upon the rock.

—Matthew 7:24–25

With little more than dogged determination and a lot of faith, Vicky decided to build her house with very limited financial resources. Seizing on a "yes, I can" inspirational moment, Vicky noticed a building project under construction in her community and asked the building constructor to draw up a plan for her dream house. With her house plan in hand, she proceeded to secure a small loan from her local bank. Empowered by her new founding, she contacted an excavating contractor to dig her foundation. It was all done at the spur of the moment with very little planning. With an attitude of "build as resources become available," Vicky is currently sitting pretty in a lovely three-story house that her son helped her finish.

However, Vicky was far from being satisfied. She became even more restless now that her temporal home has been completed, so she embarked on a new construction—her spiritual house. Barely literate, she decided to know God personally by studying his Word, but she could barely read. She spent long hours sounding out the vowels and pronouncing simple Bible passages until she taught herself to read the scriptures all by herself. She proudly displayed to me her time-worn, liquid-smeared Sunday missal Catholic manual, which she used as her textbook. "God works in mysterious ways his wonders to perform."

God is working diligently to bring all his children into a saving relationship with himself, and he accepts them where they are, regardless of their religious affiliation. "My Father has been working until now, and I have been working" (John 5:17). God is hard at work, using instruments beyond our knowledge in bringing his children from all religious persuasions to know him as Savior and Lord. "And other sheep that I have which are not of this fold; them also I must bring, and they will hear My voice; and there will be one flock and one Shepherd" (John 10:16).

The Holy Spirit is also very busy urging all to build a lasting relationship with God. Before his death, Jesus made an urgent request of the Father on our behalf. "And I will pray the Father, and He will give you another Helper, that He may abide with you forever . . . I will not leave you orphans; I will come to you" (John 14:16, 18). Our loving Father has placed at our fingertips the resources needed for a meaningful relationship with him, and here is a sampling of the goodies that will help build our character: "But the fruit of the Spirit is love, joy, peace, longsuffering, kindness, goodness, faithfulness, gentleness, self-control" (Gal. 5:22–23). The building material is here and within easy access for a deeper relationship with God. All that is required of us is to rise and use the building material provided to us.

Have you begun your building project yet? Is your spiritual house in order? Are you ready for translation? Are you ready to meet your God if you are called home tonight? Time is not our ally; let us ask God for the will to begin building our spiritual house.

July 24

Sing to the Lord a New Song

Sing to the Lord a new song! For He has done marvelous things; His right hand and holy arm has gained Him the victory.

—Psalm 98:1–2

His melodious songs can be heard about twenty miles away, but this time, his tune has a special sense of urgency. He must convince the girls that he has the maturity and discipline to raise a family. Other whales click, quack, and chirp, but the mighty humpback is a true maestro (master musician). It is not known why humpbacks sing. We can guess the motive behind their mystery tunes, which you can help me with. Since only the males sing, maybe it's a love song, a song to court a mate, or a song to denote location. Could it be a song to demonstrate dominance or seniority or just another humpback singing in a talent show? Whatever is their motive, their songs are sweet, intense, powerful, impressive, and melodious. Keep on singing, humpbacks. We're listening.

Humans sing also. When we sing, it's usually when we're happy, and we make others happy with our songs. We sing to please others. We sing to learn things. We sing for pleasure. We sing in contest with others to discover who has the sweetest melody. We sing out of a sense of duty to our nation. Some sing for their dinner (making money), but believers sing with purpose—to praise God, to honor him, and to glorify our God, who has been so mighty good to us. And this is a song worth singing: "I will bless the Lord at all times; His praise shall continually be in my mouth. My soul shall make its boast in the Lord, the humble shall hear of it and be glad. Oh, magnify the Lord with me, and let us exalt His name together . . . The righteous cry out, and the Lord hears, and delivers them out of all their troubles. The Lord is near to those who have a broken heart, and saves such as have a contrite spirit" (Ps. 34:1–3, 17–18).

While it is always good to thank God for narrow escapes from sickness, accidents, or even death, God deserves our praise at all times, whether in good times or bad. "I will praise you, O Lord, with my whole heart; I will tell of all Your marvelous works. I will be glad and rejoice in You; I will sing praise to Your name,

O Most High" (Ps. 9:1–2). The abundance of God's blessings is all around us. When trouble strikes—and it will—we must not despair but see it as an occasion to glorify the God we serve. God said of the pharaoh, "For this very purpose I have raised you up, that I may show My power in you, and that My name may be declared in all the earth" (Exod. 9:16). Does God use adversity to bring honor and glory to his name? Of course. The Psalms were born out of affliction. They are the excruciating and bitter experiences of God's people triumphing over difficult circumstances. They composed the Psalms for our benefit.

Sometimes the glory of God runs ahead of us, and we must pause and give him thanks for his goodness and mighty works in our behalf as in this case: "For we have heard how the Lord dried up the water of the Red Sea for you when you came out of Egypt, and what you did to the two kings of the Amorites who were on the other side of Jordan, Sihon and Og, whom you utterly destroyed" (Josh. 2:10). We thank God for what he has done, what he is doing in our behalf, and what he will do for us. Have you praised and thanked God lately for drying up your Red Sea (obstacles)? Does he still work wonders in your life? Are you aware of his miraculous works in your life?

July 25

It's All Over

Do not be unequally yoked together with unbelievers, for what fellowship has righteousness with lawlessness? And what communion has light with darkness? And what accord has Christ with Belial?

—2 Corinthians 6:14–15

He called by phone, and the tone of his voice suggested urgency. He even proposed marriage, but Vicky would have none of it. The shenanigan was over; the lies, the double-talk, the deceptions are all over. Vicky finally got it right; her spiritual eyes had been opened. She claimed Christ as Savior and Lord and wanted to live right and do his will, so Mr. Unreliable and his procrastinations had to go.

Christ and Satan's kingdoms are mutually exclusive (cannot both be true). They can never unite, can never be at peace, and do not have the same agenda. While we must interact with the world for business, social, and other pressing necessities, we should not get entangled in the world's agenda. Let's define *world* from a scriptural perspective: any set of values that are in opposition to the kingdom of God is of the world. "Do not love the world or the things in the world. If anyone loves the world, the love of the Father is not in him. For all that is in the world—the lust of the flesh, the lust of the eyes, and the pride of life—is not of the Father but is of the world" (1 John 2:15–16). The apostle John has not left us guessing about the transience (short-livedness) of the world. "And the world is passing away and the lust of it; but he who does the will of God abides forever" (1 John 2:17). Is there anything more permanent in this world than God and his Word?

As we approach the end of the age, the lines of moral behavior are becoming extremely blurred. Behaviors that were once morally unacceptable are gradually being worked into our psyche, and since we have been forewarned, we therefore should be forearmed. "But know this, that in the last days perilous times will come: for men will be lovers of themselves, lovers of money, boasters, proud blasphemers, disobedient to parents, unthankful, unholy, unloving, unforgiving, slanderers, without self-control, brutal, despisers of those that are good, traitors, headstrong, haughty, lovers of pleasure rather than lovers of God, having a form of godliness but denying its power" (2 Tim. 3:1–5). Doesn't this quote sound like an article on the nightly news or the morning paper?

God's people have always been distinct and identifiable throughout the ages. Abraham and other Bible patriarchs refused to conform to the customs of their idolatrous neighbors. Unlike their neighbors, they walked with a God whom they could neither see nor transport but nonetheless was real and very present with them. We serve such a God, the very God Abraham served, and he is with us even when we do not perceive him. When the pressure to conform to worldly standards escalates, he is faithful and provides sufficient strength when the temptation increases.

The darkest period of the night precedes morning; likewise, the wanton immorality prevailing in our days is indicative of Jesus's soon return. "Now when these things begin to happen, look up and lift up your heads, because your redemption draws near" (Luke 21:28). This world, with all its glittering arcades and fancy extravaganzas, is gradually coming to an end. Have you noticed? Even those oblivious to Bible prophecy are noticing the signs. Are you walking in tune with the Lord?

July 26

The Blood of Abel

And He said, what have you done? The voice of your brother's blood cries out to Me from the ground.

—Genesis 4:10

Captured at gunpoint and forced to carry AK-47 machine guns, the little child soldiers are forced to terrorize the communities where their aunts and mothers reside. While these children are emotionally scarred for life, few of their abusers have been caught, let alone brought to justice. Heinous crimes too horrible to describe are being committed daily, and in some cases, the perpetrator may choose to escape justice by taking his own life, leaving grieving families and baffled law enforcement officers scrambling for answers. Those enforcing the law are hardly the only ones confused and alarmed by the rising tide of iniquity. "Why do You show me iniquity, and cause me to see trouble? For plundering and violence are before me; there is strife, and contention. Therefore the law is powerless, and justice never goes forth. For the wicked surround the righteous; therefore perverse judgment proceeds" (Hab. 1:3–4).

When the law of the land is slow to act or may not act at all and may choose to look the other way, when interest groups with their deep pockets circumvent the legal system, is there anything we can trust? The Word of God is our only course of comfort, hope, and security. "Though a sinner does evil a hundred times, and his days are prolonged, yet I surely know that it will be well with those who fear God, who fear before Him. But it will not be well with the wicked; nor will he prolong his days, which are as a shadow, because he does not fear before God" (Eccles. 8:12–13).

When justice evades the child of God, and resources to fight corruption are nonexistent, we must appeal to a higher authority. "Then Pilate said to Him, are you not speaking to me? Do you not know that I have power to crucify You, and power to release You? Jesus answered, you could have no power at all against Me unless it had been given you from above" (John 19:10–11).

Even if justice fails as it may and we appeal to a higher court and find no justice here on this earth, we must be careful to live without animosity toward our abusers. In fact, Jesus has given the perfect formula that can cause us to heal and live a normal life without being traumatized by the past. "You have heard that it was said, you shall love your neighbor and hate your enemy. But I say to you, love your enemies, bless those who curse you, do good to those who hate you, and pray for those who spitefully use you and persecute you" (Matt. 5:43–44). There is power in praying for your tormentor. It brings glory to God when others see the image of Jesus being reflected in you. It gives you power over your abuser since you are no longer controlled by him. With that said, we can safely conclude that by not retaliating, Stephen, Paul, and the long list of martyrs will soon have their day in court. Are you still harboring old grudges and grievances? Being free entails not allowing another person's unkind action keep you in bondage.

"Beloved, do not avenge yourselves, but rather give place to wrath; for it is written, vengeance is mine, I will repay says the Lord" (Rom. 12:19). Hang on in there, dear saint. Justice is just around the corner. Do not, by any means, avenge yourself.

July 27

Help! Help! Help!

Behold He who keeps Israel shall neither slumber nor sleep.

—Psalm 121:4

I turned and twisted and shuffled from one side of the bed to the other but to no avail; sleep did not come to me until the blaring, loud music was turned off at 5:30 a.m. The first night of our dream vacation was an absolute disaster. We found ourselves inadvertently trapped smack in the center of a Caribbean carnival celebration. The monstrous ten-foot speakers pulsating unintelligible loud music kept us awake till the wee hours of the morning. When I could no longer tolerate the loud blasts emanating from the blaring speakers, I called the local police to have things toned down, but my many calls went unanswered. I tried the capital police, who attempted to contact their local subordinates, but to no avail; they were fast asleep. Finally, at about 1:00 a.m., I gathered the courage and approached a young man sitting on a stool (the DJ and the source of my sleeplessness) and kindly asked him to tone down the music. He did lower it somewhat, and finally, I had some sweet sleep.

Sleep is very essential to us humans, but God never sleeps and is accessible to us all day, every day and is very much awake. Is he always alert to the cry of his people? But of course. "He who keeps Israel shall neither slumber nor sleep" (Ps. 121:4). The sun rises and sets, and few take notice. Tender blades of grass provide fuel for animals, benefiting man. The seasons roll in and out, providing us with a variety of temperature changes. Animals raise their families when food supply is abundant to preserve their species. Is God wide awake at the wheels? Has he put the world on cruise control, or has he delegated his responsibilities to nature? No. Everything conceivable, however minute, is upheld by God. "The heavens declare the glory of God; and the firmament shows His handiwork. Day unto day utters speech and night unto night reveals knowledge. There is no speech nor language where their voice is not heard" (Ps. 19:1–3).

Besides supervising nature and overseeing an infinite universe, God is busy listening to and answering the prayers of his people. Take notice: "Now while I was speaking, praying, and confessing my sins and the sins of my people Israel, and presenting my supplication before the Lord my God for the Holy Mountain of my God, yes while I was speaking in prayer, the man Gabriel, whom I had seen in vision at the beginning, being caused to fly swiftly, reached me about the time of the evening offering" (Dan. 9:20–21). Did you catch this? While the prophet was still in prayer, the angel Gabriel was instantly dispatched to assist him in understanding the vision, and he made it in time for the evening sacrifice held at 3:00 p.m. God is just a prayer away.

God is ever ready to hear, assist, and answer the prayers of his children. No one understood this better than David. When found in constant tight spots fighting the battles of the Lord, he called on God very often to deliver him. "If it had not been the Lord who was on our side, when men rose up against us, then they would have swallowed us alive. When their wrath was kindled against us; then the waters would have overwhelmed us, the stream would have gone over our soul" (Ps. 124:2–4).

Seeing that our God is everywhere at all times, his shop never shuts, and he is in the prayer-answering business, shouldn't we pray and call on him more often?

July 28

Background Noise

But take heed to yourselves, lest your hearts be weighed down with carousing, drunkenness, and cares of this life, and that Day come on you unexpectedly. For it will come as a snare on all those who dwell on the face of the whole earth.

—Luke 21:34–35

We were talking to each other within hearing range but could not hear a word from the other because of the background noise. The expressions on our faces revealed our utter frustration at being within talking range yet unable to hear each other. We live in the tristate DC region and sometimes go for afternoon strolls at Gravelly Point Park in Washington DC, but when the noisy Boeing 737 is taxiing down the runway for takeoff, you can forget about talking; communication is nearly impossible.

Today's technological inventions, innovations, and achievements are disrupting the normal functions of the family. Mom has made dinner, but everyone is in their own high-tech world, so she must send a mass text to assemble family members to the dinner table. While dinner is being eaten, Suzan has one eye on the food and the other on her smartphone; she periodically checks her instrument for the latest text message.

Is today's technology affecting the way we interact with each other? Scientists think as we delegate more of our chores to machines, the biggest losers are ourselves. In his article in *Psychology Today*, Brain Bootcamp asks the question "Is technology fracturing your family?" Well, it's a no-brainer; it already has. The smartphones, iPads, and laptops are making us lonelier, more insular (uninterested in other happenings), less interactive with each other and the world in general.

While we thank God for modern technology, which is facilitating the spread of the everlasting gospel, we must be careful that technology does not become a background noise hindering us from hearing the voice of God. "Give ear to my words, O Lord, consider my meditation. Give heed to the voice of my cry, my King and my God, for to You will I pray. My voice You will hear in the morning, O Lord; in the morning I will direct it to You, and I will look up" (Ps. 5:1–3). Whether in the morning, at noon, or in the evening, God is expecting to hear from his earthbound children, but the noise of technology is deafening, hindering that communication and distracting us from true devotion to our God. Who hasn't fallen in the trap of spending enormous quantities of time listening to music on YouTube? Do I plead the Fifth Amendment? Yes. I am guilty as charged, but I am a reformed offender.

"Turn your eyes upon Jesus, look full in his wonderful face, and the things of earth will grow strangely dim in the light of his glory and grace." The songwriter has just given us the solution to our perplexing modern dilemma. Turning our full attention to God and his kingdom will detach us from the dross of worldliness. Turn off the gadgets and the background noises, pick up the good old-fashioned Bible, and give thanks to the God of the universe. Let us not make gods of the instruments with which he has blessed us.

With all the noise and distractions around us, we are in mortal danger of not hearing the still small voice of the Holy Spirit. "He who has ears to hear, let him hear!" (Matt. 13:9).

July 29

Consecrate Me, Lord

As they ministered to the Lord and fasted, the Holy Spirit said, separate to Me Barnabas and Saul for the work to which I have called them.

—Acts 13:2

Their work in the community bore testimony of their service to God. On a crisp Sabbath morning, Rudulph (name changed) was ordained as an elder of his local church, together with two other counterparts ordained as deacons. Elders were notorious in Bible times for their honesty, integrity, and humility, and my friend Rudulph is uniquely qualified for this office. Knowing him since childhood, it was no surprise to me when he was called by his peers for this servant leadership position. While I tip my hat in affirmation to him, we must recognize that his work in building the kingdom of God has just begun.

"I charge you therefore before God and the Lord Jesus Christ, who will judge the living and the dead at His appearing and his kingdom. Preach the word! Be ready in season and out of season. Convince, rebuke, exhort, with all longsuffering and teaching" (2 Tim. 4:1–2). While this charge is applicable to all believers, an elder's life is woven in the fabric of service to the church and is empowered by this charge to fulfill his ministry.

"This is a faithful saying: if a man desires the position of a bishop he desires a good work. A bishop must be blameless, the husband of one wife, temperate, sober-minded, of good behavior, hospitable, able to teach; not given to wine, not violent, not greedy for money, but gentle, not quarrelsome, not covetous; one who rules his own house well" (1 Tim. 3:1–4). This code of ethics is particularly high to elders by virtue of their visible role among the community of believers. In essence, this standard is applicable to all officers employed in the Lord's vineyard.

The Holy Spirit cannot and will not work in an unclean vessel. "I beseech you therefore, brethren, by the mercies of God, that you present your bodies a living sacrifice, holy, acceptable to God which is your reasonable service. And do not be conformed to this world, but be transformed by the renewing of your mind that you may prove what is good and acceptable and perfect will of God" (Rom. 12:1–2).

Even if one isn't an elder, a deacon, or some other officer in the church, Paul's instruction to live a consecrated life is what Christianity is all about. After all, did not Jesus set the example for us? "Do you know what I have done to you? You call Me Teacher and Lord, and you say well, for so I am. If I then, your Lord and Teacher have washed your feet, you also ought to wash one another's feet. For I have given you an example, that you should do as I have done to you" (John 13:12–15).

The call for sacrificial and holy living has always been the criteria God's people have been called to attain, but it is even more necessary today as we witness a general decline in moral and ethical behavior. "But you are a chosen generation, a royal priesthood, a holy nation, His own special people that you may proclaim the praises of Him who called you out of darkness into His marvelous light" (1 Pet. 2:9). We must stand in the gap and uphold the bloodstained banner of Christ's righteousness in our lives. Can God depend on you and me to make a difference in the life of someone else by our holy living?

July 30

Where Do You Stand?

And it came to pass, when Joshua was by Jericho, that he lifted his eyes and looked, and behold, a man stood opposite him with his sword drawn in his hand. And Joshua went to Him and said to Him, are You for us or for our adversary?
—Joshua 5:13

He was in sympathy with both sides of the conflict. Therefore he wore a coat of the Confederacy and the pants of the Union and ended up being shot to shreds by both sides in the conflict. The late great Martin Luther King once said, "If you don't stand for something, you will fall for anything." In the shifting sands of today's ethical and moral standards, the Word of God is the only sure foundation to build on. "The grass withers, the flower fades, but the word of the Lord stands forever" (Isa. 40:8). The Bible is still God's manual for holy living; without it, society will simply disintegrate. Written by holy men under the inspiration of the Holy Spirit, the sacred scriptures is the only relevant guide for holy living. As the saying goes, "Don't leave home without it."

The Ten Commandments are the jewels in the crown of God's will, and they are the origin of all human laws. Nations have woven their principles into their laws and have enacted them as a good moral restraint on their citizens. Its laws governing health, diet, hygiene, business, reparation, disposal of waste, and the family's code of ethics were ahead of any law of its time. The Ten Commandments do not contain all the above-mentioned units, but in general, the whole body of God's laws does. The Bible is the very Word of God and has stood the test of time. Should we now question its authority and authenticity? I will not argue against it.

"I understand more than the ancients, because I keep Your precepts. I have restrained my feet from every evil way, that I may keep Your word. I have not departed from Your judgments, for You Yourself have taught me. How sweet are Your words to my taste, sweeter than honey to my mouth! Through Your precepts I get understanding; therefore I hate every false way. Your word is a lamp to my feet and light to my path" (Ps. 119:100–105).

During the darkest period of the earth's history, God-fearing men from all walks of life have peered into its sacred pages for guidance and solutions to circumstances beyond their control. The Bible was a source of comfort and reference to Abraham Lincoln as he presided over a nation torn apart by Civil War. In the closing moments of the Second World War, the Bible was often quoted by leaders on both sides of the conflict as they sought ways to bring the conflict to an end. Although slaveholders misinterpreted its precepts to suit their misguided interests, the Negro slaves found great comfort in appropriating its precious promises and latching on to the eternal values within its sacred pages. Etched on the building of the United Nations in New York are these words: "They shall beat their swords into plowshares, and their spears into pruning hooks; nation shall not lift up sword against nation neither shall they learn war anymore" (Isa. 2:4). The Bible's ideal is that instruments used for war will be more profitable when they are converted into farming tools such as tractors, shovels, hoes, and combines to feed the earth's masses.

While the Bible condemns the wicked, it brings peace and offers hope to the penitent. It is not a time to harbor doubt and have reservations about the sacred authority of the Bible. Have you made it your code of conduct? Long live the Bible, the Word of God!

July 31

A City on a Hill

You are the light of the world, a city that is set upon a hill cannot be hidden.
—Matthew 5:14

Driving up a narrow steep village road at about a forty-five-degree angle while slipping and sliding is not for the fainthearted. My sister lives in Dominica, a tropical paradise where steep, meandering roads pose a challenge to the fittest human specimen. From her vantage point at the extreme south of the island, she has an excellent view of the Caribbean Sea to the west and the Atlantic Ocean to the east. On the porch of her hillside mansion, she observes the fishermen plying their trade and bringing in their much-anticipated catch. The cruise ships loaded with pleasure-seeking passengers whiz past her wandering gaze in the very waters where pirates played the game of life and death. After absorbing the breathtaking beauty of the village complemented by the verdant greenery of the countryside and the rolling waves of the Atlantic Ocean, we concluded that the rough climb to her mansion was worth it all.

My sister's home on the hilltop is typical of our Lord saying, "You are the light of the world, a city that is set on a hill cannot be hidden." Should the lighthouse stop shedding its lifesaving beams to mariners plying the oceans? Obviously not. By virtue of the marvelous light God has blessed us with, we cannot and should not suppress the amazing revelation bubbling inside of us. Someone once said, "If

God has done something amazing in your life, then you should let someone else know about it."

"Then they said to one another, 'We are not doing right. This day is a day of good news, and we remain silent. If we wait until morning light, some punishment will come upon us. Now therefore, come, let us go and tell the king's household'" (2 Kings 7:9). Those were the words of four leprous outcasts who stumbled on a bounty of much-needed food. Should they keep the good news to themselves while their fellow men starve from hunger? We are obligated to tell our fellow men of the wonderful things the Lord has done for us. When an ant or honeybee stumbles on a good fortune, the entire colony is informed and shares in the bonanza. Should we do any less?

"And when He got into the boat, he who had been demon possessed begged Him that he might be with Him. However, Jesus did not permit him, 'Go home to your friends, and tell them what great things the Lord has done for you, and how He has had compassion on you'" (Mark 5:18–19).

The city-on-a-hill metaphor was captured in Daniel's vision. "You watched while a stone was caught out without hands, which struck the image on its feet of iron and clay, and broke them in pieces . . . And the stone that struck the image became a great mountain and filled the whole earth" (Dan. 2:34–35). This stone is the kingdom of God, and its principle of sharing and broadcasting the gospel enabled the early church to swallow up the Roman Empire with the good news. The light is too marvelous to contain among ourselves; we must spread the good news. "Then I said, I will not make mention of Him, nor speak anymore in His name. But His word was in my heart like a burning fire shut up in my bones; I was weary of holding it back, and I could not" (Jer. 20:9). The parable of the light is to be shared with everyone. What are you doing to spread the good news far and wide? Are you confessing Christ to your friends? Do they know what you believe in?

August 1

The Best Kept Secret

Immediately his ears were opened, and the impediment of his tongue was loosed, and he spoke plainly.
Then He commanded them that they should tell no one;
but the more He commanded them, the more widely they proclaimed it.
—Mark 7:35–36

There are no large electronic signs pointing to its presence, but it's there. After paying a small fee for entry into a warm sulfuric water pool, you're in a virtual paradise. Many North Americans and Europeans are oblivious to its existence, but on the tiny Caribbean island of Dominica, hot sulfur springs saturate the island jungles and provide exhilarating, therapeutic baths to gleeful visitors. Its warm sulfuric concoction is one of the most thrilling, exciting, and exhilarating baths ever since Roman times.

Soaking in one of its many exotic warm pools was a gentleman from Boston. I asked how he discovered this island paradise, and he remarked, "Dominica is the best kept secret in the Caribbean." Dominicans want development but fiercely guard their homeland paradise against the advancing ravages of commercial tourism.

Jesus was in a dilemma of similar kind. He did not want unwanted publicity during the infancy of his ministry, but the more he tried to avoid this unwanted attention, the more his work bore testimony of who he really was—the Messiah of the world. After his resurrection, a daring plan was hatched to suppress the obvious, but the plan backfired and embarrassed the planners. "Tell them, His disciples came at night and stole Him away while we slept. And if this comes to the governor's ears, we will appease him and make you secure. So they took the bribe and did as they were instructed" (Matt. 28:13–15). But this plan of deception was doomed from the start. Who can ever explain the mystery of the empty tomb? "He is not here, for He is risen" (Matt. 28:6).

Jesus Christ's birth, ministry, and death had never been a secret; the news was first heralded from the Garden of Eden. Eve thought she had given birth to the Christ when she expressed these words: "I have acquired a man from the Lord" (Gen. 4:1). However, her hopes would be shelved for several centuries later until the fullness of time had come. Now we have a risen Christ, whose life and ministry we must publish to every nation, kindred, tongue, and people. "Go quickly and tell His disciples that He is risen from the dead, and indeed He is going before you into Galilee; there you will see Him" (Matt. 28:7). The command "go and tell" is even more urgent than before in the wake of the earth's final events. Jesus is coming again.

The message of present truth to the early disciples was a risen Christ to disprove the propaganda of the enemies of the gospel. By contrast, our present truth stipulates we must tell the whole world of our soon-coming King. At present, his arms of mercy are extended in love and forgiveness to a rebellious planet. The church must be trumpeting the good news of Jesus's soon return to anyone who cares to listen.

In gratitude to the One who healed him, the mute man published far and wide the tidings of the gracious Healer who had restored to him the gift of speech (Mark 7:31–37). Are we under the same obligation to spread the news of the One who has rescued us from a life of sin and certain destruction? Should we use every given opportunity as a springboard for spreading the good news? "How can we escape if we neglect such great a salvation?" (Heb. 2:3).

August 2

Expressing Interest?

Seek the Lord while He may be found, call upon Him while He is near. Let the wicked forsake his way, and the unrighteous man his thoughts; let him return to the Lord, and He will have mercy on him; and to our God for He will abundantly pardon.

—Isaiah 55:6–7

I candidly admit I am a voracious quick eater with a healthy appetite. Regrettably, I've never actually mastered the art and discipline of chewing my food. (Shame on me.) However, it's not unusual on our frequent trips to the restaurant that I finish my meal way ahead of my wife and express interest in her half-eaten meal. Admittedly, I am met with rebuffs and gestures of unbelief from my wife concerning my interest in her half-eaten meal. God, on the other hand, honors only the requests that are in the best interest of his children. He gives and gives and keeps on giving. God always expresses genuine interest in the sincere petition of his children.

"And the Lord spoke to Manasseh and his people, but they would not listen. Therefore, the Lord brought upon them the captains of the army of the king of Assyria, who took Manasseh with hooks, bound him with bronze fetters, and carried him off to Babylon. Now when he was in affliction, he implored the Lord his God, and humbled himself greatly before the God of his fathers, and prayed to Him; and He received his entreaty, heard his supplication, and brought him back to Jerusalem into his kingdom" (2 Chron. 33:10–13).

The Lord has a very short memory of our past iniquities. In fact, as long as we confess and forsake our sins, he chooses not to remember them at all. "For I will be merciful to their unrighteousness, and their sins and their lawless deeds I will remember no more" (Heb. 8:12). God never embarrasses his people; our dark, secretive past is safe with him, and he will never disclose it to another unless it is for our own edification.

The Lord abounds in patience and is extremely merciful. He looks for the tiniest flicker of remorse and repentance in any person and stands ready to administer forgiveness upon request. But Israel was less than genuine in their relationship with God as evidenced by their history of backsliding and broken promises. "Nevertheless they flattered Him with their mouth, and they lied to Him with their tongue; for their heart was not steadfast with Him, nor were they faithful in His covenant. But He being full of compassion, forgave their iniquity, and did not destroy them. Yes, many a time He turned His anger away, and did not stir up all His wrath; for He remembered that they were but flesh, a breath that passes away and does not come again" (Ps. 78:36–39). We must constantly remind ourselves that we are reliving ancient Israel's experience in our modern-day experience. Are we any different from them? Are we not modern spiritual Israel? Are we not experiencing the same temptations at the shopping malls? Do we really make graven images out of our electronic toys? Lord, have mercy on us.

The wonder of wonders is that God still expresses interest in us. "The Lord has appeared of old to me, saying; Yes, I have loved you with an everlasting love; Therefore with loving kindness I have drawn you" (Jer. 31:3). It is God who always expresses interest in his creatures as cited here. "Then the Lord God called to Adam and said to him, 'Where are you?'" (Gen. 3:9). The question remains, will we joyfully respond to his gestures of love, or will we spurn his outstretched arms and amazing love?

August 3

A Mother to the Motherless

A father to the fatherless, a defender of widows, is God in His holy habitation. God sets the solitary in families; He brings out those who are bound into prosperity; but the rebellious dwell in a dry land.

—Psalm 68:5–6

Because of her compassion and motherly traits, Vicky was handed malnourished children by mothers/fathers near the end of their rope. She took them all in, fed them, raised them, schooled them, and sent them on their way to adulthood. Vicky does not run an institution, nor is she a woman of means, but what she lacks in wealth she makes up with magnanimity and love. Several grown foster children call her Mom because of her maternal love and care for them in their time of need. God never fails in rewarding the good works we do to others. Although material blessings have passed Vicky by, she lives comfortably in her home, surrounded by the pleasant memories of yesterday and a bright future of eternal life in God's coming kingdom.

"I was eyes to the blind, and I was feet to the lame. I was a father to the poor, and I searched out the case that I did not know. I broke the fangs of the wicked, and plucked the victim from his teeth" (Job 29:15–17). As long as we walk on this sin-infested planet, opportunities will abound to touch the lives of those in need, and these unique situations of human need will give recipients a true portrait of the God we serve. They may conclude from our actions and attitude whether God is a harsh and austere being or a kind and loving one who takes the time to alleviate their suffering. "Then His fame went throughout all Syria; and they brought to Him all sick people who were afflicted with various diseases and torment, and those who were demon possessed, epileptics, and paralytics; and He healed them" (Matt. 4:24).

The early disciples adopted the very format Jesus utilized in establishing the kingdom of God in the hearts of men. The results were astounding as the Holy Spirit magnified himself through the witness of the apostles. "And through the hands of the apostles many signs and wonders were done among the people. And they were all with one accord in Solomon's Porch . . . And believers were increasingly added to the Lord, multitudes of both men and women" (Acts 5:12, 14).

It takes only one person who is led by the Holy Spirit to change the course of history. Mother Teresa became the voice and hands to the orphans of Calcutta, India. Florence Nightingale was hope to the wounded of the Crimean War at a time when more soldiers died from untreated minor infections than grave bodily injuries. Martin Luther King brought out the best in us all with his timely words, unshackling the chains on both the oppressed and the oppressors. Who knows whether you are the next servant leader to emerge to pick up the mantle and make a difference in this world?

The great avalanches begin with a small disturbance of a single snowflake. A ripple in the water may be small but turn into a colossal wave. You may very well be that next ripple. From your first small attempt to alleviate human suffering (ripple effect), God will give you encouragement to take your next big step. Is this a challenge? Oh yes, it is. Challenges bring out the best in us. Who hasn't been challenged to jump to the next level and did it successfully? Life would be meaningless without challenges. Go for it.

August 4

Like Father, Like Son Part 1

Jesus said to him, "Have I been with you so long, and yet you have not known Me, Philip?"

—John 14:9

She did not know her grandparents, but the nose, the eyes, and the cheeks were the exact portrait of them. I'd never met Juliet before, but her facial features gave her identity away and carried me back to my childhood days growing up with her uncle, my contemporary. Juliet looked strikingly similar to a childhood friend of mine. I couldn't help asking if she was related to a particular family, to which she answered in the positive. She was indeed the daughter of a childhood contemporary of mine. Having left the country before she was born, I'd never laid eyes on her before, but the characteristic imprints of her grandparents, whom I knew, were all over her face. Jesus was no different as the Son of God; he was the exact image of his Father.

"Most assuredly, I say to you, the Son can do nothing of Himself, but what He sees the Father do; for whatever He does, the Son also does in like manner. For the Father loves the Son, and shows Him all things that He Himself does; and He will show Him greater works than these that you may marvel" (John 5:19–21).

Jesus is the very God who led the children of Israel on eagles' wings. "You have seen what I did to the Egyptians, and how I bore you on eagles' wings and brought you to Myself" (Exod. 19:4). Jesus was the very rock that Moses struck and the refreshing cool water that the children of Israel drank. "And they all drank the same spiritual drink. For they drank of that spiritual Rock that followed them, and that Rock was Christ" (1 Cor. 10:4). Jesus was the heating apparatus in the pillar of fire by night and the air-conditioning cloud by day. "And the Lord went before them by day in a pillar of cloud to lead the way, and by night in a pillar of fire to give them light, so as to go by day and night" (Exod. 13:21). But alas, our memory is not good at remembering God's mighty acts in our behalf in times past and his good intentions toward our future. "And you shall remember that the Lord your God led you all the way these forty years in the wilderness, to humble you and test you, to know what was in your heart, whether you would keep His commandment or not . . . Your garment did not wear out on you, nor did your foot swell these forty years. You should know in your heart that as a man chastens his son, so the Lord your God chastens you" (Deut. 8:2, 4–5).

Since God's intentions toward his creatures are good and for their benefit, Jesus continued where he left off in the Old Testament. Having clothed himself with the garment of humanity, he announced his ministry to the world: "The Spirit of the Lord is upon Me, because the Lord has anointed Me to preach good tidings to the poor; He has sent Me to heal the brokenhearted, to proclaim liberty to the captives, and the opening of the prison to those who are bound; to proclaim the acceptable year of the Lord and the day of vengeance of our God" (Isa. 61:1–2).

Still working as a Trio of One, the Father sent Jesus to this earth, and the Holy Spirit authenticated his ministry by dwelling in him. "And he saw the Spirit of God descending like a dove and alighting upon Him. And suddenly a voice came from heaven, saying, 'This is My beloved Son, in whom I am well pleased'" (Matt. 3:16–17).

August 5

Like Father, Like Son Part 2

Now when they saw the boldness of Peter and John, and perceived that they were uneducated and untrained men, they marveled. And they realized that they had been with Jesus.

—Acts 4:13

Juvenile male lions are evicted from the pride by their mean-tempered dads as soon as they begin growing their mane (bearded face and puberty). Their dads do to them what was done to them by their dads, and the cycle continues. It's tough when your dad is more interested in getting you out of his sight than training you with the values you need for life. Sadly, this type of behavior is not restricted to lions only; sons often join their fathers in jail because of neglect and lack of interest. Thankfully, the relationship between Jesus and his followers is the strongest bond on planet Earth.

"I have manifested Your name to the men whom You have given Me out of the world. They were Yours, You gave them to Me, and they have kept Your word. Now they have known that all things which You have given Me are from You. For I have given to them the words which You have given Me; and they have received them, and have known surely that I came forth from You; and they have believed that You sent Me" (John 17:6–8). The Lord had just prayed for his disciples and, in so doing, revealed to us that the same level of affection that exists between the Godhead should exist among us, his modern disciples.

All cultures are plagued by cultural biases. Even the apostles of Christ showed the ugly side of their perceived cultural superiority, but in Christ, we move beyond that, don't we? Christ's followers should be distinguished by their sincere love for one another. After all, Jesus couldn't have put it more succinctly. "By this all will know that you are My disciples, if you have love for one another" (John 13:35). If only we could get beyond the elementary exercise of loving our fellow humans without reservations. If we don't, how can we move on to the more strenuous exercise of loving God whom we cannot see?

"A new commandment I give to you, that you love one another; as I have loved you, that you also love one another" (John 13:34). Love is definitely the test of discipleship, and without mincing words, I affirm that if we can't love as Jesus loves, we are not fit to be his disciples. We must come to love everyone as Jesus loves—without conditions, without strings attached, and without reservations—if we intend to make it to heaven.

"In this is love, not that we loved God, but that He loved us and sent His Son to be the propitiation for our sins. Beloved, if God so loved us, we also ought to love one another" (1 John 4:10–11). Love is an active principle, which constantly seeks new people or objects to affect. Someone once said, and you may have repeated it yourself, "If you love me, show it." We sometimes have strange ways of showing love to one another, but here is the embodiment of true love. "Love suffers long and is kind; love does not envy; love does not parade itself, is not puffed up; does not behave itself rudely, does not seek its own, is not easily provoked, thinks no evil; does not rejoice in iniquity but rejoices in the truth; bears all things, believes all things, hopes all things, endures all things" (1 Cor. 13:4–7). "Go and do likewise!" Love the unlovable, even those who defraud you.

August 6

When God Hears

Because your heart was tender, and you humbled yourself before God when you heard His words against this place and against its inhabitants, and you humbled yourself before me, and you tore your clothes and wept before me, I also have heard you.

—2 Chronicles 34:27

Few things are anticipated more on planet Earth than the first intelligible words of a baby. Being a grandparent, I find myself constantly asking, "How is his vocabulary doing?" Finally, the day arrived when the little guy could actually say the words "mommy" and "daddy," and he reserved the special name Papa for me and Mama for his grandma. The voice of his children praying, whether in joyful thanksgiving or agonizing petition, is music in the ears of God and is worth more than its weight in gold to our God. Like a mother hovering over the crib of her infant child, God anxiously waits, listening to the requests being directed to him.

"If My people who are called by My name will humble themselves, and pray and seek My face, and turn from their wicked way, then I will hear from heaven, and will forgive their sin and heal their land. Now My eyes will be open and My ears attentive to prayer made in this place" (2 Chron. 7:14–15). Since God is in the saving business, his ears and eyes are always on the alert for genuine signs and sounds of repentance; and when he hears and sees what he likes, like the prodigal son's father, he cannot contain himself. "But the father said to his servants, bring out the best robe and put on him, and put a ring on his hand and sandals on his feet. And bring the fatted calf and kill it, and let us eat and be merry; for this my son was dead and is alive again; he was lost and is found. And they began to be merry" (Luke 15:22–24).

This is no fluke or an accidental behavior; God is actually like that. He genuinely wants all his creation to be eternally secure. After all, that's why he created us. He is offended when we spurn his grace. "Behold, the Lord's hand is not shortened that He cannot save; nor His ear heavy that it cannot hear. But your iniquities have separated you from your God; and your sins have hidden His face from you, so that He will not hear. For your hand is defiled with blood and your fingers with iniquity" (Isa. 59:1–3).

The Lord is anxious to have this sad chapter of sin arrested, closed, and finally erased from memory. Even nature is groaning under the staggering weight of sin. "For we know that the whole creation groans and labors with birth pangs together until now. Not only that, but we also who have the firstfruits of the Spirit, even we ourselves groan within ourselves, eagerly waiting for the adoption, the redemption of our body" (Rom. 8:22–23). Are you disgusted with sin and the behavior of sinners?

Even though we long to go home to meet the Lord, there are just a few more precious souls to be gathered in. "Now the Lord spoke to Paul in the night by vision, do not be afraid, but speak, and do not keep silent, for I am with you, and no one will attack you to hurt you; for I have many people in this city" (Acts 18:9–10). Our friends, children, neighbors, and family members who are tilting toward God are to be prayed for and gathered in. Will you remember them in prayer daily?

August 7

Revival in the Land Part 1

For in the eighth year of his reign, while he was still young, he began to seek the God of his father David;
and in the twelfth year he began to purge Judah and Jerusalem of the high places, the wooden images, the carved images, and the molded images.

—2 Chronicles 34:3

Betty (name changed) couldn't explain it, but the many invitations she received to the parties and nightclubs went unheeded. The thrill and excitement for these events are gone; she simply has no desire for these amusements anymore. Betty now shuns the easy sleazy money that comes by exploiting the foolish and gullible. She has a new hobby now. Can you take a guess? It's Bible study. Her friends are mystified by her sudden change of lifestyle, but she absolutely loves her Bible studies and can't have enough of them.

Betty is one of many specimens God is using to demonstrate the transformation that takes place when he is in control of our lives. Young king Josiah, son of the apostate king Amon, embraced revival and reformation with a passion and tenacity that is worthy of emulation and commendation. At his command, "they broke the altars of the Baals in his presence, and the incense altars which were above them he cut down; and the wooden images, the carved images, and the molded images, he broke in pieces, and made dust of them and scattered it on the graves of those who had sacrificed to them. He also burned the bones of the priests on their altars, and cleansed Judah and Jerusalem" (2 Chron. 34:4–5). He even got rid of all the bad magazines, videos, and CDs of his predecessor.

Revival is the rebirth of the spiritual life, but true revival is always accompanied by reformation. The mere fact that we have been revived is the first step, and then comes the second step—the reformation, which by definition entails carrying out the works of the revival. Besides destroying the false system of worship, King Josiah proceeded to repair the temple that had fallen in disrepair, restore corporate worship, and rededicate Levites to their order. "So all the service of the Lord was prepared the same day, to keep the Passover and to offer burnt offering on the altar of the Lord, according to the command of King Josiah" (2 Chron. 35:16).

Revival is never complete without reformation; they actually go hand in hand. How can one claim to be revived if he or she is unwilling to give up his or her toys (idol)? "And many who had believed came confessing their deeds. Also, many of those who had practiced magic brought their books together and burned them in the sight of all" (Acts 19:18–19). Another example stands out: "So they gave Jacob all the foreign gods which were in their hands, and earrings which were in their ears; and Jacob hid them under the Terebinth tree which was by Shechem" (Gen. 35:4). Here's another follow-up to true revival: "Moreover Josiah put away those who consulted mediums and spirits, the household gods and idols, all the abominations that were seen in the land of Judah and in Jerusalem, that he might perform the words of the law which were in the book [Torah, Bible] that Hilkiah the priest found in the house of the Lord" (2 Kings 23:24).

It's good that we repent, but reformation must follow repentance. Revival must be deep, and reformation must be sincere, accompanied by remorse, introspection, reparation where necessary, confession of wrongs committed, and finally rejoicing in the Lord for a new life. Lord, purge us by your Holy Spirit and give us true revival and reformation in our lives. It can only happen as a result of sincere prayer. Keep on praying for it; it will come when God wills.

Lacking Wisdom? Ask

Then God said to Solomon, because this was in your heart, and you have not asked riches or wealth or honor or the life of your enemies, nor have you asked long life—but have asked knowledge for yourself, that you may judge My people over whom I have made you king—wisdom and knowledge are granted to you.

—2 Chronicles 1:11–12

Mother was illiterate, but you would not have known it. She spoke English fairly well, raised us well-mannered, and ran a little business with thrift and efficiency. She must have prayed the prayer of Solomon early in life. Where could she have acquired such skill, wisdom, and discipline to deal with me and my nine other siblings? Mother Emelia was no pushover by any means. She may have been of a mild and quiet nature, but when pushed to her limits, she could ruin the day of a juvenile delinquent (me) quite easily.

"If any of you lacks wisdom, let him ask of God who gives to all liberally and without reproach, and it will be given to him. But let him ask in faith, with no doubting, for he who doubts is like a wave of the sea driven and tossed by the wind" (James 1:5–6). Educators relentlessly push their students to attain wisdom, but can it be found outside God? "Where can wisdom be found? And where is the place of understanding?" The elements confess complete ignorance and deny any association with it. "The deep says, it is not with me; and the sea says, it is not with me. It cannot be purchased for gold, nor can silver be weighed for its price." Maybe destruction and death know something about it since they lure many to eternal death and ruin. "Destruction and death say, we have heard a report about it with our ears." But where is it? Are we getting any closer? Wisdom begins by acknowledging God. "To establish a weight for the wind, and apportion the waters by measure . . . Then He saw wisdom and declared it; He prepared it, indeed, He searched it out. And to man He said, Behold the fear of the Lord, that is wisdom, and to depart from evil is understanding" (Job 28:12, 14–15, 22, 25, 27–28).

Simply put, the tireless search for wisdom is within everyone's grasp. One is counted wise when he or she acknowledges God as the Savior. "The fear of the Lord is the beginning of wisdom." And since the fear of the Lord is the beginning of wisdom, the opposite is also true. Those who choose to deny the sovereignty of God are unwise. "The fool has said in his heart there is no God. They are corrupt, they have done abominable works" (Ps. 14:1). We give credit to the great academic minds, past and present, who have revolutionized communication, medicine, commerce, travel, and food production; but without acknowledging the sovereignty of God, they are mere fools, denying the obvious.

In civilizations past, believers in God were distinguished among their peers by their outstanding wisdom, which they always attributed to God. Daniel, Joseph, Mordecai, and Moses all have one thing in common; they fulfilled the following verse: "He made him ruler over his house, and ruler of all his possessions, to bind his princes at his pleasure, and teach his elders wisdom" (Ps. 105:21–22). Anyone who submits to the lordship of Jesus Christ is wise; to do otherwise is foolish. We give thanks to God for making us wise to accept the saving knowledge of the plan of salvation.

August 9

Thoughts Shape Action

As a man thinks in his heart, so is he.

—Proverbs 23:7

The human brain is an astonishing and very complex organism. It makes millions of calculations each day; it connects names to faces, makes sense out of chaos, recalls events in time of need, and can even show affection, to name a few of its chores. Jermaine has been seeing Sally for a while now (his angel, so he thinks); the more he daydreams and thinks about her, the more the *M* word is shaping up in his mind. Finally, gathering all his strength reserve, he initiates a conversation with Sally and pops the magical question.

What took him so long? Jermaine's daydreaming thoughts blossomed into interesting conversations; dates ensued, followed by flowers and eventually an engagement ring. To no one's surprise, Jermaine and Sally walked into the sunset of marital bliss.

Recognizing the brain as the command and control center of all our actions, Paul counsels, "Finally brethren, whatever things are true, whatever things are noble, whatever things are just, whatever things are pure, whatever things are lovely, whatever things are of good report, if there is any virtue and if there is anything praiseworthy—meditate on these things" (Phil. 4:8). The brain or the heart, as the Bible commonly refers to it, is the origin of all our actions; however, there are a few exceptions—unintended and accidental situations. "When you cross the Jordan into the land of Canaan, then you shall appoint cities to be cities of refuge for you, that the manslayer who kills any person accidentally may flee there" (Num. 35:10–11). The cities of refuge offered sanctuary to those who killed others unintentionally. Note that there was no premeditated intent to kill. Cities of refuge are symbolic of Christ, our refuge, who absorbed all our guilt and died in our place to give us a second chance to make things right with God.

Barring accidental incidents and mental illnesses, the mind is held responsible for actions perpetrated. "You have heard that is was said to those of old, 'You shall not commit adultery.' But I say to you that whoever looks at a woman to lust for her has already committed adultery with her in his heart" (Matt. 5:27–28).

The mind has the capacity to doom the body long before the act is consummated or perpetrated. Lord, have mercy on us all. Who shall be able to stand? In this age of pernicious split-second advertisements, we are often deceived into buying things without reading the fine prints. Have mercy on us. We are often abused and exploited by crafty snake oil salesmen who hide the fine prints and cleverly disguise warnings into legal language we do not understand. Have mercy on us, Lord. We are swept off our feet by those who promise much but deliver little once elected or, worse, betray our trust. Have mercy on us, O Lord. Lest we forget, God—who alone is able to read our thoughts—takes into account our motives, something no other being is capable of doing.

Although our thoughts shape our actions, God is gracious, long-suffering, and abundant in mercy and will make a way of escape for his children. He will not allow the righteous to fall prey to temptation without providing adequate strength to match. "For You, Lord, are good, and ready to forgive, and abundant in mercy to all those who call upon You. Give ear, O Lord, to my prayer, and attend to the voice of my supplication" (Ps. 86:5–6).

August 10

Make the Crooked Path Straight

Then they said to him, who are you, that we may give an answer to those who sent us? What do you say about yourself? He said, I am the voice of one crying in the wilderness:
Make straight the way of the Lord.

—John 1:22–23

Manholes are welded shut, sharpshooters are positioned on rooftops, and buildings along the travel route are secured to facilitate the president's travel. He is usually safely cocooned in the Beast, one of the three specially designed vehicles that transport him. Before any presidential visit, an elite team of security service agents are dispatched to secure the travel route and ensure the president's safety. The security chiefs, to their credit, have prevented the nightmare of bad things happening to any president while in office. To date, no modern president has been assassinated since JFK, thanks to the hard work of these well-trained agents.

The security format used to ensure presidential travel is nothing new; it was borrowed from antiquity. Whenever a king or person of high rank traveled, squads of road repairers and military personnel were dispatched to level steep hills, clear trees, and cut grass and bushes to make the route safe. John the Baptist was assigned such a mission to prepare the way of our Lord before he began his public ministry. God left nothing to chance; he wanted the world to know that his provision for salvation was a reality and that the Messiah was actually dwelling among men. John quotes from the prophet Isaiah, "The voice of one crying in the wilderness. Prepare the way of the Lord; make straight in the desert a highway for our God. Every valley shall be exalted and every mountain and hill brought low; the crooked places shall be made straight and the rough places smooth" (Isa. 40:3–4). John's preaching ignited a genuine revival that prepared the people for Jesus's teaching. "Then he said to the multitudes that came out to be baptized by him, 'Brood of vipers! Who have warned you to flee from the wrath to come? Therefore bear fruits worthy of repentance' . . . So the people asked him. Saying, 'What shall we do then?' He answered and said to them, 'He who has two tunics, let him give to him who has none; and he who has food, let him do likewise'" (Luke 3:7–8, 10–11). John's mission of preparation was coming to an end, but Jesus's had only begun.

Another Elijah will prepare people's hearts just before Christ's Second Coming. "Behold, I will send you Elijah the prophet before the coming of the great and dreadful day of the Lord. And he will turn the hearts of the fathers to the children and the hearts of the children to the fathers, lest I come and strike the earth with a curse" (Mal. 4:5–6). But who is this Elijah? Is it a resurrected Elijah or another John the Baptist? Neither. God will raise in our age a people with the power of Elijah and a judgment message of John. This movement will preach relevant truths with the courage, boldness, and dynamism of Elijah and, like John the Baptist, point men to a kind, loving, and caring Redeemer.

Are you part of this movement that preaches the truth as John the Baptist without fear, even if it imperils your neck? Someone rightly said, "Evil flourishes when good people do nothing." The crooked ways will be straight when we demonstrate by precept and example the righteousness of Christ resident in us. What better way to make the rough places straight than by treating others with genuine love and compassion?

August 11

Long Live the King

There let Zadok the priest and Nathan the prophet anoint him king over Israel; and blow the horn, and say, Long live king Solomon!

—1 Kings 1:34

Long live the king! Long live the king! Prince Adonijah rebelled against the command of his father and against the will of God by proclaiming himself king. After his big party crashed and his hopes of becoming king dashed, Prince Adonijah and his fellow conspirators fled in every direction. During the chaos in the palace, young Solomon demonstrated exceptional skill, wisdom, and judgment and was appointed by God to be the next king of Israel. But his selection did not go well with his ambitious bigger brothers. Brothers Absalom and Adonijah led separate failed military rebellion to be king despite God's choice of Solomon through the mouth of the prophet Nathan. The two rebel brothers were inspired by another rebel who showed utter contempt for God and his divine authority.

"How are you fallen from heaven, O Lucifer, son of the morning? How are you cut down to the ground, you who weakened the nations! For you have said in your heart: I will ascend into the heaven, I will exalt my throne above the stars of God; I will also sit on the mount of the congregation on the farthest sides of the north; I will ascend above the heights of the clouds, I will be like the Most High" (Isa. 14:12–14).

The spirit of Lucifer thrives in all who willfully rebel against established law and righteous authority. God rules through established authority and civil government whose governance is based on the rule of law. Any attempt to thwart this ordained principle is subverting God's established formula of governance. "Let every soul be subject to the governing authorities. For there is no authority except from God, and the authorities that exist are appointed by God. Therefore, whoever resists the authority resists the ordinance of God and those who resist will bring judgment upon themselves" (Rom. 13:1–2).

Whether the system of government is monarchical, democratic, or dictatorial, the people of God (being subjects of a better country) must comply with civil and federal government as long as they do not conflict with the law of God. God is the Creator of peace, obedience, order, and discipline; and since his people embrace the same values he espouses, there should be no resistance by his people to established authority. Being citizens of democratic states, we reserve the right to make our voices heard by lawful protests and by installing or defeating political leaders at the polls. What better place to do this than in the voting booth, where we cast our vote against those who despise the sacred truths we hold dear.

We are forbidden, however, to join forces with anyone in instigating, fermenting, destabilizing, and leading a revolution. This is not our calling. The people of God have a different agenda in building the kingdom of God with or without the blessings and cooperation of the authorities. We should work with governments wherever possible, but if their agenda collide with our kingdom values, we should part ways. Then who should we obey, God or Caesar? "And Peter and the other apostles answered and said, we ought to obey God rather than man" (Acts 5:29). Long live the eternal King!

August 12

The Slow Wheels of Justice

Now therefore do not hold him guiltless, for you are a wise man and know that you ought to do to him;
but bring his gray hair down to the grave with blood.

—1 Kings 2:9

Our home phone rings consistently between 7:00 and 8:30 p.m. We know who's at the other end of the line. Can you guess who? Telemarketers are on the prowl for new customers. Confession is good for the soul. Can you keep a secret? Shhh! I used to hang up my phone before a word came out of their carefully rehearsed speech but not anymore. I learned there is a better way since we are to be courteous to all. This is an opportunity that can be utilized in witnessing to them about our soon-coming Savior.

We all carry a mental list of those who have caused us much injury and pain. Memory would not allow David to forget when he was on the run for his life, only to be met by a rogue and vain-cursing subject. "Come out! Come out! You bloodthirsty man, you rogue . . . So now you are in your own evil, because you are a bloodthirsty man!" (2 Sam. 16:7–8). Now wait a minute. Is he addressing his king, the king of Israel this way? Let's see David's restraint: "Then Abishai the son of Zeruiah said to the king 'Why should this dead dog curse my lord the king? Please let me go over and take off his head!'" (2 Sam. 16:9). David's magnanimity shines through: "Let him alone, and let him curse; for so the Lord has ordered him. It may be that the Lord will look on my affliction, and that the Lord will repay me with good for his cursing this day" (2 Sam. 16:11–12). Well, the little guy was not quite through with David just yet but pursued him, cursing him and pelting stones at the king as he went.

David did nothing to avenge himself; he simply left his case in the hands of the Almighty. Do you have someone in your life like Shimei—someone who jabs and elbows you at any given opportunity? Welcome to the school of character building; your instructor is the Holy Spirit. The list of former students who graduated here and moved on to postgraduate studies is impressive. David graduated ahead of his class and was rewarded by his professor with top honors. After all, despite his foibles, "David was a man after God's own heart" (Acts 13:22). All the prophets graduated from the school of affliction with top honors. Jonah had some problems, but he made it. Affliction is absolutely necessary in being an effective witness for God; it keeps us humble. Believers were imprisoned; others were persecuted and even killed for the testimony of Jesus.

"And what more shall I say? For the time would fail me to tell of Gideon and Barak and Samson and Jephthah, also of David and Samuel and the prophets: who through faith subdued kingdoms, worked righteousness, obtained promises, stopped the mouths of lions, quenched the violence of fire, escaped the edge of the sword, out of weakness were made strong, became valiant in battle, turned to fight the armies of the aliens. Women received their dead raised to life again. Others were tortured, not accepting deliverance, that we might obtain the better resurrection" (Heb. 11:32–35).

Stay in this school, my friend. It is a good school; you will learn much here. I am a student here myself, and I am learning every day. God develops our faith muscles by putting us through a battery of tests. You'll graduate soon; hang on in there with your cranky neighbor, coworker, and spouse. Jesus is coming soon to liberate us.

August 13

No Place Like Home

The wolf and the lamb shall feed together, the lion shall eat straw like the ox, and dust shall be the serpent's food. They shall not hurt nor destroy in my holy mountain, says the Lord.

—Isaiah 65:25

Some creatures have developed ingenious ways of raising a family. After pairing, Mrs. Toucan takes up residence in a hollow tree where her mate cements her in with mud, leaving only a tiny hole to deliver her meals. The delivery picks up steam when the eggs are hatched. She's not picky but has a delicate taste for fresh fruits of all kind. She loves nuts, particularly Brazilian, although an occasional lizard or two will do. The family is growing fast and needs much protein. The sanitation situation is impeccable. Mom keeps the home squeaky-clean by expelling all garbage through the waste disposal system. She keeps the youngsters clean and healthy by methodical grooming. In a few days, the chicks will be pulled from the safety and comfort of home by an invisible force to fend for themselves. Once grown, they are not invited back home. Mom and Pops might have plans to raise a new family.

Unlike some animals that are evicted from their home, we are invited to a home where there will be no evictions. The saved will live in peace and comfort forever. Dream with me of a place where the sun never sets and the roses never fade. "Then I, John, saw the holy city, New Jerusalem, coming down out of heaven from God, prepared as a bride adorned for her husband" (Rev. 21:2). Nothing on this earth can fully prepare the eye for the surprise awaiting the saints when they see their eternal home. From the prophets' limited glimpse of heaven in vision, human language is inadequate in describing its glorious beauty.

The foundation and city walls are built from precious stones, very much like the ones locked behind glass an inch and a half thick at a Smithsonian museum. "The foundations of the wall of the city are adorned with all kinds of precious stones: the first foundation was jasper, the second sapphire, the third chalcedony, the fourth emerald, the fifth sardonyx, the sixth sardius" (Rev. 21:19–20). But wait, that's not all; the streets are paved with pure gold. You can even build your bed and furniture from the fine stuff.

"And he showed me a pure river of water of life, clear as crystal, proceeding from the throne of God and of the Lamb. In the middle of its street, and on either side of the river, was the tree of life, which bore twelve fruits, each tree yielding its fruit every month. The leaves of the tree were for the healing of the nations. And there shall be no more curse, but the throne of God and of the Lamb shall be in it, and His servants shall serve Him" (Rev. 22:1–3).

I plan to be there in that blissful country. How about you? What is described here is only a limited view of the real place called the New Jerusalem. Our view of eternal things is still distorted by the dross of earthliness. "For eyes have not seen, nor ears heard, nor have entered into the heart of man the things which God has prepared for those who love Him" (1 Cor. 2:9). There is plenty of good room in the Father's house. Have you decided yet where you intend to spend your future? Certainly not in this sin-cursed earth, I hope. As someone said, "If you miss heaven, you missed it all."

August 14

The Wonder of Wonders

For scarcely for a righteous man will one die; yet perhaps for a good man someone would even dare to die. But God demonstrates His own love towards us, in that while we were still sinners, Christ died for us.

—Romans 5:7–8

Anthropologists use it every time, and it works like a magnet. Whoever wants to make entry into a tribe or civilization must either befriend natives or shower them with gifts. Love and kindness are universal principles; they are practiced even before the visitor learns the language of his host. We are enthralled (delighted) when someone intentionally chooses to shower us with love and affection. We are captivated by love and can hardly contain ourselves, especially when the feeling is mutual, but God's love is different from ours. He loves us even when the relationship is one-sided. God is love, and what's even more amazing is that he loves us just the way we are. He loves us in our mess and where we are and lifts us to where he wants us to be. Someone needs to hear this once more; therefore I'll repeat it. God loves you and me just the way we are.

"In this is love, not that we loved God, but that He loved us and sent His Son to be the propitiation for our sins. Beloved if God so loved us, we also ought to love one another" (1 John 4:10–11). A young man once said to his prospective suitor, "Honey, I will swim the widest ocean just to see your face, and I will climb the highest mountain just to feel the warmth of your hand. I will see you hopefully tomorrow, if it doesn't rain." Amazingly, God's love is not like that; it is inexhaustible. He keeps on loving and giving regardless of our attitude toward him.

The easy part of love entails showering affection on our friends and loved ones, but God commands us to go just a little further. He wants us to lavish love profusely on everyone, including those we deem undeserving of it. "For if you love those who love you, what reward have you? Do not even the tax collectors do the same and if you greet your brethren only, what do you do more than others? Do not even the tax collectors do so?" (Matt. 5:46–47). By loving those who will not love us or have the capacity to do so, we are demonstrating God's love in action.

We may have read many fanciful novels on love and romance, but nothing outshines Calvary. Calvary is the ground zero of love. Ground Zero became sacred ground when Americans and citizens of other nations resolved not to allow hate to triumph over the power of love. Calvary portrays an all-powerful God, allowing himself to be humiliated in the worst possible way to save the very creatures who were tormenting him. "Father, forgive them, for they do not know what they do" (Luke 23:34).

Calvary put a new definition on *love*; all incentives, gestures, and overtures made to others in the name of love must be weighed by what transpired at the cross. "A new commandment I give you to you that you love one another; as I have loved you that you also love one another. By this all will know that you are My disciples, if you have love for one another" (John 13:34–35). Go and do likewise. Love everyone irrespective of their shape, size, race, or national origin; that's the Jesus way of loving. Go out there and make Jesus proud of you. Love everybody, even your enemies.

August 15

Is Anyone Listening?

Now the Lord spoke to Paul in the night by a vision, do not be afraid, but speak, and do not keep silent; for I am with you, and no one will attack you to hurt you; for I have many people in this city.

—Acts 18:9–10

A sweet singer has just begun a melodious tune, but he is not alone; his neighbors have the same idea, but his song drowns the melody of the other singers. Is it because he carries a relevant message? "I have a dream that one day my three little children will not be judged by the color of their skin but by the content of their character." Since Martin's dream was present truth in a racially divided America, it prevailed and drowned all the other voices that were injurious and subversive to the dignity of colored people.

The kingdom message of present truth is medicine to a world teetering on the brink of self-destruction. "How beautiful are the feet of those who preach the gospel of peace, who bring glad tidings of good things" (Rom. 10:15). The gospel of Jesus is glad tidings, but it causes great discomfort to those intent on going in the path of least resistance (wickedness). The off-and-on diet programs do more harm than good to our physical health, and we know it, but some people—hopefully not you—prefer believing a lie than facing the truth. Truth dictates we must be selective in the types of food we eat, but who wants to hear that? Just as an athlete must deny himself or herself unhealthy foods, likewise, anyone desirous of maintaining good health must practice self-restraint. Stay away from bad foods. This is not a popular saying, and few humans have the guts to speak this truth. Why would anyone consciously eat poisonous foods?

We want good health, and who doesn't? At the same time, we also want to eat and drink the things that are unhealthy to us. We can't have both. "You cannot serve God and mammon" (Matt. 6:24). Our supermarkets, with their overabundance of finger-licking produce, are not making life any easier for us. There is a better solution than the one Solomon cites here:

I search in my heart how to gratify my flesh with wine, while guiding my heart with wisdom, and to lay hold on folly, till I might see what was good for the sons of men to do under heaven all the days of their lives. I made my works great, I built myself houses, and planted myself vineyards, I made myself gardens and orchards, and I planted all kinds of trees in them . . . Then I looked on all the works that my hands had done and on the labor in which I had toiled; and indeed all was vanity and grasping for the wind. (Eccles. 2:3–5, 11)

What a terrible conclusion to arrive at. What a terrific waste of resources.

Thank god there is a better way. Nothing satisfies the soul like Jesus: "Your fathers ate the manna in the wilderness and are dead. This is the Bread which comes down from Heaven, that one may eat of it and not die. I am the living Bread which comes down from heaven. If anyone eats of this Bread, he will live forever; and the Bread that I shall give is My flesh, which I shall give for the life of this world" (John 6:49–51). Have you gotten yourself a supply of this fresh bread while it is still available, or are you satisfied with your moldy, stale bread? Nothing tastes better than the bread that came down from heaven, Jesus Christ. Have you eaten of this bread lately?

August 16

Satisfied

He shall see the labor of His soul, and be satisfied. By His knowledge My righteous Servant shall justify many, For He shall bear their iniquities.

—Isaiah 53:11

Lewis and Clark did not live to see the transformation of the West, the by-product of their curiosity. They could not have envisioned the towering walls of the Hoover Dam and the Silicon Valley, which leads the world in technological research. Los Alamos, with its hush-hush, don't-see-don't-tell inventions, would have brought great pride to them had life permitted them to live and see the reward of their adventure. York would have been disappointed with his people's slow progress, and Sacagawea would recoil in horror that her people still live in isolation on reservations. They all were true pioneers, and we owe them a lot for launching themselves into the unknown to see what lay beyond the eastern shores of America. We glow in satisfaction of their tremendous achievement.

But no one was more satisfied than God the Father on resurrection morning. God has emotions as well; after all, we were made in his image. He was at the tomb watching the developments, allowing the kingdom of darkness to have their little power play (hockey terminology). On Sunday morning, there was a deep rumbling in the tomb; something was happening. Matthew explained, "And behold there was a great earthquake; for an angel of the Lord descended from heaven, and came and rolled back the stone from the door, and sat on it" (Matt. 28:2). What an amazing sight it must have been; the grave—once a scene of disappointment and mourning—now transformed into a spectacle of triumph, of life over death, of victory over defeat, of righteousness over sin. Hallelujah! And you know who was dancing with joy? God himself. The earth was finally reunited with the heavenly family, never to be separated.

The Father couldn't wait; he wanted to see the spoils of victory. He wanted to see his saints once held captive by the icy tentacles of death. "Then, behold, the veil of the temple was torn in two from top to bottom; and the earth quaked, and the rocks were split, and the graves were opened; and many bodies of the saints who had fallen asleep were raised; and coming out of the graves after His resurrection, they went into the holy city and appeared to many" (Matt. 27:51–53).

Who can be more satisfied than God in seeing the transformation of character that one experiences after submitting to the cross of Calvary? "What man of you, having a hundred sheep, if he loses one of them, does not leave the ninety-nine in the wilderness, and go after the one which was lost until he finds it, he lays it on his shoulders, rejoicing . . . I say to you likewise there will be more joy in heaven over one sinner who repents than over ninety-nine just persons who need no repentance" (Luke 15:4–5, 7). And that's precisely what God did with the resurrection of Christ. He reunited the earth with the unfallen universe. God is well satisfied you've come home, and there is rejoicing over every sinner who repents. However, there are many others who are yet to hear of the wonderful name of Jesus Christ. Will you pray that the Lord recruit more workers in his vineyard so that the billions who are not saved will have the same opportunity you've had? Lord, make me a vessel to use in your vineyard.

August 17

Numbered with Transgressors

And He was numbered with the transgressors, and He bore the sin of many, and made intercession for the transgressors.

—Isaiah 53:12

Dietrich Bonhoeffer was swallowed up in the killing machine of the Nazi concentration camp system. He was hanged just two weeks before American GIs broke into the camp and brought the madness to an end. Bonhoeffer was a thorn Adolf Hitler desperately wanted to get out of his side. His love for humanity would not allow him to be silent in the wake of Nazi atrocities against Jews and other dissenters. Dietrich did something extraordinary of his time; he identified with the victims as his Lord did, something intolerable to the Nazis and embarrassing to the well-respected silent church leaders who were content with just looking on.

Bonhoeffer's sympathy for Jewish suffering can be traced to his tenure as a Sunday school teacher at a black Harlem church where he struck an affinity with African American leaders and Reinhold Niebuhr. It was there he developed an interest in the Social Gospel. Upon returning to his native Germany, his public speaking was directed at the abuse of the Nazi regime, and he became a headache that Adolf Hitler could do without. He sealed his testimony with his blood and was numbered as a transgressor, a disturber of the peace (www.dbonhoeffer.org).

Bonhoeffer picked up the baton Jesus handed him as his passion grew for the Jews and the marginalized people who were being systematically murdered by the Nazi regime. Needless to say, he ran headlong into trouble with government officials and the silent religious establishment as Jesus his Lord did. "Now it happened, as He was dining in Levi's house that many tax collectors and sinners also sat together with Jesus and His disciples; for there were many and they followed Him. And when the scribes and Pharisees saw Him eating with the tax collectors and sinners, they said to His disciples, how is it that He eats and drinks with tax collectors and sinners?" (Mark 2:15–16). Everyone is precious in Jesus's eyes. The slave is just as beloved as his master; the captain and the cook stand equal. They stand toe to toe at the foot of the cross. Jesus is the tide that lifts all people, including you and me. He took us to the banquet table even though we were dressed in rags and were not on the original list of invited guests.

Peering through the future, Jesus predicted a time when his disciples would be persecuted for the very values he espoused and articulated. Spreading the gospel as Jesus did will always run into opposition with a determined enemy and his surrogates intent on keeping you and me out of the kingdom of God. "They will put you out of the synagogues; yes the time is coming that whoever kills you will think that he offers God a service" (John 16:2). The early disciples counted it an honor to suffer for Christ's sake. Are you preparing yourself if that situation arises to seal your testimony with your blood? We must view obedience to God more worthwhile than remaining alive and going along with the status quo. "And they overcame him by the blood of the Lamb and by the word of their testimony, and they did not love their lives to the death" (Rev. 12:11). Do you love God and his kingdom to the extent that you will give your life for his cause? God goes with you, my friend, and be faithful even unto the very end.

August 18

When Opportunities Come Knocking

Therefore take the talent from him, and give it to him who has ten talents. For to everyone who has, more will be given, and he will have abundance; but from him who does not have, even what he has will be taken away.
—Matthew 25:28–29

They detected the movement of a school of fish in the bay, and suddenly, there was a mad scramble to their boats to encircle the fish with their nets. Several energetic burly young men raced to their boats; whoever got there first began encircling the fish with their nets. They expended enormous amounts of energy in encircling what they thought would be the catch of a lifetime, but the fish simply escaped them. Who wants to be dinner on the table of another? Not even fish. The joy and excitement of the hunt turned into gloom and dismay. "What happened?" I asked one fisherman close to me. "The fish outsmarted us this time" was his remark.

A school of very big tuna fish came calling on the very doorsteps of the fishermen, but they did not have the right equipment or the skill to capitalize on the opportunity. As I thought about the fishermen's missed opportunity, it dawned on me how often the Lord Jesus quite literally throws opportunities and situations conducive to our spiritual growth at us, but our slow perception and awareness fail in capitalizing on them. Where some might see only barren rocks, another sees a stone-processing plant. Where some see only trash, another sees a waste-processing facility. One man's garbage might be another man's treasure. "If any of you lacks wisdom let him ask of God, who gives liberally and without reproach and it will be given to him" (James 1:5).

"When Ephraim was a child, I loved him, and out of Egypt I called My son . . . I taught Ephraim to walk, taking them by their arms; but they did not know that I healed them. I drew them with gentle cords, with bands of love, and I was to them as those who take the yoke from their neck. I stopped and fed them" (Hosea 11:1, 3–4). God is constantly making these wonderful overtures to us every day throughout our lifetime. Isn't God simply amazing? Lord, help us be attentive when we perceive you are talking to us. Help us be more sensitive to those who are smiling but deep within are hurting real bad. Lord, help us use our life experience to dissuade those intent on making the dreadful choices we made. Lord, one more thing, help us love those we do not like.

God has blessed some with the ability to grow businesses. Whatever they touch turns into gold; they have the proverbial Midas touch, but he has not left us empty-handed. Opportunities abound in making a difference in the lives of those around us. "When He ascended on high, He led captivity captive and gave gifts unto men . . . He Himself gave some to be apostles, some prophets, some evangelists, and some pastors and teachers, for the equipping of the saints for the work of the ministry for the edifying of the body of Christ" (Eph. 4:8, 11–12). Do you know you are a gifted person and have been endowed with many gifts by Jesus? Oh yes, you sure are. You are specially equipped to do something great. You must find out from Jesus, who is the giver of every good gift, what you're good at. You go ahead and grab a hold of your opportunity and just do it. God be with you, dear friend. Give the glory to God, to whom it belongs. Amen and amen.

God's Impeccable Timing

So the king said, who is in the court? Now Haman had just entered the outer court of the king's palace to suggest that the king hang Mordecai on the gallows that he had prepared for him.

—Esther 6:4

The acceleration is good and the athleticism impeccable, but the dunk is terrible; the basketball doesn't go into the net. Regardless of how many times the ball bounces around the rim, once it enters into the net, the shot is perfect. Conversely, the opposite is true. Whatever distance the shot may have been tried, if it doesn't enter the net, the shot is no good. God is perfect, and his timing is always impeccable. We may have missed a terrible accident by a split second or made it to a successful job interview with minutes to spare without considering that the God who knows the number of hair on our head had it all figured out. He is always hard at work in our behalf.

Haman, the prime minister of Persia, has just walked into the king's court to ask of him an urgent request—the head of his avowed enemy, Mordecai the Jew, and the total destruction of his people. "There is a certain people scattered and dispersed among the people in all the provinces of your kingdom; their laws are different from all other people's and they do not keep the King's laws. Therefore it is not fitting for the king to let them remain. If it pleases the king, let a decree be written that they be destroyed, and I will pay ten thousand talent of silver into the hands of those who do the work" (Esther 3:8–9). Haman was blissfully unaware of the fact that God created time and arranges situations and circumstances to suit his purpose. "Daniel answered and said: 'Blessed be the name of God forever and ever, for wisdom and might are His. And He changes the times and the seasons; He removes kings and raises up kings; He gives wisdom to the wise and knowledge to those who have understanding. He reveals deep and secret things; He knows what is in the darkness, and light dwells with Him'" (Dan. 2:20–22).

We sometimes attribute too much to chance, although the Bible acknowledges that chance happens to men, but God's involvement in the lives and circumstances of his people is not left to chance. "But when the fullness of time of the time had come, God sent forth His son, born of a women, born under the law, to redeem those who were under the law, that we might receive the adoption of sons" (Gal. 4:4–5). God works within and outside our time schedule in saving people, and his timing is always precise and flawless. He arranges time and events that will lead to our good and ultimately to our conversion. An invitation to a meeting, the reading of spiritual books, the reading of the Bible, the hearing of a radio/television sermon, and more have all been carefully coordinated by God to lead us to Jesus Christ.

What a relief in knowing that while we cannot see or control the evil being directed or planned against us, God is in total control, deflecting them from us. Realizing that death was dogging his every footstep, Martin Luther King said, "I am not worried about the future. I am not fearing any man. Mine eyes have seen the glory of the coming of the Lord." Anything that touches us has been screened by God, and a way of escape has been made in our behalf. Therefore don't worry; just be happy.

August 20

This Far and No Farther

Where were you when I laid the foundation of the earth? Tell Me if you have understanding . . .
When I said, this far you may come, but no further, and here your proud waves must stop!
—Job 38:4, 11

Three years after the terrible tsunami that devastated Japan, debris from the disaster are washing up on the West Coast and on some Pacific islands. Intent on detecting the next tsunami, scientists have installed monitoring equipment to keep tabs on ocean behavior, but can they predict with certainty when these monster calamities will occur? Although God did not create natural disasters; He has total control over them.

"Now when He got into a boat, His disciples followed Him. And suddenly a great tempest arose on the sea, so that the boat was covered with the waves. But He was asleep. Then His disciples came to Him and awoke Him, saying, Lord, save us! We are perishing! But He said, why are you fearful, O you of little of faith? Then He arose and rebuked the winds and the sea, and there was a great calm" (Matt. 8:23–26). The entrance of sin threw the balance of nature out of alignment. The seasons gradually turned to the extremes of bone-chilling cold and sweltering heat. After the flood, things really took a turn for the worse; rivers overflowed their banks, oceans were formed, rugged cliffs and jagged rocks emerged, barren deserts and mountains were formed in the aftermath of the receding waters. The Grand Canyon, Old Faithful, and all the other natural wonders of the world were formed after the flood of Noah.

Animal behavior adapted to suit their new environment in the wake of this global phenomenon. Predation began after man's sin, and over time, animals began developing unique capabilities to catch their prey. The spider designed its fabulous and intricate net not only for sleep comfort but also for catching prey. Cheetahs developed their long, slender frames not to run marathons but to catch their favorite prey.

Despite the apparent dysfunction in nature, God is in absolute control, and nothing escapes his all-knowing, all-seeing, and ever-present being. "Then the word of the Lord came to him, saying, get away from here and turn eastward, and hide by the Brook Cherith, which flows into the Jordan. And it will be that you shall drink from the brook, and I have commanded the ravens to feed you there" (1 Kings 17:2–4). God oversees the order of nature and commands the birds to feed the man instead of the man feeding the birds.

In other instances, he saves everyone in the company of his trusted servants. "Men you should have listened to me, and not have sailed from Crete and incurred this loss . . . For there stood by me this night an angel of God to whom I belong and whom I serve, saying, do not be afraid, Paul; you must be brought before Caesar; and indeed God has granted you all those who sail with you. Therefore take heart, men, for I believe God that it will be just as it was told me" (Acts 27:21, 23–25). Is God in control even when nature seems to be in rebellion against the will of her Creator? "Can you bind the cluster of Pleiades, or loose the belt of Orion? Can you bring out Mazzaroth in its season? Or can you guide the Great Bear with its cubs?" (Job 38:31–32). God runs his universe with the help of no one since no one was around when he created it. He is in absolute control of the minutest atom on the Great Barrier Reef. God runs his universe, not nature.

August 21

It Is Finished

So when Jesus had received the sour wine, He said, "It is finished!"
And bowing His head, He gave up His spirit.

—John 19:30

The Brooklyn Bridge is a technological monument of human engineering. It was completed in 1883 to connect Manhattan to Brooklyn; it has survived the many rumors of its imminent collapse and still carries millions to their destinations. Its completion revolutionized travel in and around New York City; pedestrians could walk from Manhattan to Brooklyn with relative ease. Motor vehicle and train traffic cut commuting time significantly. Among the many significant accomplishments of the bridge—and there are many—none is as remarkable as its effect on cutting down travel time.

With the words "It is finished," two worlds were connected; a bridge was built connecting the earth to heaven. Jesus began his High Priest ministry after his ascension in our behalf. All humanity has direct access to the throne of God through the ministry of Christ Jesus. The road to heaven has been paved with the spilt blood of our Lord and Savior, Jesus Christ. "Now this is the main point of the things we are saying: we have such a High Priest, who is seated at the right hand of the throne of the majesty in the heavens, a Minister of the sanctuary and of the true tabernacle which the Lord erected, and not man" (Heb. 8:1–2).

Our Lord Jesus Christ is a member of the human race, fully God and fully man; he is very familiar with our weakness, our tears, our fears, our pain, and our sorrows and is now representing us before the throne of God. And he also is an expert in legal affairs; after all, he created all laws—natural, civil, moral, health, and ceremonial laws. Besides, he is abundant in mercy as cited here. "When Jesus had raised Himself up and saw no one but the woman, He said to her, 'Woman where are those accusers of yours? Has no man condemned you?' She said, 'No one Lord.' And Jesus said, 'Neither do I condemn you; go and sin no more'" (John 8:10–11).

Can we find a more compassionate attorney to represent us in heaven than our merciful and considerate Savior? Is he not familiar with every weakness in our anatomy, being a human himself? Capitalizing on this high-profile representation, the writer to the Hebrews eloquently states, "Seeing then that we have a great High Priest who has passed through the heavens, Jesus the Son of God, let us hold fast our confession. For we do not have a High Priest who cannot sympathize with our weaknesses, but was in all points tempted as we are, but without sin. Let us therefore come boldly to the throne of grace that we may obtain mercy and find grace to help in time of need" (Heb. 4:14–16).

The words "It is finished" sealed the fate of Satan and inaugurated a new beginning. "What do you conspire against the Lord? He will make an utter end of it. Affliction will not rise up a second time" (Nah. 1:9). God will root out every vestige of sin and ensure that it will never raise its ugly head ever again. I have resolved to be ready and help others get ready for that great heavenly reunion. How about you? Are you getting ready, staying ready, or not interested in getting ready at all?

August 22

No More Rash Vows

Again you have heard that it was said to those of old, you shall not swear falsely, but shall perform your oaths to the Lord. But I say to you, do not swear at all neither by heaven, for it is God's throne nor by the earth for it is His footstool . . . but let your yes, be yes, and your no, no.

—Matthew 5:33–35, 37

Many hearts have been broken, elections lost, hopes dashed, and lives ruined as a result of rash vows. Daimler-Benz and Chrysler Corporation were a wonderful couple. They had a steamy romance that blossomed into wedlock; they invited many guests as the business world watched their flamboyant marriage. With high-powered attorneys looking on, they signed papers and made many interesting promises to each other, which proved too costly to keep. When tough times came and financial losses began piling up at Chrysler, the marriage fell apart, and they went their separate ways.

Rash vows have been with us for quite some time now. We make them out of passion, on the spur of the moment, without thinking; but once they are made, God expects us to keep them, however difficult the circumstances. "And Jephthah made a vow to the Lord, and said, 'If you will indeed deliver the people of Ammon into my hands, then it will be that whatever comes out of my house to meet me, when I return in peace from the people of Ammon, shall surely be the Lord's and I will offer it up as a burnt offering'" (Judg. 11:30–31). Unfortunately for Jephthah, his only child and virgin daughter came bouncing from the house to greet her victorious dad returning home from battle. Jephthah began pulling off his hair as he realized the predicament he was in. Thankfully for him, God does not accept or condone human sacrifices, but he lost the opportunity of having genetic descendants since she was his only child and a virgin at best.

"When you make a vow to God, do not delay to pay it; for He has no pleasure in fools. Pay what you have vowed, it is better not to vow, than to vow and not pay" (Eccles. 5:4–5). There are always witnesses when a vow is taken. Dealing with stubborn Israel, God called on the earth, mountains, and trees as witnesses. In like manner, in the absence of human witnesses, God is always an unseen witness to our good intentions gone bad. "When you beget children and grandchildren and have grown old in the land, and act corruptly and make a carved image in the form of anything, and do evil in the sight of the Lord your God to provoke Him to anger, I call heaven and earth to witness against you this day, that you will soon perish from the land which you cross over the Jordan to possess, you will not prolong your days in it, but will be utterly destroyed" (Deut. 4:25–26). O Lord, help us. What modern convenience haven't we idolized?

Our love to our heavenly Father will prevent us from reneging on our commitment to him, especially as it relates to our financial obligation to his kingdom, but I must add that we are mortals, and mortals do get weary in well-doing. However, this text provides us a shot in the arm. "Jesus said to him, if you can believe, all things are possible to him who believes. Immediately the father of the child cried out and said with tears, 'Lord I believe, help my unbelief!'" (Mark 9:23–24). Help our unbelief, Lord. Most times, we mean well, but our human weaknesses fail us. Does Jesus take our weaknesses into account? "He knows our frame; He remembers we are dust" (Ps. 103:14).

August 23

Few against Many

Whom have you reproached and blasphemed? Against whom have you raised your voice and lifted your eyes on high? Against the holy one of Israel.
—Isaiah 37:23

Secular academia has declared God is dead, but they are not the first in defying the very One in whom they live and move and have their being. Unfortunately, power, intelligence, fame, and fortune have blinded men to the overall sovereignty of God. At the peak of his power, King Nebuchadnezzar made this astonishing statement in defiance against God: "Now if you are ready at the time you hear the sound of the horn, flute, harp, lyre and psaltery in symphony and all kinds of music, and you fall down and worship the image which I have made, good! But if you not worship, you shall be cast immediately into the midst of a burning fiery furnace. And who is the god who shall deliver you out of my hands?" (Dan. 3:15).

The pharaoh, king of Egypt, echoed similar defiance. "And Pharaoh said, 'Who is the Lord that I should obey His voice to let Israel go? I do not know the Lord, nor will I let Israel go'" (Exod. 5:2). Fighting against God is always a losing proposition as the pharaoh and the Egyptians found out. "Then Pharaoh's servants said to him, 'How long shall this man be a snare to us? Let the men go, that they may serve the Lord their God. Do you not yet know that Egypt is destroyed?'" (Exod. 10:7).

Defying God in ignorance is one thing, but mocking the Almighty intentionally is quite a different story as this gentleman discovered. "Then the Rabshekeh said to them, Say now to Hezekiah, thus says the great king of Assyria: What confidence is this in which you trust? . . . Thus says the king: Do not let Hezekiah deceive you, for he will not be able to deliver you; nor let Hezekiah make you trust in the Lord, saying, the Lord will surely deliver us; saying this city will not be given into the hand of the king of Assyria" (Isa. 36:4, 14–15).

As always, when God's people are in dire trouble and pray to him, he is ever ready to deliver. Hezekiah prayed to the Lord, and God heard him. "Now therefore, O Lord our God save us from his hand, that all the kingdoms of the earth may know that you are the Lord, you alone" (Isa. 37:20). After hearing the prayer of his servant, God delivered a personal message to the king of Assyria. "Then the angel of the Lord went out, and killed in the camp of the Assyrians one hundred and eighty-five thousand; and when people arose early in the morning, there were the corpses—all dead" (Isa. 37:36).

God is always a majority. Even if the whole world is arrayed against us, we should do as the prophet advised Israel. "Stand still, and see the salvation of the Lord, which He will accomplish for you today. For the Egyptians whom you see today, you shall see again no more forever. The Lord will fight for you and you shall hold your peace" (Exod. 14:13–14). "Where the two and the three are gathered together in My name, I am in their midst of them" (Matt. 18:20). We are confident of the battle's outcome; we are on the winning team, and the game is in the final seconds of the fourth quarter. Are you engaged in the battle? Are you a player or a spectator? Are you winning in Christ?

August 24

Set Your House in Order

In those days Hezekiah was sick and near death. And Isaiah the prophet, the son of Amoz, went to him and said to him, "Thus says the Lord: set your house in order, for you shall die and not live."

—Isaiah 38:1

The U.S. Navy SEALs train rigorously. They are handed difficult assignments around the world, which they perform with flawless precision. They train in extreme heat that could induce heat stroke and in bone-chilling cold that could jolt one into hypothermia and even death. They are trained to make lifesaving decisions under difficult conditions, all in honor of the country they love and serve. They will not hesitate in executing the command of the president even when it necessitates giving their lives to save others. They scoff at death since the honor of the country is greater to them than life itself.

God looks at death differently from how we do; while we view it as something to be dreaded or a cessation of all life, God sees it as a temporary nap. "Oh, that You would hide me in the grave, that You would conceal me until Your wrath is past that You would appoint me a set time, and remember me! If a man dies, shall he live again? All the days of my hard service I will wait until my change comes" (Job 14:13–14). Whether one sleeps for a thousand years or but for one moment, the sleeping believer and the unsaved lost are oblivious to the passage of time. What is most important in this life is not the length of one's life but how that time allotted him was spent in the service of God.

Through the ages, many saints have slipped peacefully to rest, embracing God's glorious promise. This wonderful promise was often quoted as believers gave their lives en masse in the amusement stadiums of Rome. "Precious in the sight of the Lord is the death of His saints" (Ps. 116:15). The Lord watches with keen interest the endurance of his saints and will not let them be exposed to any situation greater than their ability to endure. Therefore it is with love born out of compassion that the Lord allows some to fall sleep. Many are taken in the prime of their youth, while others are spared the agony of a debilitating long sickness. God knows what is best for his children and commissions his angels to gently lay the head of the fallen to their rest and mark their graves for that "great getting-up morning." We need not fear death; Jesus has the keys to unlock the graves and set their victims free.

"Behold, I tell you a mystery. We shall not all sleep, but we shall all be changed, in a moment, in the twinkling of an eye, at the last trumpet. For the trumpet will sound, and the dead will be raised incorruptible, and we shall be changed. For this corruptible must put on incorruption, and this mortal must put on immortality . . . O death, where is your sting? O Hades where is your victory?" (1 Cor. 15:51–53, 55).

Since death is more real than the payment of taxes, should we go kicking and screaming at its silent approach, or should we set our house in order, for we all will die someday should the Lord delay his coming? Thanks be to God, death is only a sleep for the saints and eternal and complete destruction to the lost. Fear not, Jesus knows where you will be laid to rest and will commission his angels to find you and your loved ones.

August 25

Comfort Ye, My People

Comfort, yes comfort My people! Says your God. Speak comfort to Jerusalem, and cry out to her, that her warfare is ended, that her iniquity is pardoned: for she has received from the Lord's hands double for all her sins.

—Isaiah 40:1–2

Ever since Pearl Harbor, U.S. presidents have become commanders in grief in the wake of national tragedies. After being informed of the full impact of a tragedy, they appear on national television to comfort a wounded nation. Since Pres. Franklin D.

Roosevelt, every U.S. president has had to appear in impromptu news conferences to refresh the spirit of a grief-stricken nation. In a recent tragedy, President Obama reassured a stunned nation with these words: "We will get through this," and we did.

God is our Comforter in Chief, and he knows just when our spirit needs refreshing. What is more comforting than to know the heavy load of sin, which has been crushing our conscience, has been forgiven? "Have mercy upon me, O God, according to Your loving-kindness; according to the multitude of Your tender mercies, blot out my transgressions. Wash me thoroughly from my iniquity and cleanse me from my sin" (Ps. 51:1–2). We need constant cleaning just as little babies. We often get messy and must constantly request cleansing from the Lord. Remember, "if we confess our sins, He is faithful and just to forgive us our sins and to cleanse us from all unrighteousness" (1 John 1:9).

Lord, comfort your people that we do not become too pessimistic under a steady barrage of negative news and hateful incidents around us. The newspapers and television broadcasters brush aside the good being done and jolt us with the criminal behavior of the worst among us. Comfort us, Lord. Let us know that you will be with us even when things seem to be falling apart all around us. "Behold, the Lord God shall come with a strong hand, and His arm shall rule for Him; Behold, His reward is with Him, and His work before Him. He will feed His flock like a shepherd; He will gather the lambs with His arm, and carry them in His bosom, and gently lead those who are with young" (Isa. 40:10–11).

Like ancient Israel, we are living our own modern version of the Exodus experience. There are pharaohs (bad habits) to confront and overcome, bitter waters (disappointments) to drink, graven images (modern technologies) to avoid, and negative mixed multitude (toxic TV shows) to deal with. But through it all, we are confident that God is with us; and by his power, we shall make it through. "When you pass through the waters, I will be with you; and through the rivers, they shall not overflow you, when you walk through the fire, you shall not be burned, nor shall the flame scorch you for I am the Lord your God the Holy one of Israel, your Savior" (Isa. 43:2–3). God is with us, my friend, and he will carry us over the finish line on his ever-secure and strong shoulders.

August 26

What Could Have Been

Oh, that you had heeded My commandments! Then your peace would have been like a river, and your righteousness like the waves of the sea.

—Isaiah 48:18

Being the older of the twins, Esau was destined to greatness. Foremost among the entitlements of the firstborn was being priest and leader of the family, but Esau was more interested in chasing game all over the plains than leading his family in worship. As the boys sat at their father's feet listening to stories of Adam,

Enoch, Abraham, Noah, and the great flood, Esau grew restless; his mind truly was somewhere else—hunting. Jacob, on the other hand, sat entranced at the wonderful stories being told.

Esau's bad decisions in life brought constant pain to his mom and dad, especially his choice of wives. "When Esau was forty years old, he took as wives Judith the daughter of Beeri the Hittite, and Basemath the daughter of Elon the Hittite. They were a grief of mind to Isaac and Rebekah" (Gen. 26:34–35). Esau's poor choices led him to choose unbelieving mates who did not worship the God his family served. His perpetual irrational decisions led him to choose a bowl of lentils over his spiritual inheritance, a choice he would regret with bitter tears. "And Esau said to his father, 'Have you only one blessing, my father? Bless me, me also, O my father!' And Esau lifted up his voice and wept" (Gen. 27:38).

The choices some make in childhood pretty much seal up their fate as adults. As we watch our children and grandchildren grow, being wiser now than before, we cringe at the decisions they make as adolescents. God had the similar reaction about Israel, his son. "Oh that they had such a heart in them that they would fear Me and always keep all My commandments, that it might be well with them and with their children forever" (Deut. 5:29). Jerusalem was a citadel among nations, a light to the Gentiles, and a grand concourse of travel from Asia to Africa. It was prized real estate sought by and fought over by many famous world conquerors, including Nebuchadnezzar, Alexander the Great, and Julius Caesar, but Israel failed to be God's nation of priests and teachers to the Gentiles. It was only during their captivity that the host nation learned of the wonders of the true God. Daniel witnessed in the palace of Nebuchadnezzar, Belshazzar, and Darius; Mordecai and Esther did the same in Persia, Joseph in Egypt, and Paul and the disciples in Rome. Why didn't they witness in times of relative peace?

We would do well not to repeat the mistakes of ancient Israel, witnessing only when in captivity. May God help us not to squander witnessing opportunities he sends our way. Do you know God strategically places people, events, and circumstances in our life to bring us to faith in him? Even the way we handle adversity can be a model to others who are watching. Remember, we are books being read by all men. As we take daily inventory of our lives, let us ask God to give us the will, foresight, and ability to use every opportunity to bring honor and glory to him. There are friends, family members, coworkers, and neighbors to tell of our gracious Lord and soon-coming King. Even when we make unwise decisions, we can use these testimonies to glorify God. Paul was not proud of persecuting the church, but he used his ignorance to God by contrasting his life before and after the Damascus experience. Even in our follies, which we should be ashamed of, we can still praise, honor, and glorify God without glamorizing sin.

August 27

Conservation Now

Then God said, Let us make man in Our image, according to Our likeness; let them have dominion over fish of the sea, over the birds of the air, and over the cattle, over all the earth and over creeping things that creep on the earth.
—Genesis 1:26–27

When in flight, they darkened the sky by their sheer numbers, but now they can only be seen behind the secure confines of a museum glass. Regrettably, we hunted them to extinction, and they are no longer with us. The passenger pigeon was indigenous to the eastern part of North America; their feeding grounds extended from Michigan to the west, Quebec to the north, and Mexico to the south. In their abundance, observers recorded flocks of migrating birds covering an area of about forty square miles. Unfortunately, they were relentlessly massacred and hunted in the absence of laws limiting how many could be harvested from the wild. No one voiced any real concern for their continued sustainability as a species. The prevailing theory of the day held that their numbers were simply inexhaustible and that nature would make up for the losses.

Gradually, the vast flocks that darkened the skies in their multiplied millions and were thought inexhaustible became less and less abundant. Over a period, it was discovered that the bird was declining in population. The few struggling nesting colonies could not replenish the massive losses suffered at the hands of inconsiderate hunters. A last fleeting effort was made to preserve the species. It was assumed that captivity might just work. The last surviving passenger pigeon died in captivity on September 1, 1914, in a Cincinnati zoo; her name was Martha, and it was thought she was twenty-nine years of age. What a sad legacy of man's stewardship of his environment. The elephants, the giraffes, the black and white rhinos, and many others are all under great threat of going the way of the passenger pigeon, and it is not too late to take action to stop their declining numbers (https://www.scientificamerican. com/article/3-billion-to-zero-what-happened-to-the-passenger-pigeon/).

"Then God said, Let us make man in Our image, according to Our likeness; let them have dominion over fish of the sea, over the birds of the air, and over the cattle, over all the earth and over creeping things that creep on the earth" (Gen. 1:26–27). Man's dominion over the animals does not include their wanton destruction; the word "dominion" expressly refers to rulership. Man is to rule over the earth just as a wise guardian would have authority over a child, to protect the toddler from the folly of infancy. A careful reading of the text will reveal that man is not given dominion over the celestial bodies (e.g., sun, moon, and stars) but the animals and plant life. Yes, we are affecting the environment by our unwise habits and bad agricultural practices. But all is not lost; we can do better and should do better as wise stewards of our environment.

"But now ask the beasts, and they will teach you; And the birds of the air, and they tell you; Or speak to the earth, and it will teach you; And the fish of the sea will explain to you. Who among all these does not know That the hand of the Lord has done this, In whose hand is the life of every living thing, and the breath of all mankind?" (Job 12:7–10). Conservation of the earth and its vast resources begins with the realization that God is the supreme Creator, and man—the highest order of his creation—has been tasked with the stewardship and supervision of the environment.

Get up. Wake up. What are you doing to protect the environment? Are you on the side of those who are polluting our environment, or are you helping to conserve it? Are you still asleep during this great revolutionary period of the earth's history? Get up and make a difference in the health of our environment. Conserve, recycle, and economize. God be with you in your approach.

August 28

Prayer Changes Things

Call upon Me in the day of trouble; I will deliver you, and you shall glorify Me.
—Psalm 50:15

His head drooped as he heard from his doctor the much-dreaded *C* word. Who wants to hear he or she has cancer? But Sammy (name changed) decided to fight this deadly disease with everything at his disposal. He pored over every available piece of information relative to his disease. He modified his diet and adopted a new attitude to cope with his new reality. Great. However, the key behind Sammy's survival lies in the fact that he has a solid group of prayer warriors supplicating to God on his behalf. Unknown to him and his family, we submitted his name to our church prayer list where a group of prayer warriors regularly prayed for his recovery. We drove up north to see our friend hoping for the best but bracing for the worst. Brace yourself for some good news. He's alive. He is alive! Thank you, God Almighty, that he is still alive.

Not only is Sammy very much alive but he also has accepted Jesus Christ as his Lord and Savior and is now rejoicing in the faith. Am I worried about his medical condition? No. If you have Jesus, you have it all. "For I know that my Redeemer lives, and He shall stand at last on the earth; and after my skin is destroyed, this I know, that in my flesh I shall see God, whom I shall see for myself, and my eyes shall behold and not another" (Job 19:25–27).

If the truth be told, people need prayer, much prayer, and we must recognize this reality and pray for them and allow God to work his wonders. Failure to realize this reality and implement prayer as a "must do" in our daily life will put us on the same course as the dodo bird. We have no other recourse; the prisons are full of creative healthy young men and women who have been used and abused by Satan. It would bring a smile to the face of God to see these dear ones turn their lives over to him. It can happen if we pray for them. Positive things happen in the community when we pray. God connects the unsaved to life-changing events when we pray. God causes people to miss disastrous situations when we pray. God shields us or cancels bad things directed against us and our loved ones when we pray. We become closer to God and more sensitive to the needs of others when we pray. We become less critical and more supportive when we pray and become willing tools in the hands of the Master Craftsman.

Finally, prayer is the key that opens heaven's storehouse. Let us examine its contents. The shelves of heaven are full of neatly wrapped packages waiting to be delivered upon request. Grace is ready and packaged to the penitent, forgiveness to those who earnestly desire it, protection against evil, and strength to the weak when we pray. But these gifts are given only upon request. "Ask and it shall be given unto you" (Matt. 7:7).

"If it had not been the Lord who was on our side, let Israel now say, if it had not been the Lord on our side, when men arose up against us, then they would have swallowed us alive. When their wrath was kindled against us, then the waters would have overwhelmed us, the stream would have gone over our soul . . . Our help is in the name of God" (Ps. 124:1–4, 8). God is among us even when we are unaware of his presence.

August 29

A Narrow Escape

The Lord is my shepherd; I shall not want. He makes me to lie down in green pastures;
He leads me beside the still waters. He restores my soul.

—Psalm 23:1–3

A South African Cape fur seal sits precariously on the nose of a great white shark, just above its snapping jaws, and this is not a circus act. He escapes this time with his life but might not be so fortunate next time. The waters surrounding South Africa are teeming with plankton and other nutrients, providing a bountiful buffet for all residents, including seals, the great white's favorite snack. It's a dangerous cat-and-mouse game being played between predator and prey as they take advantage of nature's bounty (https://www.pinterest.com/pin/844493653576703/).

The highly developed countries are the economic engines of the world economy, but economic development comes at a high price. It takes a heavy toll on citizens, and the workers swimming these waters of economic development are showing signs of breakdown. The most common symptoms are stress, drunkenness, oppressive poverty, premature death, suicide, overwork, exploitation, selfishness, burnout, office romances and tired eyes behind the wheels. Like the Cape seal, we are forced to coexist in a dangerous neighborhood with others who make fun at the law. We need help.

Because the Lord is our shepherd, he will safely navigate us through these shark-infested waters. Reflecting on the dangers of his time, David affirms, "Yea, though I walk through the valley of the shadow of death I will fear no evil; for You are with me; Your rod and Your staff, they comfort me. You prepare a table before me in the presence of my enemies; You anoint my head with oil my cup runs over. Surely goodness and mercy shall follow me all the days of my life and I shall dwell in the house of the Lord forever" (Ps. 23:4–6).

God has not left us to the cruel antics of Satan. He has assured us, "He who touches you, touches the apple of His eyes" (Zech. 2:8). "The poor man cried out, and the Lord heard him and saved him out of all his troubles. The angel of the Lord encamps all around those who trust in Him and delivers them" (Ps. 34:6–7). When the righteous cry for help, God is already there. His purpose knows no haste or delay.

Even when we are blissfully unaware of God's presence, he is with us. Like an anxious patient before an impending surgery or a nervous student about to take an unscheduled exam, we are saddled with fear, worry, and anxiety, but God is always there to calm us down. "And the Lord, He is the One who goes before you. He will be with you, He will not leave you nor forsake you; do not fear nor be dismayed" (Deut. 31:8). What a wonderful promise to treasure as we live in a society beset by crime, stress, financial hardships, and economic and political turmoil. Get a good night's rest. God is in control; he will never leave us or desert us. "A thousand may fall at your side, and ten thousand at your right hand; but it shall not come near you. Only with your eyes shall you look and see the reward of the wicked. Because you have made the Lord who is my refuge, even the Most High, your dwelling place, no evil shall befall you, nor shall any plague come near your dwelling; for He shall give His angels charge over you, to keep you in all your ways. In their hands they shall bear you up" (Ps. 91:7–12).

August 30

The Temple of the Lord

Now therefore, please be careful not to drink wine or similar drink and not to eat anything unclean.

—Judges 13:4

The car began swerving from the right to the left side of the road, sometimes almost brushing against the guardrail. Could he be sick? Certainly, if he were, he would have stopped and dialed for medical assistance. The most common culprit for this type of behavior is alcohol consumption. Numerous scientific research studies have confirmed that alcohol consumption impairs the mind and judgment; it renders one vulnerable to accidents, abuse, loss of memory, and even death. But God is always ahead of the game, and he gave specific instruction to his people concerning substance abuse and unclean foods.

"Or do you not know that your body is the temple of the Holy Spirit which is in you, whom you have from God, and you are not your own? For you were bought at a price; therefore glorify God in your body and in your spirit, which are God's" (1 Cor. 6:19–20). God choose to dwell in the heart instead of magnificent temples; therefore our bodies have become receptacles to inhabit the Most Holy God.

During the Exodus economy, God directed his people to build him a sanctuary so that he could dwell with them. "And let them make Me a sanctuary that I may dwell among them" (Exod. 25:8). The sanctuary was a visual teaching aid to Israel on how God deals with the sin problem. But since the sacrifice of Jesus Christ, the human body has become the primary residence of the living God, replacing the temple of old. The ceremonial law came to an end, meeting its fulfillment in the cross of Jesus Christ. "Having wiped out the handwriting of requirements that was against us, which was contrary to us. And He has taken it out of the way, having nailed it to the cross" (Col. 2:14). The Passover became null and void at the cross, meeting its fulfillment in Jesus. Every lamb slain pointed to him—the real atonement for the sins of the world.

In response to the woman of Samaria's insistence of a central place of worship, Jesus remarked, "Woman, believe Me, the hour is coming when you will neither on this mountain, nor in Jerusalem, worship the father . . . But the hour is coming, and now is, when the true worshipers will worship the Father in spirit and in truth, for the Father is seeking such to worship Him" (John 4:21, 23). There are worshippers of the true God in hostile enemy territories where they dare not openly confess the name of Jesus for fear of persecution and even death, but God accepts their worship, and they are members of his universal church.

Since our bodies are the temple of the living God, we must be careful of the foods we eat, the liquids we ingest, the clothes we wear, what we listen to, and what we watch on the big screen. "Now the Lord spoke to Moses and Aaron saying to them, speak to the children of Israel, saying, these are the animals which you may eat among all the animals that are on the earth" (Lev. 11:1–30, Deut. 14:1–28; space would not allow us to include the whole list, but the information is there for the taking in the above texts).

The motive behind laws is always to keep citizens safe. If we obey God's law, not only will we enjoy a healthier standard of living but we will be pleasing God as well. Have a healthful day. Don't ignore God's laws; obey them.

August 31

Awake! Awake!

Behold I tell a mystery; we shall not all sleep, but we shall be changed, in a moment, in the twinkling of an eye, at the last trumpet. For the trumpet will sound, and the dead will be raised incorruptible, and we shall be changed.

—1 Corinthians 15:51–52

Alaska's wildlife has had to adapt to deal with its severe cold. Wolves grow thicker coats of fur during winter, whales add on thick layers of insulating blubber to cope, and others hibernate or migrate to warmer climates, but the wood frog does not invest in any of these measures; he does not have to. He stays put; he doesn't go anywhere. Why bother expend much energy in migrating to a warmer climate when you can freeze solid during winter and then thaw out when spring arrives? Amazingly, as the temperature begins freezing, the frog expels water out of its cells and replaces it with an antifreeze substance. He then freezes solid, suspends all activity, does not go into hiding, remains anywhere in the open, and waits patiently for the arrival of spring. As the snow melts, he thaws out and resumes life where he left off. Isn't God amazing? (http://www.latimes.com/science/sciencenow/la-sci-sn-alaskan-frozen-frogs-20140723-story.html).

The wood frog's entombment in his icy habitat reminds us of the words of Jesus. "Therefore My Father loves Me, because I lay down My life that I may take it again. No one takes it from Me, but I lay it down of Myself. I have power to lay it down, and I have power to take it again. This command I have received from My Father" (John 10:17–18). Mercy, justice, and love kissed one another as Jesus rested peacefully in Joseph's tomb, and the Father was right there with his Son, observing the proceedings. As the prophetic time clock hit the last second, the Father shouted, "Awake! Awake!" Jesus emerged from the tomb victorious, crushing the head of the devil, Satan (Gen. 3:15).

But Christ's resurrection is a precursor to the great resurrection of Daniel's prophecy. "And at that time your people shall be delivered, everyone who is found written in the book. And many of those who sleep in the dust of the earth shall awake, some to everlasting life, some to shame and everlasting contempt" (Dan. 12:1–2). Death and Hades (the grave) will involuntarily yield the sleeping saints as angels are dispatched to wake them from their slumber. Those martyred for the testimony of Jesus, some devoured by wild beasts, others burned at the stake will all rise with a glow on their face, ready to meet their Savior.

Two trains are scheduled to depart the earth's train station. The announcer is giving the departure time; let's listen. "Blessed and holy is he who has part in the first resurrection. Over such the second death has no power, but they shall be priest of God and of Christ, and shall reign with Him a thousand years" (Rev. 20:6). Consequently, the other train is delayed for a thousand years and is headed in the opposite direction, to a dreadful destination. "The sea gave up the dead who were in it, and Death and Hades delivered up the dead who were in them. And they were judged, each one according to his works. Then Death and Hades were cast in the lake of fire. This is second death" (Rev. 20:13–14). By all means, do not book a ticket on that dreadful train; its destination is hell and everlasting fire, and you don't want to be there.

Which train are you booked on? I have requested a window seat for sightseeing. I want to see Jesus, my Lord, and cast my crown at his feet. Do you have your ticket?

September 1

Abundant in Mercy

He has not dealt with us according to our sins, nor punished us according to our iniquities.
For as the heavens are high above the earth so great is His mercy towards those who fear him.

—Psalm 103:10–11

If you live beyond the ripe old age of five, you will become the victim of someone's clenched fist, cruel joke, or assassination of character. What do you do? Ask for relocation to a gentler planet? The U.S. Constitution, the document that has become a model for the free world, has its hidden flaws and biases. Laws, lawmakers, and law enforcement agencies have in the past failed in their administration of justice. History is replete with laws crafted to disenfranchise certain people groups of their God-given rights. Quite recently, men who served long prison sentences for wrongful convictions were asked by reporters, "Do you harbor ill will toward those responsible for your long years of suffering?" They all emphatically replied no. Why would anyone want to drag resentment and bitterness around for another day?

God created a perfect system of laws. He created the natural law, which regulates the earth and the planets both in and out of our solar system (Gen. 1:3–6). Then he made the health law (hygiene, diet, preventive care), which we all benefit from (Lev. 11:1–30). Would anyone wish or desire to abolish the health law, which deals with cleanliness, health, sanitation, and disposal of waste? The civil law, whether drafted in the jungles of Amazonia by indigenous people there or from the lofty halls of Congress, has the divine imprint on them. Just laws are designed to create order and eradicate chaos in society.

Another law, once very significant but no longer relevant, is the ceremonial law. This law was given by God to Moses, and it contained the ceremonies of how sin was pardoned before the cross of Jesus. Once Jesus died on the cross, the Passover and all the other holy days met their fulfillment in Christ and came to an end at the cross of Calvary. "Having wiped out the handwriting of requirements that was against us, which was contrary to us. And He has taken it out of the way, having nailed it to the cross" (Col. 2:14). The ceremonial laws were a teaching aid leading to Christ. Once Jesus died, they met their fulfillment and were no longer necessary. They played their part in pointing to Christ, the real sacrificial Lamb.

Jesus was the fulfillment of the Passover lamb slain on every day of the Passover feast. The sanctuary and all its impressive rituals were transferred to a different venue. "Wherefore also He is able to save to the uttermost those who come to God through Him, since He lives to make intercession for them. For such a High Priest was fitting for us, who is holy, harmless, undefiled, separate from sinners and became higher than the heavens; who does not need daily, as those high priests, to offer up sacrifices, for His own sins and then for the people's, for this

He did once for all when He offered up Himself" (Heb. 7:25–27). Jesus is now our High Priest, representing us in heaven. Do we really deserve to be forgiven? No. But God is love. "The Lord, the Lord God, merciful and gracious, longsuffering, and abounding in goodness and truth, keeping mercy for thousands, forgiving iniquity and transgression and sin" (Exod. 34:6–7). Thank you, Lord, for saving us, undeserving as we are.

September 2

I Have Sinned

Have mercy upon me, O God, according to your loving kindness;
according to the multitude of Your tender mercies, blot out my transgression.
Wash me thoroughly from my iniquity and cleanse me from my sin.
—Psalm 51:1–2

It was a perfect vacation for our family. All the events planned transpired with flawless precision until, two days before our departure to the U.S., old split-foot (the devil) struck. News of the arrest of a young family member caught with a lot of cannabis with intent to distribute sent a sad pall on everyone. We could not abandon him in his moment of distress, so we did what families do—form a circle around his wagon with smart legal representation. At court and with family members looking on in somber silence, the young man expressed remorse for dragging his family into this fine mess. After much prayer and an amazing legal team, he got away with only a slap on the wrist for punishment and a stern warning. "Do not come back here before me!" the judge thundered.

When the young man pled guilty and threw himself at the mercy of the court, several thoughts ran through my mind. "For all have sinned and fall short of the glory of God" (Rom. 3:23). We all stand guilty of grievous, atrocious sins before a holy God. Like my young grandnephew, we cannot defend our actions because we were caught red-handed, with the evidence to verify our guilt. He couldn't deny the cannabis that he possessed (displayed in a plastic bag), nor can we deny the evidence of our crimes committed against our God.

"There is none righteous, no not one; there is none who understands; there is none who seeks after God. They have all turned aside; they have together become unprofitable; there is none who does good, no, not one" (Rom. 3:10–12). The prognosis does not look good for us standing on the witness stand before a righteous and holy God, but wait a minute, something amazing is happening. Isaiah is shouting something to us. "But He was wounded for our transgressions, He was bruised for our inequities; the chastisement for our peace was upon Him, and by His stripes we are healed" (Isa. 53:5). This is too good to be true, but it is true. Jesus's death cancels the debt of our sins and clothes us in his perfect righteousness.

But wait, this is not all; the news gets even better. "For we do not have a High Priest who cannot sympathize with our weaknesses, but was in all points tempted as we are, yet without sin. Let us therefore come boldly to the throne of grace that we may obtain mercy and find grace to help in time of need" (Heb. 4:15–16). Jesus walked in our shoes. He knows our weakness and sympathizes with us when we fall, but there is something we must do.

"If we confess our sins, He is faithful and just to forgive us our sins and to cleanse us from all unrighteousness" (1 John 1:9). It all begins with admission of guilt. Someone rightfully said, "If you can confess it, Jesus will forgive it." It's that simple, isn't it? But it is easier said than done. Sometimes we just love being miserable. Misery loves company. The devil is trying very hard to have us share his fate. Don't believe him; he is a loser destined to the flames of hell. Lord, I cast my sin-plagued body into your merciful arms; give me the strength to overcome sin when it comes calling at my door. In Jesus's name, amen.

September 3

You Are the Man

Why have you despised the commandment of the Lord, to do evil in His sight? You have killed Uriah the Hittite with the sword . . . of the people of Ammon. Now therefore, the sword shall not depart from your house, because you have despised Me.

—2 Samuel 12:9–10

Believing they can never be caught, scam artists often expand their criminal enterprise. They rent lucrative offices and hire new employees to lure more victims into their trap with promises of high returns on their investments. *American Greed*, which airs on CNBC on Sundays in our area, depicts in raw detail how creative con artists have become in separating us from our hard-earned money. Relentless in their hunt for new streams of cash, these heartless con artists steal from friends, retirees, total strangers, the greedy, other family members, and even their moms and dads to keep up their lavish lifestyle.

As always, every day may belong to the mouse, but all the cat needs is one day, and it's all over. There is a day of reckoning coming when no one can delay the hand of justice. In beautiful allegorical language, the prophet Nathan recites a story of total greed and depravity as a wealthy man exploits his poor neighbor by stealing his only possession. What made the crime so heinous is that the rich man had many sheep but chose to steal his neighbor's only lamb, leaving him with nothing. Nathan wisely allowed David to display his horror and disgust for such a vile crime, only to inform him that he was, in fact, that villain. Having pronounced judgment on himself, including his own death sentence, David threw himself and fell prostrate at the feet of a merciful God. Is there a little David in us, a little mischief maker in us sometimes? Absolutely.

"The heart is deceitful above all things and desperately wicked; and who can know it? I the Lord, search the heart, I test the mind, even to give every man according to his ways, according to the fruit of his doings" (Jer. 17:9–10). Charles Wesley, upon seeing a staggering drunkard, said, "Had it not been for the grace of God, here go I." Paul declared himself the chief of sinners while reflecting on his pre-conversion experience. "This is a faithful saying and worthy of all acceptance, that Christ Jesus came into the world to save sinners, of whom I am chief" (1 Tim. 1:15). No evil is beyond the human heart to accomplish; it is only the Spirit of God abiding in us that prevents us from being totally swept away in the tide of immorality.

David demonstrated more zeal in his repentance than in the cover-up of his sins and confessed. "Have mercy upon me, O God, according to Your loving kindness; According to the multitude of your tender mercies, blot out my transgressions. Wash me thoroughly from my iniquity and cleanse me from my sin" (Ps. 51:1–2). David emptied his heart from "iniquity" (intentional, flagrant, willful sins) and requested a new heart and a right spirit from God. "Create in me a clean heart, O God, and renew a steadfast spirit within me. Do not cast me away from Your presence, and do not take Your Holy Spirit from me" (Ps. 51:10–11). Never trust yourself. Do not place confidence in the arm of flesh, for it will fail you every time. Cast all your cares on him, for he cares for you.

September 4

Good Worker but Raise Denied?

And you know that with all my might I have served your father.
Yet your father has deceived me and changed my wages ten times, but God did not allow him to hurt me.

—Genesis 31:6–7

Big corporations are making record profits, but hiring new workers is not on their agenda just yet. They are making more with less. *Why bother hire new workers?* they muse. Is it any wonder that the Wall Street index is breaking through the ceiling while the unemployment numbers barely move downward? Businessman Laban has bequeathed his dubious formula to his modern-day pals. "Thus I have been in your house twenty years; I served you fourteen years for your two daughters, and six years for your flock, and you have changed my wages ten times. Unless the God of Abraham and the fear of Isaac, had been with me, surely now you would have sent me away empty-handed" (Gen. 31:41–42). God is wide awake at the wheel; he never slumbers or sleeps. Though you are underappreciated on the job, he has recognized your services already.

While a few small companies are leading the charge in rewarding their employees with a $15 minimum pay raise, the successful corporate giants that are more capable of providing this necessary obligation to employees remain neutral and on the sidelines. We commend the few generous small employers who treat their employees as family and give them a salary proportionate to their skill level. We give tribute to them.

We may never get the recognition, the awards, or the justice that is due to us on this earth, and that's more reason to fix our gaze on eternal things. Go ahead and ask for your raise anyhow since you have been an exceptionally productive and reliable worker. However, whether you receive the raise or not, we should work with the mentality that we are working for the Lord; and essentially, we are. "Bondservants, obey in all things your masters according to the flesh, not with eye service, as men pleasers, but in sincerity of heart, fearing God. And whatever you do, do it heartily as to the Lord and not to men, knowing that from the Lord you will receive the reward of the inheritance; for you serve the Lord Jesus Christ" (Col. 3:22–24).

Boy, this is just what I needed to hear. If like me, you are currently working for a boss whose vocabulary does not contain complimentary words like "Good job," "I appreciate your hard work," or "Thank you for giving the project top priority," the subsequent text will bring nourishment and refreshment to the soul. Consider this, dear friend: the inheritance of the wicked will soon be evaporated in the flames of hell. Be faithful in your sphere of work, and in due time, God will triumph in his cause.

"Come now, you rich, weep and howl for the miseries that are coming upon you! Your riches are corrupted, and your garments are moth-eaten. Your gold and silver are corroded, and their corrosion will be a witness against you and will eat your flesh like fire. You have heaped up treasure in the last days. Indeed the wages of the laborers who mowed your fields, which you kept back by fraud, cry out; and the cries of the reapers have reached the ears of the Lord of Sabaoth."

Who said God is not in control? The Bible is as relevant as tomorrow's headline news. Concerning that pay raise, well, God's dividend is multiplied in the tens of billions.

September 5

Revival in the Land Part 2

And it shall come to pass in the last days, says God, that I will pour out of My Spirit on all flesh;
Your sons and your daughters shall prophesy, your young men shall see visions, your old men shall dream dreams.

—Acts 2:17

A shrill cry punctuates the stillness of the night. Baby Jerome is demanding food again; he is hungry. Mom shuffles from underneath her covers and ambles to the refrigerator to fetch a bottle for the little milk drinker. He does this continuously throughout the week with little consideration of poor Mom's baggy eyes. "If you then, though you are evil, know how to give good gifts to your children, how much more will your Father in heaven give the Holy Spirit to those who ask Him!" (Luke 11:13).

Herein lies the problem of the twenty-first-century church. We do not ask or are not consistent enough in asking for the outpouring of the Holy Spirit. We must approach this request with a special sense of urgency when we pray. When something is of importance to us, it occupies the forefront of our minds. The same is true in our approach to spiritual things. If we truly desire the baptism of the Holy Spirit, this concept will occupy our walk, our talk, and our conversation with God and others. And the scripture has not left us ignorant of how this request can be attained.

> Then He said to them, suppose one of you has a friend, and he goes to him at midnight and says, friend, lend me three loaves of bread, because a friend of mine on a journey has come to me, and I have nothing to set before him. Then the one inside answers, don't bother me. The door is already locked, and my children are with me in bed. I can't get up and give you anything. I tell you, though he will not get up and give him the bread because he is his friend, but because of the man's boldness he will get up and give him as much as he needs. So I say to you, ask and it will be given to you, seek and you will find, knock and the door will be opened to you. (Luke 11:5–9)

Did you notice the neighbor's persistence?

I will be first in declaring my guilt for not being persistent and consistent in requesting the baptism of the Holy Spirit. God is more eager to give it than we are ready to receive it. But we can learn a thing or two from baby Jerome, who will not let Mom sleep until she feeds him, and the man who pounded on his neighbor's door until the neighbor could no longer ignore the request of his friend. There is much work to be done in us before the infilling of the Holy Spirit can be materialized. There are bad habits to overcome, sins to confess, relationships to be amended, much praying to be realized, and a persistent attitude to be attained. What are you waiting for? Don't you pray for things that are important to you? Begin praying for the infilling of the Holy Spirit.

Dear Jesus, cleanse my mind to think more like you, and forgive me for all conscious and unconscious sins. Instill in me an appetite, a hunger, and a passion for the lost, even for the radicals who wage jihad on the innocent. Strip from me all the trimmings of worldliness. Let your will become my will. And one last thing, Lord, give me humility of soul that I will be careful to give you all the praise and glory for what you will do through me and with me. Amen.

September 6

The Language of Tears

Then Elkanah her husband said to her, why do you weep?
Why do you not eat? And why is your heart grieved?
Am I not better to you than ten sons? . . . And she was in bitterness of soul, and
prayed to the Lord and wept in anguish.
—1 Samuel 1:8, 10

We were happy and excited about her soon-to-be bundle of joy, but joy turned into sorrow when an abnormality was discovered. That prepared us for what would follow. The tear-filled eyes, the blank stares, the long naps, and the lack of laughter are very familiar to a God who walks in our shoes. "Therefore, when Jesus saw her weeping, and the Jews who came with her weeping, He groaned in the spirit and was troubled. And He said, 'Where have you laid him?' They said to Him, 'Lord, come and see.' Jesus wept" (John 11:33–35).

We do not know which loss carries more pain (and, women, you are better adapted in bearing pain than us men)—a barren woman's many attempts at having a child or a mother's miscarriage. God understands both: "He was despised and rejected by men, a Man of sorrows and acquainted with grief. And we hid, as it were, our faces from Him; He was despised, and we did not esteem Him. Surely He has borne our griefs and carried our sorrows; yet we esteemed Him stricken, smitten by God, and afflicted" (Isa. 53:3–4).

Nothing surprises God. He has seen it all. Being all knowing, all powerful, and all seeing, He foresaw the emergence of evil and equipped us with the necessary strength to cope. In Christ Jesus, we can triumph over our circumstances. Besides equipping us in his strength, he walks with us every step of the way, ensuring that the burden of grief, sorrow, and sometimes despair doesn't overwhelm us. "I taught Ephraim to walk, taking them by the arms; but they did not know that I healed them. I drew them with bands of love, and I was to them as those who take the yoke from their neck. I stooped and fed them" (Hosea 11:3–4). God does that and more for us every day.

No one feels the pain that sin has caused more than God himself. It hurts God to see the pain and degradation of mankind. How much God would have loved to intervene and save man from this terrible nightmare called sin, but his justice dictates that punishment must accompany disobedience of his holy law; therefore he mourns and weeps with us. The greatest pain comes to God when his creatures choose to be separated from him. Standing on a hill overlooking the city of Jerusalem just days before its leaders murdered their only Savior and foreseeing the carnage of the Roman slaughter, the occupation, and the destruction, Jesus wept. "O Jerusalem, Jerusalem, the one who kills the prophets and stones those who are sent to her! How often I wanted to gather your children together, as a hen gathers her chicks under her wings, but you were not willing!" (Matt. 23:7).

The pain, the grief, the illness, and the wayward children may not be explained to us, nor will it ever make sense to us, but God understands and sympathizes with us. He helps us walk, and if we are unable, he carries us in his arms like little lambs. It will soon be over in a little while; therefore hold on to Jesus and be faithful.

September 7

My Alabaster Box

A woman came to Him having an alabaster flask of very costly fragrant oil, and poured it on His head as He sat at the table.

—Matthew 26:7

The spectacular hunt with its great pomp and ceremony has netted only a handful of small fish, not even enough to satisfy a child, and the tribe will go hungry tonight. But the tribal chief does something absolutely astounding; in keeping with tribal courtesy to guests, he prepares the meager catch for the two anthropologists residing among them. The guests eat their fish, dinner while the hunter-gatherers, still hungry, contemplate their strategies for the next fishing expedition. What more can anyone ask from someone who has so little and has given you his all? This fish meal will not be remembered for its size or taste but for the generosity of those who prepared it (*National Geographic*).

"How can I repay the Lord for all His goodness to me?" (Ps. 116:12). We can't repay God, and we should not try to; salvation is absolutely free with no strings attached. However, a heart won over by the gracious love of Jesus cannot remain passive, indifferent, and unresponsive to the One who has done so much for us. "This is love; not that we loved God, but that He loved us and sent His Son as an atoning sacrifice for our sins" (1 John 4:10).

My two-year-old grandson rewarded my persistent begging by giving me a little piece of his granola bar—a huge sacrifice to him since he was still caught up in the selfish world of infancy. But I appreciated his generosity and complimented him profusely for his selfless act. The Lord delights in our acts of generosity motivated by fervent love.

What does the Lord requires of us since he owns everything and needs nothing? A life submitted to Jesus in total surrender is the most precious gift anyone can give to the Lord. Just as a spouse would forgo the expensive gifts in favor of intimate time spent with the other, likewise, Jesus craves intimacy with his people. "With what shall I come before the Lord and bow down before the exalted God? Shall I come before Him with burnt offerings, with calves a year old? Will the Lord be pleased with thousands of rams, with ten thousand rivers of oil? Shall I offer my first born for my transgression, the fruit of my body for the sin of my soul? He has shown you, O man, what is good. And what does the Lord require of you? To act justly and to love mercy and to walk humbly with your God" (Mic. 6:6–8).

Gifts of generosity are always welcomed, but if they are not actuated by a deep and abiding love for God and fellow men, forget about it; it is all in vain. My alabaster box to Jesus requires giving my heart to him in response to the wonderful things he has done in my life. Also, my love for him will extend horizontally to my fellow men. We all have sweet, fragrant ointment that we can pour on Jesus's head and feet. Whatever you hold precious, dedicate it to Jesus, and it will be counted as your alabaster box of ointment. Mary showed us how this can be done. What is your alabaster box?

September 8

One Thing You Lack

Jesus looked at him and loved him. One thing you lack, He said. Go sell everything you have and give to the poor, and you will have treasure in heaven. Then come, follow Me.

—Mark 10:21

Shaquille O'Neal is someone you'd love to have on your basketball team. He's big, tall, and intimidating; gets a lot of rebounds; and discourages opponents from driving to the basket. Upon his entry into the NBA, the three-hundred-pound gentle giant shattered and destroyed several basketball backboards with his thunderous dunks. The NBA had to install reinforced backboards in all its arenas to accommodate the big guy. He dominates the paint at will and lets those intent on driving to the basket be aware that they might just run into a freight train.

As dominating and intimidating as Shaq may be, he has a weakness. He's terrible at the free throw line. When the game is on the line, the big fellow has to be pulled out of the game and for good reason; opponents foul him purposely, knowing he'll miss his free throws. Every now and then, he'll rattle one or two in; but for the most part, he misses the greater part of his attempts. However, his weakness certainly does not affect his game; he goes on to win several NBA championships on different teams and is headed for the NBA Hall of Fame.

Shaq is not the only one saddled with weaknesses; we are all partly weak and partly strong. "And Jacob called his sons and said, gather together, that I may tell you what shall befall you in the last days" (Gen. 49:1). Under the inspiration of God, Jacob gave his sons an accurate historical profile of each (son) tribe, complete with their strengths, weaknesses, compliments, affirmations, and rebukes. It was said of Reuben, "Unstable as water, you shall not excel" (Gen. 49:4). Reuben, Jacob's firstborn, committed incest with his stepmother, which disqualified him for the inheritance of the firstborn. His descendants did not fare any better; they were the first to be drawn into idolatry and rebellion and did not produce any prominent spiritual leader in Israel. Conversely, it was said of Judah, "The scepter shall not depart from Judah, nor a lawgiver from between his feet until Shiloh comes" (Gen. 49:10). The tribe of Judah produced all the kings of the southern kingdom, including Christ, the King of kings and the Lord of lords.

Since a chain is as strong as its weakest link, the evil genius Satan loves to throw our embarrassing moments at us, but Jesus will have none of it. "He has not observed iniquity in Jacob, nor has He seen wickedness in Israel" (Num. 23:21). With all our weakness, foibles, and sins, God sees what we can become in Christ and not who we are in our present struggles. Like the rich young ruler, we lack one thing to be complete in him, but we are confident that "he who begun a good work in you will complete it until the day of Jesus Christ" (Phil. 1:6). As long as we remain plugged in Jesus, our salvation is never in doubt. "Now to Him who is able to keep you from stumbling, and to present you faultless before the presence of His glory with exceeding joy, to God our Savior, Who alone is wise, be glory and majesty, and power, both now and forever. Amen" (Jude 24–25). Your victory is never in doubt if you allow Jesus to fight your battles with you.

September 9

The Born-Again Night Visit

Jesus answered and said to him, most assuredly, I say to you, unless one is born again, he cannot see the kingdom of God.

—John 3:3

Darkness provides cover for a host of shy creatures, and nature has obliged by rewarding them with her bounty while the day-shift animals are fast asleep. However, some creatures have adapted well to work both day and night shifts, giving them an edge over their counterparts. Humans also have learned to capitalize on this opportunity, and Nicodemus took full advantage of this occasion by posing this intriguing question to Jesus at night. "How can a man be born when he is old. Can he enter the second time into his mother's womb and be born?" (John 3:4).

The term "born twice, die once" or "die once and born twice" may sound like a play on words, but it is pregnant with truth. All living creatures emerge as a result of being born or hatched. Humans are born naturally only once; however, upon acceptance of Jesus as Lord and Savior, one is born again, this time into the kingdom of God. For emphasis, there is only one natural birth; and to the child of God, a spiritual birth at conversion is the more important of the two. God has promised to give all his faithful children who endure to the end everlasting life, and isn't that good news? Accept Jesus and live; reject him and die the everlasting death in hell.

"Most assuredly, I say to you, unless a grain of wheat falls into the ground and dies, it remains alone; but if it dies, it produces much grain" (John 12:24). Just as the grain of wheat must die as a seed and be transformed into a brand-new plant, likewise, when one comes to Jesus, the old man of sin with all its lust is strangled and laid to rest in the watery grave. A brand-new person emerges, not a perfect person but a person with a new attitude, a person with a new sense of direction. "Therefore, if anyone is in Christ, he is a new creation; old things have passed away; behold, all things have become new" (2 Cor. 5:17).

Having explained the natural and spiritual birth, the other factor to be dealt with is the natural and everlasting death. What happens at death? "For the living know that they shall die but the dead know nothing, and they have no more reward, for the memory of them is forgotten. Also their love, their hatred, and their envy have now perished; nevermore will they have a share in anything done under the sun" (Eccles. 9:5–6). This is the death the saved of all ages will be raised from. "Behold, I tell you a mystery; we shall not all sleep, but we shall be changed, in a moment, in the twinkling of an eye, at the last trumpet, for the trumpet will sound, and the dead will be raised incorruptible, and we shall be changed" (1 Cor. 15:51–52). Brother, sister, friend, please don't miss this part.

Being born twice and dying once has eternal benefits. "And there shall be a time of trouble, such as never was since there was a nation, even to that time. And at that time your people be delivered, everyone who is found written in the book. And many of those who sleep in the dust of the earth shall awake, some to everlasting life, some to shame and everlasting contempt" (Dan. 12:1–2). If you die only once, you are doomed to hell; but if you die to sin as the seed does and die the natural death, you will be raised in Christ to live eternally. "Precious in the eyes of the Lord are the death of His saints" (Ps. 116:15).

September 10

The Bitter Water of Marah

Now when they came to Marah, they could not drink the waters of Marah, for they were bitter. Therefore the name of it was called Marah.

—Exodus 15:23

West Virginia's government declared tap water safe to drink again. Understandably, residents were nervous about drinking tap water, considering what they'd been through. On January 9, 2014, poisonous chemicals found their way into West Virginia's drinking water. The result left officials in a very uncomfortable position as residents converged in shopping centers snatching up bottled water as soon as they became available. The hospitality industry was hit particularly hard as restaurants watched their clientele dwindle to a mere trickle. Thanks to early detection, to date, no one has been hurt, but the experience left a bitter taste in the mouths of West Virginians (https://www.nytimes.com/2014/01/11/us/west-virginia-chemical-spill.html?_r=0).

Israel had a similar experience with bitter water during their Exodus experience. God was testing them to see what kind of people they really were. "And you shall remember that the Lord your God led you all the way these forty years in the wilderness, to humble you and test you, to know what was in your heart, whether you would keep His commandments or not" (Deut. 8:2).

The bitter water of Marah comes in different situations today, but the basic principle remains the same. It is only a test. What do you do when the water you choose to drink turns bitter? How do you handle losing your home to foreclosure? (May it never happen to you, but it can.) How do you react to losing a child or a spouse? You have just discovered that the used car you bought is a lemon, and sorry, no refunds; how do you react? The result of a medical test is due, and you are obviously very nervous. Are you ready to accept the limitations that accompany the results? "So He humbled you, allowed you to hunger, and fed you with manna which you did not know nor did your fathers know, that He might make you know that man shall not live by bread alone; but man lives by every word that proceeds from the mouth of the Lord" (Deut. 8:3).

God's children are not immune from the tragedies of life; good and bad things befall all the children of humanity without exception or discrimination. Job puts it rather bluntly when urged by his wife to curse God and die. "You speak as one of the foolish women speaks, shall we indeed accept good from God and shall we not accept adversity? In all this Job did not sin with his lips" (Job 2:10).

Isn't it refreshing to know that our God weighs and screens the trials and obstacles that life throws at us? Our God takes no delight in causing pain, tears, and distress to his people. Let us be aware that there are rules to games and even conflicts, but Satan has thrown the rule book out the window and hurts even helpless babies and the aged. But God abides by his righteous character and law and must stay in the game and abide by the rules of the game. We may have to gulp down some more bitter water before it's all over, but through it all, "God is our refuge and strength a very present help in time of need therefore we will not fear even though the earth is removed" (Ps. 46:1–2). Regardless of what the devil throws at you, God is in control and will not allow you to be overwhelmed.

September 11

Finders Keepers?

One of the two who heard John speak, and followed Him, was Andrew, Simon Peter's brother.
He first found his own brother Simon, and said to him, "We have found the Messiah" (which is translated, the Christ).

—John 1:40–41

He was so cute that the children adored him; he blended perfectly in our family, but we knew he was lost, and his owner must be desperately searching for him. Brandy was a playful dog trying to connect with anyone who would show him affection. He looked healthy and well cared for and soon became the center of affection at home. After about a week, it became clear to me that his owner must be having sleepless nights searching for him. We placed an advertisement in the local paper, and Brandy was returned to his grateful owner.

Finding something of value is not necessarily yours; it may belong to someone else, and you are obligated to return it to its rightful owner regardless of how significant or insignificant it may seem to you. However, there is something we all can keep when found. "Or what woman, if she loses one coin, does not light a lamp, sweep the house, and search carefully until she finds it? And when she has found it, she calls her friends and neighbors together, saying, rejoice with me for I have found the piece which I lost" (Luke 15:8–9).

Salvation is certainly something that calls for great rejoicing when it is found, but it is God who does the searching; it is he who conveniently places himself in our path. "What man of you, having a hundred sheep, if he loses one of them, does not leave the ninety-nine in the wilderness, and go after the one which is lost until he finds it? And when he has found it. He lays it on his shoulders, rejoicing. And when he comes home, he calls together his friends and neighbor, saying to them, rejoice with me, for I have found my sheep which was lost" (Luke 15:4–6).

The extent of the search mounted by the owner of the lost item determines its value. Was an advertisement placed in the local paper? Were the neighbors informed? Were posters with a photograph placed in visited places? God agonizes over every stubborn rejection of his love, grace, and mercy as depicted here. How could he give up on his creation, beings created in his very image and likeness? Yes, our loving God goes through this crisis over every unrepentant sinner who spurns his love. "How can I give you up Ephraim? How can I hand you over, Israel? How can I make you like Admah? How can I make you like Zeboiim? My heart churns within Me; my sympathy is stirred" (Hosea 11:8).

The story is told of a young man from a well-to-do family who ran away from home and ended up on the streets of Washington, DC. His family saw footage of him on a newsclip and immediately contacted the TV station and related to them his story. The family rejoiced as the young man came back home to hugs, kisses, and Mama's homemade pies. Thank you, Jesus, for relentlessly searching for us in the pubs, casinos, and nightclubs. Thanks for not giving up on us in spite of our, well, stubbornness. Thanks for loving us just the way we are.

September 12

Come See a Man

The woman then left her water-pot, went her way into the city, and said to the men, come, see a Man who told all things that I ever did. Could this be the Christ?
—John 4:28–29

The most decorated Olympian athlete might be your neighbor; that's if you live in the city of Baltimore. Swimming sensation Michael Phelps has shattered thirty-nine world records to amass an astonishing twenty-eight medals, of which twenty-three are gold, three silver, and two bronze. Swimming athletes are weary of him showing up in Japan, the site of the next Olympic event. He might decide to bag some more gold for his collection. He draws extra attention from a sport-hungry media eager to drive up their rating. The crowds swell up at his events to see the athlete of the century in action (http://www.npr.org/sections/thetorch/2016/08/14/489832779/if-michael-phelps-were-a-country-where-would-his-gold-medal-tally-rank).

But someone greater than Michael Phelps lived in Israel in the first century, and the crowds flocked to see him wherever he went. Obviously, the Jewish leadership became very worried about their slipping grip over the masses and sought every occasion to destroy him. But wasn't that a good thing for the people to meet their long-promised Messiah? Were the leaders on the right side of history by forbidding the people to welcome their Messiah? "The Pharisees therefore said among themselves, you see that you are accomplishing nothing. Look, the world has gone after Him!" (John 12:19). To their dismay, they realized their influence on the people was decreasing as Christ's influence began to increase, and that posed a mighty headache to them.

The woman at the well, a Gentile, had a different perception of Jesus from the Jewish leadership. She wanted the world to know about Jesus and became a missionary to her people. With this running appeal to the men of her town and to the people of the entire world, she shouted, "Come see a man who told all things that I ever did. Could this be the Christ?" (John 4:29). As Jesus shone the spotlight on the deep secrets of her life, it became clear to her that she was talking to no ordinary traveler but the Messiah of the world. She surrendered her life to him and hurried to spread the news of the wonderful thing that had just happened to her. She forgot her waterpot and became a missionary to her people. Through the testimony of this faithful witness, many Samaritans came to know Christ as Savior and Lord. "And many of the Samaritans of the city believed in Him because of the word of the woman who testified, He told me all that I ever did" (John 4:39).

Who can be a missionary? We all can. We may never see the teeming masses of India, the City of Lights of France, or the towering skyscrapers of New York City, but we can be a beacon of light to our friends. "Come, see a man who told me all things that I ever did." Don't be worried about what to say; God will put the right words in your mouth. "But when they deliver you up, do not worry about how or what you should speak. For it will be given to you in that hour what you should speak" (Matt. 10:19).

You probably have heard this saying at some time: "Charity begins at home." Whoever coined this phrase should be given an award. Our area of immediate impact will be among those who know us best. The Holy Spirit will impress on the hearts of friends and neighbors that your change is real. Go out there and do likewise.

The Big Shout

And it shall come to pass, when they make a long blast with the ram's horn, and when you hear the sound of the trumpet that all the people shall shout with a great shout;
then the wall of the city will fall down flat. And the people shall go up every man straight before him.

—Joshua 6:5

Locked gates, standing armies, towering walls, and obstinate kings—not a problem; our God is able and up to the task. The residents of Jericho watched scornfully as the Hebrews silently marched around their city. Seven priests blowing the ram's horn preceded the ark; the army marched silently behind them without muttering a sound. Day after day, they marched around the city once and retreated to their camp. "And the seventh time it happened, when the priests blew the trumpets that Joshua said to the people: Shout, for the Lord has given you the City!" (Josh. 6:16). "And the walls came tumbling down." Whoever wins a battle by silently marching around his or her enemy's property? Our God delights in doing the seemingly impossible. "Some trust in chariots, and some in horses; but we will remember the name of the Lord our God" (Ps. 20:7).

Everything in biblical times has its modern-day parallel. For Israel to get to their earthly Canaan, they had to go through Jericho and a host of naughty kings intent on denying them their desired objective. Likewise, there are giants standing in our way even now as we march to our heavenly Canaan, but we cannot conquer them with silent marches and blaring trumpet; this calls for a different strategy. Our enemies have now become institutionalized; they are part of our modern-day culture. Can you name a few? They include sports, compulsive shopping, TV entertainment, and acquisition of toys, but God has not left his people defenseless. "Now to Him who is able to keep you from stumbling, and to present you faultless before the presence of His glory with exceeding joy, to God our Savior, who alone is wise, be glory and majesty, dominion and power, both now and forever" (Jude 24–25). This verse may be a closing benediction, but it is loaded with strength and affirmation. Jesus can and will prevent us from falling. Amen! Isn't he "the same yesterday, today and forever" (Heb. 13:8)? God is more than able to keep us faultless.

To be victorious over sin, every member of the body must be surrendered to the lordship of Jesus Christ. Boy, this is so elementary, but it is the starting point in the Christian journey. You don't attend seminars on how to overcome sin; you just stay plugged into Jesus. And this is how it is done: "If you abide in Me, and My words abide in you, you will ask what you desire, and it shall be done for you. By this My Father is glorified, that you bear much fruit; so you will be My disciples" (John 15:7–8). Abiding in Christ involves doing what Jesus did. But what did Jesus do? He involved himself in the lives of others by ministering to them.

It never fails; by helping others, we become strong—strong enough to gain victory over these stubborn habits seeking to destroy us. But we cannot yell out that big shout quite yet; it must be saved until we are safe on the other side in our heavenly Canaan. Many athletes have lost games by celebrating prematurely; it is not over until it's all over. "Not that I have already attained, or am already perfected; but I press on, that I may lay hold of that for which Christ Jesus has also laid hold of me" (Phil. 3:12).

September 14

Faithful to Me

Fear not, for I am with you; be not dismayed for I am with you . . .
I will uphold you with My righteous hand.

—Isaiah 41:10

A fierce public opinion battle is wagging among animal lovers about which animal is truly man's best friend. Is it a horse or a dog? Now hold your horses—I mean, your dog. I am not an advocate for either; I'll just let the facts speak for themselves. Historians confirm that a special bond existed between Alexander the Great and his horse, Bucephalus; it faithfully carried him to the gates of his enemies and all the way to world conquest. However, dogs have proved their value in sniffing out harmful substances and have become an instant success, indispensable to both the police and the military. And it came as no surprise that decommissioned Gulf War soldiers fought tooth and nail to have their companion dogs returned to them after their service, but the army thinks otherwise. There is no question that these fine animals are lovable, adorable, and quite charming, performing many outstanding services to their masters, especially the physically challenged. Stories abound of horses rushing into battle, oblivious to personal safety to please their masters. Dogs are also renowned for providing comfort and help to the disabled and, in some instances, saving or alerting their masters of imminent danger.

God is the Commander in Chief of love. He loves unconditionally. Who is deserving of his love? Certainly not us. When our self-esteem plummets, he says reassuringly to us, "Be strong and of good courage, do not fear nor be afraid of them; for the Lord your God, He is the One who goes with you. He will not leave you nor forsake you" (Deut. 31:6). Because the Lord goes with me and is a reliable partner, I have no fear for the future. There are risks everywhere, and it gives us the chills just thinking of the many impaired people behind the wheels of vehicles zooming past us at speeds of over 65 mph. But "God is our refuge and strength, a very present help in trouble. Therefore, we will not fear, even though the earth be removed, and though the mountains be carried into the midst of the sea" (Ps. 46:1–2).

The evenhandedness of God can be seen in his dealing with his avowed enemies. "But I say to you, love your enemies, bless those who curse you, do good to those who hate you, and pray for those who spitefully use you and persecute you, that you may be the sons of your Father in heaven; for He makes His sun rise on the evil and on the good, and sends rain on the just and on the unjust" (Matt. 5:44–45). Other gods are renowned for favoring the strong over the weak, the rich over the poor, and the good-looking over the less good-looking, but it is not so with our God. He is "a father to the fatherless, a defender of widows, is God in His Holy habitation. God sets the solitary in families; He brings out those who are bound into prosperity; but the rebellious dwell in a dry land" (Ps. 68:5–6). Is there any god like our God?

Regardless of the storm that confronts us, we are assured God will be right there with us, walking in the minefield with us and directing our footsteps. We are absolutely confident our God has the capacity to handle any situation that comes our way. God has vowed never to leave or abandon his children, whom he bought with his own blood.

September 15

No Regrets

For thus says the Lord, Who created the heavens, Who is God, Who formed the earth and made it, Who has established it, Who did not create it in vain, Who formed it to be inhabited:
I am the Lord, and there is no other.

—Isaiah 45:18

I was deceived, robbed, and exploited; and to add insult to injury, my down payment was nonrefundable. We went to a neighboring state auction to purchase a car to make a quick (buck) profit. Boy, were we surprised by the turn of events! At this particular auction, you were not allowed to inspect the cars, but you could bid on them as they came rolling down past the fast-talking auctioneer. The car we bought was a total lemon; it was written off by an insurance company, bought by the auction, patched up, and sold to unsuspecting folks like me. The broken frame rail was patched up with aluminum foil, smoothed up a little, and painted over to make it look presentable. While driving away from the auction, the front of the vehicle bounced up and down like a bouncing ball. After extensive repairs and vehicular registration, the profit-making venture evaporated into thin air and ballooned into a colossal loss. Do I have regrets? Of course. Have I been burned by other adventures in life? Yes. Who hasn't been? But life continues.

Only God has no regrets. There is no need for regrets with God since he gets everything right the first time; there is no do-over with God. He is omniscient, meaning he sees everything from A to Z, and nothing is hidden from his all-seeing eyes. He is omnipotent—all powerful with absolute control over everything; after all, he created everything. God is omnipresent; he is everywhere and is bigger than the universe he created. But man sinned and changed the entire landscape of God's creation.

God reacted to the Fall of man with these words: "And the Lord was sorry that He had made man on the earth and He was grieved in His heart" (Gen. 6:6). God was pained in his heart toward the downfall of man. He felt sorry for man's depravity and the terrible consequences that would follow. But God is immutable, meaning not subject to change. As any good parent does, he did what is characteristic of him; he loved man even more. "But where sin abounded, grace abounded much more" (Rom. 5:20).

The latter part of the text of Isaiah 45:18 is equally forceful as the opening; God did not create the earth in vain in spite of the mess we made of it. He actually "formed it to be inhabited." The Fall of man did not change God's attitude toward his creation, and this is obvious in God's passionate love for mankind. In spite of man's apparent sinfulness, he is still the apple of God's eyes. "The Lord has appeared of old to me, saying: Yes, I have loved you with an everlasting love; Therefore with loving kindness I have drawn you" (Jer. 31:3).

God's love is everlasting and unconditional. He loves us whether we are good or bad. He has no favorite and does not have any grandchildren. His love is not contingent on our obedience, even though he said, "If you love me, keep my commandments." His love is manifested whether we are obedient or not. As one little kid demonstrates by opening his arms as wide as he could, "God loves me this much." Be aware that God loves us this much that he emptied heaven of its most expensive gift in our behalf. No regrets. You're worth more than you think.

September 16

Apples and Onions

And the Lord commanded the man saying, of every tree of the garden you may freely eat;
but of the tree of the knowledge of good and evil you shall not eat, for in the day that you eat of it you shall surely die.

—Genesis 2:16–17

The contraband that was not detected by the scanning machines was sniffed out by the dog. Away with these expensive scanning machines, and give the job to our furry friends. Not so fast, though. Dog trainers tell us to ignore a bad behavior and reward a positive one. But how does this principle hold up in the grand scheme of things, God's Word, the Bible? The scripture says, "If you are willing and obedient you shall eat of the good of the land; but if you refuse and rebel, you shall be devoured by the sword; for the mouth of the Lord has spoken" (Isa. 1:19–20). Does God really ignore our bad behavior?

You may call it carrot and stick or apples and onions, but the principle remains the same. If you're obedient, you're rewarded; if you disobey, you're punished. It is that simple. "So the Lord said to Cain, why are you angry? And why has your countenance fallen? If you do well, will you not be accepted: and if you do not do well, sin lies at your door. And its desire is for you, but you should rule over it" (Gen. 4:6–7).

God operates on a "love through obedience" principle, and this theme runs deep throughout the Bible as cited in the following verse: "Now it shall come to pass, if you diligently obey the voice of the Lord your God, to observe carefully all His commandments which I command you today; that the Lord your God will set you high above all nations of the earth. And all the blessings shall come upon you and overtake you, because you obey the voice of the Lord your God" (Deut. 28:1–2).

God will not force, beg, cajole, or coerce anyone into obedience to him; it must be a conscious decision made through love. The principle of making man in his image and likeness offers man the option to make decisions free from compulsion and free from force and fear. We love God because he first loved us. To do otherwise is to show disloyalty to the One who created us and deserves our worship.

How can anyone resist being serenaded by God's love every day and continue to rebel against the One who is doing all the loving? However, to those who do respond to this love through the obedience principle, the reward is not disappointing, and the carrots are tantalizingly sweet. "And I heard a loud voice from heaven saying, Behold, the tabernacle of God is with men, and He will dwell with them, and they shall be His people. God Himself will be with them and be their God. And God will wipe away every tear from their eyes; there shall be no more death, nor sorrow, nor crying. There shall be no more pain, for the former things have passed away" (Rev. 21:3–4). There is absolutely nothing on this planet comparable to being with God and spending the rest of eternity with him. "Eyes have not seen, nor ear heard, nor entered into the heart of man the things which God has prepared for those who love Him" (1 Cor. 2:9). You don't want to miss out on heaven. If you do, you'll be pulling out your hair with regrets in hell's fire.

September 17

Our Bread and Water Sure

And there will be sign in the sun, in the moon, and in the stars; and on the earth distress of nations, with perplexity, the sea and the waves roaring; men's heart failing them for fear and the expectations of those things which are coming on the earth, for the powers of the heavens shall be shaken.

—Luke 21:25–26

The ecosystem is breaking apart under the staggering assault of human economic development. How long will it last? Not very long, according to recent scientific analysis. Smoke-belching chimneys are spewing toxic chemicals into the atmosphere. Climate change has intensified the destructiveness of monster storms, and tornadoes are wreaking unimaginable damage of more than tens of billions of dollars in damage to property. Millions of acres of farmlands are being ruined and rendered unproductive by bad agricultural practices. The depletion of fisheries and the pollution of rivers and oceans are already posing a major threat to the nutrition of millions around the globe. New diseases are emerging, while long-dormant old ones are making a comeback with stubborn resistance to drugs. While all these dark clouds are gathering, the world's population is exploding by the minute. It may look like a scene from a science fiction movie, but this is the real world we are living in. Is anyone in control?

"The earth is the Lord's and all its fullness, the world and those who dwell therein. For He founded it upon the seas, and established it upon the waters" (Ps. 24:1–2). Yes, the earth is still the Lord's, and he takes full ownership of it, even though it is far different in its present form from when he first gave man ownership over it. The scriptures describe the earth under a withering assault from mankind: "Lift up your eyes to the heavens, and look on the earth beneath for the heavens will vanish away like smoke, The earth will grow old like a garment, and those who dwell in it will die in like manner" (Isa. 51:6).

Even though the prognosis does not look good for the restoration of the ecosystem and the environment, God has a million ways of providing for his children. Did he not feed Israel in a hot and barren desert devoid of any food and water? Did he not use ravens to ferry dinner to the hungry prophet Elijah. Did he not feed five thousand with five loaves and two fish? Is he not the Lord of nature, and is everything not at his disposal to use as he sees fit? Is he not very near to his children, especially when they are in need and facing distress? "He who walks righteously and speaks uprightly, he who despises the gain of oppressions, who gestures with his hands refusing bribes, who stops his ears from hearing of bloodshed, and shuts his eyes from seeing evil: He will dwell on high; his place of defense will be the fortress of the rocks; bread will be given him, his water will be sure" (Isa. 33:15–16).

We have nothing to fear except we forget the way the Lord has led us in the past. Even while hanging on the cross, Christ made provision for his widowed mom. Shall he do any less for us? "When Jesus therefore saw His mother, and the disciple whom He loved standing by, He said to His mother, woman, behold your Son! Then He said to the disciple, behold your mother! And from that hour that disciple took her into his own home" (John 19:26–27). God will take care of you and will meet your needs.

September 18

Our God Is Greater

And when the people of Ashdod arose early in the morning, there was Dagon, fallen on its face to the earth before the ark of the Lord. So they took Dagon and sit it in its place again.
And when they rose early the next morning, there was Dagon fallen again on his face to the ground before the ark of the Lord.

—1 Samuel 5:3–4

In recent times, there has been a steady rise in suicide among famous celebrities; they either die by accidental overdose or intentionally take their own life. The god of this world offers fame and quick success to the talented and then snuffs out their lives in their moments of vulnerability. "The thief does not come except to steal, and to kill and to destroy, I have come that they may have life, and that they may have it more abundantly" (John 10:10). Thanks be to God for showing us the better way as opposed to the utter futility of life apart from him. "For a day in Your courts is better than a thousand. I would rather be a doorkeeper in the house of my God than dwell in the tents of wickedness" (Ps. 84:10).

The true motive of Satan is quite obvious; he is feverishly working to have many people go to a godless grave as himself. But God offers men life—real life, eternal life with him forever—and that is mighty good news, my friend. "For I know the thought that I think towards you, says the Lord, thoughts of peace and not of evil, to give you a future and a hope. That you will call upon Me and go and pray to Me, and I will listen to you. And you will seek Me and find Me, when you search for Me with all your heart. I will be found by you says the Lord" (Jer. 29:11–14).

Besides our God being great, he has every good intention toward us; he wants us to be saved in his kingdom. Therefore it should come as no surprise to us if certain doors of opportunities remain shut to us. God, who knows the end from the beginning and the beginning from the end, is intent on protecting us from the monsters lurking behind closed doors. And God knows these monsters are fully intent on devouring us. When we pray, we should thank God not only for our daily bread and the nice things he has given but also for the monsters we requested but were denied to us.

Because our God is great and is the God of gods and the King of kings, we will extol his name to all around us. The children of this world are unabashed and bold in their iniquitous practices; they air their private lives in public so all could see. Therefore why should we be shy in proclaiming the good news of our soon-coming King? "And let us not grow weary while doing good, for in due season we shall reap if we do not lose heart" (Gal. 6:9). Are you engaged in doing positive things wherever God has placed you? He will pour his Spirit only on those who are already engaged and working for the salvation of their fellow men. Get busy; brighten the corner where you are.

September 19

Rain in the Forecast

Then it came to pass the seventh time, that he said, there is a cloud, as small as a man's hand, rising out of the sea! So he said, go up, say to Ahab, prepare your chariot, and go down before the rain stops you.

—1 Kings 18:44

The weather forecast that day called for a dry, muggy day, but don't say this to the prophet Elijah. His forecast was different; it included rain and lots of it. At the word of the prophet, it had not rained in Israel for more than three years and with good reason. The Phoenician god Baal, which was Israel's favorite false god, was supposedly a rainmaker, a thunder producer, a master of fertility, and an agricultural specialist. Elijah challenged the god Baal to produce rain for his worshippers. But alas, neither Baal nor his prophets were able to produce one drop of moisture.

"Whatever the Lord pleases He does, in heaven and in the earth, In the seas and in all deep places. He causes the vapors to ascend from the ends of the earth; He makes lightning for the rain; He brings the wind out of His treasures" (Ps. 135:6–7). But there is another kind of rain that the Lord delights in pouring over his people. "And it shall come to pass in the last days, says God, that I will pour out of My Spirit on all flesh; Your sons and your daughters shall prophesy, your young men shall see visions, Your old men shall dream dreams. And on My menservants and on My maidservants I will pour out My Spirit in those days and they shall prophesy" (Acts 2:17–18).

The Holy Spirit is already being poured on believers the world over. Laypeople untrained in evangelism are being used mightily by the Holy Spirit to promulgate the gospel of Jesus Christ to their native people. Electronic tools have been devised that allow truth seekers to listen silently to the gospel within the privacy of their homes, and isn't that good news? We may never know the hundreds of thousands who are silently following and learning about Christ via the Internet because it is too dangerous to openly profess Christ in public. Lives are being changed, decisions are being made, and destinies are being decided for God.

The harvest is fully ripe, but the laborers are few; let us pray for the baptism of the Holy Spirit to stimulate our lives and the worldwide church. Without the pouring of the former rain, Pentecost would not have been possible. The disciples would not have been equipped to speak in tongues, bypassing their native tongue to speak to the multilingual audience gathered. Without the former rain, the audience would not have responded favorably to the extent that over three thousand were baptized that day.

Do you see why we need the pouring of the latter rain? But before we pray for it, we must pray for genuine revival in our lives. We must confess our sins and ask Jesus for the faith that will triumph over the temptations of this world. In the interim, we must immerse ourselves in the study of God's Word and must engage ourselves wholly in the service of the local church, and the Holy Spirit will come in full measure when God wills. And let us be intentional in asking God to use us wherever we are needed the most. One last thing, pray this prayer with me: Lord, save us at any cost to ourselves.

September 20

Your Love Inspires Me

Therefore the Lord brought upon them the captains of the army of the king of Assyria, who took Manasseh with hooks, bound him with bronze fetters and carried him off to Babylon.

—2 Chronicles 33:11

He was too busy to listen to his conscience. There were gang meetings to attend, drugs to sell, and fights to win, but it all came to an end with the deafening sound of a police siren. Sitting in jail and with the prospect of spending the rest of his life in prison, Jonas (name changed)—like Manasseh—found God through repentance. "Now when he was in affliction, He implored the Lord his God and humbled himself greatly before the God of his fathers, and prayed to Him; and He received his entreaty, heard his supplication, and brought him back to Jerusalem into his kingdom. Then Manasseh knew that the Lord was God" (2 Chron. 33:12–13). Brought him back to his kingdom? Are you kidding me? After all this guy did to provoke God? Yep. God is altogether different from us. That's why he is God.

If anyone deserved to be left rotting in jail, by all accounts, Manasseh qualified for this punishment, but God's mercy always runs ahead of his judgment anyway. The history of Manasseh's violent and bloody antics is given in 2 Chronicles 33:2–7, and it is not pretty, but God is merciful and altogether loving to the sons of men and always sees the better angel in us. "He has not dealt with us according to our sins nor punished us according to our iniquities. For as the heavens are high above the earth, so great is His mercy towards those who fear Him; as far as the east is from the west, so far has He removed our transgressions from us. As a father pities his children, so the Lord pities those who fear Him" (Ps. 103:10–13).

You cannot outrun God's love and mercy; they will outrun you and overtake you. As long as there is a genuine desire to turn away from sin, God goes to work regardless of how gruesome one's past may have been. However, the converse is sadly true; if the conscience is dead and shows no remorse or desire for repentance, God has no choice but to respect the decision one makes for his or her life.

Isn't God amazing? He buries our dark past and issues us a clean, blank slate to begin life anew. "For I will be merciful to their unrighteousness, and their sins and their lawless deeds I will remember no more" (Heb. 8:12). This is too good to be true, but it is true. Does everyone know this? I do not know. Can we tell everyone about the amazing grace of our God? The news gets even better. Here's what the Bible says concerning God's intention toward mankind. "For the grace of God that brings salvation has appeared to all men, teaching us that, denying ungodliness and worldly lust we should live soberly, righteously, and godly in the present age" (Titus 2:11–12). God has extended mercy to every child of Adam. Those who accept his offer of grace and repent will be saved.

We can conclude from this saying that however limited one's understanding of God may be, he (God) puts the truth in a language appropriate to one's understanding and offers him or her a choice between life and death. One consciously decides between doing what is right and continuing to walk in iniquity. Where human witness is not possible, God uses dreams, visions, nature, and the witness of the Holy Spirit to draw in his children. Isn't God amazing? "For God did not send His Son into the world to condemn the world but that the world through Him might be saved" (John 3:17).

September 21

To Tell or Not to Tell

Then they said to one another, we are not doing right. This day is a day of good news, and we remain silent. If we wait until morning light, some punishment will come upon us.
Now therefore, come, let us go and tell the king's household.

—2 Kings 7:9

The difference between a full refrigerator and an empty one boils down to having a job, and Tiana has just landed herself a brand-new job to augment the state of her refrigerator. Months of poring over Internet job listings are over. There is a sparkle in her eyes and a smile on her face, and she is on the proverbial cloud nine. *Job market, here I come,* she seems to say with a bounce in her steps. If the Lord has blessed you, should you keep it a secret? Not to these guys in our story.

Four lepers are deciding whether to remain in a city on the brink of starvation or surrender to the enemy. Let's hear it from them: "If we say, we will enter the city, the famine is in the city, and we shall die there. And if we sit here, we die also, Now therefore, come, let us surrender to the army of the Syrians. If they keep us alive, we shall live; and if they kill us, we shall only die" (2 Kings 7:4). God is about to do something hilarious for his people, and he has chosen four lepers as his instrument and mouthpiece. As undeserving and unfaithful as Israel was, God was still married to them and could not endure to see his people humiliated by every Joe Blow passing by.

The invading Syrian army hears an imaginary battle noise (sent by God) and runs away, leaving turkeys on the grill, bread and glasses of juice on the table, lots of cash, and every kind of designer clothes behind. But alas, there is no one to take advantage of the bounty left by the fleeing Syrians. However, God is never left without witnesses; four brave lepers are good enough for the task of heralding the good news to a skeptical king.

God has an urgent last day message that he badly wants to broadcast far and near to a worldwide audience. Are you up to the task? "Then I saw another angel flying in the midst of heaven, having the everlasting gospel to preach to those who dwell on the earth to every nation, tribe and tongue and people saying with a loud voice, fear God and give glory to Him for the hour of His judgment has come; and worship Him who made heaven and earth the sea and springs of water" (Rev. 14:6–7).

This message calls on men to totally surrender their lives to God because the long-delayed judgment has begun. Embedded in the three angels' message is "worship." Christ told the woman of Samaria, "You worship what you do not know; we know what we worship, for salvation is of the Jews" (John 4:22). Many, like the woman of Samaria, are worshipping something they think is God but is not God. "Salvation is of the Jews." In other words, the Jews have the correct system of worship. The third angel announces the fall of Babylon, the enemy of ancient Israel and God's modern true church. Fallen are the false systems of worship because they distract men from true worship to God on the day he has ordained as his holy Sabbath day.

God is looking for bold and brave people to herald the good news of the gospel to the world. Can he count on you? Where can I sign up? First, thank God for being chosen, but being chosen entails a heavy responsibility to others. Then proceed to your local church for baptism, training, and your assignment.

September 22

Comfort, Yes, Comfort My People

Comfort, yes, comfort my people! Says your God. Speak comfort to Jerusalem and cry out to her, that her warfare is ended, that her iniquity is pardoned; for she has received from the Lord double her sins.

—Isaiah 40:1–2

Vietnam vets came back home demoralized, confused, and defeated and melted away into a nation torn by the nagging question why are we at war? War should never be the first option to resolve disputes but should always be a card on the table if all other measures fail. Some wars are perfectly justifiable. A war for independence, though sometimes gruesome, is quite necessary since colonialism is demoralizing to any people. Colonial powers are usually reluctant in granting political independence to their colonies. And of course, nations and people are entitled to self-defense and self-determination, don't they? This brings us to the question asked by millions of mothers all through the ages. Why do we have all these senseless wars? Have you ever been engaged in any kind of warfare?

Understanding the origin and nature of sin will give us an insight into why some wars are necessary and are perfectly justified. "And war broke out in heaven: Michael and His angels fought with the dragon; and the dragon and his angels fought, but they did not prevail, nor was a place found for them in heaven any longer" (Rev. 12:7–8). God's kingdom was under attack by a disgruntled angel named Lucifer. When all attempt to have him renounce his revolt failed, he—along with one-third of his sympathizers—was forcefully banished from heaven. "Your heart was lifted up because of your beauty; You corrupted your wisdom for the sake of your splendor, I cast you to the ground, I laid you before kings, that they may gaze at you" (Ezek. 28:17). Having been expelled from heaven, Satan decided to avenge his expulsion by wreaking havoc on God's creation. Has he been successful? Yes, but his days are numbered.

The war begun in heaven is now being waged with full intensity for the allegiance of your soul and mine. "And Elijah came to all the people, and said, how long will you falter between two opinions? If the Lord is God follow Him; but if Baal, follow him. But the people answered him not a word" (1 Kings 18:21). This relentless war for the soul continues even after a person surrenders to Christ. Even in the heat of conflict, there are usually moments when the warring parties take a break to rest and restock their inventories; but in the fight against evil, there is no break. Our only break and comfort in this life is the peace of Jesus Christ. "Peace I leave with you, My peace I give to you; not as the world gives do I give to you. Let not your heart be troubled, neither let it be afraid" (John 14:27). The anxiety and fear of this life will soon be over because Christ is in control, and our soul is at peace with God. Isn't that good news?

Upon receiving Jesus as Savior and Lord, we become heir to all the promises made to Abraham, Isaac, and Jacob. God's Word is his bond; whatever he promised, he delivers. "For he waited for the city which has foundations, whose builder and maker is God" (Heb. 11:10). Should we give up now when we know the outcome of the battle is in our favor? And this, my friend, is good reason for us to continue fighting the good fight of faith, even if we are denied a favorable outcome in this life.

September 23

Mining the Word

Your word I have hidden in my heart that I might not sin against you.
—Psalm 119:11

As he lay dying with his sons at his bedside, he whispered faintly of a buried treasure in the ground somewhere near the house, but he slipped away without giving any further specifics. After burying their father, the sons launched an energetic assault on the soil in search of the buried treasure, but it soon became apparent that this elusive treasure might not exist at all. Bill threw away his digging tools and walked away in disgust, but Tom took an altogether different approach. "Why not cultivate the soil and grow some crop since I have done all this digging?" To his amazement, the hidden treasure was in the richness of the soil. While Bill walked away from wealth, his brother Tom embraced it and, with hard work and dogged determination, became wealthy.

"The grass withers, the flower fades, but the word of our God stands forever" (Isa. 40:8). The U.S. dollar is the currency of choice and is the medium by which international trade is conducted. It is reliable and is backed by the promise "I will pay my debt on time, and I will not default on my payment." Because of its reliability, it has weathered catastrophic wars and thrived in the aftermath. Its presence is everywhere, stabilizing jittery markets, facilitating trade, and encouraging innovation. Can another currency or precious commodity provide a better "bang for the buck"? Absolutely. The Word of God stands head and shoulders above the U.S. dollar and any other world currency and anything living or dead.

"And He said to me, 'Son of man can these bones live?' So I answered, O Lord you know. Again He said to me, prophesy to these bones, and say to them, O dry bones, hear the word of the Lord! Thus says the Lord God to these bones: surely I will cause breath to enter you and you shall live" (Ezek. 37:3–5). The Word of God has the capacity to do anything, including bringing the dead back to life again.

In times past, the Word of God came to prophets and prophetesses in visions, dreams, and audible communication; but now to hear God's voice, we must read the Bible. It is through the reading of the Word that God speaks to us; ideas are formulated, decisions made, errors avoided, and lives changed. We must not rush through this process; it is different from reading the morning paper. Chew on it well, and then swallow it hook, line, and sinker, doubting nothing. We may wish to hear God's audible voice, but we can hear from him through the reading of his Word.

"Thy word is a lamp to my feet and a light to my path" (Ps. 119:105). Jesus was able to deflect Satan's temptation because he had a profound grasp on the scripture. He who spoke the worlds into existence had to learn like any child of humanity at Mom's feet. Once the scripture is committed to memory, it can be retrieved at any given moment for use; but if it is not stored, it would be the equivalent of going to the bank without an account and expecting to withdraw funds. When we invest in studying the scriptures, we will be better prepared to give a reason for the hope within us. "But sanctify the Lord God in your heart, and always be ready to give a defense to everyone who asks you a reason for the hope that is in you, with meekness and fear" (1 Pet. 3:15).

September 24

The Name

And God said to Moses, I AM WHO I AM. And He said, thus you shall say to the children of Israel, I AM has sent me to you.

—Exodus 3:14

What is the meaning or experience behind your name? Were you named after a famous person, a family member, a plant, or an experience? Everyone has a name, and it is used to identify us and to differentiate us from others. When sitting in a doctor's office or emergency room, you submit to the protocol of signing your name and wait patiently for your turn to be called. Hopefully, a nurse with a pad in hand makes the much-anticipated announcement, and only you will arise and respond to your name and no one else. Amazing, isn't it? A name is very purposeful since God invented it and allowed Adam to name his wife, his descendants, the creatures, and everything living (Gen. 2:20).

Many people change their name, choosing to erase a horrible past from memory, but God's name remains the same. He is changeless and timeless and is the same "yesterday, today and forever" (Heb. 13:8). God's name "I Am" is defined in Hebrew as "Yahweh," from which we derive our English word "Lord." It also means self-existent, which comprises eternity past, eternity present, and eternity in the future, and this truth is simply mind-boggling.

Now let's try to analyze what we just read. Everything around us, visible and invisible, was created at some point by God, but the thought that our God owes his existence to no one is a sobering truth. God is the origin of all life. He created life for his honor and glory, and he himself was not created by any other entity. God existed from eternity past, is the source of all life, and is the maker of all things, whether thrones or dominion, principalities or power. Every now and then, Jesus demonstrated to his disciples who he was and where he came from. "And they feared exceedingly, and said to one another, who can this be, that even the wind and the sea obey Him!" (Mark 4:41). As one songwriter puts it, "No water can swallow the ship where lies the Master of ocean and earth and skies; they all shall sweetly obey thy will. Peace! Peace be still" (Horatio R. Palmer).

In conversation with some skeptical Jewish leaders, Jesus made this bold declaration: "Most assuredly, I say to you, before Abraham was, I AM" (John 8:58). No one can apply this statement to himself without being a raving maniac, a madman, or God himself; and Jesus, being the very embodiment of God, had every right to make this bold declaration. Essentially, Jesus is God, along with God the Father and God the Holy Spirit. They are one. "Hear O Israel, the Lord our God, the Lord is one" (Deut. 6:4).

Because we are followers of God and recipients of his love and mercy, we are obligated to represent him well to a skeptical world. As his ambassadors, we must portray God as a merciful Father and a friend of sinners—a title he loves dearly. A great sermon fades away with the passage of time, but a kind deed done to another in the name of God is etched in the corridors of the mind forever, and that's what Jesus was noted for. Is it any wonder he was called "the friend of sinners"? Go and do likewise. Love everybody as Jesus did, even your enemies.

September 25

Going through Samaria

He left Judea and departed again to Galilee. But He needed to go through Samaria.
—John 4:3–4

Jesus left Judea (Florida) and headed on Highway 95 for Galilee (Canada), but he needed to pass through Samaria (Maryland) on some pressing business. The Jews assiduously avoided all contact with the Samaritans as evidenced by the parable of the good Samaritan. Our Savior stated categorically that he was "not sent except to the lost sheep of the house of Israel" (Matt. 15:24). How could he ignore the harvest of Samaritan souls waiting for the kingdom? Well, he did both in one mighty swipe. While he intended to save his own nation, his outstretched arms were wide open and very accessible to the whole world, even to Pontius Pilate.

Jesus remarked to his disciple that his missionary agenda was ordained by the Father, who sent him. "For I have come down from heaven, not to do My own will, but the will of Him who sent Me, this is the will of the Father who sent Me, that of all He has given Me I should lose nothing but should raise it up at the last day" (John 6:38–39).

God's plan for the salvation of mankind includes everyone. God promised Abraham, "In your seed shall the nations of the earth be blessed, because you have obeyed My voice" (Gen. 22:18). God's providence called for the Jewish nation to be a land of evangelists, proclaiming the good news of the gospel to the nations around her, but for the better part of their history, Israel was plagued by idolatry. Misguided national pride and blind fanaticism rendered the Jews incapable of fulfilling their mandate.

It may appear that Jesus was harsh in his dealing with the Gentiles, but he was teaching a very important lesson to his disciples. By imitating their attitude toward their Gentile neighbors, he was showing them everyone has equal access to the grace and mercy of God. Nothing Jesus did was accidental. He went into town via the local road, not the highway, and intentionally struck a conversation with the woman of Samaria, breaking a local taboo, for the Jews had no communication with the Samaritans.

Jesus was on the hunt for every soul sincerely searching for a better way. He arranges circumstances and situations for anyone seeking him to find him. "I love those who love Me, and those who seek Me diligently find Me" (Prov. 8:17). This text is applicable to everyone, including those who exist outside the perimeters of Israel and the church. God has a mechanism for saving souls in the absence of human witness. Will the masses who lived outside the borders of Israel be totally lost? Of course not. "For when the Gentiles, who do not have the law, by nature do the things in the law, these, although not having the law, are a law to themselves" (Rom. 2:14). This is good news to the teeming millions who lived outside Israel, who have never heard of the wonderful name of Jesus but followed and obeyed the voice of their conscience, leading them to live a life against the evil and corrupt culture of their time.

Our Savior still makes detours into town to seek and save those who are lost and directs his people to do the same. "For God so loved the world that He gave His only begotten Son, that whoever believes in Him should not perish but have everlasting life" (John 3:16).

September 26

No Thanks, Not Intimidated

That Sanballat and Geshem sent to me, saying, come, let us meet together among the villages in the plain of Ono.
But they thought to do me harm. So I sent messengers to them, saying, I am doing a great work, so that I cannot come down.
Why should the work cease while I leave and go down to you?

—Nehemiah 6:2–3

They were outnumbered, outgunned, and overwhelmed but stood their ground, refused to surrender, and eventually won the war. The American army was surprised by a well-coordinated attack by the Germans in the Ardennes forest. Some 250,000 German troops and hundreds of tanks broke through and attacked thinly held American positions. Low on ammunition and under constant heavy fire, some 6,500 GIs were captured in the initial stage of the battle, but the United States regrouped and responded with a ferocious barrage of aerial bombardment, and they snatched victory from the jaws of defeat (www.history.com/topics/world-war-ii/battle-of-the-bulge).

Intimidation is a desperate tool of last resort the devil uses when all other measures seem to fail, but the believer should know when not to expose himself or herself to foolish risks. According to the scripture, the devil suggested to Christ the following: "Then the devil took Him up into the holy city, set Him on the pinnacle of the temple, and said to Him, 'If You are the Son of God, throw Yourself down. For it is written: He shall give His angels charge over you, and, in their hands they shall bear You up, least you dash Your foot against a stone'" (Matt. 4:5–6). This scripture-misquoting devil conveniently left out sections of the Psalm and wanted Jesus to presume on his Father's mercy.

Isn't it refreshing to know that we are covered 24/7 by the Almighty's arm? "Yea though I walk through the valley of the shadow of death, I will fear no evil for You are with me; Your rod and Your staff, they comfort me" (Ps. 23:4). The rod is the shepherd's defense against would-be thieves of his sheep, both human and wild beast. As long as we remain within the confines of God's will, we are safe; but if we deviate from the straight and narrow path, we make ourselves vulnerable to the temptations of Satan. "And the people spoke against God and against Moses: Why have you brought us up out of Egypt to die in the wilderness? For there is no food and no water, and our soul loathe this worthless bread. So the Lord sent fiery serpents among the people; and many of the people of Israel died" (Num. 21:5–6). The Lord simply withdrew his protection, and the serpents knew the address of the complainers. But God always leaves the door open for repentance and reconciliation. A bronze serpent was set up, a symbol of a loving and forgiving Savior.

When Satan cannot get us by coercion, cajoling, or trickery, he uses intimidation, but we need not fear; he cannot force us into sin. God does not violate our power of choice; neither can Satan. We are always safe when we trust in God's Word, know the boundary is God's law, and remain safely within its confines. The devil can huff and puff, but he cannot throw our house down as long as we trust in God and insulate ourselves in his Word. "Your word is a lamp unto my feet and a guide to my path" (Ps. 119:105).

September 27

Moved by Compassion

So Jesus had compassion and touched their eyes.
And immediately their eyes received sight, and they followed Him.
—Matthew 20:34

They sit around a rectangular table cracking jokes and having plenty of fun, but a serious mission of mercy is taking shape at their fingertips. With colorful yarns and hooks, these female angels weave lovely delicate blankets for cancer patients. Upon completion of their project, these lovely ladies assemble with their leader and donate their precious investment to an organization dedicated to the care of terminally ill cancer patients.

Jesus set the precedent, and he enjoins all believers to follow: "But when He saw the multitudes, He was moved with compassion for them, because they were weary and scattered, like sheep having no shepherd" (Matt. 9:36). Because Jesus expressed his compassion for mothers/fathers grieving the loss of an only child, lepers ostracized by society, and many other shunned social groups, he was able to win their confidence with the message of the gospel. Is it any wonder why children, soldiers, marginalized people, demoniacs, the wealthy, and the poor alike found a friend and a hero in Jesus?

Our Savior's compassion led him to immediate action in alleviating the suffering of his fellow citizens. Jesus fed multitudes. He affirmed the broken, cleansed lepers, restored speech, brought back hearing, returned sight, and gave dignity to the abused; and in so doing, he prepared them for the reception of the gospel. The Chinese say, "If you give a man a fish, he will be back the next day for another one. But if you teach him how to fish, you have broken his cycle of dependency." Some are perpetually trapped in a never-ending cycle of poverty and need a fish. The writer of the book of James puts it rather bluntly. "If a brother or sister is naked and destitute of daily food, and one of you says to them, depart in peace, be warmed and filled, but you do not give them the things which are needed for the body, what does it profit?" (James 2:15–16).

Educators tell us time and again that kids do not learn on an empty stomach; the same is true of adults. They are turned off if we are able to help but choose to ignore their needs. Although the Word of God is an exquisitely sharp tool that slices through joints, bones, and marrow; it is handicapped when the necessary groundwork for successful evangelism has not been followed. Christ studied the needs of his audience and, being God, knew whether the physical or spiritual need came first. The Holy Spirit will always impress the evangelist which should come first, the Bible or a loaf of bread.

"A certain woman of the wives of the sons of the prophets cried out to Elisha, saying, your servant my husband is dead, and you know that your servant feared the Lord. And the creditor is coming to take my two sons to be his slaves. So Elisha said to her, what shall I do for you? Tell me, what do you have in the house? And she said, your maidservant has nothing in the house but a jar of oil" (2 Kings 4:1–2). Elisha blessed the jar of oil to the extent that the woman went and borrowed containers from her neighbors and friends to store the proceeds from the miracle. God points out the needs of others to us for a reason—that we may influence that life with love and compassion and hopefully lead them to Christ. Christ's method is the only model of success. It worked wonderfully for him then, and it can for us today. Go and do likewise.

September 28

Jerusalem, Judea, and Samaria

But you shall receive power when the Holy Spirit has come upon you; and you shall be witnesses to Me in Jerusalem, and in all Judea and Samaria, and to the end of the earth.

—Acts 1:8

Sputtering, misfiring, and burning more fuel than usual, my 1996 Mazda B3000 labored with great difficulty to get me from point A to point B; but with a few new spark plugs, oil, and some other tender loving care, it roared back to life again. Every now and again, it becomes necessary to take your vehicle to the shop for a makeover, unless you can do it yourself. The makers of automobiles recommend a tune-up for maximum performance; failure to do this will result in underperformance or permanent damage to your vehicle.

Knowing the limits of our human performance even with good intentions, Jesus remarked, "Behold, I send the Promise of My Father upon you; but tarry in the city of Jerusalem until you are endued with power from on high" (Luke 24:49). While Christ was still with his disciples, he gave vital hints concerning his death and resurrection, but it went straight over the heads of his worldly-minded disciples. After his death, they would need a new teacher to direct them since their Lord would no longer be with them.

They would need empowerment and lots of it to carry the gospel to the entire world, and this necessitated prayer and fasting to patch up old squabbles. "These all continued with one accord in prayer and supplication with the women and Mary the mother of Jesus, and with His brothers" (Acts 1:14). Peter and the other disciples put behind them their less than valiant crucifixion experience and sincerely implored God to forgive them and fill them with the power of the Holy Spirit. Being conscious of their weaknesses and failings, they were now ready to be insulated in God's strength.

"When the Day of Pentecost had fully come, they were all with one accord in one place. And suddenly there came a sound from heaven, as of a rushing mighty wind, and it filled the whole house where they were sitting. Then there appeared to them divided tongues of fire, and one sat upon each of them" (Acts 2:1–3).

The first phase of their mission began right where they were defeated a few weeks previously. The gloating priests had to witness the dynamic resurrection power of Jesus Christ, the multitudes who were recipients of his miracles had to be harvested, and Jerusalem and the infant church had to be the springboard to Samaria and beyond.

Jesus invested much time in Samaria, and its residents (Gentiles) brushed aside their grievance against the Jews and embraced the Samaritan woman's message with these words: "Then they said to the woman, 'Now we believe, not because of what you said, for we ourselves have heard Him, and we know that this is indeed the Christ, the Savior of the world'" (John 4:42). When the church is fully aroused, men will brush aside their indifference and embrace the gospel.

The Holy Spirit who empowered these once-timid men to stand boldly before kings, councils, and emperors stands ready to equip you today. Do you see a need today for the power of the Holy Spirit in our lives to evangelize the world? Lord Jesus, prepare us for the reception of the Holy Spirit. Amen.

September 29

What Is Your Name?

Then He asked him, what is your name? And he answered saying, "My name is Legion; for we are many."
—Mark 5:9

Legion operated his office of terror from a graveyard, and anyone coming to bury their dead or lay a rose on the tomb of a loved one was fair game. Having given demons a little opening in his life, they now controlled him. He had little in common with his fellow men and chose to make his home among the dead rather than the living, but something was stirring inside of him. Every once in a while, he dreamed of deliverance from his demonic tormentors, but the demons shut the door of opportunity every time.

Like anyone held captive for a long time and sensing an opportunity for freedom, Legion bolted in the direction of Jesus. However, when he opened his mouth to ask a petition of Jesus, the demons spoke for him, but Jesus would have none of it and commanded the evil spirits to depart permanently. "And He said to him, 'Come out of the man, unclean spirit!'" (Mark 5:8).

Lurking in the guise of drug addiction, gambling addiction, and all other addictions affecting our society are the same demons oppressing and terrifying their host. By choosing the worst specimen, Jesus demonstrated that no one is beyond full and complete restoration. "For the Son of Man has come to seek and save that which was lost" (Luke 19:10).

God is actively seeking his children. Some are on street corners; others are in drug-shooting alleys, the exercise parlors, the barbershops, and the supermarkets. "Then Jesus entered and passed through Jericho. Now behold, there was a man named Zacchaeus who was a chief tax collector, and he was rich. And he sought to see who Jesus was, but could not because of the crowd, for he was of short stature. So he ran ahead and climbed up a tree to see Him, for He was going to pass that way" (Luke 19:1–4). Amazingly, Jesus stopped at the base of the tree and said these inviting words: "Zacchaeus, make haste and come down, for today I must stay at your house" (Luke 19:5). Jesus sought him.

Jesus was intentional in his encounter with people. He either sought them out or placed himself in their path for an encounter that would bring change to them. Legion was no exception. Though he was tormented by a legion of demons, Jesus had a rendezvous with him and found him. A Roman legion consisted of 5,400 soldiers, but the demons, however numerous, could not damper Legion's enthusiasm for salvation. He wanted a clean break from his horrible past. Do you desire a clean break from sin and a new life in Jesus?

When Jesus saves, he gives us a new identity, and our name is etched in the Lamb's Book of Life. "He who has an ear, let him hear what the Spirit says to the churches. To him who overcomes I will give some of the hidden manna to eat. And I will give him a white stone, and on the stone a new name written which no one knows except him who receives it" (Rev. 2:17).

Every reminder of this miserable existence on the earth as we know will be erased from memory. Our old name that is associated with the torturous past will not be brought to mind. "And God will wipe away every tear from their eyes; there shall be no more death, nor sorrow, or crying. There shall be no more pain, for the former things have passed away" (Rev. 21:4). Thank God for a new beginning just around the corner.

September 30

It Pays to Serve Jesus

If your brother, a Hebrew man, or a Hebrew woman, is sold to you and serves you six years, then in the seventh year you shall let him go free from you.
—Deuteronomy 15:12

There is hardly a slave story with a happy ending; however, this one does. I am a personal slave to Jesus Christ, and I am absolutely happy about my state. God has never intended for one person or people group to dominate or subjugate another. Man is given the mandate to rule over the earth and exploit its bounty but never to enslave another. "Then God blessed them, and God said to them, be fruitful and multiply; fill the earth and subdue it; have dominion over the fish of the sea, over the birds of the air, and over every living thing that moves on the earth" (Gen. 1:28). Man's domination extends to nature (the earth) and the elements (verse 27).

As God's steward, everything is placed under man's control, including the elements. The power to harness fire, wind, water, and other resources is not new.

However, with the emergence of sin, nature and her resources became stubbornly resistant to man's control.

> Then to Adam He said, because you have heeded the voice of your wife, and have eaten from the tree of which I commanded you, saying, you shall not eat of it: "Cursed is the ground for your sake; in toil you shall eat of it all the days of your life. Both thorns and thistles it shall bring forth for you, and you shall eat the herb of the field. In the sweat of your face you shall eat bread till you return to the ground, for out of it you were taken; for dust you are, and to dust you shall return." (Gen. 3:17–19)

By choosing to obey the serpent (the medium of the devil), man became a slave to sin and Satan. However, God was not caught napping. He had a plan to redeem man from the tyranny of sin. "All who dwell on the earth will worship him, whose name have not been written in the Book of Life of the Lamb slain from the foundation of the world" (Rev. 13:8). The term "slain from the foundation of the world" implies that, just as Isaac was good as dead when he submitted himself to be the sacrificial lamb, likewise, Jesus became the sacrificial Lamb for man and was marked for death even before he created the world.

But God did not leave us to the whims of Satan. He gave us choices. "And if it seems evil to you to serve the Lord, choose for yourselves this day whom you will serve, whether the gods which your fathers served that were on the other side of the river, or the gods of the Amorites, in whose land you dwell. But as for me and my house we will serve the Lord" (Josh. 24:15). Everyone must make a conscious decision whether to serve Jesus or not. Salvation is not an entitlement handed from one generation to another; neither is it an inheritance. It must be accepted personally by someone.

When one submits to the lordship of Jesus Christ, he or she becomes a slave to God as Joshua attested and Paul confirmed. "Paul, a bond-servant of Jesus Christ, called to be and apostle, separated to the gospel of God" (Rom. 1:1). Paul affectionately called himself a slave of Jesus Christ since he had given himself completely and voluntarily to God. Can you think of a better master to serve other than the Lord Jesus Christ? His biddings are always enabling. Gladly will I submit to his yoke. "For My yoke is easy and my burden is light" (Matt. 11:30).

October 1

Time of the End

But you, Daniel, shut up the words, and seal the book until the time of the end; many shall run to and fro, and knowledge shall increase.

—Daniel 12:4

Daniel was a very busy man. He was a full-time scripture-writing prophet and chief executive to three successive kings—Nebuchadnezzar, Belshazzar, and Darius. Though he had a reputation for explaining difficult mysteries and dreams, this one was a brain buster and proved to be quite challenging to him. The angel cautioned him, "Therefore seal up the vision, for it refers to the days in the future" (Dan. 8:26).

Seeing in vision the rise and fall of empires and the terrifying firepower of weapons used by armies in warfare, Daniel was overwhelmed. He could not digest everything he saw. He saw many things in vision, from stone-throwing catapults assaulting city gates to F-16 fighter-bombers dropping their lethal ordinance on cities and was mystified. He had problems understanding the intricacies of Wall Street and all the complexities associated with our advanced society, but that wasn't all. He saw the emergence of a religious political power persecuting the saints and influencing the nations. He got very sick trying to understand the whole thing. "And I, Daniel, fainted and was sick for days; and afterward I arose and went about the king's business. I was astonished by the vision, but no one understood it" (Dan. 8:27). And the angel in mercy told him, "Therefore seal up the vision, for it refers to many days in the future" (Dan. 8:26).

We are in the end-times. What Daniel and the other prophets saw in vision and could not understand is front-page news in our day. We have gotten used to hearing reports of monster storms, terrifying tornadoes, disappearing airplanes, wars, and dwindling food and water reserves. The grim reports don't move an eyebrow anymore. No one can deny that something catastrophic may happen any day now; even the skeptics are beginning to change long-held positions on climate change. How do the last days affect our Christian behavior?

"Therefore, since all these things will be dissolved, what manner of persons ought you to be in holy conduct and godliness, looking for and hastening the coming of the day of God?" (2 Pet. 3:11). "Occupy till I come" is Jesus's mandate to every believer. This translates into being ready and helping others get ready, but helping others get ready comes at a cost. It takes our time and lots of it. It takes resources and lots of it also, and we must be willing to pour all our effort into the harvest field.

"Now learn the parable of the fig tree: when its branch has already become tender and puts forth leaves, you know that summer is near. So you also, when you see all these things, know that it is near, even at the doors" (Matt. 24:32–33). Does anyone need to be reminded that we are living minutes to midnight in the earth's history? Can you see where all this madness of gender change is leading to? Morality is being dictated by the shifting tide of popular culture. "Truth forever on the scaffold, wrong forever on the throne,— / Yet that scaffold sways the future, and, behind the dim unknown, / Standeth God within the shadows, keeping watch above His own" (James Russell Lowell). God has not abandoned this planet but is in firm control of it. We are commissioned to be faithful to the very end, and in so doing, we will help reap the earth's harvest.

October 2

The Lord Is with You

And the Angel of the Lord appeared to him, and said to him, "The Lord is with you, you mighty man of valor."

—Judges 6:12

It is not complicated, nor is it rocket science; just believe it. Regardless of what you are going through, God is with you throughout life's struggles, and he will never abandon you. As a couple in a loving and caring relationship are confident of each other's love, likewise, we should be confident of God's love and never doubt his favor on us. "By this I know that You are well pleased with me, because my enemy does not triumph over me" (Ps. 41:11). Thank God for this affirmation. Because we have pledged our allegiance to Jesus, we have become objects of Satan's wrath, but God has not left us defenseless. He has given us some effective weapons to neutralize Satan's attack. Foremost in this arsenal of weaponry are prayer, fasting, faith, and self-control. The devil hates it when we pray; he just can't stand it, for he knows he is losing control in our decision making. But time spent in prayer is worthwhile since we are imperfect and mistake prone.

Has anyone escaped being disciplined by God since we are sinners by nature and by choice? "My son, do not despise the chastening of the Lord, nor be discouraged when you are rebuked by Him; for whom the Lord loves He chastens, and scourges every son whom He receives. If you endure chastening, God deals with you as with sons; for what son is there whom a father does not chasten?" (Heb. 12:5–7). While no one enjoys being disciplined, it is further indication that God is very interested in our spiritual development and is actively transforming our character into his image. We are tempted to squirm and whine as little kids protesting every whipping, but every stroke is measured with love and is necessary for keeping us safe in the straight and narrow path.

The parable of the Good Shepherd leading his flock into a green pasture is a fitting representation of our dependency on God and his ability to lead and protect us and provide for our needs. "The Lord is my shepherd, I shall not want. He makes me lie down in green pastures, He leads us besides the still waters, He restores my soul. He guides me in the paths of righteousness for His name's sake" (Ps. 23:1–3). Even in lean times, God has guaranteed that our bread and our water will be sure. Whether we are employed or underemployed, God is wonderfully gracious in providing for all our needs. "I have been young and now I am old; yet I have not seen the righteous forsaken, nor his descendants begging bread" (Ps. 37:25). How many times have we been down to our very last dollar or last can of beans only to see God do what he does best, work wonders in behalf of his people? Do you see God's leading in any particular department of your life?

"Through the Lord's mercies we are not consumed, because His compassions fail not. They are new every morning; Great is Your faithfulness" (Lam. 3:22–23).

Whether you are financially secure or struggling like most of us, this offers much comfort: "His compassions fail not. They are new every morning"—not every week, month, or year but every morning. God overwhelms us with his love, his mercy, and his grace. Thank you, Jesus, for loving us despite our unloveliness.

October 3

Outflanked and Outnumbered but Still Victorious

And it happened on the same night that the Lord said to him, "Arise, go down against the camp, for I have delivered it into your hand.
But if you are afraid to go down, go down to the camp with Purah your servant, and you shall hear what they say; and afterwards your hand shall be strengthened to go down against the camp."

—Judges 7:9–11

With nothing but guts and daring boldness, fifteen hundred Greek soldiers held at bay the one-hundred-thousand-plus Persian soldiers at a narrow pass at Thermopylae. Having conquered everything in his neighborhood, Xerxes—the Persian king—set his sight westward toward the bickering city-states of Greece, but he was resoundingly defeated at sea and land by the smaller but more resourceful Greeks. This victory provided the stepping stone for Alexander the Great's Greek conquest and world domination (http://www.ancientgreece.co.uk/war/home_set.html).

"Some trust in chariots, and some in horses; but we will remember the name of the Lord our God" (Ps. 20:7). God fills the earth with his huge presence; he is a majority all by himself. Those who muster the courage to fight against Satan and his interest in the name of God will always have the victory. God is renowned for fighting for the underdog, and when we embrace his kingdom principles, this makes us even more formidable. "When they were few in number, indeed very few, and strangers in it. When they went from one nation to another, from one kingdom to another people, He permitted no one to do them wrong, yes He rebuked kings for their sakes, saying, 'Do not touch My anointed ones, and do My prophets no harm'" (Ps. 105:12–15).

Israel's constant enemies were the Moabites, Ammonites, Philistines, and many surrounding nations, but our enemies are modern and are well camouflaged in everyday disguises. We must go to war against an enemy who furnishes us with convenient excuses for forsaking the assembly of church service. Every day we muster the strength and courage to go to work, but on Sabbath, paralysis sets in;

we either oversleep or can't find the strength to wake up and worship our Maker. What a shame!

Lord, help us overcome the enemy of infrequent prayer, which translates into little prayer, little power. "The effective, fervent prayer of a righteous man avails much. Elijah was a man with a nature like ours, and he prayed earnestly that it would not rain; and it did not rain on the land for three years and six months" (James 5:16–17). Our prayers allow us to keep the channel of communication open with God while staying focused on the task of saving souls for God's kingdom.

Ignorance of God's Word, if the believer is literate, is the chief enemy of the Christian, and it must be fought at every turn. In the Savior's battle with Satan, he used the scripture at every turn to defeat Satan. "But He answered and said, it is written, 'Man shall not live by bread alone, but by every word that proceeds from the mouth of God'" (Matt. 4:4). Jesus knew the scriptures and memorized them. After all, did he not speak them into existence? How can we be victorious in our daily life if we don't read the Bible to discover God's requirements for our life?

Like Caleb of old, we should have no fear of overcoming the enemy, for God is with us. "Let us go up at once and take possession, for we are well able to overcome it" (Num. 13:30). In God's strength and by his grace, we will overcome and conquer.

October 4

If This Isn't Love, What Is?

What do you think? If a man has a hundred sheep, and one of them goes astray, does he not leave the ninety-nine and go to the mountains to seek the one that is straying?

—Matthew 18:12

We often take them for granted, but their job description involves running into burning buildings to rescue trapped victims. Putting others first and their personal safety last seems to be their motto. It is always heart-wrenching to hear of firemen fatality. They perform their dangerous job every day without much drama, fanfare, or publicity. Part of their training consists in making lifesaving decisions under difficult circumstances while blinded by smoke, seared by heat, and weighed down with heavy equipment. They often run back into burning building to save pets from the flames. What bravery!

While we admire the fireman for his bravery, devotion, and passion for putting his life at risk to save others, we must understand that Christ's sacrifice for humanity is without parallel. He left the security of heaven, the adoration of the angels, the unity and oneness with God to seek and save a planet in rebellion. What makes this venture even more astounding is that, as God, Jesus foresaw his rejection and ultimate humiliation, but his love for humanity urged him to move forward with the plan of salvation, even at his personal risk. He saw the reward (you and me) of his sacrifice and was satisfied.

By taking upon himself the guilt of every sinner who ever lived, on that fateful day, Jesus could not see beyond the cross; as a matter of fact, he could not even sense the presence of his Father. He who once said, "I am in the Father and the Father in me," could not detect the company of his Father during this trying ordeal. The stress, the betrayal, the pain, the mental torment, and the uncertainty were overwhelming.

"And about the ninth hour Jesus cried with a loud voice, 'My God, My God, why have You forsaken Me?'" (Matt. 27:46). This cry of anguish is the feeling every unrepentant sinner will experience at the judgment—eternal separation from God, the source of all life. But God did not forsake his only beloved Son. He was right there at the cross with him. Where else could he be? The heaven of heavens cannot contain him; he's everywhere, including Calvary. The plan to save mankind had to run its full course without any intervention from anyone, including God. "God demonstrates His owns love towards us, in that while we still sinners, Christ died for us" (Rom. 5:8).

Here is the most exciting part:

> What man of you, having a hundred sheep, if he loses one of them, does not leave the ninety-nine in the wilderness, and go after the one which is lost until he finds it? And when he has found it, he lays it on his shoulders, rejoicing. And when he comes home, he calls together his friends and neighbors, saying to them, rejoice with me, for I have found my sheep which was lost! I say to you likewise there will be more joy in heaven over one sinner who repents than over ninety-nine just persons who need no repentance. (Luke 15:4–7)

If you love Jesus, you will serve him. When we love someone, hopefully of the opposite sex, we quickly seek to partner with that loved one. Likewise, if we love God, we will set our hearts to find him and propose to him. Lord Jesus, please be my Savior and forgive me of my sins. Come into my heart and save me. Amen.

October 5

The Touch of Faith

For she said to herself, if only I may touch His garment, I shall be made well, . . . and the woman was made well from that hour.

—Matthew 9:21–22

Susan (name changed) was in robust health until she felt a lump in her breast. "Oh, please don't let it be, dear God," she muttered. Since her family had no history of breast cancer, she did not feel it necessary to visit her doctor immediately. However, when her checkup was due, a CAT scan confirmed she had full-blown breast cancer. Survival instinct kicked in; she sought treatment, joined a prayer group, and immersed herself in ministering to others. Friends, family, and colleagues prayed regularly for her, in addition to long hours spent on her knees, seeking for a miraculous healing. She altered her diet and initiated a robust workout program to contain the beast—cancer.

Susan did everything right; not only did she touch the hem of the Master's garment but she also embraced it and wrapped herself around it. We stand in solidarity with Susan as she struggles through prayer and medical science to overcome this silent killer. We may never fully understand down here why bad things happen to good people, but we can find comfort in God's Word, which brings peace, hope, and nourishment to our souls. "Now as Jesus passed by, He saw a man who was blind from birth. And His disciples asked Him, saying, Rabbi, who sinned, this man or his parents, that he was born blind? Jesus answered, neither this man nor his parents sinned, but that the works of God should be revealed in him" (John 9:1–3).

Our hearts go out to anyone suffering with a debilitating or terminal illness. You have our outmost and dearest compassion and prayer. Sin and sickness do not choose their victims, and no one, including believers, has immunity from them. However, there are golden nuggets to be derived from Jesus's statement, "That the works of God should be revealed in him." What work does God want to reveal in us? Let's ask Paul. "And lest I should be exalted above measure by the abundance of the revelations, a thorn in the flesh was given to me, a messenger of Satan to buffet me, lest I be exalted above measure. Concerning this thing I pleaded with the Lord three times that it might depart from me. But He said to me, 'My grace is sufficient for you, for My strength is made perfect in weakness'" (2 Cor. 12:7–9). We do not know what that thorn in the flesh was, and speculation is an attempt in futility, but this we do know: Paul was dealing with some discomfort so debilitating that he called it a thorn in the flesh. Whatever it was, it was painful and uncomfortable, and he sought God in prayer for its removal but was denied.

But here is the clincher: "My grace is sufficient for you, for My strength is made perfect in weakness." God utilizes thorns and roses as he sees fit to bring glory to his name through our weak human vessels. Can God reach others through our pain and suffering? Can we ask Job? "Then Job arose, tore his robe, and shaved his head; and he fell to the ground and worshipped. And he said, 'Naked I came from my mother's womb, and naked shall I return there. The Lord gave, and the Lord has taken away; blessed be the name of the Lord" (Job 1:20–21).

Be courageous, dear friend, and give God the glory. He is working in you and with you to reach others. You may never know on this earth whose life your suffering touched for Jesus. Who would have thought the thief on the cross would be an inspiration at all? Yet he was. Praise God in your suffering.

October 6

Lord, Remember Me

And we indeed justly, for we receive the due reward of our deeds; but this Man has done nothing wrong. Then he said to Jesus, Lord remember me when You come into Your kingdom.

—Luke 23:41–42

A thief being a role model? This one certainly has been. He repented of his sins, and though he did not live to enjoy his newfound faith, his legacy lives on. Thieves are reviled in every culture, and interestingly, the thief at Calvary was reaping the reward of his criminal past. Over here in the West, some white-collar thieves are adored, envied, venerated, and sometimes rewarded with their ill-gotten gain by a lack of will or resources to prosecute them, but not so in primitive cultures, where they usually have brief life spans. Residents of ancient cultures had little tolerance for them; justice was usually swift and very harsh.

We do not know if the thief had any contact with Jesus before his execution, but this we do know: he saw in him righteousness and godliness on display under the most horrible provocation and taunting. He had seen enough to believe Jesus was indeed who he said he was—the Messiah of the world. And with a contrite heart and in bitterness of soul, he requested forgiveness and was given immediate assurance of being in God's kingdom.

The thief on the cross represents a broad class of people who will yield to Christ during their final hour. They may be your prison inmate who may never experience freedom outside prison walls but are rejoicing in their newfound faith. And how about career criminals who, like the thief on the cross, may have had a relationship with God but were swept astray by their criminal activities; they will make their peace with God and enjoy a seat around God's table. The terminally ill preparing for death can find courage that Jesus does accept sincere last-minute confessions. How can we forget the millions who were mortally wounded in battle and, with life slowly ebbing away, bravely submitted themselves to Jesus?

Despite his criminal past, the thief's experience provides a shining path to the cross where the Savior stands with open arms, ready to receive all who come to him with no questions asked. "But I said to you that you have seen Me and yet do not believe. All that the Father gives Me will come to Me, and the one who comes to Me I will by no means cast out" (John 6:36–37). This is tremendous hope for all people, for we all have had a questionable past; if the truth be told, we probably would not want to hang around to view the history of our life on display. Thanks be to God because our past is erased and forgotten forever.

God is loving and kind and does not bring up our past to embarrass us once we confess and forsake our sins. "Who is a God like unto You, pardoning iniquity and passing over the transgression of the remnant of His heritage? He does not retain His anger forever because He delights in mercy. He will again have compassion on

us, He will subdue our iniquities. You will cast our sins into the depth of the sea"
(Mic. 7:18–19).

Every sinner who repents reflects the sentiment of the thief on the cross.
"Lord remember me when you come into your kingdom." And Jesus always affirms.
"Assuredly I say to you today, you will be with Me in Paradise" (Luke 23:42–43).

October 7

I Want to Be First

Then the mother of Zebedee's sons came to Him with her sons, kneeling down and
asking something from Him.

—Matthew 20:20

Both Cook and Peary claimed to have been the first to set foot on the North
Pole, but since there was no independent body there to verify either man's claim,
the mystery continues. No place on earth is as forbidding as the North Pole.
The temperature fluctuates between 32 degrees in summer and -45 degrees in
winter. With few places left to conquer on the earth and bragging rights at stake,
proponents of both explorers are in a virtual war about who made it first to the
North Pole. However, historians have discredited both claims since there was no
independent party there to verify either claim (www.smithsonianmag.com/history/
who-discovered-the-north-pole).

The desire to be first runs deep in our human psyche. No one cares to
remember who finishes second, third, or last in a race, but the eyes of the world
are riveted on the winner. And with this "winner takes it all" attitude, Mary—the
mother of disciples James and John—presented her boys to Jesus and made an
urgent request to Christ. "And He said to her, what do you wish? She said to Him,
grant that the two sons of mine may sit, one on Your right hand and the other on
the left, in Your kingdom" (Matt. 20:21). Nothing wrong with that request, right?
Mary was just securing her boys' future, but Jesus's reply wasn't very encouraging
to her ego.

"But Jesus answered and said, You do not know what you ask. Are you able to
drink the cup that I am about to drink, and be baptized with the baptism that I
am baptized with? They said to Him, we are able" (Matt. 20:22). Really? Jesus did
not disappoint his misguided disciples; he worked with them, and when they were
spiritually mature, he equipped them with the power of the Holy Spirit on the day
of Pentecost. James fulfilled Christ's ideal by becoming the first apostle to seal
his testimony with his blood; his brother, John the Revelator, was banished to the
isle of Patmos (Acts 12:2, Rev. 1:1). They both drank the bitter cup they ignorantly
requested.

While Jesus was visibly present with his disciples, it was not his duty to award
favors to anyone. However, he complimented many who recognized and identified
him as God (Matt. 16:17). He paid tribute to the Roman soldier who expressed

profound faith in his mastery over sickness, something the Jewish leadership failed to admit (Matt. 8:8).

But when it comes to salvation, does it really matter who is first or last? If one has a large ego and being first really matters, be the first to initiate a revival and reformation in your family and church. Be the first to take the higher road when tempted to retaliate. Be the first to say, "I am sorry, forgive me." Always be the first to say, "Good morning. How are you? Isn't it a wonderful day God has made?"

Jesus reminds us to be first in seeking him. "But seek first the kingdom of God and His righteousness, and all these things shall be added to you" (Matt. 6:33). Of all the things we may be pursuing, let's make Jesus first on our agenda. Because he is God, give him your best. I love the Lord because he first loved me.

October 8

Lazarus, Come Forth!

I am the resurrection and the life. He who believes in Me, though he may die, he shall live.

—John 11:25

Dormant through the harsh winter, farmer Brown's seeds are beginning to break out. Their quest for life propels them to shatter kernels and burst open soil to feast on the nutritious sunlight. They are not disappointed; nature obliges with consistent showers of drenching rain to greet their thirsty buds. Their long night of waiting is over; life has begun in earnest for a new generation of herbs, trees, and shrubs. Their produce is simply delicious, and you will one day sample some of their succulent offerings on your dinner table. This is the resurrection of a dead seed transitioning itself into a vibrant tree.

Jesus is the source of all life and the key to the resurrection as well. All who believe in him and submit to his lordship, though they may sleep in the dust of the earth, shall break forth on resurrection morning with triumph on their lips. "O death where is your sting? O Hades, where is your victory?" (1 Cor. 15:55). The resurrection of Lazarus and all who preceded him from the Old Testament era symbolizes a greater harvest awaiting the call of the Life Giver. "For the Lord Himself will descend from heaven with a shout with the voice of the Archangel, and with the trumpet of God and dead in Christ will rise first" (1 Thess. 4:16). It is noteworthy to point out that Paul referenced the resurrection of the dead as a future event. The saints of old, who are very much dead and asleep in their graves, will be raised and, together with the living righteous, will be granted eternal life by our Lord. Without question, this has been the anticipation of every saint from Adam to our generation. Our mortal bodies will give way to immortality. "Behold I tell you a mystery: we shall not all sleep, but we shall all be changed, in a moment, in the twinkling of an eye, at the last trumpet. For the trumpet will sound, and the dead will be raised incorruptible, and we shall be changed. For this corruptible must put on incorruption, and this mortal must put on immortality" (1 Cor. 15:51–53).

Every new blade of grass emerging from the slumber of winter reminds us of what is just around the corner, the glorious resurrection of the saints. We recall the saints who were lost at sea, and their remains were never recovered; they will be reconstituted with a vibrant eternal body. And those torn by wild beasts in the Colosseum of Rome will arise totally whole. They will be unmindful of the suffering they endured but thankful to God for standing with them during their terrible ordeal. And how can we forget those of whom pain was a constant companion? Their bodies have been ravaged by debilitating spasms of pain and suffering; they will actually inherit pain-free brand-new bodies. Babies denied the privilege of growing up to fulfill their dreams on earth will have every opportunity to grow up in an environment where death is no more.

Thank you, Jesus, for unlocking the graves and setting our captives free. Those of us who had close encounters with death can appreciate these words: "For I know that my Redeemer lives, and He shall stand at last on the earth; and after my skin is destroyed, this I know, that in my flesh I shall see God, whom I shall see for myself and my eyes shall behold, and not another" (Job 19:25–27). Get ready and stay ready. The next face you gaze on could be that of Jesus.

October 9

Cast Your Net over There

But Simon answered and said to Him, Master, we have toiled all night and caught nothing;
nevertheless at your word I will let down the net.

—Luke 5:5

Some of the world's most successful predators have a one-in-ten chance of making a successful kill, and to some unfortunate ones, the odds are even higher. When prey is scarce, it does matter how many attempts result in a successful meal. The predator must have a timely meal, and expending energy on failed attempts weakens the beast even more. Every failed attempt saps the strength, and if food is not forthcoming, the beast will succumb to weakness and eventually starve to death.

Peter and the disciples were nursing a fruitless night of fishing in their favorite location. They could see and smell the fish but somehow could not entice the little guys into their net. How frustrating! At what point does one pack it in and do something different? How does one know when to change direction or regroup and come back with renewed energy? Should I pour more precious time and resources into this venture? Someone famously said, "Success is one more attempt from complete failure."

Giving up is not an option to the believer. Is Jesus ever late? Is he ever delayed? As always, his roving eyes caught his disciples' frustration, and he showed up on the scene of the failed catch with these words: "Launch out into the deep and let down your nets for a catch" (Luke 5:4). Are you ready for their response? "Master, we have toiled all night and caught nothing; nevertheless at Your word I will let down the net" (Luke 5:5). Would you have answered differently if you were in Simon Peter's shoes? In what way do we doubt and limit God's ability to do incredible things in our lives?

It did not fully dawn on Peter that he was talking to the One who made and designed fish and crafted the ecosystem. Jesus knows all about fish, their habitat, where they feed, where they rest, and where they assemble day or night. And since Jesus is Lord over nature, which includes fish, they dutifully obeyed his command. Let's see what happened to Peter and his buddies. "And when they had done this, they caught a great number of fish, and their net was breaking. So they signaled to their partners in the other boats, and they came and filled both the boats, so that they began to sink" (Luke 5:6–7). What can Jesus do when we submit our weak faith to him? He is ready to give us the catch of our life, but most often, he is not consulted, not invited, or ignored completely. However, the Bible does not leave us in doubt. It says, "In all your ways acknowledge Him and He shall direct your paths" (Prov. 3:6).

Acknowledging Jesus's mastery over creation and over the simple things of life, a humbled Peter fell down at the Master's feet and exclaimed, "Depart from me, for I am a sinful man, O Lord!" (Luke 5:8). Once he acknowledged his limitations in fishing, despite his many years of plying the waters of the lake of Gennesaret, Peter succumbed at the feet of Jesus, a disciple ready for service. But Peter was hardly a finished product for the showroom, nor are we; Jesus worked with Peter in very much the same way he is working with us today. Are you open to advice even if you are an expert in your field? "Humble yourselves in the sight of the Lord and He shall lift you up" (James 4:10).

October 10

Are Your Eyes Open?

When He came to the disciples and found them sleeping, and said to Peter, could you not watch with Me for one hour?

—Matthew 26:40

North American black bears and grizzlies hibernate during the winter, and scientists are at a loss in understanding this mysterious and intricate behavior. During their long sleep, they intermittently wake up, give birth, nurse their young, and fall asleep again without taking in any nourishment until winter breaks. Though sleep is very important and necessary for properly balancing our human anatomy, some serious emergencies in life compel us to forgo our desire for a well-deserved nap.

"Then He took with Him Peter and the two sons of Zebedee, and He began to be sorrowful and deeply distressed. Then He said to them, My soul is exceedingly sorrowful, even to death. Stay here and watch with Me" (Matt. 26:37–38). With the sins of the entire world cast on his shoulders, Jesus sought power through prayer in the garden of Gethsemane, but he needed human companionship, as we all do, when facing times of crisis. Though divine, his humanity craved for solidarity from his close friends and associates, but could they keep their eyes open? We may have heard this commonly used phrase: "Where there is a will, there is a way."

We modern-day disciples need to stay wide awake and on our knees if we hope to be ready for the trials and tribulations ahead. Our Savior showed us how to prepare for the coming crisis. "Now in the morning, having risen a long while before daylight, He went out and departed to a solitary place; and there He prayed" (Mark 1:35). Lord, give us the will and tenacity to pray like you did. Your values and principles are being attacked from every direction. The family is under siege by hostile forces. Any attempt to condemn immorality is hailed as being antisocial. Righteousness and virtue are ridiculed, while infidelity, vice, and immorality are glamorized and accepted as the new normal. The paycheck expires without accomplishing its desired objective, and employers want more from us while paying less and less. We need help.

Dear Lord, keep our eyes open to eternal values, where "rust and moth do not corrupt and where thieves do not break in and steal" (Matt. 6:20). Lord, keep us wide awake to stand in the gap and pray for our children who are being targeted with violent adult songs, videos, and movies. We will keep our eyes open and pray that our schools remain a place where children can learn and aspire to be all that they can be without the threat of someone lurking out there to harm them.

We have much to watch and pray about, don't we? The challenges to live a blameless life may be daunting and overwhelming, but we serve a mighty God who makes the impossible possible. "O our God, will You not judge them? For we have no power against this great multitude that is coming against us; nor do we know what to do, but our eyes are upon you" (2 Chron. 20:12).

Are you awake to the threat facing the believer in today's society? Are you on your knees often, or are you driven there by circumstances beyond your control? Do you have your eyes open and focused on Jesus? I pray that you do.

October 11

Why Not Me?

Now when he was in affliction he implored the Lord his God, and humbled himself greatly before the God of his fathers.

—2 Chronicles 33:12

Stacy (name changed) was determined to enjoy life to the fullest. She made no effort to tone down her frequent casino and party binges until a slippery ice patch did her in. She fell and injured her pelvis. Her doctor tried to buoy her spirit, but he knew it was serious. The nature of the fracture called for a long period of recuperation. "Why me?" she moaned and sighed as reality began setting in. Being flat on her back and with no place to go, Stacy had lots of time for introspection and reflection. In her hour of need and despair, she remembered the God of her childhood and surrendered her life to Christ. From the confines of her hospital bed, Stacy began a new mission to anyone venturing on her space. Her nightclub buddies who came calling were pleasantly surprised to discover an energetic preacher of righteousness in Stacy.

God has not limited himself in what he must do to get our attention. He has a wide variety of tools in his inventory and knows which one works best for different people. Very much like sheep, we are prone to stray, and only God knows whether we desire to be found or not. Nevertheless, driven by his intense love and unrelenting desire for our spiritual and physical well-being, he pursues us anyway. Leaving no stone unturned, God influences situations and circumstances to make his point understood.

God threw Paul down from his horse and had him blind for three days to turn him around. A receptive Paul was willing to listen then. "And Ananias went his way and entered the house; and laying his hands on him he said, 'Brother Saul, the Lord Jesus, who appeared to you on the road as you came, has sent me that you may receive your sight and be filled with the Holy Spirit" (Acts 9:17). The proud Nebuchadnezzar was taught a lesson in humility by temporarily losing his sanity and kingdom until he realized God was the ultimate ruler and was seeking to save his soul. "And at the end of the time, I Nebuchadnezzar, lifted my eyes to heaven, and my understanding returned to me; and I blessed the Most High and praised and honored Him who lives forever" (Dan. 4:34). An overconfident David had to learn brokenness all over again. Being in the church is no guarantee that we are secure. David had a rude wake-up call by the prophet Gad, all in an effort to save his soul. After his great sin with Bathsheba, David was given a choice to choose one of three punishments: "And David said to Gad, I am in great distress. Please let me fall into the hand of the Lord, for His mercies are very great; but do not let me fall into the hand of men" (1 Chron. 21:13).

When we stray over into the devil's playground, God allows adverse situations to affect us to bring us to salvation. After the dust has settled and you make it to the pearly gates, ask to push the rewind button, and you will discover that every stripe, every tear, every speeding ticket, and every fine had redemptive intent and outcomes. "And we know that all things work together for good to those who love God, to those who are the called according to His purpose" (Rom. 8:28). God had to disable Stacy to get her attention. Has he done the same to you?

October 12

Stay on the Ship

Paul said to the centurion and the soldiers, unless these men stay in the ship, you cannot be saved.
Then the soldiers cut away the ropes of the skiff and let it fall off.

—Acts 27:31–32

When her minivan burst into flames in an open enclosure with lions watching with much interest, Helen was sternly commanded by park rangers, "Do not leave the van. It is safer in there." Smoke was really billowing out of her Fiat van, and her two children were getting frantic, but Helen Clements was again ordered to stay in the burning vehicle while park rangers try to corral a reluctant pride of lions into their enclosure. Fortunately, the incident had a happy ending. With a few seconds to spare, a jeep swooped in to rescue the family, leaving behind a hungry and disappointed lion pride. Twelve-year-old Charlie moaned about leaving her cell phone on the dashboard, while nine-year-old George grabbed his teddy bear and was glad to be out of the burning vehicle (http://www.dailyrecord.co.uk/news/longleat-lion-enclosure-fire-mother-3434711).

Paul's cautionary advice in our memory text reflects a continuous theme in the Bible. Stay in the church regardless of the issues affecting her; it is always safer in here than in the world. Where can we flee for safety? Is it in the embrace of the devil or in the camp of the enemy? Staying in the church is not only a good idea but it's also the only idea. The ark of Noah was the only vehicle pulling out of the madness of the antediluvian (preflood) world. Did it make perfect sense to be in the ark? "And God said to Noah, the end of all flesh has come before Me, for the earth is filled with violence through them; and behold I will destroy them with the earth. Make yourself an Ark of gopher wood; make rooms in the ark, and cover it inside and outside with pitch" (Gen. 6:13–14). Noah's family may have initially questioned his sanity in building a boat in the middle of nowhere, but they followed his instruction, helped build the ark, and were saved.

The church is the only institution that will survive the coming catastrophe. Are you on the inside? Do you know the Captain?

> Then the sky receded as a scroll when it is rolled up, and every mountain and island was moved out of its place. And the kings of the earth, the great men, the rich men, the commanders, the mighty men, every slave and every free man, hid themselves in the caves and in the rocks of the mountains, and said to the mountains and rocks, "Fall on us and hide us from the face of Him who sits on the throne and from the wrath of the Lamb! For the great day of His wrath is come, and who shall be able to stand?" (Rev. 6:14–17)

The looming catastrophe long foretold by prophets of old is here. "But know this, in the last days perilous times will come: For men will be lovers of themselves, lovers of money, boasters, proud, blasphemers, disobedient to parents, unthankful, unholy, unloving, without self-control, brutal despisers of good" (2 Tim. 3:1–3). With these signs fulfilling fast and the end of the world already on us, this is no time to think about quitting on Jesus and abandoning the ship. Where will you go? Is there any safety outside the house of God? Get a grip on Jesus, and stay in the church. "Unless these men stay in the ship, you cannot be saved" (Acts 27:31). Stay on board the ship; it is the safest place to be in a boisterous storm.

October 13

You Are Rich Part 1

Do not lay up for yourselves treasures on earth, where moth and rust destroy and where thieves break in and steal;
but lay up for yourselves treasures in heaven, where neither moth nor rust destroys and where thieves do not break in and steal.

—Matthew 6:19–20

They stare at these rare treasures locked behind one-and-a-half-inch-thick glass. Nonetheless, the admirers of these rare treasures, mostly women, dream of wearing some sparkling jewels around their neck someday. The Smithsonian Institution National Museum of Natural History houses the largest trove of rare treasure in the United States. It is the place of choice for viewers of these precious jewels who would love to have them but do not have the means to purchase them. Its exotic exhibits draw huge crowds from the United States and all over the world; they gaze in wonder at its priceless and infinite inventory. I must confess, I am a secret admirer myself, but God has even better goodies in store for his people. Do you know you can acquire some of these rare jewels someday soon?

Historians and economists agree that it is not the resources of the United States that make her the greatest nation in the world; it is her laws, the Constitution, the free enterprise system, her ingenuity, her thirst for knowledge, and her freedom of expression. God has treasures that surpass all others, and it is housed in each one of us. "The kingdom of heaven is like treasure hidden in a field, which a man found and hid; and for joy over it, he goes and sells all that he has and buys that field" (Matt. 13:44). The knowledge of God is priceless; it is superior to any other body of knowledge.

Jesus continues to place invaluable primacy on his Word even today. "Again the kingdom of heaven is like a merchant seeking beautiful pearls, who when he has found a pearl of great price went and sold all that he had and bought it" (Matt. 13:45). No wonder believers are bubbling all over with joy, knowing the glorious future that awaits them. Paul puts it succinctly. "But we have this treasure in earthen vessels, that the excellence of the power may be of God and not of us" (2 Cor. 4:7). God has entrusted to weak, fallen, erring beings his priceless truths, and that is remarkable, isn't it? We are the vehicles, the conduits, and the channels of his rich grace, mercy, and love to a sin-sick world, and that makes us very wealthy indeed.

The fact that we are channels of this wonderful body of truths should make us more careful in our walk with God and eager to share him with our fellow men. "But I discipline my body and bring it into subjection, lest when I have preached to others, I myself should become disqualified" (1 Cor. 9:27). Oh yes, and this warning comes from the prince of the apostles himself. We can lead others to Christ and be disqualified in the end if we are not deeply attached to Christ. Nothing short of

100 percent commitment will do. God will not accept divided service. "You cannot serve God and mammon."

Are you conscious of the priceless body of truths that we possess and represent? I will be more diligent in living these principles in my life so that others can see Jesus in me. I will commit myself to these principles and enjoin others to do the same. The treasure of God's love is in you, and the truth you espouse is priceless and is yours to keep. Amen.

October 14

You Are Rich Part 2

For every beast of the forest is mine, and the cattle upon a thousand hills.
I know all the birds of the mountains, and the wild beasts of the field are Mine.
If I were hungry, I would not tell you; for the world is Mine, and all its fullness.
—Psalm 50:10–12

They are fabulously wealthy, and their toys include fast and expensive cars, custom-made Learjets, and specially designed luxurious yachts; but without God, it will all go up in smoke. God has blessed some with the uncanny ability to amass wealth and lots of it. They are blessed with the knowledge of acquiring wealth or may have grown in the right environment that breeds success. We tip our hats to them, and society needs them; history bears evidence that, in every society, capital is concentrated in the hands of a few powerful men, and we accept that.

Though we should strive to be financially secure down here, our most valuable treasure is the One who beautifies the soul. Speaking to the Laodicean church, Jesus affirmed, "I counsel you to buy from Me gold refined in the fire, that you may be rich; and white garments, that you may be clothed, that the shame of your nakedness may not be revealed; and anoint your eyes with eye salve, that you may see" (Rev. 3:18). Jesus placed emphasis and priority on a different kind of treasure. Someone who takes a needy child to a ball game, cares about an immigrant, feeds the homeless, checks on the sick and elderly, shovels snow, cuts the grass of neighbors, works with challenging students, or involves himself or herself in voluntary service is fabulously wealthy.

Investing in the bank of heaven not only makes sense but also will solely stand the intense scrutiny of an all-wise God. "Do not lay up for yourselves treasures on earth, where moth and rust destroy and where thieves break in and steal; but lay up for yourselves treasures in heaven, where neither moth nor rust destroys and where thieves do not break in and steal. For where your treasure is, there your heart will be also" (Matt. 6:19–21).

God is not minimizing the importance of wealth, for when the church was in dire need, Nicodemus, Lydia, and Joseph of Arimathea stepped up to the plate and utilized their wealth in the work of God (John 19:39, Mark 15:43). God wants his people to be the head and not the tail. He is the giver of every good and perfect gift. God desires his people to be wealthy. But true gems and pearls are formed under the crucible of trials and affliction. "Search me, and know my heart; try me and know my anxieties; and see if there is any wicked way in me, and lead me in the way everlasting" (Ps. 139:23–24).

Not only are treasures developed under trying times but we also can obtain them by caring for and standing up for the downtrodden. Martin Luther King died penniless or probably with very little money in the bank, but would anyone question his priceless legacy to the world? Those who determine not to care for the poor will themselves die poor. True wealth in God's sight is our love for our fellow humans, including the disadvantaged, and care for the downtrodden. We bring nothing into this world, and we certainly will take nothing with us when we make our exit, but the righteous will awake to an eternal inheritance with God. In our pursuit of wealth, we need to ponder this sobering thought: "But seek first the kingdom of God and His righteousness, and all these things shall be added unto you" (Matt. 6:33). You are truly rich if you have Jesus abiding in your heart.

October 15

Those Left Behind

How the mighty have fallen in the midst of the battle!
Jonathan was slain in your high places. . . Tell it not in Gath, proclaim it not in the streets of Ashkelon, lest the daughters of the Philistines rejoice, lest the daughters of the uncircumcised triumph.

—2 Samuel 1:25, 20

Grieving fluctuates from "I can't believe it" to "He's at rest now" or "At least he's not suffering anymore." The passing of a loved one is always traumatic and delivers a crushing blow to the family of the deceased. It is even more painful if the deceased was very young or had just begun a career. No family, however rich and famous, has immunity from the tentacles of the Grim Reaper. Some do not like being reminded of death, but we all, without exception, will depart this life someday. As one thoughtful theologian affirms, "This ceremony [meaning the eulogy] is not for the deceased but for the living."

The Bible declares that the dead are absolutely and positively dead and are not anywhere else except in their graves. "The living know that they will die; but the dead know nothing, and they have no more reward, for the memory of them is forgotten. Also their love, their hatred, and their envy have now perished; nevermore will they have a share in anything done under the sun" (Eccles. 9:5–6). The dead are in their graves awaiting the resurrection. Any sightings of supposedly deceased people play into the hands of the power of darkness. Remember the devil's little white lie: "Ye shall not surely die." They did die, not immediately, but the dying process began then.

In an effort to win over Caesar's loyalists, Mark Antony claimed that his heart was in the coffin with Caesar, but was Caesar really in the coffin or his corpse? "Then the dust will return to the earth as it was, and the spirit return to God who gave it" (Eccles. 12:7). When the spirit vacates the body, the remains are actually dust and nothing more. We pause for reflection after a national tragedy or the untimely death of a loved one. *That could have been me*, we often say to ourselves. More often than not, we dismiss the thought as too unpleasant to dwell on. Given the fact that tomorrow is promised to no man, isn't it prudent to prepare for the unexpected approach of death by making our peace with God now? Some discover too late that death always keeps its appointment and is never late or delayed.

Jesus underscores the tragedy of sudden death by citing these two examples in his teaching: Pilate had brutally slaughtered some unfortunate Galileans, and a tower tragically fell and killed some worshippers. Jesus asks, "Do you suppose that these Galileans were worse sinners than all other Galileans, because they suffered such things? I tell you, no; but unless you repent you will all likewise perish" (Luke 13:2–3).

In essence, Jesus was saying, "Is your soul right with God?" If you were to depart this life tonight, would you be safe and secure in the arms of Jesus? Not asking this very crucial question will not make it go away. Resurrection morning will not be a surprise to the child of God; this is the moment we've been waiting for all through our lives. This is the event the whole universe has been anticipating. How can we dread the coming of Jesus Christ as Lord of lords and King of kings when it is to put an end to sin and death? Are you making the necessary preparations to meet our soon-coming King? God is always convenient to those who seek him. "I love those who love Me, and those who seek Me diligently will find Me" (Prov. 8:17).

October 16

Down but Not Out

For man does not know his time: Like fish taken in a cruel net, Like birds caught in a snare, So the sons are snared in an evil time, When it falls suddenly upon them.
—Ecclesiastes 9:12

A little confession is good for the soul. Can you keep a secret? Don't tell anyone; this is between you and me. Bank executives actually met in their elegant boardrooms and intentionally handed over toxic and bad loans to their unsuspecting customers. Needless to reiterate, as soon as these toxic loans were handed over to the customer, they exploded in their hands like firecrackers. The economic meltdown of 2008 took a bite out of our savings, home value, and financial estates. No one escaped it unscathed except those who perpetrated this great fraud and prepared for it. They were rewarded with their ill-gotten gain, and to date, no one has gone to jail for the crime of the century. The believer is not immune from the troubles of life, like everyone else; he suffers from the greed, bad decisions, and excesses of the rich.

It is refreshing to know that Jesus has equipped us with tools to confront these terrible crises head-on. "We are hard-pressed on every side, yet not crushed; we are perplexed, but not in despair; persecuted, but not forsaken; struck down, but not destroyed" (2 Cor. 4:8–9). We should never quit while running in the race of life; if we stumble, we gather ourselves, get up, and continue the race. God has embedded in the believer the spirit of the great Conqueror, Jesus Christ, so that we would reflect on how God has delivered us in times past. The road of life is never paved with all positive experiences as the Hebrews in Nebuchadnezzar's court found out. "If that is the case, our God whom we serve is able to deliver us from the burning fiery furnace, and He will deliver us from your hand, O king. But if not, let it be known to you, O king, that we do not serve your gods, nor will we worship the gold image which you have set up" (Dan. 3:17–18). When we place our full confidence and trust in God, we will brace ourselves and wait for the consequences, whether affirmative or negative. God will use us in any way he sees fit to bring glory to his great name.

Do not be surprised if through your righteous living you have become the object of Satan's wrath. "Be sober, be vigilant; because your adversary the devil walks about like a roaring lion, seeking whom he may devour" (1 Pet. 5:8). Since we cannot stand out of the devil's way, our only safety is in Jesus Christ. "The name of the Lord is a strong tower; the righteous run to it and are safe" (Prov. 18:10). Because we have built our faith on the sure foundation of Jesus Christ, we are safe and secure in him.

While politicians tell us that our best days are ahead of us, the Bible differs with their rosy assessment. "But know this, that in the last days perilous times will come, for men will be lovers of themselves, lovers of money, boasters, proud, blasphemers, disobedient to parents, unthankful, unholy, unloving, unforgiving, slanderers, without self-control, brutal, despisers of good" (2 Tim. 3:1–3). Will these bad behaviors ever stop? Will world conditions improve? Will the damage done to the global ecosystem be reversed? Certainly not. But these events should help us grow stronger in Christ as we see the days approaching. "Now when these things begin to happen, look up and lift up your heads, because your redemption draws near" (Luke 21:28).

October 17

I'll Be Back Someday

The thief does not come except to steal, and to kill, and to destroy.
I have come that they may have life, and that they may have it more abundantly.
—John 10:10

Even in her grief, she hugged the mother of the man who killed her family. Pastor Ruimar and his family of five left Andrews University to pursue their dream of being missionaries in Palau. This lovely family from Brazil charmed many friends from the community, including the first lady of the nation, who was delighted to have them from halfway across the world. One eventful night, a drunken intruder turned their world upside down by systematically killing everyone who woke up to investigate the noise he was making. Ten-year-old Melissa was kidnapped but was finally released by the killer (http://www.adventistsaffirm.org/article/129/ previous-issues/volume-18-number-2/the-de-paiva-forgiveness-story).

The Palau nation was horrified by this gruesome and senseless crime. A state funeral was granted to the family, and the national flag was flown at half-mast, but what transpired at the four-hour-long funeral service belongs to the ages. Pastor Ruimar's mom, Mrs. O. DePaiva, having met previously with the family of the murderer, walked up to the microphone unannounced and invited the killer's mom and family to come forward. She embraced them publicly and absolved the family from all guilt. She implored the Palauan community not to blame the whole family for the crime of one errant, drunken member. The entire audience was stunned in silence by this moving gesture as tissue papers were dabbed to tear-filled eyes.

Mrs. Ruimar's gesture typifies the great example set by our Savior while hanging on the cross. "Father, forgive them, for they do not know what they do" (Luke 23:34). Calvary continuously demonstrates the triumph of love over hate and righteousness over evil. Mahatma Gandhi remarked, "If we all avenge ourselves, we all would be sightless, toothless, and with missing limbs," referencing the "eye for an eye, tooth for a tooth" law. Hate has absolutely no place in the healing of broken families. Hate imprisons and separates; love, on the other hand, restores ruptured relationships, liberates those once imprisoned by guilt, gives peace to the victimized, and allows one to sleep peacefully even when victimized.

Joseph had every reason to be bitter about being sold as a slave by his brothers. He was falsely accused by his master's wife and thrown in jail for a crime she invented, but he chose to dwell on the positive by forgiving his tormentors and allowing God to work his will through him. When the dust settled and the curtain folded, Joseph's love conquered hate, and his righteousness triumphed over evil. When asked where she would like to live, ten-year-old Melissa (survivor) had no second thought. "Here in Palau," she remarked.

The conquering spirit of love swallowed up the Roman Empire as Christians went to their deaths exchanging their love for the empire's hatred. The cheering spectators were mystified by the dignity and courage displayed by the Christians as they faced death. Many in the stands inquired about the God of the Christians. Some of the spectators who took their stand for Christ met the same grim fate of their slain brethren. Jesus warned, "Then they will deliver you up to tribulation and kill you, and you will be hated by all nations for My name's sake . . . But he who endures to the end shall be saved" (Matt. 24:9, 13).

October 18

The Best in the Business

For three in heaven bear witness: the Father, the Word, and the Holy Spirit;
and these three are one.

—1 John 5:7

Three engineers are busy surveying the landscape, but their junior partner seems
a bit puzzled and hesitant. He hasn't been involved in a building project of this
magnitude, but in time, he'll learn. Winter is approaching fast, and there is a lot of
work to be done, food to be harvested, and repairs to be made to the home, and a
cleanup of the surrounding area is top priority. Mom and Pop decide to repair the
leaky dam with a mixture of mud and weed while little Junior fetches small twigs and
emulates his parents. Having secured the leak in the dam, they turn their attention
to felling trees and fortifying the outer lining of the lodge. After a tree is felled, the
choice part must be stored for winter's meal, while the leaves and tiny branches go
toward repair material for the dam.

Little Junior, a son from last year's litter, doesn't know it yet, but his mom is
pregnant, and soon he will be tapped for babysitting duties. With the bulk of the
work done, the family exercises a little more prudence by storing extra food just in
case winter is extended. Amazingly, the family has survived, with the addition of
two kits to show for their investment. The beavers' industry has benefited several
neighbors, including the bald eagle, which regularly snacks on fish in Junior's pond
(*National Geographic*).

A beaver's work is never done; he stays busy hauling twigs and branches to
patch his lodge and dam. However busy the beaver may be, his Creator, God, is even
busier, answering prayers and overseeing the functioning of the earth, the other
planets, and the universe at large. The earth's climate is regulated precisely at the
right temperature to facilitate the growth of plants and the freezing of the Arctic
and Antarctic. The animals never have to worry where their next meal is coming
from; their meals are delivered in a timely manner every day. Some attribute this
intricate efficiency to chance and nature, but even nature needs a little tweak every
once in a while. "The heavens declare the glory of God; and the firmament shows
His handiwork. Day unto day utters speech, and night unto night reveals knowledge.
For there is no speech nor language where their voice is not heard" (Ps. 19:1–3).
Nature gives thanks and praise to God for performing his function so flawlessly.

God is busy every day with us mankind, and his task is made even more
complex by our stubborn attachment to this world and its delicacies. Here is the
extent through which God will go to save a hesitant but willing soul. "When the
morning dawned, the angels urged Lot to hurry, saying, 'Arise, take your wife and
two daughters who are here, lest you be consumed in the punishment of the city.'
And while he lingered, the men took hold of his hand, his wife's hand and the hands
of his two daughters, the Lord being merciful to him, and they brought him out

and set him outside the city" (Gen. 19:15–16). In like manner, all three members of the Godhead are very busy saving us, sometimes dragging us out while we're still kicking and screaming out of unhealthy relationships and self-induced troubles, all in a day's work. God is good, isn't he? He is busy every day saving stiff-necked sinners like you and me. He saves even the hesitant who willingly desires salvation.

October 19

In God We Trust

Trust in the Lord with all your heart and lean not on your understanding; in all your ways acknowledge Him, and He shall direct your paths.
—Proverbs 3:5–6

Fearing that the nation was losing its grip on God as the guiding force behind the republic, a worried minister M. R. Watson wrote to Treasury Secretary Salmon P. Chase, strongly urging him to print "In God we trust" on the U.S. currency. This sentiment was also expressed by numerous people as the nation became embroiled in the throes of the Civil War, but this change necessitated an act from Congress, which happily obliged. The change appeared first on the two-cent coin in 1864 and later on paper currency in 1957 (www.allabouthistory.org/in-god-we-trust.htm).

God was front and center in the nation formed by fleeing religious and economic refugees from Europe. They set up shop here and built educational institutions deeply rooted in the "In God we trust" policy, but as the nation became prosperous and more secularized, adherence to religious principles was tossed out of the institutions. Regrettably, secular movements have successfully peeled away prayer from schools and religious icons from national parks, and now they are fighting furiously to separate Christ from Christmas and God from Thanksgiving. What are they up to, and what will they do next?

With the nation progressively sliding into immorality and degradation, we have a stark choice to make. "No one can serve two masters; for either he will hate one and love the other, or else he will be loyal to one and despise the other. You cannot serve God and mammon" (Matt. 6:24). Television entertainment is becoming more sensual, graphic, and seductive; the stock market is riddled with corruption and is tantamount to going to the casino to gamble. What else hasn't been corrupted? Not much, but the Word of God still maintains its freshness and relevance over the passage of time; it is still totally pure. It has survived the many attempts of false scholars calling into question its authenticity. "Knowing this first that no prophecy of Scripture is of any private interpretation, for prophecy never came by the will of man, but holy men of God spoke as they were moved by the Holy Spirit" (2 Pet. 1:20–21).

While everything around us is falling apart and becoming corrupt, we must solidify our hold on Jesus, and David shows us how to do it. "As for you, Solomon, know the God of your father, and serve Him with a loyal heart and with a willing mind; for the Lord searches all the hearts and understands all the intent of the thoughts. If you seek Him He will be found by you; but if you forsake Him, He will cast you off forever" (1 Chron. 28:9).

God is very convenient to us. He sometimes comes to us in the form of good friends, dreams, visions, nature, reading material, audiovisual equipment, and good old conscience. However, when these tools fail to get our attention, he has other means that may be unpleasant but necessary to save us. God will leave no stone unturned in saving humans. His Holy Spirit lovingly persuades us throughout our lifetime, providing us opportunities for salvation. "Some trust in chariots, and some in horses; but we will remember the name of the Lord our God" (Ps. 20:7).

October 20

In His Sanctuary Part 1

Your way, O God is in the sanctuary; who is so great a God as our God?
—Psalm 77:13

The president and the Oval Office are inextricably bound together; they need each other. The office has a hallowed presence, the scene of many great and significant world events. Each president brings his personal charm, traits, characteristics, and office rearrangement to the room. Congress may pass laws, but without the presidential signature, which usually occurs in the Oval Office, they are dead on arrival. The room is elegant and stately but simple. Unlike other countries, which may have palatial office space for their heads of state, the founding fathers intended to keep the man and his office very simple.

God's office space from which he rules and supervises the universe is in his sanctuary. Like the sacredness that marks the Oval Office, God needed a holy office to work on the character of his people. He therefore instructed Moses to build him a sanctuary, and he personally designed every facet of the building. "And they shall make an Ark of acacia wood; two and half cubits shall be its length, a cubit and a half its width and a cubit and half its height. And you shall overlay it with pure gold, inside and out you shall overlay it, and shall make on it a molding of gold all around" (Exod. 25:10–11). The quality of the material suggests the status of the One who resides in the office, and the God of the universe will have nothing less than the best.

The sanctuary itself is fully loaded with illustrative symbolisms of the plan of redemption. The tabernacle consists of a tent with two divisions: the holy place where the daily ministry is conducted and the most holy where the yearly ministry is done. The ark is the only item of furniture of the most holy place and is totally overlaid with pure gold. Two cherubim with outstretched right wings toward each other are looking down on the mercy seat, which in turn illuminates the brilliant Shechinah, the glory of God. On the inside of the ark are the Ten Commandments, a bowl of manna, Aaron's rod, and the books of the law (Torah) (Heb. 9:3–5).

The mercy seat, as its name implies, represents the approach to God himself. Every repentant sinner (you and me included) who throws himself on the mercy seat obtains pardon from God. "Let us therefore come boldly to the throne of grace, that we may obtain mercy in time of need" (Heb. 4:16). By dwelling in his sanctuary (our bodies), God is accessible to us every hour of every day. The ancient sanctuary and all its furnishings were designed to separate the sinner from his sins and enable him to be reconciled with God. The sanctuary teaches how God dealt with sin before Calvary.

After his resurrection, Jesus took residence in the heavenly sanctuary and now abides in the most holy place, where he is forever making intercession for us in the presence of God. "For we do not have a High Priest who cannot sympathize with our weaknesses, but was in all points tempted as we are, yet without sin" (Heb. 4:15). Jesus is this wonderful High Priest, and he is the only one qualified to plead on our behalf. He walked in our shoes, knows when we ache, and lived a blameless life while being hounded daily by Satan. He is also aware of the intensity with which we are tempted by Satan, and when we succumb to sin, he is faithful and just to forgive us and cleanse us from unrighteousness (1 John 1:9). The only sins not forgiven are the ones we do not forsake. Lord, be merciful to us.

October 21

In His Sanctuary Part 2

And let them make me a Sanctuary that I may dwell among them.
—Exodus 25:8

The sanctuary was in the center of the Israeli encampment, and everything revolved around it. God's presence was always there visibly in multiple manifestations, sometimes hovering over the encampment in a pillar of cloud by day for cooling and a pillar of fire by night for warmth. Always present at the mercy seat was his dazzling glory manifested through the Shechinah. Only the officiating high priest had access to the most holy place, but the other apartment, the holy place, was equally important, for it was there that the daily ministry was conducted.

The holy place housed three critical items of furniture: the golden lampstand, the table of shewbread, and the altar of incense. The golden lampstand had to be lit every day and supplied with oil. Both the light and oil are symbolic of the Holy Spirit, which was later described by Jesus in the parable of the ten virgins. Jesus himself stated, "I am the light of the world," and of course, David reiterated this fact with these words: "Thy word is a lamp to my feet and a light to my path" (Ps. 119:105). Interestingly, Jesus assumed ownership of being both the Word of God and the light of the world (John 1:1–3, 8:12). He is the Word who created light (John 1:1).

Symbolic of Jesus's twelve disciples and the twelve tribes of Israel is the table of shewbread, which consists of two sets of six loaves. The loaves were eaten only by the priest in the same way we study and assimilate the Bible or ingest the bread at Communion. Having consecrated themselves to the teaching and spiritual nourishment of Israel, the priests ate the holy bread to distribute it later in the form of teachings, sermons, counseling, and discipleship.

Positioned to the left of the golden lampstand and to the right of the table of shewbread was the altar of incense. It performed a critical function; special gums (which no one could burn or duplicate on the pains of death) were burned on its altar, which always represented the prayer and supplications of God's people. As the holy smoke wafted its way upward to God, the sinner would receive assurance that his petition was being addressed by a patient, loving, and caring God. The altar also received the droplets of blood that the priest sprinkled on it. Both the blood and the altar are symbolic of Christ. The blood of the sacrifice represents the spotless blood of Christ and the altar his broken body, always a symbol of mercy.

While other Levites assisted the high priest in his ministry, only he could officiate and function as our intermediary. "Then I turned to see the voice that spoke with me. And having turned I saw seven golden lampstands, and in the midst of the seven lampstands One like the Son of Man, clothed with a garment down to the feet and girded about the chest with a golden band" (Rev. 1:12–13). Jesus is attired as our High Priest in the sanctuary in heaven. He officiates there as our intercessor before God.

Aren't you glad that the One who walked in our shoes, slept in our bed, wore a human body, and understands our pain is our mediator? That should encourage us to take all that ails us to him in prayer. Jesus, a member of the human race, is our High Priest. Think about it. Thank you, God Almighty. Glory! Hallelujah! Jesus is our High Priest. Have you confessed everything to him? Are you holding back any sin in your bosom, in your closet? If you confess it, he will forgive it.

October 22

In His Sanctuary Part 3

And they brought Him to a place called Golgotha which is translated, Place of a Skull . . . And when they crucified Him, they divided His garments, casting lots for them to determine what every man should take.

—Mark 15:22, 24

The outer court of the sanctuary, with its wide courtyard, completely surrounds the tent of meetings and represents Calvary. It is the busiest part of the sanctuary. Upon entry into the outer court, two items of furniture are visible: the laver and the altar of burnt offering. The laver is a basin in which the high priest takes a ritual washing to symbolize his cleansing from sin. In the outer court, all the sacrifices are offered and eventually burned on the altar. All officiating priests must wash themselves before performing their duties.

After the priest's ritual washing, sinner X walks into the sanctuary with his lamb on his shoulders. Before the beast is tied up, the sinner confesses his sins on the head of the innocent lamb. Assistant Y to high priest Z hands sinner X a knife, and he proceeds to take the life of the innocent animal. Priest Y collects the blood and hands it over to high priest Z, who goes into the holy place and sprinkles some droplets on the altar of incense. The carcass of the lamb is then prepared for the burning, and as the smoke wafts upward to God, the sinner is forgiven, and his sins are transferred to the most holy place.

This activity continues throughout the day. Moreover, worshippers with high socioeconomic standing offer bulls, reflective of their affluence, while the poor utilize lambs and turtledoves, and the poorest of the poor offer fine flour (Lev. 5:11). Interestingly, God accepts the offerings of his people as long as they are accompanied by confession, genuine repentance, and forsaking of all sins (1 John 1:9).

It is by no coincidence that Jesus, our Lord, functions in all three aspects of the sanctuary transaction. "For He made Him who knew no sin to be sin for us, that we might become the righteousness of God in Him" (2 Cor. 5:21). On that fateful Thursday night, the entire sin of past, present, and future generations were laid on the Savior. He took our place at the execution block while we gained life through his death. Christ was treated as a sinner and punished as one to satisfy God's righteous law.

Being the symbol of every lamb slain from Adam to the cross, Jesus willingly submitted himself as the sacrifice for our sins. "The next day John saw Jesus coming toward him, and said, 'Behold! The Lamb of God'" (John 1:29). Because Jesus was the slain Lamb even before the foundation of the world, we find forgiveness in him when we confess and forsake our sins. "For it is not possible that the blood of bulls and goats could take away sins" (Heb. 10:4). No blood of angels or any other intelligent creature could portray God's amazing love for his wayward children.

Having completed the function of sinner and lamb, Jesus now officiates as our High Priest in the sanctuary in heaven. "We have such a High Priest who is seated at the right hand of the throne of the Majesty in the heavens" (Heb. 8:1). The earthly sanctuary was a visual aid in describing how God takes care of sin, but after the resurrection of Jesus, he ascended to heaven, where he now stands officiating on our behalf. "If we confess our sins He is faithful and just to forgive our sins and cleanse us from all unrighteousness" (1 John 1:9). Have you confessed everything to him? Everything?

October 23

The Firstfruits

Speak to the children of Israel, and say to them:
when you come into the land which I give to you, and reap its harvest, then you shall bring a sheaf of the first fruit of your harvest to the priest.
—Leviticus 23:10

The wheat crop was healthy and bountiful, more than farmer Simeon expected, but he dared not harvest the crop before choosing a few choice sheaves for the wave offering. This ritual was designed to impress on the mind that God is the Creator and Sustainer of all things and deserves the first and the best of everything we possess. "And you shall remember the Lord your God, for it is He who gives you power to get wealth, that He may establish His covenant which He swore to your fathers, as it is this day" (Deut. 8:18).

Every Old Testament ritual, including the law of the firstfruits, was filled with rich illustrative and symbolic meaning, depicting God's sovereignty over nature and our lives. Obedience to this principle of putting God first and foremost would not only banish selfishness but also establish God in his rightful place as Lord and Savior of our lives. The firstfruits ordinance has a much broader meaning that transcends its agricultural symbolism. "But now Christ is risen from the dead, and has become the first-fruit of those who have fallen asleep" (1 Cor. 15:20). In much the same way, the firstfruits of the crop represent a greater harvest to come; likewise, the resurrection of Jesus Christ is symbolic of the spectacular resurrection of all believers who have fallen asleep in Jesus. "For this we say to you by the word of the Lord, that we who are alive and remain until the coming of the Lord will by no means precede those who are asleep. For the Lord Himself will descend from heaven with a shout, with the voice of the archangel, and with the trumpet of God, and the dead in Christ will rise first. Then we who alive and remain shall be caught up together with them in the clouds to meet the Lord in the air. And thus we shall always be with the Lord" (1 Thess. 4:15–17).

It's interesting to note that Paul referred to the sleeping saints as "the dead in Christ." Yes, they are very much dead and not in heaven as some erroneously assume. Because they are dead and asleep in their graves awaiting the call of the Life Giver, that's the reason for the great resurrection. After all, if they were already in heaven, what's a resurrection for? Christ will resurrect the dead saints and translate the living.

Many have been resurrected in both the Old and the New Testaments, only to die again, but candidates of the resurrection, which Paul referenced in the above text to the Thessalonians, will never die again. It is also noteworthy to point out that many were resurrected from their graves at the death of Christ. Could they have been part of a special resurrection? "Then behold, the veil of the temple was torn in two from top to bottom; and the earth quaked, and rocks were split, and the graves were opened; and many bodies of the saints who had fallen asleep were raised; and coming out of the graves after His resurrection, they went into the holy city and appeared to many" (Matt. 27:51–53).

Which would you prefer, being raised from the dead or personally witnessing the Second Coming of Jesus Christ? Either one is fine with me. I just want to be with my Lord. Let us make every effort to be among the saved.

October 24

No Deceptions, Period

But let your Yes be Yes, and your No, No.
For whatever is more than these is from the evil one.
—Matthew 5:37

The black drongo bird of the African plain has perfected many different calls, some of which he uses to trick his neighbors to his advantage. While feeding, his noisy meerkat neighbors always post a guard to detect danger from land and sky. When the meerkats stumble on a feast, which usually includes tasty scorpions and delicious beetle larvae, sensing his opportunity, the drongo lets out a warning call identical to the meerkats' guard, which sends everyone scrambling to the underground den for safety. In the wake of their hasty departure, the drongo feasts on their lunch undisturbed. Upon reentry to the surface, the lookout guard seems puzzled that the colony fled with no apparent danger in sight. They don't have to look very far. The drongo is suffering the after-effects of a hasty meal and a full stomach. The drongo's tactics is equivalent to crying "fire" in a crowded theatre and then swooping in to pick up the gold chains and wallets once the crowd has bolted for the exits.

That may be perfectly legal and legitimate for the drongo and all other animals practicing deception to earn a living, but it is illegal, forbidden, and ungodly for us. Because we answer to a higher authority and are ambassadors for Christ to the world, we must be scrupulously honest in our dealings with our fellow men. The Bible does not gloss over the sins of its heroes; it records their foibles as they happened. It neither justifies nor condones their sins but records them that we may take heed as we walk in Christ.

Besides Jesus, who is our supreme example and didn't sin even by a wink of the eye, the life of Daniel stands out. "So the governors and satraps sought to find some charge against Daniel concerning the kingdom; but they could find no charge or fault, because he was faithful; nor was there error or fault found in him. Then these men said, 'We shall not find any charge against this Daniel unless we find it against him concerning the law of his God'" (Dan. 6:4–5). May this be said about all of us; after all, the same grace that was available to Daniel is also available to us.

Respect others' property. Another example of sterling integrity under fire shines forth in the character of Joseph. "And it came to pass after these things that his master's wife cast longing eyes on Joseph, and she said, 'Lie with me.' But he refused and said to his master's wife, 'Look, my master does not know what is with me in the house, and he has committed all that he has to my hand. There is no one greater in this house than I, nor has he kept back anything from me but you, because you are his wife. How can I do this great wickedness, and sin against God?'" (Gen. 39:7–9). What a man! What integrity!

God has never abandoned his faithful children when under attack by Satan, and he will move heaven and earth to ensure corresponding strength is available to us for the trial. However, he cannot stop us from sinning if we are intent on doing wrong. "Let no one say when he is tempted, I am tempted by God; for God cannot be tempted by evil, nor does He Himself tempt anyone. But each one is tempted when he is drawn away by his own desires and enticed. Then, when desire is conceived, it gives birth to sin; and sin when it is full-grown, brings forth death" (James 1:13–15). May God help us as we aspire to live exemplary lives as Daniel and Joseph.

October 25

Others May, but We Can't

Whoever abides in Him does not sin.
Whoever sins has neither seen Him nor known Him . . .
Whoever has been born of God does not sin, for His seed remains in him;
and he cannot sin because he has been born of God.
—1 John 3:6, 9

Jerry (name changed) is choking his old sinful nature by the minute. He simply cannot muster the will to have another drink; somehow it doesn't have the zing, nor does it appeal to him anymore. Something is happening inside of him, and it is called conversion. Jerry is a burly construction worker, and it was not unusual for him to spend long afternoons at the neighborhood bar sipping drinks until his face begins to turn red, but thanks to his praying mom and a rude awakening, Jerry has had a change of heart and of lifestyle. The swirling purple and red lights of a cop's car resulted in multiple drunk-driving tickets and several hundreds of dollars in fines. Rehabilitation classes were not free either, but they have given Jerry a new impetus to change his reckless lifestyle. Set on his new course, Jerry dismisses the urges to the bar and all the trouble associated with it. He wonders what took him so long.

"Whoever abides in Him does not sin. Whoever sins has neither seen Him nor known him" (1 John 3:6). After coming to faith in Christ, the believer does not intentionally continue in sin. The Holy Spirit ensures this by providing a clear alternative to a life of sin. He initiates a new and wonderful package filled with goodly things ready to be opened by the believer. In exchange for the fleshly lust, which hounded the Jerry of old, the new Jerry now snacks on delicious fruits. "But the fruit of the spirit is love, joy, peace, longsuffering, kindness, goodness, faithfulness, gentleness, self-control" (Gal. 5:22–23). And who in their right mind would go back to taste the sour grapes of nicotine, alcohol, gambling, and idol worship of every kind? Embedded in the believer's package are all these tasty virtues, including the one Jerry lacked initially, self-control. By abiding in Christ, we are partakers of all the fruits of the Spirit, which enable us to walk circumspectly in Jesus Christ.

These juicy fruits do not grant us blanket immunity from temptation; we must constantly battle the old fleshly lust that comes calling every once in a while. "But put on the Lord Jesus Christ, and make no provision for the flesh, to fulfill its lusts" (Rom. 13:14). However, Jerry must be alert and ready to say no when the drinking urge pops up; dwelling on previous experiences with alcohol will only revive the old habit of the past. We shouldn't romanticize sin or daydream about it.

But we all have our Achilles' heel, and it varies from one person to another. One must know his strengths and weaknesses and must remain on Christ's turf while avoiding the devil's playground. In essence, while sinners may enjoy sinning and look forward to it, we can't. The Spirit of God will not allow us to enjoy sin. Sin is breaking God's law. Should we enjoy breaking God's law of grace and liberty? Of course not, a resounding no. "What shall we say then? Shall we continue in sin that grace may abound? Certainly not! How shall we who died to sin live any longer in it?" (Rom. 6:1–2).

October 26

Is God Still Speaking Today?

God who at various times and in various ways spoke in time past to the father by the prophets, has in these last days spoken to us by His Son, whom He has appointed heir of all things, through whom also He made the worlds.

—Hebrews 1:1–2

Having squandered earlier opportunities to turn his nation around and staring disaster in the face, a vacillating king Zedekiah inquired, "Is there any word from the Lord?" Here is someone who has been regularly receiving God's instruction, through his prophet Jeremiah. "But neither he nor his servants nor the people of the land gave heed to the words of the Lord which He spoke by the prophet Jeremiah" (Jer. 37:2).

Our day and age are typical of biblical times. Nothing has changed very much except our clothes, toys, and gadgets. Exploitation of the poor by the rich continues, and the strong crush the weak and mightily oppress them. Capitalists express little interest in their employees beyond the little payment they dole out to them, much of which are inadequate at best to cover their living expenditures, let alone save for a rainy day. But God is watching with keen interest and is about to act. "Come now, you rich, weep and howl for your miseries that are coming upon you! Your riches are corrupted, and your garments are moth-eaten. Your gold and your silver are corroded, and their corrosion will be a witness against you and will eat your flesh like fire. You have heaped up treasure in the last days. Indeed the wages of the laborers who mowed your fields, which you kept back by fraud, cry out; and the cries of the reapers have reached the ears of the Lord of Sabaoth" (James 5:1–4).

It may appear that God is silent about the apparent chaos and dysfunction of society, but he is very much active and wise in his governance. He is giving everyone a fair opportunity at salvation. "For this is good and acceptable in the sight of God our Savior, who desires all men to be saved and come to a knowledge of the truth" (1 Tim. 2:3–4). God is not going to turn the tables around or reverse the trend of society. He continues extending opportunities to everyone to embrace the waves of grace and mercy. He is very much in control.

God has never abandoned the planet he created, nor has he failed to leave communication channels open for dialogue with mankind. In times past, he communicated with his people through dreams, visions, and the personal appearance of Jesus in the flesh, but now he speaks to us through his Word, the Bible. "The grass withers the flowers fades, but the word of God abides forever" (Isa. 40:8).

Do we want to hear God's voice? Really?

> Then He said, "Go out, and stand on the mountain before the Lord." And behold, the Lord passed by, and a great and strong wind tore into the mountains and broke the rocks in pieces before the Lord, but the Lord was not in the wind; and after the wind an earthquake, but the Lord was not in the earthquake; and after the earthquake a fire, but the Lord was not in the fire; and after the fire a still small voice. So it was, when Elijah heard it, that he wrapped his face in his mantle and went out and stood in the entrance of the cave. Suddenly a voice came to him, and said, "What are you doing here, Elijah?" (1 Kings 19:11–13).

God's voice is still soft and tender to his people, and as always, it can be heard through your conscience. Can you hear his voice today? Are you still listening? What are you doing about it?

October 27

Enduring the Storm

But he who endures unto the end the same shall be saved.

—Matthew 24:13

They saw the Allied planes flying overhead, heard bombs falling nearby, and heard the sound of liberating gunfire coming ever closer to their camp. But many could not hold on; they slipped into silence just minutes before liberation. On July 23, 1944, Soviet forces liberated Majdanek, followed by the British liberation of Bergen-Belsen, and then U.S. forces liberated Buchenwald and Dachau. Horrified by what they found, the Allies immediately embarked on a campaign to save as many inmates as they could. But some were too malnourished; they died of starvation even as the abundance of food overran the camp. They were so close to being saved, but their emaciated bodies were beyond recovery and did not permit them to survive (Jewish Virtual Library).

Are we feeling the turbulence of the approaching storm? Absolutely. When a monster storm is approaching, fishermen secure their boats to safe heavens. Merchants board up their stores. Shoppers stockpile on necessities. Cruise liners get out of the way. Thousands of flights in the path of the storm are cancelled. Even the U.S. Navy takes evasive action in securing its ships to safer waters. Weather forecasters remain at their jobs for the duration of the storm, informing the public of the safest course of action.

The Bible has been accurate in predicting the rise and fall of empires and has given a detailed account of our looming storm. However, it is not the aim of God and the prophets to terrify us with bad news. Knowing the future, God reveals events long before the calamity occurs. "I beheld the earth, and indeed it was without form, and void; and the heavens they had no light. I beheld the mountains, and indeed they trembled, and all the hills moved back and forth. I beheld, and indeed there was no man, and all the birds of the heavens had fled. I beheld and indeed the fruitful land was a wilderness, and all its cities were broken down at the presence of the Lord" (Jer. 4:23–26). John and other apocalyptic (last day events) prophets saw the same event and described it in familiar language. "I looked and when He opened the sixth seal, and behold, there was a great earthquake, and the sun became black as sackcloth of hair and the moon became like blood. And the stars of heaven fell to the earth, as a fig tree drops its late figs when it is shaken by a mighty wind. Then the sky receded as a scroll when it is rolled up, and every mountain and island was moved out of its place" (Rev. 6:12–14).

These events will precede the Second Coming of Jesus Christ to this earth. And as sure as the earth is beneath our feet, these signs will come to pass just as the Bible predicts. This leads us to the all-important question: how do we get ready and stay ready for the approaching storm? First, we must be securely fastened to Jesus, for everything that can be shaken will be shaken. Second, we must be plugged into his Word for our daily nourishment and be tuned into the Holy Spirit, which is our only sure footing during the storm. "For in the time of trouble He shall hide me in His pavilion; in the secret place of His tabernacle He shall hide me; He shall set me high upon a rock" (Ps. 27:5). The formula for being ready has not changed with the passage of time; read your Bible, pray for the infilling of the Holy Spirit, and stay busy working in God's vineyard, and you will be ready.

October 28

Ask for It

And I will pray the Father, and He will give you another Helper, that He may abide with you forever.

—John 14:16

Having suffered the indignity of being without electricity during last year's terrible winter storm, Steve is well prepared this year. He has invested in a generator, but it comes at a cost. Besides being noisy and expensive, there is the ever-present danger of carbon monoxide poisoning if the generator is placed in the house or too close to it, but the benefits are quite rewarding. He can relax in comfort during winter's chilly days without the hassle of waiting on the power brokers to hook him on to the power source.

Did you know there is a greater power to be had as the believer begins to grow in Christ? Are you also aware that this power will not fall indiscriminately like rain but must be requested?

> Ask, and it will be given to you: seek, and you will find; knock, and it will be opened to you. For everyone who asks receives, and he who seeks finds, and to him who knocks it will be opened. For what man is there among you who, if his son asks for bread, will give him a stone? Or if he asks for a fish, will give him a serpent? If you then being evil, know how to give good gifts to your children, how much more will your Father in heaven give good things to those who ask Him! (Matt. 7:7–11)

The population explosion of modern times far outpaces our modest ability to spread the gospel to the entire world. We most definitely stand in need of the power of the Holy Spirit to empower the body of believers into action. "Behold, I send the Promise to My Father upon you; but tarry in the city of Jerusalem until you are endued with power from on high" (Luke 24:49). Just as a motor vehicle lays dormant and immobile in our driveway until we turn on the ignition switch, likewise, we remain dormant, powerless, and ineffective until we receive the power of the Holy Spirit.

If you are being impressed to reach your neighbor, friend, spouse, or family member for Christ, this qualifies you to pray for a refreshing of the Holy Spirit. "But you shall receive power when the Holy Spirit has come upon you; and you shall be witnesses to Me in Jerusalem, and in all Judea and Samaria, and to the end of the earth" (Acts 1:8). Any desire to witness for Christ is a gentle nudging from the Holy Spirit.

Language, nationalism, lack of resources, and other obstacles are easily overcome by the Spirit's power. "And there were dwelling in Jerusalem Jews, devout men, from every nation under heaven. And when this sound occurred, the multitude came together and were confused, because everyone heard them speak in his own language. Then they were all amazed and marveled, saying to one another, 'Look are not all these who speak Galileans?'" (Acts 2:5–7).

When we commit our lives and our resources to God's service, he will move mountains out of our way. We cannot take anything for granted; we must implore God every day for a fresh baptism of the Holy Spirit. "And it shall come to pass afterward that I will pour out My Spirit on all flesh; your sons and your daughters shall prophesy, and your old men shall dream dreams, your young men shall see visions. And also on My menservants and on My maidservants I will pour out My Spirit in those days" (Joel 2:28–29). Are you praying for the Spirit's refreshing in your life each day?

October 29

Submission to God's Will

> Then Jonathan, Saul's son arose and went to David in the woods and strengthened his hand in God. And he said to him, "Do not fear, for the hand of Saul my father shall not find you. You shall be king over Israel, and I shall be next to you. Even my father Saul knows that."
>
> —1 Samuel 23:16–17

In a clear message of defiance, over thirty-five thousand marathoners chanting the "Boston strong" slogan would attempt to cross the finish line of this year's marathon. But the true spirit of magnanimity to the city was already displayed when the Red Sox dedicated their championship trophy to the city and its residents. Recalling the events of that awful bombing, the very best of the human spirit was on full display to the world as neighbors, doctors, bystanders, and first responders put aside their own agenda and rushed in to help mend broken bones and wounded spirits.

We don't have to look very far to find someone in dire distress. Upon learning that his best friend, David, had been anointed by God to be king over Israel, Prince Jonathan—heir to the same throne—unselfishly threw his full support behind the future kinship of David, to the chagrin of his father, Saul. "Then Saul's anger was aroused against Jonathan and he said to him, 'You son of a perverse, and rebellious woman! Do I not know that you have chosen the son of Jesse to your own shame and to the shame of your mother's nakedness? For as long as the son of Jesse lives on the earth, you shall not be established, nor your kingdom'" (1 Sam. 20:30–31).

Jonathan's submission to the will of God reflects a decision made by the preincarnate Christ before the foundation of the world was laid. "Sacrifice and offering You did not desire, but a body You have prepared for Me. In burnt offering and sacrifices for sin You had no pleasure. Then I said, behold, I have come, in the volume of the book it is written of Me, to do your will O my God" (Heb. 10:5–7).

The will of God called for a rescue operation of the planet even before the earth was created. Jesus willingly volunteered at great risk to himself. Lying aside his immense frame and compressing his divinity into a tiny human body, Jesus subjected himself to both Roman and Jewish laws and died in our place. Besides subjecting himself to human authority, his daily routine involved submitting to and fulfilling the Father's will, which is the reconciliation of a rebellious planet with the family of God.

Nearing the end of his mission on earth, the Savior's face was irrevocably set toward the cross. His humanity shuddered and shrank from the task ahead, but his Spirit prevailed. "O my Father, if this cup cannot pass away from Me unless I drink it, Your will be done" (Matt. 26:42). Thank you, Jesus, for complying with your Father's will; even when your body was revolting against the cross, you remained focused on our salvation. Thank you so much.

When we accept Jesus into our lives as Lord and Savior, we submit every member of our anatomy to him, including our will. His will becomes our will. Every day we must prayerfully reflect the aspiration of Jesus while he was here on earth. "For I have come down from heaven, not to do My own will but the will of Him who sent Me" (John 6:38). Have you made God's will your top priority? I did. Have you?

October 30

Ransom Paid in Blood

And they sang a new song, saying:
You are worthy to take the scroll and to open its seals; for You were slain, and have redeemed us to God by Your blood out of every tribe and tongue and people and nation.

—Revelation 5:9

A thriving, grotesque business was in operation in the Horn of Africa. Pirates seized unsuspecting ships at will, held their crew hostage, and demanded a hefty ransom for their release. To their utter misfortune, they hijacked a ship with an American captain in command. What usually ended up in a quiet exchange of cash for hostages by less able nations became a full-blown international crisis once a U.S. national was involved.

An elite team of Navy SEALs was secretly dispatched to the troubled area and made quick work of the pirates. A relieved and tired captain Richard Phillips was delighted to see the American insignia emblazoned on the SEALs uniform. They pledge allegiance to the commander in chief of the United States Army and will go anywhere, anytime to do the nation's bidding (mobile.nytimes.com/2009/04/13/world/africa/13pirates.html).

Sin, instigated by Satan, is holding humanity hostage. A little baby who could very well be the inventor of a medicine to cure and eliminate cancer is himself afflicted with the disease. A husband walks off on his family in pursuit of a greener pasture. A hardworking senior who saved prudently for retirement is swindled of her life's savings by a smooth-talking con artist. A teen from a gated community has to be institutionalized for cocaine addiction. These heart-wrenching stories are real and happen to real people. They happen to neighbors, friends, coworkers, and even to family members.

But what does the hijacker want? What are his demands? "I will ascend into heaven, I will exalt my throne above the stars of God; I will also sit on the mount of the congregation on the farthest sides of the north; I will ascend above the heights of the clouds, I will be like the Most High" (Isa. 14:13–14). The creature who wanted his Creator's job was ousted from his position in heaven and has become a menace to society and the world. Do you know at this very moment he may be knocking at your door?

"Therefore rejoice, O heavens, and you who dwell in them! Woe to the inhabitants of the earth and the sea! For the devil has come down to you, having great wrath, because he knows that he has a short time" (Rev. 12:12). Having been dealt a mortal blow at Calvary, Satan is as a wounded wild beast on a mission to destroy as many lives as he possibly can. "Be sober be vigilant; because your adversary the Devil walks about like a roaring lion, seeking whom he may devour" (1 Pet. 5:8).

We have nothing to fear because Satan has been defeated, and the price of our ransom has been paid in full by the blood of Jesus Christ. We are redeemed. Thank God Almighty because we have been redeemed. All that is required of us is to hold on firmly to Jesus. "Abide in Me, and I in you. As the branch cannot bear fruit of itself, unless it abides in the vine, neither can you, unless you abide in Me" (John 15:4).

Since the ransom has been paid, God jealously guards his people, and none can be lost except by his or her own choice. "Those whom You gave Me I have kept; and none of them is lost except the son of perdition, that the Scripture might be fulfilled" (John 17:12). The outcome of our salvation is sure. Jesus has won the conflict.

October 31

The Double Portion

And so it was, when they had crossed over, that Elijah said to Elisha, Ask! What may I do for you, before I am taken away from you? Elisha said, Please let a double portion of your spirit be upon me.

—2 Kings 2:9

He could have asked to be famous and to be powerful; that too followed, but he asked to be equipped with power to continue the great work his master started. Elisha was divinely appointed to be the mouthpiece of God to the nation as his master's ministry was drawing to a close, but there was one final test for the young prophet-elect. What would the rookie prophet ask for?

The prophet Elijah was a dynamic leader and an excellent orator who challenged adulterous Israel to turn back to God. Elijah's résumé was impressive, but none of that mattered to Elisha; he just wanted to do God's will with the same zeal and dynamism that accompanied his master, Elijah. By requesting a double portion of Elijah's spirit, Elisha demonstrated his zeal for God and his kingdom, and nothing short of the dynamic power that accompanied Elijah would satisfy him.

Elisha, however, got more than he requested. "Then he took the mantle of Elijah which had fallen from him, and struck the water and said, 'Where is the Lord God of Elijah?' And when he struck the water, it was divided this way and that; and Elisha crossed over" (2 Kings 2:14). Make no mistake about it; it was not

Elijah who granted the request. God stands ready with package in hand to give to those who ask.

> On that night God appeared to Solomon, and said to him, ask! What shall I give you? . . . Now give me wisdom and knowledge that I may go out and come in before this people; for who can judge this great people of yours? Then God said to Solomon: because this was in your heart and you have not asked riches or wealth or honor or the life of your enemies, nor have you asked long life, but have asked wisdom and knowledge for yourself, that you may judge My people over whom I have made you king. Wisdom and knowledge are granted you; and I will give you riches and wealth and honor, such as none of the kings have had who were before you, nor shall any after you have the like. (2 Chron. 1:7, 10–12)

Priority matters in God's work where there is a determination to work hard in the Master's vineyard. God never fails in granting the necessary resources to undertake the gospel-preaching assignment. Stories abound of simple laypeople who simply wanted to do God's will in an exceptional way, and God overlooked their lack of formal education and granted them above and beyond what they requested.

What are you praying for these days—a new sports car, a fat bank portfolio, more shoes and toys? God laments over these prayers. "If my people who are called by my name will humble themselves, and pray and seek My face and turn from their wicked ways, then I will hear from heaven, and will forgive their sin and heal their land" (2 Chron. 7:14).

It cannot be overemphasized; we need to talk and pray very often about God drenching us with his Holy Spirit. Pray for it morning, noon, and night. God is more willing to give to us than we are willing to ask. Ask and you shall receive.

November 1

Comfort in the Psalms

How lovely is Your tabernacle, O Lord of host! My soul longs, yes, even faints for the courts of the Lord;
my heart and my flesh cry out for the living God.

—Psalm 84:1–2

The Psalms are a collection of songs, testimonies, thanksgiving, and heart-wrenching experiences of God's people. The book was composed of songs by multiple authors, with David being its main contributor. Like us, the psalmists were battered and buffeted by life's storms, and they were inspired by God to edit their experiences so that we may profit from them. Were they discouraged? Oh yes. Did they have bad days? Yes, of course. Were they ever overwhelmed by their weakness? Yes, but they conquered in the end. Were they ever depressed? Yes. Can you detect depression here? "Why are you cast down, O my soul? And why are you disquieted within me? Hope in God; for I shall yet praise Him, the help of my countenance and my God" (Ps. 43:5).

When trials and troubles roll in like the waves of the ocean, what better place to find refuge than in the secure arms of the Almighty.

> The Lord is my light and my salvation; whom shall I fear? The Lord is the strength of my life; of whom shall I be afraid? When the wicked came against me to eat up my flesh, my enemies and foes, they stumbled and fell. Though an army may encamp against me, my heart shall not fear; though war may rise against me in this I will be confident. One thing I have desired of the Lord that I will seek: that I may dwell in the house of the Lord all the days of my life, to behold the beauty of the Lord. (Ps. 27:1–4)

It is refreshing to know that we can keep our focus on Jesus, even when waves of trouble and perplexities come crashing at our feet. David was constantly outnumbered by his enemies and continuously watched by Saul's spies. How did he survive his enemies' constant harassment? "I waited patiently for the Lord; and He inclined to me . . . He also brought me up out of a horrible pit, out of the miry clay and set my feet upon a rock and established my steps" (Ps. 40:1–2).

No trial or affliction takes God by surprise; he has seen it all, he knows all about us, and he is waiting to unleash legions of angels at our request. "Many are the afflictions of the righteous, but the Lord delivers him out of them all" (Ps. 34:19). God knows how to deliver us from trouble, but he cannot prevent us from being tempted. We all must choose to deny the sins of the flesh and live a life pleasing to God.

We would miss the beauty of the Psalms if we fail to mention how the psalmists, with the help of God, turned tragedy into triumph, weeping into joy, and defeat into victory. David suffered horrendous family loss, but his faith in God never wavered. The sons of Korah witnessed their rebellious father being swallowed up by a sinkhole in a failed rebellion, but they were spared, thanks to the justice of God. They went on to write Psalms. "The son shall not bear the guilt of the father, nor the father bear the guilt of the son. The righteousness of the righteous shall be upon himself, and the wickedness of the wicked shall be upon himself" (Ezek. 18:20). They looked forward to that great day when pain and suffering would be no more. "Weeping may endure for a night but joy comes in the morning" (Ps. 30:5). *Night* here can be classified as everything that could go wrong in this life, but there is the joy of resurrection morning when this old body will give way to a glorious immortal body, when we will live eternally with God, our Maker. Comfort ye, my people.

November 2

The Coming Kingdom

You watch while a stone was cut out without hands, which struck the image on its feet of iron and clay, and broke them in pieces.

—Daniel 2:34

A flash of light followed by a sonic boom exploded over the Russian skies, setting off alarms in automobiles, shattering windows, damaging buildings, and injuring 1,200 people. What made it more interesting is that it was caught on film, and real people suffered injuries (www.pbs.org/newshour/rundown/fireballs-crash-to-earth-after-meteorite-streaks-across-russian-skies). It was not the rock of Nebuchadnezzar's dream; it was but a mere meteorite. When the rock referenced in the book of Daniel is unleashed, it will demolish the earth's civilization, wipe out its evil occupants, and usher in God's eternal kingdom of peace.

The ancients placed tremendous value and importance on dreams; they believe the gods communicated with them through such medium. God used precisely the same mode of operation to inform the pharaoh of his part in the divine plan. "And Pharaoh said to Joseph, I have had a dream, and there is no one who can interpret it. But I have heard it said of you that you can understand a dream, to interpret it" (Gen. 41:15). Joseph then recognized why he was dragged down to Egypt as he unfolded God's plan to the heathen monarch. "This is the thing which I have spoken to Pharaoh. God has shown Pharaoh what He is about to do" (Gen. 41:28).

God's dream to the pharaoh called for a shelter to the Israelites from a withering famine, while in Nebuchadnezzar's dream a big stick was given to Babylon to smack a backsliding Israel down to its knees. However, Nebuchadnezzar's dream revealed much more to him than the demise of his kingdom, along with Medo-Persia, Greece, and Rome. It ushered in God's glorious reign of righteousness. Curious and notable in the vision of the metallic image is the stone (God's kingdom) crashing into the feet of the image, destroying it completely, and replacing it with an entirely new civilization.

We are living in the very toes of that image. "And as the toes of the feet were partly of iron and partly of clay, so the kingdom shall be partly strong and partly fragile . . . And in the days of these kings the God of heaven will set up a kingdom which shall never be destroyed; and the kingdom shall not be left to other people; it shall break in pieces and consume all these kingdoms, and it shall stand forever" (Dan. 2:42, 44).

God is building his kingdom with real people—people from every culture of the world. Some are becoming citizens of this kingdom even as you are reading this material. God utilizes the electronic media, the printed page, personal witnessing, and other methods we know nothing about in reaching the lost. He is inviting the willing to assist him in his worldwide movement to broadcast the good news of the everlasting gospel far and wide. "Go therefore and make disciples of all the nations, baptizing them in the name of the Father and the Son and the Holy Spirit teaching them to observe the things that I have commanded you and lo, I am with you always even to the end of the age" (Matt. 28:19–20). Are you up to the task? Are you a citizen of this kingdom? Do you have Jesus as your passport? Have you packed your bags yet? Ready to go? God bless you.

November 3

When Civil Disobedience Isn't a Crime

Then the king of Egypt spoke to the Hebrew midwives, of whom the name of one was Shiphrah and the name of the other Puah;
and he said, "When you do the duties of a midwife for the Hebrew woman, and see them on the birth stools, if it is a son, then you shall kill him;
but if it is a daughter then she shall live."

—Exodus 1:15–16

Civil laws are usually humane and well-intentioned toward the well-being of citizens. In modern times and even in wartime, laws call for the proper treatment of enemy prisoners. They must be fed, clothed, medicated, and not tortured. Even the most brutal and skeptical of the nations have added their signatures to humane laws and agree to uphold them. However, when these laws are flaunted and violated by the authorities, who should speak on behalf of the victims, who are on the receiving end of these atrocities? Should believers look the other way, not wanting to get involved in the prickly matters of state? "Evil flourishes when good people do nothing." "Not a sermon, just a thought" (Joshua Nozzi). Adolf Hitler was very happy when the church said nothing and did nothing while the Jews were systematically being exterminated.

Moses, Caleb, Joshua, Aaron, and others of their generation were the beneficiaries of the first civil act of disobedience done by midwives Shiphrah and Puah. They were told explicitly by the Egyptian monarch to abort Jewish boys in an effort to cap the fast-growing Jewish population. They stared the fat paychecks and enticing bonuses in the face, looked at each other, and decided simultaneously, "Thanks, but no thanks" (Exod. 1:15).

Followers of Jesus report to a higher authority as compared with their work buddies. We cannot facilitate, lend our support, or remain silent when programs or unjust laws discriminate against other humans on the basis of age, race, gender, nationality, or political affiliation. Therefore it is with much thought that we reveal to the powers that be; we can no longer stand idly by or participate in programs designed to discriminate against other humans. "But Peter and John answered and said to them, 'Whether it is right in the sight of God to listen to you more than to God, you judge'" (Acts 4:19). Of course, it is always safe and right to obey God rather than man. Wherever the laws of God and man come into conflict, we should never hesitate to put God first. "And Peter and the other apostles answered and said, 'We ought to obey God rather than men'" (Acts 5:29).

To those contemplating making a difference in the lives of others by standing up against injustice directed against the weak, old, voiceless, and oppressed, I say you have been chosen for this moment, and God is with you. You will be walking in the legacy of an extraordinary group of people who became great by refusing to go along with the status quo. They made a difference by challenging unjust long-standing laws, cultural taboos, and social norms. Abraham Lincoln took the gas out of institutionalized slavery and paid dearly with his life. Martin Luther King made us take a better look on who we are as a nation, and who can forget Rosa Parks, who stood up by sitting down?

As the salt of the earth, we are supposed to make a difference in the spot where we are placed. If there is no change in your office, school, neighborhood, or workplace, ask Jesus to make you salty and renew your first love before it's too late. "I counsel you to buy from me gold refined in the fire, that you may be rich; and white garments that you may be clothed, that the shame of your nakedness may not be revealed; and anoint your eyes with eye salve, that you may see" (Rev. 3:18). Make a difference where you are.

November 4

Tribute to Mother Eve

To the woman He said: I will multiply your sorrow and your conception; in pain you shall bring forth children; your desire shall be for your husband, and he shall rule over you.

—Genesis 3:16

She was a first-time mom eagerly awaiting the delivery date of her first child. What might the massive bulge in her belly yield? Could he be the messianic child spoken about by God in Genesis 3:15? Though driven from their Garden of Eden home, Adam and Eve were not abandoned by God. He continued being their spiritual advisor and teacher, talking to the first family face-to-face (Gen. 4:6–7). The Bible does state he came walking to them in the cool of the evening, something that seems to have been habitual (Gen. 3:8).

All mothers instinctively instruct their little girls in the delicate art of love, homemaking, and motherhood, and Eve was not different. Being the first human mom, she was specially equipped to teach her children all the lessons she learned at the feet of her divine Teacher. They were given the oral Word of God, the Bible, which they taught to their children. Listen to Eve's jubilant expression thinking she had conceived the Christ child they were promised. "I have acquired a man from the Lord" (Gen. 4:1). She must have had prior knowledge that a Savior would be born to save her, Adam, and the world.

Not enough tribute has been paid to Eve, our maternal grandmother. No more finger-pointing at the great and noble grandmother because she was deceived, but Adam was the intentional sinner. He was the one who fumbled the ball, and he was the one whom God called on to give an account of their misstep. Putting behind us the sad saga at the tree of knowledge of good and evil, let us pay some tribute to Mother Eve and give her the honor due to her motherhood.

Your grateful children—comprising many nations, tongues, and peoples—wish to express our thanks to you for the rich diversity in culture, race, and language you have given us. We do not see this as a barrier or an impediment but as a catalyst to know one another better and to be sensitive to the needs of others. The curiosity we inherited from you have led some in our midst to probe into the unknown; some have discovered new frontiers and cures for diseases, and others have invented incredible flying machines, which have opened up new ways of travel and communication to us. Your genes have enabled some of us to become legal scholars, instituting laws for the smooth functioning of the government and society.

Thanks for the wonderful feminine traits you passed on to women that influence and refine us all, for we do know that "the hand that rocks the cradle influences the throne." We see this principle at play in the presidency of Barack Obama and Abraham Lincoln, whose lives were influenced by their insightful mothers who kept their adrenaline for wisdom and knowledge ablaze. We thank God for using you as a channel to instill in us the very fine virtues that have enabled us to maintain healthy and happy relationships with our spouses and others over the years.

God created you specifically with the intent of giving birth to a wide diversity of children, including us living in the twenty-first century. After all, if all the trees of a forest were of one size, shape, or color, what beauty would there be in that? And if all the lovely roses were of one size, shape, or color, what beauty would there be in that? We thank God for you and eagerly look forward to meeting you and Grandpa Adam after we've had dinner with our Lord and Savior, Jesus Christ. Please meet us at the tree of life, where we can sample all the delicious fruits of the garden without any ill effects. With love, your earthly children.

November 5

Tribute to All Mothers

Who can find a virtuous wife? For her worth is far above rubies.
The heart of her husband safely trusts her; so he will have no lack of grain.
She does him good and not evil all the days of his life.

—Proverbs 31:10–12

Everyone believes it, but no one has said it with more emotion and conviction than Kevin Durant. In a moving MVP award ceremony, Durant departed from the formal protocol to focus the attention on the true MVP of his life, his mom. Choking words and fighting back tears, he thanked his mom for remaining hungry overnight so that he and his brother might have enough to eat. The wave of emotion, empathy, and sympathy aroused from this tribute has been monumental. Now advertisers are very interested in him and his mom to sell their brand of produce, but moms all through the ages and all over the world have been performing this unique innate behavior unrecognized by their society. Isn't it fitting for someone to pay tribute to moms for their heroics?

We give tribute to these magnificent moms past and present not because they married famous men but because their prudent heroics affected their societies and history in general. Tribute to you, great Grandmother Eve, mother of all living, for the privilege of being your sons and daughters. As the first lady of the race, you were adventurous, smart, savvy, beautiful, and creative. All that we are, we owe to you, dear mother, since you made significant contributions to our personality.

Tribute to Sarah, who gave hope to the barren. One can still do great things late in life after all; you became a mom at age ninety. Successful careers have been launched well into midlife because of your example. You gave us a good sense of humor so that we can laugh and poke fun at ourselves. You were beautiful in every respect, but what captivates us the most is the beauty of character resident in you. Rebekah, Rachel, Leah, and all subsequent mothers, as well as those having difficulty conceiving, hold you in high esteem.

Tribute to Miriam, the first female prophet of the Most High God, who led Israel in songs of triumph in the wilderness. "Then Miriam the prophetess, the sister of Aaron, took the timbrel in her hand; and all the women went out after her with timbrels and with dances. 'Sing to the Lord, for He has triumphed gloriously! The horse and its rider He has thrown into the sea'" (Exod. 15:20–21).

Tribute to Huldah, a contemporary of the prophet Isaiah and a relative of Jeremiah, who was a rock of stability and a teacher in Israel (2 Kings 22:14). Tribute to Deborah; when Barak, the military commander of Israel, got cold feet and refused to go into battle without the prophetess present, Deborah remarked, "No problem, I'll be there." Tribute to her for putting her life on the line for God's cause and the love of her nation (Judg. 4:8–9).

We give tribute to Ruth, who changed the map of the Middle East simply by being the great-great-grandmother of King David, the warrior king. "Entreat me not to live you, or turn back from following after you, for wherever you go, I will go; and wherever you lodge, I will lodge; your people shall be my people, and your God will be my God. Where you die, I will die, and there I will I be buried. The Lord do so to me, and more also, if anything but death parts you and me" (Ruth 1:16–17). We give tribute to Rahab, Tamar, the prophetess daughters of the evangelist Philip, and all the other famous women not mentioned here for lack of space; they are examples worthy of emulation. Give tribute to the woman in your life, will you?

November 6

Doing it God's Way

Then his brothers also went and fell down before his face, and they said, Behold, we are your servants. Joseph said to them, do not be afraid, for am I in the place of God?

—Genesis 50:18–19

Most victims of violent crimes are traumatized to the extent that they do not wish any future contact with their abuser. And that's their right, for no victim should be forced or coerced into doing it. However, others see in it a sense of closure and healing if the perpetrator expresses remorse and repentance. However, a tiny segment of victims has taken forgiveness to a higher level by meeting with the perpetrator in a controlled environment and allowing him to express remorse for his crime.

Joseph, son of Jacob's favorite wife, Rachel, was being groomed to take over leadership of the family's business. The brothers seethed in anger as Joseph related to them his dream that they would bow before him one day. He related to them another dream about the entire clan, including Mom and Pop, bowing before him and paying him homage. Jacob had seen enough. "So he told it to his father and his brothers; and his father rebuked him and said to him, 'What is this dream that you have dreamed? Shall your mother and I and your brothers indeed come to bow down to the earth before you?' And his brothers envied him but his father kept the matter in mind" (Gen. 37:10–11).

A sequence of events transpired in which Joseph was sold into slavery by his brothers. *That will effectively put an end to his dreams*, they thought, but even in slavery, Joseph continued to thrive until he became the prime minister of Egypt. A terrible famine struck the land, and his brothers came to buy grain to feed their households; Joseph recognized them and tested them for signs of genuine repentance. They (the elder brothers) passed an agonizing test, after which Joseph revealed to them that it was God's plan for the sequence of events to unfold as they did. "But as for you, you meant evil against me; but God meant it for good, in order to bring it about as it is this day, to save many people alive. Now therefore, do not be afraid; I will provide for you and your little ones. And he comforted them and spoke kindly to them" (Gen. 50:20–21).

Part of the healing process calls on the victim to forgive the perpetrator, and this is much easier said than done, but it comes from the One who designed the human body. "If your enemy is hungry, feed him; if he is thirsty, give him a drink; for in so doing you will heap coals of fire on his head. Do not be overcome by evil, but overcome evil with good" (Rom. 12:20–21). Jesus's way is totally and diametrically opposed to the ways of the world. Forgiveness may sound weak and foolish to some, but it is the best way to bring peace and redemption to the soul. Love always conquers hate. "You have heard that it was said, 'You shall love your neighbor and hate your enemy.' But I say unto you, love your enemies, bless those who curse you, do good to those who hate you, and pray for those who spitefully use you and persecute you'" (Matt. 5:43–44).

Hate destroys, but love always builds. Forgiveness helps the victim to move beyond the terrible experience; nonforgiveness sticks the victim to the past. Even when the wound is healed, the scar remains, and only God can bring relief and healing to the soul. Jesus forgave his enemies, so why can't you? Give it a try. Go and do likewise.

November 7

I Trust Your Judgment

Again, if two lie down together, they will keep warm;
but how can one be warm alone? Though one may be overpowered by another, two can withstand him. And a threefold cord is not quickly broken.
—Ecclesiastes 4:11–12

Janna had to attend special classes to conquer her fear of flying. Some are terrified of height, creepy critters, spiders, snakes, closed spaces, and large bodies of water. Others even fear barking dogs, but kind people and organizations have emerged to the rescue by helping people confront their fears and overcome them. Three things are important in overcoming fear: acknowledgement, confrontation, and conquering.

Acknowledgment is key to this venture. Therefore before Janna attempts to conquer her fear mountain, she must first acknowledge that she does need help in this area. While Janna has no problem admitting that she has fear of heights, she has difficulty accepting that she is a sinner. No one will admit being a sinner unless prompted by the Holy Spirit. It is contrary to our sinful nature to acknowledge our true standing before God, and this varies with each person. Some are very close to God and are enjoying a healthy relationship with their Maker, while others are on life support. If you are on life support spiritually (and that's where most of us are), let's take a fresh look at opening the door of our hearts to a familiar friend. "Behold, I stand at the door and knock. If anyone hears My voice and opens the door, I will come in to him and dine with him and he with Me" (Rev. 3:20). We may have read this text a thousand times before, but it is always inviting. Jesus desires intimacy with us. He longs to sit and dialogue with his children, but it's all up to us to swing open the door and let him in.

The U.S. Army is big on trust. At boot camp, soldiers work in a variety of settings to establish trust. They cooperate with one another in solving problems. Needless to say, their lives will depend on trusting one another's judgment. Janna might be nervous, but she must trust her instructor implicitly if she desires victory over her fear of flying. Likewise, we must put our absolute and complete trust in Christ. Is there any other way besides trusting in Christ? "So they rose early in the morning and went out into the Wilderness of Tekoa; and as they went out,

Jehoshaphat stood and said, 'Hear me, O Judah and you inhabitants of Jerusalem: believe in the Lord your God, and you shall be established; believe His prophets, and you shall prosper'" (2 Chron. 20:20). Belief and trust are twins in the Christian vocabulary; they are joined to the hip. Where you see one, the other is not far behind. Belief is more than an intellectual knowledge about God; it is trusting and obeying his Word. After all, the devil believes and trembles.

Confrontation is the hardest part in overcoming fear because it brings you into contact with whatever you are fearful of, and that's the part God enjoys. "When you pass through the waters, I will be with you; and through the rivers, they shall not overflow you. When you walk through the fire, you shall not be burned nor shall the flame scorch you. For I am the Lord your God, the Holy One of Israel" (Isa. 43:2–3). God is with you as you confront your fears.

Now claim your victory over whatever you may have been fearful of; Jesus has assured us that he will be with us every step of the way, including when that nauseating feeling punches you in the stomach. Mighty person of valor, God is with you. Do not fear.

November 8

Revival in the Land

And it shall come to pass afterward that I will pour out my Spirit on all flesh;
Your sons and your daughters shall prophesy, your old men shall dreams, your men shall see visions.

—Joel 2:28

The record-breaking winter has given way to a much-anticipated spring, and mayors around the nation are delighted. They can now rest comfortably at night without worrying about finding new funds for snow removal. Spring triggers explosive growth in buds eager to fill the landscape with their beautiful leaves and flowers. The birds too; those who did not migrate have a head start in carving up territories to attract mates. The animals time their family raising to coincide with the abundant spring buffet.

During biblical times, spring was a much-anticipated event; it brought torrential rain to stimulate the growth of agricultural crop. Livestock benefited from the abundant fresh green grass springing up everywhere. "Then I will give you the rain for your land in its season, the early rain and the latter rain, that you may gather in your grain, your new wine, and your oil. And I will send grass in your fields for your livestock, that you may eat and be filled" (Deut. 11:14–15). The early rain came at the end of March and the beginning of April. It moistened the earth, allowing seeds to crack open their kernels and sink their roots into the nutrient-rich soil.

Pentecost marked the pouring out of a different kind of rain. "When the Day of Pentecost had fully come, they were all with one accord in one place. And suddenly there came a sound from heaven as of a rushing mighty wind, and it filled the whole house where they were sitting" (Acts 2:1–2). Having sown the seed of the kingdom of God in the hearts of men during his earthly ministry, Jesus's promise of the Comforter was being fulfilled in the lives of the disciples on the day of Pentecost. Interestingly and by no coincidence, Jesus's promise coincides with another promise made several centuries ago. "And it shall come to pass afterward that I will pour My Spirit on all flesh; your sons and your daughters shall prophesy, your old men shall dream dreams, your young men shall see visions. And also on My menservants and on My maidservants I will pour out My Spirit in those days" (Joel 2:28–29).

Glorious were the results of the Pentecostal revival; the sick were healed, the dead were raised back to life, the demons were cast out, thousands were converted, and the church experienced prodigious growth. It is noteworthy to point out that conditions were met for the outpouring of the Holy Spirit at Pentecost. "These continued with one accord in prayer and supplication" (Acts 1:14). The disciples met continuously, praying and confessing their sins with fasting for the outpouring of the Holy Spirit. And when he came, he outfitted them for the task ahead. Are you praying and fasting for the outpouring of the Holy Spirit in your life, in your congregation, and on the worldwide church?

Lord, prepare us, and pour out your Spirit on our thirsty souls; let it moisten and crack the kernel of indifference that imprisons our love and dedication to you. I confess all my known sins. Give me strength to supplement my weakness. Here I am. Do with me what is best for your service. In Jesus's name, amen.

November 9

One Person, Two Natures

Then Saul sought to pin David to the wall with the spear, but he slipped away from Saul's presence; and he drove the spear into the wall.
So David fled and escaped that night.

—1 Samuel 19:10

Promotion one day and attempted assassination the next, all in a day's work for King Saul, bent on destroying his servant David. Ever since the killing of Goliath by David, Saul sensed a genuine threat to his throne and dynasty by the people's favorite, David. "So the women sang as they danced, and said: Saul has slain his thousands, and David his ten thousands. Then Saul was very angry, and the saying displeased him; and he said, 'They have ascribed to David ten thousands, and to me they have ascribed only thousands. Now what more can he have but the kingdom?' So Saul eyed David from that day forward" (1 Sam. 18:7–9). For the rest of his life, Saul spared no effort to kill David, who saved Israel from certain defeat—a job Saul should have done himself as commander of the Lord's army.

You may have heard the term "Jekyll and Hyde," which the *World English Dictionary* defines as a person with split personalities, one good and the other evil. Author Robert Louis Stevenson wrote a novel about these two interesting characters. Moreover, Paul's description of our dual nature comes very close to the Jekyll and Hyde character embedded in us.

> For I know that in me (that is, in my flesh) nothing good dwells; for to will is present with me, but how to perform what is good I do not find. For the good that I will to do, I do not do; but the evil I will not to do, that I practice. Now if I do what I will not to do, it is no longer I who do it, but sin that dwells in me. I find then a law, that evil is present with me, the one who wills to do good . . . But I see another law in my members, warring against the law of my mind, and bringing me into captivity to the law of sin which is in my members. (Rom. 7:18–21, 23)

Simply put, sin has created Jekyll and Hyde personalities in all of us, and only Jesus can deliver us from this evil nature. Our mood swings can be near catastrophic to the ones we love. Had it not been for the restraining power of Jesus in our lives, we would self-destruct. "O wretched man that I am! Who will deliver me from this body of death? I thank God through Jesus Christ our Lord! So then, with the mind I myself serve the law of God, but with the flesh the law of sin" (Rom. 7:24–25).

It is essential to know that the carnal nature (unconverted nature) is entirely controlled by Satan and will never by itself submit to God, but God has not left anyone to grope their way in thick darkness unassisted. "He has shown you, O man, what is good; and what does the Lord require of you but to do justly, to love mercy, and to walk humbly with your God?" (Mic. 6:8). Amazingly, God's nature in us gets the victory every time we submit to the small still voice of the Spirit, saying to us, "This is the way, walk in it" (Isa. 30:21). Cheer up. God has ensured victory for us in Christ Jesus. The weakest of us can overcome in his great strength.

November 10

Strength through Weakness

Yes, he struggled with the angel and prevailed; He wept, and sought favor from Him.
—Hosea 12:4

Even though he repented of his sins, the memory of his hideous past paralyzed him with fear. He couldn't go backward, and ahead of him, a danger was looming larger by the minute. Overwhelmed by fear and uncertainty, Jacob divided his family into two bands and hoped for the best while preparing for the worst. God, however, had one final test for his broken and penitent servant. He allowed the accuser, Satan, one last opportunity to prove the faithfulness of Jacob. With his back hunched and his head buried in his hands, Jacob turned to the only one who could relieve his pain and mental anguish. While in agonizing prayer, he felt a hand clutching his shoulder.

Mistaking the hand to be that of his brother, Esau, Jacob sprang into a fight that would change his life and destiny. In the thick cover of darkness, the two men fought fiercely and relentlessly, with neither one willing to accept defeat and surrender to the other. As night gave way to day, the assailant touched Jacob's hip and immediately disabled him, but Jacob tightened his grip firmer on his divine assailant. God tested the resolve of his wrestling partner a little bit more. "And He said, 'Let Me go, for the day breaks,' but he said, I will not let You go unless You bless me! So He said to him, what is your name? He said, Jacob. And He said, your name shall no longer be called Jacob, but Israel; for you have struggled with God and with men, and have prevailed" (Gen. 32:26–28).

Was God defeated? Of course not, but Jacob developed that night the overcoming faith that you and I will need to be victorious over sin in the flesh and cross over the finish line. Make no mistake about it; we all will be called to endure what the Bible calls "Jacob's trouble." To some, it might be sooner than they expect, but it represents a period of intense struggle with evil and great uncertainty before divine deliverance is granted. On a prophetic note, just before the return of Christ, when evil is at its zenith, when all the restraints that hold men's behavior in check expire, the wicked will attempt to destroy the righteous. Then God's people will have no other recourse but huddle themselves in prayer and supplication, earnestly requesting from God forgiveness for their sins.

"Then I saw another angel ascending from the east, having the seal of the living God. And he cried with a loud voice to the four angels to whom it was granted to harm the earth and the sea, saying, do not harm the earth, the sea, or the trees till we have sealed the servants of our God on their foreheads" (Rev. 7:2–3). The sealing process is ongoing now. God is putting his mark of ownership on the foreheads (minds) of his people. This means all likable sins will have been confessed and put away.

Jacob's name, which previously meant "deceiver," was changed to Israel; then he was transformed, and his weakness became his strength. His limp, a sign of his struggle with Christ, evoked sympathy and compassion from Esau, his brother, and the estranged brothers fell on each other's neck kissing and embracing. Is anything too hard for God?

Time is short. We all can see that the storm clouds of disasters long foretold are on us; we cannot cuddle unconfessed sins any longer. We must shore up our weak defenses and wrestle unrelentingly with God to make bulwarks from our weakness.

November 11

Jehovah Jireh, My Provider

And my God shall supply all your needs according to His riches in glory by Christ Jesus.

—Philippians 4:19

The arctic fox has developed ingenious methods of keeping himself well fed even in the lean months of winter. During the plentiful days of summer, when his favorite prey are nesting, he stocks his freezer with lots of their freshly laid eggs, but his supply never carries him all through the bitter days of winter. When his supply of eggs runs out, as it often does, he seeks out his neighbor the polar bear and shadows his every move at a safe distance. When the bear settles in at his dinner table, the fox patiently waits his turn, usually after the bear takes a nap; he sneaks in and eats his fill. Unlike other relationships that have mutual benefits, this one is completely one-sided; the bear does not need the fox since he is the sole boss at the top the food chain, but the fox needs the bear. God does not need us, but we sure do need him. We simply cannot exist without him.

"I know all the birds of the mountains, and the wild beasts of the field are Mine. If I were hungry, I would not tell you; for the world is Mine and all its fullness" (Ps. 50:11–12). It is from a heart flowing with gratitude for what Christ has done for us that we worship you, great God. You are our Creator and Provider, and we count it all joy to know and serve such a wonderful God as you. Who is a God like unto you?

You told us we should never worry about our needs because you are more willing to give than we are able to ask, but remind us, dear Lord, as we sometimes forget.

> And you shall remember that the Lord your God led you all the way these forty years in the wilderness, to humble you and test you, to know what was in your heart, whether you would keep His commandments or not. So He humbled you, allowed you to hunger, and fed you with manna which you did not know nor did your fathers know, that He might make you know that man shall not live by bread alone; but man lives by every word that proceeds from the mouth of the Lord. Your garments did not wear out on you, nor did your foot swell these forty years. (Deut. 8:2–4)

What a timely reminder to our fears and anxieties of our twenty-first-century existence. We really are not in control; God is. We are in the proverbial wilderness experience, and God is leading and directing us to our heavenly Canaan. Is he oblivious to our need for a job, a pay increase, good health, children, mates, or housing? Absolutely not. Again, we always find comfort in the scriptures, which brings nourishment to our souls. "Therefore I say to you, do not worry about your life, what you will eat or what you will drink; nor about your body, what you will put on. Is not life more than food and the body more than clothing? Look at the birds of the air, for they neither sow nor reap nor gather into barns; yet your heavenly Father feeds them. Are you not of more value than they? Which of you by worrying can add one cubit to his stature?" (Matt. 6:25–27).

We often forget that God is in total control of the entire universe, and if we are the apple of his eye as the Bible affirms, then surely he will take care of us. As memory recalls, if a honeybee burdened by pollen stumbles, he notices; will he not notice our needs? Does he want us to petition him for our needs? But of course.

November 12

When I Am Afraid

Whenever I am afraid, I will trust in You. In God I will praise His word, In God I have put my trust; I will not fear. What can flesh do to me?

—Psalm 56:3–4

Dad was in the pool with arms extended, beckoning his reluctant little girl to jump into his arms and join him in the pool. She walked gingerly to the edge of the swimming pool, saw the scary deep blue water, shook her head from side to side, and bolted away in fear. However, Dad was persistent, and he lovingly coaxed her back to the edge of the pool with sweet, charming words. This time, the little girl's focus was not on the scary deep blue water but on the strong, cuddly arms of her dad. She took a deep breath, closed her eyes, jumped into his strong arms, and was safe. Should we keep our eyes on Jesus or the troubles of this life?

Fear is real, and the giants of the faith have had their fair share of fear. Even the fearless David conceded, "I am a reproach among all my enemies, but especially among my neighbors, and I am repulsive to my acquaintances; those who see me outside flee from me. I am forgotten like a dead man, out of mind; I am like a broken vessel, for I hear the slander of many; fear is on every side; while they take counsel together against me, they scheme to take away my life" (Ps. 31:11–13). This is reality, friends of mine; we live in an evil and broken world, but the devil does not have the final word, nor does he have the last laugh. God does.

Moses had good reason to fear going back to Egypt, for a bounty was placed on his head for murdering an Egyptian foreman. He bristled at the thought of going back to that dreadful palace, but he was commanded by God to do just that—go back to Egypt—and he did. As courageous as Elijah was, he also was overcome with fear by a threat from Queen Jezebel. Peter was fearful as he removed his eyes from Jesus and saw the horrible possibilities of life outside his safe arms. Even the prince of the apostles, Paul, had his bouts with fear as he described the constant perils that dogged his footsteps (2 Cor. 11:26–27).

Fear is real, and a moderate dose of it is healthy for our continuous existence. Fear informs us that a particular situation poses real harm and danger to our well-being. I must be fearful of a lion and take the necessary measures to protect myself; otherwise, I'll be on its dinner menu, but we cannot allow ourselves to be paralyzed and consumed by our fears. Let us do what David did when confronted by his fears. "But as for me, I trust in You, O Lord; I say, 'You are my God' my times are in Your hand; deliver me from the hand of my enemies and from those who persecute me, make your face to shine upon your servant; save me for Your mercies' sake" (Ps. 31:14–16).

Our fears are of a different kind these days. Unlike ancient Israel, which faced continuous extinction from her neighbors, we face the possibility of a collapse of the financial institutions due to greed, fluctuations in the housing market, joblessness, homelessness, hunger, sickness, and loneliness; but through it all, our God is more than able. He has a proven record of snatching his people from the jaws of the enemy. We trust completely and implicitly that he will "supply all of [our] needs according to His riches in glory" (Phil. 4:19). Do not fear, little flock, for it is his desire to see you through.

November 13

The Perfect Match

Now let it be that the young woman to whom I say, "Please let down your pitcher That I may drink," and she says yes, "Drink, and I will also give your camels a drink," let her be the one You have appointed for Your servant Isaac. And by this I will know that You have shown kindness to my master.

—Genesis 24:14

The hormones are churning, and hips and goatees are being developed, sending the insecure scrambling to their mirrors for reassurance. Once upon a time, choosing a mate was no simple ordeal; it was a parental obligation to find a suitable mate for the stumbling, mistake-prone, difficult-to-please generation. How times have changed! Dating services and Internet chat rooms have replaced what is supposed to be one of the most important decisions one makes, the choosing of a mate for life.

Can we ever get it right? Statistics reveal that very few of us successfully choose the right mate on the first attempt. The marriage institution is disintegrating, with fewer people opting to marry; more are choosing to cohabit these days. How can we fail to condemn the sham called same-sex marriage? Does such a thing as same sex exist in nature? While younger couples are more inclined to work out the kinks in their relationships, boomers abandon ship (marriage) in favor of a greener pasture. Marriage is taking a beating these days, but it still remains the glue that holds society together. How about imitating what worked best in the past?

While it may appear to be a story of love at first sight, the love relationship that blossomed between Ruth and Boaz was engineered by the shrewd mother-in-law Naomi. Ruth clearly would be too bashful to devise the plan on her own. "And Naomi said to Ruth her daughter-in-law, it is good, my daughter, that you go out with his young women, and that people do not meet you in any other field" (Ruth 2:22). Naomi pushed Ruth into the circle of Boaz, and under her clever tutelage, Ruth ended up being the first lady of Bethlehem and the maternal ancestor of King David and our Lord Jesus Christ.

Mom and Pop may not know it all, but they sure do know a whole lot more than their self-assured, know-it-all children. Though Isaac was about sixty years of age, Abraham felt it was his obligation and duty to arrange his son's marriage, and it was not short of drama either. Consider the awesome responsibility placed on Eliezer, his chief steward, to find Ms. Right for Isaac. "So Abraham said to his oldest servant of his house, who ruled over all that he had, 'Please, put your hand over my thigh, and I will make you swear by the Lord, the God of the earth, that you will not take a wife for my son from the daughters of the Canaanites, among whom I dwell; but you shall go to my country and to my family, and take a wife for my son Isaac'" (Gen. 24:2–4).

Parents owe it to their children, whether they appreciate it or not, to provide the best advice, arrangements, and a start in life. In the end, it all boils down to the children's trust in their parents and submission to their wise advice. Many a broken heart would have been avoided if only we had taken the advice of our parents, but suffice to say, God is a good healer of broken hearts, and he continues to heal our aching heart every day. Has he healed yours lately? Parents, create an atmosphere that will facilitate your children's making good choices. Children, involve your parents in your decision making for a mate. They know a whole lot more than you think.

November 14

Dig Deep; It's There

For by grace you have been saved through faith, and that not of yourselves; it is the gift of God; not of works, lest anyone should boast.

—Ephesians 2:8–9

New drilling technologies have allowed the United States to begin making some noise on the once-exclusive oil-rich market, and it is getting a lot of attention and respect from friends and foes alike. Drilling at incredible depths with a new invention (fracking), the United States is poised to dramatically change the oil geographical landscape and emerge as a reputable oil-producing country. Wow! How did this happen? Technology. "Fracking is the technique that creates fractures in rock and rock formations by injecting fluids into cracks to force them open to release their rich deposits" (http://www.bbc.com/news/uk-14432401).

There is usually more to it than this simple explanation since trade secrets are not usually posted on YouTube or in the news media anyway. However, there is no denying that the new technology has enabled U.S. engineers to dig deeper and rotate their drills to unimaginable depths and in many different angles to pry the oil loose.

The Bible teaches that it takes faith unmixed with doubt to get monumental things accomplished. "And when He had come into the house, His disciples asked Him privately, 'Why could we not cast it out?' So He said to them, 'This kind can come out by nothing but prayer and fasting'" (Mark 9:28–29). How woefully unprepared the disciples were when confronted with the crisis of casting out a demon from a young boy. Although Christ had empowered them previously to cast out demons and work other miracles, their constant bickering and infighting rendered them impotent as they faced their daily challenges from without. We often allow ourselves to be blindsided and distracted by the allurements of the world that we fail to prepare for the great evangelical opportunities that surround us.

God sends opportunities everywhere we go that can bring honor and glory to his name, but we do not exercise the faith to capitalize on those occasions. We should ask for the faith of Abraham, the patience of Job, the meekness of Moses, the courage of David, and the wisdom of Daniel to make a difference in the lives of those around us. We realize this request calls for much prayer and fasting, and we may not have mastered those disciplines yet, but are we willing to start somewhere? Lord, instill in us a desire to dig deeper than we have ever dug before. Give us the discipline and tenacity to pray and to read your Word when we don't feel inclined to.

Help us, O Jesus, to sense the nearness of your coming so that we may be prepared for the great coming crisis. "So you also, when you see these things happening, know that it is near—even at the doors!" (Matt. 24:33). But alas, we must confess that we do not have what it takes to live through the turbulence of the final day events. That's why we are earnestly requesting of you, dear God, to give us the power and discipline to stay on our knees. Lord, help us dig deeper where we have never dug before so that we may tap into your rich power reserve that will enable us to raise the sick, cast out demons, and heal those plagued with drug addiction, alcoholism, prostitution, gambling, and pedophilia. Empower us, dear Lord, to bring your work to completion here on earth. Amen.

November 15

I Can't Fix It, but You Can

Moreover Manasseh shed much innocent blood, till he had filled Jerusalem from one end to another, besides his sin by which he make Judah sin in doing evil in the sight of the Lord.

—2 Kings 21:16

Manasseh did much damage to God's cause beyond his capacity to repair it. He could never return the missing fathers whom he killed to their families, nor could he bring back all those he led astray, but he did what he should; he repented of his sins, and God accepted him. Manasseh is not alone in this respect. There are numerous people who have inflicted irreparable damage to innocent victims, only to spend the rest of their days in jail or, worse, hiding somewhere, enjoying the protection of like-minded predators.

But if we are to be candid with ourselves, we will admit that we do not see the entire picture; only God does. Humans have always questioned the justice of God, but he is very patient with his erring children. "Yet the house of Israel says, the way of the Lord is not fair. O house of Israel, is it not My ways which are fair, and your ways which are unfair?" (Ezek. 18:29). And that's where we must concede our limited understanding of things to God's all-knowing vast mind. "But if a wicked man turns from all his sins which he has committed, keeps all my statutes, and does what is lawful and right, he shall surely live; he shall not die none of the transgressions which he has committed shall be remembered against him; because of the righteousness which he has done, he shall live" (Ezek. 18:21–22). The following verse gives us a better understanding of the reason why God is ever so gracious in receiving sinners. Your life is not defined by your past but by your intention for the future. Do you have repentance of your sins on your agenda?

"Do I have any pleasure at all that the wicked should die? Says the Lord God, and not that he should turn from his ways and live?" (Ezek. 18:23). Regardless of how wicked you were or how far you have sunk down into iniquity, it matters not to God; he freely forgives and forgets. This, however, does not absolve one from his debt to society; law and justice must be enforced and be fully carried out to its full extent.

The poor guys or girls may never be able to put back together all the lives they have ruined. Neither was the thief on the cross able to restore all the loot he had stolen from others, but he was nonetheless accepted on the basis of his repentance. Had he lived beyond that day, he would have been liable to society, whether by confinement or reparation. Since God is in the soul-saving business, he prioritizes in rescuing as many souls from death as possible while allowing the physical circumstances to dictate reparations and other situations. One may never be able to undo the damage he or she has inflicted on others and society at large, and God accepts this reality also.

Was Paul able to restore Stephen back to life? Was David able to restore Uriah, or Moses the Egyptian foreman? Of course, the answer is a resounding no. It is good that God is a wise and discerning Judge and will take all the circumstances of an incident into consideration in judging the victim and the assailant. "Great and marvelous are your works, Lord God Almighty! Just and true are your ways, O King of the saints! Who shall not fear You, O Lord, and glorify Your name?" (Rev. 15:3–4).

November 16

The Word of the Lord
Is the Best Course

Now therefore, I beg you, swear to me by the Lord, since I have shown you kindness, that you also will show kindness to my father's house, and give me a true token, and spare my father, my mother, my brothers, and my sisters, and all that they have, and deliver our lives from death.

—Joshua 2:12–13

The scarlet cord dangling from her window looked simple, but it became a gateway to life for Rahab and her family. Putting her life on the line by hiding the Israeli spies, Rahab extracted a promise from the spies that when the city of Jericho is destroyed, she and her family would be saved. The word was given that her entire family would be saved under one condition: they all had to abide within the confines of her house. "So it shall be that whoever goes outside the doors of your house into the street his blood shall be on his own head, and we will be guiltless. And whoever is with you in the house, his blood shall on our head if a hand is laid on him" (Josh. 2:19). They waited patiently and confidently behind the door where the scarlet cord of promise hung, and they were saved. Just as the Word of God through the spies provided the only lifeline out of certain destruction for Rahab and her family, it certainly is the only way out for us in this sin-infested, pleasure-seeking, idol-loving world. The Word of God is our compass and chart for moral living, and as long as we follow its life-giving precepts, we are safe. "Thy word is a lamp to my feet and a light to my path" (Ps. 119:105).

During times of difficulty and uncertainty, the Word of God is the safest course to follow. Men's words will fail, however well-intentioned they may be. Couples fail in their vows to each other. Business partners break their word and pay huge settlements to each other for breach of trust. Nations cheat and violate treaties they signed, but our God will never violate or alter his word to us. That is a promise we can count on and hold near and dear to our heart. "And the Lord, He is the One who goes before you. He will be with you, He will not leave you nor forsake you; do not fear nor be dismayed" (Deut. 31:8).

"Do not despise prophecies. Test all things; hold fast what is good" (1 Thess. 5:20–21). The word of God comes in many forms, sometimes in gentle rebukes, stunning denunciations, well-intentioned encouragements, and the advice of parents, friends, mates, and companions. We must be careful to listen diligently and not throw away the baby with the bathwater. We may not always like what we hear, but the word of God is always faithful and is always designed for our good.

Who likes to hear unfavorable opinions anyway? King Ahab of Israel wanted Jehoshaphat, king of Judah, to join him in battle against the king of Syria, but Jehoshaphat objected after hearing the carefully devised talking points of Ahab's court prophets: "Is there not still a prophet of the Lord here, that we may inquire of him?" (1 Kings 22:7). Ahab's answer was equally stunning. "There is still one man, Micaiah the son of Imlah, by whom we may inquire of the Lord; but I hate him, because he does not prophesy good concerning me, but evil" (verse 8). Be careful what you ask for. The word of God is the best and surest course even when it defers from our well-planned intentions. Needless to reiterate, they went ahead with their plans anyway, and the result was disastrous. Ignoring God's word is never a wise and safe proposition. Amen.

God at His Finest, Saving People

Artaxerxes, king of kings, to Ezra the priest, a scribe of the Law of the God of heaven: Perfect peace, and so forth.
I issue a decree that all those of the people of Israel and the priests and Levites in my realm who volunteer to go up to Jerusalem, may go with you.

—Ezra 7:12–13

No plagues fell from the skies, no Moses or Aaron was among them, no Red Sea parted for them, no falling manna either; but pregnant with hope for the future, the exiles inched their way toward Jerusalem, their destination. Humbled but not deflated, Ezra and his fellow captives lumbered in long lines back to their broken down city to rebuild and restore their nation. The challenges ahead would be daunting and monumental, but they were confident that God would take them through, around, above, and under any obstacle thrown at them. Tired feet were waxed strong and weary spirits revived as the exiles meditated on the prayer of their elder statesman Daniel. "O my God incline Your ear and hear; open Your eyes and see our desolations and the city which is called by Your name; for we do not present our supplications before You because of our righteous deeds, but because of Your great mercies. O Lord, Hear! O Lord, forgive! O Lord, Listen and act! Do not delay for Your own sake, my God, for Your city and Your People who are called by your name" (Dan. 9:18–19).

While the nation battled dissenters from within and hostile enemies from without, its leaders remained focused on the massive building project. The temple, center of Jewish life, was given first priority. Broken down walls must be repaired promptly to ward off thieves and troublemakers. Homes demolished by years of warfare and neglect had to be restored quickly to house new arrivals. Civil and religious institutions must be established simultaneously, along with other projects. It was a massive undertaking.

But before a hammer could be lifted, leaders Zerubbabel, of the first wave of exiles, and ultimately Ezra and Nehemiah all directed their attention to God's many promises of mercy as evidenced in the prayer of Solomon.

And when they return to You with all their heart and with all their soul in the land of their enemies who led them away captive and pray to You towards their land which You gave to their fathers, the city which You have chosen and the temple which I have built for Your name; then hear in heaven Your dwelling place their prayer and their supplication, and maintain their cause, and forgive Your people who have sinned against You, and all their transgressions which they have transgressed against You and grant them compassion before those who took them captive, that they may have compassion on them. (1 Kings 8:48–50)

Like Israel of old, we are building God's kingdom here on planet Earth. Different people have been commissioned to repair the breaches made in God's law. Have you been assigned to undertake a part in God's vineyard or work in your local church? Where do you fit in? Are you part of the problem or part of the solution? Are you repairing the breaches made in God's law by upholding it and pointing men to the better way? Are you downsizing your worldly aspirations to prioritize the programs of the kingdom and the saving of souls? Pray that God will send you and more workers into the harvest field.

November 18

Inspiration from the Cross Part 1

And when they had come to the place called Calvary, there they crucified Him, and the criminals, one on the right hand and the other on the left.

—Luke 23:33

He was one of Rome's tough, bulldog law enforcers and had executed many troublesome rabble-rousers, but this assignment puzzled him. Commander Marcus had gone out on many daring military campaigns for Rome and did not earn his rank by being nice to prisoners. However, this disgraceful trial and condemnation of the innocent Jesus was eating away at his conscience. He was totally confused by the blind hatred of the Jewish leaders toward Jesus but equally mystified by the testimonies of those healed by the gentle Teacher. In his briefings from his superior, Marcus became acquainted with the criminal history of the two thieves, which was validated by the testimony of witnesses. But the third man, Jesus, did not have a criminal past; as a matter of fact, he was pronounced innocent by Governor Pilate. Being at a loss in handling this strange sequence of events, he decided to follow the situation as it unfolded.

"After this, Jesus, knowing that all things were now accomplished, that the Scripture might be fulfilled, said, 'I thirst'" (John 19:28). Centurion Marcus was in a dilemma. Water would work against what he intended to do—end life. He therefore offered Christ the best alternative, pain-numbing alcohol. Jesus accepted their offering but remained focused with the destiny of billions hanging in the balance (John 19:29–30).

Besides his physical desire for a drink of water, Jesus's words "I thirst" represents the sinner's need of the water he possesses, but he was unable to drink from it himself. While in the throes of death, Christ's wish for water was denied; the Father could not intervene now. Every step of his mission had been preordained; his way was irreversible. "I have trodden the winepress alone, and from the peoples no one was with Me" (Isa. 63:3). God was totally silent because Jesus could not be spared the second death. That was what he came here to do, to die in our place. Jesus had to die the death of a sinner to satisfy the just requirement of God's law so that we may inherit the life that was his.

While his enemies continued to taunt and heap on the abuses, Jesus's pain intensified, and he cried with a loud, agonizing voice, "My God, My God why have You forsaken Me?" (Matt. 27:46). It felt like Jesus was forsaken, but was he really? Jesus received no answer from God, even though the Father was right there with him, but we have been given unequivocal assurance of being heard by our heavenly Father. "Before they call, I will answer; and while they are still speaking, I will hear" (Isa. 65:24).

Looking down at the soldiers casting lots over his garment, Jesus cried, "Father forgive them, for they do not know what they are doing" (Luke 23:34). Jesus's vicarious death paid the price of our salvation, including those of his tormentors. Had they repented of their sins, they would have been forgiven. Even Centurion Marcus, the presiding officer of the execution, received grace, and his admission of Christ's divinity brings hope to many struggling under difficult situations. "By this you know the Spirit of God: Every spirit that confesses that Jesus Christ has come in the flesh is of God" (1 John 4:2).

The thief on the right made his peace with Jesus, and the Savior set him on the right course. Jesus replied, "Assuredly, I say to you, today you will be with Me in Paradise" (Luke 23:43). Jesus stands ready and waiting for you to get it right. What's holding you back?

November 19

Inspiration from the Cross Part 2

Pilate answered, "Am I a Jew? Your own nation and the chief priest have delivered You to me. What have You done?"

—John 18:35

Commander Marcus may have been briefed by fellow centurions who saw Christ or were beneficiaries of his miracles themselves, but nothing prepared him for this event that would have such universal ramifications to the world. The crucifixion is taking its toll on the Savior's endurance. To breathe, he must push himself upward on his legs, which were nailed together. Gravity, plus his body weight, dragged him downward, and breathing was becoming extremely labored.

During this rhythmic motion, he blurted out, "Woman, behold your son." This must have been a crushing moment to Mary, witnessing the execution of her only Son in the flowering stage of his manhood. Like the other disciples, she may not have understood the prophetic importance of this moment and its significance to salvation, but reality was absolutely clear. Her Son was hanging on a Roman cross and was conscious of everything swirling around him, even the social security needs of his mother.

"Woman behold your Son! Then He said to the disciple, Behold your mother! And from that hour that disciple took her to his own home" (John 19:26–27). In death, Jesus committed the care of his mother to John, the writer of the fourth gospel. In so doing, he enjoined all children to honor their parents and make their final days as pleasant as possible by providing for their needs as they advance in age. The total absence of Joseph since the nativity seems to suggest that Joseph, his stepfather, had been dead, and Mary would need some sort of social assistance.

Gathering his last ounce of energy, Jesus cried out, "'It is finished!' And bowing His head, He gave up the spirit" (John 19:30). What is finished? The bitter cup that he dreaded was drunk in full. He successfully accomplished his mission on earth. Satan's reign as the prince of terror of this world was at an end. Salvation was made available to everyone, even to the vilest sinner. Judgment day was established, and the end of sin and Satan was in sight.

But wait, what does the Father have to say of this whole ordeal? "This is My Beloved Son in whom I am well pleased" (Matt. 3:17). These words of affirmation were spoken by God at the beginning of Christ's ministry and at the Mount of Transfiguration near the close of his ministry (Matt. 17:5). Can there be any doubt that God was absolutely ecstatic about the conclusion of the whole event? God breathed a deep sigh of relief as the Savior rested in the tomb until Sunday morning.

"And behold, there was a great earthquake; for an angel of the Lord descended from heaven, and came and rolled back the stone from the door, and sat on it. His countenance was like lightning, and his clothing as white as snow. And the guards shook for fear of him, and became like dead men. But the angel answered and said to the women, Do not be afraid, for I know that you seek Jesus who was crucified. He is not here; for He is risen, as He said. Come and see the place where the Lord lay" (Matt. 28:2–6). Jesus died so that you and I could live. What a Savior is Jesus, our Lord! Will you tell everybody, including your closest associates, of his amazing love to them?

November 20

Movement of God's People

For thus says the Lord: After seventy years are completed at Babylon, I will visit you and perform My good word toward you, and cause you to return to this place.
—Jeremiah 29:10

Almost everyone on the earth wishes to make the West (Europe and America) home. They cross barren deserts to freedom or drift for days across shark-infested waters on rickety boats, and the most daring ones attempt stowing away in the wheel compartment of airplanes. But Ahmed's family is fortunate; they are refugees awaiting repatriation into the United States. For once, Ahmed anticipates putting behind him the carnage of war and is looking forward to being in school at last and meeting new friends when he crosses the oceans.

Like Ahmed, we are witnessing horrific crimes and some very disturbing trends, but the Bible predicts that things are going to get a whole lot worse. Could we be living in the end of time? "But when you hear of wars and rumors of wars, do not be troubled; for such things must happen, but the end is not yet. For nation will rise against nation, and kingdom against kingdom. And there will be earthquakes in various places, and there will be famines and troubles. These are the beginnings of sorrow" (Mark 13:7–8).

War has always been with us. In the past, wars were localized, having very little effect on those living beyond its borders, but that has changed significantly. Because of advanced communication and the interdependency of global economies, wars send shockwaves around the world, instilling fear and uncertainties in world markets. Of course, if any event threatens to destabilize the free flow of oil from Middle Eastern nations, we feel the reverberation at gas-filling stations and supermarkets.

While the last day events are taking place, God is using this opportunity to gather his people in. Ahmed and his family will be ministered to by a loving church family that will help them make a smooth transition into their new culture. Most significantly, God is moving on the hearts of volunteers from developing countries to take up positions as teachers, aids, workers, and missionaries in foreign lands. God is raising up a new generation of Hudson Taylor, David Livingstone, and Florence Nightingale.

Even amid the bad events of the earth, God is very much at work gathering his people in. Are you involved in his great work? Do you see him at work in your life and in the life of others? "But Jesus answered them, 'My Father has been working until now, and I have been working'" (John 5:17). God is very busy, always busy, working and connecting the dots together that will bring us to the foot of the cross.

Is God moving in your neighborhood, in your city, and in your village? If you can't discern his movement, then pray and ask him to integrate you just where he is hard at work. Hint: serving others as Jesus did not only help the person in need but also enrich and refresh our spiritual experience. It allows us to join God in saving souls, and as someone remarked wisely, "The soul you save might be your very own."

November 21

The Exodus

Then the children of Israel journeyed from Rameses to Succoth, about six hundred thousand men on foot, besides children.
A mixed multitude went up with them also, and flocks and herds—
a great deal of livestock.

—Exodus 12:37–38

Secular historians have flatly denied the Jewish Exodus from Egypt; they claim to have found not a single shred of evidence or artifact corroborating the biblical story. They assert the Israeli Exodus was a postexilic myth written to glue the nation together. Are we surprised by this community's claim, which denies the very existence of God, the Creation, and salvation through Jesus Christ? Consider the source.

Since no one was around when this world was created, it takes faith to believe any theory postulated by anyone. And many theories from antiquity exist relative to the creation of this world. Among all these antiquated theories, the Word of God empathetically states, "But without faith it is impossible to please Him, for he who comes to God must believe that He is, and that He is the rewarder of those who diligently seek Him" (Heb. 11:6). We approach God on the premise of faith that he is the Creator and that we are the creature. The creature must always submit to the wisdom and authority of the Creator; failure to do this amounts to treason at best and insurrection at worst.

Also, the Bible teaches about a second *exodus* (biblical definition, "going out"), which is well on its way right now. This time, the exodus is to get out of Babylon. "And I heard another voice from heaven saying: 'Come out of her My people, lest you share in her sins, and you receive of her plagues'" (Rev. 18:4). Babylon of old was the archenemy of God's people, Israel, in times past, and its reemergence in Bible prophecy represents a revival of its antagonism against God's people of modern times.

For us to flee Babylon, we must understand what constitutes modern Babylon. Babylon represents confusion and is derived from the word "Babel," the monument of defiance against God (Gen. 11:1–7). Babel's civilization transitioned into Babylon with apostasy and spiritualism at its core. Modern-day Babylon has the same characteristics—belief in the spirits, praying to dead saints, apostasy (living in a state of godlessness), and embracing Sunday sacredness as God's Sabbath. In general, Babylon constitutes following and living under the influence of the pope and his papal institutions.

Today God is calling on his people to forsake these false systems of worship for the worship of the true God. "You worship what you do not know; we know what we worship, for salvation is of the Jews. But the hour is coming, and now is, when the true worshipers will worship the Father in spirit and in truth; for the Father is seeking such to worship Him" (John 4:22–23). It is sad but true, as Jesus confirmed, that many are worshipping not knowing who they are worshipping. Paul later referenced the same thought: "For as I was passing through and considering the objects of your worship, I even found an altar with this inscription: TO THE UNKNOWN GOD. Therefore, the One whom you worship without knowing, Him I proclaim to you" (Acts 17:23).

God is calling his people from the churches that were once beacons of light and hope but have now compromised the truth and lowered their standards to accommodate and pacify the masses. If you are hearing God's voice, it is time to get out of Babylon.

November 22

Waging War on Bad Habits

And the Lord said to Joshua, do not fear them, for I have delivered them into your hand;
not a man of them shall stand before you.

—Joshua 10:8

The city-dwelling monkeys of India have become experts at snatching food from unsuspecting residents. From their perch on rooftops, they study the weaknesses of their victims and then swoop in for their ill-gotten prize. They are entrenched in their bad habits and may very well be beyond rehabilitation. They have developed an elaborate system of lookout spies who keep an eye out for danger. Once a home or a car is invaded, it's a free-for-all; every monkey is on its own to sort out an escape route. The victim is usually left wielding a frying pan or shaking their fist in anger, saying, "Monkey thieves" (https://www.vice.com/en_us/article/monkeys-are-taking-over-india).

The Westminster Kennel Club puts on the best dog show on the entire planet. Dogs participating in their event have been meticulously trained, primed, and groomed for the tournament. They look smart and poised, and having been flawlessly streamlined, they run with class and graceful dignity. Their owners expect great things from them tonight as they give them a trial run to acquaint them with what is expected of them on their big night. "No bad poise or misbehavior please, guys. This is it."

Animal misbehavior may be overlooked, but humans are accountable to their fellow men because their actions may severely affect the lives and well-being of others. We often need help in the department of behavior modification, but the Bible offers this sobering reality: "Can the Ethiopian change his skin, or the leopard his spots? Then may you also do good who are accustomed to do evil" (Jer. 13:23). Unaided by the spirit of God, we are perpetually and hopelessly stuck in our evil ways. Paul improves on this point a little further: "Therefore you are inexcusable, O man, whoever you are who judge, for in whatever you judge another you condemn yourself, for you who judge practice the same things. And do you think this, O man, you who judge those practicing such things, and doing the same, that you will escape the judgment of God? Or do you despise the riches to His goodness, forbearance, and longsuffering, not knowing that the goodness of God leads you to repentance?" (Rom. 2:1–4). Absolutely true. It is the goodness of God that softens our callous hearts that makes repentance possible.

Even with the act of repentance, we must be willing to constantly submit ourselves at the foot of the cross and plead for mercy, for we are virtually at war with our carnal nature. No one has simplified this concept better than Paul. "For the good that I will to do, I do not do; but the evil I will not to do, that I practice . . . But I see another law in my members, warring against the law of my mind, and bringing me into captivity to the law of sin which is in my members. O wretched man that I am! Who will deliver me from this body of death? I thank God—through Jesus Christ our Lord!" (Rom. 7:19, 23–25). However well-intentioned, without God, we are hopeless.

There should be no enjoyment of sin on our part. When we do sin, remorse should drive us on our knees, supplicating for grace, strength, and mercy in time of need. Finally, we must declare an all-out war on sin, especially the ones that entrap us most easily. We must, like Jacob, ask God to strengthen our vulnerable soft spots. "My grace is sufficient for you, for my strength is made perfect in weakness" (2 Cor. 12:9).

November 23

Full Speed Ahead

Brethren, I do not count myself to have apprehended; but one thing I do, forgetting those things which are behind and reaching forward to those things which are ahead. I press toward the goal for the prize of the upward call of God in Christ Jesus.
—Philippians 3:13–14

Low tide impeded their landing at Normandy, causing the landing crafts to disgorge the troops prematurely. Meanwhile, the waiting enemy welcomed them with fierce artillery barrages and blistering bursts of machine gun fire. This was D-day, folks, and there was no turning back; we were taking the fight to the enemy. The closely guarded secret was no longer a secret. The long-awaited invasion by the Allies to liberate Western Europe from the tyranny of Axis domination has begun in earnest, but things hardly went as planned. With much improvisation and substantial versatility, the Allies accomplished their goal in establishing a beachhead and ultimately defeated the enemy.

We are allied with the kingdom of heaven and are under strict orders to press forward unrelentingly toward the goal for the prize in Christ Jesus. Usually, there is a prize at the end of a goal; and to attain the prize, we must first reach the goal. "I beseech you therefore, brethren, by the mercies of God, that you present your bodies a living sacrifice, holy, acceptable to God, which is your reasonable service. And do not be conformed to this world, but be transformed by the renewing of your mind, that you may prove what is that good and acceptable and perfect will of God" (Rom. 12:1–2). God's ideal for his people has always been holy living, but without the intervention of the Holy Spirit, this goal is practically impossible.

God wants us to be a living sacrifice, which implies continuous living and denial of self. The term "sacrifice," as defined by Google, connotes someone giving up something of value to someone superior. This terminology fits precisely with what we are called on to do daily. Presenting our bodies as living sacrifices entails daily self-surrender, daily suppressing the desire to sin, and daily walking and cooperating with God. In essence, the believer does not live for himself but for his Lord.

"I have been crucified with Christ; it is no longer I who live but Christ lives in me; and the life which I now live in the flesh I live by faith in the Son of God, who loved me and gave Himself for me" (Gal. 2:20). By virtue of our surrender and commitment to Christ, we are crucifying ourselves daily by starving the desires and lusts of the flesh. Because we engage in these acts of self-mortification, it is no longer us who live but Jesus living in us.

But wait, the news gets even better. Remember, a handsome reward always follows a hard-fought battle. "Do not fear any of those things which you are about to suffer. Indeed, the devil is about to throw some of you into prison, that you may be tested, and you will have tribulation ten days. Be faithful until death, and I will give you the crown of life" (Rev. 2:10). This crown of life is no ordinary crown; it is everlasting life with the source of all life—God the Father, God the Son, and God the Holy Spirit. This, my friend, is reason enough to give up any and all things for the crown that never fades away.

November 24

No Turkey yet Thankful

Now at the dedication of the wall of Jerusalem they sought out the Levites in all their places, to bring them to Jerusalem to celebrate the dedication with gladness, both with thanksgiving and singing, with cymbals and stringed instruments and harps.
—Nehemiah 12:27

Thanksgiving in the United Stated and its territories is a grand event. Although there is nothing unusual about the day itself, the preparation leading to its celebration is maddening. Across the nation's airports and train stations, the rush hour is on to get home in time for this grand dinner. In the supermarkets, hordes of shoppers are snatching up the birds with eager frenzy and great delight. On the highways, give yourself an extra hour in travel time. What's all the rush about? It's Thanksgiving Day, an all-American holiday intended to give thanks to God for all his bounty to the nation.

Can we give thanks even when there is no turkey on the table and the only item in the refrigerator is a bottle of water? "In everything give thanks; for this is the will of God in Christ Jesus for you" (1 Thess. 5:18). Now wait a minute, Paul, not so fast. Should I give thanks even when I am famished and nothing seems to be going right for me? The scripture is absolutely clear and wonderful. Here are some compelling reasons why we should praise God and give thanks in spite of our situation. "The dead do not praise the Lord." Are you beginning to get it? It's obvious. They are dead, and therefore they cannot praise God. "Nor any who go down into silence" (Psalm 115:17). Wouldn't you rather be praising God on an empty stomach than being silent in some tomb somewhere? Of course, I'd rather be alive praising God than to be silent in a graveyard.

Paul had much to complain and gripe about, yet he didn't. Let's see how he handled his adversity.

> In labor more abundant, in prisons more frequently, in deaths often. From the Jews five times I received forty stripes minus one. Three times I was beaten with rods; once I was stoned; three times I was shipwrecked; a night and a day I have been in the deep; in journeys often, in perils of robbers, in perils of my own countrymen, in perils of the Gentiles, in perils on the city, in perils in the wilderness, in perils in the sea, in perils among false brethren, in weariness and toil, in sleeplessness often, in hunger and thirst, in fasting often, in cold and nakedness. (2 Cor. 11:23–27)

Jacob didn't fare any better with his father-in-law. "Thus I have been in your house twenty years; I served you fourteen years for your two daughters, and six years for your flock, and you have changed my wages ten times. Unless the God of my father, the God of Abraham and the Fear of Isaac, had been with me, surely now you would have sent me away empty-handed. God has seen my affliction and the labor of my hands and has rebuked you" (Gen. 31:41–42). The lot of godly men and women has never been easy. We are hounded at every step by an enemy bent on making us miserable and who is actively seeking ways to destroy us. But we are never forsaken: "Through the Lord's mercies we are not consumed, because His compassion fails not. They are new every morning, great is your faithfulness" (Lam. 3:22). Here is another compelling reason why we should praise God always: he is always faithful. When we are tempted to complain, let volleys of praise burst forth from our mouths. Turn your complaints into praise to God.

November 25

Giving Thanks on Thanksgiving Day

> In everything give thanks; for this is the will of God in Christ Jesus for you.
> —1 Thessalonians 5:18

"Grant clemency to the turkey! Grant clemency to the turkey!" My honorable friend of many years, residing in the great state of New Jersey, texted me this urgent message on Thanksgiving Day. "Grant clemency to the turkey," he pleaded. He claimed that the bird was totally innocent and did not deserve to be executed. Whatever your views are on Thanksgiving, the Bible is absolutely clear on this subject; we are admonished to give thanks always under all conditions, even when in pain. What have you been thankful for lately? How do you thank God when he does something extraordinary for you?

My 1996 Mazda B3000 is an old workhorse; it failed emission inspection miserably for the past three years in succession. I was forced by MVA to make cosmetic repairs, which I did not need and which I could ill afford. A hefty $500 repair bill would get you a waiver to comply with state regulations. However, this year and quite unexpectedly, my vehicle passed inspection with flying colors, and not a dime was spent on repairs. I remarked to myself, *God, you are full of humor.* I went to the inspection station expecting my vehicle to fail since I hadn't done any repairs to it, and quite unexpectedly, it passed. The emission inspection experience by itself is a test of our Christian virtues, especially if your vehicle is as old as mine. Hallelujah to our God for doing the unexpected! Is this a chance occurrence?

How do we give thanks when things don't go according to plan, when our prayers go unanswered, or when we receive the dreaded unfavorable news from our physician? "Now He who searches the heart knows what the mind of the Spirit is, because He makes intercession for the saints according to the will of God. And we know that all things work together for good to those who love God, to those who are called according to His purpose" (Rom. 8:27–28). Let's try to analyze verse 27. It says that God searches the heart and knows the operations of the Holy Spirit, who intercedes on our behalf. Therefore armed with the information of what the Holy Spirit sees in our future or the good he desires for us, whatever the outcome of our struggle, we should glorify God. In everything, give thanks. Trials are always packaged with corresponding grace to cope.

Having said that, we can draw from the experience of those who have trodden this difficult path of pain and tragedy. Let's see how Job handled his share of turmoil. After watching the stock market crash, with his fortune evaporating before his eyes and his children killed in a tornado, Job had plenty to complain and gripe about, but he didn't. "Naked I came from my mother's womb and naked shall I return there. The Lord gave, and the Lord has taken away; blessed be the name of the Lord. In all this Job did not sin nor charge God with wrong" (Job 1:21–22).

Few have tasted the bitter cup handed to Job. God chose him for this special assignment because God is collecting jewels for his museum. When trials come calling—and they will—could they be your opportunity for giving thanks and a possible entry into God's museum of faith? Will you pray and ask for the discipline to stand up for God even under difficult conditions, like Job? When tempted to complain, give thanks instead. In all things, give thanks.

SHOW ME YOUR WAYS LORD

November 26

Down but Not Out

I have fought the good fight, I have finished the race, I have kept the faith. Finally, there is laid up for me the crown of righteousness, which the Lord, the righteous Judge, will give to me on that Day, and not to me only but also to all who have loved His appearing.

—2 Timothy 4:7–8

She fell and was almost run over by a competitor, but she got up quickly, began running again, overtook her four hustling contestants, and won the race. Competing in a six-hundred-meter race, Heather Dorniden was the lead runner when something terrible happened. She fell while still in the lead, with the hustling runner behind her barely miss smashing her head. But what transpired next would be talked about for ages. She sprang back up and went into overdrive, overtaking the first runner, then the second, ultimately the third, and finally the fourth by a hair. Where most fall and stay fallen, true champions rise and run again, ignoring the hand dealt to them by life's circumstances (http://nhne-pulse.org/heather-dorniden-the-runner-who-didnt-give-up/).

The crowd was electrified with applause, and sports commentators were at a loss for words to describe what they had just seen. Every now and again, we need to be reminded of brave men and women beset by physical and mental impediments digging deep into their souls to succeed. We need to be reminded constantly that God can barrel through, over, under, and around any mountain of obstacles. If he chooses, he can take us around the obstacle as he did the children of Israel to test them and see what they were made of. "And you shall remember that the Lord your God led you all the way these forty years in the wilderness, to humble you and test you, to know what was in your heart, whether you would keep His commandments or not" (Deut. 8:2).

Sometimes God chooses to go in the midst of fire with his people to demonstrate his sovereignty over all. "Then King Nebuchadnezzar was astonished; and he rose in haste and spoke, saying to his counselors, 'Did we not cast three men bound into the midst of the fire?' They answered and said to the king, 'True O King.' 'Look!' he answered, 'I see four men loose, walking in the midst of the fire; and they are not hurt, and the form of the fourth is like the Son of God'" (Dan. 3:24–25).

At other times, he chooses not to deliver, and that's the hard part to deal with. "So he sent and had John beheaded in prison . . . When Jesus heard of it, He departed from there by boat to a deserted place by Himself" (Matt. 14:10, 13). Obviously, Jesus could have saved John; but while on earth, he submitted himself to the Father's will and remained subject to his leading.

We expect to be delivered from every pain, trial, and tribulation, but it will be helpful to remember Job's experience. God needs future Hall of Famers who can take the best the devil has to offer and rise above their circumstance and be a testimony of what is expected of those who desire to follow Christ. Being a believer in Christ is not lying on a bed of roses or sailing on balmy seas; sometimes the waters do get rough and boisterous, and we sometimes perish doing God's service, like John the Baptist. "And do not fear those who kill the body but cannot kill the soul. But rather fear Him who is able to destroy both soul and body in hell" (Matt. 10:28). Job was not told why he was being used as a model for all future suffering saints. God just used him as he saw fit.

November 27

Victory in the Back of the Book

And he showed me a pure river of water of life, clear as crystal, proceeding from the throne of God and of the Lamb . . .
And there shall be no more curse, but the throne of God and of the Lamb shall be in it, and His servants shall serve Him.

—Revelation 22:1, 3

The sixteenth and the forty-fourth presidents have much in common. They both lost a parent early in childhood and were raised by the surviving parent and stepparent. They both overcame the odds stacked against them to become president. Both attributed their success to insightful mothers, who showered them with lots of love and kept them focused on the straight and narrow path. Both men must be credited for their incredible hard work, making good choices that ultimately landed them at the top of the world.

Things did not go well for the first family in the garden; their attempt at garden management ended in disaster when they opened their door to a complete stranger in the form of a slithering snake. Although given the operating manual for the smooth functioning of the Garden of Eden, Adam obeyed the voice of a total stranger who wrestled the garden away from him. He ultimately became a servant to the intruder. "So He drove out the man; and He placed cherubim at the east of the garden of Eden, and a flaming sword which turned every way to guard the way to the tree of life" (Gen. 3:24).

Things went from bad to worse as man degenerated into evil. "Then the Lord saw that the wickedness of man was great in the earth, and that every intent of the thoughts of his heart was only evil continually. And the Lord was sorry that He had made man on the earth, and He was grieved in His heart" (Gen. 6:5–6).

To save the human species, God had to destroy those beyond reform and start all over again. "And God said to Noah, the end of all flesh has come before Me, for the earth is filled with violence through them; and behold, I will destroy them with the earth. Make yourself an Ark of gopher wood; make rooms in the ark and cover it inside and outside with pitch" (Gen. 6:13–14). Despite God's great acts of mercy and grace to save the race, man became progressively worse as sin of every description multiplied.

However, God wasn't caught napping. He invented a bold plan by calling Abraham and his seed, Israel, as a nation of priests and evangelists to broadcast his saving grace to the world. But his prophet messengers were ill-treated, persecuted, and eventually killed. "Since the day that your fathers came out of the land of Egypt until this day, I have even sent to you all My servants the prophets, daily rising up early and sending them. Yet they did not obey Me or incline their ear, but stiffened their neck" (Jer. 7:25–26).

Just when it seemed like all was hopelessly lost, God did something extraordinarily wonderful. He sent his Son to pay the penalty for our sins. "For God so loved the world that He have His only begotten Son, that whoever believes in Him should not perish but have everlasting life" (John 3:16). Let the celebration begin; happiness is a choice we make daily. We can choose to be happy or be miserable. We choose life with Jesus because he loved us and died in our place. We are not powerless to the circumstances that surround us. We can call on our Maker who is just a prayer away. Despite what life throws at us, we are more than conquerors through him, who loves us.

November 28

Dignity among Thieves

A new commandment I give to you; that you love one another as I have loved you, that you also love one another.

—John 13:34

Police in Sicily, Italy, stumbled on a Mafia code of conduct and arrested a wanted mob boss in the process. Dubbed the Ten Commandments of the Cosa Nostra, it details the code of operation and acceptable moral behavior for a healthy crime organization. The crime commandments read as follows:

1. Never look at the wives of your friends.
2. Avoid pubs and nightclubs.
3. Keep up your appointments.
4. Never be seen with a cop.
5. Respect your wife.
6. Never steal money from members within the organization. (http://www. digitaljournal.com/article/245975)

Believers of Yahweh in every age have been distinguished from others by following a different code of conduct. Their unselfish love for God and their fellow men has set them apart from others. Jesus pointed that out succinctly with this statement: "You shall love the Lord your God with all your heart, with all your soul, and with all your mind. This is the first and great commandment. And the second is like it: you shall love your neighbor as yourself. On these two commandments hang all the Law and the Prophets" (Matt. 22:37–40). The vertical relation with God will inevitably flow horizontally to one's neighbor, friend, and even enemy.

Jesus invites us to love one another as he loves us, but how does Jesus love? "Greater love has no one than this, than to lay down his life for his friends" (John 15:13). And who understands this concept better than the U.S. military. They will literally move mountains if need be to retrieve a missing or fallen comrade, and time is of no consequence in bringing to rest a fallen comrade. They are trained in the art of caring for the wounded and covering one's back, looking for the safety of others. Even mobsters express love to one another.

Should the modern disciples of Yahweh do any less? Love does not come naturally to us, for humans are selfish by nature. Love must be cultivated, and anyone who exhibits true love is motivated by God, for after all, "God is Love" (1 John 4:8). The converse is also true. "If someone says, I love God, and hates his brother, he is a liar; for he who does not love his brother whom he has seen, how can he love God whom he has not seen?" (1 John 4:20).

Love always seeks the best interest of others. "Love suffers long and is kind; love does not envy; love does not parade itself, is not puffed up; does not behave rudely, does not seek its own, is not provoked, thinks no evil; does not rejoice in iniquity, but rejoices in the truth; bears all things, believes all things, hopes all things, endures all things. Love never fails" (1 Cor. 13:4–8).

If you are not yet on the love train, get on board; you have nothing to lose and everything to gain by loving others as Jesus did. Love even your enemies.

November 29

We Need Each Other

Two are better than one, because they have a good reward for their labor.
For if they fall, one will lift up his companion.
But woe to him who is alone when he falls, for he has no one to help him up.
—Ecclesiastes 4:9–10

If you thought being alone is a good idea, this story will probably change your mind. Mr. G. was a ten-year-old male goat rescued from a hoarder who could barely take care of herself, let alone the dozens of animals found on her property. On a tip from concerned neighbors, the authorities were called in and raided her residence. In an effort to give each animal a comfortable existence, Mr. G. was taken to a California animal shelter for a happy retirement; but for six days, he refused to eat and lay depressed in a corner, barely lifting his head. Tasty treats and ingenious attempts to lift him out of his depression all failed. Someone struck on the golden idea of bringing Mr. G.'s old buddy Jellybean, the donkey, to join him at the shelter. Immediately, upon sensing the arrival of his old buddy, Mr. G. got up and rushed to greet his old friend. He promptly ended his long fast with a delicious meal with his favorite old friend (https://www.animalbliss.com/mr-g-and-jellybean/).

God did not make man to live as hermits. "And the Lord God said, it is not good that man should be alone; I will make him a helper comparable to him" (Gen. 2:18). It is okay to have friends and be friendly. Statistics have shown that those who lavish love on pets, companions, and others live longer and enjoy a better quality of life; developing friends is a lifelong intentional venture. "A man who has friends must show himself to be friendly but there is a friend who sticks closer than a brother" (Prov. 18:24).

Making friends is quite simple; it is not rocket science, nor is it a complicated affair. In some instances, all it takes is a twitch of the facial muscle, and a genuine smile is formed. Helping others is another good way of making friends. "A friend is born out of adversity." The old adage is always true: "You will know who your real friends are when trouble strikes."

We are encouraged to make friends; after all, how will the gospel commission be carried out to the world if we are friendless? We must develop relationships with the specific purpose of reaching others for Christ. Jesus chose twelve disciples, who in turn introduced their friends and families to him. "One of the two who heard John speak, and followed Him, was Andrew, Simon Peter's brother. He first found his own brother Simon, and said to him, 'We have found the Messiah' (which is translated, the Christ). And he brought him to Jesus" (John 1:40–42). The big secret, which is no secret at all, states that friendship is still the most effective catalyst by which the gospel commission is carried out. No one will invite us into their space unless we have developed a relationship with them.

Mr. G. survived his terrible ordeal because he had a relationship with Jellybean, but woe is him who has no friends or not intent on forming relationships. Again, the old adage still holds true: "One hand can't clap." The meal always tastes better when enjoyed with a friend, doesn't it? Go out there and make friends; smile and make a difference in the lives of hurting people.

November 30

Averting a Disaster

Then Abigail made haste and took two hundred loaves of bread, two skins of wine, five sheep already dressed, five seahs of roasted grain, one hundred clusters of raisins, and two hundred cakes of figs, and loaded them on donkeys.
—1 Samuel 25:18

The class jubilation turned into shock and horror when the *Challenger* exploded in a ball of fire. Just seventy-three seconds into the flight carrying teacher Christa McAuliffe, the shuttle broke apart. An O-ring malfunction of a seal on the right solid rocket booster was the culprit. Those old enough still remember where they were when the gut-wrenching news was displayed on television worldwide. The Rogers Commission, which was delegated by President Reagan, made the troubling discovery. It stated that NASA was familiar with the failure of the O-ring system but chose to ignore it, hoping it would go away. Problems usually never go away on their accord; they must be fixed. The space program was grounded for thirty-two months to iron out the kink (nypost.com/2016/01/I-could-have-died-on-the-challenger).

The cure is always more expensive, more time-consuming, and more painful than prevention. Abigail wisely chose the latter, the prevention, and boy, how timely was her action. Upon learning that her husband acted foolishly by being mean and disrespectful to Israel's future king, Abigail took matters into her own hands. Without her husband's consent, she marshaled a small army of servants, complete with food and refreshments for David and his men. Her decisive action not only saved her household but also saved an unthinking David from avenging himself. "Then David said to Abigail 'Blessed is the Lord God of Israel, who sent you this day to meet me! And blessed is your advice and blessed are you, because you have kept me this day from coming to bloodshed and from avenging myself with my own hand. For indeed, as the lord God of Israel lives, who kept me back from hurting you, unless you had hurried and come to meet me, surely by morning light no males would have been left of Nabal!" (1 Sam. 25:32–34).

No one will question that threats against life and property are on the increase. We owe it to the victims and to society at large to have the aggressors making those threats explain themselves in a court of law. A student would not feel good about himself if he knows his buddy is planning to do some mischief at school and does nothing to alert the authorities about it. Christians are aware of the wonderful news of the Second Coming of Christ. Are you telling your friends about it? Do as Abigail did; do something about it.

You probably have heard of the classic anecdote "We have some good news and some bad news, but first, the bad news." Things are getting from bad to worse despite the optimism of campaigning politicians. The poor are indeed getting poorer, and the deck of cards is rigged in favor of the well-to-do. Meteorologists are at a loss in trying to explain the erratic behavior of weather conditions, but we have hope. Jesus is coming again. How soon? Real soon. Very, very soon. Are you ready?

"And there will be signs in the sun, in the moon, and the stars; and on the earth distress of nations, with perplexity, the sea and the waves roaring; men's heart failing them for fear and expectation of those things which are coming on the earth for the powers of the heavens will be shaken" (Luke 21:25–26). The only way to avert this coming disaster is to be covered by the blood of Jesus. We are ambassadors of this good news and must tell our friends how they can be saved from the coming catastrophe.

December 1

Ladies, Gentlemen, Fasten
Your Seat Belts

The Lord is your keeper; The Lord is your shade at your right hand.
The sun shall not strike by day, nor the moon by night.
The Lord shall preserve you from all evil. He shall preserve your soul.
—Psalm 121:5–7

The SUV in which the family was traveling flipped over multiple times at speed of over sixty-five miles per hour, but Jody (name changed) and her family escaped with only minor bruises. Numerous studies have credited seat belts for saving untold millions of lives, and Jody's family, fortunately, has confirmed this argument. Conversely, the statistics are grim for those who forgot or didn't see the need of buckling up. The federal government has inflicted tough penalties on those who put themselves and others at risk by not wearing their seat belts. Safety belts work, and you better get used to wearing them.

Our God has been way ahead of Detroit auto makers in installing safety devices for the good of his people. He has equipped us with safety devices to keep us safe while zooming past the obstacles on life's busy highways. "The Lord will establish you as a holy people to Himself, just as He has sworn to you, if you keep the commandments of the Lord your God and walk in His ways. Then all peoples of the earth shall see that you are called by the name of the Lord and they shall be afraid of you" (Deut. 28:9–10).

Contrary to the opinion of some that commandment keeping, or obedience to the law as it was called in the Bible, is restrictive and cumbersome, God thinks the opposite. The law is there to keep us safe from the dangers that lurk in the unknown. When the buggy and horse-drawn carriages were invented, there was no need for seat belts; but with the emergence of faster vehicles, seat belts became standard in all vehicles, necessary to keep us safe in the event of a crash. God's laws have always been there; they keep us safe from sin. "What shall we say then? Is the law sin? Certainly not! On the contrary, I would not have known sin except through the law. For I would not have known covetousness unless the law had said, 'You shall not covet' . . . Therefore, the law is holy, and the commandment holy and just and good" (Rom. 7:7, 12).

God's laws cover a whole spectrum of laws, of which the Ten Commandments is only a part. There is the natural law that was introduced at Creation. Remember, "He spoke, and it was done; He commanded, and it stood fast" (Ps. 33:9). God created the natural law by simply speaking things into existence. The rivers, seas, stars, animals, seasons, and all nature were set in their course by the word of the Lord.

By telling Adam what was wholesome for food and what was not, God brought the health law into existence, and its full content is given in Leviticus 11:1–47 and Deuteronomy 14:1–21. However, health is more than just eating a wholesome meal; it covers hygiene, rest, work exercise, prevention, and many other medical, ethical, and scientific issues.

With such an advanced, complex, and technological society as we have now, what would we do without civil laws? Every society, however primitive, needs them to keep order. While civil laws are loathed by criminals, law-abiding citizens, including you and me, hold them in high regard. The Levitical law was given by God to Moses as a shadow of things pointing to the coming of the Messiah; when the Messiah arrived, their usefulness expired (Lev. 23:4–44). Last but not least are the Ten Commandments, spoken by God himself and which are still relevant. God's laws are there to protect us from harm and danger. As long as we comply with them, we are safe. What would we do without them? Can you imagine a world without laws? Do you see God's law as a constraint on your freedom or as a barrier to keep you safe from immorality?

December 2

Ladies, Gentlemen, Start Your Engines

Forgetting those things which are behind and reaching forward to those things which are ahead, I press toward the goal for the prize of the upward call of God in Christ Jesus.

—Philippians 3:13–14

Colleges and universities tap generals, CEOs, journalists, and other highly talented speakers to deliver motivational speeches to their graduates. Graduations have become a much-anticipated affair in recent years; everyone wants to know who is going to deliver a knockout address. The graduates have shed precious blood, sweat, and tears in successfully completing their various courses of study and are anxiously waiting to jump-start their careers, but they need a boost. Can they get it all from a motivational speech?

"Be diligent to present yourself approved to God, a worker who does not need to be ashamed rightly dividing the word of truth" (2 Tim. 2:15). Companies love to present their employees as sharp, smart, eager, and helpful, but they should credit the Bible for their employees' work ethics. We are admonished to work for our employers as if we own the company, and essentially, we do. If the company sinks, we sink also. We have a stake in the company because if it succeeds, we will also succeed. "Bondservants, obey in all things your masters according to the flesh, not with eye service, as men pleasers, but in sincerity of heart, fearing God. And whatever you do, do it heartily, as to the Lord and not to men, knowing that from the Lord you will receive the reward of the inheritance; for you serve the Lord Christ" (Col. 3:22–24). Although this scripture text was written about two thousand years ago, it sounds very much like a modern-day graduation address.

Believers in Christ are model citizens demonstrating good moral ethics to the world. We are ambassadors of virtue, even if it appears to be on the decline. The one whom we represent does not change with the times, nor does he modify his Word to suit the shifting public debate. Believers must say what they mean and mean what they say. We should never be ashamed of standing on the side of righteousness, for righteousness will always triumph over iniquity. Therefore should we be ashamed of aligning ourselves under God's banner of truth? It is always helpful to remember Jesus's saying in this regard. "Enter by the narrow gate; for wide is the gate and broad is the way that leads to destruction, and there are many who go in by it. Because narrow is the gate and difficult is the way which leads to life, and there are few who find it" (Matt. 7:13–14).

Whether you are a babe in Christ or a mature older believer, we need to project the winning message of a risen and soon-coming King. Did not Christianity conquer the first-century world by storm? "And Jesus came and spoke to them saying, 'All authority has been given to Me in heaven and earth. Go therefore and make disciples of all nations, baptizing them in the name of the Father and of the Son and of the Holy Spirit, teaching them to observe all things that I have commanded you; and lo, I am with you always, even to the end of the age.' Amen" (Matt. 28:18–20). Go out there, and don't be shy; we carry a winning and a powerful message. Spread the good news.

December 3

Been in the Dumps Lately? Part 1

And he said, I have been zealous for the Lord God of Host;
because the children of Israel have forsaken Your covenant, torn down Your altars, and killed Your prophets with the sword.
I alone am left; and they seek to take my life.
—1 Kings 19:14

Been in the dumps lately? Having a pity party for yourself? Don't feel alone. We've all "been there, done that" at some time in our life, but this is no time for having a pity party for oneself with translation coming up. No doubt, being a full-time prophet and professor of the school of the prophets, compounded with Jezebel's threat, may have taken a toll on Elijah. But it's also interesting to see how tenderly God addressed his depressed child. Notice that God did not reprove or chastise his tired prophet in his moment of weakness; he simply ministered to him. Is there something to be learned from this approach? "Then as he lay and slept under a broom tree, suddenly an angel touched him and said to him, arise and eat. Then he looked, and there by his head was a cake baked on coals, and a jar of water. So he ate and drank and lay down again" (1 Kings 19:5–6).

Only a loving God who knows the limit of endurance in his children can act in such a compassionate manner. Elijah just had a great victory over the forces of Baal and was probably drained from the encounter. To add insult to injury, he took Jezebel's threat very personally. "Then Jezebel sent a messenger to Elijah, saying, 'So let the gods do to me, and more also, if I do not make your life as the life of one of them by tomorrow about this time" (1 Kings 19:2). Of course, Jezebel was still fuming in anger about the slaying of her false prophets by Elijah, being commissioned by God to root out idolatry from Israel.

Knowing the glorious future in store for his tired prophet, God tenderly commanded, "Go and return on your way to the Wilderness of Damascus; and when you arrive, anoint Hazael as king over Syria. Also you shall anoint Jehu the son of Nimshi as king over Israel. And Elisha the son of Shaphat of Abel Meholah you shall anoint him in your place" (1 Kings 19:15–16). Something must be brewing since Elijah is being replaced by Elisha, but whether Elijah knew of his soon-coming translation or not, he obediently complied.

Those who are tirelessly engaged in ministry must take time out to replenish their reserves or run the risk of burnout as prophet Elijah did. Even Jesus recognized the need to take time out. "Then the apostles gathered to Jesus and told Him all things, both what they had done and what they had taught. And He said to them, 'Come aside by yourselves to a deserted place and rest a while.' For there were many coming and going, and they did not even have time to eat" (Mark 6:30–31).

But even when one is well rested, the devil never gives up on his favorite tool— discouragement—and that we must guard against. We must constantly request of God fresh energy, fresh zeal, and new determination for the battles ahead. After all, even new mechanical parts wear out in time, but we are confident; we serve a God who knows our frame better than we do and understands that we are dust. "As a father pities his children, so the Lord pities those who fear Him. For He knows our frame; He remembers that we are dust" (Ps. 103:13–14). Even when we neglect to take proper care of ourselves and suffer the consequence of stress and burnout, God is always there to offer us the cake of bread and jar of water. Come apart and rest awhile, will you?

December 4

Been in the Dumps Lately? Part 2

And David said in his heart, "Now I shall perish someday by the hand of Saul. There is nothing better for me than that I should speedily escape to the land of the Philistines; and Saul will despair of me, to seek me anymore in any part of Israel."
—1 Samuel 27:1

The mountain men of Alaska are a rugged bunch; some of them frown at tilling the ground, preferring instead to chase after big game, but the wily moose—which is their favorite prey—is no pushover. He is big, bad-tempered, and mean-spirited when molested; he can easily trample a hunter without giving him a second glance. But more often than not, he becomes stew in the hunter's pot. Anxiety, depression, stress, and pressure can kill you. Don't be a victim to these bad guys. Listen to your doctor.

Who hasn't felt threatened on the job by an overzealous boss under pressure to meet the company's deadlines or goals? The constant pressure to give more while receiving less places one in a never-ending race to compete with more energetic rivals across the world, but our job is hardly the sole contributor to our high levels of stress and depression. Before the grind of the job, many have to deal with hectic traffic commute, whether it's the crowded trains, irregular buses, problematic cars, distracted drivers, traffic light malfunctions, or accidents. Any one of these scenarios can ruin one's day even before he gets to the job, but when it rains, it pours. And modern-day workers have to delicately balance many pressing issues to make a living, thus contributing to their high level of stress. Welcome to the world of multitasking.

Health is a major concern for the middle class and the poor of any culture; a few days of sickness could very well endanger one's ability to meet their financial obligations. Besides the threat of being sick, most workers are underpaid and are under great stress to keep up with inflation (rising prices).

Needless to reiterate, the lack of money is the chief contributor of stress to anyone espousing our Western culture. The need to have money to be fed, clothed, and housed is another factor of stress, and many are left devastated after paying the bills, wondering where the paycheck has gone. But all is not lost, though. We cannot and must not allow ourselves to be traumatized by our fears and circumstances that are beyond our control. We serve a big God who moves mountains and makes ways out of no way. Your circumstance can and will change. If you are contributing 100 percent to your company, then muster the strength and request a raise in salary. You may have to take some additional courses at your local college to show your competence or simply look for another a job that will meet your financial obligations. God works in mysterious ways; he sometimes places people in jobs to make a difference in the lives of others, and that may necessitate you taking a pay cut to be of service to others. Service to God, whether on the job or in the church, transcends job opportunities and monetary gains. We invest in people, not in banks.

Although problems in the workplace and poor living conditions may never go away, Jesus supplies us with corresponding grace, strength, and patience to cope with daily stress. Fortunately for David, the character in our opening text, God did not allow him to be overwhelmed by his difficulties but removed the irritable pain (Saul) out of the way. He can and will do the same for us if we keep trusting in him. Everything will be all right. God is in control.

Forgiven

Then behold, they brought to Him a paralytic lying on a bed.
When Jesus saw their faith, He said to the paralytic, Son be of good cheer;
your sins are forgiven you.

—Matthew 9:2

No one, however pious and well-intentioned, can say to another, "Your sins are forgiven." Forgiveness of sins is God's prerogative since only God can actually forgive sins. Because Jesus is God, the One in whom we live and move and have our being, he alone reserves the right to forgive whoever he deems worthy of it.

"Nevertheless the solid foundation of God stands, 'The Lord knows who are His, let everyone who names the name of Christ depart from iniquity'" (2 Tim. 2:19). Since forgiveness is the only way whereby reconciliation can be effected, the person to whom forgiveness is being extended must have a contrite heart, and even that requires an act of God. It is God who does the heart softening. "Or do you despise the riches of His goodness, forbearance, and longsuffering, not knowing that the goodness of God leads you to repentance?" (Rom. 2:4). Without the gentle nudging of the Holy Spirit, the natural man would never feel sorry for his sins, let alone ask forgiveness for them.

Andrew is coming from a horrible past, and who doesn't have a horrible past? He is delighted to know that Jesus has cut—yes, literally cut—sacks of baggage that were weighing him down. He no longer has to look over his shoulders at the sight of former rivals, nor does he have to take another route at the approach of someone whose money he swindled. Yes, since he belongs to a new Master and has been forgiven, he can now embark on a journey of repairing fractured relationships wherever possible.

Here's what forgiveness can lead to: "Then Zacchaeus stood and said to the Lord, 'look, Lord, I give half of my goods to the poor; and if I have taken anything from anyone by false accusation, I restore fourfold'" (Luke 19:8). It might not be possible to right every wrong one has committed, but the believer must begin rebuilding the bridges he burnt down unless the other party is not interested in his reconciliation gestures.

Having been a recipient of God's generous act of mercy, Andrew must extend that mercy to his fellow men as outlined in the following parable: "Then his master, after he had called him, said to him, 'You wicked servant! I forgave you all that debt because you begged me, should you not also have had compassion on your fellow servant, just as I had pity on you?'" (Matt. 18:32–33).

To have peace with God, we must forgive those who hurt us in the past and might still be hurting us now. Don't take their injury to our body personally, for even Jesus, the apostles, and the prophets were attacked. But God says, "For he who touches you touches the apple of His eye" (Zech. 2:8). Our Savior was brutally whipped and still asked forgiveness for his tormentors. He harbored no ill feelings against his tormentors and bade us to do the same. When the believer can bring himself or herself to praying for his or her tormentors, he or she is walking in the path where Jesus walked. "Father forgive them for they know not what they are doing" (Luke 23:34). We are called on to love everyone and bear no grudge against anyone. Love as Jesus loved. In due time, God will take care of your tormentors.

December 6

Fighting Our Battles with Us

Then I said to you, "Do not be terrified, or afraid of them.
The Lord your God, who goes before you, He will fight for you, according to all He did for you in Egypt before your eyes."
—Deuteronomy 1:29–30

When the game is on the line with a few seconds left, Coach K. is the man you want coaching your team. He is the winningest basketball coach ever, and opponents are usually astonished at his remarkable brilliance in executing the game plan. His 903 victories took him past his mentor Bobby Knight, but Coach K., as he is affectionately called, is a national treasure and a true legend. He took Duke University to four NCAA championships, eleven Final Fours, twelve Atlantic Coast Conference (ACC) titles, and thirteen ACC tournament championships. But Coach K. wasn't through; he had bigger fish to catch. He coached the U.S. national basketball team, winning Olympic gold medals in 2008, 2012, and 2016 and later another gold coaching the U.S. FIBA World Championship team (http://www.espn.com/blog/statsinfo/post/_/id/122317/few-have-coached-more-nba-players-than-mike-krzyzewski).

As impressive as Coach K.'s résumé might be, and it is, he has been defeated on many occasions by better teams, but there is One among us who knows no defeat at all, and that's the One we want coaching us to victory. When confronted with trivial obstacles, God usually reminds his people of his miraculous acts on their behalf. But as Israel of old, we falter at the slightest sniff of trouble. "Nevertheless you would not go up, but rebelled against the Lord your God; and you complained in your tents, and said, 'Because the Lord hates us, He has brought us out of the land of Egypt to deliver us into the hand of the Amorites to destroy us'" (Deut. 1:26–27).

As we cross our wilderness, we certainly do not want to repeat the mistakes of ancient Israel. Yes, the issues we face are very real and threatening, and every generation has had to face their fair share of trouble, but God is on our side, and he has the winningest record in the game. When confronted with overdue bills, eviction, failing health, an inevitable divorce, or worse, this text is helpful: "We are hard pressed on every side, yet not crushed; we are perplexed, but not in despair; persecuted, but not forsaken; struck down, but not destroyed" (2 Cor. 4:8–9). God is with us always.

Israel's fixation on their present inconveniences hindered them from focusing on the strength of their mighty God and their glorious future ahead. They complained about everything from their diet to their burning thirst and their hunger, even the strength of their enemies. We should never magnify our problems and present difficulties as if to say our God is impotent. Don't we serve a God who delights in making the impossible possible? "God is our refuge and strength, a very present help in trouble. Therefore we will not fear, even the earth be removed, and though the mountains be carried into the midst of the sea; though the waters roar and be troubled, though the mountains shake with its swelling. There is a river whose streams shall make glad the city of God . . . God is in the midst of her" (Ps. 46:1–5). God can do anything but fail and is delighted when we ask him to move mountains out of our way.

Are you intimidated by your troubles and obstacles? Call on the name of the Lord. Hand over your troubles to Jesus. Get out of the way and let God work for you. "Stand still and see the salvation of your God" (Exod. 14:13).

December 7

Give Thanks Even in Chaos

I will bless the Lord all times; His praise shall be continually be in my mouth.
My soul shall make its boast in the Lord;
the humble shall hear of it and be glad. O magnify the Lord with me, and let us exalt His name together.

—Psalm 34:1–3

Politicians have the uncanny ability of putting a good spin on things even when things are falling apart all around them. Airline personnel usually don't give us the bad news until things have been stabilized and brought under control. Who delights in hearing bad news anyway? I hate to disturb your rosy optimism of the future, but things are going to get awfully bad here on planet Earth. However, God is in control. Life is a mixture of good and bad, so we must savor the good moments while asking God for strength to cope when things begin falling apart around us. Who can bring beauty out of ashes? Need we ask? Only God can make sense of all this madness swirling around us.

The most beautiful songs were written under very painful conditions. Where does one get the inspiration to write a song after the tragic death of a loved one, a failed relationship, losing a job, or battling a terminal disease? David's desire to bless the Lord at all times was written while on the run for his life. He was hunted relentlessly by King Saul and had to flee to a hostile neighboring state to seek asylum, yet he blessed the Lord. His situation was bleak, but he decided to bless the Lord his God anyway.

When Alexander the Great crossed the Alps in pursuit of world conquest, harsh winter decimated his army, including his prized war elephants; he did not lament his temporary setback but pressed on to subjugate his enemies. Julius Caesar was always outnumbered by his enemies; nevertheless, he placed his hope in the Roman Army, the best fighting military machine of the day, and won. Things did not go well for the Allies on the first day of the D-day invasion; the losses were horrendous, and the troops were pinned down by withering enemy fire, but turning back was not an option. They pressed on despite the losses, and the rest was for the history books.

Rafael Nadal is famous for his come-from-behind victories, and the French Open was no exception. Staring elimination in the face, he got his confidence back, stabilized his game, and went on to win the French Open title. Tighten up your belt, Christian friend; we're taking the fight to the enemy in the name of Jesus and putting old Satan to flight. Satan does not have the last hurrah; God does. Every now and then, we must take a quick look at the book of Revelation to stabilize our game. We will win the war against evil. "And I heard, as it were, the voice of a great multitude, as the sound of many waters as the sound of mighty thunderings, saying, Alleluia! For the Lord God Omnipotent reigns! Let us be glad and rejoice and give Him glory, for the marriage of the Lamb is come, and His wife has made herself ready" (Rev. 19:6–7).

Even if you are hounded by the henchmen of hell, God is absolutely Almighty, and his cause will ultimately prevail. We must choose to give God thanks even under every difficult condition as David, Paul, and Job did. Do not lament over your troubled circumstances, get up, "stand still and see the salvation of your God." I choose to give God thanks; lamenting over spilled milk won't get me anywhere. I will give thanks even when things don't go as planned, and I hope you do the same also.

December 8

Increase Our Faith, Lord

And the apostles said to the Lord, increase our faith.
—Luke 17:5

Fukushima Daiichi is still a ghost town devoid of any living thing, except for a few stray domestic animals and resident wildlife. However, the Japanese government is intent on changing that image. The government is trying its best to reassure a jittery public that the decontamination process is progressing nicely. Yasuhiro Sonoda, member of the parliament, took some journalists to task by drinking a glass of water from the nuclear power plant, a bold move considering what transpired there. Even though the water was thoroughly decontaminated, his quivering lips revealed his unease. True faith trusts and believes completely (www.bbc.com/news/world-asia-pacific-15533018).

We join the apostles in requesting a sharp increase in our faith, but it comes at a cost. Are you ready to pay the price? "By faith we understand that the worlds were framed by the word of God, so that the things which are seen were not made of things that are visible" (Heb. 11:3). This is the starting point of faith: we must believe God made the world from absolutely nothing, but this belief will land you in trouble in a heartbeat if you express it in public in today's scientific world. Your increased faith will cause others to eye you with hate and, worse, persecution. "By faith Abel offered to God a more excellent sacrifice than Cain, through which he obtained witness that he was righteous, God testifying of his gifts; and through it he being dead still speaks" (Heb. 11:4). Abel's faith excited the jealousy and hatred of his brother Cain, who slew him.

By faith, Abraham cooperated with God by separating himself from negative family influences and became a nomad for the rest of his life, still looking for the city whose Builder and Maker is God. God did not disappoint his faithful prophet; he had glimpses of the heavenly city and was content with being a sojourner here on the earth.

Moses's faith ran him afoul with the agenda of the pharaoh. "By faith Moses, when he became of age, refused to be called the son of Pharaoh's daughter, choosing rather to suffer affliction with the people of God than to enjoy the passing pleasures of sin, esteeming the reproach of Christ greater riches than the treasures in Egypt; for he looked to the reward" (Heb. 11:24–26). Faith will allow us to prioritize eternal values over present-day toys, fads, and fashion. Inventions come and fade away; God abides forever.

An increase of faith will cause us to obey God rather than the king, even when it involves spending the night with hungry lions or being thrown in a fiery furnace. "And what more shall I say? For time would fail me to tell of Gideon, and Barak and Samson and Jephthah, also of David and Samuel and the prophets: who through faith subdued kingdoms, worked righteousness, obtained promises, stopped the mouths of lions, quenched the violence of fire, escaped the edge of the sword, out of weakness were made strong, became valiant in battle, turned to fight the armies of the aliens" (Heb. 11:32–34).

Do you still want an increase in your faith? Are you prepared to handle what an increase of faith might entail? Whether you realize it or not, we all will need an increase in faith. That's what will get us over the hump. You better submit your faith request while it is still early. Lord, give me the patience of Job, the faith of Abraham, and the moral strength of Joseph to handle the trials that accompany this request. Amen.

December 9

Learning to Walk All over Again

And Enoch walked with God; and he was not, for God took him.
—Genesis 5:24

His body is frail and fragile, and surgery is the only option to save his life. Family and friends gather in the visitor's lounge with somber faces, expecting news, good news hopefully; but in the interim, they must wait. Jeremy (name changed) is the innocent party in a drink-and-drive accident. He was extricated by first responders and airlifted to the nearest medical trauma center barely hanging on to life. The diagnosis is not what the family anticipated; Jeremy has suffered spinal cord injury and may never walk again.

But Jeremy is fortunate to have a praying church family who relentlessly intercedes with God on his behalf; his prognosis looks wonderful after surgery. However, before Jeremy could roller-skate in his favorite park, he must undergo therapy, take baby steps, and learn how to walk all over again.

Heather was blinded by what she called love at first sight and married the first guy who showed up on her radar screen. However, after two years, two kids, and numerous scars both physical and emotional, Heather has had enough; and to add insult to her injury, she was booted out of her apartment for being penniless and behind on her rent.

Interestingly, Heather and Jeremy have much in common. They are both young and in trouble, with much of their life ahead of them, but they must first take baby steps as they learn to walk all over again. Fortunately for them, they belong to caring communities of believers, which overwhelm them with love, therapy, tenderness, and many other niceties.

How does one learn to walk again after being badly bruised by the devil and his agents? Simple. You trust in the goodwill of the divine Healer. The great achievers of our time credit someone who said a kind word or did a good deed that refreshed their spirit. Hardly anyone in need turns down a kind gesture of goodwill. This is the opening that Jesus wants to turn a life in his direction. Are you aware that performing a kind deed to someone gives you the opening to introduce that person to our Lord and Savior, Jesus Christ? When you extract my teeth, fill my hungry belly, dig me a water well, or educate my child, I am ready. Tell me anything that's on your mind. This, my friend, is walking with God and teaching others how to walk with him, especially the vulnerable.

Sometimes we take walking for granted; if the muscles are not stimulated by stress, we might lose the ability to walk. It is only by adding stress (walking) to the limbs that we maintain mobility. Gen. Colin Powell made famous these words: "If you don't use it, you'll lose it." This is particularly true of our spiritual gifts; it is only as we use our gifts to bless others that the Lord entrusts us with more capabilities. "For to everyone who has, more will be given, and he will have abundance; but from him who does not have, even what he has will be taken away" (Matt. 25:29).

December 10

Covered by Grace

But Noah found grace in the eyes of the Lord.
—Genesis 6:8

Though Shoichi Yokoi and his army lost the war, he and ten other buddies refused to surrender. They did not take advantage of the amnesty extended to all combatants but fled to the hills to continue the war. Once there, they lived in a state of constant battle readiness until they succumbed to disease and aging, but Yokoi survived barely by subsistence living. For twenty- seven years, he survived in a cavelike dwelling in the ground until he was discovered by two villagers. Realizing he was discovered, Yokoi immediately kicked into battle readiness and went on the offensive, swinging punches, but his weak and emaciated frame was quickly overpowered by the two younger and stronger men. They bound him and carried him back to the village. Upon questioning, it was soon discovered that he was a Japanese soldier who had survived the war (http://www.history.com/this-day-in-history/japanese-soldier-found-hiding-on-guam).

The villagers informed him that the war was over some twenty-seven years ago, but Shoichi would have none of it; he refused to believe it. They informed the Japanese government of his dilemma, which produced a next of kin to convince him that the war was indeed all over; but he thought he was being tricked into submission. However, with a little pressure and the promise of a better life, Yokoi reluctantly decided to return home.

Yokoi's attitude is reflected in the mind-set of some modern believers—the reluctance to evangelize a lost world. "Also I heard the voice of the Lord, saying: 'Whom shall I send, and who will go for us?' Then I said, 'Here am I! Send me.' And He said, 'Go and tell this people'" (Isa. 6:8–9). Someone needs to go and tell the eight billion Yokois of this world that there is grace and general amnesty to all from God, that forgiveness is there for the asking with no question asked.

"Jesus is coming again" is the glaring, familiar theme of the Bible, and to those acquainted with its language, this is the best message to pierce the human ear. But to the masses who have never heard of the wonderful news of a resurrected and soon-coming Christ, we are obligated to show them a better way to escape the tyranny of sin and enslavement to Satan. Regardless of your past, you qualify for this "go and tell" mission. As a matter of fact, the most effective missionaries are those like Paul and Mary who were steeped in sin.

"In this the love of God was manifested toward us, that God has sent His only begotten Son into the world, that we might live through Him. In this is love, not that we love God but that he loved and sent His Son to be the propitiation for our sins" (1 John 4:9–10). Jesus's blood has been offered in sacrifice for everyone, from Adam down to the very last sinner who will walk the face of the earth. The big question remains whether the sinner will accept the free offer of grace and turn from a life of disobedience to that of obedience to God. I am grateful to Jesus for saving a wretch like me.

> And you He made alive, who were dead in trespasses and sins, in which you once walked according to the course of this world, according to the prince of the power of the air, the spirit who now works in the sons of disobedience, among whom also we all once conducted ourselves in the lusts of the flesh, fulfilling the desires of the flesh and of the mind and were by nature children of wrath just as the others. But God who is rich in mercy because of His great love which He loved us even as we were dead in trespasses, make us alive together with Christ (by grace you have been saved)." (Eph. 2:1–5)

Share this good news with a friend.

Where Are the Nine?

So Jesus answered and said, were there not ten cleansed?
But where are the nine? Were there not any found who returned to give glory to
God except this foreigner?

—Luke 17:17–18

Because of their disease, they were separated from the general public; and to
add insult to their injury, they had to cry, "Unclean, unclean," when approaching
anyone. But they found a friend in Jesus. Leprosy was the most dreaded disease
before the advent of modern medicine; it was both hideous and repulsive. Upon
affliction, the sufferer was isolated in a containment camp where contact with
the public was restricted. "And Azariah the chief priest and all the priests looked
at him, and there, on his forehead, he was leprous; so they thrust him out of that
place, because the Lord had struck him. King Uzziah was a leper until the day of
his death. He dwelt in an isolated house, because he was a leper; for he was cut off
from the house of the Lord. Then Jotham his son was over the king's house, judging
the people of the land" (2 Chron. 26:20–21). Not even the king was exempt from
the harsh treatment the leper received upon detection of this dreaded disease. The
leper was cut off from family and friends and spent his days in isolation.

It is rather interesting to note the relief and joy the ten lepers experienced
when they were declared clean by the priests. But wait a minute, where have they all
gone? Have they all forgotten their kind benefactor except for this one immigrant
among them? "And one of them, when he saw that he was healed, returned, and
with a loud voice glorified God, and fell down on his face at His feet, giving Him
thanks. And he was a Samaritan" (Luke 17:15–16).

Shall we forget where the Lord found us and what he has done for us? "Enter
His gates with thanksgiving, and into His courts with praise. Be thankful to Him and
bless His name. For the Lord is good; His mercy is everlasting, and His truth endures
to all generations" (Ps. 100:4–5). God has been mighty good to us considering the
direction we were heading before coming to faith in Jesus. He saved us from a life
full of mischief and indignities not fit to mention for fear of glamorizing sin. When
we see the path some of our friends have chosen, we can truly say, as a famous
songwriter puts it, "Had it not been for the grace of God, there go I."

The life of the believer is one of continuous praise and thanksgiving to God
not only for what he has done but also for what he is now doing in our life. "Then
King David went in and sat before the Lord; and said: 'Who am I, O Lord God? And
what is my house, that You have brought me this far? And yet this was a small thing
in Your sight, O Lord God; and You have also spoken of Your servant's house for a
great while to come. Is this the manner of man, O Lord God?" (2 Sam. 7:18–19).

Like David, the immigrant Samaritan leper broke down in thanksgiving and
gratitude before God, who had been mighty good to him. He was saved first from

the tyranny of sin that destroys the soul and second from the dreadful disease of leprosy, which disfigured his physical body. Regrettably, we spend little time on our knees in thankfulness to God for all his blessings. Very much like the nine unthankful lepers, some believers walk away without much of a second glance of our gracious Benefactor. How often do you thank God for saving you from yourself or from your huge ego, for keeping your family safe from the terrible unknown, or for just showing you a better way of life? How often do you thank him? Always? Sometimes? Never? Give thanks to him, for he is worthy to be praised.

December 12

Think Eternity

Do not lay up for yourselves treasures on earth, where moth and rust destroy and where thieves break in and steal;
but lay up for yourselves treasures in heaven, where neither moth nor rust destroys and where thieves do not break in and steal.
For where your treasure is, there your heart will be also.
—Matthew 6:19–21

Are you looking for inspiration and motivation? Look no further. Despite David's roller-coaster and colorful lifestyle, he meets the criteria of being a successful and sincere man of God.

> And David prepared iron in abundance for the nails of the doors of the gates and for the joints, and bronze in abundance beyond measure. . . . And David said to Solomon: My son, as for me, it was in my mind to build a house to the name of the Lord my God; but the word of the Lord came to me, saying, "You have shed much blood and have made great wars; you shall not build a house for My name, because you have shed much blood on the earth in My sight. Behold, a son shall be born to you, who shall be a man of rest; and I will give him rest from all his enemies all around . . . He shall build a house for My name." (1 Chron. 22:3, 7–10)

No time for sulking in being passed over for this awesome privilege of building the much-anticipated temple. Upon learning that he was disqualified for building the Lord's house, David's zeal was unabated; it went from good to excellent. We may have good intentions relative to what we deem essential for the work of God, but it is God's prerogative to use our zeal and talent as he sees fit. David made the preparations; he won the wars and subjugated Israel's enemies, but it took Solomon's wisdom to actually execute the building project.

How many self-declared enthusiasts have rushed into building projects with neither the skill nor experience or preparation for the task ahead? They would do well to copy David's example. He was passionate about building God's kingdom here on earth, and he did in part, but it was for another to carry his work to its full completion. Do you have a vision for building the kingdom of God here on this earth? Consult Jesus, and he will tailor-make a project for you.

Building the kingdom can take various shapes and forms. As we noticed, David provided the resources for the project, but that was hardly all that was needed. It takes more than resources to build the kingdom. That's where our talents come into sharp focus. "When He ascended on high, He led captivity captive, and gave gifts unto men. . . . And He Himself gave some to be apostles, some prophets, some evangelists, and some pastors and teachers, for the equipping of the saints for the work of the ministry, for the edifying of the body of Christ, till we all come to the unity of the faith and of the knowledge of the Son of God, to a perfect man to the measure of the stature of the fullness of Christ" (Eph. 4:8, 11–13).

Do you see yourself in this grand scheme of things in the above text? If you think you are not a skilled worker at all, there is still a place for you in God's vast vineyard. There is a phrase in ministry called "ministry of presence," and everyone qualifies for this ministry. "But Moses' hands became heavy; so they took a stone and put it under him, and he sat on it. And Aaron and Hur supported his hands, one on one side, and the other on the other side; and his hands were steady until the going down of the sun" (Exod. 17:12). You can support those in ministry by your encouragements, prayers, cupcakes, and pumpkin pies.

December 13

Absolute Authority

When the Lord saw her, He had compassion on her and said to her, "Do not weep." Then He came and touched the open coffin, and those who carried him stood still. And He said, "Young man, I say to you, arise."

—Luke 7:13–14

If you were a widow in biblical times, your social security would significantly diminish at the death of your spouse. To add to that hardship, the death of an only son meant the widow was at the mercy of friends and neighbors for support, but the Savior's compassion is limitless in restoring to mankind what the enemy has stolen. He goes about this work of restoration with absolute authority. Who gave him this authority? "Most assuredly, I say to you, the Son can do nothing of Himself, but what He sees the Father do; for whatever He does, the Son also does in like manner. For the Father loves the Son and shows Him all things that He Himself does; and He will show Him greater works than these, that you may marvel" (John 5:19–20).

All three members of the Godhead have been heavily involved in the restoration of man ever since the Fall. Having laid his life into the safekeeping of his Father,

Jesus faithfully followed every assignment handed him from God the Father and God the Holy Spirit. It was with this confidence that Jesus told the skeptical Jews, "My Father has been working until now and I have been working" (John 5:17). God is hard at work, providing for the needs of eight billion of us and the innumerable habitable planets in our solar system and beyond.

Despite his business with the universe, he is our High Priest in the heavenly court, interceding on our behalf. We can rest in confidence that when we sin (and we sin willfully and inadvertently), our sins are covered by his blood, but God goes further than this. The Holy Spirit is also hard at work permeating the thoughts of those who do not know God with impressions of the better way of life. Those acquainted with the way of salvation, he does not ignore but leads and guides them to acts of more fruitful labor.

Christ has set the guideline for us in ministry; we must never be timid or hesitant in doing the Father's will. We have at our disposal the same power made available to Jesus while here on the earth. "All authority has been given to Me in heaven and on earth. Go therefore and make disciples of all nations, baptizing them in the name of the Father and of the Son and of the Holy Spirit, teaching them to observe all things that I have commanded you and lo, I am with you always, even to the end of the age" (Matt. 28:18–20).

From where do we get our power, authority, and confidence? Is it not from a deep abiding trust in what God can do in us when we are fully surrendered to his will? "Behold, I send the promise of My Father upon you; but tarry in the city of Jerusalem until you are endued with power from on high" (Luke 24:49). We must operate with the same zeal and enthusiasm as the early disciples, but some of us become weary in well-doing. Our sharpness sometimes becomes dull, and we are hesitant in utilizing the formidable power of God available to us. When the temporal seems to be gaining precedence over the spiritual, it's time to fall at the feet of Jesus supplicating for an infilling of the Holy Spirit. "Ask and it shall be given to you, seek and you shall find, knock and the door will be opened to you" (Matt. 7:7).

December 14

Where Is Your God?

As the deer pants for the water brooks, so pants my soul for You O God.
My soul thirst for God, for the living God.
When shall I come and appear before God?
My tears have been my food day and night, while they continually say to me, where is your God?

—Psalm 42:1–3

The workplace reeks with profanity and vulgarity, and like a caged animal, I am trapped, and must endure the filthy language with no relief and nowhere to go.

This type of behavior may not be visibly apparent in your workplace, but in the ones I have been exposed to, it is business as usual. The colorful and obscene vocabulary is the norm and not the exception. Janet, my upwardly mobile friend, confirms my assertion. Her boss also engages in colorful profanity while directing and interacting with them. Is there any place one can find solace and tranquility and enjoy unbroken fellowship with their Maker?

We have every reason to be happy on the job despite its challenges. Here are some compelling reasons for our happiness: we serve a God who abounds in mercy, love, and grace, and because we are beneficiaries of these awesome gifts, we are obligated to broadcast this dynamic message to the world. However, there are those who may be tempted to ask, "Where is your God?" They need not look very far. God's presence should be easily discernible in our interactions with our acquaintances.

The playing field here on earth is not always level; there are peaks and valleys, ups and downs, feasts and famines, and it is during these low points in life that the presence of God is appreciated the most. Let's draw a mental picture of David being hunted like a wild animal and is extremely thirsty. However, water in the Judean wilderness is a rare and precious commodity; nevertheless, he uses water as a metaphor to illustrate his longing for God. He equates his fellowship with God as a deer longing for a drink of water and cries, "When shall I come and appear before God?" (verse 2). Being on the run is taking a heavy toll on the psalmist's desire to participate in corporate worship. He simply doesn't know when the opportunity might present itself for some meaningful time with the saints in worship (through no fault of his). He laments that his tears have become his food while his enemies stab him with these poisonous words: "Where is your God?"

It is at such low moments that we should recall the tangible victories God has given us in times past. The car was almost repossessed, but the title is now yours. You thought this old illness might just do you in someday, but you are still alive and kicking. How about that child you were worried about and spent many sleepless nights wondering about? After all, he or she turned out all right.

Even with all these impressive victories in life, like ancient Israel, we sometimes worry and invite the clouds of doom and discouragement to hover over us again. You are not alone. After an impressive victory over the prophets of Baal at Mount Carmel, one would think the prophet Elijah was safe and secure, but a threat on his life by the wicked queen Jezebel sent him scurrying from the contest. Thank God because he is always available to his erring children. "Call upon me in the day of trouble; I will deliver you, and you shall glorify me" (Ps. 50:15). That's why when we assemble before God for corporate worship, our faces should reflect victory and happiness on the inside. God resides in us and not in the church.

December 15

Return, Rebuild, and Claim

And I will cause the captivity of Judah and the captivity of Israel to return, and will build them, as at the first.
And I will cleanse them from all their iniquities, whereby they have sinned against me; and I will pardon their iniquities, whereby they have sinned, and whereby have transgressed against me.

—Jeremiah 33:7–8

The guns of World War II fell silent on both the European and Pacific theatres of operation. Hundreds of thousands of troops packed their bags and headed home to waiting moms, wives, families, and friends. Treaties were signed and prison camps emptied except for the vilest of the vile, those convicted of horrible war crimes. Everywhere there was joy, parades, celebrations, healing, and liberation. Former enemies could look one another in the eyes and shake hands, swearing never again to resort to war to settle trivial differences.

As we all know too well, treaties down here on earth are as fragile as the paper on which they are written, but there is a day coming when God will lay hold on the prison gate (the grave) and rip it apart, freeing all the sleeping saints from its gristly embrace.

> For if we believe that Jesus died and rose again, even so them also which sleep in Jesus will God bring with Him. For this we say unto you by the word of the Lord, that we which are alive and remain unto the coming of the Lord shall not prevent them which are asleep. For the Lord Himself shall descend from heaven with a shout, with the voice of the archangel, and with the trump of God; and the dead in Christ shall rise first: Then we which are alive and remain shall be caught up together with them in the clouds, to meet the Lord in the air: and so shall we ever be with the Lord. (1 Thess. 4:14–17)

Every saint from Adam has been looking with eager anticipation to the day when the captivity of sin will be overturned, the graves unlocked, and the captives released. The righteous shall be given immortal bodies, and never will they have any urge to sin anymore. At the pronunciation of the words "It is done" by God, the fate of everyone will be sealed for the ages with the decision they have made.

"He that is unjust, let him be unjust still: and he which is filthy, let him be filthy still: and he that is righteous, let him be righteous still: and he that is holy, let him be holy still" (Rev. 22:11).

However, these words will be music to the ears of the righteous, who have been yearning for liberation from sin. By virtue of our corrupt nature, we have been trapped in this sinful mortal body. When we die, though righteous, we are held captive by death in the grave; but at the Second Coming of our Lord and Savior, Jesus Christ, our situation will be reversed permanently. Everything that was against us will be reversed; bodies once ravaged by pain and sickness will spring to vigorous health. Children snatched from their mothers' arms by death will be reunited with them. The ears of the deaf shall hear the melodious songs of the birds, and the blind shall gaze on the spectacular beauty of the fragrant rose. Frowns and wrinkles will give way to eternal youth and vigor, and time as we know it will be a thing of the past. Eternity, here we come.

The future of the righteous is a glorious one; every other earthly achievement doesn't even come close in comparison. Have you purchased your ticket? Have you made your reservations yet? Have you accepted Jesus as Savior and Lord?

December 16

No More Playing Church

They went out from us, but they were not of us; for if they had been of us, they would no doubt have continued with us; but they went out, that they might be made manifest, that none of them were of us.

—1 John 2:19

The monarch butterfly is a king in his own right; he is bright orange and very toxic and is certainly not on anyone's buffet menu. He is native to North America but vacations in Mexico during the winter. His bright orange color is broken by black and a sprinkled patch of white along the border of his wing. The viceroy butterfly is a copycat of the king; though he looks very much like the monarch, he is certainly not the king. Since the monarch has no known predators, the viceroy mimics his distant relative's characteristics to avoid being on someone else's dinner table. The nerve of him. Mimicry (imitation) is not relegated to animals only; the early church encountered the same problem. "For I know that after my departing shall grievous wolves enter in among you, not sparing the flock" (Acts 20:29). We are hearing very strange teachings these days that are not supported by the Bible nor the writings of credible church teachers. Could these false teachers indeed be copycats, mimicking the behavior of the true Teacher? Should we be surprised? Should we even give them an audience?

"For the time will come when they will not endure sound doctrine; but after their own lusts shall they heap to themselves teachers, having itching ears; and they shall turn away their ears from the truth, and shall be turned into fables" (2 Tim. 4:3–4). We have been warned and should not be surprised when churches and people set aside the Bible to establish their own standard of righteousness.

The Word of God is the only safe standard of righteousness for all believers; it has guided the ship of Zion through the ages. "All scripture is given by inspiration of God, and is profitable for doctrine, for reproof, for correction, for instruction in righteousness: That the man of God may be perfect thoroughly furnished unto all good works" (2 Tim. 3:16–17). The scripture is still God's standard for right and wrong, just as the Constitution is the standard to which all local and state laws conform. Any attempt to replace, set aside, or trivialize the Holy Scriptures is tantamount to establishing one's own standard of righteousness; and that is treason, contrary to the government of God, and against the integrity of the scripture.

Though everything around us is changing, God and his Word remain unchanged, and that's the safest course to follow. "Heaven and earth shall pass away, but My words shall not pass away" (Matt. 24:35). We live in an age where everything is being challenged, when wrong is being accepted as the new normal, even by those who should know better. However, anyone attempting to change the Word of God will incur God's personal wrath unmixed with mercy (Rev. 14:10).

God never fails, nor has he had to alter, change, or amend his Word or creation. He is the only unchanging Being in a constantly changing universe. He makes change but remains changeless himself. His Word is the guide for life and is our only safe route to salvation. If you are playing church, stop it; it's unsafe and unwise, and it will get you nowhere. It's time to wake up and take your relationship with God seriously. God bless you, my friend. Amen.

December 17

Exonerated and Restored

And the Lord restored Job's losses when he prayed for his friends. Indeed the Lord gave Job twice as much as he had before.

—Job 42:10

A bomb went off in Atlanta's Centennial Olympic Park, killing 1 and injuring 111 persons. But before anyone was arrested, the press already had a suspect to fit the crime. Richard Jewell, a local security guard, reported a suspicious device to the authorities that turned out to be a bomb. In the aftermath of the bombing, Jewell assisted authorities with the evacuation of people from the park, but he came under suspicion by an aggressive press and an impatient law enforcement agency eager for an arrest. Because of his familiarity with law enforcement, Jewell fit the profile of a lone bomber. His life was turned upside down by twenty-four-hour news coverage of him and his family. Though he was not charged with a crime, he was tried and condemned in the domain of public opinion. After many thorough searches of his home, it became evident to the authorities that they had implicated the wrong man. However, not very far, the real killer, Eric Rudolph—no stranger to law enforcement—was savoring his victory in gaining the attention of the nation (http://www.cnn.com/2007/US/08/29/richard.jewell/). How do you gain your reputation back after being found guilty even before being tried?

Count it an honor to lose everything for the cause of Christ. "And when they had called for the apostles and beaten them, they commanded that they should not speak in the name of Jesus, and let them go. So they departed from the presence of the council, rejoicing that they were counted worthy to suffer shame for His name" (Acts 5:40–41). In every age, defenders of the gospel have had to stand up for the cross of Christ and defend their belief in him to the world, regardless of the consequences.

Joseph was tried and found guilty without a shred of evidence pointing to his guilt (Gen. 39:7–20). It was futile to defend his good name, and he did not even try. Who would believe the word of a slave against the integrity of his mistress? He was sentenced to hard labor without the possibility of parole, but he was not forgotten. Someone was following his case from the tribunal of heaven, and his fortune was reversed. His righteous stand was honored in heaven, and his example is a great victory against the modern-day hanky-panky office romance.

John the Baptist suffered a similar fate and was thrown in jail without trial, except that his preaching offended the first lady of the land. Unfortunately, she was in an adulterous relationship with King Herod while her husband was still alive. John's righteous rebuke of the unholy affair offended the first lady and cost him his head. Though not mentioned by name, he is definitely in Hebrews 11 Hall of Faith.

Serving God comes at a cost, and Thomas Shepherd reminds us, "Must Jesus bear the cross alone and all the world go free? No, there is a cross for everyone, and there's a cross for me." You may not get restoration or vindication down here on earth, but the day is coming when Jesus will make all things straight. Don't expect exoneration by human courts. Jesus has already restored us by absorbing our guilt on the cross.

December 18

Lift Your Head

Lift up your heads, O you gates! And be lifted up, You everlasting doors!
And the King of Glory shall come in. Who is the King of glory?
The Lord strong and mighty, The Lord mighty in battle.

—Psalm 24:7–8

Little baby Arlene's (name changed) parents have left nothing to chance; they have decided to dedicate her to the service of God. In anticipation of this event, family and friends from out of town have come to lend their support. Cuddled in the warm embrace of Mom's bosom, baby Arlene doesn't know it yet, but she is the center of attraction. Like the prophet Samuel and many other great Bible characters, she is being dedicated exclusively to God's work.

David was not a perfect man by any stretch of the imagination, but God's kingdom was paramount on his agenda. After establishing himself by subduing his enemies and completing his palace, he cast a longing eye on the tabernacle of God, which was housed in the home of Obed-Edom. He thought, *This is not right*: "Now it came to pass when the king was dwelling in his house, and the Lord had given him rest from all his enemies all around, that the king said to Nathan the prophet, 'See now, I dwell in a house of cedar, but the ark of God dwells inside tent curtains'" (2 Sam. 7:1–2).

Bible scholars believe Psalm 24 was a musical composition by King David celebrating the arrival of the ark of God to the city of Jerusalem. Although God dwells in heaven, his Shechinah was reflected on the mercy seat in the earthly sanctuary. David, under inspiration, called on the gates to recognize this magnificent moment by lifting their heads, but since gates are lifeless objects, we must conclude that the creatures within the vicinity of the gates were being urged to lift their heads. The gates were divided into two choruses: singers A and singers B. Group A asked the rhetorical question (for emphasis), not that they didn't know but to maximize the effect of the moment, "Who is the King of glory?" Who can fail to hear the overwhelming refrain "The Lord strong and mighty, the Lord mighty in battle"?

Ellen White, my favorite Christian writer, juxtaposes this scene to when Christ returned to heaven from his conquest of sin and death. Before the gates of the everlasting city, one angel calls the gates (other angels) to attention as the King of glory (Jesus Christ) receives his victory parade, but the other angel pretends not to know and asks, "Who is the King of glory?" Don't you know, the other affirms, "The Lord strong and mighty, the Lord mighty in battle" (Ps. 24:8, SDA Bible Commentary).

We serve a great God, a majestic God, the God who owns the entire universe; we have nothing to be ashamed, afraid, or timid about. It is okay to praise God with emotion even if others may seem a little disturbed. "Now as the Ark of the Lord came into the City of David, Michal, Saul's daughter, looked through the window and saw King David leaping and whirling before the Lord; and she despised him in her heart" (2 Sam. 6:16). God accepted the worship of David in contrast to Michal, who offered him none.

We are looking forward to the reenactment of Psalm 24 in Victory Boulevard when the gates shall be called to attention as the King of glory rides past with his legions (you and me included). Are you in his army? Have you donned your uniform yet? What are you waiting for? Get on board; if you are indecisive, this train is too good to miss. It is real. Get on board.

December 19

It Is the Seventh that Matters Part 1

And Elisha sent a messenger unto him, saying, go and wash in the Jordan seven times, and your flesh shall come again to you, and you shall be clean.

—2 Kings 5:10

Bill and Jenifer have been married for seven years now, but friends close to the family could tell something was missing in their home. They had been trying unsuccessfully to have a baby. With Jenifer's biological clock running out, they had few options left: adopt or opt for in vitro fertilization. They chose the latter. With their financial resources running dangerously low, they began to hope again for their bundle of joy.

Hope was the driving force that kept Jenifer and Bill confident that if they did all that was within their power, God and medical science would do the rest. Fortunately for them, their faith was rewarded with the conception of a healthy baby girl. Their disappointment gave way to hope and, finally, joy as Mom and Pop hovered over the crib of their bundle of joy.

However hopeful one may be, if that hope is not transformed into action and compliance, it is altogether useless as we shall see. "And the Syrians had gone out on raids, and had brought back captive a young girl from the land of Israel. She waited on Naaman's wife. Then she said to her mistress, if only my master were with the prophet who is in Samaria! For he would heal him of his leprosy. And Naaman went in and told his master saying, this and thus said the girl who is from the land of Israel. Then the King of Syria said, go now and I will send a letter to the king of Israel" (2 Kings 5:2–5).

Naaman was an amazing man; verse 5 says he was "great and honorable." Despite him being on the wrong side of God's army, the Lord had given victory to Syria through him. When told by the prophet's messenger to dip in the Jordan seven times, Naaman was obviously furious; but his servants' advice to their master suggested that he was both approachable and rational. "My father, if the prophet had told you to do something great, would you not have done it? How much more then, when he says to you, 'Wash and be clean'?" (2 Kings 5:13). Far from being arrogant, the general meekly humbled himself and complied with the prophet's command. "So he went down and dipped seven times in the Jordan, according to the saying of the man of God; and his flesh was restored like the flesh of a little child, and he was clean" (2 Kings 5:14).

The general's initial hope was dashed by disappointment when he felt he was treated poorly by the prophet who did not even come out to meet him personally.

However, his disappointment gave way to faith and hope when he realized he was still a leper in need of cleansing. He complied with the word of God through the prophet and received not a skin appropriate to his age but a baby's brand-new skin. When we comply with God's requirements in the order he has directed, blessings will follow. As long as it is within our power to perform God's bidding, he will accept nothing short of full compliance to his word. Are you tempted to give partial obedience to God's commandments? How about God's law that goes against your beliefs and lifestyle? Can you pick and choose which commandment you like to obey as in a lunch buffet? Have you decided to obey God's law or the traditions of your church? May God be with you, my friend, as you plan to do what Naaman did—obey and live.

December 20

It Is the Seventh that Matters Part 2

Thus the heavens and the earth, and all the host of them, were finished.
And on the seventh day God ended His work which He had done, and He rested on the seventh day from all His work which He and done.
Then God blessed the seventh day and sanctified it, because in it He rested from all His work which God had created and made.

—Genesis 2:1–3

God's favorite number is seven: there are seven plagues, seven trumpets, seven churches, seven years of plenty, and seven days of the week, and many other sevens in the Bible. Is God giving us a clue by his constant use of the number seven that the seventh day means more to him than any other day? Whereas seven is the number of perfection and completion, the Lord God blessed the seventh day, set it apart for holy use, and made it holy just by resting from his labor. He set it aside as a memorial of his creation. By resting on the seventh day from his creation activity, God identified which day is the Sabbath and commanded all his creation everywhere to stop, cease their gainful employment, and worship him on that day.

Was it a test to Naaman to dip seven times in the river Jordan? Of course, it was, and Naaman's example speaks to us who are coming to faith in Jesus Christ; we must follow God's instructions just as they are prescribed. It is never safe to follow man's instructions instead of God's. Our safety lies in obeying God's specific commands as they are outlined. It is only from the Word of God that we are able to differentiate between true and false and reject the false standards of the world. We can't just do anything, say anything, eat anything, and expect to slide our way into the kingdom of heaven. "Enter by the narrow gate; for wide is the gate and broad is the way that leads to destruction, and there are many who go in by it" (Matt. 7:13).

Had Naaman chosen to dip seven times in another river besides the Jordan, he would have taken just a mere bath and nothing more. The healing power was not in the Jordan but in his faith to believe God's word and comply with it. Here is another example of faith and compliance: "When He had said these things, He spat on the ground and made clay with the saliva; and he anointed the eyes of the blind man with the clay. And He said to him, go wash in the pool of Siloam . . . So he went and washed, and came back seeing" (John 9:6–7). Again, the blind man was sent not to any pool in Jerusalem but to a specific pool, Siloam by name.

We know it was a specific river, and also, a specific number of times Naaman was told to wash. "So he went down and dipped seven times in the Jordan, according to the saying of the man of God; and his flesh was restored like the flesh of a little child and he was clean" (2 Kings 5:14). Five or six times did not bring the healing; it was only after the seventh dip that he became clean. Again, we must point out that the healing virtue was in his willingness to fulfill God's command to the fullest. The blind man and Naaman were healed by their faith and works (compliance); likewise, we must obey God's Word and comply with his command to rest on the seventh day, Sabbath, as he has prescribed.

God's modern-day children need to be informed of this simple truth—the Sabbath of the Lord is still the seventh day and not the first. If you do not know which day the Sabbath is, this text will help. "Then they returned and prepared spices and fragrant oils. And they rested on the Sabbath according to the commandment. Now on the first day of the week, very early in the morning, they, and certain other women with them, came to the tomb bringing in the spices which they had prepared" (Luke 23:56–24:1). The Sabbath is the day between Friday and Sunday. Do you plan to comply and observe the Sabbath as Jesus, the prophets, and his disciples did?

May God be with you in your Sabbath observance.

December 21

A King Is Born

Where is He who has been born King of the Jews?
For we have seen His star in the East and have come to worship Him.
—Matthew 2:2

The delivery room is full, not with medical staff or anxious grandparents but with doting livestock and angels. It was meticulously planned before the entrance of sin to this planet that the Creator/King of the universe would reconcile the wayward planet Earth with the family of God. "But when the fullness of time had come, God sent forth His Son, born of a woman, born under the law, to redeem those who were under the law, that we might receive the adoption as sons" (Gal. 4:4–5).

Recently, the third in line to the British throne, Prince George Alexander Louis, was born in a royal hospital with an anxious nation looking on with great delight. The news was announced to the world that mother and son were doing just fine. With the best of medical care and the nod of his approving parents, Prince George received his official royal title, His Royal Highness of Cambridge.

By contrast, the King of kings was born in obscurity in an animal feeding trough without fanfare or publicity. His parents had little time to digest the fantastic news of being selected to be the parents of the Messiah/King when they were told to flee to Egypt to avoid persecution by the jealous and murderous king Herod. Both Joseph and Mary, being descendants of Judah and David, fulfilled the Old Testament scripture with flawless accuracy. Joseph taught Jesus the trade of carpentry; yes, even Jesus had to be taught like any other child of Adam.

The child who was called the carpenter's son by his townsfolk had more than carpentry on his mind. The Old Testament prophecies concerning the Christ were being fulfilled in quick succession as an old man walked into the temple where Mary and Joseph were dedicating the child to the Lord and made this astonishing prophecy, "Lord now you are letting Your servant depart in peace, according to Your word; for my eyes have seen Your salvation which You have prepared before the face of all peoples, a light to bring revelation to the Gentiles, and the glory of Your people Israel" (Luke 2:29–32).

Of course, Jesus preexisted with God the Father and God the Holy Spirit. It was predetermined in the heavenly council that should man sin, which he did, Jesus would be our substitute to incur the wrath of God to reconcile man with God, allowing him to be just and merciful at the same time. God could not sweep man's sin under the rug and pretend it didn't exist, nor could he ignore it and remain a just and holy God. Justice called for the swift destruction of the violators of his holy law. But God did something altogether marvelous. He incurred his own wrath against sin through the death of his own Son to save mankind. With this sweeping act of mercy, God was both accepting and forgiving on the one hand, while punishing and administering judgment on the other. Thank you, Jesus, for taking my place at the execution block.

"For God so loved the world that He gave His only begotten Son, that whoever believes in Him should not perish but have everlasting life. For God did not send His Son into the world to condemn the world, but that the word through Him might be saved" (John 3:16–17). The beauty of Christmas is accepting the life and sacrifice of Jesus and calling on others to do the same. After all, he came that we might have life and have it more abundantly (John 10:10).

December 22

Joy to the World

Then the angel said to them, do not be afraid for behold, I bring you good tidings of great joy which will be to all people.

—Luke 2:10

The distant singing once far away got closer and closer until the singers (carolers) were on our doorsteps and finally in our living room. It was indeed joy to a ten-year-old to listen to the sound of delightful carols being sung from the comfort of one's bed. The custom of the Seventh-Day Adventist Church brought much joy to the inhabitants of my village with a nightly serenade of angelic singing. The sweet melodies wafted from house to house as the singers made their way to whoever felt inclined to host them. Father was the kind of person who did not pass on a good opportunity. Our door was flung wide open to them, and in came the group singing, "Joy to the world, the Lord is come. Let earth receive her King. Let every heart prepare him room and heaven and nature sing, and heaven and nature sing, and heaven and heaven and nature sing" (Isaac Watts).

Christmas brings a lot of joy to many hearts, but sadly, its joyous celebration does little to help alleviate the pain inflicted on the vulnerable. Victims of violence, widows, and those once engaged in happy marriages but now with undesirable outcomes need a lot of comfort. Singles betrayed by flirtatious suitors and the elderly approaching their sunset years need to feel the joy that Christmas brings. There is much reason to be joyful. The sun still shines, the ground is still beneath your feet, and God is madly in love with you. What more could you ask for? But there is something that is far better than a house full of presents; it's the Savior's embrace. "But when he was still a great way off, his father saw him and had compassion, and ran and fell on his neck and kissed him" (Luke 15:20). Although this narrative relates to the prodigal son, it applies to any child of God who feels lost, neglected, and lonely.

Around the Christmas season and in every season, God has been a champion for the oppressed, the marginalized, the homeless, the lonely, the poor, the victimized, and the neglected. "A father to the fatherless, a defender of widows, is God in His holy habitation. God sets the solitary in families; He brings out those who are bound into prosperity; but the rebellious dwell in a dry land" (Ps. 68:5–6). While it is indeed true that God is a champion for the poor and neglected, he uses us as his instruments in bringing comfort to those in need.

The apostle James presses home the point further: "If a brother of sister is naked and destitute of daily food, and one of you says to them, depart in peace, be warmed and filled, but you do not give them the things which are needed for the body, what does it profit?" (James 2:15–16). Saying "merry Christmas" to someone in need is not good enough. Let us bring the joy of Christ into their lives by addressing their needs and then wish them a happy Christmas. Those in need are within easy reach; they may be your next-door neighbor, a total stranger, someone without a permanent address, or a sick person. As of this writing, I am searching for someone whom I can minister to during this wonderful season. Merry Christmas to you and your family. Touch somebody with your love.

December 23

It's Christmas Time Again

But you Bethlehem Ephrathah, though you are little among the thousands of Judah, yet out of you shall come forth to Me the one to be ruler in Israel, whose goings forth are from of old, from everlasting.

—Micah 5:2

Another teenager was pregnant out of wedlock again, and the villagers were not amused. But this was no ordinary teenager; she was Mary, the mother of the newborn King. The Christmas story is about the birth of the Christ child to a recently married couple whose world had been turned upside down by news of this unusual and unexpected pregnancy. They were still busy checking out the local motels, trying to find a suitable room to rest and relax before going to pay their taxes in the morning, when the contractions came with all its intensity and urgency. Just about any place would suffice to deliver the baby, but no respectable room was found for the King of the universe to be born that night. His parents could no longer tolerate the indifference of the innkeepers, so they settled in an animal shelter. "And she brought forth her firstborn Son, and wrapped Him in swaddling clothes, and laid Him in a manger, because there was no room for them in the inn" (Luke 2:7). What an irony! No room for the Creator/King in a town full of residents dwelling in comfortable houses.

The Savior's coming was no secret to Bible students; it was pronounced by the prophets and anticipated by truth seekers living in Old Testament times. "Now after Jesus was born in Bethlehem of Judea in the days of Herod the king, behold, wise men from the East came to Jerusalem, saying, where is He who has been born King of the Jews? For we have seen His star in the East and have come to worship Him" (Matt. 2:1–2). It was not by coincidence that these truth seekers came searching for the King. Balaam, a non-Israelite prophet, made this exciting reference to the coming Christ. "I see Him, but not now; I behold Him but not near; a Star shall come out of Jacob; A Scepter shall rise out of Israel" (Num. 24:17). Christmas came to Bethlehem, and its residents were ignorant about him, but wise men came searching and found a skeptical and confused king Herod scratching his head for answers. The King was born in Bethlehem that night, and the wise men were not disappointed; they, along with the shepherds, were invited guests.

"Joy to the world, the Lord is come. Let earth receive her King. Let every heart prepare him room and heaven and nature sing." The songwriter had good intentions in urging men to receive the King, but regrettably, most folks seem to prefer Christmas without the Christ. In the true spirit of Christmas, which had its humble origin in an animal shelter (by design), when we buy gifts for friends and loved ones, let us be mindful of those who cannot afford to return the favor.

Christmas is a time of joy, a time for giving, a time for sharing, and a time for showering others with our love and affection. However, we must never forget the needy, the marginalized, the suffering, the sick, and the physically challenged. "For if you love those who love you, what reward have you? Do not even the tax collectors do the same?" (Matt. 5:46). Surprise yourself; give a precious gift to someone who is completely undeserving or someone who could ill afford to return the favor.

Go out there, enjoy the Christmas season, and enjoy the lights, the songs, and the shopping if you are able, being mindful that Christ is the reason for the season. Without Christ, Christmas is a meaningless shopping extravaganza. Merry Christmas to you.

December 24

Christ, Peace, and Christmas

I do not pray for these alone, but also for those who will believe in Me through their word; that they all may be one, as you, Father, are in Me, and I in You; that they also may be one in Us, that the world may believe that You sent Me.

—John 17:20–21

Nothing captures the heart of the nation as the lighting of the national Christmas tree. With beaming dignitaries present and the nation holding its breath, the first family flips the switch to the Christmas tree to the applause of thousands gathered for this joyous event. It has been the delight of presidents, following the example of Pres. Calvin Coolidge, to warm the heart of the nation by lighting the nation's tree. It's a symbol of national unity. The diversity of colors on the tree reflects the richness of the nation's cultural heritage and the unique contributions of its sons and daughters, both free and bound.

Christmas brings warmth and togetherness. It is a time eagerly anticipated by kids of all ages (myself included) because of the songs, the lights, the carols, and—who can forget?—the shopping. Little children learn to be very persistent and quite demanding as the day approaches. Of course, the inventors of high-tech equipment have not made it easy for parents to stay within their budget. Which parent wants to see a grumpy or disappointed child at Christmas? But is this all there is to Christmas?

Without Christ, there would be no Christmas at all. None. Zero. The message of Christ's centrality to Christmas is somehow lost in the hustle and bustle of shopping except for the occasional Christian carol. The central message of Christmas has not changed with the passage of time. "For there is born to you this day in the city of David a Savior, who is Christ the Lord. And this will be the sign to you: You will find a Babe wrapped in swaddling clothes, lying in a manger" (Luke 2:11–12). This, without question, is the most wonderful news ever announced to mortals. The Savior is born; the long-promised anointed One is with us and in human flesh. Have you met him yet?

This little baby who grew up to be Jesus, the Christ, was God's Christmas Day present to our fallen world. The angels chosen for this mission put on their best musical performance. Listen as they sing: "Glory to God in the highest, and on earth peace, good will towards men" (Luke 2:14). Though the angels were commissioned to say nice things regarding the coming of Christ as a baby, they stuck to the basics: "peace on earth and good will towards men" was the message they announced. This world cannot have peace since it does not know the Prince of Peace, but we have his peace. "Peace I leave with you, My peace I give to you; not as the world gives do I give to you" (John 14:27). The peace Jesus gives looks beyond this troubled world and sees a world where God dwells with his people, including you and me. It is a world free from alcohol and tobacco and anything that defiles, where the inhabitants will not say, "I am sick."

The message of Christmas coincides with Christ's promise. "Let not your heart be troubled, you believe in God, believe also in Me. In My Father's house are many mansions; if it were not so I would have told you. I go to prepare a place for you. And if I go and prepare a place for you, I will come again and receive you to Myself; that where I am, there you may be also" (John 14:1–3). Have you made a conscious decision to follow the Lord Jesus wherever he leads? Happy are you then.

December 25

Season's Greetings

Glory to God in the highest, And on earth peace, goodwill towards men.
—Luke 2:14

Christmas came in a spectacular fashion for the Gaines family. The neighborhood Calvary Baptist Church came by to spread the Christmas joy. They came with some good stuff, brought the children Christmas gifts, spread the table with nice, delicious food, and sang some Christmas carols. Capitalizing on the season of goodwill, a few days later, a local TV channel took up position as the church brought a carefully wrapped package and sat it at the front door of the family. Mr. Gaines and his three children began ripping away the box wrappings when suddenly his soldier wife, Jamee, sprang up and flung herself into his arms. Jamee Gaines served with the Oklahoma National Guard in Afghanistan and was on a two-week furlough from the battle front (ABC News).

The greatest gift to our world came wrapped up in swaddling rags lying in a manger (Luke 2:7). The shepherds were elated, the livestock were curious, and the ruling elites overlooked and were thoroughly confused. Jesus was born. Where was he born? Don't you know? In Bethlehem. What a glorious event! Angels dispatched from heaven for this special occasion broke out into harmonious anthems of praise. "Glory to God in the highest, and on earth peace, goodwill toward men!" (Luke 2:14).

The birth of Jesus gives the Christian world an excellent platform to broadcast the good news of salvation. Like the hub of a bicycle to which all the spokes are anchored, all the prophetic forecasts met their fulfillment in his birth, ministry, and death. His coming brought the gift of salvation to every soul on earth, making it possible for rebellious humanity to be reunited with God's universal family. In some ancient cultures where suppression of Jesus's divinity is encouraged by state religions, merchants eagerly welcome the Christmas spirit and the rich profit that accompany its celebration. Would it not be wonderful to let our non-Christian friends know there is much more to Christmas than just presents and gifts and profits? Let them know that Jesus is the reason for the season.

"Peace on earth and goodwill towards men" was the angels' wish to mankind. But the peace of God is more than the absence of war, it is not the secession of strife, it is not even a peace treaty document, nor is it rest or serenity. The peace of God entails being forgiven and accepted into the family of God. At conversion, the sinner experiences peace and quiet confidence that gives him or her the assurance that he or she can "come boldly to the throne of grace, that we may obtain mercy and find grace to help in time of need" (Heb. 4:16).

All claims of having peace without the Prince of Peace are bogus; there can be no peace without the Prince of Peace. "There is no peace, says the Lord for the wicked" (Isa. 48:22). Real peace comes when Jesus is abiding in the heart. Is your surrounding tumultuous? Are you surrounded by treacherous friends? Are you living with a difficult spouse? You can still have the peace of Jesus even if all the above situations are existing in your life. We can be in the most perilous situation on the earth and still display the peace and quiet confidence of Jesus on our faces. Lord, give me your peace today and forevermore.

December 26

Just Say the Word

The centurion answered and said, Lord, I am not worthy that You should come under my roof. But only speak a word, and my servant will be healed. For I also am a man under authority, having soldiers under me. And I say to this one, Go and he goes;
and to another, Come and he comes, and to my servant, Do this, and he does it.
—Matthew 8:8–9

My friend keeps his car sparkling clean; not one iota of dirt can be seen in the interior of his car. He keeps a polishing cloth and cleaning agent ready to destroy any dirt invading the interior of his automobile. Of course, this makes me quite nervous and a little bit unworthy to use his vehicle. I must confess, and confession is good for the soul, that I am completely the opposite of him. I do not make cleaning my automobile an absolute priority as he does. I am more concerned about how the engine functions and getting from point A to point B.

The centurion felt totally unworthy to have the God of all flesh under his roof. How was he able to understand the intricate dimension of Jesus's authority, something the Jewish leaders dismissed with disdain? "Now when He came into the temple, the chief priests and the elders of the people confronted Him as He was teaching, and said, 'By what authority are You doing these things? And who gave You this authority?'" (Matt. 21:23). "In the abundance of water, the fool is thirsty" (Bob Marley). The Jewish religious leaders had mountains of evidence authenticating Jesus's divine authority, but they chose to be naive and, in so doing, made themselves willfully ignorant of his mission on earth. Quite to the contrary, a Gentile who was not privy to the scriptures, who was not raised in church, and who did not attend Sabbath school readily accepted Jesus and saw God at work in his ministry. How did he come to know this truth? Did he have a refreshing from the Holy Spirit? "No one can come to Me unless the Father who has sent Me draws him, and I will raise him up at the last day" (John 6:44).

The centurion's depth of faith and his grasp of the authority of Jesus caused the Savior to stop and marvel about why his countrymen persistently refused to believe and accept the obvious. "And when Jesus heard it, He marveled and said to those who followed, 'Assuredly, I say to you, I have not found such great faith, not even in Israel'" (Matt. 8:10).

The centurion had seen and heard enough. The evidence was overwhelming: the sick were healed, the blind received their sight, and the dead were raised to life. He probably knew some of the people healed and was privy to their testimonies of a changed life and restored health. *I must seek an audience with this Teacher,* he said to himself. *But how? I am a Gentile and, worse, a hated Roman oppressor.* But the urgency of the moment propelled him forward.

His request reflects our heart's condition: Lord, I am not worthy that you should come under my roof. Speak the word, and my soul will be healed. The heart is the origin of every sinful thought, and it does get messy at times. "The heart is deceitful above all things, and desperately wicked; Who can know it?" (Jer. 17:9). But "search me, O God, and know my heart; Try me and know my anxieties; and see if there is any wicked way in me, and lead in the way everlasting" (Ps. 139:23–24). I stand unworthy in your presence, Lord. Wash me thoroughly in your blood and clean me up. Amen and amen.

December 27

Even so, Come, Lord Jesus

He who testifies to these things says, surely I am coming quickly, Amen. Even so come Lord Jesus.

—Revelation 22:20

Anyone seeking attention to oneself craves the company of the president of the United States. Some believe their association with him will enhance their status quo. His presence anywhere commands attention and curiosity. Those fortunate enough to have him in their company can look back at some newspaper or video with nostalgia for being in his company. For security reasons, some of his national trips are not disclosed to the public. He sometimes frustrates his security team by making impromptu stops at local eateries to munch on his favorite snack, but nowhere is his presence appreciated more than in times of national crisis. Somehow we've come to depend on the president to have the last word, to simplify complexities, to inform us, to clear falsehood, to protect citizens, and to comfort the hurting. When he takes time from his busy schedule to visit a constituency hit by some tragedy, whether natural or man-made, he carries with him the sympathy of the nation to those affected. "We share your pain. We're in this together."

If you have access to the news media, you will discover that our planet is under siege; it is being bombarded 24/7 by bad news. While there is no doubt more good news than bad, it seems the bad news always dominate the day and grab the headlines. Aren't you tired and homesick for heaven? Don't you wish sometimes you didn't have to punch a time clock/card, see your boss's face, or work so hard for so little? Well, believe it or not, Jesus is coming soon; he has his hand on the doorknob and can swing the door wide open and make his appearance any day now. "Then the sign of the Son of Man will appear in heaven, and then all the tribes of the earth will mourn and they will see the Son of Man coming on the clouds of heaven with power and great glory. And He will send His angels with a great sound of a trumpet, and they will gather together His elect from the four winds from one end of heaven to the other" (Matt. 24:30–31).

The first-century believers literally believed Christ was coming in their day, and they preached the gospel to everyone of that era. Like them, we have been commissioned with the same obligation to reach everyone in our generation with the gospel. Even though the population explosion far outpaces our capacity to spread the gospel, let us leave that problem to the Holy Spirit. He will sort things out in his own way.

In the midst of the daily deluge of bad news, God offers us something that is absolutely astounding—everlasting life to believers. "For God so loved the world that He gave His only begotten Son that whosoever believes in Him should not perish but have everlasting life. For God did not send His Son into the world to condemn the world, but that the world though Him might be saved" (John 3:16–17). Can anyone with sanity turn down such an offer? But wait, it gets even better, and the human mind is limited in trying to analyze it. "Eye has not seen, nor ear heard, nor have entered the heart of man the things which God has prepared for those who love Him" (1 Cor. 2:9).

Eternal life in the presence of God is something we just cannot afford to miss. Lord, impute your values in me, divest me of the things that are temporal, and implant in me kingdom-building principles. Take away from me anything that is against your will. Amen.

December 28

Harassed and Hassled
but Vindicated

Therefore I take pleasure in infirmities, in reproaches, in needs, in persecutions, in distresses for Christ's sake. For when I am weak, then I am strong.
—2 Corinthians 12:10

Just when defeat seemed inevitable, God showed up big-time and snatched victory from the jaws of defeat. Harry (name changed) left his job disappointed, exasperated, dejected, and deflated, but God wasn't about to let a wicked accusation against his servant go unchallenged. Items usually went missing at Harry's job, and when they did, he and his fellow employees would get a suspicious glance from management. But God delights in showcasing the trustworthiness of his faithful children, and this was no exception. While the devil busies himself accusing the brethren, God, on the other hand, prefers to defend the integrity of his faithful children. "Then the Lord said to Satan, 'Have you considered My servant Job that there is none like him on the earth, a blameless and upright man, one who fears God and shuns evil? And still he holds fast to his integrity, although you incited Me against him, to destroy him without cause'" (Job 2:3).

Poor Harry, he had no way of proving he was a loyal, faithful, and productive employee, but he did what the Bible recommends: he took his plight to the throne of grace and asked God to defend his integrity and use circumstances and situations to his glory. Interestingly and by no coincidence, when payday arrived, Harry was inadvertently paid an extra hundred dollars. Upon realizing the error, he immediately returned the unintended bonus to a stunned secretary. Her boss, sitting nearby, showed no emotion or gratefulness. The message behind the unintended bonus was abundantly clear; Harry was no thief but an ambassador of Christ in the workplace. "But as for you, you meant evil against me; but God meant it for good, in order to bring it about as it is this day, to save many people alive" (Gen. 50:20).

Hurling accusations against God's people is nothing new. It happened to Daniel, who was accused of disloyalty to the king by disgruntled fellow employees. Joseph suffered a similar injustice, landing him a lengthy prison sentence without the possibility of parole. Has Satan changed his tactics? When the believer cannot be overwhelmed by guile or intimidation, Satan uses his favorite weapon, false accusation. "Many are the afflictions of the righteous, but the Lord delivers him out of them all" (Ps. 34:19).

The tried and proven method of achieving spiritual growth, when all else fail, is through trials and tribulations, and if the trials help us keep our eyes on Jesus, it's all for our good. God will give us the overcomer's faith to triumph over obstacles in our way. "For to this you were called, because Christ also suffered for us, leaving us an example, that you should follow His steps: Who committed no sin, nor was deceit found in His mouth, who, when He was reviled, did not revile in return; when He suffered, He did not threaten, but committed Himself to Him who judges righteously" (1 Pet. 2:21–23).

Someone once said, "God will never lead us in any direction that we would not like to be led." While it is painful and uncomfortable being verbally assaulted, bear it as a badge of honor, for Jesus himself was falsely accused. In due time, God will exonerate you. Spiritual growth takes place when we do not retaliate against the wrong committed against us. Be patient; in due time, God will clear up your good name.

December 29

A Better Day Is Coming

Then the Lord said to him, this is the land which I swore to give Abraham, Isaac, and Jacob, saying, "I will give it to your descendants."
I have caused you to see it with your eyes, but you shall not cross over there.
—Deuteronomy 34:4

In 1976, Yoni Netanyahu led an elite squad of 100 commandos to retake a hijacked Israeli airliner. He and his troops liberated the hijacked aircraft from terrorists in Entebbe, Uganda. Tragically, the lieutenant colonel who led the operation did not survive to receive the gratitude of a grateful nation. He was shot during the waning moments of the operation. However, the mission was flawless in its execution; and when the dust settled, 102 out of 106 passengers survived and were flown back to Israel. Unfortunately and regrettably, Yoni was the only casualty of his squad and did not make it back to savor this remarkable feat of the triumph of good over evil (https://www.theguardian.com/world/2016/jun/25/entebbe-raid-40-years-on-israel-palestine-binyamin-netanyahu-jonathan-freedland).

"Then the Lord spoke to Moses and Aaron, because you did not believe Me, to hallow Me in the eyes of the children of Israel, therefore you shall not bring this assembly into the land which I have given them" (Num. 20:12). An unguarded moment of anger and indiscretion cost Moses the honor of leading the children of Israel into the Promised Land. God will not overlook sin or lower his standard of integrity expected of his leaders. There was a golden opportunity to point the people to God, their sole Provider, and Moses and Aaron blew it. "And Moses and Aaron gathered the congregation together before the rock, and he said unto them, hear now, rebels; must we fetch you water out of this rock?" Who was this rock that Moses referenced, and who did the water represent? Who provided the water and food for Israel? Was it Moses and Aaron or God? The answer is obvious; it is God, but Moses took the credit and furthermore called God's people rebels—out of anger, of course. "They angered Him also at the waters of strife, so it went ill with Moses on account of them. Because they rebelled against His spirit, so that he spoke rashly with his lips" (Ps. 106:32–33).

God understands we are fallen humans and works through us anyway despite our shortcomings. "And we know that all things work together for good to those who love God, to those who are called according to His purpose" (Rom. 8:28). Though he fumbled the ball at Kadesh, God had better things in store for his faithful servant. Whereas Moses was supposed to speak to the rock, he angrily struck it twice and destroyed the symbolism of Christ, the Rock being struck (killed) only once. However, God took his erring servant and made him symbolic of the saints who will be raised to life at the coming of the Lord. The Lord personally buried Moses and resurrected him at a time known only to Providence (Deut. 34:5–6, Jude 9).

We take great comfort in the fact that, in spite of our failings and shortcomings, God works through us even when we fall flat on our faces. God works even better when things go wrong for us. Was he not able to work his will through the captivity of a slave girl in Naaman's house? Did he not use Joseph's captivity to humble his proud brothers and reveal his will to the pharaoh? We should not sin intentionally, but even when we do, God can bring some good out of our mistakes. Some have shed the blood of martyrs, only to be convicted by the testimony of the victims they murdered, and went on to become Christians themselves. God can use any disadvantage to his advantage in saving souls.

December 30

A Calm during a Storm

Teacher, do You not care that we are perishing?

—Mark 4:38

Tossed like a paper boat in the angry Atlantic and with a broken mast, the Moravians looked calm, serene, peaceful, and totally unafraid. John Wesley, by contrast, was frantic, afraid, frightful, and panicky (Ellen G. White, *Triumph of God's Love*). What a difference; veteran seamen cowered in fear during the ferocious storm while their Christian counterparts, exposed to the same element, remained calm and totally composed.

Men you should have listened to me, and not have sailed from Crete and incurred this disaster and loss. And now I urge you to take heart, for there will be no loss of life among you, but only of the ship. For there stood by me this night an angel of the God to whom I belong and whom I serve, saying, "Do not be afraid, Paul, you must be brought before Caesar; and indeed God has granted all those who sail with you." Therefore take heart, men for I believe God that it will be just as it was told me. (Acts 27:21–25)

Since God has absolute control of everything, including nature, why then should we fear at the least approach of danger? Make no mistake about it; a healthy dose of fear is good for survival. After all, had it not been for a moderate amount of fear, many of us would not have survived to fight another day. We learn early in life when to run and when to fight. We all need some degree of fear just as a little child needs to fear the red-hot, glowing fire. "And do not fear those who kill the body but cannot kill the soul. But rather fear Him who is able to destroy both soul and body in hell" (Matt. 10:28). This kind of fear implied here refers to a childlike trust and a healthy reverence for God.

Someone benefits from our being afraid, frantic, and unsettled. While God says, "Fear not," Satan suggests to be fearful always. Fear invites paralysis, and paralysis prevents us from moving forward to follow clear given instructions. "And Saul the son of Kish was chosen. But when they sought him, he could not be found. Therefore they inquired of the Lord further, 'Has the man come here yet?' And the Lord answered, 'There he is, hidden among the equipment.' So they ran and brought him from there" (1 Sam. 10:21–23). Why was Saul hiding on his big inauguration day?

This is not a time to be fearful. What if David had given in to his fear? Israel would have lived in perpetual bondage to the Philistines. What if Gideon had given in to his fear? Midian and the enemies of Israel would have triumphed, and the cause of God would have languished for want of an effective leader. What if Nehemiah had given in to his fear and wavered in the wake of the threats made on his life by Tobiah and Geshem? What if Shadrach, Meshach, and Abednego had given in to their fear of the fiery furnace? Nebuchadnezzar would never have come to a saving knowledge of the true God. We cannot and must not give in to fear since we have such a great cloud of witnesses.

It is not uncommon to doubt. After all, doubt has plagued the most noble of us at some point, but God is faithful and has promised, "Fear not, for I am with you; Be not dismayed, for I am your God. I will strengthen you, Yes I will help you, I will uphold you with My right hand" (Isa. 41:10). "For God has not given us a spirit of fear, but of power and of love and of a sound mind" (2 Tim. 1:7). Do not fear, my friend. God has won the battle, and victory is assured.

December 31

On Holy Ground

Then He said, do not draw near this place, take your sandals off your feet, for the place where you stand is holy ground.
—Exodus 3:5

The bush erupted in flames but was not consumed. Moses stood transfixed by this amazing sight. Of course, being a shepherd, he was used to seeing lightning bolts ignite clusters of dry bush in the wilderness; but unlike other bushes, this one was different because the fire did not consume its host. Moses's curiosity got the better part of him, and he decided to take a peek, and from the bush, he heard the voice of God: "Take your sandals off your feet, for the place where you stand is holy ground" (Exod. 3:5).

The throne room of God gives us the closest insight into his holiness. "In the year King Uzziah died, I saw the Lord sitting on a throne, high and lifted up, and the train of His robe filled the temple. Above it stood seraphim; each one had six wings: with two he covered his face, with two he covered feet and with two he flew. And one cried to another and said: Holy, Holy, Holy, is the Lord of host; the whole earth is full of His glory" (Isa. 6:1–3).

God's throne room is saturated with glory and majesty, and that glory illuminates everything that is close to him. His glory is brighter than ten thousand noonday suns; Moses's face had to be veiled after his encounter with the Almighty on Mount Sinai (Exod. 34:35). The angels never failed in exclaiming, as they flew back and forth, "Holy, holy, and holy is the Lord of Hosts." These holy creatures glowed in radiance in the immediate presence of the One who is altogether lovely.

John the Revelator, who was exposed to the same vision, exclaimed, "God is light and in Him there is no darkness at all" (1 John 1:5).

Because God is absolutely radiant, holy, magnificent, and wonderful, shouldn't we approach him with utmost reverence, joy, gladness, and thanksgiving? The psalmist gives us a clue. "Enter into His gates with thanksgiving and into His courts with praise. Be thankful to Him, and bless His name, for the Lord is good; His mercy is everlasting and His truth endures to all generations" (Ps. 100:4–5). When we approach God, like the angels, we must do so humbly yet conscious that he is merciful and approachable.

Praising God is a voluntary act of worship; no creature is ever coerced or forced into this exercise. Are the angels ever bored or listless in praising God? Of course not. In the presence of God, there is virtue, love, joy, happiness, life, vigor, and vitality. How could anyone be bored in the presence of the One who manufactures joy? Alas, our present sinfulness hinders our total appreciation of eternal things. What a revelation it will be on resurrection morning when the scales are lifted from our eyes! God will give us a new perspective of eternal things when the human family leads the chorus around God's throne, singing this song: "Moses the servant of God and the song of the Lamb" (Rev. 15:3). Then the angels will listen with folded wings as we sing the song of how God delivered us from sin and degradation; we will sing how you and I made it over into heaven.

To be with Jesus in heaven, we must practice holy living down here. God dwells in the temple of our hearts. Every day we must erect the family altar and worship him. Have you erected an altar for him in your heart?

Index

CPSIA information can be obtained
at www.ICGtesting.com
Printed in the USA
LVHW091223050119
602465LV00003B/32/P

9 781543 459722